# Motor Learning and Performance

**Second Edition**


Richard A. Schmidt, PhD

Principal Scientist
Exponent Failure Analysis Associates, Inc.

Professor of Psychology
University of California, Los Angeles

Craig A. Wrisberg, PhD

Professor of Sport Psychology
Coordinator of Mental Training Services for Men's and Women's Athletics
University of Tennessee, Knoxville

Human Kinetics

**Library of Congress Cataloging-in-Publication Data**

Schmidt, Richard A., 1941-
Motor learning and performance / Richard A. Schmidt and Craig A. Wrisberg. -- 2nd ed.
p. cm.
Includes bibliographical references.
ISBN 0-88011-500-9
1. Motor learning. 2. Perceptual-motor learning. 3. Motor ability. I. Wrisberg, Craig A. II. Title.
BF295.S249 2000
152.3'34--dc21 99-28368
CIP

ISBN: 0-88011-500-9



**Acquisitions Editor:** Judy Patterson Wright, PhD; **Developmental Editors:** C.E. Petit, JD, and Anne M. Heiles, DMA; **Assistant Editors:** Phil Natividad, Laurie Stokoe, and Jan Feeney; **Copyeditor:** Judy Peterson; **Proofreader:** Erin Cler; **Indexer:** Gerry Lynn Messner; **Graphic Designer:** Robert Reuther; **Graphic Artist:** Kathleen Boudreau-Fuoss; **Photo Editor:** Clark Brooks; **Cover Designer:** Jack W. Davis; **Photographer (cover):** ALLSPORT; **Illustrator:** Mic Greenberg except where otherwise noted. Line drawing on page 61 by John Hatton; **Printer:** United Graphics/Dekker

Printed in the United States of America 10 9 8 7 6 5 4

**Human Kinetics**
Web site: www.humankinetics.com

*United States:* Human Kinetics, P.O. Box 5076, Champaign, IL 61825-5076
800-747-4457
e-mail: humank@hkusa.com

*Canada:* Human Kinetics, 475 Devonshire Road, Unit 100, Windsor, ON N8Y 2L5
800-465-7301 (in Canada only)
e-mail: orders@hkcanada.com

*Europe:* Human Kinetics, Units C2/C3 Wira Business Park, West Park Ring Road
Leeds LS16 6EB, United Kingdom
+44 (0) 113 278 1708
e-mail: hk@hkeurope.com

*Australia:* Human Kinetics, 57A Price Avenue, Lower Mitcham, South Australia 5062
08 8277 1555
e-mail: liahka@senet.com.au

*New Zealand:* Human Kinetics, P.O. Box 105-231, Auckland Central
09-523-3462
e-mail: hkp@ihug.co.nz

To the memory of
Virginia S. Schmidt and Allen W. Schmidt,
as a small thanks for all the skills they taught me

**—Richard A. Schmidt**

To Madelyn G. Wrisberg and Arthur P. Wrisberg
for their unfailing love and encouragement
throughout my life

**—Craig A. Wrisberg**

# Contents

PART II

## Principles of Human Skilled Performance 53

## PART III

## PART IV

## Integration and Applications 287

# Preface

Moving—from the time you wake up to the time you go back to sleep for another night, you hardly ever stop moving. You walk, eat, maybe wash the dishes, drive a car, ride a bike, open your books—and those are just the routine kinds of everyday movements. Parents or teachers may have helped you learn some of those movements, while others you picked up by trial and error. Some of you may move under disabling conditions, making otherwise simple actions difficult to perform. At times you're called upon to perform considerably more skillful actions. Like professionals in the work environment (that is, dentists, surgeons, airplane pilots, or jewelers), you may use complex movements to play a sport, dance, or spend time in recreational pursuits. The skilled performance of these more complicated actions requires years of practice, often under the watchful eyes of teachers, coaches, or other types of movement practitioners.

How people learn to move poses a fascinating set of questions. We have written this book to help you learn more about the fundamental processes underlying human movement. You'll discover how humans learn skilled actions and how principles of motor (movement) performance and learning can be useful in teaching, coaching, rehabilitation, and the design of performer-friendly equipment and work environments (a field known as ergonomics, or human factors engineering). We designed this book so that you don't need prior knowledge of physiology, psychology, statistical methods, or other basic sciences to understand the text. It is an introductory text for undergraduates in fields ranging from physical education, exercise and sport science, kinesiology and biomechanics, ergonomics, or psychology to physical and occupational therapy.

## Mission, Method, and Conceptual Model

In this second edition we combine a conceptual model of human performance with a problem-based learning approach. Our intention is to ask the kinds of questions that challenge you to seek solutions to practical issues of motor performance and learning. You'll find a variety of exercises and activities that guide you to actively connect the concepts and principles you are reading about with real-world problems and situations. As you respond to these open-ended applications, you will learn to ask important questions that are relevant to finding a solution. These include such questions as Who is the person? What is the motor task the person must perform? Where and under what conditions does this person want to be able to perform this task? You may come to realize that, although a lot of scientific information is available on motor learning topics, it is often impossible to get all the facts you think you need about a particular issue! So sometimes you must provide support for your decisions based only on the information you do have available; you must learn to discuss the logic for and limitations of your solutions when you don't have all the necessary information.

When you have finished studying this book, we hope you will understand many of the fundamental principles of motor performance and learning and also be familiar with the supporting literature or research results for each. If you have this knowledge, a solid grasp of the conceptual model of the human performer, and some problem-based working strategies for instructing others in skill movements, you should be able to help individuals who want to learn or relearn just about any motor skill.

## Organization

Before embarking on your studies in *Motor Learning and Performance*, you'll want a view of the landscape ahead (see the "road map" in figure 1). In part I (chapters 1 and 2), you'll find background information about motor behavior, along with definitions of some of the foundational terms used throughout the book. Chapter 1 presents a general overview of the book and

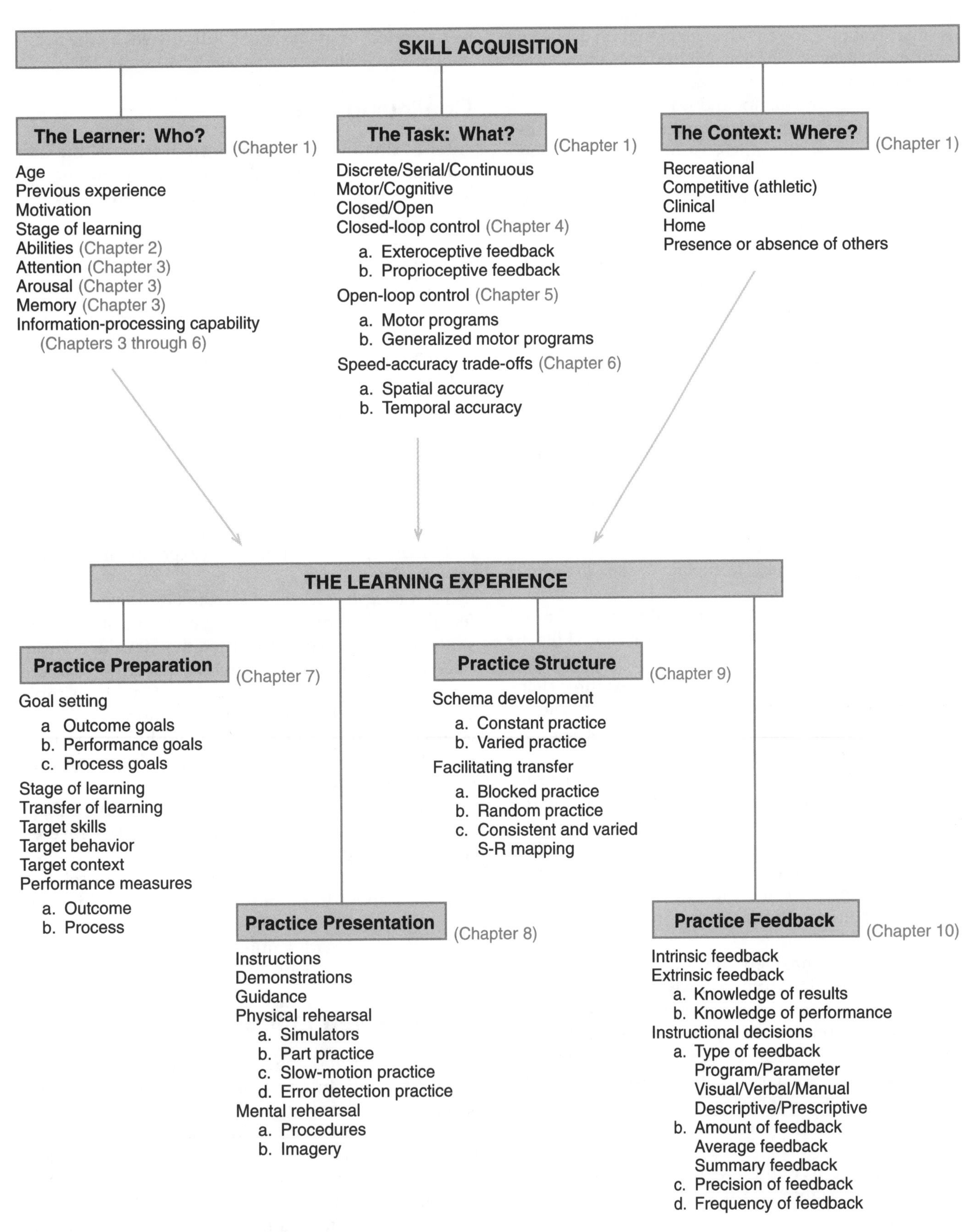
SKILL ACQUISITION
The Learner: Who?
(Chapter 1)
Age
Previous experience
Motivation
Stage of learning
Abilities (Chapter 2)
Attention (Chapter 3)
Arousal (Chapter 3)
Memory (Chapter 3)
Information-processing capability
(Chapters 3 through 6)
The Task: What?
(Chapter 1)
Discrete/Serial/Continuous
Motor/Cognitive
Closed/Open
Closed-loop control (Chapter 4)
a. Exteroceptive feedback
b. Proprioceptive feedback
Open-loop control (Chapter 5)
a. Motor programs
b. Generalized motor programs
Speed-accuracy trade-offs (Chapter 6)
a. Spatial accuracy
b. Temporal accuracy
The Context: Where?
(Chapter 1)
Recreational
Competitive (athletic)
Clinical
Home
Presence or absence of others
THE LEARNING EXPERIENCE
Practice Preparation
(Chapter 7)
Goal setting
a Outcome goals
b. Performance goals
c. Process goals
Stage of learning
Transfer of learning
Target skills
Target behavior
Target context
Performance measures
a. Outcome
b. Process
Practice Structure
(Chapter 9)
Schema development
a. Constant practice
b. Varied practice
Facilitating transfer
a. Blocked practice
b. Random practice
c. Consistent and varied
S-R mapping
Practice Presentation
(Chapter 8)
Instructions
Demonstrations
Guidance
Physical rehearsal
a. Simulators
b. Part practice
c. Slow-motion practice
d. Error detection practice
Mental rehearsal
a. Procedures
b. Imagery
Practice Feedback
(Chapter 10)
Intrinsic feedback
Extrinsic feedback
a. Knowledge of results
b. Knowledge of performance
Instructional decisions
a. Type of feedback
Program/Parameter
Visual/Verbal/Manual
Descriptive/Prescriptive
b. Amount of feedback
Average feedback
Summary feedback
c. Precision of feedback
d. Frequency of feedback

**Figure 1** A road map for providing instructional assistance.

its organization, along with an explanation of the key features that recur. Chapter 2 introduces the concept of motor abilities—the genetic equipment people bring with them to performance and learning—and the importance of this concept to practitioners, whether teachers, coaches, therapists, or human factors engineers.

In part II (chapters 3 through 6) we begin to build the conceptual model of human performance. The building occurs in layers. We start with a simple information-processing model, and we gradually add elements to that model. Chapter 3 discusses the information-processing approach, along with some factors that influence how individuals can (a) identify important stimuli in the environment, (b) select the most appropriate action in response, and (c) produce that action. In chapter 4 the role of feedback in controlling movements is explored, and chapter 5 explains the concept of the motor program and its role in the control of rapid actions. Chapter 6 then describes some of the important principles of motor control and accuracy. By the time you finish part II, you can expect to have a reasonably coherent view of how the human motor system functions and be able to explain the key principles of skilled performance.

Part III demonstrates how to apply the conceptual model from part II to the learning of motor skills. In chapter 7 we provide a framework to help you define individuals' learning experiences. The next three chapters explain how professionals can prepare for, structure, and provide feedback, respectively, for learners during these experiences.

In part IV we propose how professional practitioners might combine the conceptual model and a problem-based learning approach to assist learners. In chapter 11 we present four case studies to illustrate this approach, and in chapter 12 we give you the opportunity to use the approach yourself in defining an instructional experience of your own choosing.

We have emphasized the topics from the vast motor behavior literature that we feel have the best potential for real-world applications. In deciding on what information to present, we considered theoretical ideas and empirical data, including competing ideas and seemingly contradictory research findings. We did not want to interrupt the flow of the book with the extensive justifications, rationales, and discussions of critical evidence that we could have included for each of our points. Rather, we hope you will find this text simple, straightforward, and readable, no matter what your background. And we have taken care to assure that every concept and principle in this book can be defended, or at least not contradicted, by the available research literature.

## Continuing Features

After evaluating the feedback from users of the first edition, we have decided to again integrate the following elements in this second edition of *Motor Learning and Performance*:

1. Preview
2. Chapter Objectives
3. Highlight Boxes
4. Conceptual Model of Human Performance
5. Chapter Summaries
6. Checking Your Understanding
7. Index

At the beginning of each chapter, a *Preview* dramatically introduces the chapter's topic by using real-life scenarios and motor skill examples. Then, the *Chapter Objectives* lists those most important outcomes that readers should understand by the end of the chapter.

Within the chapters, *Highlight Boxes* (in the green or teal shading) describe important experiments and concepts in detail.

The *Conceptual Model of Human Performance* is a defensible, coherent, personal viewpoint about how skills are performed and learned that developed from over 25 years of basic research by Dr. Dick Schmidt. Graphically shown in figures, it starts with a simple view of the performer as an information processor; gradually builds; and concludes with a larger, integrated, conceptual model showing a framework for explaining human performance.

At the close of each chapter you can find a *Summary* to help you recall important concepts covered within the chapter.

*Checking Your Understanding* poses lists of self-test questions about important concepts covered in each chapter.

The *Index* provides quick access to topics and to names used in the book.

## Features New in This Edition

We have blended many new elements into this second edition. In an attempt to share updated information in a meaningful way, you'll find a variety of exercises, thought-provoking questions, and activities. In particular, we have added features that will help you become more involved with the process of learning and better understand how to apply the information in real-life situations. In addition to the learning aids retained from the first edition, we have added the following features in this new edition:

1. Overview
2. Running Glossary
3. It Depends
4. Special Tidbits
5. Application Exercises
6. Case Studies (in chapter 11 only)
7. Culminating Project (in chapter 12 only)

The *Overview* contains a brief summary of the purpose of the chapter and the content to be covered in that chapter.

The *Running Glossary* both lists and defines new terms in the margins on the page that the new term is discussed in the text. For easy reference, sometimes the glossary terms are repeated when they are discussed in later chapters.

*It Depends* requires you to identify important factors you think might contribute to solving motor performance and learning problems. You'll soon find out that most answers require some qualification, depending upon the person, the task, and the context of the performance or learning situation. In addition, you'll find out that there is no one "right" answer, rather some are better than others because they are based on more substantiated evidence, or consider relevant factors, or . . . (here's where your brainpower fits in).

From time to time within a chapter, you'll notice *Special Tidbits*—interesting facts and quotes that provide supplemental information and enliven particular topics. These are given individual topic names and set off in the book's design.

To round out the chapter, four *Application Exercises* test your ability to use a problem-based approach in finding reasonable solutions to problems typically encountered in teaching; coaching; rehabilitation; ergonomics, or human factors, and other everyday motor performance and learning situations.

Two special new features constitute part III of *Motor Learning and Performance.* Four extensive *Case Studies* (see chapter 11) demonstrate both practical problems and potential solutions. Many more specific problems may be found in the *Study Guide.*

The *Culminating Project* (see chapter 12) then challenges *you* to apply all of the concepts covered in the second edition, by selecting a problem of your own choice to solve.

## Supplements

Several new supplements were designed to work in tandem with this new edition, both for students to better understand and apply information and for instructors to structure effective learning experiences while using the second edition of *Motor Learning and Performance:*

1. Study Guide (paperback)
2. Instructor Guide (software), including a test bank and selected graphics

### To the Student

The *Study Guide* that accompanies the second edition of *Motor Learning and Performance* further challenges you to utilize a problem-based learning approach in seeking solutions to performance and learning problems. When you have completed the *Study Guide for Motor Learning and Performance,* you should have a working knowledge of how to use the Conceptual Model of Human Performance to solve problems as well as new insights into how best to tackle the culminating project presented in chapter 12 of the textbook. The chapters in the *Study Guide* correspond to the first 10 chapters in the textbook and follow a consistent format:

1. Key Concepts
2. Key Terms
3. Review Questions
4. Problem-Solving Exercises
5. Worksheets for Your Solution

The *Key Concepts* briefly summarize the chapter's most important concepts and points. Somewhat like a running glossary, the *Key Terms* lists those terms needed to effectively complete the activities and answer the problems posed in the chapter.

The *Review Questions* require you to demonstrate your understanding of key concepts by applying them to specific problems.

The *Problem-Solving Exercises* challenge you to analyze the strengths and weaknesses of two different student responses to three different problems, then to create your own solutions to these problems. There is no "one, correct answer"—rather, you need to justify your answer based on pertinent motor learning and performance principles and concepts.

The three *Worksheets for Your Solution* (per chapter) are templates to help you organize your thoughts in creating a viable working strategy, providing support for your decisions, and listing suggestions for solving the problem.

### To the Instructor

An ancillary package (software) is available for instructors who choose to adopt the second edition of *Motor*

*Learning and Performance*. The package includes these components:

1. Instructor guide
2. Test bank
3. Graphics

## Acknowledgments

We would like to express sincere thanks to a number of people who helped us put this edition of the text together. Acquisitions editor Judy Wright and developmental editors Charlie Petit and Anne Heiles provided invaluable assistance in helping us shape the conceptual framework for the book. Judy offered many good ideas and frequent pep talks during the writing process; Charlie and Anne suggested many changes that have made the book more reader friendly. Tim Lee, Craig Morrison, and John Halbert served as reviewers on earlier drafts of the manuscript and contributed many helpful comments. We particularly thank John Halbert for the idea that led to the road map in figure 1. Several individuals gave us useful information and valuable examples from their professional experiences in coaching (Dave Parrington), physical therapy (Nancy Fell and Lisa Kenyon), and fire fighting (Jerry Harnish). Joe Whitney "raised the bar" for doctoral students by picking up many of Craig Wrisberg's faculty assignments so that Craig could devote considerably more uninterrupted time to the task of writing. Finally, Gwen B. Gordon and Sue R. Wrisberg lent a good deal of emotional support during this undertaking—and we greatly appreciate their patient acceptance.

*Richard A. Schmidt, Westwood, California*
*Craig A. Wrisberg, Knoxville, Tennessee*

# PART I

# An Introduction to Motor Performance and Learning

# Getting Started

## Chapter Outline



## Chapter Objectives

**When you have completed this chapter, you should be able to**

understand the many aspects of the definition of "skill,"

◆

explain the relationship between motor performance and motor learning,

◆

discuss the problem-based approach to motor performance and learning, and

understand the organization and design of this book.

## Preview

From the 1970s into the 1990s, David Kiley (see facing photo) earned the title "King of Wheelchair Sports" by winning five gold medals in the 1976 Paralympic Games in Canada, climbing the highest mountain in Texas, and playing on the U.S. Men's Wheelchair Basketball team five times, as well as by being a top competitor in tennis, racquetball, and skiing. In contrast with Kiley's remarkable feats, most individuals perform motor skills under considerably less dramatic conditions, though not without meeting their own challenges. Paper carriers toss newspapers from moving bicycles onto front porches (some with more accuracy than others), skiers break legs and then must adapt to their environment while wearing casts or using crutches, motorists drive automobiles along busy streets filled with pedestrians and other vehicles, a child takes his first swing at a baseball or attempts her first soccer kick, and senior citizens are faced with the reality that what was once the simple task of walking is no longer possible without the aid of a cane or a walker. These and many other examples indicate that motor skills are an important part of human existence. How well people perform motor skills and how they develop and use those skills in such a variety of situations are the primary focus of this book.

## Overview

The capability to perform skills is a prominent feature of human existence. Without having the capacity for skilled performance, people could not type pages such as this one, nor could they read or modify them. However, since there is both an abundance and variety of skilled movements, it is important for students of exercise science, human factors (or ergonomics), physical and occupational therapy, the performing arts, physical education, or coaching to be knowledgeable about the mechanisms that underlie motor performance and learning.

Franklin M. Henry (1904–1993) teaching at the University of California at Berkeley.

Human skills take many forms, of course, from those that emphasize the control and coordination of large muscle groups in relatively forceful activities, as in soccer or tumbling, to those in which the smallest muscle groups must be tuned precisely, as in typing a term paper or repairing a watch. In this book we focus on the full range of skilled behavior because many movements share the same features, regardless of whether the task is performed in a competitive sport situation, a physical rehabilitation setting, a military or industrial environment, or a common "everyday" location.

All of us are born with some skills, and we only need a little maturation and experience to produce those skills in nearly complete form. Walking and running, chewing, balancing, and avoiding painful stimuli are examples of these relatively innate behaviors. To achieve proficiency in other skills, we need considerably more practice. Only then are we able to detect important environmental features (and ignore others) and produce the kinds of movements that result in consistent goal achievement. Thus, our lives as human beings are characterized

### Franklin M. Henry, Father of Motor Skills Research

Prior to World War II and during the 1950s and 1960s, considerable effort was being directed to the study of people's performance of military tasks such as piloting an aircraft. Most of this research was conducted by experimental psychologists who examined relatively fine motor skills. At that time, little attention was devoted to the study of gross motor skills, such as those that occur in sport and other performance contexts (e.g., dance and music).

A notable exception was the work of Franklin M. Henry at the University of California at Berkeley. Henry, a PhD trained in experimental psychology but working in the Department of Physical Education, introduced a new tradition of laboratory experimentation in the field of motor skills. He primarily studied gross motor skills, many of which involved actions of the whole body. Such movements were more representative of the kinds of tasks seen on the playing fields and in gymnasia. Faithful to his training in experimental psychology, Henry used laboratory-type tasks—many of which he designed and constructed himself in his workshop—that enabled him to conduct more rigorous investigations of skill performance. During his career, Henry examined a number of important research topics, such as the underlying basis for differences in people's performances and the role of motor programs in the control of rapid movements. We will review some of Henry's ideas in greater detail in chapters 2 and 5.

Many of Henry's students who were schooled in this new tradition (including Dick Schmidt) later began their own research programs and mentored other students (including Craig Wrisberg). By the 1970s and 1980s, Henry's direct and indirect influence on the fields of physical education and kinesiology was widespread, earning him the title "Father of Motor Skills Research."

by the performance of skills and the learning of skills. In this book both of these phenomena—motor performance and motor learning—are examined.

We begin this first chapter by discussing a number of concepts that are foundational to an understanding of motor performance and learning. First we examine the concept of motor skill and discuss several skill classification systems, along with three of the key characteristics of skill performance. Next we discuss the relationship between motor performance and motor learning and show how both processes are occurring simultaneously when individuals engage in motor behavior. Then we describe the problem-based approach to motor performance and learning that we will be emphasizing throughout the book. Finally, we describe the logic behind our organization of the text as a whole and the design of individual chapters.

# Motor Skill: What Is It?

Motor skill can be conceptualized in one of two ways. First, skills can be seen as tasks, such as archery, billiards, or carving a turkey. Viewed this way, skills can be classified along a number of dimensions or according to prominent characteristics. Second, skills can also be viewed in terms of the features that distinguish higher-skilled performers from lower-skilled performers. In the following sections, we examine each of these conceptualizations of skill in more detail.

© Tom Roberts

Throwing and catching a softball are examples of a discrete skill.

## A Task Perspective: Skill Classification

One way to view the concept of skill is as an act or task. The issue here is to determine prominent characteristics of motor tasks that practitioners can use to distinguish one from another. Three characteristics that have been used to classify tasks include the way the task is organized, the relative importance of motor and cognitive elements, and the level of environmental predictability surrounding skill performance.

### *Skills Classified by Task Organization*

One scheme for classifying skills concerns the way the movement is organized. At one end of this classification system is the **discrete skill**, which is a task that is characterized by a defined beginning and end and that often is very brief in duration. Discrete skills include tasks such as throwing or kicking a ball, firing a rifle, or flipping the controls on a pinball machine. Discrete skills are prominent in the context of many sports and games, especially those involving the distinct acts of hitting, kicking, jumping, throwing, and catching.

**discrete skill**—A skill task that is organized in such a way that the action is usually brief and has a well-defined beginning and end.

Sometimes discrete skills are strung together to form more complicated actions. These skills are classified as **serial skills**, suggesting that the order of the elements is in some sense crucial to successful performance. Shifting the gears of a manual transmission car is an example of a serial skill; it may have three, four, or sometimes five

**serial skill**—A type of skill organization that is characterized by several discrete actions connected together in a sequence, often with the order of the actions being crucial to performance success.

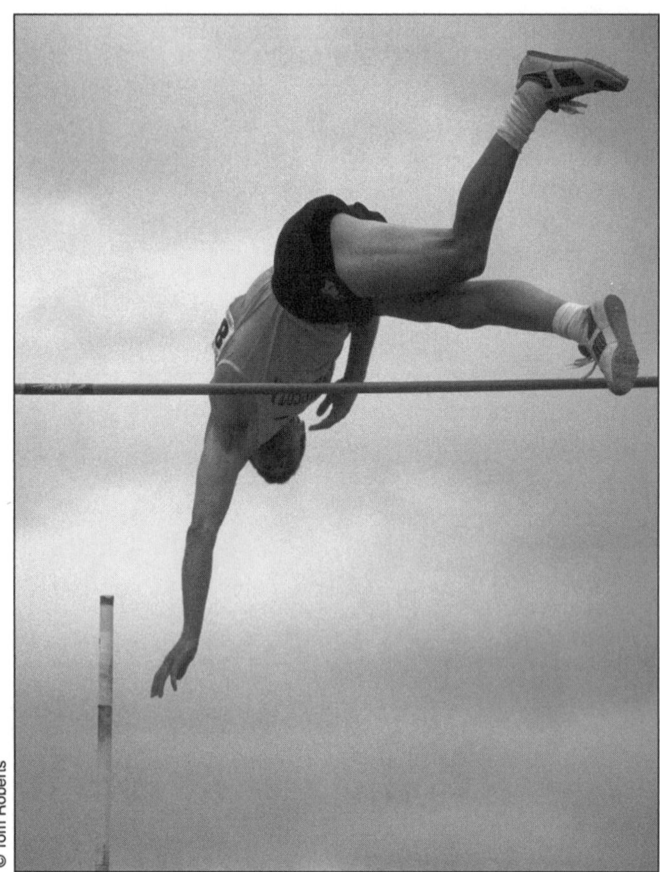


Pole vaulting involves a series of actions and can be viewed as a serial skill.

elements (discrete gearshift, clutch, and accelerator actions) connected in a particular sequence. You might think of other examples of serial skills, such as performing a gymnastics routine and following the sequential gates during a downhill ski race. Serial skills differ from discrete skills in that the circumstances of movement production require a somewhat longer time, yet each movement element retains a discrete beginning and end. During the learning of serial skills, individuals initially focus on the separate elements of the task. Later on, after considerable practice, they are able to combine the elements to form one larger, single element. This allows the accomplished performer to control the entire action almost as if it were a single, discrete movement (e.g., the smooth, rapid way a race car driver shifts gears).

A final category of skills in this system is for those organized in a way that suggests no particular beginning or end. These skills, referred to as **continuous skills**, are often repetitive or rhythmic in nature, with the ongoing stream of action flowing on for many minutes. Examples of continuous skills include swimming, running, skating, and cycling. For these types of skills, either the performer or some environmental barrier or marker (e.g., a pool wall or a finish line) determines the duration of the activity. Still another form of continuous skill is the "tracking" task, which requires performers to use limb movements to maintain contact with a target. Steering a car is a good example of a continuous tracking task, with operators making steering wheel movements that allow them to keep the vehicle in contact with the roadway.

For a capsule summary of the distinguishing characteristics of discrete, serial, and continuous skills, see table 1.1.

**continuous skill**—A skill organized in such a way that the action unfolds without a recognizable beginning and end in an ongoing and often repetitive fashion.

### *Skills Classified by the Relative Importance of Motor and Cognitive Elements*

A second type of classification system emphasizes the relative importance of motor and cognitive elements in task performance. With a **motor skill** the primary determinant of movement success is the quality of the movement itself, with less emphasis

**motor skill**—A skill for which the primary determinant of success is the quality of the movement that the performer produces.

**Table 1.1**
**Discrete-Serial-Continuous Skill Dimension**

| Discrete skills<br>Distinct beginning and end | Serial skills<br>Discrete actions linked together | Continuous skills<br>No distinct beginning or end |
|---|---|---|
| *Throwing a dart* | *Hammering a nail* | *Steering a car* |
| *Catching a ball* | *Gymnastics routine* | *Swimming* |
| *Sit-to-stand transfer* | *Brushing teeth* | *Ice skating* |

being given to the perceptual and decision-making aspects of the task. For example, a high jumper in the sport of track and field knows exactly what to do (jump over the bar). The challenge for this individual is to produce movements that maximize vertical height.

On the other hand, with a **cognitive skill** the nature of the movement is less important to success than is the decision or strategy about which movement to make. For example, in the game of chess it matters little whether the pieces are moved quickly or smoothly; the challenge is to decide which piece to move and where to move it in order to maximize the chances of winning.

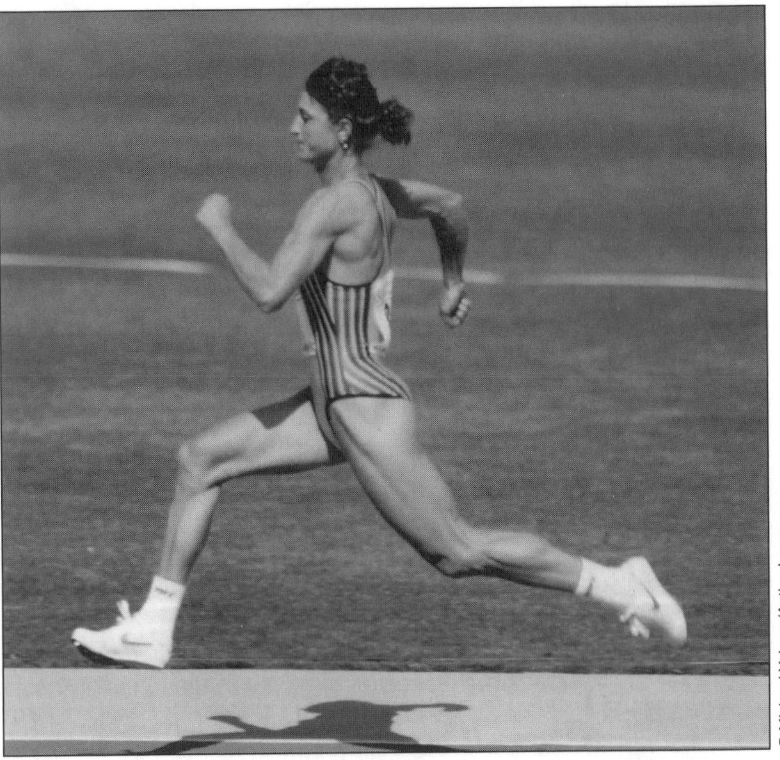



Running has repetitive movements and can be called a continuous skill.

In short, then, a cognitive skill is one that mainly emphasizes "knowing what to do," whereas a motor skill mainly emphasizes "doing it correctly." Note that we have inserted the word "mainly" in the previous sentence. This is because "purely" motor skills and "purely" cognitive skills are actually at the opposite ends of a continuum, with most skills lying somewhere in between (see table 1.2). Thus, the more appropriate approach to classifying skills according to this system is to consider the *degree* to which cognitive (and perceptual) elements (i.e., knowing what to do) and motor elements (i.e., doing it correctly) contribute to successful goal achievement—which may be the reason why motor skills are sometimes referred to as "psychomotor skills" or "perceptual-motor skills."

**cognitive skill**—A skill for which the primary determinant of success is the quality of the performer's decisions regarding what to do.

For example, an individual beginning physical therapy after having knee surgery may need to think more about what to do when walking (e.g., heel strike, balanced posture) because she can no longer produce the movement automatically. After considerable treatment, however, the patient may not have to think as much about what to do, thus making the movement more of a "motor" skill. In a similar vein, a person who is just beginning to learn a new skill (e.g., three-ball juggling) may spend a great deal of time deciding what to do, whereas after many practice sessions the individual "just performs" the movement without much thought. Rarely, however,

**Table 1.2**

**Motor-Cognitive Skill Dimension**

| Motor skills ← | | → Cognitive skills |
|---|---|---|
| **Decision making minimized<br>Motor control maximized** | **Some decision making<br>Some motor control** | **Decision making maximized<br>Motor control minimized** |
| *High jumping* | *Playing quarterback* | *Playing chess* |
| *Weight lifting* | *Driving a race car* | *Cooking a meal* |
| *Changing a flat tire* | *Walking in a busy airport terminal* | *Coaching a sport* |

## Gentile's Two-Dimensional Classification System for Physical Therapy Settings

In an attempt to provide physical therapists with a tool for evaluating patients' motor skills and for determining appropriate treatment activities, Gentile (1987) developed a two-dimensional classification system that considers both the requirements of the action and the demands of the environment. The possible requirements of the action consist of body transport and object manipulation. Environmental demands include the degree to which the regulatory conditions of a person's movements are stationary or in motion and the extent to which the regulatory conditions are the same from one performance attempt to the next. Generally speaking, regulatory conditions for closed skills (e.g., hitting a golf ball) are stationary, while those for open skills (e.g., hitting a baseball) are in motion.

A simplified version of Gentile's system is shown in table 1.4. The two components of each dimension (shown at the top and left sides of the table) are combined in various ways to form 16 possible task versions. As you can see, the complexity of task variations increases as you move from the top left side to the bottom right side of the table. A task classified in the top left box would be one for which no movement, or only a simple movement, is required. Regulatory conditions are stationary, and they remain the same from one attempt to the next. An example might be the task required of a patient who is asked to maintain an erect posture or, while in an erect posture, to lift the right arm to shoulder level. The patient always performs the task in the same closed environment, such as in the office of the physical therapist. A task classified in the lower right box would be one that requires the patient to manipulate some object while transporting the body and in response to a regulatory stimulus that is in motion. In addition, the regulatory stimulus is different from one attempt to the next. An example might be the task required of a patient who is asked to toss and catch a beanbag with a partner while the patient is walking. On each occasion the patient performs this task, her partner tosses the beanbag in a different way (e.g., one time with a higher trajectory, another time with a slower speed, etc.).

While Gentile designed her classification system for use by physical therapists, her notion of combining several classification systems to achieve a more precise description of task demands is one that can be mimicked by movement practitioners in other settings (e.g., sport, performing arts, industry, the military).

do either cognitive or motor elements become entirely unimportant to performance. Even highly skilled individuals—who are able to perform complex movements with little thought—are sometimes required to think about what to do, such as the split-second tactical decisions required of sailors during the America's Cup race.

### *Skills Classified by the Level of Environmental Predictability*

**open skill**—A skill performed in an environment that is unpredictable or in motion and that requires individuals to adapt their movements in response to dynamic properties of the environment.

**closed skill**—A skill performed in an environment that is predictable or stationary and that allows individuals to plan their movements in advance.

A third way to classify motor skills is to consider the extent to which the environment is stable and predictable throughout performance. An **open skill** is one that is performed in an environment that is variable and unpredictable during the action. Examples include defending against a fast break in basketball and engaging an opponent in wrestling. In situations like these, it is difficult for the performer to effectively predict the future moves of others (and hence the future responses to them). A **closed skill**, on the other hand, is one that is performed in an environment that is stable and predictable. Examples include gymnastics routines and swimming in an empty lane in a pool. As is the case for "motor" and "cognitive" skills, these "open" and "closed" skill designations actually represent the end points of a spectrum, with the circumstances surrounding most forms of skill performance lying somewhere between low (i.e., open) and high (i.e., closed) degrees of environmental predictability.

The open-closed skill classification system emphasizes the relative demands placed on the performer to respond to moment-to-moment variations in the environment. For skills that lie closer to the "closed" end of the continuum (e.g., golf, bowling, knitting a sweater), the environment waits to be acted upon. Thus, the performer can evaluate environmental demands in advance, organize the movement without time pressure, and carry out the action without any need for sudden adjustments. For skills that are closer to the "open" end of the continuum (e.g., hitting ground strokes in tennis, fielding a ground ball in baseball or softball, shooting the rapids in white-water canoeing), the performer must utilize the processes of perception, pattern recognition, and decision making to adjust the movement, often in a short amount of time, in response to changing environmental conditions. The essential features of open and closed skills are summarized in table 1.3.

Each of these classification systems addresses a particular dimension of motor tasks. However, practitioners should probably consider several systems simultaneously when attempting to determine the demands of a task or to evaluate the capabilities of a performer. A good example of this type of multidimensional

**Table 1.3**
**Open-Closed Skill Dimension**

| Closed skills ← | | → Open skills |
|---|---|---|
| **Predictable environment** | **Semipredictable environment** | **Unpredictable environment** |
| *Gymnastics* | *Walking a tightrope* | *Soccer* |
| *Typing* | *Steering a car* | *Wrestling* |
| *Cutting vegetables* | *Crossing the street* | *Chasing a rabbit* |

**Table 1.4**
**An Extension of Gentile's Two-Dimensional Classification System**

| Environmental Demands ↓ / Action Requirements → | Neither body transport nor object manipulation | Object manipulation only | Body transport only | Both body transport & object manipulation |
|---|---|---|---|---|
| **Neither regulatory variability nor context variability** | *Maintaining standing balance* | *Writing on a blackboard* | *Walking on a city sidewalk* | *Walking on a city sidewalk while pulling a wagon* |
| **Context variability only** | *Using sign language* | *Dealing a deck of cards* | *Playing a game of hopscotch* | *Twirling streamers in rhythmic gymnastics* |
| **Regulatory variability only** | *Standing on a moving escalator* | *Standing in place while dribbling a basketball* | *Walking on a moving escalator* | *Dribbling a soccer ball while in motion without a defender* |
| **Both regulatory variability & context variability** | *Balancing on alternate feet while on a moving escalator* | *Playing a video-arcade game (with joysticks)* | *Running through a crowded airport* | *Dribbling a soccer ball against a defender* |

approach to skill classification in physical therapy settings is described in the highlight box on page 8. Some non-therapeutic examples are illustrated in table 1.4.

## A Performance Proficiency Perspective: Characteristics of Skill Performance

We can also view the concept of motor skill in terms of the features that distinguish higher-skilled performers from lower-skilled ones. There are many qualities of skilled performance we could consider (and, in fact, we do consider them in chapter 7), but for now let's turn to the definition of skill proposed by the psychologist E.R. Guthrie (1952), which captures three of the essential features of skilled behavior. According to Guthrie, skill "consists in the ability to bring about some end result with maximum certainty and minimum outlay of energy, or of time and energy." (p. 136)

When we talk about motor skills, we are talking about movements that are performed with a desired environmental goal in mind, such as holding a handstand in gymnastics or eating a meal with the use of a prosthetic hand. Movements having no particular environmental goal, such as idly tapping your fingers, are not skills. Individuals who are more proficient in achieving a particular movement goal usually demonstrate one or more of the qualities we next discuss, which are mentioned in Guthrie's definition: maximum certainty, minimum energy expenditure, and minimum movement time.

### *Maximum Certainty of Goal Achievement*

One quality of skill proficiency is movement certainty. To be "skilled" implies that a person is able to meet the performance goal, or "end result," with *maximum certainty*. For example, many people might throw a dart into the "bull's-eye" of a target. But this action, by itself, does not ensure that those people are skilled dart players. For most of them, such an outcome is the result of one lucky throw in the midst of hundreds of others that are not so lucky. Only those individuals who show that they can produce the goal with a high degree of certainty, on demand, without luck playing a very large role, can be considered skilled. This is one reason why people admire the champion athlete who, with but one chance or only seconds remaining in the game, produces the skilled action that achieves the goal and brings the victory.

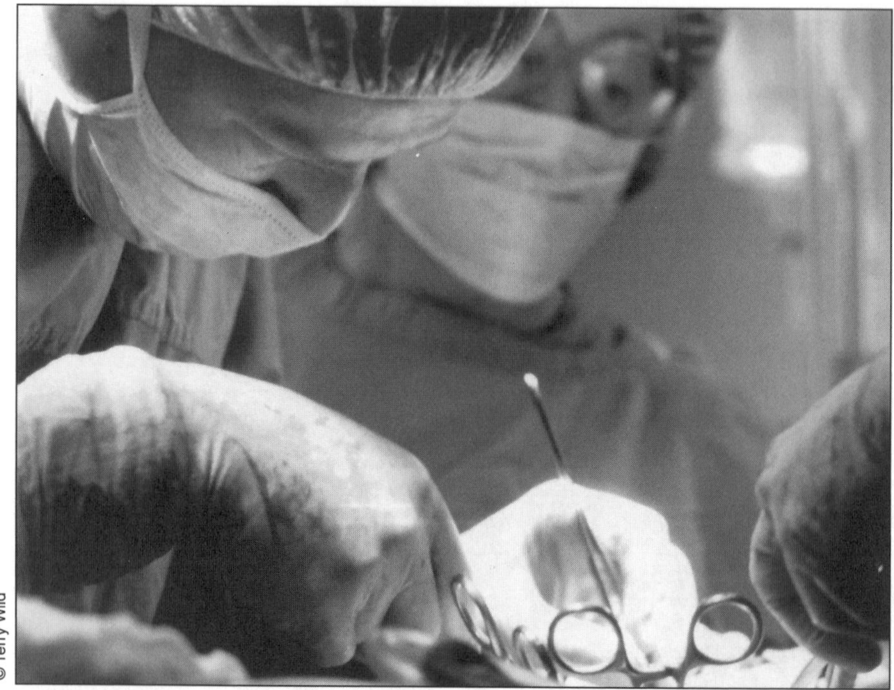
© Terry Wild

The skilled performance of surgery requires maximum certainty of movement.

### *Minimum Energy Expenditure*

A second quality of skill proficiency is the minimization, and occasionally conservation, of the energy required for performance. For some skills this is clearly not the goal. In the shot put, for example, the only goal is to heave the shot the maximum distance. But for many other skills the *minimization of energy expenditure* means the reduction or elimination of unwanted or unnecessary movement. This characteristic is crucial for those performers who must conserve energy to achieve success. Examples include

## IMPROVED SKILL PROFICIENCY IS REFLECTED BY INCREASES IN CERTAINTY, DECREASES IN ENERGY EXPENDITURE, AND SOMETIMES DECREASES IN MOVEMENT TIME

A person decides that she wants to learn how to snow ski. She loves the outdoors and knows that if she just could ski, it would open a whole new dimension of nature to her. The individual has read magazine articles on the subject and has watched numerous TV programs showing the performance of skilled skiers in both recreational and competitive settings.

She decides to spend the money for lessons at a nearby ski school, and enrolls for classes. The first day is discouraging. It's all she can do to put on her gear and just stand up! When she falls—which is quite often—it takes her several minutes to get back on her feet. Even though the teacher tries to keep instructions simple, the woman feels overwhelmed by all the information. Her teacher tells her not to feel too bad because all beginners experience similar frustrations.

After several days of classes, the novice skier begins to notice that she is able to do simple skills, turning and stopping, with some consistency—and she doesn't fall as much! Within a few weeks, she enjoys the thrill of her first successful run—with no falls—on the beginner's slope. By the end of that day, she completes several more runs by herself with only a couple of mistakes. The individual realizes that she is enjoying more of the scenery while she skis because she doesn't have to pay as much attention to her movements. She is not as tired at the end of her lessons as she was when she first began taking them, and she looks forward to fine-tuning her skills even more in the future. She is moving toward her goal of independent recreational skiing in the great outdoors.

the skilled triathlete who holds an efficient pace or the skilled wrestler who saves strength for the last few minutes of a match. The minimum-energy notion also implies that skilled individuals are able to organize their actions in a way that reduces the mental demands of the task. Performers who produce their movements in an automatic fashion can direct their thoughts to other features of the activity, such as the strategy used by a race car driver or the creative expression chosen by a ballet dancer. Minimization of energy expenditure is an important goal for individuals at the lower end of the skill spectrum, including those with disabling conditions such as multiple sclerosis. Among some people with disabilities, movements of any kind must be performed as efficiently as possible for survival reasons.

### Minimum Movement Time

A third quality of skill proficiency is the *reduced time* (or increased speed) in which the goal is achieved. Many sport performers, such as sprinters in track, swimming, and cycling, have minimum time as their primary competition goal. Skilled individuals in other activities are more effective when they execute their movements more quickly, such as the quick jab of the boxer or the crisp pass of the point guard in basketball. Minimizing time, however, can be a problem during the performance of some tasks. For example, the typist who speeds up the production of keystrokes on a computer may produce more errors in word processing. Or, the farmer who attempts to increase the speed of stacking hay bales in a barn may burn more energy. When we view the concept of skill in terms of movement proficiency we must remember that individuals often have to balance and optimize several qualities of performance in order to achieve their desired goal.

## The Chicken and the Egg: Motor Performance and Motor Learning

**motor performance**—The observable attempt of an individual to produce a voluntary action. The level of a person's performance is susceptible to fluctuations in temporary factors such as motivation, arousal, fatigue, and physical condition.

**motor learning**—Changes in internal processes that determine an individual's capability for producing a motor task. The level of an individual's motor learning improves with practice and is often inferred by observing relatively stable levels of the person's motor performance.

As we mentioned earlier, the concepts of motor performance and motor learning are two of the prominent themes of this book. In many ways, these concepts are difficult to distinguish—in much the same way as it is difficult for us to answer the old question, "Which comes first, the chicken or the egg?" Each time an individual attempts a motor task, the person displays some level of performance. If the action that the person produces is representative of the individual's typical performance (uncontaminated by temporary factors such as fatigue, anxiety, boredom, etc.), it might also be considered to be representative, to some extent, of the person's level of learning of the task.

There are some primary differences between the concepts of motor performance and motor learning. **Motor performance** is always observable, and it is influenced by many factors (e.g., motivation, attentional focus, fatigue, physical condition). **Motor learning**, in contrast, is an internal process that reflects the level of an individual's performance capability and may be estimated by relatively stable performance demonstrations. In order for people to learn a motor task, however, they must engage in performance attempts or practice. As a result of this practice, people's capability for producing the desired action improves (i.e., motor learning). The best way for practitioners to assess the motor learning of individuals is to observe people's motor performance. If the individual's level of performance proficiency is relatively stable over several observations and under different sets of circumstances, the practitioner can assume that the performance is an accurate reflection of the person's level of motor learning.

Two phenomena that illustrate the intimate connection between motor performance and motor learning are related to the stages of learning and the concept of implicit learning. We discuss each of these phenomena in the following sections.

IT DEPENDS . . .

Movement practitioners must estimate an individual's level of learning by observing various aspects of the individual's performance. To illustrate the difficulty associated with this task, we suggest that you spend some time at a local recreational area and observe the performance of a particular individual (unbeknownst to the person, of course). As you watch this individual perform, what aspects are you looking for that might tell you something about the individual's level of learning? Be as specific as possible when describing each aspect.

### The Stages of Performance and Learning

A number of scholars have attempted to define the performance characteristics of individuals at different stages of the skill-learning process. In table 1.5 we present several of these representations. Viewed as a whole, the information contained in table 1.5 offers a nice depiction of the activities of individuals during early and later stages of learning, along with some of the observable motor performance characteristics.

**Table 1.5**
**Theoretical Depictions of the Stages of Motor Learning and Associated Motor Performance Characteristics**

| Reference | Early stage of learning → | | Later stage of learning |
|---|---|---|---|
| *Fitts and Posner (1967)* | *Cognitive (trial and error)* | *Associative (homing in)* | *Autonomous (free and easy)* |
| *Adams (1971)* | *Verbal motor (more talk)* | | *Motor (more action)* |
| *Gentile (1972)* | *Getting the idea of the movement* | | *Fixation/diversification (closed or open skill)* |
| *Newell (1985)* | *Coordination (acquire the pattern)* | | *Control (adapt the pattern as needed)* |

**Associated Motor Performance Characteristics**

| Early learning → | | Later learning |
|---|---|---|
| *Stiff-looking* | *More relaxed* | *Automatic* |
| *Inaccurate* | *More accurate* | *Accurate* |
| *Inconsistent* | *More consistent* | *Consistent* |
| *Slow, halting* | *More fluid* | *Fluid* |
| *Timid* | *More confident* | *Confident* |
| *Indecisive* | *More decisive* | *Certain* |
| *Rigid* | *More adaptable* | *Adaptable* |
| *Inefficient* | *More efficient* | *Efficient* |
| *Many errors* | *Fewer errors* | *Recognizes errors* |

In all cases, early learning is characterized by attempts on the part of the individual to get an idea of the movement (Gentile, 1972) or understand the basic pattern of coordination (Newell, 1985). In order to do this, individuals must do a considerable amount of problem solving, involving the exercise of cognitive (Fitts & Posner, 1967) and verbal (Adams, 1971) processes. Performance during the early stage of learning is characterized by considerable inaccuracy, slowness, inconsistency, and stiff-looking motor activity. Individuals lack confidence and are therefore hesitant and indecisive in their mannerisms. Even when they do something correctly, beginners are not sure how they did it.

Depending on a number of factors, such as the abilities, motivation, and previous experiences of individuals and the difficulty of the task, people eventually reach the stage of learning where their performance becomes more accurate and consistent. At that point, they have a pretty good idea of the general movement pattern, and now they begin the process of refining, modifying, and adapting that pattern to meet particular environmental demands. Gentile (1972) contends that if the task to be learned is a closed skill, individuals profit most from rehearsal experiences that take place under a fixed set of regulatory conditions (i.e., fixation). If, however, the task to be learned is an open skill, individuals refine their movements better under a diverse set of regulatory conditions (i.e., diversification). The ten-pin bowler's challenge is to produce the same action under relatively invariant conditions, while the soccer goalie attempts to learn ways to adapt his movements to a wide variety of environmental events.

Only after considerable practice do a few individuals reach the stage of learning that is characterized by virtually automatic movement production. Fitts and Posner (1967) call this stage the "autonomous stage," while Adams (1971) labels it the

## LEARNING ABOUT LEARNING FROM WATCHING CHILDREN

It is great fun to watch a group of children at play. It also teaches us something about the way humans learn skills. At first a child observes a playmate or an adult doing something—like swinging on a swing, sliding down a slide, or throwing and catching a ball. The child then attempts her own imitation of the task. If she has some degree of success or finds the movement challenging or enjoyable—or if she hears praise from a parent or friend—she may continue to engage in the task. The child may even achieve some degree of success at something simple (e.g., sliding down the slide feetfirst) and choose to repeat that action for several attempts. Once she feels reasonably confident, the child may attempt another, more difficult, variation of the movement (e.g., sliding down the slide headfirst) or may decide to do something altogether different (e.g., swinging on the swings).

The general progression of skill learning seems to be from the foundational to the sophisticated (Haywood, 1993). As individuals achieve one level of skill, they move to the next. If the task is throwing a ball, the child may throw and chase the ball many times before he has achieved sufficient skill to begin throwing it to a partner. Catching comes even later because it involves the additional skills of visual tracking, anticipation, accurate hand placement, and timed grasping. If a skilled adult is throwing to the child, the latter may benefit from seeing and attempting to catch a ball that is coming at nearly the same speed and trajectory each time. In any case, considerable experience of throwing and catching in a variety of situations over a long period of time will be required before the child is able to pick up any type of ball and play a successful game of throw and catch with someone else.

While adults bring a greater amount of past experience to learning situations than do children, their performance progresses in much the same way—starting with the basic skills, they gradually incorporate the more advanced "details" that allow them to execute their movements with greater accuracy, consistency, and diversity.

"motor stage," suggesting a proportionately greater emphasis on motor as compared to cognitive aspects of the task. The performance of individuals who reach this level of skill proficiency is characterized by all of the qualities we mentioned in our earlier discussion of Guthrie's (1952) definition of skill. In addition, these individuals are able to detect and correct errors in their movements, if and when errors do occur.

It is sometimes difficult for practitioners to determine exactly when individuals progress from one stage of learning to the next. However, you should be able to use the motor performance characteristics shown in table 1.5 to make reasonable inferences about an individual's level of motor learning. You should also be able to use this information to decide what forms of instructional assistance are most appropriate for individuals at the different stages of learning.

**implicit learning**—Improvements that occur in an individual's capability for correct responding as a result of repeated performance attempts and without the person's awareness of the components of the task that prompted the improvements.

## Implicit Learning

Another phenomenon, **implicit learning**, illustrates the close relationship between motor performance and motor learning. When individuals set a goal to learn a motor task, they typically begin to practice their movements. In this way, they use motor performance as a vehicle for determining the appropriate pattern of movement, for refining that pattern, and for making that pattern more controllable. As a result,

## IT DEPENDS . . .

Can you pick out the differences in people's performances? Observe the performances of a variety of people in a group setting (e.g., playing volleyball at a picnic, performing a line dance at a country-western dance club, playing racquetball at a local recreational facility or health club). Focus in on two or three of the individuals who appear to differ the most from each other in skill proficiency. Using table 1.5, indicate those specific aspects of the people's performances that distinguish them the most from each other.

individuals begin to observe explicit (i.e., obvious) changes in a number of performance characteristics they are targeting for improvement (see table 1.5). However, they sometimes experience performance improvements for which they have no awareness or explanation.

There is research evidence suggesting that repeated motor performance experiences can increase a person's level of motor learning, even when the individual is oblivious to the components of the task that are producing the change. In several of these studies, participants' learning of a repeated segment of a tracking task was found to be superior to their learning of other segments that were randomly presented (Magill, Schoenfelder-Zohdi, & Hall, cited in Magill, in press; Pew, 1974; Wulf & Schmidt, 1997). When interviewed after the experiment was over, none of these individuals indicated being aware of the fact that one of the movement segments had been repeated.

Results such as these underscore the likelihood that every time individuals engage in motor performance, some type of motor learning is going on. We've all heard the adage "practice makes perfect." In the realm of motor skills, repeated motor performance "makes" motor learning. The crucial question for practitioners is, "What types of repeated motor performance produce the *most effective* motor learning?" The challenge for practitioners is to design the types of performance experiences that lead to the "perfecting" of the *desired* action—whether it be intentional learning or implicit learning. In order to meet this challenge, practitioners need to be able to ask the right questions and then devise answers that will allow them to assist

## HOW "SMART" IS THE MOTOR SYSTEM?

Several clinical studies of individuals who have suffered permanent memory deficit following brain surgery suggest that the motor system is capable of organizing movements even when individuals can't remember having performed them before. In one longitudinal study conducted by Milner, Corkin, and Teuber (1968), an adult male patient was reportedly able to learn and continue to produce a number of motor skills, even though he could not remember the previous performance occasions. This individual was eventually employed in a rehabilitation center where he performed a variety of tasks, including one that involved the mounting of cigarette lighters on cardboard frames, for which he achieved a high degree of skill. In another case study (Gardner, 1975), a patient with severe amnesic symptoms was found to be able to learn and recall piano melodies even though he couldn't remember any of the teaching sessions. Studies such as these seem to indicate that the motor system requires little more information than that pertaining to the movement goal and the environmental context in order to organize an effective response.

learners in achieving their goals. In the next section, we discuss the problem-based approach to motor performance and learning in greater detail.

## A Problem-Based Approach to Motor Performance and Learning

In 1981 the prominent educator Arthur Combs contended that "Tomorrow's citizens must be problem solvers, persons able to make good choices, to create solutions on the spot. Effective problem solving is learned by confronting events, defining problems, puzzling with them, experimenting, trying, searching for effective solutions." (1981, p. 369) We believe this viewpoint is more relevant today than it was then, and that is why, in this book, we encourage a problem-based approach to learning. The key ingredient of **problem-based learning** is the capacity to ask the right questions. For the movement practitioner who wants to be able to assist learners, three important questions to ask are simply Who? What? and Where?

**problem-based learning**—An approach to learning that presumes that the key to understanding is the ability to ask the right questions.

### Asking the Right Questions

In order to be an effective practitioner you have to be able to ask the right questions. If you can do this you should be able to determine the most appropriate teaching and therapeutic applications for just about any instructional situation. The reason we believe you need to be able to ask the right questions is that the solutions to most problems dealing with people's motor performance or learning depend on a number of things.

These "things" include the person you are assisting, the task you are assisting the person to learn, and the context(s) in which the person wants to eventually be able to perform the task. Put more simply, these factors can be put in the form of three

### The Strength of Problem-Based Learning

In the current information age, approaches to learning are shifting from the older traditions that emphasize the acquisition of subject matter to newer views that stress the importance of effective problem solving. Today's learners must be able to accurately define problems and sort out the available information they need to propose workable solutions. Sometimes individuals are required to solve problems without the benefit of all the necessary information—either because the available information does not suggest clear-cut answers or because the facts are conflicting. A problem-based learning approach teaches individuals how to tackle problem scenarios in the most effective manner possible. It teaches them that there is usually no single correct answer to a problem, but that the better solutions are the ones that are defensible and, wherever possible, supported by existing scientific evidence.

As Arthur Combs, the prominent humanist, suggests, "Effective problem solving is learned by confronting events, defining problems, puzzling with them, experimenting, trying, searching for effective solutions. Problem solving is using your brain and all the resources you can command to search for solutions. It is a creative process not tied to any particular subject. One can solve problems effectively in any area of human endeavor." (1981, p. 370)

For prospective movement practitioners, problem solving means asking the kinds of questions that are relevant to an instructional situation. Questions like "Who is the learner? What is the individual's learning goal? What is the learning task? What are the cognitive, perceptual, and motor demands of the task? Where does the person want to be able to perform the task once he or she learns it?" are the kinds of questions you are going to continually confront as you work through the various activities in this book.

questions: Who? What? and Where? (see figure 1.1). *Who* is the person you are assisting (child, athlete, therapy patient, senior citizen). *What* is the task the person wants to be able to perform (catching a ball, executing a complex gymnastics routine, using a wheelchair, playing croquet). *Where* is the context in which the person wants to be able to perform the task (during a noon recess with a number of other children, at a piano recital or dance concert, in the dining hall at a nursing home, at a golf course with a foursome of friends, on a basketball court in front of thousands of spectators).

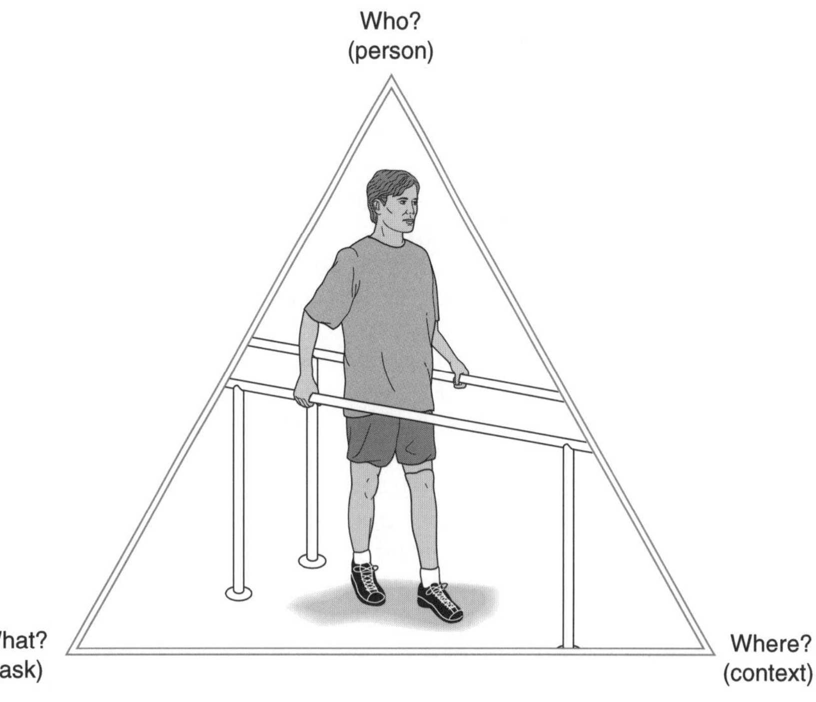


**Figure 1.1** Movement practitioners continually ask three basic questions to assist people in motor learning: Who? What? and Where?

### *Who?—The Person*

The most important component of any motor performance situation is the person performing the skill. Each individual possesses innate abilities, a particular maturational level, previous movement experiences, a level of motivation and emotions, and perhaps some form of handicapping condition that predisposes him or her to a certain degree of performance proficiency. If the person possesses the requisite perceptual-motor abilities (a concept we will discuss in more detail in the next chapter), has achieved a satisfactory level of maturation, has had previous movement experiences that are relevant to performance of the task, is motivated to excel, and is capable of maintaining an emotional level that is optimal for task performance, then that person's skill achievement should be higher than it would be if one or more of the previous conditions were not satisfied.

### *What?—The Task*

The nature of the task to be performed is a second important component that practitioners need to consider. Some tasks place a considerable emphasis on sensory-perceptual factors, such as the demands placed on the tennis player to detect the speed and direction of an approaching ball or those placed on the ice hockey goalie to analyze the pattern of motion of opposing players during a rush up the ice. Sensory-perceptual events such as these generate decisions concerning what the performer should do and how he or she should do it. Accurate decision making is another element that can determine the degree of performance success (e.g., what type of return shot the tennis player should attempt to hit, or how the goalie should handle a shot on goal). Finally, of course, is the element of movement execution. For some tasks, motor control or production factors are the principal determinant of

 IT DEPENDS . . .

Three elements that are important to the performance of many motor tasks are sensory or perceptual elements, decision-making elements, and motor control elements. Can you think of an example of each type of element for one of the following tasks: a goalie in a soccer game, a jockey in a horse race, a skater at a crowded recreational ice rink?

### A CLOSER LOOK AT THE COMPONENTS OF MOVEMENTS

If we take a closer look at the movements we produce, we see that several possible components are involved. First, there is the postural component, which supports most of our actions—for instance, the arms of an expert archer provide a stable platform that promotes accurate shooting. Physical therapists, particularly those who specialize in the pediatric and neurologic areas, are very aware of the essential nature of postural components for motor control. For these specialists, the head, neck, and trunk are the starting points and building blocks of most therapeutic treatments. A second component of movements is the locomotor component, which we use to transport our bodies to locations where we perform other skills, such as when a waiter carries a tray of food from the kitchen to the table in a restaurant. Finally, our movements sometimes contain a manipulation component, which we couple and coordinate with postural and locomotor components or which is occasionally the major focus of a skill, such as the finger and wrist movements of a neurosurgeon.

performance success (e.g., how skillfully the triple jumper executes the three-component movement sequence or how skillfully the concert pianist performs a piece of classical music). For other tasks, the response itself may come at the end of a sequence of perceptual and decision-making activities but is still an important ingredient of goal achievement. Even if the situation is correctly perceived and the appropriate movement decision is made, the performer will not be effective in meeting the environmental goal if he or she cannot execute the actions properly (e.g., the tennis player must be able to accurately produce the return shot and the goalie must be able to successfully execute the "save" maneuver).

### *Where?—The Target Context*

A third important component of motor performance and learning is the context in which the movement is to be performed (i.e., the target context). Where does the learner intend to perform the task he or she is trying to learn? Will it be in the presence of spectators or alone in a gymnasium? Will time pressure be an issue or will the individual be able to take all the time he or she needs to produce the desired movement? An important part of problem-based instruction involves providing the learner with opportunities to perform the desired movement in a context that is similar to the one(s) he or she wants to be able to eventually perform the task in.

Throughout this book, we challenge you to become a *participant in the problem-solving process*. In the next section, we discuss the ways we will be helping you achieve a clear understanding of the concepts of motor performance and motor learning and learn to utilize the problem-based approach.

## Developing Your Understanding of Motor Performance and Learning

Because motor skills make up such a large part of our lives, scientists and educators have been trying for years to understand the basis of skill performance and the factors that influence skill learning. The results of research studies offer important information for professional educators and movement practitioners in a number of areas. For individuals in the fields of exercise science, kinesiology, physical education, and physical medicine and rehabilitation, the results suggest ways of designing skill instruction that lead to movement success for persons in a variety of life situations. For coaches, the findings offer information about ways to structure practices that produce more consistent skill execution and that give athletes an advantage in competitive situations. For human factors practitioners, the information suggests principles of skills training that can enable individuals to operate machines and other types of equipment effectively and safely. For physical and occupational therapists, the results provide ideas for assisting individuals who are trying to relearn movements they have lost or have had compromised as a result of injury, stroke, birth defects, and the like. In light of recent initiatives in health care reform, a knowledge of motor performance and learning principles would appear to be more important than ever for therapists who must provide effective treatment in a shorter time, with fewer patient visits, and at a lower cost.

Although all of these settings are different and the physical capabilities of the learners in each may vary widely, the principles that lead to successful application are generally the same. In this book we discuss the important generic principles of motor performance and motor learning that have emerged from the results of scientific studies.

In the next chapter we discuss the concept of individual differences in the movement capabilities of people. These are the inherited abilities (or, in some cases, disabilities) people bring with them to performance or learning situations. In chapter 2 we illustrate how a person's abilities can influence his or her potential for performance success. Later, in parts II and III of the book, we present the important principles of motor performance and motor learning, respectively. Even though these two phenomena are not easily separated, we temporarily treat them separately to help you more clearly comprehend the principles of each and then eventually grasp the connection between the two.

You might wonder whether we shouldn't address the concept of motor learning before turning our attention to the concept of motor performance (perhaps reasoning that a person has to learn a skill before she or he can be expected to perform it). However, we have chosen to discuss performance principles before discussing learning principles for two reasons. First, much of the research examining the processes underlying simple motor performance has been used as the basis for principles of motor learning. Second, it is the literature on motor performance that allows us to construct a conceptual model of human performance that illustrates how the human

## SO YOU THINK YOU WANT TO BE A MOVEMENT PRACTITIONER

One way to get an idea of the demands of a professional occupation is to ask the opinion of people who are working in the profession. To help you understand the challenges that face movement practitioners, we suggest you interview a person who provides instructional or therapeutic assistance on a regular basis (e.g., a physical education teacher, a youth sport coach, a physical therapist, an occupational therapist, a dance or music teacher). Ask the person to respond to each of the following questions:

- What do you like most about teaching people skills?
- What do you like least about teaching people skills?
- What is the easiest part of your job?
- What is the toughest part of your job?
- What is the biggest challenge you face when you are trying to help an individual improve his or her skill?

Summarize the person's comments and then discuss your own thoughts and feelings.

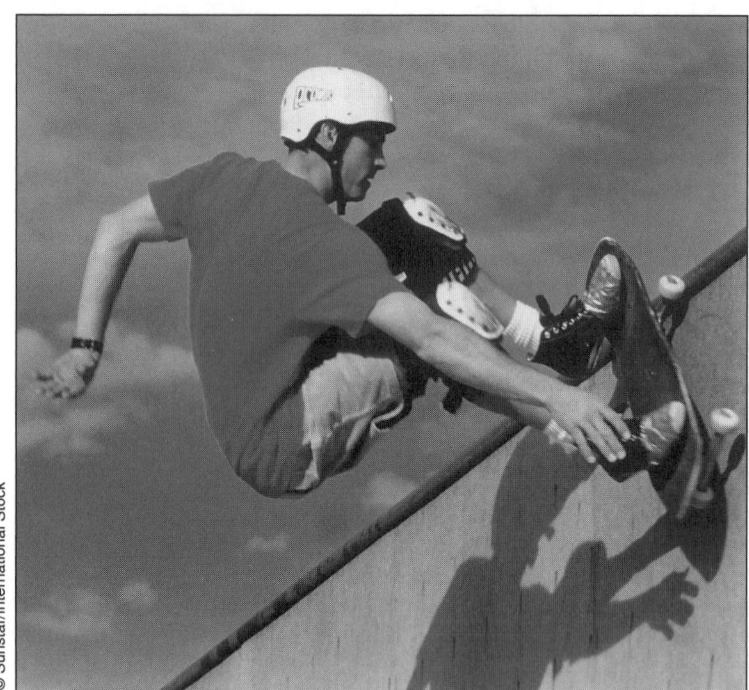

© Sunstar/International Stock

The model of human performance attempts to account for how people learn and perform such complex motor skills as skateboard maneuvering.

perceptual-motor system works, how individuals interact with their environment during skilled movement, and how additional factors (such as task complexity, types of feedback, practice structure, and the presence of others) can influence the performance and learning of skills.

In summary, then, we focus on two separate but related themes in parts II and III of the book. In part II we discuss the components and principles of motor performance. These include the nature of information processing (chapter 3), the ways individuals use sensory information to control their movements (chapter 4), the role of motor programs in movement production (chapter 5), and the determinants of accuracy in rapid movements (chapter 6).

In part III we turn our attention to issues related to the learning of motor skills and to some of the principles practitioners should remember when assisting learners. In chapter 7 we discuss the concept of the learning experience and describe methods practitioners might use in evaluating the progress of learners. In the remainder of part III, we discuss the principles and techniques practitioners should consider when supplementing the learning experience (chapter 8), structuring the learning experience (chapter 9), and providing feedback during the learning experience (chapter 10). As we progress through parts II and III we will also be building a conceptual model of human performance to help you understand the interrelationships of the various mechanisms and principles of motor performance and motor learning.

### Building a Conceptual Model of Human Performance

**model**—A tentative description of a system that accounts for many of its known properties; models facilitate people's understanding of systems and promote practical applications.

In order to provide effective instructional assistance for learners, you need to have a relatively consistent overall viewpoint, a "big picture," a conceptual **model** of human performance. During some of your prior educational experiences you have likely been introduced to various types of models. In chemistry, you may have used Styrofoam balls and wooden sticks to build models that attempt to approximate the structure of atoms and molecules. If you have had a class in physiology, you have probably been introduced to the plumbing-and-pump model of the human circulatory system.

The model of human performance we begin constructing in part II of the book is an "information-flow" type of model, which postulates that individuals use information of various kinds to perform and learn skills. As we build the model we first depict how sensory information enters the system through receptors (chapter 3). In subsequent chapters we explain how performers process, transform, and store this information, and how they use it to make decisions and plan their actions. Finally, we discuss several features of movement execution like the process of movement initiation and the activities that occur while the action is unfolding (e.g., the control of muscular contractions and the detection and correction of errors). By the end of part II you should have a good understanding of the components of the conceptual model of human performance and be able to identify which components are most essential for the production of different types of movements. In part III we discuss various dimensions of the motor learning process and suggest which components of the model are modifiable with practice—which of them, thus, contribute to skill acquisition.

### Applying the Problem-Based Approach to Skills Instruction

In part IV of the book we illustrate how movement practitioners can use the conceptual model of human performance and the important principles of performance and learning to devise a working strategy for providing instructional assistance. In chapter 11 we discuss the components of the working strategy and then demonstrate how practitioners in four different settings (teaching, coaching, rehabilitation, and firefighter training) might use the strategy to design and structure learning experiences for individuals. In chapter 12 we provide you with the opportunity to demonstrate your own ability to use the working strategy to design a learning experience for a person, task, and situation of your choosing.

By that time you should have a good comprehension of the important principles of motor performance and learning, an understanding of the conceptual model of human performance, and the capability of using a problem-based approach to assist individuals in achieving their movement goals. We hope you enjoy your experience.

## Summary

Motor skills are an important and often fascinating aspect of our lives. What we know about skills has come from a variety of scientific disciplines, and the results of this research are useful to practitioners in a variety of settings, such as teaching, coaching, rehabilitation, and industrial or technical environments.

A skill may be viewed from a task perspective and classified according to dimensions such as the following:

- The organization of the task
- The relative importance of motor and cognitive elements
- The level of environmental predictability

Skill can also be conceptualized as the level of proficiency demonstrated by a performer. Qualities associated with high levels of performance proficiency include the following:

- Maximum certainty of goal achievement
- Minimum energy expenditure
- Minimum movement time

The concepts of motor performance and motor learning are difficult to distinguish. This is because repetitions of motor performance are required for individuals to achieve higher levels of motor learning, and the level of learning can only be estimated by observing a person's motor performance. Motor performance is susceptible to fluctuations in temporary factors such as fatigue, boredom, anxiety, and motivation. Performance repetitions sometimes produce increases in learning that are beyond the awareness of the individual. Motor learning is an internal process, the level of which reflects an individual's capability for producing a movement at any particular point in time. Different performance characteristics are evident at different stages of learning.

A problem-based approach to performance and learning presumes that there are many factors that contribute to successful movement production. Practitioners who use this approach emphasize the importance of asking the right questions, including "Who is the learner? What are the demands of the learning task (i.e., sensory-perceptual or decision-making factors, movement production)? Where is the task going to eventually be performed?"

## From Principles to Practice

Check your understanding of the material in this chapter by responding to the following questions and then completing the application exercises. In each case, see if you can identify the most relevant questions or issues and then propose a solution based on the concepts and principles discussed in the chapter.

### Checking Your Understanding

1. Discuss the concept of motor skill from a task classification perspective and from a performance proficiency perspective, and then explain how each perspective might be used by a person who is coaching a youth soccer team.
2. Explain the concepts of motor performance and motor learning, and discuss two movement characteristics a physical therapist might look for to determine if a stroke patient is learning how to walk with a cane.
3. Explain why a problem-based approach to motor performance and learning is an effective strategy for movement practitioners.

### Application Exercise #1

Since you have more experience with the sport of bowling than he does, your friend wants you to critique his performance.

*It Depends*

- How strong is your own knowledge of and skill in the sport of bowling?
- What is your friend's stage of learning?
- What are some movement characteristics you would look for in order to infer your friend's skill level?

*Strategy*

Assist your friend by accurately identifying the movement characteristics that are associated with various levels of bowling performance and then by observing his performance to determine his proficiency in each.

*Response Example*

- Ask your friend to tell you what he thinks are the strong and weak points of his performance.
- Ask several expert bowlers what characteristics they would look for to determine a person's skill level.
- Make a list of those characteristics and see whether you can identify them when you watch your friend bowl.
- See how stable your friend's performance is by watching him bowl on several different occasions.
- Compare your friend's performance with that of other bowlers, and see if you can identify differences in their movement characteristics.

### Application Exercise #2

Your neighbor asks you to help her coach a youth soccer team. She would especially like for you to help her identify the movement characteristics that are important for performance success.

*It Depends*

- How knowledgeable and skilled are you in the sport of soccer?
- How old are your neighbor's players?
- How much previous soccer experience do the players have?
- What movement characteristics distinguish soccer players at different skill levels?

*Strategy*

Gather as much information as you can about your neighbor's players and about the movement characteristics you should look for in their soccer performance. Practice observing players of all skill levels to improve your capability of identifying the important characteristics. Using a checklist of the movement characteristics, observe your neighbor's players on several occasions to see how well you can assess each player's skill level.

### Application Exercise #3

Your exercise science professor gives your class an assignment in which you are to visit a local hospital in order to observe physical therapists performing functional evaluations on new patients.

*It Depends*

- What information would you like to have from the therapists?
- What characteristics of patients' movements are the therapists looking for?
- What criteria would you use if you were performing the patient evaluations?

*Strategy*

Read as much as you can about the process of functional evaluation, observe the therapists as they perform their evaluations, and take notes on the things you hear them say and see them do. Use Gentile's two-dimensional classification system (see table 1.4) to classify the functional performance of several of the patients. Ask one or two of the therapists if they would be willing to tell you the types of characteristics they look for when performing evaluations.

## Application Exercise #4

Your cousin is thinking about taking scuba lessons so he can go diving with his friends. He asks you for your opinion.

*It Depends*

- Is your cousin an experienced swimmer?
- Is he claustrophobic?
- Does he know the mental and physical requirements of the task of scuba diving?
- Does he know the essential movement characteristics of skilled divers?

*Strategy*

Assist your cousin in evaluating his own skills and motivation for learning to scuba dive. Determine the nature of the demands of this sport and the movement characteristics that skilled divers are expected to demonstrate. Encourage him to consider whether his capabilities, motivation, and future prospects for success in scuba diving are sufficient to warrant his enrollment in a course of instruction.

2

# Individual Differences and Motor Abilities

## Chapter Outline



## Chapter Objectives

**When you have completed this chapter, you should be able to**

understand the concept of individual differences,

discuss the fundamental nature of motor abilities,

discuss several things practitioners should remember about people's abilities,

explain how a practitioner might use the concept of motor abilities to classify skills and perform task analyses, and

discuss the difficulties inherent in predicting a person's future performance success based on assessments of the individual's abilities.

## Preview

You are amazed when your friend, who has no previous golf experience, suddenly takes up the game and nearly beats you. Her proficiency is about as good as yours, and you have been practicing golf seriously for several years. Your friend continues to improve, while you seem stuck at your present skill level. She is clearly different from you in terms of the capability for playing golf, and she will eventually be much better. Why? What are the underlying differences between the two of you? Does this mean your friend will be better than you in other activities as well?

## Overview

Everyone knows that people differ in many ways. In some cases these differences are due to things individuals have little control over, such as gender, age, race, and cultural background. Occasionally these factors influence people's motor performance and learning. In this chapter we examine some of the characteristics individuals bring with them to a performance situation that can influence their levels of goal achievement. First, we discuss the concept of individual differences, focusing more specifically on the notion of abilities, which are largely inherited capabilities that underlie people's performance. Next we describe several theoretical notions about the fundamental nature of people's abilities and discuss the relative merits of each. Then we suggest several things practitioners should remember about people's abilities and discuss ways practitioners might utilize the notion of abilities to classify skills and perform task analyses. Last we discuss the difficulties inherent in predicting the future success of individuals based solely on estimates of their abilities.

## The Concept of Individual Differences

**capabilities**—Characteristics of individuals that are subject to change as a result of practice and that represent a person's potential to excel in the performance of a task.

It doesn't take a genius to recognize that people are different. Folks come in all sizes and shapes. They represent different ages, racial groups, genders, and cultural backgrounds. Some individuals have disabilities of a physical or mental nature. People have different temperaments, social influences, and types of life experiences. In addition to these kinds of differences, individuals possess other **capabilities** that can influence the quality of their motor performance. Some of the possible factors that contribute to differences in people's movement performance are shown in table 2.1.

When Dick Schmidt was a boy, a guy by the name of Charlie Breck used to infuriate him. Charlie could throw a baseball faster and hit it farther, dribble and shoot a

© Jean Higgins/Unicorn Stock Photos

People come in all sizes and shapes.

**Table 2.1**
**Individual Difference Factors That Can Contribute to Differences in People's Movement**

| Factor | Examples |
|---|---|
| *Abilities* | *Finger dexterity, stamina, trunk strength* |
| *Attitudes* | *Open, closed, or neutral to new experiences* |
| *Body type* | *Stocky, tall, short, lean, muscular, round* |
| *Cultural background* | *Ethnicity, race, religion, socio-economic status* |
| *Emotional makeup* | *Boredom, excitement, fear, joy* |
| *Fitness level* | *Low, moderate, high* |
| *Learning style* | *Visual, verbal, kinesthetic* |
| *Maturational level* | *Immature, intermediate, mature* |
| *Motivational level* | *Low, moderate, high* |
| *Previous social experiences* | *One-on-one, small group, large group* |
| *Prior movement experiences* | *Recreational, instructional, competitive* |

basketball better, and run faster than all the other kids his age. Charlie clearly had something the rest of his peers did not, and he used it well to become a fine team sport athlete in high school.

Dick took great pleasure in one fact: he was a much better gymnast than Charlie. While Charlie struggled, Dick was a master at performing a kip on the horizontal bar, and Dick could tumble circles around Charlie. Other kids were far better than either Dick or Charlie in activities like riflery, cross-country running, or swimming. It seemed like each person had the capability of performing certain kinds of skills but little ability to do others.

Why is it that some people perform certain activities better than other people? And why is it that a particular person performs some activities better than she or he performs others? Are people born with special capabilities or do they develop them with practice? Can an individual's capabilities be measured and evaluated? If practitioners knew something about individuals' capabilities, would it help them provide better instructional assistance in teaching, coaching, and other human performance situations?

These questions related to individuals' capabilities form the basis of a research approach within psychology and motor behavior that examines differences in people's behavioral abilities. This type of inquiry is referred to as **individual differences** research. Contrary to an **experimental approach**, in which scientists focus on principles common to all people, a **differential approach**, such as the one used to examine the question of individual differences, focuses on factors that make people different from each other.

Individual differences are defined as stable, enduring differences among people that contribute to differences in task performance. The key words in this definition are *stable* and *enduring*. For example, if one person sinks a long golf putt and a second person misses the same putt, this doesn't necessarily mean that the first person's

**individual differences**—Differences in people's performance that are due to differences in their stable and enduring abilities.

**experimental approach**—A method used by scientists to examine variables that influence individuals' performance or behavior in a uniform way.

**differential approach**—A method used by scientists to examine differences in the abilities of individuals.

### WHAT MAKES PEOPLE SUCCESSFUL ON SOME TASKS AND NOT ON OTHERS?

Have you ever stopped to think about why people are good at different activities and what it is that makes some individuals such capable performers? It is a well-established fact that with sufficient practice of a task everyone improves his or her skill level. Beyond this, however, the very best performers seem to possess the right combination of attributes they need to achieve high levels of skill. Skilled gymnasts not only are strong and powerful, but they also seem to possess a level of coordination that allows them to perform incredible stunts. In the sport of track and field, sprinters seem to possess attributes that are different to some extent from those of distance runners and throwers. While concert pianists and ballet dancers likely possess some common abilities (e.g., rhythmic ability), they are gifted with other abilities that are unique to their respective art forms (e.g., leg power is needed for the ballet dancer but is relatively unimportant for the pianist). If all other factors are held constant (e.g., motivation, previous experience), differences in the patterns of people's abilities often determine which individuals become the more accomplished performers.

putting abilities are superior to the second's. However, if the first person consistently outperforms the second under a variety of circumstances, we can say more confidently that there are individual differences in the two people's abilities.

Research on individual differences is concerned with two things. First, there is the matter of identifying the underlying *abilities* that contribute to differences in people's skilled performance. Scientists who conduct this type of research attempt to measure and describe as many different abilities as possible. Second, there is the challenge of estimating or predicting a person's future (or potential) skill level at a particular sport, occupation, or everyday task based on his or her abilities.

## Abilities and Capabilities

Scientists who study individual differences in human performance generally use the notion of **abilities**, defined as inherited, relatively enduring, stable traits of the individual that underlie or support various kinds of activities or skills. Abilities, for the most part, are thought to be genetically determined and essentially unmodified by practice or experience. They represent the "hardware" that individuals bring with them to performance or learning situations.

**abilities**—Stable, enduring traits that, for the most part, are genetically determined and that underlie individuals' skilled performance.

There appear to be many kinds of abilities spread throughout the human perceptual-motor system. They range from visual acuity and color vision to body configuration (height and build), numerical ability, reaction speed, manual dexterity, kinesthetic sensitivity, and so on. Some abilities support the acts of perception and decision making, others underlie the organizing and planning of movements, and still others contribute to the actual production of the movement and to the evaluation of feedback.

Scientists have identified some 20 to 30 cognitive and motor abilities so far, and they anticipate discovering more in the future. They assume that all individuals possess all of the abilities but that people differ with respect to the strength of various abilities. For example, one individual might have very poor kinesthetic sensitivity but very good visual acuity, whereas another person might have a low level of eye-hand coordination but a high level of static balance.

Researchers investigating individual differences assume that a particular subset of abilities is important for the performance of each type of task. For example, threading a needle probably requires a high level of near visual acuity and arm-hand steadiness, but not much lower-body strength. Power lifting, on the other hand, requires little or no near visual acuity or arm-hand steadiness, but requires a great deal of lower-body strength.

An important practical implication of this relationship between abilities and performance is that, if a person possesses high levels of the abilities important to the performance of a particular task, that individual should be able to perform the task at a higher level than another person who possesses lower levels of the important abilities. This is probably part of the reason that Charlie Breck was better at hitting a baseball than Dick Schmidt, while Dick was better at tumbling than Charlie. Because a person has an effective pattern of abilities for performing one type of task, however, does not mean that the individual will possess an effective pattern for performing another task, unless the two tasks require essentially the same subset of underlying abilities.

## Abilities Versus Skills

**skill**—The capability of producing a performance result with maximum certainty, minimum energy, or minimum time; developed as a result of practice.

How often have you heard people in everyday conversation use the terms *abilities* and *skills* almost interchangeably? For example, they might say, "That woman has a lot of basketball ability" when they see the person demonstrating a high level of **skill**. It is useful, however, to distinguish between the concepts of abilities and skills. The scientist would probably say that the person has a lot of *skill* in playing

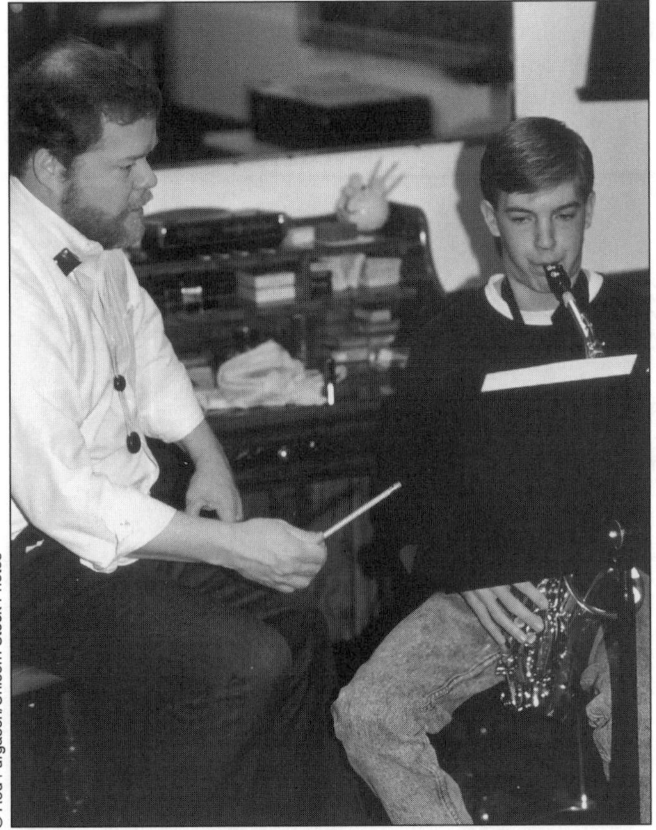



The abilities that a musician needs are, in large measure, specific to the instrument played.

Skills are capabilities that are chiefly developed as a result of practice.

basketball. In contrast to most people's more casual view, movement scientists differentiate the two concepts: they consider abilities to be, for the most part, genetically determined and largely unmodified by practice or experience, whereas they think of skills as capabilities that are chiefly developed as a result of practice.

As we mentioned earlier, abilities can be considered the basic "equipment" people are born with. Other analogies for abilities might be the hardware in a computer or the cards a person is dealt in a game of bridge. The more sophisticated the computer hardware, or the better the hand of cards, the greater the *potential* for performance success. However, the most sophisticated computer in the world is useless without software programs that are capable of maximizing its performance. Similarly, holding great cards does not guarantee success, unless the individual knows how to play them. Skills, then, reflect a person's proficiency in performing a particular task, such as playing a bridge hand or playing the quarterback position in American football.

People who possess high levels of the subset of abilities important for a particular task *and* who spend many hours practicing the task usually achieve the highest performance levels. For example, Peyton Manning, former all-American quarterback at the University of Tennessee, appears to have excellent visual-perceptual abilities, but he has also spent many hours watching game films in order to identify the patterns of his opponents' movements. Similarly, Manning seems to have a good deal of arm strength, but he has also devoted a considerable amount of practice time to improving his passing skills. The pattern recognition capabilities and passing skills that Manning has developed and that contribute to his outstanding performance as a quarterback are likely the result of both the pattern of his inherited abilities and the countless hours he has devoted to practicing the necessary tasks.

In summary, then, the level of skill that individuals can ultimately achieve depends on the abilities they bring with them to the task situation and on the quantity and quality of their practice experiences. For a review of some of the important differences between the concepts of abilities and skills, see table 2.2.

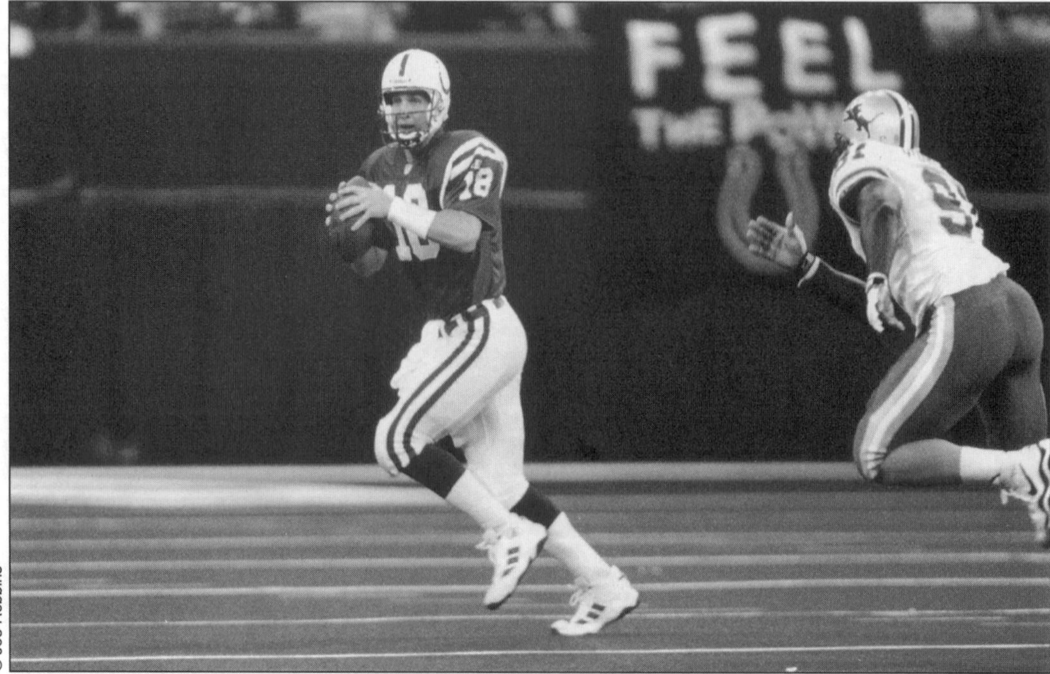




Quarterback Peyton Manning's pattern recognition and passing skills result from inherited abilities and countless hours of practice.

**Table 2.2**
**Some Important Distinctions Between Abilities and Skills**

| Abilities | Skills |
|---|---|
| *Inherited traits* | *Developed with practice* |
| *Stable and enduring* | *Modified with practice* |
| *Few in number* | *Many in number* |
| *Underlie the performance of many different skills* | *Depend on different subsets of abilities* |

## Abilities as Limiting Factors for Performance

Practitioners need to remember that people's abilities influence the level of skill they are able to achieve. Craig Wrisberg will never become a skilled gymnast, regardless of how much time he devotes to practice, because he does not have the proper body configuration or perceptual-motor abilities that contribute to task performance—not to mention the fact that he's too old. Similarly, individuals who are color-blind will never be very proficient in identifying wildflowers, people without digital dexterity will not feel comfortable playing the guitar, nor will someone without good balance abilities be a very effective tightrope walker or balance beam performer.

While it is true that the level of a person's abilities limits her or his ultimate level of performance proficiency, it is a mistake for practitioners to make final judgments about a person's potential for skill achievement on the basis of observing the individual's performance during the early stages of practice. As you will read later in this chapter, several factors that contribute to improvements in performance, including the subset of important underlying abilities, can change as people practice. Sometimes people who are less impressive during early practice sessions later become the more skilled performers.

## How Should Practitioners Conceptualize the Notion of Abilities?

Since people's abilities appear to have the potential to influence performance and skill achievement, it is important for practitioners to have a general conception of the nature of these abilities. Historically, several theoretical views of abilities have been proposed. In the next few sections we briefly discuss each of these.

A frequent challenge for movement practitioners is finding ways to assist individuals who must compensate for deficiencies in their abilities when they are learning or relearning a skill. What factors might practitioners consider in order to assist each of the individuals described in the following scenarios: (a) a 10-year-old female who consistently misses a tennis ball when it is hit to her, (b) a 60-year-old male with paralysis of his preferred hand due to stroke who is trying to relearn the task of opening a bottle of wine, and (c) a 42-year-old female with a loss of vision in one eye who is trying to learn to crochet.

## Correlation: The Language of Individual Differences

An important statistical concept for understanding the nature of abilities is the *correlation,* which is a way of measuring the strength of a relationship between people's performance scores on two tasks. To illustrate this concept, let's assume that we obtain performance scores for a large group of individuals (usually 100 or more in number) on two different tasks (task X and task Y). We want to determine the extent to which the level of performance on one task is similar to that on the other task as well as the type of relationship that exists between the people's performance on the two tasks.

In figures 2.1a and 2.1b, we present special graphs called scatterplots, which show the task-X performance of our hypothetical group on one axis and their task-Y performance on the other. Each person's score on the two tasks is represented as a single dot on the graphs. If the dots tend to lie along a line (referred to as the line of best fit), then we can say that the task-X and task-Y performances of the individuals in this group are closely related. In figure 2.1a, this relationship is positive. In other words, those individuals with higher scores on task X tend to be the same individuals with higher scores on task Y. The scatterplot in figure 2.1b shows a negative relationship: people with higher scores on task X are the ones with lower scores on task Y.

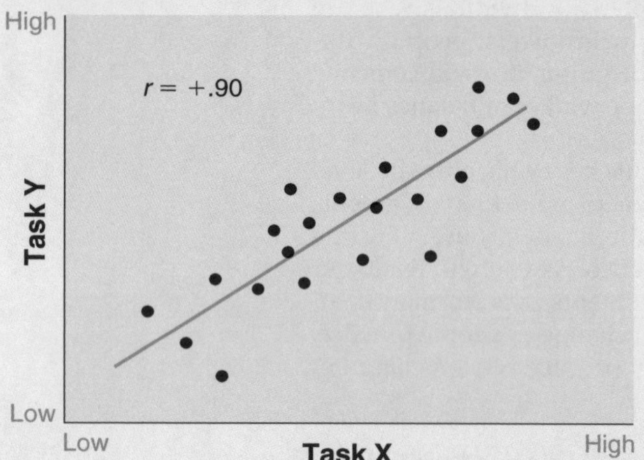


**Figure 2.1a Showing a strong, positive relationship.**

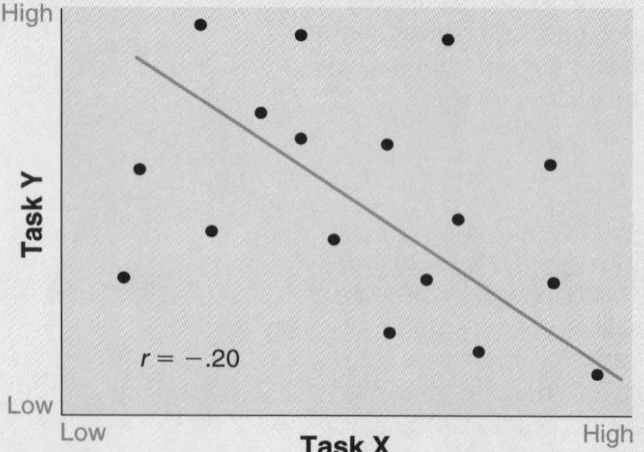


**Figure 2.1b Showing a weak, negative relationship.**

The statistic that is used to measure these relationships is the Pearson product-moment correlation coefficient (abbreviated *r*), which can range in value from −1.0 to +1.0, with a + or − sign signifying a positive or negative correlation, respectively. It's important to remember that the size and the sign of the correlation coefficient represent different aspects of the relationship. The size of the correlation coefficient indicates the strength of the relationship between people's performance on the two tasks; that is, how close the individual dots are to the best-fitting line passing through them. The algebraic sign (+ or −) of the correlation coefficient indicates the direction of the relationship between people's performance on the two tasks; that is, if a high value for one task is associated with a high value for the second task, then the relationship is positive, and if a high value for one task is associated with a low value for the second task, then the relationship is negative. If the dots are close to the line, as in figure 2.1a, then the correlation coefficient is close to a value of 1.0 (in this case, $r = +.90$, indicating a strong, positive relationship). If the dots lie relatively far from the line, as in figure 2.1b, then the correlation is closer to zero (in this case, $r = -.20$, indicating a relatively weak, negative relationship). A correlation of near zero would produce a graph with the dots scattered about it in a random way, in more or less of a shotgun pattern. The line of best fit would have no slope, and we could conclude that performance on task X is not meaningfully related to performance on task Y.

The extent to which the two tasks share common elements is indicated by the squared correlation coefficient. For example, if we square the correlation of −.20, we can conclude that the two tasks have $-.20^2 = .04$, or 4%, of their elements in common (i.e., in this case, virtually nothing). If there is a strong correlation between people's performance on two tasks (e.g., $r = \pm .80$ or more), the squared correlation tells us that the tasks have a greater percentage of common underlying features. Scientists who study perceptual-motor skills assume that these features are the abilities that underlie performance on the two tasks in question. The stronger the correlation, the more abilities shared by the two tasks. The weaker the correlation, the fewer the shared abilities; that is, the abilities underlying performance on one task are different and separate from those underlying performance on the other.

### *A Singular Global Ability*

One of the earliest views about human abilities was that "they" (i.e., abilities) were actually an "it" (i.e., ability). Proponents of this notion believed that a singular, global ability was the basis for all skill performance (Brace, 1927; McCloy, 1934). Perhaps not surprisingly, the concept of a **general motor ability** was popularized around the same time that theorists in the field of cognitive or intellectual functioning were proposing the existence of a general mental ability, known as intelligence and measured by the intelligence quotient, or IQ.

**general motor ability**—An early, and incorrect, view that a single global ability was the basis for all motor behavior.

At first glance, the concept of general motor ability appears to be a reasonable one. It is certainly consistent with people's observation that some individuals—think of Charlie Breck, mentioned earlier—seem to be successful at performing most of the popular sport tasks, whereas other people are unsuccessful at performing any of these activities. Doesn't it make sense to conclude that the all-around athlete must have a very high level of general motor ability, while individuals who can't do anything very well have little or none?

If the idea of a singular general motor ability is valid, then we should always expect a high correlation between people's performances on any two motor tasks (see the highlight box for more details). In other words, individuals who possess high levels of general motor ability should always produce high levels of performance on any two tasks, whereas a person who possesses moderate or low levels of general motor ability should always produce moderate or low levels of performance, respectively.

The fact is that the available research suggests little support for the general motor ability notion. An excellent example of this research is a study by Drowatzky and Zuccato (1967). In this study, people's performance on six different balance tasks was examined. The correlations between their performance on each pair of tasks are presented in table 2.3. Notice that all of the correlations are quite low, with the highest being for the bass stand and the sideward stand ($r = .31$).

What makes these results particularly damaging for the general motor ability notion is that the tasks Drowatzky and Zuccato examined in their study involved

## THE MYTH OF MOTOR INTELLIGENCE

During the 1920s, theorists in motor behavior proposed a concept similar to that of mental intelligence that presumably reflected the general capability of individuals to *learn* new movement skills (Brace, 1927). This concept, labeled motor educability, received little support in subsequent motor learning studies and gradually faded from view in the professional literature. Interestingly, the validity of the concept of *mental* intelligence is now being questioned by people who argue that IQ tests do not predict an individual's capacity to learn.

**Table 2.3**
**Correlations Among Six Tests of Static and Dynamic Balance**

| | Stork stand | Diver's stand | Stick stand | Sideward stand | Bass stand | Balance stand |
|---|---|---|---|---|---|---|
| *Stork stand* | — | *.14* | *–.12* | *.26* | *.20* | *.03* |
| *Diver's stand* | | — | *–.12* | *–.03* | *–.07* | *–.14* |
| *Stick stand* | | | — | *–.04* | *.22* | *–.19* |
| *Sideward stand* | | | | — | *.31* | *.19* |
| *Bass stand* | | | | | — | *.18* |
| *Balance stand* | | | | | | — |

Adapted by permission from Drowatzky & Zuccato, 1967.

various types of balancing activities, encompassing a relatively narrow range of human motor performance. The correlations they obtained suggest that there isn't even a general ability for balancing. Rather, it appears that different balance tasks require a separate ability for controlling posture. In summary, then, these and the findings of other studies (e.g., Fleishman & Parker, 1962; Lotter, 1960) offer no support for the notion that movement abilities are packaged in a singular, general motor ability.

How similar do two tasks have to be for practitioners to assume that the tasks require the same subset of abilities? Rank in order each of the following pairs of tasks according to the extent to which you think each pair shares similar underlying abilities. (The pair you rank #1 is the pair you think requires the greatest number of similar abilities, the pair you rank #2 is the pair you think requires a slightly lower number of similar abilities, and so on.)

Rank

____ The overhead smash in badminton and tennis
____ The breaststroke and the backstroke in swimming
____ The fastball and the slider in baseball pitching
____ Playing the violin and playing the saxophone
____ Splitting wood with an axe and hanging Sheetrock plasterboard
____ Driving a car and flying a plane
____ The back handspring and the iron cross in gymnastics
____ The serve and the volley in tennis
____ Putting and driving a golf ball
____ The spike and the jump serve in volleyball

For the pair you ranked #1 and the pair you ranked #10, indicate the underlying abilities you think the two tasks share in common and the underlying abilities you think they do not share.

© Tom Roberts

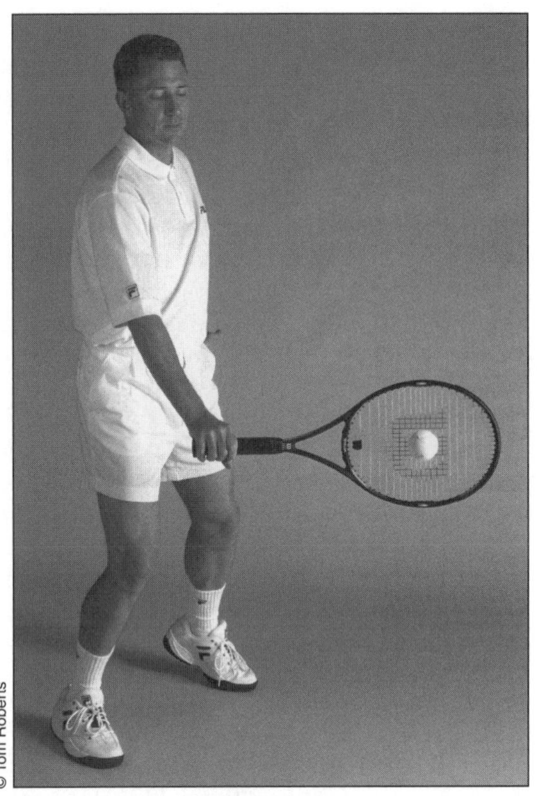
© Tom Roberts

How are the abilities required for the serve and the volley in tennis similar and different?

CLEO

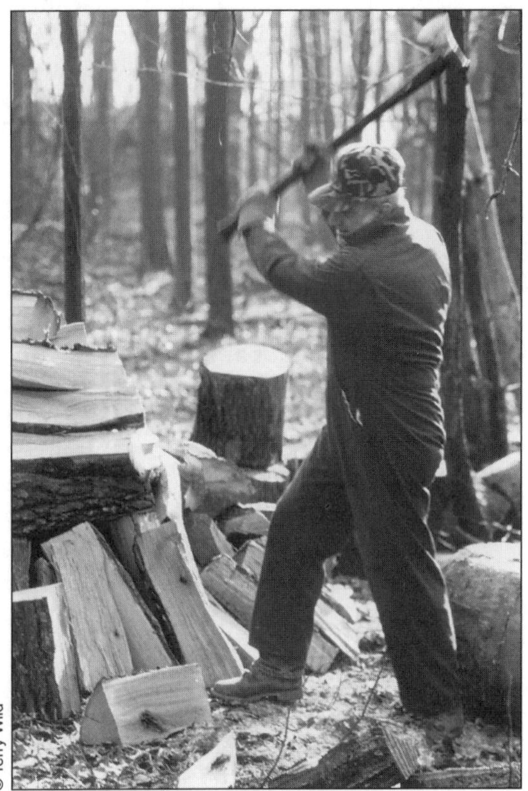
© Terry Wild

How are the abilities required for hanging Sheetrock plasterboard and chopping wood similar and different?

### Many Specific Abilities

The most vocal opponent of the general motor ability notion was the late Franklin Henry (see the highlight box on page 4). Henry proposed that movement behaviors are based not on a singular global ability but on a very large number of specific abilities, perhaps thousands (Henry, 1958/1968; 1961). These abilities are independent of each other. Henry contended that an individual's performance on any given task, such as fly fishing, is based on hundreds of different abilities, some of them strong, some of them weak.

According to Henry's **specificity hypothesis**, a champion tennis player is an individual who has inherited high levels of the particular abilities relevant for playing tennis. However, there is no guarantee this person would also be a strong springboard diver, since the particular abilities underlying springboard diving are entirely different from those underlying tennis performance. The best guess is that the individual would be an average springboard diver, with no special advantage. According to Henry's view of specificity, there should be no correlation between people's performance on any two tasks since the tasks have no shared abilities. Clearly, the correlations obtained in the studies we mentioned in the previous section (see table 2.3) are much more supportive of Henry's specificity view (e.g., Drowatzky & Zuccato, 1967; Fleishman & Parker, 1962) than they are of the general motor ability notion.

**specificity hypothesis**—A view proposed by Franklin Henry that a large number of specific, independent, and different motor abilities are the basis for every type of motor performance.

### Groupings of Abilities

As we indicated previously, Henry's specificity hypothesis predicts that there should be no correlation (i.e., $r = 0$) between people's performance on two different skills. However, most of the available evidence shows that the correlations, while sometimes quite low, are usually greater than zero. Such findings suggest that there are *some* common abilities that underlie the performance of different tasks. If this is true, what might these abilities be like?

One possible answer to this question surfaced during the 1950s and 1960s in a series of studies by Edwin Fleishman and his colleagues that were conducted on young American military personnel (Fleishman, 1964, 1965; Fleishman & Bartlett, 1969). Fleishman used a statistical technique called *factor analysis* to identify some of the groupings of abilities that underlie people's performance on different motor tasks.

Fleishman's conception of abilities, like Henry's view, is that abilities are independent of each other. The major differences between Fleishman's and Henry's notions include the total number of presumed abilities, the number of abilities that are involved in the performance of tasks, and the extent to which the same abilities are important to the performance of different tasks. In Fleishman's view, the total number of abilities and the number of abilities that are involved in the performance of tasks are considerably smaller than that postulated by Henry. In addition, Fleishman contends that two separate tasks may require *some* of the same underlying abilities for successful performance, particularly when the requirements of the two tasks are similar. This is because the abilities proposed by Fleishman are more general in nature than those proposed by Henry.

Fleishman (1964) groups abilities into two larger categories, labeled "perceptual-motor abilities" and "physical proficiency abilities." These groupings, along with examples of the kinds of skills for which each might be useful, are presented in table 2.4. While this list of abilities is useful, we need to interpret it with some caution because it is based solely on the performance of younger, male participants in tasks that require the manipulation of various types of apparatus while in a sitting position. Therefore, it is presently unclear as to whether the same abilities would surface if other types of participants or tasks were examined.

More recent research by Keele and his colleagues (Keele & Hawkins, 1982; Keele, Ivry, & Pokorny, 1987; Keele, Pokorny, Corcos, & Ivry, 1985) has revealed several

**Table 2.4**

## Groupings of Abilities Proposed by Fleishman (1964)

**Perceptual-motor abilities**

*Multilimb coordination*—The ability to coordinate the movement of a number of limbs simultaneously. This ability is probably important when serving a tennis ball or playing the drums.

*Control precision*—Requires highly controlled movement adjustments, particularly where larger muscle groups are involved. An example is the task of a person who must operate a bulldozer or other types of earthmoving equipment, requiring careful positioning of the arms and feet.

*Response orientation*—Involves quick choices among numerous alternative movements, more or less as in choice reaction time. An example is the task of a goalie in hockey, where the type of shot on goal is often uncertain.

*Reaction time*—Important in tasks where there is a single stimulus and a single response, where speed of reaction is critical, as in simple reaction time. An example is the sprint start in a 100-m dash.

*Rate control*—Involves the production of continuous anticipatory movement adjustments in response to changes in the speed of a continuously moving target or object. Examples include the tasks of high speed auto racing and white-water canoeing.

*Manual dexterity*—Underlies tasks in which relatively large objects are manipulated with the hands and arms. An example is dribbling a basketball.

*Finger dexterity*—Involves tasks requiring the manipulation of small objects. Examples include threading a needle and eating spaghetti with a fork and spoon.

*Arm-hand steadiness*—The ability to make precise arm and hand positioning movements where strength and speed are not required. A waiter who carries trays of food and dispenses the contents without incident exemplifies this ability.

*Wrist-finger speed*—Involves rapid movement of the wrist and fingers with little or no accuracy demands. An example is playing the bongo drums.

*Aiming*—A highly restricted type of ability that requires the production of accurate hand movements to targets under speeded conditions. An example is the task of hitting a target with a rapid throw of a dart.

**Physical proficiency abilities**

*Explosive strength*—The ability to expend a maximum of energy in one explosive act. Advantageous in activities requiring a person to project themself or some object as high or far as possible. Also important for mobilizing force against the ground. Examples of tasks requiring explosive strength include the shot put, javelin, long jump, high jump, and 100-m run in the sport of track and field.

*Static strength*—Involves the exertion of force against a relatively heavy weight or some fairly immovable object. Tasks requiring static strength include near maximum leg and arm presses in weight lifting, as well as moving a piano.

*Dynamic strength*—The ability to repeatedly or continuously move or support the weight of the body. Examples include climbing a rope and performing on the still rings in gymnastics.

*Trunk strength*—Dynamic strength that is particular to the trunk and abdominal muscles. Tasks requiring trunk strength include leg lifts and performing on the pommel horse in gymnastics.

*Extent flexibility*—The ability to extend or stretch the body as far as possible in various directions. An example of a task requiring extent flexibility is yoga.

*Dynamic flexibility*—Involves repeated, rapid movements requiring muscle flexibility. Ballet dancers and gymnasts need high levels of dynamic flexibility.

*Gross body equilibrium*—The ability to maintain total body balance in the absence of vision. Circus performers who attempt to walk across a tightrope while blindfolded require this ability.

*(continued)*

**Table 2.4** *(continued)*

**Physical proficiency abilities** *(continued)*

*Balance with visual cues*—The ability to maintain total body balance when visual cues are available. This ability is important for gymnasts who perform on the balance beam.

*Speed of limb movement*—Underlies tasks in which the arm(s) or leg(s) must be moved quickly, but without a reaction-time stimulus, to minimize movement time. Examples include throwing a fast pitch in baseball or cricket or rapidly moving the legs when tap dancing or clogging.

*Gross body coordination*—The ability to perform a number of complex movements simultaneously. Individuals needing this ability include ice hockey players who must skate and stickhandle at the same time or circus performers who try to juggle duckpins while riding a unicycle across a tightrope.

*Stamina*—The ability to exert the entire body for a prolonged period of time; a kind of cardiovascular endurance. Individuals requiring stamina include distance runners and cyclists.

Reprinted by permission from Fleishman, 1964.

**Table 2.5**

**General Coordination Factors Identified by Keele and His Colleagues**

*Movement rate*—Similar to Fleishman's speed of limb movement, this ability applies more to situations in which a series of movements must be made at a maximum speed. Examples include typing or keyboarding.

*Motor timing*—Important for the performance of tasks in which accurately timed movements are essential. Examples include most open sport skills as well as driving an automobile in traffic, stepping on a moving escalator, and playing drums in a band.

*Perceptual timing*—Underlies tasks in which accurate judgments about the time course of perceptual events is required. Examples include judgments of the timing of a musical score by a ballet dancer or a vocalist, the timing of a partner's movements in pairs dancing or of a horse's movements in equestrian competition, or judging the speed of a moving object such as a ball in tennis, cricket, or soccer.

*Force control*—Important for tasks in which forces of varying degrees are needed to achieve the desired outcome. Examples include changes in mood or emphasis when playing musical instruments such as the piano or violin and performing sport tasks such as billiards, figure skating, and floor exercise in gymnastics.

additional abilities beyond those that Fleishman suggested (see table 2.5). These abilities include a variety of general coordination factors such as movement rate (measured by repetitive tapping), motor timing (measured by timed tapping), perceptual timing (measured by a person's ability to judge the duration of time intervals between events), and force control (measured by button presses of various magnitudes with the finger and forearm).

An important outcome of Keele's work has been the discovery of consistent levels of task performance *within* individuals (i.e., similar levels of timing performance by the same person when using the finger, thumb, wrist, forearm, and foot) but considerable differences in performance *between* individuals. These results suggest that there may be a general "timekeeping" ability that underlies the performance of a variety of timing tasks. And this notion has support from laboratory studies that show more consistent timing performance among professional pianists than among nonpianists

## A GENERAL TIMING ABILITY MAY NOT EXIST FOR ALL TIMING TASKS

Researchers Robertson et al. (in press) have recently found that timing processes may not be shared across a wide variety of motor tasks; rather, timing ability may be specific to the task in question. In several experiments, these researchers found low correlations between individuals' performance on tapping and drawing tasks. They proposed that different types of timing processes exist for different types of tasks. For example, tapping tasks that require a general timekeeping ability (because performers must be able to estimate time intervals) rely on a timing process that differs from the one people need for the timing of movement production processes (e.g., drawing tasks). These researchers point out that the results of experiments supporting the notion of a general timing ability are based on individuals' performance of *one* of these types of tasks (Franz, Zelaznik, & Smith, 1992; Ivry & Hazeltine, 1995; Keele & Ivry, 1987)—but not both. Taken together, the results of these studies argue against *both* a strict version of the specificity hypothesis of motor abilities (Henry, 1968) and a strong model of a central common timing process for movement production (Ivry & Hazeltine, 1995).

(Keele et al., 1985) and among nonhandicapped children compared with children classified as motorically "clumsy" (Williams, Woollacott, & Ivry, 1992). How general this time keeping ability might be remains to be determined however (see the box at the top of this page).

### *How Many Ability Groupings Might There Be?*

It is important to note that neither Fleishman nor Keele has examined the performance of whole-body coordinated movements, such as those found in many real-world activities. Until such movements are studied systematically, we can only guess how long the final list of ability groupings might be.

## What Should Practitioners Remember About People's Abilities?

What we know of the nature of motor abilities suggests several possible applications. First, practitioners should expect individuals to bring different patterns of abilities with them to a performance or learning situation. Second, practitioners should realize that the pattern of any individual's abilities will facilitate that person's performance on some tasks more than it does on others. Finally, practitioners should remember that the pattern of each person's abilities is only one of the factors that contributes to the individual's overall performance. In the following paragraphs, we discuss each of these applications in more detail.

## IT DEPENDS . . .

Have you ever thought about what some of your own dominant abilities might be? List three movement activities for which you feel particularly skilled. What abilities do you think you possess that allow you to perform these skills so well? Feel free to borrow from the lists offered by Fleishman (table 2.4) or by Keele and his colleagues (table 2.5). Are any of these abilities important to the performance of more than one of the tasks you have listed? If so, which abilities are they?

### *Expect Individuals to Bring Different Patterns of Abilities With Them to Performance or Learning Situations*

Practitioners should expect to see differences in the patterns of people's abilities and should attempt to determine the basis of those patterns before providing instructional assistance. For example, a tennis instructor who is assisting two individuals may notice that one makes more consistent contact with the ball and the other covers the court better. Based on these observations, the instructor tries to determine the patterns of abilities that allow each of these individuals to perform the way he or she does.

For the first person, the pattern might include speed of limb movement, reaction time, perceptual timing, motor timing, and force control. All of the abilities in this pattern are separate and independent, and various combinations probably contribute more or less to his racket control in different situations. For example, reaction time and speed of limb movement are more important in situations where the approaching ball is traveling at a high rate of speed, whereas perceptual and motor timing are more important when the person has to respond to balls approaching at different speeds.

For the second person, the pattern of abilities might include reaction time, response orientation, speed of limb movement, and explosive strength. Subjectively, each of these abilities involves rapid actions. However, each also represents a different way of producing fast movements. In order to determine which of these abilities might be underlying this person's rapid court coverage, the instructor must be able to identify the particular circumstances in which the individual demonstrates this behavior. If she exemplifies the behavior more when she is running after a shot than when she is responding to a ball hit directly at her, the instructor might conclude that the individual's court coverage is due more to speed of limb movement and explosive strength than to reaction time and response orientation.

## DIFFERENT PERCEPTUAL ABILITIES MAY UNDERLIE THE PERFORMANCE OF SIMILAR-APPEARING MOTOR TASKS

Research by Beals et al. (1971) suggests that the relationship between selected perceptual abilities and motor performance may be quite task specific. First, these researchers obtained the field goal and free throw shooting percentages of college basketball players, using game statistics for a single season. Then they tested each of the players to determine levels of the following visual abilities: static visual acuity (the perception of fixed visual objects), dynamic visual acuity (the perception of moving visual objects), size constancy (the perception of objects of different sizes), and depth perception. Subsequent correlational analysis revealed that dynamic visual acuity was the only ability that contributed significantly to field goal shooting performance and that static visual acuity was the only ability that was significantly associated with free throw shooting accuracy. Interestingly, some studies in ecological psychology (Gibson, 1966, 1979) have also shown that optical-flow patterns are different depending on whether a performer or the environment is dynamic and moving (as in most field goal shots) or whether the performer or environment is static and stationary (as in the free throw shot). The results also suggest that, even within a single sensory modality (i.e., vision), different perceptual abilities may be required for the performance of similar-appearing motor tasks.

## HOW CAN MOVEMENT PRACTITIONERS HELP PARENTS?

Practitioners who understand the nature of motor abilities can assist parents in three important ways. First, they can encourage parents to provide their children with a broad range of movement experiences early in life. This allows children to discover those activities that are best suited to their abilities. Second, practitioners can instruct parents to observe how well their child performs different activities. In this way parents may be able to identify the child's dominant pattern of underlying abilities and encourage the child in the direction of activities for which he or she might experience the greatest success and enjoyment. Third, practitioners can caution parents that many factors (e.g., body size, achievement motivation, motor abilities) can influence the performance of people at different times and levels of maturation. Therefore, parents should not be surprised if their child performs some activities better at a younger age than at an older age and vice versa. Parents should remain flexible and allow their child to pursue those activities the child enjoys performing the most—at any age.

### *Realize That an Individual's Pattern of Abilities Will Facilitate That Person's Performance More on Some Tasks Than on Others*

If a practitioner can estimate the patterns of an individual's abilities, he or she might consider which activities the person's abilities are more suitable for—and which they are not. After doing this, the practitioner can tailor assistance more appropriately to the individual's needs. This usually means creating practice experiences that challenge individuals to work on those aspects of performance for which their abilities are not as suitable.

Most people know which activities better fit their abilities. They come to these conclusions as a result of experiences with a variety of tasks, some of which they perform well (and sometimes quite easily) and others with which they struggle. Because most people enjoy success rather than failure, they tend to repeat those activities for which they are most well suited or on which they demonstrate the most skill. However, individuals perform certain aspects of the various activities better than they do other aspects. In the case of the two individuals in the tennis example we mentioned on page 40, the man demonstrates better racket control, while the woman demonstrates better court coverage. To become complete players, each individual must practice those aspects of the activity for which they are less well suited. A challenge for practitioners, then, is to find creative ways to encourage learners to work on their weaknesses when they would rather repeat the things they do well.

### *Remember That Each Person's Pattern of Abilities Is Only One of the Factors That Contributes to That Individual's Overall Performance*

People's abilities are an important part of their performance, but practitioners need to remember that abilities do not constitute the only part. Other factors can influence how individuals perform, including the types and amount of their previous movement experiences, body configuration, and a variety of personal characteristics.

Beginning at an early age, some people have more opportunities to participate in movement activities than do other people. If a child's parents are particularly supportive of athletics or other forms of performance activities, the child is likely to be exposed to a wide variety of movement forms beginning at an early age. As a result, the child gets valuable movement experiences and extensive rehearsal opportunities. As the child's skill level improves, she or he is more likely to join groups of similarly skilled individuals (e.g., sport teams, dance or musical groups), resulting in opportunities for more advanced movement experiences. Children who are not exposed to movement activities at any early age will not have this wealth of experience, and they may demonstrate lesser skill, giving observers the false impression that they have lower levels of motor abilities.

Body configuration is another factor that can influence an individual's performance. Bigger, stronger children who mature at an earlier age have an advantage when it comes to the performance of a number of physical skills (e.g., throwing, jumping, striking). As a result, observers may assume that these children have a wider range of motor abilities than do kids who are smaller, weaker, or physically immature. Body configuration can also affect the preferred performance of adults in such activities as basketball, ballet, gymnastics, and springboard diving.

Another factor that can contribute to individuals' performances is personal characteristics. People differ with respect to traits like achievement motivation, competitiveness, risk taking, and vigor. Thus, some individuals may demonstrate higher levels of motor performance because they possess personal characteristics that are important for successful motoric activity.

### *Performance Success Is Due to a Combination of Factors*

It is important for movement practitioners to remember that performance differences at any given time are due only in part to differences in participants' motor abilities. A good illustration of this point may be found in a study by Deshaies, Pargman, and Thiffault (1979). These investigators attempted to determine the extent to which 14 different variables representing physiological-anthropometric, psychological, and motor skill factors were associated with the ice hockey performance of 116 Quebec Junior Major League players, ages 16 and 17 years. They found that a combination of four variables (forward skating speed, achievement motivation, visual-perceptual speed, and anaerobic power) differentiated the higher-skilled from the lower-skilled players. A closer look at these variables suggests that superior ice hockey performance is due to a *combination* of perceptual-motor abilities, motivation, and task-specific skill. Using a similar approach, Landers, Boutcher, and Wang (1986) found that the variables of relative leg strength, reaction time, depth perception, body type, imagery usage, confidence, and focus on past mistakes differentiated the shooting performance of above-average and average archers. It is probably not stretching matters to suggest that various combinations of stable and unstable factors differentiate the performance of individuals in practically every type of motor skill.

## MOOD IS SOMETIMES IMPORTANT TO PERFORMANCE

In addition to motor abilities, other factors can contribute to differences in people's performance. One of these factors is the mood of the individual. In the 1970s Dr. William Morgan of the University of Wisconsin used the "Profile of Mood States" inventory to assess the mental health of successful and unsuccessful candidates for the 1974 U.S. Olympic crew team and for the 1972 and 1976 U.S. Olympic wrestling teams. Morgan (1979) found that successful candidates (i.e., those who made the team) scored higher on vigor and lower on depression, anger, fatigue, and confusion than did their less successful counterparts. These findings indicate that mood is one factor that can differentiate the performance of sport participants.

In some skill-learning situations, practitioners must assist a number of performers simultaneously. Based on what you have learned so far about the nature of people's underlying abilities, what advice might you offer a skill instructor who has been hired to teach a group of people differing in their patterns and levels of underlying abilities? Assume that all the instructor knows is that some folks seem to have low levels of the abilities important to skilled performance, while others possess moderate or high levels.

## How Abilities Contribute to the Performance of Skills: A Toolbox Analogy

A helpful analogy practitioners can use to conceptualize the role of abilities in motor performance is that of the toolbox. When a person is born, he or she inherits a "toolbox" of abilities. Individuals use these abilities to perform the nearly infinite number of tasks they must face during the course of their lives. The different abilities in the toolbox are like different tools that a builder uses to complete various tasks (e.g., installing a sink and faucet, framing a door or window, laying brick or stone). Each ability is designed to do a particular kind of job (e.g., coordinate several limbs at the same time or respond quickly to a single stimulus), in much the same way that tools are designed to perform different functions (e.g., cutting, striking, twisting, smoothing). Any particular movement skill or task (such as jumping over a fence or playing the trumpet) requires a certain set of abilities, and people use different combinations of their abilities for different tasks.

This point is illustrated in figure 2.2. At the top of this diagram, we show some of the abilities that we previously displayed in tables 2.4 and 2.5 (space does not permit a complete depiction of all the abilities). At the bottom of the figure is a list of selected movement skills for which these abilities might be more or less relevant. For two of the skills, race car driving and playing the position of quarterback in American football, we indicate several underlying abilities that might be important for performance. Notice that race car driving requires a different pattern of underlying abilities than does quarterbacking. However, the tasks of race car driving and quarterbacking have at least one ability in common (i.e., reaction time). This figure illustrates two important points. The first

*(continued)*

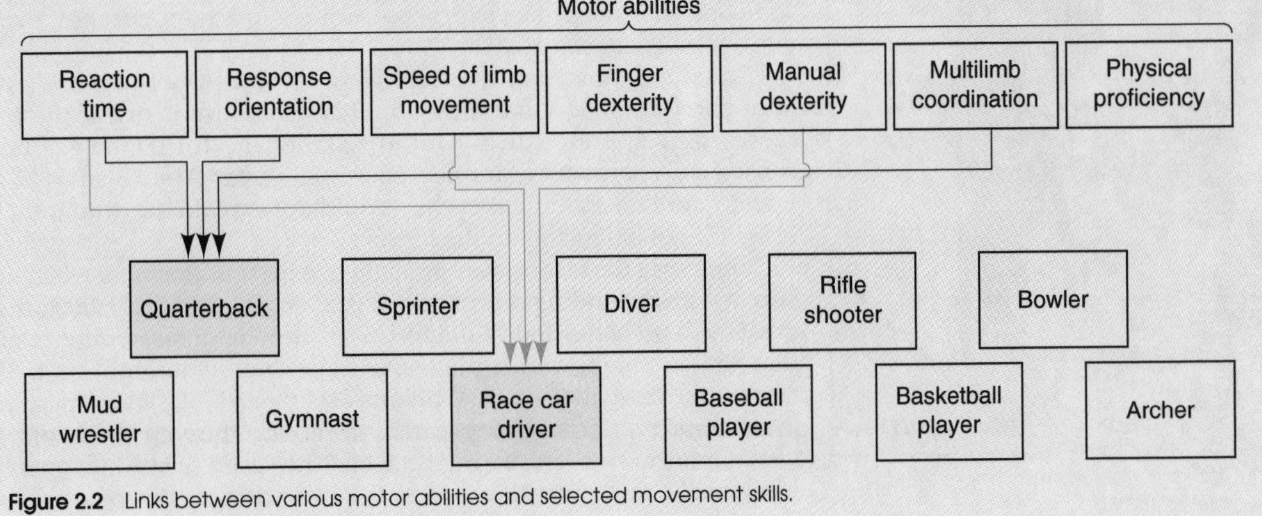


**Figure 2.2** Links between various motor abilities and selected movement skills.

(continued)

is that different skills rely on different combinations of underlying abilities. The second point is that different skills might possibly use one or more of the same abilities.

Another aspect of the toolbox analogy is that the "quality" or levels of people's abilities differ (e.g., some people inherit higher levels of movement speed than do other people), in much the same way that the quality of tools in a toolbox may vary (e.g., an industrial-grade power tool is of a higher quality than a home power tool). The pattern of people's stronger or more dominant underlying abilities predisposes them to perform certain types of tasks more effectively. Individuals who possess high levels of the abilities that are important to the performance of a particular task (e.g., playing the flute, three-ball juggling, throwing the javelin) can be expected to perform better on that task than would people who possess lower levels of the relevant abilities.

## How Might Practitioners Utilize the Notion of Abilities?

**task analysis**—A useful method for classifying motor tasks. First the various components of the task are identified and then the types of abilities that underlie task performance are estimated.

Up to this point, we have focused mainly on the concepts of individual differences and motor abilities, presenting what we believe is the most appropriate interpretation of each concept and suggesting some things to keep in mind when analyzing the possible influence of people's abilities on their motor performance. Now we look at several uses practitioners can make of these notions of abilities to assist individuals who are trying to learn or perform skills. These applications include skill classification, task analysis, and the possible prediction of future performance success.

### *Skill Classification and Task Analysis*

In chapter 1 we discussed some skill classification systems (open vs. closed skills; serial, continuous, discrete skills; etc.). Skills can also be classified by analyzing the various components or demands of the task and then considering the types of abilities that underlie task performance. By using a **task analysis** approach, practitioners can determine which movement components to emphasize during instruction. You can see an abbreviated example of this method in figure 2.2, which is discussed in more detail in the highlight box that began on page 43.

Practitioners who classify skills in this way can do so either informally or formally. On an informal level, practitioners can make an educated guess about task components and underlying abilities based on their own knowledge or experience. If they do not have a sophisticated understanding of the task, practitioners can solicit the advice of someone who does (e.g., expert performers, teachers, coaches, therapists, movement scientists).

Highly skilled performers may not know how they do what they do.

Remember, however, that highly proficient performers may not know how they do what they do. This is because many of the processes that operate during highly skilled performance are nonconscious. A pertinent example comes from research by Polanyi (1958), who found that champion cyclists could not explain the fundamental principles of balancing on the bicycle.

Sometimes the informal comments of expert performers are inconsistent with the findings of controlled research. For example, the former great baseball batter Ted Williams is well known for his frequent claim that he was able to watch the seams of the ball rotate right up to the moment of bat-ball contact (Williams & Underwood, 1988). This comment conflicts with what research has revealed about the length of visual information-processing time and the speed of eye movements. In cases like this, practitioners must exercise due caution before using the advice of experts.

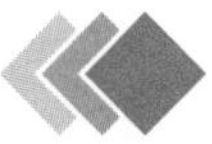

## SPORTPROFESSIOGRAMS

Sport psychologists in the former Soviet Union amassed large amounts of scientific data during the 1960s and 1970s from which they compiled lists of the most important physical characteristics and psychological traits of successful performers in different sports. For each sport, the psychologists combined the traits and qualities of the leading athletes, including psychological, physical, and emotional components. They also obtained input from coaches as to the task requirements of various sports and activities. Each task analysis of this type resulted in a profile, termed a *sportprofessiogram,* of the "ideal" superior athlete (Rodionov, 1978). The sportprofessiogram represented an estimate of the basic abilities and personal characteristics needed to achieve success in important competitions. A less formal version of this approach (referred to as a "scouting report") is used by many college and professional coaches in the United States and other countries to estimate the characteristics needed for superior performance. Instruments like these are often used to select individuals for participation in different sports and to identify deficiencies that the coach should target for specialized training.

A more formal approach to task analysis involves the use of flowcharts and other relatively inexpensive questionnaires. By using instruments such as these, practitioners can obtain the responses of expert performers in a more systematic and reliable fashion than if they simply ask these individuals, "Tell me what you think." The flowchart method has been implemented effectively in many military and industrial situations and appears to have good potential application for a variety of other performance settings.

A modified example of a flowchart developed by Fleishman and Stephenson (1970) is shown in figure 2.3. Using this chart, practitioners ask an expert to begin at "start" and then answer the "yes/no" questions in an ordered sequence. If the task in this example were pitching a baseball, an expert might respond "yes" to the first and second questions, "no" to the third question, and "yes" to the fourth question, leading the practitioner to the conclusion that the expert feels that the task of pitching primarily requires speed of arm movement, an ability that involves rapid movement of the arm in order to minimize movement time.

### *Possible Prediction of Performance Success*

You might be thinking that another way practitioners can utilize the notion of motor abilities is to predict the future performance success of individuals based on their dominant pattern of abilities. Predictions like this seem to be a part of so many aspects of our lives. Insurance companies, for example, attempt to predict the likelihood that we will have an automobile accident based on our age, sex, kind of car we drive, and our driving record. In industry, a personnel director attempts to predict which of several applicants for a job will be most successful after a year's training and experience. In sports, a coach attempts to predict which participants in a youth sport program will be the best athletes in the future. In rehabilitation

## IT DEPENDS . . .

Use the flowchart shown in figure 2.3 to determine the dominant ability for one of the following tasks: high-speed auto racing, serving a tennis ball, or neurosurgery.

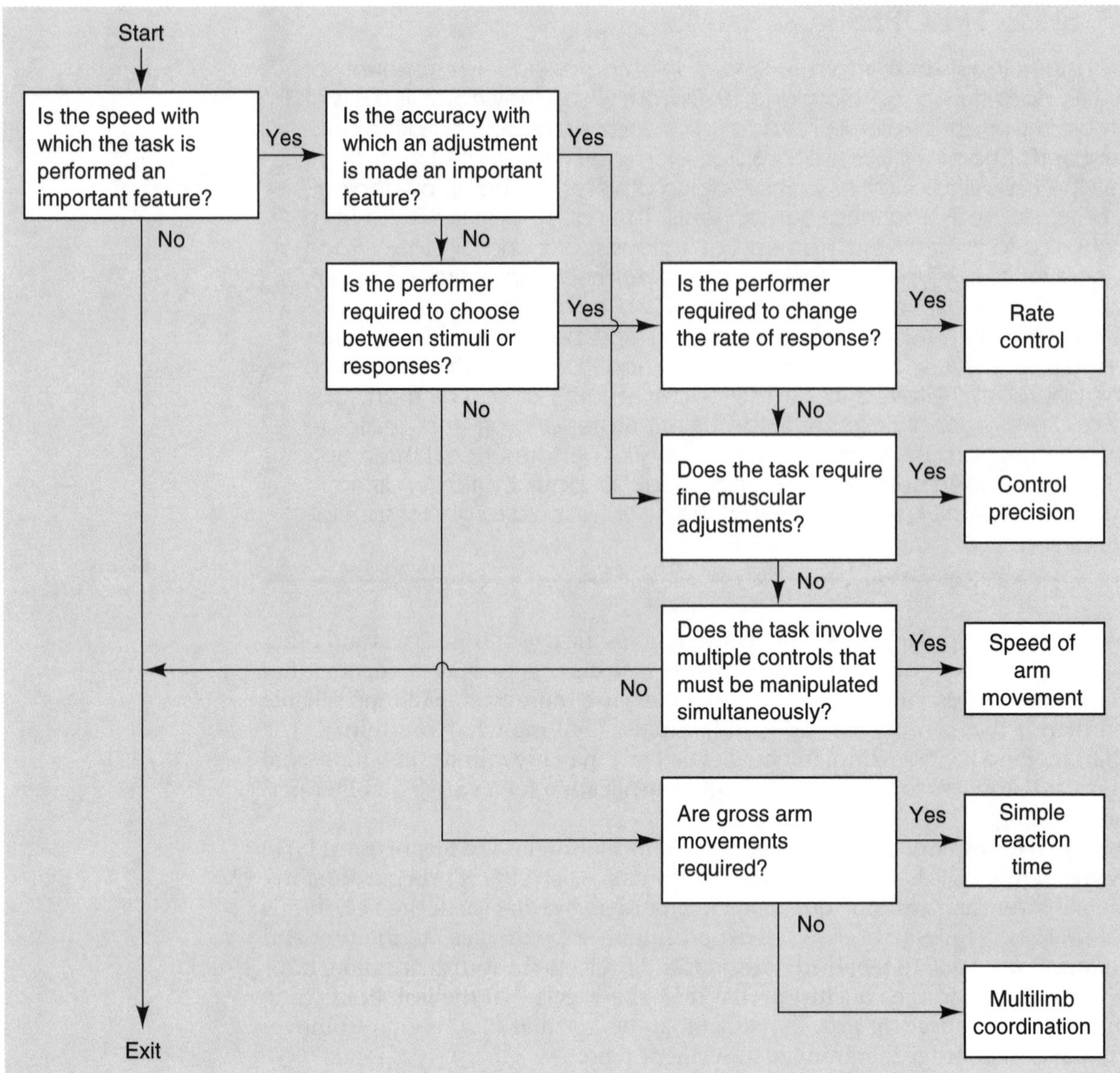


Figure 2.3 A flowchart for interviews with expert performers helps you map out a task analysis.

settings, therapists evaluate their patients in order to predict outcomes, establish goals, and estimate length of stay in therapy.

An important phenomenon that movement practitioners need to consider before attempting to predict an individual's future skill performance is the changing pattern of abilities that underlies task performance over the course of practice and experience. For beginners, considerable mental activity is involved in deciding what to do, remembering what comes after what, and figuring out the instructions, rules, strategies, and the like. With a little experience, however, individuals learn the intellectual parts of the task, and the need for effective mental activity (supported by cognitive abilities) is replaced by a greater emphasis on movement production (supported by abilities that are more "motor" in nature).

Consider an activity like soccer. Let's assume that we know which abilities underlie the performance of soccer skills for beginners and for expert performers. The hypothetical subset of abilities needed for beginning-level performance is shown

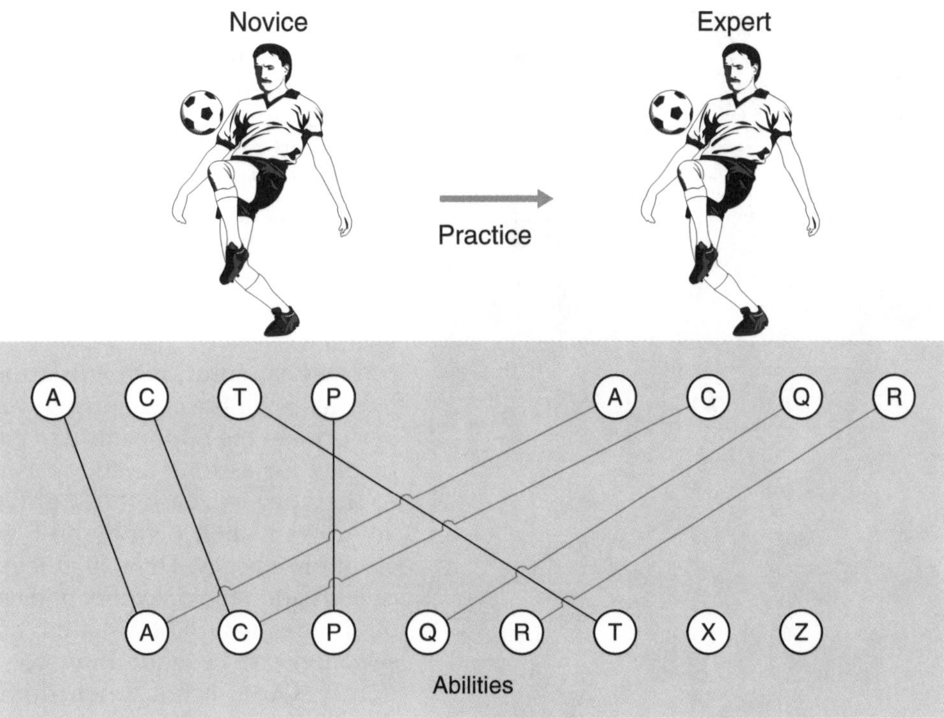


Figure 2.4 The pattern of abilities important for successful performance of a task changes over the course of practice.

just below the picture of the individual on the left side of figure 2.4. (We are labeling the abilities with the letters A, C, T, and P; in reality, they could be any of the abilities shown in tables 2.4 and 2.5). With training, however, the pattern of supporting abilities gradually changes. As shown on the right side of figure 2.4, the important abilities for expert performance are A, C, Q, and R. Notice that two of the abilities, A and C, are important for both novice and expert performers. However, two other abilities, T and P, become less important with practice and are replaced by abilities Q and R, which are not important during the early stages of practice. Perhaps abilities T and P are cognitive abilities, which drop out after a sufficient level of rehearsal experience. Still other abilities that individuals bring with them to the performance situation, X and Z, are never important to the performance of soccer skill. Remember from our earlier discussions that the abilities themselves do not change because abilities are by definition genetically defined and not modifiable by practice. It is the use or importance of these abilities that changes with practice.

Perhaps you are beginning to see the problems associated with trying to predict a person's future success based on the person's performance during the early stages of practice. Simply put, the person may have high levels of the pattern of abilities that contribute to good beginning-level performance—but there is little way of knowing whether the person possesses high levels of the necessary abilities important for later performance.

To put this problem in a real-world perspective, consider the common situation in youth sports in which a large group of youngsters is invited to try out for a particular team or activity. After a relatively brief tryout period of a few hours, the coach informs some of the youngsters that they have been selected to remain on the team. The coach thanks the others and tells them to "try again next year." In addition to the devastating effect the coach's decision might have on those who are "cut" from the activity, the coach very likely has made the mistake of releasing some people

Deneve Feigh Bunde/Unicorn Stock Photos

The early practice stage is not adequate as the basis for judging a person's potential.

who would eventually become the better performers. Referring to figure 2.4 again, assume that the people who are successful during the tryout are the ones with high levels of abilities A, C, T, and P. After extensive practice, these individuals may not be the more proficient performers unless they also possess high levels of abilities Q and R.

The best solution in situations like this is for the coach to allow all performers the opportunity to participate for as long as they desire, so that they can each move gradually toward their own highest levels of proficiency. Then, high levels of skill and stable, expert patterns of abilities may be evaluated, and selections can be made more confidently. Quite often when this is done, the less skilled participants eventually "deselect" themselves anyway, at a much lower risk to their self-esteem, because *they* realize that their abilities are not appropriate for proficient performance of the activity.

There are several reasons why predicting future success is so difficult. First, the patterns of abilities underlying the successful performance of tasks are generally not very well understood. Coaches, trainers, and instructors usually have some ideas about innate characteristics that are important to task performance, such as a person's need to be strong and flexible

## PREDICTING FUTURE PERFORMANCE SUCCESS IS A DIFFICULT TASK

In 1974 Schmidt and Pew attempted to design a test battery for predicting whether a person had the abilities to be a successful dental technician—an individual who makes appliances for the mouth (e.g., crowns, bridges, artificial teeth, etc.). The final battery was comprised of four tests that estimated about 25% of the abilities important for successful performance. While somewhat higher levels of estimation have been reported for test batteries that predict the performance of airplane pilots (Fleishman, 1956) and American football players (McDavid, 1977), no predictive tests have been able to account for all of the necessary abilities. Thus, it appears that predicting future performance on the basis of people's abilities alone is, at best, an imperfect science.

in gymnastics. Beyond this, predicting abilities is like a guessing game. In addition, it is difficult for practitioners to determine how many abilities are important to task performance and which ones are more important for various skill levels. Finally, even when practitioners think they know more of the abilities, they may not have a complete understanding of them (e.g., what does "quickness" mean?) and may have a difficult time measuring them.

## Summary

People differ in numerous ways. Many of the factors that make people different also contribute to differences in people's movement performance. For example, people differ in their abilities, which are defined as stable, genetically determined traits. The concept of abilities is different from that of skill, which deals with the proficiency of a person's performance on a task. Theoretical views about abilities include the general motor ability notion, the specificity of abilities hypothesis, and the notion of fundamental abilities. The latter view appears to have the broadest scientific and anecdotal support and presumes that

- a considerable number of independent, fundamental abilities exist, perhaps as many as 50 or more;
- different combinations of these abilities underlie the performance of different tasks;
- some abilities play a dominant role in task performance, whereas others have a lesser role; and
- some abilities may be important for a number of different tasks.

Practitioners can use the notion of abilities to classify tasks according to the important abilities underlying task performance. First, the practitioner performs a task analysis to determine the requirements of the task, and then he or she attempts to identify the important abilities that are necessary to meet those requirements. Once this is done, the practitioner can design learning experiences that allow individuals to capitalize on their stronger abilities and practice activities to compensate for their weaker abilities.

Generally, practitioners should avoid making predictions about an individual's future performance success based on the person's performance during initial practice for the following reasons:

- The patterns of abilities necessary for successful performance change with practice; therefore, individuals who do well early in practice may not be the ones who do well later on.
- The patterns of abilities underlying the successful performance of tasks may be large in number and not well understood.
- Even when the majority of relevant abilities are known, they may be difficult to measure accurately.

## From Principles to Practice

Check your understanding of the material in this chapter by responding to the following questions and then completing the application exercises. In each case, see if you can identify the most relevant questions or issues and then propose a solution based on the concepts and principles discussed in the chapter.

### Checking Your Understanding

1. Distinguish the concept of *abilities* from that of *skill*. Why is this distinction an important one for movement practitioners to be aware of?
2. Explain the logic of statistical correlation in language a friend or family member might understand. What are two important aspects of the notion of abilities that have been discovered by researchers who have used a correlational analysis?
3. How does Fleishman's conception of abilities differ from that of Henry? In what way does Fleishman's notion strike a balance between the general motor ability notion and Henry's concept of specificity?
4. What role do motor abilities play in the performance of individuals?
5. How might practitioners use the notion of abilities to classify motor tasks?
6. What factors should practitioners be aware of when trying to predict the future performance success of an individual?

### Application Exercise #1

A friend of yours has a teenage daughter who wants to learn how to drive a stick shift (manual transmission) car. Your friend is worried because her daughter has never had much success performing motor skills. She asks you if you think her daughter has the necessary abilities to successfully operate a car.

*It Depends*

- Does the daughter have 20/20 (corrected) vision?
- Does she have any physical or mental impairments?
- What are the requirements for effective operation of a stick shift car?
- What abilities are important for the performance of this task?
- How might the abilities of your friend's daughter be estimated?

*Strategy*

Determine the requirements for safe operation of a stick shift car and estimate the level of the daughter's abilities to achieve successful performance.

*Response Example*

- Perform a task analysis by identifying the requirements of stick shift vehicle operation from the time a person enters the vehicle until the time the individual turns off the engine.
- If necessary, solicit the input of expert drivers to perform the task analysis.
- Use Fleishman's classification system to estimate the pattern of abilities that appear to be necessary for skillful performance of the various tasks involved in driving a stick shift car.
- Ask people who know your friend's daughter if they think the daughter has any deficiencies in the relevant abilities for driving.
- If it appears that she does, indicate activities to which the daughter may need to devote particular attention when practicing her driving in order to compensate for the deficiencies.

### Application Exercise #2

A friend of yours wants to take up golf. He knows that you are a pretty good golfer and asks your opinion about his prospects for success.

*It Depends*

- How old is your friend?
- Does he have any handicapping conditions?
- What other sport or movement activities does your friend enjoy doing?
- What are the requirements of the golf swing?
- What abilities does your friend possess that might contribute to successful performance?

*Strategy*

First, perform a task analysis to determine the requirements of the different activities in the game of golf. Use Fleishman's classification system to estimate the abilities that might underlie the performance of each activity. If necessary, solicit input from a club pro or other golf expert for either task. Observe your friend's performance during an initial practice session and then discuss your impressions of the activities he performs better and those he seems to struggle with. Target for additional rehearsal those activities for which the two of you feel his abilities are less well suited.

## Application Exercise #3

Your roommate is the volunteer coach of a soccer team comprised of 5- and 6-year-old girls. She wants you to help her with the team in the area of skill development.

*It Depends*

- What are the different skills your roommate wants to target for player development?
- What are the task requirements of each of the skills?
- What are the skill levels of the different players?
- What abilities might underlie performance of each of the skills?
- How might the players' abilities be estimated?

*Strategy*

Assist your roommate in determining the task requirements of the different skills she wants her players to develop. If necessary, seek the assistance of other knowledgeable youth soccer coaches. Estimate the abilities that might contribute to successful performance of each skill. You and your roommate independently observe the players as they attempt to perform the selected skills. Compare your notes in order to estimate the strengths and weaknesses of each player. Design practice experiences that allow individuals to receive specialized instruction and additional rehearsal on tasks for which they appear to have the greatest difficulty.

## Application Exercise #4

A 4-year-old boy who was born prematurely has a sensory-integration problem that makes balancing activities difficult for him. For this reason he is reluctant to attempt balancing tasks such as walking up and down the stairs. The activity the boy enjoys most is jumping. In fact, he appears to possess an unusual degree of vertical jumping ability. A physical therapist is trying to assist the boy in improving his balancing skills, and she asks you for advice.

*It Depends*

- Are there other motor skills or games the boy enjoys performing?
- What are the requirements of the different balancing activities?
- What are the boy's most profound sensory impairments?
- Does the boy perform some balancing activities better than others?
- In what way does the boy's impairment impact on his performance of balancing tasks?

*Strategy*

Assist the therapist in determining the requirements of different balancing tasks and the potential impact the boy's impairment might be having on his performance of each. Ask the therapist which types of activities, in addition to vertical jumping, the boy performs best. During several therapy sessions, observe the boy as he engages in activities of his own choosing. Discuss with the therapist each of your views as to the relevant underlying abilities for each of these activities. Assist the therapist in creating practice experiences that maximize the boy's strengths. Consider modifying some of the more difficult balancing tasks so that they contain some of the components of the tasks with which the boy is more successful.

# PART II

# Principles of Human Skilled Performance

3

# Processing Information and Making Decisions

## Chapter Outline



## Chapter Objectives

**When you have completed this chapter, you should be able to**

understand the nature of at least three information-processing stages,

◆

be familiar with the principles of reaction time and the factors that affect it,

◆

understand how attention influences performance, and

◆

appreciate how three discrete components of human memory affect one's retention of motor skills.

## Preview

While a basketball player is dribbling downcourt, she spots an open teammate breaking for the basket. She knows that a very quick pass is needed, so she throws the ball with extra speed. Unfortunately, the pass is intercepted by an opposing player. Why did the offensive player not accomplish her goal? Did the passer's quicker-than-usual execution produce an inaccurate pass? Did she not see the opposing player? Did the excitement of potentially making a basket affect her attention? What other options did she have in this situation? Was her action the "best" choice to take?

## Overview

Certainly a major concern for the skilled performer is the evaluation of information, leading to decision making about future action. In this chapter we describe some of the principles of information processing that are most relevant to skilled performance. We also begin the construction of the conceptual model of skills, based on an information-processing perspective. We then discuss the decision-making part of the model, with particular emphasis on the ways that information is coded, stored, and used in decision making. Finally, we cover several topics that deal with the processing of information: reaction time and the factors that affect it, decision making under stress, the concept of attention as it relates to performance, and the various ways memory is used in motor performance situations.

In the last chapter we talked about the abilities that people bring with them to motor performance situations—the abilities or "hardware" they are born with. In this chapter, we begin to address the processes that people use when they attempt to produce skilled movements. For those of you who are training to work with persons who are physically or mentally challenged, you will find that the performance problems these people encounter on a regular basis are often due to impairments in one or more of these "software" processes.

Few would argue that in addition to producing effective movements, one of the most important features of a highly skilled performer is being adept at deciding what to do (and what not to do) in particular situations, sometimes when there is little time to decide. After all, the most elegant soccer pass is ineffective if it is intercepted by an opponent. And the most beautifully executed throw to first base is ineffective if the ball should have been held or thrown somewhere else instead. Similarly, the smoothest movement of an instrument control is ineffective if the airplane is steered toward rather than away from a flock of birds.

# Information-Processing Approach

Some psychologists explain the process of learning motor skills with a model that treats a human being as an information processor similar to a computer. In this model, the individual begins to perform operations on information when he or she first receives it ("input"). The person continues to process the input using a variety of operations during several stages. Finally, he or she produces a response ("output"). Figure 3.1 depicts this process with a simple flowchart. Some psychologists hold that input acts upon the learner; others contend that the learner actively selects input from the environment. The best answer probably combines these approaches.

**input**—The information that individuals receive for processing.

## Sources of Input

In information-processing studies, **input** is usually represented by a stimulus that the experimenter presents to the research participant (e.g., a light is illuminated or a sound is produced). Under these conditions participants need only sense the presence of the stimulus in order to begin processing a response to it. While such forms of input are occasionally found in naturally occurring environments (e.g., the firing of the starter's gun in track or swimming, the illumination of a traffic light at an intersection or of an emergency lamp on an instrument panel), input more often exists in the context of a multitude of environmental stimuli. In these situations, the input a person "picks out" for processing is, to a large extent, determined by the person doing the "picking." Although most psychologists agree that the search process is an active one, they differ in how they explain the way humans deal with environmental information. For example, Gibson (1966, 1979) contends that individuals pick up information directly through their sensory systems. With increasing experience, individuals become more adept at perceiving and acting upon the information. Critics of this view (e.g., Williams, Davids, Burwitz, & Williams, 1992) point out that additional factors—such as the role of memory—must be considered in order to understand how people deal with the available information. In any case, the

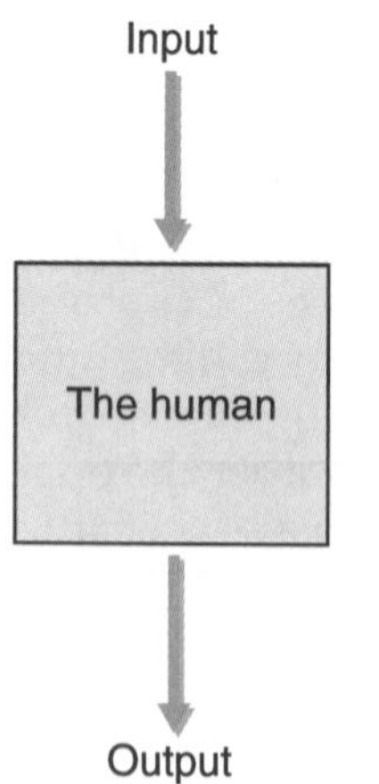


Figure 3.1 The simplest model of the information-processing approach to human performance.

## What Is Relevant?

Recent research by Williams and Davids (1998) illustrates nicely how more experienced and less experienced individuals pick up different aspects of the same environmental information. In this study one group of soccer players possessed more than 13 years of playing experience, while another had approximately 4 years' experience. All players viewed films showing life-sized sequences of soccer plays that ended with a pass by a member of the opposing team. They were told to imagine themselves as a covering defender or "sweeper" whose task it was to stop the advance of the approaching opponent(s). Some scenes involved one offensive player and one defensive player; others consisted of three offensive and three defensive players. Players were told to step on foot pads (which were located in the floor to their left, right, front, and back) to indicate when and how they would attempt to intercept the opponent's pass. The experimenters also obtained data about eye movement, as well as concurrent verbal reports, from the players in order to determine the location of their visual attention during both types of sequences.

The study's results revealed that the more experienced participants' foot responses were more rapidly initiated than those of their less experienced counterparts. The eye movement and verbal report data additionally suggested that the types of information extracted were different for the two groups. In the one-on-one situation, the more experienced participants fixated longer on the opponent's hip, while less experienced players spent more time watching the opponent's feet and the ball. The more experienced players also alternated their fixations more often between the opponent's hip and lower leg than did their less experienced counterparts. In the three-on-three scenario, the more experienced players allocated less attention to the opponent with the ball than did participants who were less experienced. More experienced players also reported shifts in their visual focus a greater percentage of the time (71%, compared with 58% for less experienced players), in spite of the fact that fixations to the left and right of the opponent with the ball were not different for the two groups. This suggests that, compared with less experienced players, the more experienced ones made greater use of vision to monitor the activities of the two offensive opponents who were not in possession of the ball.

Taken together, these findings imply that more experienced individuals use their organization of task-specific knowledge to extract the information that contributes the most to a quick and accurate response for each type of situation. In contrast, less experienced individuals tend to fixate longer on the more "obvious" aspects of environmental information (e.g., the feet of the opponent with the ball), irrespective of situational circumstances.

existing research suggests that experience influences the way individuals extract information from the environment (see the highlight box at the top of this page).

## Three Information-Processing Stages

A major goal of psychologists interested in the control of motor skills is to understand the specific nature of the processes in the box labeled "the human" in figure 3.1. While there are many ways to approach this problem, the one that has been used most often by psychologists assumes that there are several discrete stages of processing through which the information must pass on its way from input to output. For our purposes, we will focus on three of these stages (whose characteristics are summarized later in this chapter in table 3.2):

**stages of processing**—Several discrete operations (stimulus identification, response selection, and response programming) that individuals perform on information between input and output; frequently examined by scientists in reaction-time experiments.

- Stimulus identification
- Response selection
- Response programming

In employing a stage analysis of human performance, some psychologists assume that whenever outside or environmental information (i.e., input) enters the system, it is initially processed in the first stage, stimulus identification. When this stage of processing is completed, the remaining information is passed on to the second stage, response selection, for further processing, the result of which is passed on to the third stage, response programming, for more processing, and so on, until an action (i.e., output) is produced. In the following sections we discuss the rationale for a stage analysis and the kinds of operations that occur during each of the stages of processing.

### *Stimulus Identification (Stage 1)*

**stimulus-identification stage**—The first stage of information processing; during this stage the individual recognizes and identifies the input.

During this first stage, the performer's task is to determine whether information, referred to as the *stimulus*, has been presented and, if it has been, to identify it. Thus, in the **stimulus-identification stage**, individuals analyze for content the environmental information from a variety of sources, such as vision, audition, touch, kinesthesis, smell, and so on. In addition, performers "assemble" the components, or separate dimensions, of this information. For example, a combination of edges and colors might be assembled to form a visual representation of a moving object, such as a ball or person. The individual also detects patterns of the object's movement, such as whether it is moving at all, the direction and speed it is moving, and so on. Such patterns become important sources of information if the desired response is to catch the ball or to avoid contact with the person. The result of this stage of processing is thought to be some representation of the environmental information, which the performer then passes on to the next stage—response selection.

IT DEPENDS . . .

The particular stimuli that performers identify in an environmental context often depend on the situation. What stimuli (e.g., the ball, teammates, opponents, the coach, the crowd, bodily sensations) do you think the basketball player in this chapter's opening preview scenario might have detected if the score was lopsided or close? If it was the first minute of the game or the last few seconds of the game? If the crowd was noisy or the crowd was silent? If she was fatigued or nonfatigued?

### *Response Selection (Stage 2)*

**response-selection stage**—The second stage of information processing; during this stage the individual decides what, if any, response should be made.

The activities of the **response-selection stage** begin once those of the stimulus-identification stage have provided the performer with sufficient information about the nature of the environment. Using this information, the performer must now decide what, if any, response should be made. If the performer decides that a response is appropriate, he or she selects one from available movements, such as catching or trapping the ball or letting it go to a teammate. Thus, in this stage

IT DEPENDS . . .

The basketball player in the preview scenario decided to pass the ball to her teammate, who was moving toward the basket. What other choices might the player have made? What if the teammate was a poor ball handler? What if the teammate was taller or shorter than the defender? What if the defender had intercepted several earlier passes? What if the score was tied and there were 20 seconds left in the game?

a translation of sorts occurs between the sensory input that has been identified (e.g., an approaching ball) and one of several possible forms of movement output (e.g., a catch, a trap, or nothing).

*Response Programming (Stage 3)*

Once the performer has decided on the movement to be made, this information is forwarded to the **response-programming stage**. In this stage the task is to organize the motor system for the production of the desired movement. Such organization includes preparing the lower-level mechanisms in the brain stem and spinal cord for action, retrieving and organizing a plan of action to control the movement, and directing the muscles to contract in the proper order and with the proper levels of force and timing to produce the movement effectively.

**response-programming stage**—The third stage of information processing; during this stage, the individual organizes the motor system to produce the desired movement.

IT DEPENDS . . .

What was the basketball player in the preview in control of once she committed to throwing the ball to her teammate? Could she change the ball's direction, path, and force at the moment of the throw in anticipation of the ongoing movement of the receiver and other players? In order to avoid repeating the same mistake, what other factors might the player consider when confronted with a similar situation?

## Output

The end result of the activity of all three information-processing stages is termed the **output**. It could be the bat swing of a baseball, softball, or cricket player; the steering adjustments of a cyclist, pilot, sailor, or race car driver; the timed movements of a dancer or a musician; or the sit-to-stand attempt of a nursing home resident. It should be noted, however, that the output a person produces might not achieve the desired goal of the movement. The batter's swing may result in a hit or a miss; the cyclist's adjustment may result in successful navigation or a painful fall; the dancer's movement may be in or out of synchrony with a partner; and the elderly person's sit-to-stand attempt may produce vertical standing, a stumble, or a return to the sitting position.

**output**—The response an individual produces as a result of information processing.

IT DEPENDS . . .

How might you explain the output produced by the basketball player in the preview? Did she fail to correctly identify the position or movement speed of the opposing player? Would a bounce pass have been more effective than one that traveled the entire distance in the air? Did she produce a force level appropriate for the distance the ball was required to travel? Can you think of other explanations for her output in this situation? Which of your explanations rely on inadequate stimulus identification? Which identify inappropriate response selection? Which focus on errors in response programming?

## Beginning of a Conceptual Model

In figure 3.2 we add the stages of processing to the simple notion of information processing shown in figure 3.1. This structure forms the first part of the conceptual model of human performance that we will be elaborating on throughout the text.

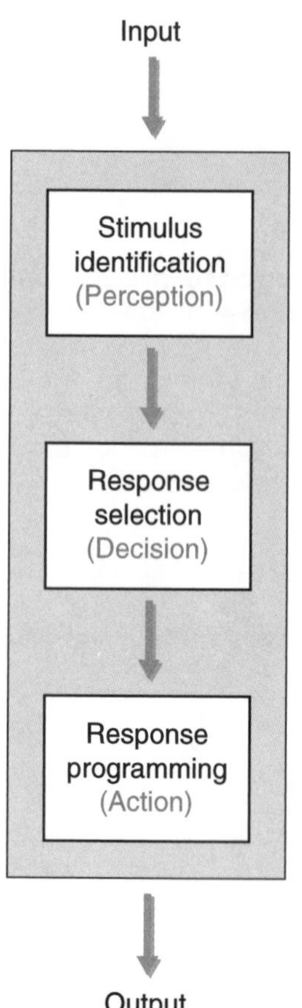


Figure 3.2 An expanded information-processing model showing the stimulus-identification, response-selection, and response-programming stages.

**reaction time (RT)**—The interval of time that elapses from the presentation of an unanticipated stimulus to the beginning of a person's response.

You might think of the first stage, stimulus identification, as *perception;* the second stage, response selection, as *decision;* and the third stage, response programming, as *action.* Let's apply these to the example of the basketball player: first, the player sees the open teammate breaking for the basket (stimulus identification, or perception); second, the player decides to throw a quick pass (response selection, or decision); third, the player throws a one-hand pass to a point ahead of her moving teammate (response programming, or action).

IT DEPENDS . . .

Errors can occur in any of the stages of processing we have just discussed. The nature of the output sometimes depends on the stage in which the error occurs. Which stage(s) of processing might contribute to each of the following output errors: A beginning dance student who is unable to walk to the beat of the music? A beginning basketball player who is unable to make more than two baskets in a 30-s time period during a continuous shooting drill? A child who is unable to catch a ball? An elderly person (octogenarian) who is unable to operate a TV's remote control?

Clearly, these stages are all located within the human information system and are not visible under usual circumstances. However, scientists have employed several laboratory methods to learn more about what goes on in these stages and to determine how long the processing of information takes in each stage. Much of this research has focused on reaction time, one of the most important measures of human performance in many situations.

## Reaction Time and Decision Making

An important performance measure, **reaction time** (abbreviated RT), indicates the speed and effectiveness of decision making. RT is the interval between the presentation of an unanticipated stimulus and the beginning of the response. It represents an actual part of some real-world tasks, such as the start in sprint races, where a starter's gun serves as a stimulus to begin. In the depiction of an old footrace shown on the next page, we see that the starter has already fired his gun by the position of the smoke. Yet the athletes all remain on the starting line, only just beginning to move. This picture emphasizes the RT delay that occurs between stimulus presentation and response initiation. A person who is able to minimize such a delay has a significant advantage in events like the 100-m dash.

In addition to reflecting processing delays in events such as the sprint start, RT also represents the time it takes an individual to make decisions and initiate actions. In many rapid skills, success depends on the speed with which the performer can detect some feature of the environment or of an opponent's movement, decide what to do, and then initiate an effective countermove. Reaction time figures importantly in sports (e.g., boxing, soccer, and stock car racing) and in nonsport activities (e.g., swatting a menacing flying insect, braking a car to avoid hitting an animal that darts across the road, or catching a can of beans that suddenly falls from a kitchen cupboard). Because RT is a fundamental component of many skills, it is not surprising that many researchers have utilized this measure as an indicator of the speed of information processing.

But RT has important theoretical meaning as well. Since RT begins when the stimulus is presented and ends when the movement is initiated, it serves as a potential measure of the accumulated duration of the three stages of processing seen in figure 3.2. Any factor that lengthens the duration of one or more of these stages lengthens RT. For

Reaction time (RT) in a footrace: the starter's gun has fired, yet the athletes are only now getting off their marks after an RT delay. (Adapted from Scripture, 1905.)

this reason, scientists who are interested in information processing use RT as a measure of the speed of processing that takes place in each of these stages. In the following section, we discuss how changes in RT inform us about some of the things that are going on in these stages.

© SportsChrome

Milliseconds of reaction time at the start of a race can be decisive in the outcome.

## Factors Influencing Reaction Time and Decision Making

Many important factors influence RT, ranging from the nature of stimulus information to the type of movement that must be performed. We consider some of these factors in this section.

### *Number of Stimulus-Response Alternatives*

Dick Schmidt's racquetball opponent has a number of good serves that all begin the same way, and Dick is often frozen for a moment, trying to decide what kind of serve is coming and how to return the serve. Why? One of the most important factors influencing the time it takes to start an action, RT, is the number of possible stimulus choices—each of which leads to a distinct response—that can be presented at a given time. In the laboratory, we generally produce this situation by presenting a subject with one of several possible stimuli, such as lights, and require the person to choose one of several possible responses, such as pressing different buttons, depending on which stimulus is presented. Situations such as this illustrate the phenomenon of **choice RT**, where the performer must identify the stimulus that is presented and then choose the response that corresponds to that stimulus. In choice RT experiments, each trial begins with a warning signal (e.g., the sound of a buzzer or tone), followed by an interval of time of unpredictable length (e.g., 2, 3, or 4 s) termed the **foreperiod**. Once the stimulus is presented (e.g., the illumination of one of the lights), the performer chooses which button to press and then presses it.

**choice RT**—The interval of time that elapses from the presentation of one of several possible unanticipated stimuli to the beginning of one of several possible responses.

**foreperiod**—The interval of time between the presentation of a warning signal and the presentation of an unanticipated stimulus.

## Hick's Law

Over a century ago Merkel (1885, cited by Woodworth, 1938) conducted choice RT experiments on himself involving 10 possible stimulus-response combinations. The stimuli were the Arabic numerals 1 through 5 and the Roman numerals I through V. Each stimulus was paired with one response key; for example, the numerals 1–5 were paired with the five digits of the right hand, and the numerals I–V were paired with the five left-hand digits. If the possible stimuli on a set of trials were the numerals 2, 3, and V (a 3-choice case), Merkel responded with either the right index finger, right middle finger, or left thumb, depending on which numeral was presented. Merkel varied the number of possible stimulus-response pairs during different sets of trials. The results of his self-experiment are shown in figure 3.3, where choice RT is plotted as a function of the number of stimulus-response alternatives. You can see that as the number of pairs increased from 1 choice (simple RT), there was a sharp rise in RT, with this rise becoming less steep as the number of pairs increased, particularly beyond 7 pairs.

Much later Hick (1952) and then Hyman (1953) discovered that the relationship between choice RT and the logarithm of the number of stimulus-response pairs was linear. This relationship has since become known as Hick's Law; it has been shown to hold for a wide variety of situations using different types of participants, different types of stimuli, and different types of movements. In fact, it is one of the most important laws of human performance. The relationship implies that choice RT increases by a constant amount every time the number of stimulus-response alternatives is doubled (e.g., from 2 to 4 or from 16 to 32). This led to an important interpretation of Hick's Law: choice RT is linearly related to the amount of information that must be processed to resolve the uncertainty about the various possible stimulus-response alternatives. Hick's Law relates to the second information-processing stage discussed previously because it pertains to the amount of information a performer must deal with before deciding what to do. The defender in a three-on-one fast break in basketball has more possible decisions to make than a defender who is guarding only one opponent. This is because she or he must decide which response is most appropriate for each of several possible things the attacking opponent(s) may do, such as dribble, pass, fake, or shoot. In a one-on-one situation the defender may disregard at least one of the options, the pass. This allows for a shorter reaction time because of one less decision to make.

Thus, RT is a measure of the time required for the participant to detect the stimulus, decide which response is appropriate, and initiate the response.

**simple RT**—The interval of time that elapses from the presentation of one unanticipated stimulus to the beginning of the response.

Generally, as the number of possible stimulus-response pairs increases, the time required to respond to any one of them (i.e., choice RT) increases. The shortest RT is found when there is only one stimulus and one response; this is referred to as **simple RT**.

Longer reaction times result from a greater number of stimulus-response (S-R) alternatives. This relationship, known as **Hick's Law**, underlies our understanding of skilled performance (see the highlight box at the top of this page). As you can see in figure 3.3, RT increases substantially when the number of alternatives is increased from one to two. RT might increase from about 190 ms with one S-R pair (simple RT) to more than 300 ms for two choices—a 58% increase in the time required to process the stimulus information and initiate a response! As the number of choices increases, RT gets longer, but the increases become smaller and smaller (e.g., the increase in RT when the number of S-R choices increases from 9 to 10 might be only 20 ms, which represents an increase of only 2% or 3%).

**Hick's Law**—Describes the stable relationship that exists between the number of stimulus-response alternatives and choice reaction time; specifically, as the number of stimulus-response pairs increases, choice reaction time increases in a linear fashion.

RT delays can be of critical importance in determining success in rapid skills, such as defending against a punch in judo, intercepting a shot in hockey, or swerving to avoid a moose that suddenly enters the narrow highway ahead of your car. The entire duration of a pitch in baseball, for instance, might be only 4/10 s, or

400 ms, and the bat swing takes 120 ms to execute. So if a batter takes an extra 100 ms to detect the speed and trajectory of the pitch, this could severely limit the chance of successful contact.

Because information-processing delays can sometimes be quite long, an important strategy in many rapid competitive activities is for performers to increase the number of stimulus-response choices their opponents must deal with in order to increase the opponents' processing delays. In softball, for example, a pitcher might increase the number of different pitches she throws in order to increase the number of choices the batter must consider. Similarly, a volleyball player who is able to set the ball to a variety of spiking positions will increase the opposing team's uncertainty about which set might actually be produced, thus delaying the opponent's response to the particular spike that is executed. Conversely, an opponent who has to deal with only a single type of pitch or set can process the stimulus very quickly and even prepare a response in advance. As a general rule, then, athletes in sports like these try to increase the number of alternatives their opponents must deal with in order to increase the opponent's information-processing delay.

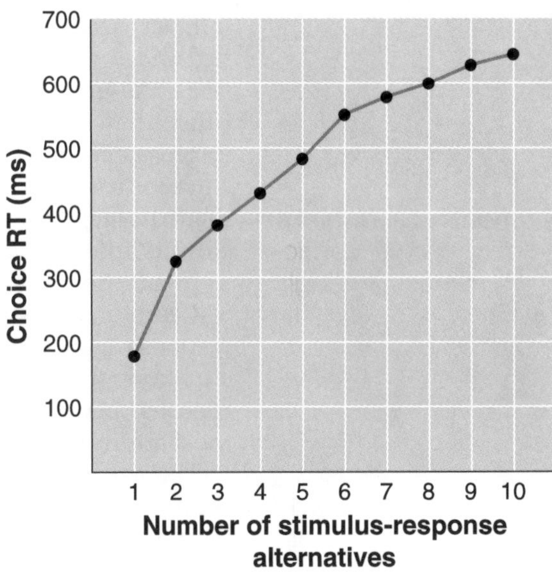


Figure 3.3 The relationship between choice reaction time and the number of stimulus-response alternatives. (Adapted from Woodworth, 1938; data obtained by Merkel in 1885.)

### *Stimulus-Response Compatibility*

An important determinant of choice RT is **stimulus-response (S-R) compatibility**, usually defined as the extent to which the stimulus and its resulting response are connected in a "natural" way. Catching an approaching ball bouncing to your right with your right hand is an example of S-R compatibility because the ball's movement (to the right) is mirrored by both the hand used to make the catch (right) and the direction the hand is moved (to the right).

**stimulus-response (S-R) compatibility**—The degree to which the relationship between a stimulus and its required response is "natural," or compatible.

In the example in figure 3.4a, the stimuli and responses are compatible because the stimulus light on the left is paired with a left-hand finger press and the stimulus light on the right is paired with a right-hand finger press. However, in the example in figure 3.4b, the relationship between stimuli and responses is not nearly so natural, or compatible.

Research has clearly established that for a given number of S-R choices, the greater the S-R compatibility, the faster the choice RT. This is assumed to be due to more rapid information processing in the response-selection stage, because more natural linkages between compatible stimuli and responses lead to faster response selection; hence, to faster RTs. The general rules regarding the number of possible stimuli and choice RT (i.e., Hick's Law) still apply to compatible stimulus-response arrangements. However, the amount of increase in choice RT with increases in the number of S-R choices is less when stimuli and responses are more compatible than when they are less compatible.

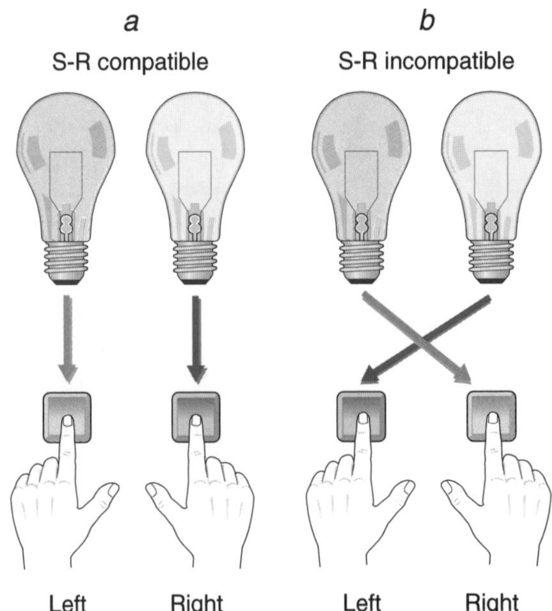


Figure 3.4 Stimulus-response compatibility. The relationship between stimulus and response is more "natural," or compatible, in the situation on the left (*a*).

### *Amount of Practice*

A highly practiced performer can overcome a lot of things, including the disadvantage of low S-R compatibility. The skilled sailboat racer almost instantly moves the tiller to the right as soon as it's clear that the boat must be turned to the left. Research has shown that two major factors affect choice RT: the amount of practice and the nature of practice. For a given number of stimulus-response alternatives, the greater the amount of practice, the shorter the choice RT. Moreover, as practice increases, the amount of increase in RT as the number of S-R alternatives increases becomes less. With extreme amounts of practice, high-level performers can produce reactions that approach automatic processing (see the section on automaticity later in this chapter); these reactions are not only very fast, but they are slowed little, if at all, as the number of S-R choices is increased.

In addition, the nature of practice is important here. As practice with the same S-R combinations increases, that is, the same stimulus always leads to the same response, choice RT becomes faster. This phenomenon is seen quite often in sporting situations when a performer produces the same responses to the same stimuli on repeated occasions. For example, the experienced boxer knows which response is most appropriate for the various punches an opponent might produce.

The nature of practice also applies to nonsport tasks. To a beginning driver, the connection between the presentation of a red light (to stop) and the response of pressing the brake pedal is very clumsy. However, after thousands of hours of driving practice, the link between the red light and pressing the brake pedal is extremely natural, leading almost automatically to the appropriate movement.

## Dealing With Decision-Making Delays

One fundamental way people cope with long decision-making delays is to anticipate. Typically, a highly skilled individual predicts what is going to happen in the environment and when it is going to happen, and thereby is able to perform various information-processing activities in advance. For example, the defensive lineman in football who anticipates that the other team is going to attempt a running play moves quickly and stops the play for a big loss. One reason he is able to do this so quickly is because he does not have to wait before he begins to select and organize his response. Thus, when the play begins he can bypass the processing activities needed to select and program his response because he has done this in advance.

Highly skilled people know which stimuli are likely to be presented, where they will appear, and when they will occur, so these people can predict the type of response that is likely to be required. This knowledge allows them to initiate their movements much sooner or at a time that is appropriate to the demands of the environment. For example, the experienced goalie predicts where and when a shot will arrive on net so that she can deflect it effectively with a well timed arm or leg movement. Because of their capability of anticipating, skilled performers seem to behave almost as if they had "all the time in the world"; they do not appear rushed, in the manner of those who are reacting to an unanticipated event. Experiments have also shown that even novice performers, when given advance information or pre-cues about characteristics of an upcoming stimulus, reduce their choice RT. Researchers presume they organize their movements in advance, completing some of the information-processing activities that are usually conducted during the response-selection or response-programming stages (Rosenbaum, 1980).

### *Types of Anticipation*

**spatial (or event) anticipation**—The capacity of a person to predict what is going to happen in a performance situation.

Anticipation can be of two general types. First, it can involve a prediction about *what* will happen in the environment, such as anticipating that a tennis opponent will hit a smash or anticipating that the driver of a car approaching yours will attempt to turn in front of you. This type of anticipation is referred to as **spatial (or event) anticipation**. Predicting what will happen in the environment allows the tennis player and the driver to organize their movements in advance, so that if the event they are anticipating does occur, they are able to initiate the appropriate response more quickly (i.e., in a time far shorter than the usual RT).

## IT DEPENDS . . .

In a social dance setting, while dancing the waltz, how can the leader signal the follower in order to avoid bumping in to another couple that unexpectedly moves directly into their path? What type of anticipation might help this couple more quickly adjust their moves? What other situations might this couple have to deal with? How might they practice to prepare for these situations?

The other type of anticipation involves predicting *when* an environmental event will occur, such as anticipating the moment that the official will drop the puck during a face-off in ice hockey or the moment that a vase that suddenly falls off a high shelf will reach your hands. This type of anticipation is usually called **temporal anticipation**. Although there is a strong advantage in knowing when some event will occur, it is probably more important for people to be able to anticipate what is going to happen in order for them to organize their movements in advance.

**temporal anticipation**—The capacity of a person to predict the time course of an event in a performance situation, or when the event is going to happen.

### *Benefits of Anticipation*

Either spatial or temporal anticipation can provide a strong advantage in the performance of many skills. However, if the person can correctly anticipate in both ways, naturally the advantage is even greater. For example, if the previously mentioned defensive lineman in American football can predict what the opponent's play is going to be (spatial anticipation) *and* the moment in time that the play is going to begin (temporal anticipation), the lineman can initiate his already prepared movement simultaneously with the snap of the ball (i.e., with no RT delay). Such a response is very likely to be effective in stopping the play.

Effective anticipation is not always easy because it requires having a great deal of knowledge about the regularities of environmental events, such as an opponent's tendencies to do particular things in certain situations. For this reason, of course, smart opponents do everything they can to prevent each other from anticipating what they intend to do and when they intend to do it. This type of strategic interplay between opponents provides one of the many fascinations of competitive sports.

Several factors affect our capability of predicting effectively. One is the regularity of the events. For example, if a racquetball player always serves the ball in the same way to her opponent's (weak) backhand side, the opponent can predict this event and counter it in various ways. Clearly, however, the receiver's capability of doing this would be minimized dramatically if the server could execute three or four different serves and did so in a random fashion. Similarly, if the center in American football always snaps the ball on the second of two rhythmical verbal signals (e.g., "hut, hut"), the defense can anticipate the moment of the snap and be highly prepared to initiate their countermovements at exactly that moment. By randomly ordering the snap count, however (e.g., using one "hut" on some plays, two "huts" on other plays, and occasionally using even three "huts"), the quarterback can keep the defensive players from anticipating temporally while still

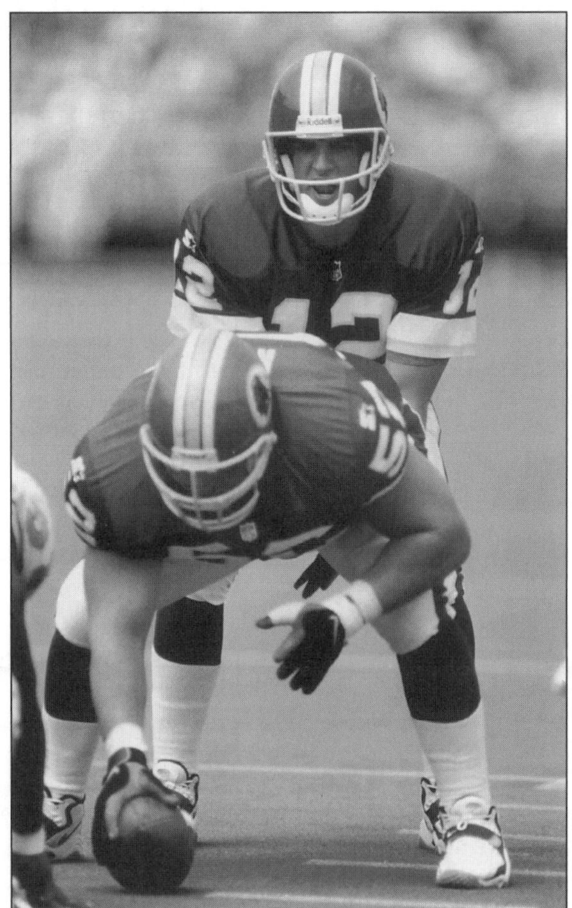



The quarterback and center respond simultaneously to the same signal.

allowing his own offensive teammates (who know the snap count) to anticipate both temporally and spatially. The goals of the offensive football team, then, are to respond as a single unit to the snap of the ball without allowing the opposing defensive players the capability of anticipating. This strategy, when executed effectively, provides the offensive players with the greatest relative advantage.

### Costs of Anticipation

There are several advantages to anticipation but, as with most things in life, there are costs as well. The primary disadvantage of anticipating is the ineffective response that occurs when the anticipation is incorrect. In American football again, if the defensive lineman anticipates that the snap will occur on the second sound, but the play begins on the third sound, the lineman could move too early, generating a penalty for his team. Similarly, if you are approaching a busy intersection in your car and the light turns yellow, you might anticipate that the driver of an approaching car with its turn signal blinking will not turn in front of you because the law says that you have the right of way. In such a case, you might depress the accelerator rather than the brake. If the other driver tries to beat the light and turns in front of you, a collision is likely to occur. Clearly, anticipating correctly can result in benefits, but anticipating incorrectly can be costly and sometimes even disastrous.

Earlier we discussed the notion that anticipating allows various information-processing activities to take place in advance of stimulus presentation. Suppose that a person has gone through these preparatory processes, but now the events in the environment change, indicating that if the prepared movement were initiated, it would be incorrect. First the individual must inhibit, or "unprepare," the already prepared movement. This takes time, of course; estimates from studies indicate that even very simple actions require somewhere around 40 ms to be halted (Schmidt & Gordon, 1977). Then the correct movement must be organized and initiated, requiring the activity of one or more of the comparatively slow information-processing stages. By the time all of this is accomplished, the opportunity for advantage has usually passed.

The situation becomes even worse if the incorrect movement is actually triggered. In this case, not only does the person have the problem of inhibiting her incorrect action and preparing the correct one, but may have an additional problem if she executes the action in the wrong direction. In that case she would be moving away from the best location and would have to reverse the momentum of her movement, two time-consuming problems. For example, a squash player may anticipate that her opponent is going to hit to the left side of the court and therefore she begins to move in that direction as the shot is made. Should the shot actually go to the right, it would be virtually impossible for the anticipating player to stop her action and move back to the right in time to return the shot.

### Strategies of Anticipation

The potential gains and losses associated with correct and incorrect anticipations give rise to important strategic elements in many rapid sport activities. For example, athletes who want to discourage their opponents from anticipating try to produce movements that are unpredictable with respect to both spatial and temporal components. Once the opponent realizes that the costs of anticipating outweigh the benefits because his anticipations tend to be unsuccessful more often than they are successful, he is forced to switch to a strategy that requires waiting for the movement to occur and then processing a response to it in a slower fashion.

Many participants of rapid sport activities organize their movements and strategies in such a way that the opponent is forced to react rather than anticipate, using the slower stages of information processing in order to prepare a response. The key to achieving this result is *randomization*—making movements that are unpredictable so that the opponent is prevented from anticipating them.

Another important strategy is to lure the opponent into an anticipation that can then be used against him. A racquetball player who moves as if she is going to hit a soft drop shot near the front wall may cause her opponent to anticipate the shot and move forward quickly to counteract it. However, when the anticipated drop shot suddenly turns out to be a passing shot, the opponent finds himself badly out of position. The effectiveness of this strategy depends on the player's convincing her opponent that she is going to do one thing (e.g., a drop shot), luring him into anticipating that action and producing a response to counteract it, and then doing something else (e.g., a passing shot) that makes him "pay the cost" of his false anticipation.

## Decision Making and Performance Under Conditions of Arousal and Anxiety

Arousal and anxiety, or motivation and stress, are common aspects of many skill performance situations. **Arousal** refers to the level of activation or excitement of a person's central nervous system, while **anxiety** deals more with the way the person interprets a particular situation and the emotions that are associated with that interpretation. If the person feels that the demands of the situation exceed her capability to meet those demands, then she will probably perceive that situation to be threatening and experience more anxiety, particularly if the outcome is important to her. Arousal levels can fluctuate for many reasons that have nothing to do with stress levels (e.g., moving from a sitting to a standing position, attending a friend's wedding, seeing a beautiful sunset). However, changes in anxiety levels are always accompanied by changes in arousal (i.e., arousal level increases when anxiety increases).

**arousal**—The level of activation or excitement of the central nervous system; varies from extremely low levels during sleep to extremely high levels during intense physical activity and excitement.

**anxiety**—A person's uneasiness or distress about future uncertainties; a perception of threat to the self (often characterized by elevated arousal levels).

Both of these phenomena are a routine part of many everyday life events (e.g., taking exams, giving a speech, interviewing for a job) and most competitive athletic contests, where the pressure to win and the threat of losing are important sources of emotional arousal and anxiety for participants. The level of arousal imposed by a situation is an important determinant of performance, particularly if the performance depends on the speed and accuracy of decision making. In this section we examine some of the effects of different levels of arousal and stress on information processing and suggest some ways performance can be enhanced under these conditions.

### Inverted-U Principle

You can think of arousal as the level of excitement or activation generated in the central nervous system—low levels of arousal being associated with sleeplike states, and high levels associated with states of agitation and extreme alertness, such as those experienced during life-threatening situations. Patients with damage to the reticular formation in the brainstem often experience difficulties associated with unpredictable shifts in arousal levels. The influence of arousal level on performance has been studied for many years with the weight of the evidence supporting the **inverted-U principle**. This principle is illustrated in figure 3.5, which shows performance level on the vertical axis and arousal level on the horizontal axis. Note that as arousal level increases from "low" to "moderate" (moving from left to right on the horizontal axis), performance level improves from "poor" to "excellent." However, as arousal level increases further from "moderate" to "high," performance level begins to fall from "excellent" back toward "poor." The inverted-U principle (illustrated by the shape of the curve in figure 3.5) states, then, that as arousal level increases (assuming that it begins at a low level) performance improves, but only to a point, usually peaking at some intermediate level of arousal. If arousal continues to increase beyond that level, performance begins to diminish.

**inverted-U principle**—Describes the relatively stable relationship that exists between arousal level and performance; specifically, as an individual's arousal level increases, the person's performance increases—but only to a point. If the individual's arousal continues to increase, performance begins to decrease.

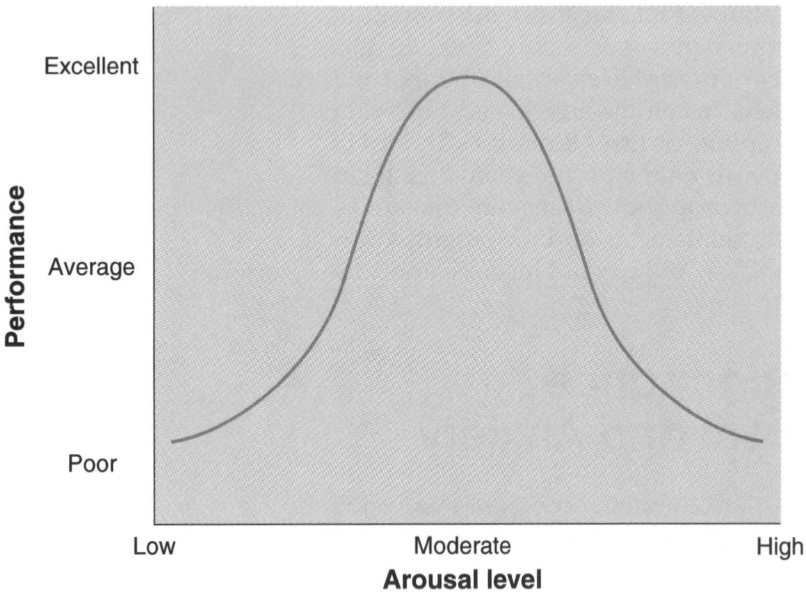


Figure 3.5 The inverted-U principle. Increased arousal improves performance only to a point, after which further increases in arousal degrade performance.

The inverted-U principle might seem surprising to many people involved with sport and coaching if they generally assume that the higher the participant's level of arousal (or motivation), the more effective the performance will be. Some coaches spend a great deal of time before competitions attempting to raise their team's arousal, and we often hear sportscasters argue that a team's performance was poor because the players were not "up" (i.e., aroused enough) for the game. Yet, this general view is contradicted by considerable experimental evidence that shows that most performance is better when the level of arousal is moderate and not too high.

Perhaps the best way to determine the level of arousal that is optimal for task performance is to consider three factors: the person, the task, and the situation (Wrisberg, 1994). First consider the person. People differ with respect to their normal range of arousal and the extent to which they perceive situations to be threatening (referred to as **trait anxiety**). That is, it is likely that individuals who normally possess higher levels of arousal are going to be more susceptible to overarousal than are persons who normally experience lower arousal levels. However, there is also evidence that different individuals perform best at different levels of arousal and that what each individual should strive to achieve is a **zone of optimal functioning**, which represents the range of arousal associated with his or her maximum performance (see Hanin, 1980, for a more detailed discussion of the zone of optimal functioning concept).

**trait anxiety**—The general disposition of an individual to perceive situations to be threatening.

**zone of optimal functioning**—The range of arousal levels associated with an individual's maximum performance.

Second, consider the nature of the task. If the task requires fine muscular control (as in archery or brain surgery) or contains important decision-making components (as in quarterbacking in American football or in piloting an airplane), then a lower level of arousal is probably needed for maximum performance (Weinberg & Hunt, 1976). On

## IT DEPENDS . . .

Consider two hypothetical individuals who are preparing to play a game of badminton, a sport that has a relatively high level of cognitive complexity and moderate motor control demands. One individual is normally an uptight, highly anxious person, and at this moment he is feeling pretty nervous because he doesn't think there is any way he can defeat his opponent. The other individual is normally laid-back, feeling little anxiety, a person who at this moment is quite sure that she can easily defeat her opponent. Knowing these facts, what do you think the precompetitive anxiety (and arousal) levels for each of these individuals might be? What level of arousal (i.e., low, moderate, high) might be the most appropriate for the game of badminton? (See figure 3.6.) What, if anything, could each of these individuals do to achieve optimal arousal? What are some things that might happen during the game that could cause shifts in the arousal (or anxiety) levels of either player? How might these shifts influence each person's performance?

© Bernardo M. Nunez/Active Images

© Tom Roberts

Activities requiring gross motor action and having little cognitive complexity benefit from a relatively high arousal level.

the other hand, skills that are dominated by large-muscle actions, without much fine motor control (such as power lifting or lumberjacking), or that have a low level of cognitive complexity (such as sprinting in track or swimming or most motor tasks that are well learned) are performed more successfully at relatively higher levels of arousal.

Finally, there is the situation to consider. As mentioned earlier, anxiety levels increase when an individual perceives a situation to be threatening. In this case, if the person perceives that the demands of a performance situation exceed his capability to meet those demands, he will experience increased anxiety and an accompanying increase in arousal level. Conversely, if the person perceives that he is easily capable of meeting the challenge of the performance situation, his anxiety (and arousal) level will be lower.

Only as practitioners consider all three of these factors (person, task, situation) can they assist individuals in achieving the level of arousal that is optimal for task performance. Figure 3.6 presents arousal-performance curves that consider the possible influence of task requirements. We show in this figure three tasks that differ with respect to type of motor control (fine, moderate, gross) and level of cognitive complexity (complex, moderate, simple). As can be seen, a task like piano playing that requires a great degree of fine motor (i.e., small muscle) control and higher cognitive demands is generally performed better when the arousal level of the participant is lower (as in the curve on the left). However, as control of the task becomes more gross motor in nature (i.e., larger muscles) and cognitive complexity is lessened (e.g., shooting a basketball, lifting a heavy weight), the optimal level of arousal required for successful performance generally becomes higher (as in the curves at the center and right of the figure).

The relationship between arousal and performance, and the factors that influence this relationship, have received considerable attention from researchers and practitioners in the field of sport psychology. An important goal of these individuals is to assist athletes in preparing for high-level performance by teaching them ways to adjust their arousal levels in order to optimally meet task requirements (Landers & Boutcher, 1998; Orlick, 1986, 1990). As a result, various arousal adjustment techniques have been developed and are being practiced by many of today's top athletes.

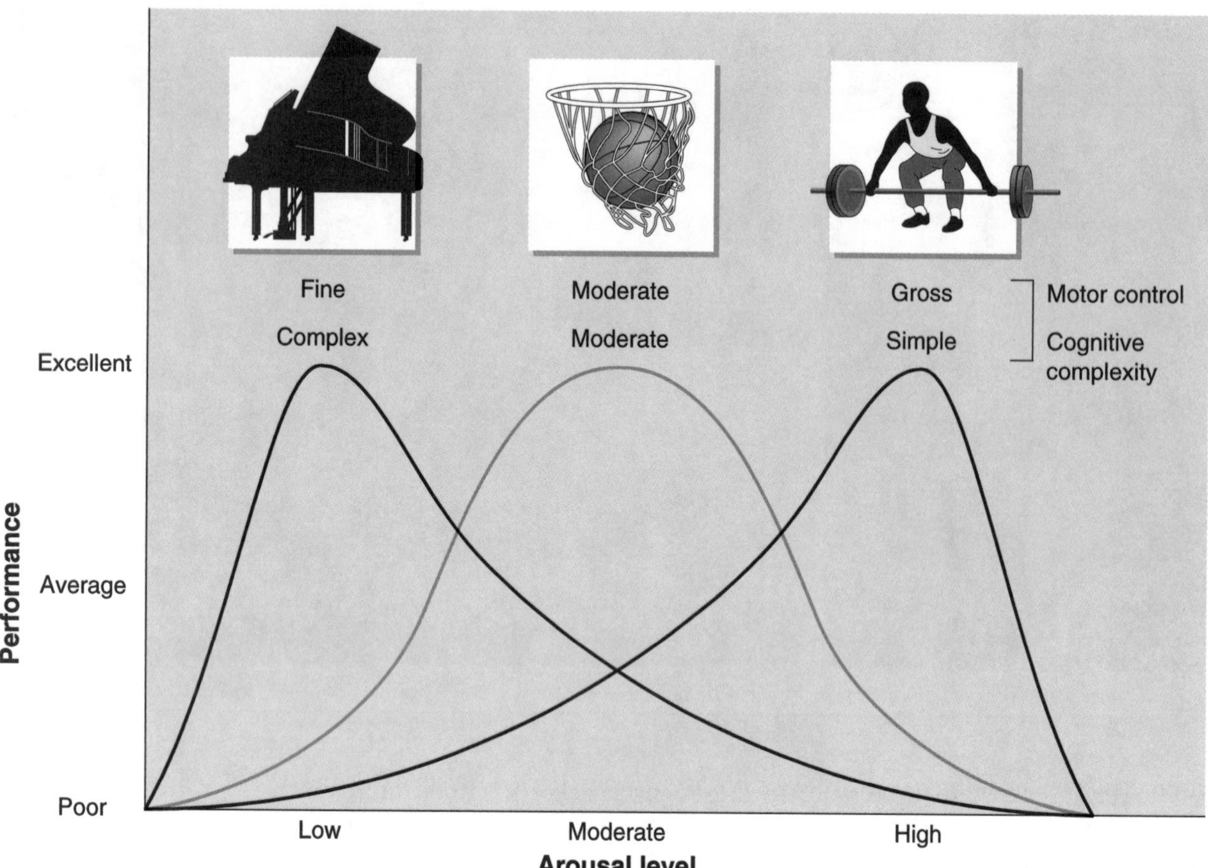


Figure 3.6 The inverted-U principle for different tasks. Optimal arousal level is higher for more simple tasks with more gross motor control.

## Information Processing Under High Arousal

During a 50-m sprint in her first big meet, a high school swimmer with a very high arousal level does a flip turn while still 3 m (10 ft) short of the end of the pool, leaving her treading water while the other competitors make the turn and finish the race. This swimmer's high level of arousal probably contributed to her faulty performance. For one thing, the processing of information changes when arousal levels are increased. We discuss next some of the ways this happens.

### *Perceptual Narrowing*

**perceptual narrowing**—The narrowing of attentional focus that occurs as a person's arousal level increases.

One important change in information processing under conditions of high arousal is **perceptual narrowing**, the tendency for people to miss certain types of information in the environment. Consider, for example, the stressful sport of deep-sea diving (e.g., Weltman & Egstrom, 1966). When the novice diver is practicing his movements on land, his arousal level is relatively low and he is able to process a number of stimuli simultaneously. However, if he attempts his dives in a swimming pool or, even more threateningly, the ocean, his arousal increases dramatically and his attention becomes more narrowly and intensely focused. The result is that he systematically detects fewer stimuli, with the majority of his attention being directed to those sources of information that are most pertinent to, or expected in, the task (e.g., the location of objects he must manipulate or diving partners he must interact with). This narrowing of attention, which can also occur when a person is under the influ-

## Managing Arousal in Athletic Competition

The following quote from 1984 Olympic gold medalist Linda Thom of Canada illustrates the way one elite athlete balances muscle and mind techniques to achieve optimal arousal in pistol-shooting competitions (Orlick & Partington, 1986).

> In competition everything is heightened including your sense of hearing. You are in a vigilant, alert mode. You aid yourself by recognizing that there are competitors. You recognize that the crowd is there, the sun is shining, and there are butterflies around the target. Then you say, "Fine, what a wonderful day for shooting, this is where we are going to produce tens, and this is how we are going to do it." The control is never relaxing totally. I mean, you can relax to a degree. Relaxation is important, but it's important for a shooter not to totally relax or you'll really become passive and that's not a good idea. You want to relax your muscles so they are not tense, but you've got to keep that something inside you, that "This is what I'm here to do" determination. You've got to keep your thoughts in that direction and not let anything interfere (p. 173).

ence of drugs or suffering sleep loss, is an important mechanism that allows the person to devote more attention to stimulus sources that are the most immediately relevant.

But perceptual narrowing has its drawbacks. It enhances performance when individuals are presented with expected stimuli, but it impairs performance when they are confronted with unexpected stimuli. For example, the perceptual narrowing that occurs with mild intoxication produces a level of automobile driving performance that is "acceptable" as long as no unexpected events occur. However, should a child suddenly dart into the street in pursuit of a ball, perceptual narrowing could result in the driver not seeing the child until it is too late.

**cue-utilization hypothesis**—An explanation for performance decrements under conditions of low and high arousal. When individuals' arousal levels are low and environmental cues are plentiful, performance is impaired because people select a greater proportion of irrelevant cues. When individuals' arousal levels are high and perceptual narrowing occurs, performance is impaired because people select fewer cues, including some that are relevant.

### *Cue-Utilization Hypothesis*

Easterbrook's (1959) **cue-utilization hypothesis** helps explain the common performance decrements that occur under conditions of low and high arousal. When arousal level is low, the perceptual field is relatively wide and the person has access to a large number of cues. However, since only a few of these cues are relevant to the task at hand (e.g., scuba diving), the performer may pick up some irrelevant cues (e.g., what other divers are wearing) and miss some of the relevant ones (e.g., undercurrents), resulting in suboptimal performance. As the arousal level rises, though,

### IT DEPENDS . . .

The player in this chapter's preview scenario threw a pass that was intercepted by an opposing defender. Is it possible that the player was experiencing perceptual narrowing? What factors may have caused perceptual narrowing? What other information or stimuli (besides the defender who intercepted the pass) might the player have missed that could have been detrimental to her performance? What are some stimuli the player may have missed that would not have degraded her performance? Can you think of other everyday situations in which perceptual narrowing might occur? What types of performance-relevant information might an individual fail to pick up under those circumstances?

attentional focus narrows onto the most relevant cues (e.g., air pressure, underwater obstacles, etc.) as more and more of the competing irrelevant cues are excluded. Therefore, proficiency improves because the performer is now mainly responding to relevant cues. However, with further increases in arousal and perceptual narrowing, some of the relevant cues are not picked up, particularly those that are not highly expected (e.g., irregular underwater currents), so performance suffers. According to the cue-utilization hypothesis, the optimal level of arousal is presumably one that produces an attentional focus narrow enough to exclude many irrelevant cues yet broad enough to pick up the most important relevant cues.

At the highest levels of arousal we find a state of hypervigilance that is more commonly referred to as panic. When inexperienced drivers lose control of their vehicles on an icy road, they often panic, applying the brakes and "freezing" at the wheel, even when they know this is the wrong thing to do. They freeze because the decision-making ability of a person in a hypervigilant state is severely limited due to an extreme perceptual narrowing and several other factors. Such a condition also degrades the physical control of movements, causing the smooth, skilled actions that are produced under more relaxed circumstances to be blocked (Weinberg & Hunt, 1976). Although hypervigilant states are relatively rare, it is not uncommon to see them in youth sports (for coaches as well as athletes!), particularly during important and close competitions. Sadly, the winner of such contests is usually the athlete or team that performs *less poorly* rather than the one that performs better!

### *Techniques for Managing Arousal Levels*

**muscle-to-mind skills**—Techniques for regulating arousal that utilize somatic activity (e.g., rhythmic breathing, muscle relaxation) to relax or energize the mind.

**mind-to-muscle skills**—Techniques for regulating arousal that utilize cognitive activity (e.g., meditation, visualization) to relax or energize the muscles.

Williams and Harris (1998) have provided a comprehensive discussion of the two major categories of relaxation and energizing techniques that individuals can use to regulate their arousal levels. The first category includes **muscle-to-mind skills**, which focus on the bodily aspects of arousal and in so doing produce a clearing of the mind as well. Most notable of these are breathing exercises and progressive relaxation techniques. The latter skills involve a brief, initial contraction of selected muscles followed by relaxation. After some practice, individuals often delete the contraction phase in order to achieve adjustments more quickly. The second category of arousal regulation techniques includes **mind-to-muscle skills**, which induce relaxation or activation of the body via cognitive activity. The most often used skills in this category are meditation and visualization. Meditation is primarily used as a relaxation technique and involves easy breathing and a passive focus of attention on something that is nonarousing, such as the words *calm* or *warm*. Visualization is used to decrease or increase arousal by creating a mental picture of either a relaxing or energizing scene, such as lying on the beach or charging up a hill.

## Attention: Limitations in Information-Processing Capacity

**attention**—Focalization and limitation of information-processing resources.

A very old idea in psychology that is still true today is that people have a limited capacity to process information from the environment or to pay attention to more than a few things at a time. In this section we discuss how the concept of **attention** is related to information-processing capabilities that place limits on human skilled performance.

As a tournament golfer is about to sink a putt that will give him the victory in a big tournament and the first prize of $500,000, his attention is distracted by a baby crying in the crowd of spectators. The sound is distracting because it enters his attentional space, a space that can handle only a limited amount of information. The baby's crying has "barged in" to this space and is interfering with other information that is more relevant to producing the golf putt. Since the space is limited in capacity, the crying may have even caused some of this relevant information to be temporarily "bumped out." In order to rectify the situation, the golfer backs away from the ball and attempts to eliminate the baby's crying from his attentional space while refilling it with only those thoughts that pertain to successful putting.

Not only is attentional capacity limited, it also seems to be serial in nature in that we usually focus first on one thing, then on another; and only with great difficulty (if at all) can we focus on two things at the same time. Sometimes we attend to external sensory events (an opponent's movements), sometimes we focus on internal mental operations (the next strategy we intend to use), and sometimes we pay attention to internal sensory information (sensations from our muscles and joints). It can be a very difficult task to try to process any combination of these types of information simultaneously (e.g., patting our head and rubbing our stomach, or driving a car while talking on a cellular phone).

Figure 3.7 shows how the fixed amount (or capacity) of attentional space (illustrated by the large circles) is divided between the space required to perform a primary or "main" task and the space that is left over to perform a secondary activity. When the main task is relatively simple (see figure 3.7a), it does not require as much attention as when it is more complex (see figure 3.7b). Therefore, more of the remaining capacity or space is left to perform the secondary task, resulting in better performance.

This notion of **limited attentional capacity** has strong implications for understanding high-level skilled performance. At the moment that most skills are performed (e.g., as in the golf putt) there is usually an abundance of available information that could occupy the participant's attentional space and be processed. Some of the information is relevant to performance (relaxing the muscles and producing the shot); some of it is not (the sound of the baby's crying). The performer's challenge is to effectively

**limited attentional capacity**—The notion that humans can concentrate on only a small amount of information at one time, which curtails the ability of people to process information.

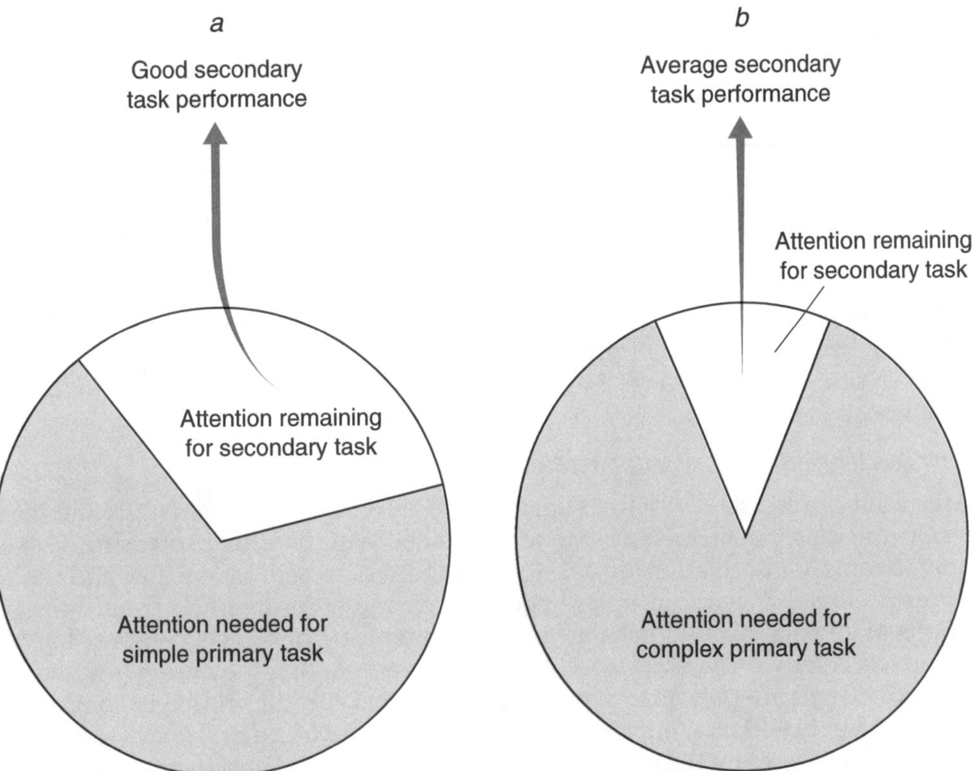


**Figure 3.7** Attention remaining for a secondary task is reduced when the primary task is more complex.

## A POSSIBLE SEQUENCE OF ATTENTIONAL SHIFTS FOR A PERSON PUTTING A GOLF BALL

One way performers can manage their attention is to handle one thing at a time, shifting their attention as needed. The following sequence illustrates possible shifts in a golfer's attention prior to and during a putt.

1. Visually focus on the position of the ball in relation to the hole.
2. Assume a comfortable stance, focusing on the feeling of balance in the legs and feet and on a relaxed but firm feel of the club in the hands.
3. Visually pick out the spot on the green that the putt will travel over.
4. Focus on breathing and on a relaxed exhalation.
5. Focus on the initiation of the club movement and the feel of a slow, smooth backswing.
6. Focus on the sight of the ball and on the feel of the club as it approaches and makes contact with the ball.
7. Focus on the sight of the spot previously occupied by the ball and on the feel of the follow-through of the club.

manage the space by making the right kinds of decisions about which information to attend to and how to handle it. Performers must also be able to *shift* attention skillfully among pertinent information in the environment, decisions about future actions, feedback from ongoing movements, and many other sources of information.

## When Do Tasks Compete With Each Other?

In this section we turn to the questions of when and under what conditions interference exists in the performance of two tasks. One way to understand this kind of interference is to revisit the stages of information processing shown in figure 3.2. Let's examine possible sources of interference or competition for available attentional capacity within each processing stage. As information moves through the stages, more interference or competition between two activities is likely. Processing can sometimes occur in parallel tracks—in other words, several things can be processed simultaneously without competing for attention—in the stimulus-identification stage. However, much less parallel processing is possible in the response-selection and response-programming stages. We develop these concepts in more detail in the following sections.

### *Stimulus Identification: Information Processing in Parallel*

**parallel processing**—A type of information processing that allows individuals to handle two or more streams of information at the same time; usually occurs during the stimulus-identification stage.

Quite a bit of research evidence suggests that information processing in the most peripheral, sensory stages can be done in parallel. With **parallel processing**, two or more streams of information are able to enter the system at the same time and can be processed together without interference: for example, information from different aspects of a visual display, such as the color and shape of objects. Support for this notion has chiefly come from laboratory studies employing the Stroop task. In this task individuals are presented with a series of visual stimuli printed in colored ink (e.g., green or black) on white cards. The stimuli consist of either irrelevant forms or of words that represent the names of colors (see figure 3.8). Participants are told that as soon as the stimulus is presented, they are to identify the *ink color* of the form or word as quickly as possible, pressing one key if the ink color is green and another if it is black. The results of these studies consistently show that RT is longer when the stimuli are the *names* of colors (see the words BLACK and GREEN on the right side of figure 3.8) than when the stimuli are irrelevant forms or symbols (see the signs on the left side of figure 3.8). These results, termed the **Stroop effect**, suggest that two stimuli—the ink color of the word (e.g., black, green) and the name of the word (e.g., GREEN)—are processed together and in parallel during the stimulus-identification stage. Since the RT is longer for the *names* of colors than for irrelevant forms, we conclude that interference occurs later, during the response-selection stage of information processing when individuals must decide which response, or keypress, to select—the one corresponding to the ink color of the word or the one representing the name of the word (i.e., GREEN).

**Stroop effect**—The label given to experimental results showing that people are able to process two stimuli in parallel during the stimulus-identification stage; however, when they do this their reaction time is longer than when they process only one stimulus.

Similar findings have been reported in studies showing that separate auditory messages delivered to the two ears can be processed together, even though one message can be ignored intentionally. Parallel processing of sensory signals has also been demonstrated in the muscles and joints associated with posture and locomotion. The standard view, then, is that sensory information can be processed in parallel during the stimulus-identification stage. Therefore, the source of interference that produces competition for attention during the performance of two separate movement tasks is presumed to lie in one of the later information-processing stages. For example, the soccer goalie may identify several stimuli simultaneously (e.g., the voices of spectators, thoughts about the game situation, and the sight of the approaching shot and several attacking players), but does not experience interference until he must select a response (e.g., to catch the ball, to deflect the ball over the goal, to head the ball toward a teammate) or program simultaneous movements (e.g., heading the ball toward a teammate while avoiding a collision with an onrushing opponent).

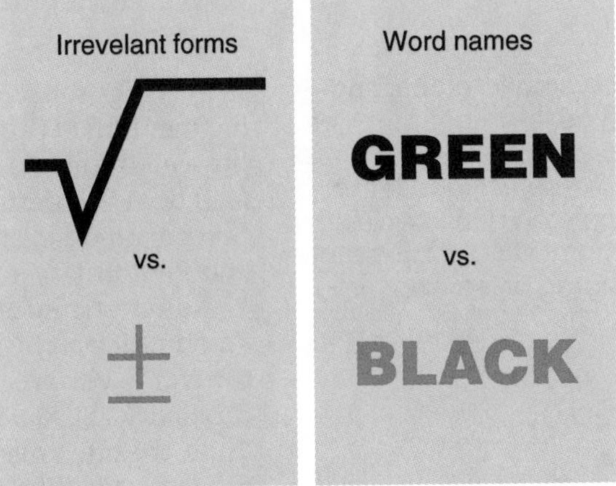


Figure 3.8 The Stroop effect. When ink color and type of stimulus conflict, reaction time to name the ink color is slowed.

### Response Selection: Controlled and Automatic Processing

Interference between tasks is never more obvious than when a person tries to simultaneously perform two actions that both require mental operations, such as dribbling a soccer ball while answering a coach's question about the best attacking strategy to use. Processing activities, such as these, are thought to be done during response selection because they deal with a choice among several possible responses. These activities are governed by **controlled processing**, which is thought to be slow; attention demanding, with interference caused by competition in response selection; serial, occurring before or after other processing tasks; and volitional, easily halted or avoided altogether. Controlled processing is relatively effortful because it requires the involvement of several conscious information-processing activities. This is particularly true for tasks that are poorly learned or completely new to the person. Having to perform two tasks at the same time, both of which require controlled processing, can completely disrupt an individual's performance due to information overload. An example might be that of a father trying to assemble his daughter's new toy with a tool he has never used before.

**controlled processing**—A type of information processing that is slow, serial, attention demanding, and voluntary; more prevalent during the early stages of learning.

In contrast to this tedious form of controlled information-processing, there is a separate, very different kind of processing that is demonstrated by highly practiced people. When asked to describe his thought process during gymnastics competition, Peter Vidmar, a 1984 Olympic silver medalist, said that he paid attention only to the first trick in his routine; the remainder of the elements occurred almost "automatically." Since the remaining elements required only minor adjustments while being run off, Vidmar was able to use his attention to focus more on the higher-order aspects of his routine, such as style and form. Clearly, his approach to this complex

**Table 3.1**
**Characteristics of Controlled and Automatic Processing**

| Controlled processing | Automatic processing |
|---|---|
| *Slow* | *Fast* |
| *Attention demanding* | *Not attention demanding* |
| *Serial* | *Parallel* |
| *Voluntary* | *Involuntary* |

**automatic processing**—A type of information processing that is fast, parallel, not attention demanding, and often involuntary; more prevalent in the later stages of learning.

gymnastics routine is fundamentally different from the type of controlled processing mentioned previously. The chief differences in these two types of processing are presented in table 3.1. In contrast to controlled processing, **automatic processing** is fast; does not demand attention, in that there is very little interference or competition for attention among tasks; parallel, with several tasks performed simultaneously; and involuntary, often unavoidable.

Automatic information processing is thought to be the result of an enormous amount of practice. Your capability to quickly recognize collections of letters, as in the words you are reading now, has come from years of practice, just as has Vidmar's capability to produce his entire gymnastics routine by focusing only on the first trick. Thus, the effectiveness of automatic processing has strong implications for both everyday tasks (like reading) as well as for high-level performance of industrial tasks (like operating an earthmoving machine) and sport skills (like gymnastics).

**production units**—Developed by individuals over practice; these units allow skilled performers to handle particular information-processing tasks in an automatic fashion.

**Production Units.** One interpretation of automaticity is that, with practice, a person develops a series of small, specialized **production units** for the handling of particular information-processing subtasks. Thus, when an individual encounters a specific stimulus, a production unit is activated to generate the appropriate output. For example, after much practice, high-level volleyball players are able to automatically recognize their opponents' movement patterns signaling the direction and type of an upcoming shot, such as a spike to the left side (e.g., see Allard & Burnett, 1985). The production units operate on these patterns and produce a particular output (the internal decision to execute a block to the left). Once this is done, the action that has been selected (i.e., the block) is detailed in the response-programming stage.

**Costs Versus Benefits of Automaticity.** Automatic performances occur when individuals process information in parallel, quickly, and without interference or competition for attention. But what if the opposing volleyball players in the previous example produce movement patterns that usually accompany a spike to the left—and then execute a play that goes to the right? On this occasion, the defender's automatic processing of the pattern would lead to a quick decision and a movement (e.g., a block) to counter the expected play (i.e., a spike to the left), a response that would fail to combat the play that actually occurs (i.e., a hit to the right).

Clearly, then, automaticity has its drawbacks as well as its benefits. Although very fast processing is advantageous to performers when the environment is stable and predictable, it can lead them to inappropriate responses and errors when the environment (or an opponent) produces a different, unexpected action at the last moment. Thus, automaticity would appear to be most effective for individuals who perform closed skills, where the environment is relatively predictable. With open skills, more stimulus patterns are possible and performers require many years of experience to develop automatic responses for each of the patterns.

**Practicing for Automaticity.** How do people develop the capability to process information automatically? Practice, and lots of it, is a very important ingredient, so individuals should not expect to see automatic processing come quickly. Practicing for automaticity is generally most effective under a **consistent stimulus-response mapping** condition; that is, where the stimulus pattern always requires the same response. For example, a red traffic light at an intersection always calls for a braking response. This is in contrast to a **varied stimulus-response mapping** condition, in which a particular stimulus may require different responses at different times or in different situations. An example of varied stimulus-response mapping may be found in homes with more than one TV. Quite often, the spatial arrangement of buttons on remote control units varies with different brands of TVs. In homes with more than one TV, channel changing may require controlled processing. To develop automaticity, viewers would need extensive practice with all of the available remote control units.

**consistent stimulus-response mapping**—A performance condition for which a given stimulus pattern always requires the same response.

**varied stimulus-response mapping**—A performance condition for which a given stimulus pattern requires different responses at different times or in different situations.

### *Response Programming: Movement Organization Occurs Serially*

A fencer moves the foil toward her opponent's shoulder but then quickly alters direction and contacts the waist instead. The opponent's speed of responding to the second move is delayed due to an initial response that she makes to the first move (i.e., the fake). Therefore, the opponent loses the point. This example suggests that some sort of interference or competition for attention exists between events that occur in the response-selection stage (Pashler, 1993, 1994). Much of the support for this notion comes from laboratory research using a **double-stimulation paradigm**. In these experiments, participants are required to respond (usually by lifting left and right index fingers off buttons) to each of two stimuli presented very close together in time (usually no more than a few tenths of a second apart). This situation is in many ways analogous to the problem facing the opponent of the previously mentioned fencer, who makes a response to the first move (the fake) and then must suddenly produce another to the second move (the thrust).

**double-stimulation paradigm**—A research design involving separate reactions to two different stimuli presented close together in time.

**Double-Stimulation Paradigm: Psychological Refractory Period (PRP).** In a typical double-stimulation study, participants might be asked to respond to a tone (stimulus 1) by lifting the right hand from a key and to respond to a light (stimulus 2) by lifting the left hand. The separation between stimuli, the **interstimulus interval (ISI)**, or the "stimulus onset asynchrony," might range from zero seconds to a few hundred milliseconds (a few tenths of a second). Yet participants are required to react to one stimulus and then to a second stimulus that follows soon after the first. Psychologists are usually interested in RT to the second stimulus (RT2) as a function of the length of the ISI.

**interstimulus interval (ISI)**—The length of time separating two stimuli in a double-stimulation paradigm; sometimes called stimulus onset asynchrony (SOA).

The general findings from this type of research are depicted in figure 3.9, where RT to the *second* stimulus is plotted as a function of the ISI. The horizontal line (control RT2) represents the RT of participants to the second stimulus when the first stimulus is not presented at all. When both stimuli are presented, the longest RT to the second stimulus (RT2) occurs when the interval between stimuli is about 60 ms in length; in this case, RT2 is more than twice as long as the control RT2. As the ISI increases, RT2 decreases, but it still is longer than the control RT2 even when the ISI reaches 200 ms or more. Clearly, the processing of the second stimulus is seriously delayed when it is presented soon after the first stimulus.

This delay in responding to the second of two closely spaced stimuli is an important phenomenon of human performance; it has been termed the **psychological refractory period (PRP)**. Apparently, in situations in which two stimuli are presented unexpectedly close together in time, the system takes in the first stimulus and begins to generate a response to it. The current understanding is that this creates a temporary bottleneck in the response-selection or response-programming stage or both (Pashler, 1993, 1994) because only one action can be organized and initiated at a time, as diagrammed in figure 3.10. Any other action (such as the organization and

**psychological refractory period (PRP)**—The delay in an individual's reaction time to the second of two closely spaced stimuli compared with the person's reaction time to the second stimulus presented by itself.

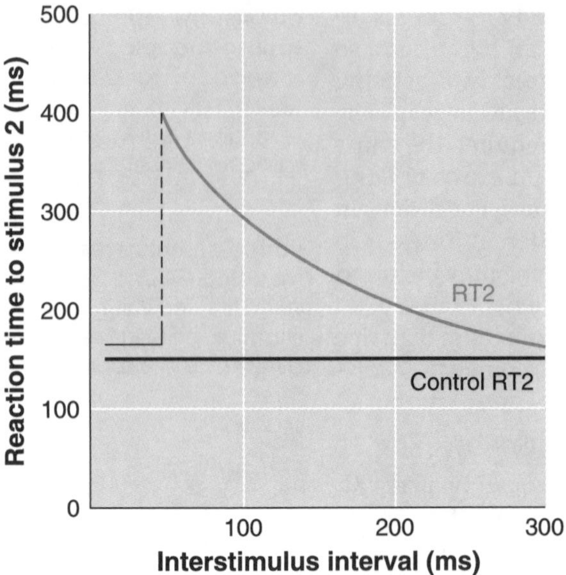


Figure 3.9 The PRP effect. Reaction time to the second of two closely spaced stimuli (RT2) is delayed, depending on the interstimulus interval (ISI).

initiation of a response to the second stimulus) must wait until the programming of the response to the first stimulus is completed. This delay is longest when the ISI is very short (approximately 60 ms) because the response-selection stage has just begun to select a response to the first stimulus; this response must then be initiated before the processing of a response to the second stimulus can begin. As the ISI increases, more programming of the first response has been completed when stimulus 2 arrives, so there is less delay in beginning the programming of the second response.

One more phenomenon is of interest here. When the ISI is extremely short, say less than 40 ms, the system responds to the two stimuli in a very different way, producing responses to both simultaneously as if they were one. This phenomenon, termed *grouping*, presumably occurs because both stimuli are detected as a single event that produces the organization and initiation of a single, more complicated action in which both limbs respond at the same time.

**The Fake in Sports: Capitalizing on the PRP.** Basketball players often use a strategy in which they fake a shot shortly before actually taking a shot. Overenthusiastic defensive players will often try to block the first "shot" (i.e., the fake), putting themselves out of position to defend against the actual shot. Players commonly use fakes in various rapid sports and games.

The phenomenon of the psychological refractory period offers a nice explanation of the underlying processes that operate when a fake is followed closely in time by another movement. In the basketball example, the player who is going to take the shot plans a single, relatively complex action that involves first making a movement intended to look like a shot (the fake), then aborting this movement, and then producing the desired movement (i.e., the shot)—performing all three actions in rapid succession. The performer organizes this sequence as a single unit, as he would any other movement in the response-programming stage. However, the defensive player assumes that the first part of the sequence, the fake, is in fact an attempt by the offensive player to shoot. The fake, then, is analagous to the first stimulus in a double-stimulation paradigm, and it triggers the defender's response (i.e., the block). Just as the defensive player is executing his response to the fake, the second stimulus (i.e., the shot) occurs—and the defender is unable to inhibit his response to the fake. Because the defensive player is unable to complete the processing of a corrective response in time, the shooter is able to produce an uncontested shot, often making the defensive player look foolish.

© Tom Roberts

In a hockey breakaway shot, the puck carrier must decide whether to shoot at the net or fake the shot and go to one side of the goalie before shooting.

Some important principles of faking in sports emerge from research examining the psychological

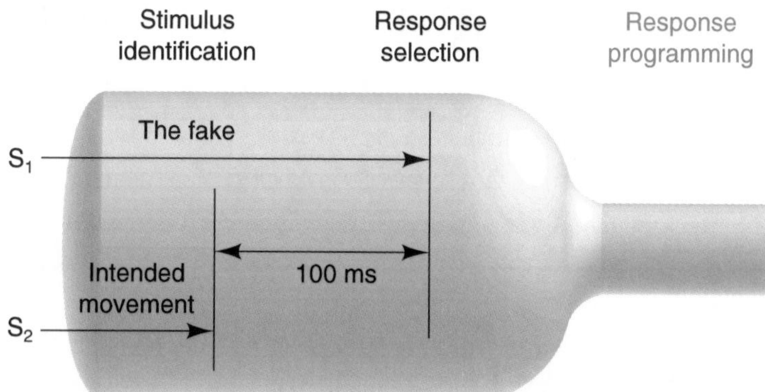


Stimulus 1 enters, followed in 100 ms by Stimulus 2. Both are processed in parallel until Stimulus 1 reaches the bottleneck in the response-programming stage, where

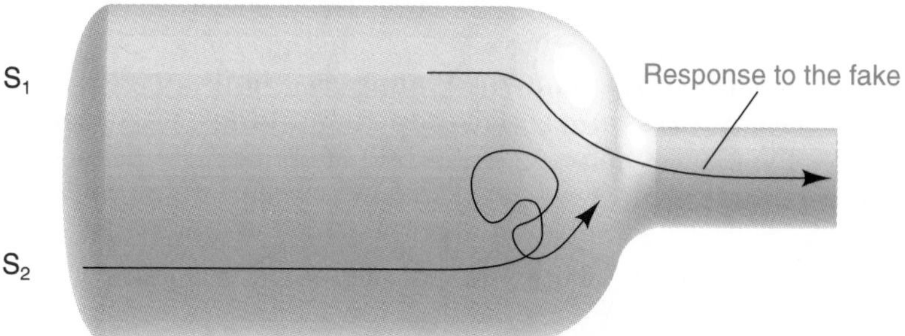


Stimulus 2 must wait until the response-programming stage is cleared for further processing, so

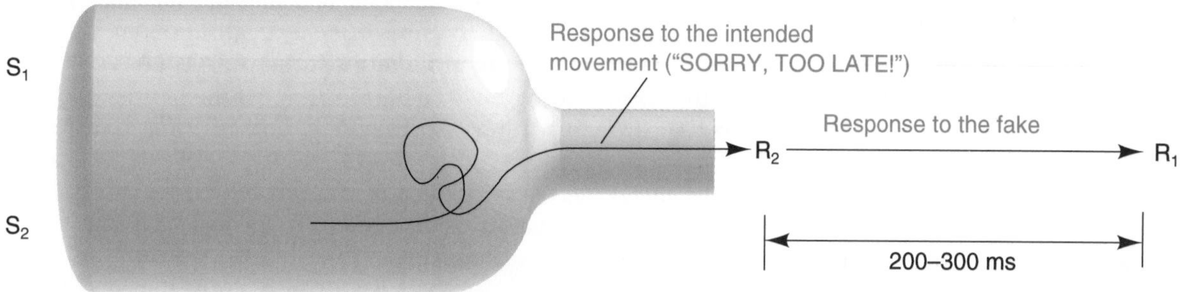


Response 1 and Response 2 are separated by far more than 100 ms.

Figure 3.10 An information-processing bottleneck in the response-programming stage.

refractory period. First, for the fake to be effective, it must look realistic and be clearly perceived to be an actual shot, so that the defensive player responds to it as if it was the expected movement (e.g., the shot). Second, the single programmed action that contains both the fake and the intended movement must be planned and executed in such a way as to separate the fake (stimulus 1) and the intended movement (stimulus 2) with the right timing in order to generate a delay in the defender's response to the intended movement. From the available research data it appears that this time should be somewhere between 60 ms and 100 ms (see figure 3.9). If it is shorter than that, the defensive player can ignore the fake and respond instead to the intended movement. If it is longer than that, the defender can respond to the

## PRINCIPLES OF EFFECTIVE FAKING IN SPORTS

For fakes to be effective they must

- appear to be identical to the expected action,
- precede the goal movement by between 60 ms and 100 ms, and
- be employed infrequently.

second stimulus with a delay that is not much longer than normal RT, and the offensive player (e.g., the shooter) will have lost the advantage of the fake.

**movement output chunking**—The act of organizing and producing several movements as a single unit; a common feature of skilled performance.

**Movement Output Chunking.** Aside from its practical applications, the PRP effect is important for understanding how movements are produced. Since two separate actions, each triggered by a separate stimulus, cannot be produced very close to each other in time, the movement control system must produce bursts or chunks of activity that exclusively occupy several hundred milliseconds each. Researchers have shown that these chunks of activity can be separated in time by no less than 200 ms (Kahneman, 1973). Thus, it is likely that when numerous chunks have to be strung together (sometimes referred to as **movement output chunking**), as in steering a car, the system produces the chunks at a maximum rate of about three per second. Researchers think that these chunks of movement are organized in the response-programming stage and then run off under the control of motor programs (see chapter 5), as shown in figure 3.11.

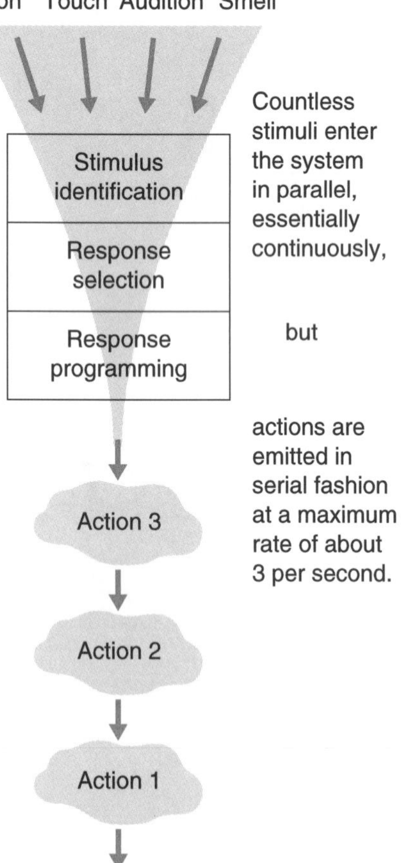


**Figure 3.11** Information from sensory stimuli is provided continuously, but responses are generated in units, or chunks (see "actions").

## When Do the Hands Compete With Each Other?

Once movements are organized they can be produced. This is not difficult, if the actions are simple. However, if the movements are complex, production can sometimes be a challenge for performers. You have undoubtedly tried to rub your stomach and pat your head at the same time and, if you are like most people, you have experienced difficulty coordinating the two hands. It's as if the hands do not "want" to do two different things, so they *both* end up *either* patting or rubbing both body parts. This classic example illustrates many important movement coordination principles concerning the kinds of movements individuals find easy to produce at the same time and those they find essentially impossible to coordinate. It also tells us about some of the principles underlying coordination of the limbs in general.

**Role of Timing and Rhythm.** An interesting aspect of many types of bimanual (using two hands) movements is that under many circumstances the hands seem to be "linked" to each other. For example, it is easy for us to make simultaneous movements of the hands if the movement pattern is the same for both hands, and even easier if the patterns for the two hands are mirror images of each other. You can experience this phenomenon by scribbling with both hands on a large sheet of paper or a blackboard. If you try this experiment, you'll see that it is extremely easy to make the "same" pattern with the left and right hands. Research that has involved more sophisticated analysis of bimanual movements has revealed that the actions of the two hands possess a common time structure, in that the muscular forces that produce the various submovements do so in the same time (or rhythm) in the two hands. The spatial structure of these movements is not so similar, how-

## The Gamma-V Experiment

Try this simple experiment. With a pencil in your left hand, practice drawing 2-in. high gamma (γ)-shaped figures relatively quickly, in one quick, continuous movement. It's best if you begin with the pencil point touching a ruler laid across the paper and finish with the pencil against the ruler again. The figures must cross over near the center and have a rounded bottom. Practice until you can do this task effectively. Now, with a pencil in your right hand, draw V-shaped figures about 2 in. high. These figures must not cross over themselves, and they must have a pointed bottom. If you are like most people, you shouldn't have too much trouble producing the γ-shaped figures and the V-shaped figures separately. Scientists assume that we use a different motor program for each figure because the temporal structure for each figure is different: down-up for the V and down-over-up for the γ.

Now try to produce the two figures at the same time, using the same hand for each figure that you used before. When you attempt this, you will find, as Konzem (1987) did, that it is a difficult task (see a sample of the results from that study in figure 3.12). Most people show a strong tendency to produce the same figure with both hands, or at least to produce certain features of each figure in both hands (e.g., a rounded bottom on the V and a next-to-nonexistent loop on the γ). They still have trouble doing this dual task effectively, even after more than 1,000 practice trials! The gamma-V experiment illustrates the fact that, even when separate programs are used to produce two figures, these programs cannot be run off at the same time without massive interference between the hands.

ever, as you can demonstrate for yourself by attempting to scribble in large strokes with the left hand and in small strokes with the right. Notice that while this spatial discrepancy is not difficult to achieve, the time structure to produce the movements remains virtually the same for both hands. Observations and laboratory analyses of similar situations have led researchers to the idea that, especially for relatively unpracticed bimanual movements, the system "prefers" to operate in a mode in which the two hands perform the same actions, or at least actions that have the same temporal (i.e., timing) structure.

We can make this point another way. It is particularly difficult for us to produce bimanual movements in which the two hands are moving in different rhythms. To experience this, try tapping a constant rhythm with your left hand while tapping as quickly as possible with your right. Researchers have shown that it is even difficult for individuals to attend to an externally produced rhythm (e.g., by listening to a metronome) while attempting to tap out a different rhythm of their own (Klapp et al., 1985). All of this suggests that the system prefers to produce simultaneous movements that have a common underlying time structure.

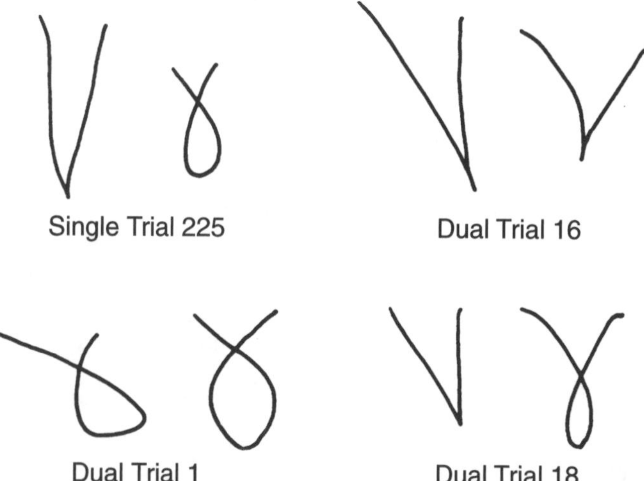


Figure 3.12 The Gamma-V Experiment. Results of attempts to draw gammas and Vs either separately (single trial) or together (dual trials) after various amounts of practice. (Reprinted by permission from Konzem, 1987.)

**One Interpretation: Output Chunking.** One important interpretation of these findings is that the motor system can effectively produce only one motor program at a time; only one action is organized at a time during the response-programming stage. In the present case, however, the focus is on the production of the movement *after* organization is completed. Fundamental here are the notions (which we develop further in chapter 6) that a single movement program has a specific temporal structure inherent to it, that only one temporal structure can be produced at any one time, and that this temporal structure provides a basis for the temporal organization of the movement for all the limbs that the system controls. Therefore, simultaneously rubbing your head and patting your stomach is difficult because it requires different temporal structures; the system tries unsuccessfully to produce different temporal structures in the two hands at the same time. Likewise, producing a Greek gamma (γ) and the letter V simultaneously presents the same problem (see the highlight box on page 81). And when a person tries to produce different tapping rhythms at the same time, one rhythm dominates, and the performance of both tasks is less effective. However, when the hands are linked together, as in scribbling, movement production is easy because both hands are controlled by the same temporal structure.

In one sense, being able to generate only one action at a time seems to be a serious limitation to human performance. From an ecological viewpoint, however, this mode of movement control is quite reasonable. If the movement apparatus of humans is organized to produce actions that are effective in solving environmental problems, such as the goalie's task of deflecting the puck or catching it, the most relevant action at that particular moment, and *only* that single action—deflecting or catching—is the one the person needs to generate. The relevant movement is "protected" from conflicting signals, which allows it to run its course uninterrupted, thus achieving the desired goal.

But how do we explain the bimanual movements of athletes, musicians, and industrial workers who perform tasks that involve independent and distinct movements of the two limbs? For example, it is difficult to see much in common between what the two hands must do during a tennis serve or while playing the violin or when operating a forklift. One possibility is that the performer learns to control the hands separately with practice, so that one hand produces a relatively well-learned pattern of actions automatically while the other hand generates its pattern using a type of controlled processing. A more likely possibility is that the system develops a more sophisticated program that is used to control both hands at the same time (Schmidt, Heuer, Ghodsian, and Young, 1998). How individuals develop this type of higher-order coordination, and what factors influence it, is one of the most puzzling problems for scientists attempting to understand motor behavior. And at present, they have found no satisfying answers. Table 3.2 summarizes the characteristics and limitations of the response-programming stage and the two stages we discussed previously.

**Table 3.2**

**Characteristics of the Sequential Stages of Information Processing**

| Characteristic | Stimulus-identification stage | Response-selection stage | Response-programming stage |
|---|---|---|---|
| *Function of stage* | *Detect, identify signal* | *Select response* | *Organize, initiate action* |
| *Effect of number of S-R alternatives* | *Minor* | *Large* | *None* |
| *Type of processing* | *Parallel* | *Parallel and serial* | *Serial* |
| *Attention required* | *No* | *Sometimes* | *Yes* |

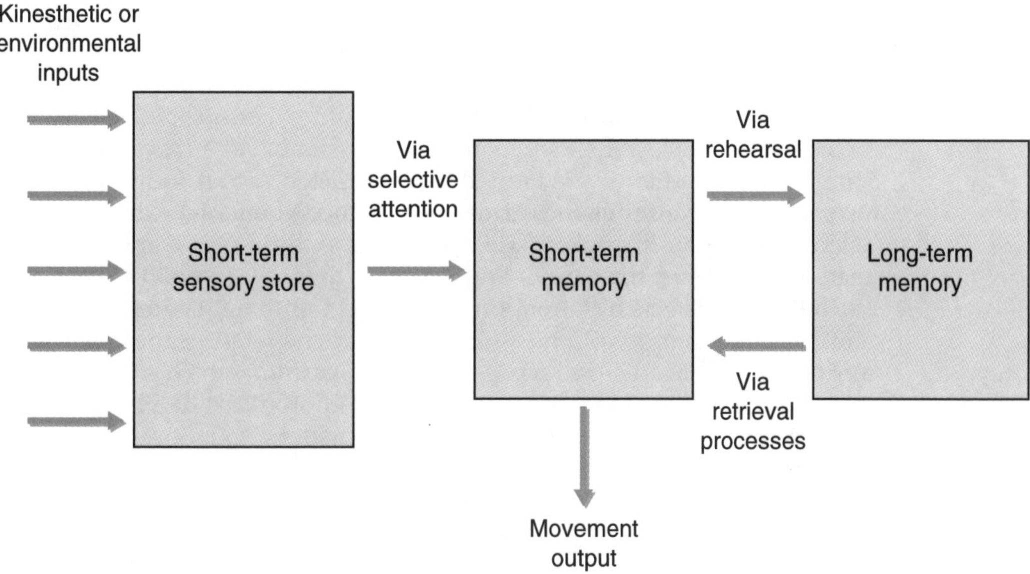


Figure 3.13 Three discrete components of human memory.

The processes we have discussed so far are presumably stored in some way in the central nervous system. However, most instances of perception, decision making, and movement production require individuals to use some type of information they have remembered from previous experiences. In the next section we discuss the general concept of memory and how this system stores information for future use.

# Three Memory Systems

**memory**—The capacity of individuals to retain and utilize information in various ways for various periods of time; comprised of three components: short-term sensory store, short-term memory, and long-term memory.

An important concept in thinking about skills is **memory**, which is usually viewed as the storage of material that results from the activities of the various information-processing stages. Psychologists have postulated at least three distinct memory systems, each of which is involved in some fashion in the processing of information that results in movement production: short-term sensory store, short-term memory, and long-term memory (see figure 3.13).

## Short-Term Sensory Store

**short-term sensory store (STSS)**—The most peripheral memory system, which holds incoming information by modality until the individual identifies it; believed to be limited in capacity and extremely brief in duration.

The most peripheral, or sensory, component of memory is the **short-term sensory store (STSS)**. As we discussed earlier, numerous streams of information are processed simultaneously and in parallel during the stimulus-identification stage. Initially stimuli enter the system and are briefly held in different STSSs according to modality (auditory, visual, kinesthetic, tactile, and so on). The information is held in these memory systems for a very short period of time, perhaps only a few hundred milliseconds, until it is replaced by the next segment or stream of sensory information. Scientists believe that STSS storage occurs prior to conscious involvement by the performer and therefore entails very little transformation of the sensory information.

## Short-Term Memory

Although a considerable amount of information passes through an individual's STSS, obviously not all of it reaches the person's consciousness. Rather, a selective attention mechanism selects some of the information in STSS for further processing (see figure 3.13), with the remainder being lost or replaced by more recent incoming information. Researchers think that the final decision regarding what information is selected for further processing relates to the information's relevance, or pertinence, to the present task. When someone says your name at a crowded party (a relevant stimulus), your attention is immediately attracted to that source of information and you select that stimulus for further processing. Many high-level sports performers selectively attend to appropriate cues as the skill unfolds—and ignore information that detracts from their goal. For example, a rugby football player attempting to catch the ball directs his attention to the object until he secures it; only then does he shift his attention to avoiding tacklers. Thus, a challenging and often difficult part of a person's skill-acquisition process involves learning which sources of environmental (e.g., the ball) or kinesthetic (e.g., the position of the hands) information to pay attention to and which (e.g., the opposing tacklers) to ignore when attempting the primary task (e.g., catching).

**short-term memory (STM)**—The memory system that allows individuals to retrieve, rehearse, process, and transfer information to long-term memory; believed to be limited in capacity and brief in duration.

People utilize selective attention to direct information into **short-term memory (STM)**. STM is thought to be a kind of temporary work space (termed "working memory" by some authors) where controlled information-processing activities can be applied to the relevant information. STM is thought to be seriously limited in capacity. If it can be likened to consciousness (which is at least reasonable to do), its "holding space" is limited to only a small number of items. Experiments have shown that, for a remarkable number of different kinds of information inputs, STM capacity is at most only about 7 ± 2 items, or "chunks" of information (Miller, 1956). The way this information is represented in STM is more abstract (less literal) than the way it is represented in STSS. Depending on the type of stimulus, the information is transformed into one of several more abstract codes (e.g., a printed word might be coded in terms of the sound of the word). We can hold information in STM only as long as we direct attention to it, such as by recycling, rehearsing, repeating the information over and over, or associating it with other items. If we direct our attention elsewhere, we forget the contents, with complete loss occurring in perhaps 30 s. A classic illustration of this phenomenon is the person who looks up a friend's phone number, then fumbles for a coin, and in only a few seconds forgets the number.

In the realm of motor skills, the brief duration of time for which unrehearsed movements are preserved in STM may also be illustrated by the situation in which a therapist guides the patient's limbs to a particular position on one occasion, only to find that the patient's memory of the position has faded from kinesthetic STM by the next attempt a few minutes later.

## Long-Term Memory

**long-term memory (LTM)**—The memory system that holds information and experiences; believed to be vast in capacity and unlimited in duration.

The third compartment of memory is **long-term memory (LTM)**, which is considered to be the storage space for very well-learned information people collect over their lifetimes. Experiments have shown that LTM is probably limitless, both in capacity and in the duration of time the information is preserved. We can all think of skills we learned long ago and have never forgotten, even after not practicing them for many years (e.g., riding a bicycle and roller skating). Probably the only reason we cannot remember someone's name or our old telephone number is because we cannot "find" it or retrieve it, not because it is no longer stored in LTM. The way individuals code information in LTM is thought to be very abstract, with elaborate connections to other stored information, perhaps by imagery and a host of other processes that scientists are only beginning to understand.

Information that we store in LTM arrives there as a result of controlled and generally effortful processing (involving things such as rehearsal and the connecting of new information to previously learned information) that takes place in STM. When we say that someone has learned something, we really mean that they have in some way processed the information in STM and transferred it to LTM. This concept also applies to the learning of movement skills, where people are assumed to process motor programs for action in STM and then store them in LTM for later execution. For many motor skills, particularly continuous ones such as riding a bicycle or swimming, research evidence and common experience tell us that retention is almost perfect after years, even decades, without intervening practice; this is quite different from the substantial forgetting we experience for well-learned verbal and cognitive skills (e.g., foreign language vocabulary). However, we do seem to more easily forget some discrete motor skills, such as gymnastics stunts, but scientists are not quite sure why.

## Summary

The human motor system can be thought of as a processor of information, with signals received from the various sense organs (input), processed through various stages, and produced as movements (output). There are three main information-processing stages:

- Stimulus-identification stage, which detects the nature of environmental information
- Response-selection stage, which decides upon the action that should be made
- Response-programming stage, which organizes the system for a response

Reaction time is an important measure of information-processing speed. Its duration is affected by the number of stimulus-response alternatives (described by Hick's Law), by the naturalness of the relationship between the stimuli and their associated movements (stimulus-response compatibility), and by the predictability of the upcoming events.

Arousal and anxiety generally show an inverted-U relationship to performance. Increases in arousal enhance performance, but only to a point; further increases beyond this optimal arousal level then diminish performance.

Attention, the general capacity to process information, is a seriously limiting factor in many performance situations. The delay in an individual's response to the second of two closely spaced stimuli (known as the psychological refractory period, or PRP) suggests that the motor system can organize and initiate only one action at a time, with a maximum rate of about three actions per second. There is potential for massive interference in the control of two-handed movements, unless individuals produce movements that have a common temporal structure.

Finally, it is useful to conceptualize three memory systems that serve as depositories for information:

- Short-term sensory store, with a large capacity for information but an extremely brief holding duration of 250 ms
- Short-term memory, with a small capacity and a holding duration of about 30 s
- Long-term memory, with a virtually unlimited capacity and holding duration

## From Principles to Practice

Check your understanding of the material in this chapter by responding to the following questions and then completing the application exercises. In each case see if you can identify the most relevant questions or issues and then propose a solution based on the concepts and principles discussed in the chapter.

### Checking Your Understanding

1. Describe the information-processing activities that might occur in the stimulus-identification, response-selection, and response-programming stages for a soccer goalie.
2. What might be a positive consequence of a correct anticipation by a pedestrian crossing a busy street? What might be a negative consequence of an incorrect anticipation?
3. Refer to the cue-utilization hypothesis to explain how the performance of a person playing a fast-action video game might deteriorate as the individual's arousal increases from a low to a high level.
4. Describe a recreational activity you participate in regularly and then indicate the level of arousal (low, medium, or high) you feel accompanies your best performance of that activity. Under what circumstances would you be concerned about being underaroused when performing the activity? Overaroused?
5. When you participate in the activity you discussed in the previous question, what things do you attend to when your performance is good? When your performance is not good? How do your answers relate to the notion of a limited attentional capacity?
6. What limitations prevent you from simultaneously producing two different hand movements, or make it very difficult for you to do so? What types of simultaneous hand movements do you find easy to perform? Why? What types of hand movements do you find difficult to perform? Why?

### Application Exercise #1

An older sister is watching her younger brother try to catch a beanbag, and she notices that the boy's eyes are focused more on her face than on the beanbag. The boy does not catch the beanbag often.

*It Depends*

- What is the boy's age and maturation level?
- What is the boy's skill level?
- How large is the beanbag?
- How far apart are the siblings standing from each other?
- Why is the boy looking at his sister's face?
- What stage(s) of information processing might be contributing to the catching errors?

*Strategy*

Determine what the boy is trying to do when he attempts to catch the beanbag. Try to identify which stage(s) of information processing might be contributing to the boy's catching problem. Suggest some things the older sister might do to increase her younger brother's catching success, and give a rationale as to why each might work.

*Response Example*

If the boy is very young or lacking experience with catching objects, he may not yet have the coordination to achieve a great deal of success. Reduce stimulus-identification demands by asking the boy to watch only the beanbag each time he tries to catch it. Reduce the demands of response selection and response programming by encouraging the boy's sister to toss the beanbag in a similar manner (i.e., speed, trajectory, etc.) each time.

### Application Exercise #2

You've been asked to help a friend coach a women's softball team. Most of the players are inexperienced with the fundamental skills involved. The season starts in three weeks.

*It Depends*

- What skills are most important for players at this level?
- What is your goal as a coach?
- What are the players' expectations?
- What are the information-processing demands of the fundamental skills (e.g., batting, catching, throwing)?
- Which processing demands should you attempt to reduce?

*Strategy*

Assess the skill levels of the players for each of the fundamental tasks. Identify the information-processing demands of each task, and determine ways to modify them in order to minimize the demands. As the players' skill levels improve, gradually increase task demands.

## Application Exercise #3

A middle-aged woman has just had arthroscopic surgery on her knee and must use crutches for the first time in her life. Questions fill her mind regarding the nature of this challenge. She knows how to walk, but she expects that crutch walking will be very little like normal walking.

*It Depends*

- What are the woman's goals?
- What are the requirements of the movement?
- What are the information-processing demands?
- Which stage(s) of processing should she give the most attention to?
- What factors might increase or decrease processing demands?

*Strategy*

Determine the requirements of crutch walking, and ask the woman which ones she is most concerned about. Identify the processing demands of those aspects of the task that present the most difficulty. Reduce information-processing demands in one or more of the stages of processing until the woman's skill level begins to improve. Gradually increase demands until she is able to use her crutches under a wider variety of circumstances.

## Application Exercise #4

A piano teacher asks his student to practice two new exercises. One requires piano key-strike movements of the fingers and thumbs while playing in time with a metronome. The other requires the same key-strike movements while accompanying the voice of a soloist from an audiotape.

*It Depends*

- What are the information-processing demands of each task?
- Which task has the greater stimulus-identification demands?
- Does the tempo of the metronome influence task difficulty?
- If the student uses one hand only, does it matter which hand she uses (i.e., dominant or nondominant)?
- What other factor must be considered if the student is required to use both hands simultaneously?

*Strategy*

Determine the information-processing demands of each task and, for each task, identify ways you might reduce those demands. For each task, indicate how you might gradually increase the information-processing demands when you see the student's skill level improving. Describe how you might modify the task to enhance the student's prospects of success when she is required to perform the task with both hands simultaneously.

4
GILBERT

# Sensory Contributions to Skilled Performance

## Chapter Outline



## Chapter Objectives

**When you have completed this chapter, you should be able to**

explain the contributions and limitations of a closed-loop control model of human skills,

understand the various ways that sensory information is used in movement control,

discuss the particular roles of vision in movement control, and

understand how sensory contributions to action are part of a conceptual model of movement control.

## Preview

The rugby player watches the ball leave her teammate's hand. With but a few tenths of a second of viewing time, the player realizes she must turn her back on the ball and cut sharply to her left to catch it. She predicts the ball's flight correctly, moves her eyes to focus on it, and times the ball's arrival into her hands. After a few steps, the player is tackled from behind, senses the ball slipping away, and compensates by grasping it with both hands, all the while trying to maintain her balance.

## Overview

Skilled performers seem to be able to receive and process vast amounts of information quickly and accurately and to make effective adjustments when necessary. How does just a brief glimpse of the ball tell the rugby player where to run? How does she know when the ball will arrive? How does she receive and process all this information?

In this chapter we focus on some of the many processes that allow performers to detect patterns of information in the environment and then use this information to determine their future actions. More specifically, we discuss how people use sensory information to plan their actions, correct their movement errors, and regulate their performance. First, we address ways in which the neuromuscular system uses sensory information in general, and then we present some of the principles of visual control of movements. Finally, we add these sensory contributions to the conceptual model of human skilled performance.

Success in skilled performance often depends on how effectively the participant detects, perceives, and uses relevant sensory information. Frequently, the successful performer is the one who most quickly detects the pattern of action of an opponent, as in rugby, or the one who senses her own body movements and positions most precisely, as in dance or gymnastics. Many coaches devote considerable practice time to activities they think will improve the speed and accuracy with which their athletes detect and process relevant sensory information. In another vein, therapists frequently work with individuals who have impaired or absent sensation involving one or more systems. These helping professionals must understand the ways people process sensory information in order to provide their patients with the most appropriate guidance and compensation activities.

## Sources of Sensory Information

**exteroception**—Sensory information that comes primarily from sources outside a person's body.

Information that might be used in the production of skilled movements arises from several basic sources, but a considerable amount comes from the environment. This source of information is typically referred to as **exteroception**, with the prefix *extero* indicating that the information "comes from outside" the body.

### Exteroceptive Information

Chief among the sources of exteroceptive information is, of course, vision. At the most fundamental level, what we see serves the important function of defining the physical structure of our environment, such as the edge of a stairway or the presence of an object blocking our path. In this context, vision provides a basis for our anticipation of upcoming events. Vision also affords us information about the movement of objects in the environment, such as the flight path and the speed of an approaching object like a ball, a subway train, or an angry dog. Another function of vision is to assist us in detecting the spatial and temporal aspects of our own movements within the environment, such as swinging a bat, stepping onto a train, or leaping over a fence. Later in this chapter we discuss some additional details about visual information.

**interoception**—Sensory information that comes primarily from sources within a person's body.

The second major source of exteroceptive information is audition, or hearing. Although audition is not as obviously involved as vision in the performance of movement skills, there are many activities for which we depend heavily on well-developed auditory skills, such as sailing, where individuals use the sound of the hull of the boat moving through the water to estimate boat speed. Audition is also an important source of sensory information for people with visual impairments.

**proprioception**—Sensory information arising from within a person's body that signals body and limb position and movement; similar to kinesthesis.

### Proprioceptive or Kinesthetic Information

The second basic source of sensory information comes from within our own body, generally termed **interoception** (e.g., hunger pangs). More relevant for motor control is information referred to as **proprioception**, with the prefix *proprio* meaning "from within the body." Examples of proprioceptive information include the positions of the joints, the forces produced in the muscles, and the orientation of the body in space (e.g., being upside down). Another type of information comes from the body's movements and is termed **kinesthesis**, with the prefix *kines* meaning "movement," and the suffix *thesis* meaning "the sense of." Kinesthesis, then, is the sense or awareness we have of the movements of our joints and the tension in our muscles during motor activity. The distinction between proprioception and kinesthesis has blurred over the years, and the terms are used almost synonymously today to refer to the collection of internal sensory information that informs us about the relative positions of our joints, the tension in our muscles, and the orientation of our bodies in space. This source of sensory information is particularly important to performers in sports such as gymnastics (i.e., for balance) and springboard diving (i.e., for orienting the body). In therapeutic settings, kinesthesis is essential for patients who are attempting to hold or alter their posture.

**kinesthesis**—Sensory information coming from the motor system that signals contraction and limb movements; related to proprioception.

Several important receptors provide the neuromuscular system with information about kinesthesis. The **vestibular apparatus** in the inner ear detects movements of the head and is sensitive to its orientation with respect to gravity. Not surprisingly, the information provided by these structures is important for posture and balance.

**vestibular apparatus**—Proprioceptive sense organs located in the inner ear that signal information about posture and balance.

Other receptors provide information about the limbs. Those located in the joints and in the surrounding joint capsules signal joint position, especially at the extremes of the limb's range of motion. Embedded within the belly of a skeletal muscle are receptors called **muscle spindles** (because of their shape), which stretch when the muscle contracts and provide information about the rate of contraction as well as the changing position of the joints. Near the junction between the muscle and the tendon are located receptors known as **Golgi tendon organs**, which signal the level of force in the various parts of the muscle. Finally, in most skin areas are found **cutaneous receptors**, including several kinds of specialized detectors of pressure, temperature, touch, and so on. These receptors are primarily responsible for providing haptic information (i.e., feel).

**muscle spindles**—Sensory receptors located in the muscles that provide the nervous system with information about changes in muscle length.

**Golgi tendon organs**—Proprioceptive sense organs located at the junction of muscles and tendons that signal information about force in the muscles.

**cutaneous receptors**—Proprioceptive sense organs located in most skin areas that signal information about pressure, temperature, and touch.

Each of these receptors provides more than one type of sensory information. For example, muscle spindles provide information about joint position, muscle velocity, muscle tension, and limb orientation with respect to gravity. Therefore, unlike vision and audition, which are unitary senses, kinesthesis includes a complex combination of inputs from various receptors that must be integrated by the central nervous system.

Because of the multiple, complex receptors involved in kinesthesis, people's perception of movement can be affected by how they produce their movements. For example, our perception (or kinesthetic "feel") of a normal, active pattern of movement, such as a kick, is different from our perception of a passive, guided action, such as when a therapist manipulates the limb of a patient. Similarly, a patient's perception of the feel associated with the action of standing up from a seated position can be distorted if the person is manually assisted during a demonstration of the movement. Many guidance techniques movement practitioners use during motor skills instruction (e.g., when the instructor moves the learner's limbs through the desired range of motion) also present kinesthetic sensations that are different from those associated with active movement. The problem with these techniques, of course, is that they create a kinesthetic feel for the person that is different from the one he or she experiences when performing the movement in an unassisted fashion.

Guidance or manual manipulation techniques are commonly used in therapy settings as well as in certain types of sport skill situations (e.g., when a therapist guides a patient's lower extremity in gait following head injury or when a swimming teacher moves the student's arms through the correct movement pattern for the breaststroke). While practitioners sometimes find such techniques to be necessary during the beginning stages of learning for defining the boundaries of the correct movement

## WHAT MIGHT A PHYSICAL THERAPIST DO?

A therapy patient is recovering from surgery on the afferent nerves of his preferred arm and hand. The sensations the patient has in his injured limb are not the same as they were prior to surgery. He is now faced with the challenge of relearning a variety of everyday manual activities (e.g., using a can opener, washing dishes, hanging clothes on a clothesline). How might a physical therapist assist the patient in recognizing the kinesthetic cues he needs to associate with successful performance? How might the therapist assist the patient in the transition to independent performance of the tasks?

**human factors**—A field of study concerned with the interaction of human characteristics and the design of things people use (tools, vehicles, etc.).

pattern (or for safety purposes), they must take care not to overuse them. To do so may distort the performer's sense of the feel associated with active movement.

Alterations in kinesthesis, however, have been exploited in positive ways by **human factors** engineers who design control mechanisms for various types of vehicle equipment and industrial machinery. For example, adding spring resistance to a car's steering system enhances the operator's feel of steering movements, making the vehicle easier to control. In a similar fashion, designing aircraft instrument knobs that differ in shape (and "feel") makes the pilot's recognition of the appropriate knob for a particular task more efficient.

Certainly, many different sources of sensory information are available for movement control. In the next sections, we focus on ways these varied sources of information are used by the central nervous system in producing skilled movements.

**comparator**—The error detection mechanism contained in closed-loop control systems; compares feedback of the desired state to feedback of the actual state.

**executive**—One of the components of a closed-loop control system; determines the actions to be taken to maintain the desired goal state.

**effector**—The component of a control system that carries out the desired action; for example, the arm is usually the effector that carries out the action of throwing a ball.

# Closed-Loop Control Systems

One way of conceptualizing how we use sensory information in the control of movements is by comparing this task to the way common physical systems use environmental information in everyday situations. Take, for example, the heating and cooling system in most homes. When the system is in operation, its goal is to maintain a desired room temperature. The mechanisms it needs to achieve this goal are a **comparator**, an **executive**, and an **effector** (see figure 4.1). The comparator, which in this example is the thermostat, senses the difference between the desired room temperature and the actual room temperature. If it detects no difference (i.e., zero error), it takes no action. However, if the comparator detects a difference, for example if the actual room temperature is lower than the desired temperature, it relays an error signal ("too cold") to the executive, or control center, which in turn issues a command to the effector mechanism responsible for carrying out the action, which in this example is the furnace. This action (the furnace running) continues until the desired temperature is once again achieved. At that point the comparator senses zero error and relays this information to the executive, which forwards it to the effector to "turn off." The process continues indefinitely, as the system attempts to maintain the temperature near the desired state.

## IT DEPENDS . . .

What types of sensory information did the rugby player in the preview use when she attempted to catch and hold on to the ball? What types of sensory information do you use when riding a bicycle? What would you do if you couldn't see? Couldn't hear? Couldn't feel your legs? What type of information would you first notice if you attempted to ride a friend's bicycle?

This kind of system is termed a *closed-loop* system because its output or action is dictated by the executive, carried out by the effector, and then routed *back* to the comparator in the form of sensory information, or **feedback**. This feedback "loop" provides the system with the necessary information to maintain the desired state.

**feedback**—Information about the actual state of a system.

People use **closed-loop control** processes for certain types of human performance, such as driving a car. Drivers use visual information about the position of the car on the road to obtain feedback about differences between the actual position of the car and the desired position. If such differences occur, the driver senses them as errors. If a correction is necessary, the driver determines the hand and arm movements needed to bring the vehicle into the correct position. The nervous system sends commands to the muscles to execute those movements, and the muscles perform them until the vehicle is once again in the desired position. As you can see in this example, the feedback that the driver uses to maintain the desired goal comes from sensory information that is both exteroceptive (e.g., vision of the car and the road) and proprioceptive/kinesthetic (e.g., the feel of the steering wheel and movement of the hands and arms). Presumably, each type of information is compared to its "desired" state (in the comparator) and any errors are relayed to the executive for correction (see figures 4.1 and 4.2). Once the system arrives at a solution, it relays the necessary action plans to the effectors (hands and arms) for execution.

**closed-loop control**—A type of control that involves the use of feedback and the activity of error detection and correction processes to maintain the desired goal; used by individuals to control slow, deliberate movements.

## Closed-Loop Control Within the Conceptual Model

In the previous chapter, we introduced a conceptual **model** of human performance that illustrates how individuals process information in three stages—stimulus identification, response selection, and response programming—in order to convert environmental input into response output (see figure 3.2). Now we expand the model by adding the mechanisms of closed-loop control shown in figure 4.1. The result is a conceptual model of human performance (see figure 4.2). This model should help you understand the processes involved in controlling relatively slow movements (e.g., a patient's positioning of a limb in physical therapy) and the processes involved in controlling relatively rapid ones (e.g., a golfer's swing). For slow movements, performers can make compensations during the action; for more rapid ones, they must wait until after the movement is completed to correct their errors.

**model**—A tentative description of a system that accounts for many of its known properties; models facilitate people's understanding of systems and promote practical applications.

Components of the closed-loop control system are highlighted in figure 4.2. When input arrives, it is processed, and a desired state is determined that defines the sensory qualities (i.e., the look, sound, and feel) of the intended movement. The desired state represents the feedback the individual should obtain if he performs the movement correctly and successfully achieves the environmental goal. A "copy" of the desired state is registered with the comparator. Commands for achieving the

### THE FOUR COMPONENTS OF CLOSED-LOOP CONTROL SYSTEMS

1. Executive—makes decisions about corrective actions needed
2. Effector—carries out those decisions
3. Feedback—information about the actual state of the system
4. Comparator, or error detection mechanism—compares expected feedback from the desired state to actual feedback from the present state and relays any difference (i.e., error) to the executive

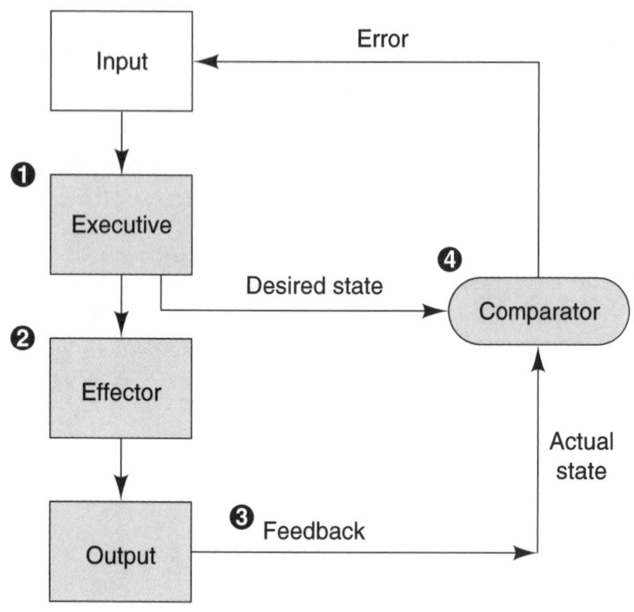


Figure 4.1 A closed-loop control system.

desired goal state are sent from the executive to an effector mechanism that consists of several components. First, there is the motor program, which produces movement commands. These commands are relayed to the lower centers in the nervous system located in the spinal cord. The result is a contraction of muscles and movement of joints. Feedback arising from this movement (e.g., a golf shot) is compared (in the comparator, of course!) to the expected sensory feedback of the desired state. Any difference between expected sensory feedback and actual sensory feedback is registered as a movement error. Should this occur, the error message is transmitted from the comparator to the executive.

When people move, various forms of proprioceptive and exteroceptive feedback information arise. Proprioceptive feedback comes from forces generated in the contracting muscles, from pressures exerted by objects in contact with the skin (e.g., the feel of the arms against shirtsleeves or the feel of the feet inside shoes), and from the joints signaling changes in body position. Exteroceptive information comes from the environment and is sensed by the receptors for vision, audition, and sometimes even olfaction (i.e., smell), generating still more feedback (e.g., the flight path of the ball, the sound of the club making contact with the ball, and the smell of the grass and dirt that are displaced by the shot).

As seen in figure 4.2, the stages of processing are an essential feature of closed-loop control. Every time an error signal goes to the executive for correction, it must pass through the stages and, as we discussed in the previous chapter, this **controlled processing** requires attention and takes time. Fortunately, closed-loop control is not the only way individuals use feedback to regulate their movements; later in this chapter we discuss various lower-level reflexlike loops, which make their own contributions to movement control.

**controlled processing**—A type of information processing that is slow, serial, attention demanding, and voluntary; more prevalent during the early stages of learning.

## The Conceptual Model and Continuous, Long-Duration Skills

The closed-loop model depicted in figure 4.2 is useful for understanding how the nervous system maintains a particular state of human motor behavior. For example, the simple act of maintaining posture in the standing position is a natural behavior that requires some form of continuous closed-loop control. Closed-loop control is also used for various learned postures, such as the one employed by skilled gymnasts when executing a handstand on the still rings. Most movement skills involving the use of various limbs require an accurate, stable posture as a platform. Without this base, people would be unable to perform movements such as throwing darts or casting a fishing lure. In these types of tasks, the comparator continually

### SEE IF YOU CAN DO IT

Models are intended to help us understand the way a phenomenon might operate. In figure 4.2 we present a conceptual model of human performance. You can test the usefulness of this model for yourself by attempting to describe how you think each of the various components of the model might operate for a person who is attempting to pour a glass of wine.

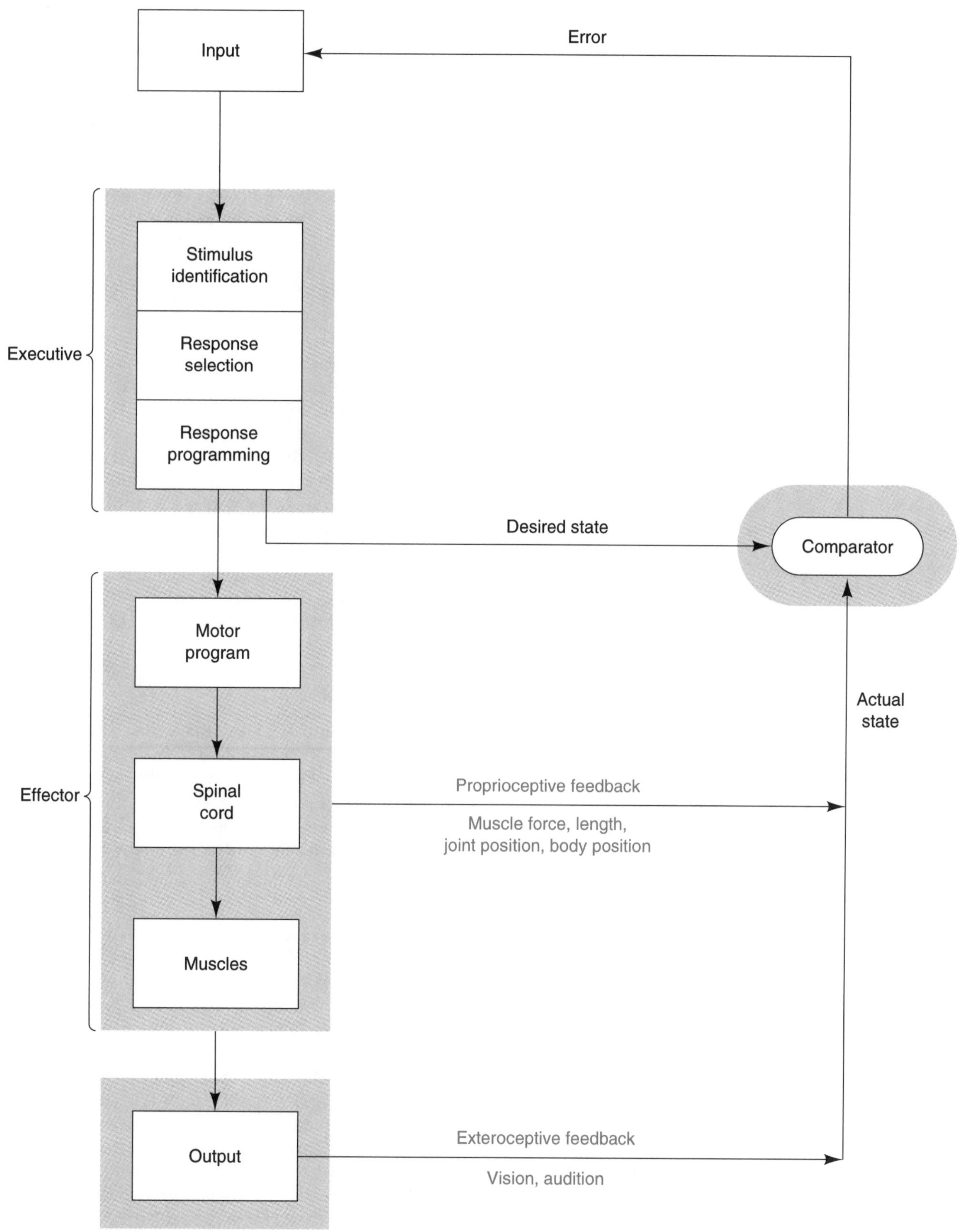


Figure 4.2 An expanded conceptual model of human performance. The elements of the closed-loop control system are integrated with the stages of processing.

evaluates the similarity or difference between the expected feedback of the correct or desired limb positions and body orientation and the actual, movement-produced feedback of the actual limb positions and body orientation. Should errors be discovered they are transmitted to the executive for appropriate corrections.

**tracking**—A class of tasks in which a moving track must be followed, typically by movements of a manual control.

Other tasks are far more dynamic. For instance, continuous **tracking** skills require the performer to operate a control device in order to follow some continuously varying target. A common example is driving an automobile, where the driver operates a steering wheel in order to keep the vehicle positioned properly on the road. Control movements are made whenever the driver visually detects an error in the car's position relative to the road. Another way performers use feedback to control an ongoing movement is evident in the experience of a distance runner competing in a 10K race. The runner compares extrinsic and kinesthetic feedback from her actual pace to an internal reference of the desired pace in order to make the necessary corrections for maintaining efficiency. There are also tasks for which the reference of correctness changes over time or during the course of action, as in a slow karate movement. These tasks and countless other examples of dynamic movements illustrate the importance of closed-loop control during much of a person's daily functioning.

Without a doubt, closed-loop models, such as the one shown in figure 4.2, are the most effective means for understanding how people control continuous, long-duration skills. They are also useful for certain types of performance applications. For example, human factors engineers have used the components of closed-loop models in designing and constructing a variety of electromechanical devices. These nonliving (often robotlike) machines are able to mimic some aspects of actual human behavior (e.g., polishing pianos) rather well (Amato, 1989). In spite of their potential for application, however, closed-loop control models are not without their limitations. We discuss these in the next section.

## Limitations of Closed-Loop Control

The expanded conceptual model shown in figure 4.2 contains a closed-loop control system that includes the three stages of information processing. Including the stages in the system is advantageous: information processing provides flexibility in movement control and allows for a variety of movement strategies and options, depending on the particular set of task and environmental circumstances. The biggest disadvantage of the closed-loop system is that it makes control very slow, particularly in the response-programming stage.

### *Rapid Tracking Behavior*

One important generalization you should remember from chapter 3 is that the stages of processing, particularly response selection and response programming, require considerable time and attention. Hence, closed-loop control systems that include these stages operate quite slowly as well. Recall that the stages of processing are critical components in reaction-time situations, where a stimulus or input requires the activity of various processing stages leading to a person's response or output (see figure 3.2). In the closed-loop control model, an error signal operates in much the same way as a stimulus or input—it is processed in the executive (containing the stages) and it leads to a response (i.e., a correction in the movement). Numerous studies of tracking performance suggest that corrections occur at a maximum rate that is relatively slow—about three per second.

In the conceptual model of the closed-loop system, corrections occur a few hundred milliseconds after the error is produced. The error is processed in the stimulus-identification stage, a movement correction is chosen in the response-selection stage, and modifications to the movement are organized and initiated in the response-programming stage. Once the correction is initiated, the movement continues in its corrected form until the next segment of error information is processed. This type of control is adequate as long as only two or three changes in the movement are required per second. If corrections must be made at a faster rate than this, performance is poor. This explains why baseball or cricket players find it difficult to intercept and catch a rapidly moving ball that is bouncing over a rough surface—the changes in direction of the object occur too quickly, leaving the performer with little time to make adequate corrections in the fielding movement.

### *Discrete Tasks of Brief Duration*

The general view of closed-loop control is also inadequate when it comes to explaining people's performance of skills that are brief in duration (e.g., the hitting, throwing, kicking, and striking tasks that are so common in many sports). Take the task of hitting a pitched baseball, for example. In performing this task, the batter first evaluates the environmental situation, particularly the path and speed of the approaching ball. He then selects a movement that is designed to achieve the goal (i.e., contact of ball with bat). Using the stages of processing, the system selects a program and organizes it for initiation. Once the program is activated, response-execution processes carry out the movement pretty much as planned. As long as the environment (i.e., the pattern of ball flight and the pitch speed) remains the same as it was when the movement was organized, the movement should be effective in achieving the goal.

But what if something in the environment suddenly changes? For example, what if the ball curves unexpectedly during its flight? Now the batter needs to alter the path of the swing or perhaps stop it altogether. A review of the conceptual model (see figure 4.2) allows us to estimate how much time it would take the batter to process this change and amend his ongoing swing. If such information must pass through the stages of processing, it would take several hundred milliseconds before the first modification in the movement could be made. And while processing of the change is occurring, the movement would continue to proceed as originally planned. If too much of the swing transpired before a correction could be made, successful contact with the ball would be unlikely.

Since closed-loop control is simply too slow to allow corrections in very rapid actions, performers must initiate a fully planned movement to achieve the goal. Therefore, the general rule is that the first few hundred milliseconds of a brief rapid movement transpire more or less without modification. As you will see later in this chapter, though, sensory information plays a more important and effective role as the duration of the movement is increased (i.e., the performer produces the movement more slowly).

More than any other observation, the sluggishness of closed-loop, feedback-based control has led scientists to propose that the production of most rapid movements depends on some form of advanced planning and programming. In this view, moment-to-moment control is a part of the preorganized program and is not dependent on the relatively slow stages of information processing the system uses during closed-loop control. (It must be pointed out, however, that feedback can sometimes act reflexively to modify movements far more quickly than indicated here. We discuss this aspect of feedback-based control later in the chapter and we explain the concept of motor program control more completely in chapter 5).

Finally, scientists assume that performers initiate rapid actions in an all-or-none fashion, in much the same way that the trigger on a rifle, when pulled, causes a bullet to fire without the possibility of modification. Once some critical point, or "threshold," is reached in the system, an internal "go" signal is delivered and the movement is initiated. Any signal given after the "go" signal has been executed is ignored by the system, and the movement proceeds without interruption. Scientists believe that this internal signal occurs during the response-programming stage, as

## The Slater-Hammel Experiment

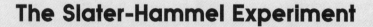

Arthur Slater-Hammel (1960) conducted an experiment in which participants were asked to hold down a reaction key with a finger while watching the sweep hand of a timer that made one revolution per second, starting and ending at the zero position. When participants lifted the finger, it caused the sweep hand to stop immediately. The participants' task was to lift the finger from the key in such a way as to stop the sweep hand at the 800-ms position—that is, 800 ms after the sweep hand started moving from the zero position. With a little practice, these individuals learned to anticipate this action and lift their fingers in time to achieve the goal. Once they had attained a good level of proficiency, participants performed additional trials on the task. On a few of these trials, the experimenter stopped the sweep hand at various locations prior to its reaching the 800-ms position. Participants were told that whenever this happened they were to keep their finger on the key—that is, to inhibit the finger-lift response. In order to determine how difficult it was for these individuals to inhibit the finger-lift response, Slater-Hammel plotted the probability of their lifting the finger at the different points the sweep hand was stopped.

His results are shown in figure 4.3. When the length of time prior to the 800-ms position was relatively long (greater than 210 ms), the probability that participants would lift their finger was practically zero (i.e., they had no difficulty inhibiting the movement). However, as the length of time decreased (i.e., the sweep hand got nearer to the 800-ms position), the probability of their lifting the finger increased, to the point that if the clock hand was stopped at 700 ms (i.e., leaving 100 ms to abort the response), the participants were almost never able to inhibit the movement. If the clock hand was stopped between 150 ms and 170 ms prior to the 800-ms position, participants were able to inhibit the movement successfully only about half the time. The most likely interpretation of Slater-Hammel's results is that the performers issued the internal "go" signal between 150 ms and 170 ms before the sweep hand arrived at the 800-ms position. This "go" signal triggered the finger-lift action and the movement occurred, even though later environmental information (i.e., stopping of the sweep hand) indicated that they should not make the movement.

Undoubtedly, you have experienced occasions where you initiated a movement and then wished you could stop it—like the times you realized that you did not have your keys just prior to slamming shut the locked door of your car or house. Perhaps you have tossed an object toward a friend just as she looked away. If you were lucky, she looked back in time to catch the pillow or the porcelain dish because, regardless of whether she did or didn't, you couldn't stop the toss once you had started it. In each of these situations you may have felt as if you planned the movement, then something happened that made you want to stop it, and then—seemingly a long time later—the movement occurred automatically, almost as if someone else were controlling it. Our view is that "someone" or "something" *is* controlling the movement after the internal "go" signal is given—and that "something" is the motor program.

### IT DEPENDS . . .

Sometimes closed-loop control is effective and sometimes it isn't. People typically use this type of control for continuous tracking tasks such as driving a car. However, closed-loop control is not always effective for this task. What are some driving situations that make this type of control more difficult? Why is it important for a driver to slow down if the road is icy or if there is heavy fog? What if a squirrel suddenly decides to cross the road? Why might the driver be unable to avoid hitting the squirrel? What, in your opinion, is the key factor that determines the effectiveness of closed-loop control in situations like these?

suggested by the results of an experiment by Slater-Hammel (1960), which we discuss in the highlight box on page 98.

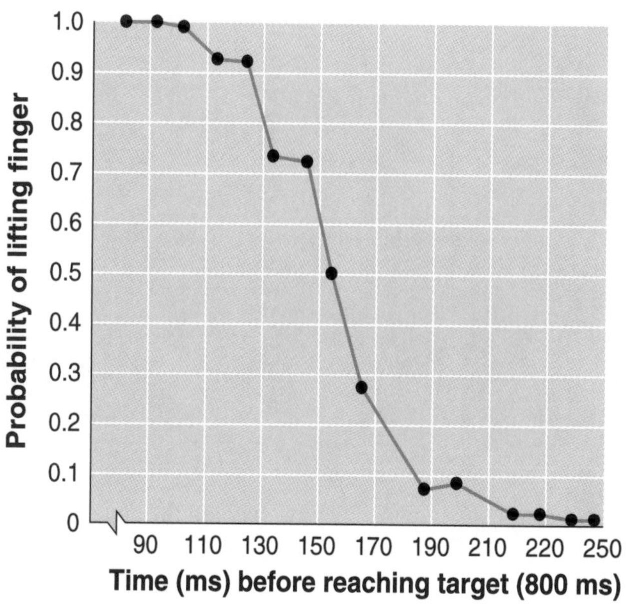

## Reflexive Modulations in Movement Skills

To this point, we have considered only one kind of closed-loop control process: the consciously controlled adjustment of performers' actions based on sensory information. However, there are other kinds of corrections that occur in our movements of which we are not aware. Relatively low-level processes lying in the spinal cord and brain stem produce these modifications to our movements. Such adjustments, which often involve no conscious control, are termed **reflexes**, because they occur in a stereotyped, involuntary, and usually rapid fashion. In this section, we discuss how these adjustments operate and the circumstances under which lower-level reflex processes can contribute to the motor control process.

**Figure 4.3** The probability of lifting the finger though the clock hand had stopped, plotted as a function of the interval of time before the 800-ms position. (Adapted by permission from Slater-Hammel, 1960.)

### Types of Compensations

Imagine that you are a participant in a simple experiment. While in a standing position, you attempt to hold one of your elbows at a right angle to support a moderate load, such as a book, in your hand. You have a measuring stick in front of you to indicate the height of the book and you are instructed to try to keep the book at a particular target position or height. While you are doing this, an experimenter is monitoring the electrical activity in your biceps muscle using **electromyography (EMG)**. Suddenly, without warning, the experimenter adds another book to the one you are holding. Your hand immediately begins to drop, but after a brief delay you compensate for the added load by bringing your hand back up to the target position.

What are the processes that contribute to these compensations? A record of the EMG might look like the one shown at the top of figure 4.4. The shaded portion

**reflexes**—Stereotyped, involuntary, and usually rapid responses to stimuli.

**electromyography (EMG)**—A device for recording the electrical activity in a muscle or group of muscles.

### THE MOST DIFFICULT PITCH TO HIT

Many baseball players believe that the change of pace is the most difficult pitch for batters to hit (*Sports Illustrated Book of Baseball,* 1960). One of the best hitters in the history of professional baseball, Henry Aaron, often said that the change of pace, or change-up, was the hardest pitch for him to hit. The secret of the change of pace is that it moves at a slower speed than most pitches, but pitchers throw it with the same arm motion they use when throwing a fastball. When the ball leaves the pitcher's hand, it looks to the batter like a fastball because the initial trajectory and spin of the seams is similar. By the time the batter realizes the ball is actually moving more slowly, he is unable to inhibit the initiation of his swing and usually completes his swing before the ball arrives. Even if the batter is able to recover in time to make contact with the ball, he does not hit it very hard because much of the swing is already completed.

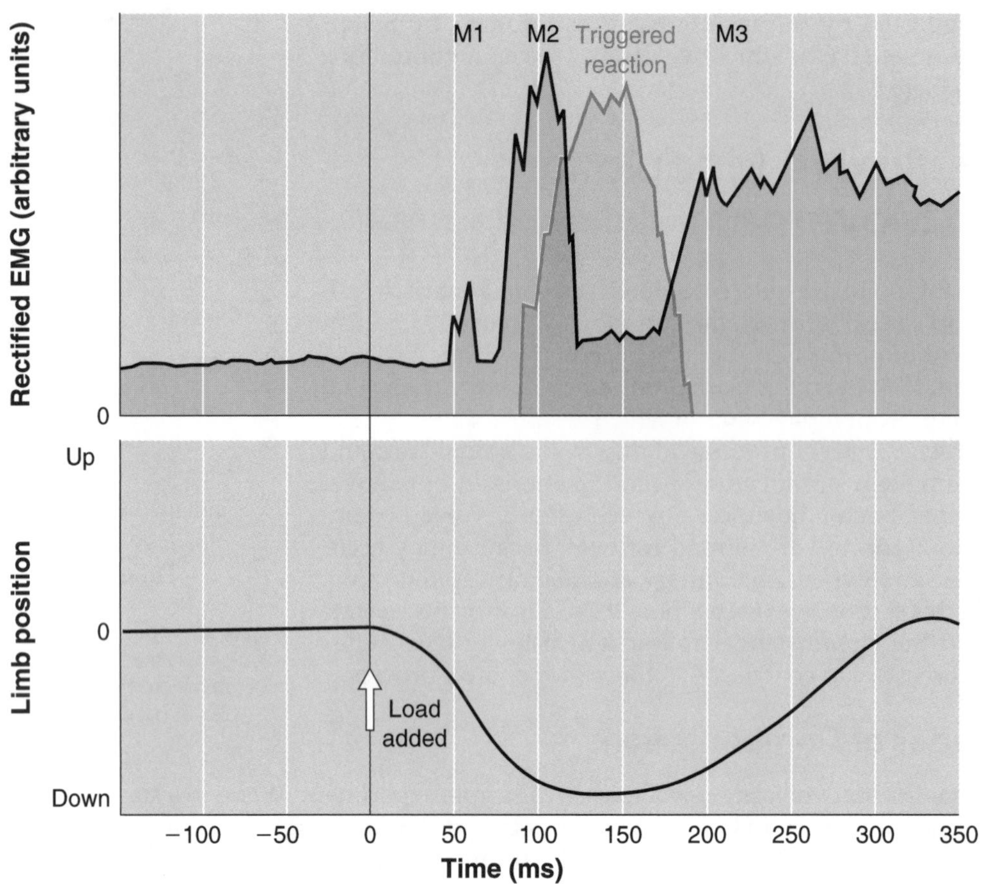


Figure 4.4 Electromyographic (EMG) responses to stretch of the biceps muscle and change in arm position when a load is suddenly applied. (© 1967 IEEE.)

at the left of the top half of the figure represents the amount of EMG activity necessary for the biceps to initially hold the limb at the target position. After the experimenter adds the second book (i.e., "load added"), several modifications to this level of activity occur, which represent the muscle's compensations for the added load:

1. M1 response, with a latency or lag of 30 ms to 50 ms
2. M2 response, with a latency or lag of 50 ms to 80 ms
3. Triggered reaction (shown hypothetically in figure 4.4 where it might be expected to occur), with a latency or lag of 80 ms to 120 ms
4. Reaction-time response (M3), with a latency or lag of 120 ms to 180 ms

### *M1 Response*

**M1 response**—The monosynaptic stretch reflex, with a latency of 30 ms to 50 ms.

The first reflexive modification is a burst of EMG activity that occurs about 30 ms to 50 ms after the load is added. This activity is brief, not resulting in very much added contraction in the muscle; the limb is still moving downward even after this response (see bottom half of figure 4.4). Sometimes called the *monosynaptic stretch reflex* or M1 reflex, the **M1 response** is one of the most rapid reflexes underlying limb control. It is prompted by the stretching of the muscle spindles when a load is unexpectedly added. The spindles relay sensory information to the spinal cord where a single connection (or synapse) is made. Then the information is routed directly back to the same muscle that was stretched, causing an increased contraction (seen as the small

EMG burst labeled M1). The latency or time of this correction is very short because it involves only one synapse (hence the term "monosynaptic") and the information has a relatively short distance to travel.

The M1 reflex is thought to be responsible for modifications in muscle contraction caused by small stretches, such as occur during postural sways or when our limbs are subjected to unanticipated outside forces. These reflex processes are nonconscious, and are therefore not affected by factors such as the number of possible stimulus-response alternatives—as described by **Hick's Law**, discussed in chapter 3. Thousands of these modifications can occur simultaneously to control functions such as our limb position and posture. Because these compensations occur at the same time, in parallel, nonconsciously, and presumably without interference, they do not require our attention and thus are automatic.

**Hick's Law**—Describes the stable relationship that exists between the number of stimulus-response alternatives and choice reaction time; specifically, as the number of stimulus-response pairs increases, choice reaction time increases in a linear fashion.

### *M2 Response*

About 50 ms to 80 ms after the experimenter adds the load, there is a second burst of EMG activity (see figure 4.4). Sometimes called the functional stretch reflex, long-loop reflex, or M2 reflex, the **M2 response** generates a higher-amplitude burst of EMG than does the M1 reflex. In addition, this response has a longer duration, so it contributes far more to movement compensation than does the M1 reflex. Like the M1 response, the M2 response arises from activity in the muscle spindles and travels to the spinal cord. However, the impulses continue further up the cord to higher centers in the brain (i.e., the motor cortex and/or the cerebellum) where they are processed. Motor impulses are then sent back down the cord to activate muscles (which in our example control the elbow). The longer travel distance and additional synapses at the higher brain levels account for some of the added latency, or time it takes the M2 response to occur.

**M2 response**—The polysynaptic, functional stretch reflex, with a latency of 50 ms to 80 ms.

The M2 response, in combination with the M1 response, is responsible for the well-known knee-jerk reflex we have all experienced at the doctor's office. We sit on an examination table, with our lower leg hanging down. The doctor taps our patellar tendon, located at the base of the kneecap. This causes the quadriceps muscle on the front of our thigh to stretch, initiating a reflex response that contracts the quadriceps and produces an involuntary extension of the lower leg.

What are some of the characteristics of the M2 response? Like the M1 response, it is not affected by the number of stimulus-response alternatives, and thus does not conform to Hick's Law. In addition, the M2 response is more flexible than the M1 response, allowing for the involvement of a few other sources of sensory information during the response. One of these sources is instructions. In our example, if the experimenter had instructed you to "let go" when he applied the added weight (rather than to "resist," as illustrated in figure 4.4), your limb would have moved to a new position without your intervention. In other words, the M2 response would not have transpired—although the M1 response would still have occurred.

Thus, we can voluntarily adjust the size or amplitude of the M2 response for a given input to generate a powerful response when the goal is to hold the joint as firmly as possible or to produce no response if the goal is to release under the increased load. This capability for variation is fortunate because it allows us to prepare our limbs to conform to different environmental demands. In skiing, for example, the performer wants her knees to be supple and to yield to sudden bumps, yet in other situations (e.g., wrestling) an athlete might not want his muscles to yield at all when his opponent applies a force to them.

In some ways, the M2 response is a unique kind of response. It is too fast to be called a voluntary response, which, as we learned in the previous section, would require 150 ms to 200 ms to be produced. Yet we can modify the M2 response voluntarily through conscious processes, such as our perception of sensory information (perhaps the nearby moguls in downhill skiing).

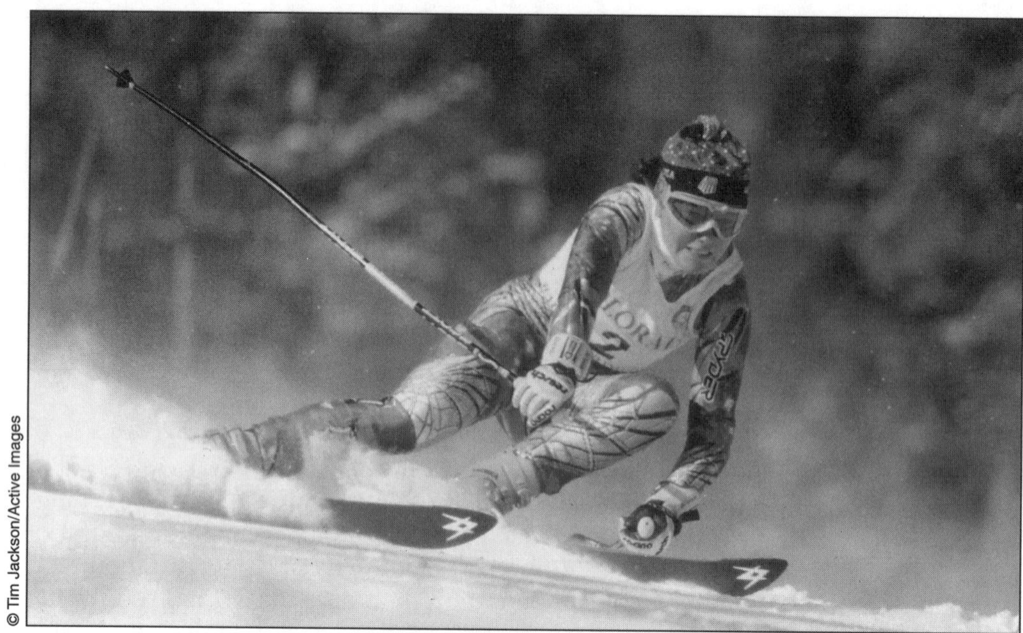


A skier can voluntarily adjust the amplitude of the M2 response to match environmental demands, making the knees supple and yielding to sudden bumps.

### Triggered Reaction

**triggered reaction**—The reaction to perturbations, with a latency of 80 ms to 120 ms; it is flexible, yet faster than the M3 response.

A third type of response (see figure 4.4) has a somewhat longer latency than the M2 response. Referred to as the **triggered reaction**, this response is also too fast to be a voluntary reaction, having a latency of 80 ms to 120 ms, but it is too slow to be an M2 (or M1) response. The triggered reaction can affect musculature that is quite far from the actual stimulation site, and it is sensitive to the number of stimulus alternatives in the same way as the conventional reaction-time response. Apparently, the triggered reaction can also be learned and can become a more or less automatic response (similar to the kind we discussed in chapter 3).

People experience triggered reactions in a number of different everyday situations, such as when an individual lifts a wineglass and it begins to slip, its red contents perhaps threatening a white carpet. These tiny "slips" generate skin vibrations that are detected by cutaneous receptors in the fingertips. The vibrations trigger several very fast compensations to stop the slip. First, there is an increase in grip force produced in the muscles of the forearm, which causes your hand to squeeze the glass somewhat tighter. There is also a decrease in force in the biceps muscle, slowing the upward acceleration of the lift and reducing the tendency of the glass to slip. These reactions, sometimes termed the *wineglass effect* (Johansson & Westling, 1984), are coordinated beautifully, being triggered as a single, unitary compensation for the slip. They are faster than reaction time, with latencies of about 80 ms, and the compensations appear to be nonconscious in that they are made even before the person is aware that the glass is slipping. Another example of the triggered reaction is found in the sport of wrestling. When a wrestler wraps his arm around an opponent's waist and the opponent attempts to escape the hold, the escape action is detected by cutaneous receptors in the forearm of the wrestler applying the hold. The resulting rapid compensations allow the wrestler to maintain the hold.

### Voluntary Reaction-Time Response (M3 Response)

**M3 response**—The voluntary reaction-time response, with a latency of 120 ms to 180 ms.

A final type of response that occurs when the experimenter unexpectedly increases the load is the voluntary reaction, sometimes called the **M3 response**. Seen as the fourth burst of EMG activity in figure 4.4, it is powerful and sustained, bringing the limb back to the desired position and holding it there. The latency of the M3 response is about 120 ms to 180 ms, depending on the task and circumstances, and it can affect all of the muscles of the body, not just those that are being stretched. The M3 response is the most flexible of all, being modified by a host of factors, such as instructions and the performer's anticipation of sensory information. Of course, the delay in the M3 response makes it sensitive to the number of stimulus-response alternatives, following Hick's Law. Underlying voluntary reactions are the stages of information processing, discussed in chapter 3 and illustrated in figure 4.2, meaning that adjustments occur in a serial fashion and require the person's attention.

## Coordinating Compensations for Unexpected Loads

The four kinds of compensations we have been discussing, along with their major characteristics, are summarized in table 4.1. An important feature to note is that as the latency of the response becomes shorter (i.e., the reaction takes less time), the response becomes systematically more rigid, or inflexible. At one extreme is the M3, or reaction-time, response, which is extremely sensitive to environmental demands but is comparatively slow. At the other extreme is the M1 response, which is practically insensitive to environmental demands but is very fast. The other two types of responses fall between these extremes. Taken together, the four types of responses illustrate a trade-off that exists between the flexibility and speed of reactions. If more flexibility is called for, more sources of sensory information must be taken into account before the action is defined. This means that more information-processing activities must occur, requiring more time.

IT DEPENDS . . .

Let's say you decide to go mountain biking on an unfamiliar trail. During your ride, it is likely that all of the responses shown in table 4.1 will occur at one time or another. Which response(s) would occur if you suddenly hit a bump? If a rabbit darted in front of you? If the steering mechanism slowly began to slip? If you hit some loose dirt and felt the bicycle sliding out from under you? What factor seems to govern the functioning of each of these responses? What might you do to diminish the activity of M1 responses, M2 responses, and triggered reactions during your ride?

**Table 4.1**
**Characteristics of Different Classes of Muscular Responses to Perturbations During Movement**

| Response type | Latency (ms) | Flexibility/ adaptability | Role of instructions | Effect of number of choices |
|---|---|---|---|---|
| *M1 response* | *30–50* | *Almost none* | *None* | *None* |
| *M2 response* | *50–80* | *Low* | *Some* | *None (?)* |
| *Triggered reaction* | *80–120* | *Moderate* | *Large* | *Moderate* |
| *Reaction-time response* | *120–180* | *Very high* | *Very large* | *Large* |

## Reflex Responses in the Conceptual Model

Now we can integrate these reflexive modifications in movement control into the conceptual model shown in figure 4.2. Figure 4.5 contains the same diagram, but it includes two reflexive pathways to give a more complete picture. The M1 loop (thin green line), carries feedback about muscle length (stretch), and perhaps muscle tension, to the spinal cord, which relays modifications directly to the muscles. This loop is fast, relatively inflexible, and represents the lowest level of feedback-based correction in movement control, having minimal contact with any of the higher brain centers.

The M2 feedback loop, the long-loop or functional stretch reflex, is illustrated by the thick green line in figure 4.5. Here information about muscle force and length as well as joint position and body position is fed back to somewhat higher centers in the brain concerned with the motor programming of the action. Once this feedback arrives, these programming processes produce minor modifications in movement commands and send this information back to the spinal cord and muscle levels. This loop is slower than that for M1 responses, but it has more flexibility because it involves a higher level of control.

### *Final Common Path*

The final common path (Sherrington, 1906) is an important principle of motor control. Contributions to movement control arise from three different sources, as illustrated in figure 4.5. First, there is the original set of movement commands from the motor program down the spinal cord to the muscles. Added to this is the contribution from the M1 response, sensitive to muscle force and length, shown by the thin green line. Finally, there is the M2 response, sensitive to limb position and movement as well as to muscle force and length, shown by the thick green line. Therefore, the final common path (or ultimate contribution) of the central nervous system to muscle action is the sum of all these separate flows of information, each with a different latency and a different type and amount of influence.

### *Loops Within Loops*

The notion of embedded feedback loops emphasizes the fact that certain closed loops operate totally "within" other closed loops. For example, the M1 response shown in figure 4.5 operates between the muscle level and the spinal cord level, exerting its influence on the control of muscle force when the performer experiences an unexpected variation in load. This loop does not have access to higher-order information about the goals of the task, but rather is restricted to the relatively "dumb" task of holding muscle length or stiffness levels constant. The M1 loop is insensitive to whether the performance goal is being achieved (e.g., whether the diver is executing the dive correctly or whether the puck being shot by the hockey player is going into the net), but it faithfully attempts to hold muscle force and length constant. Any information about goal achievement or lack of such is processed in the "outer" loop (shown in black on the right side of figure 4.5), which includes the activity of the comparator and, if there is an error signal, the information-processing stages to select a totally new action.

### *Role of Movement Time*

**movement time (MT)**—The interval of time that elapses from the beginning to the end of a person's movement.

The relative roles of these responses depend on the duration of the movement the person is trying to produce, as shown in figure 4.6, a through d. The quickest of human actions has a **movement time (MT)** of only 40 ms or so (see figure 4.6a). That is the amount of time required, for example, to strike a blow in boxing. For this movement, the "outer" feedback loop and the M2 response (with a latency of 50 ms to 80 ms; shown as the thick green line in the inner loop) are incapable of completing their processing activities in time to modify the boxer's punch once it is initiated.

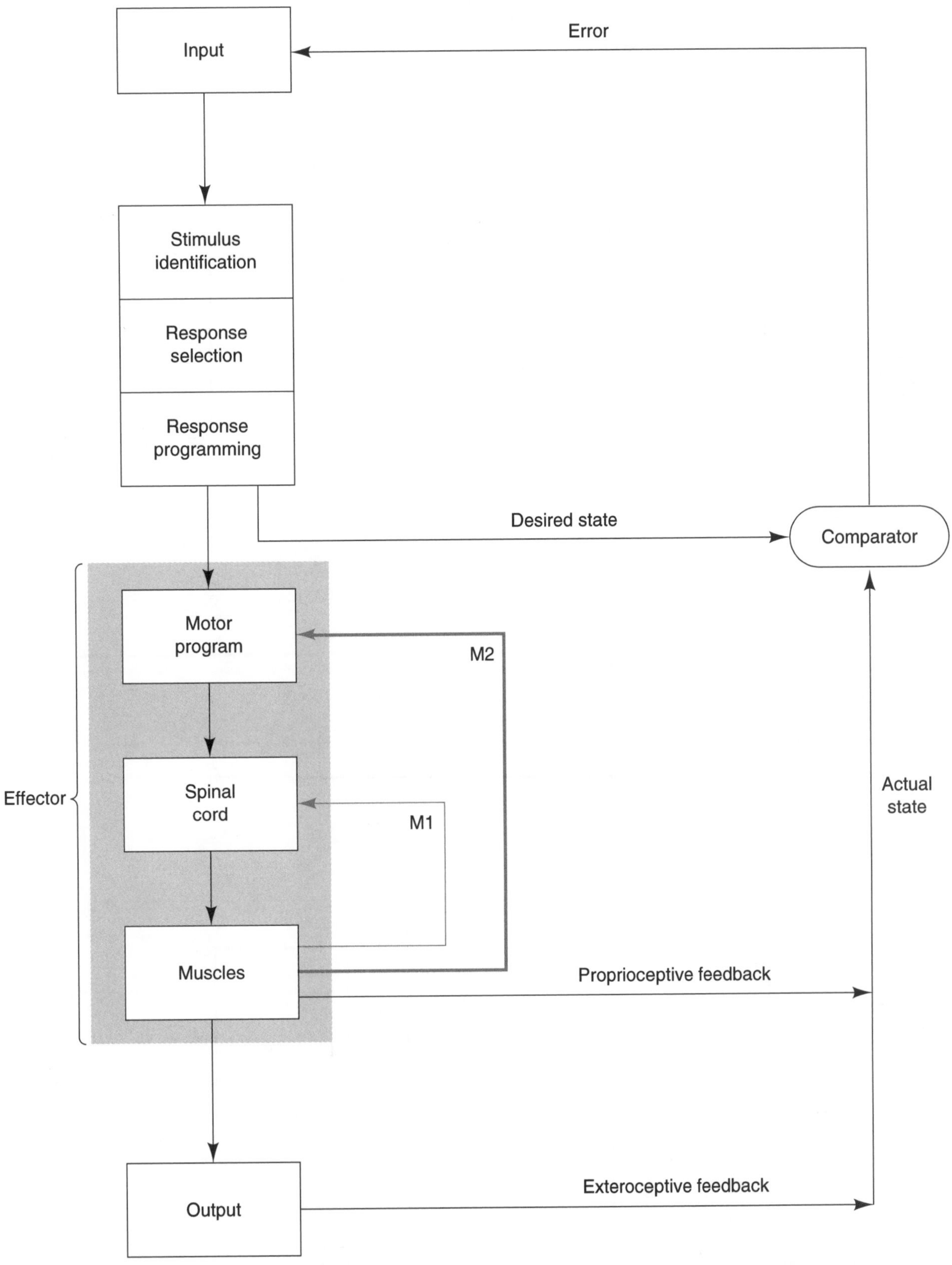


**Figure 4.5** The conceptual model of human performance expanded further, here by adding M1 and M2 feedback loops, shown by the thin and thick green lines, respectively.

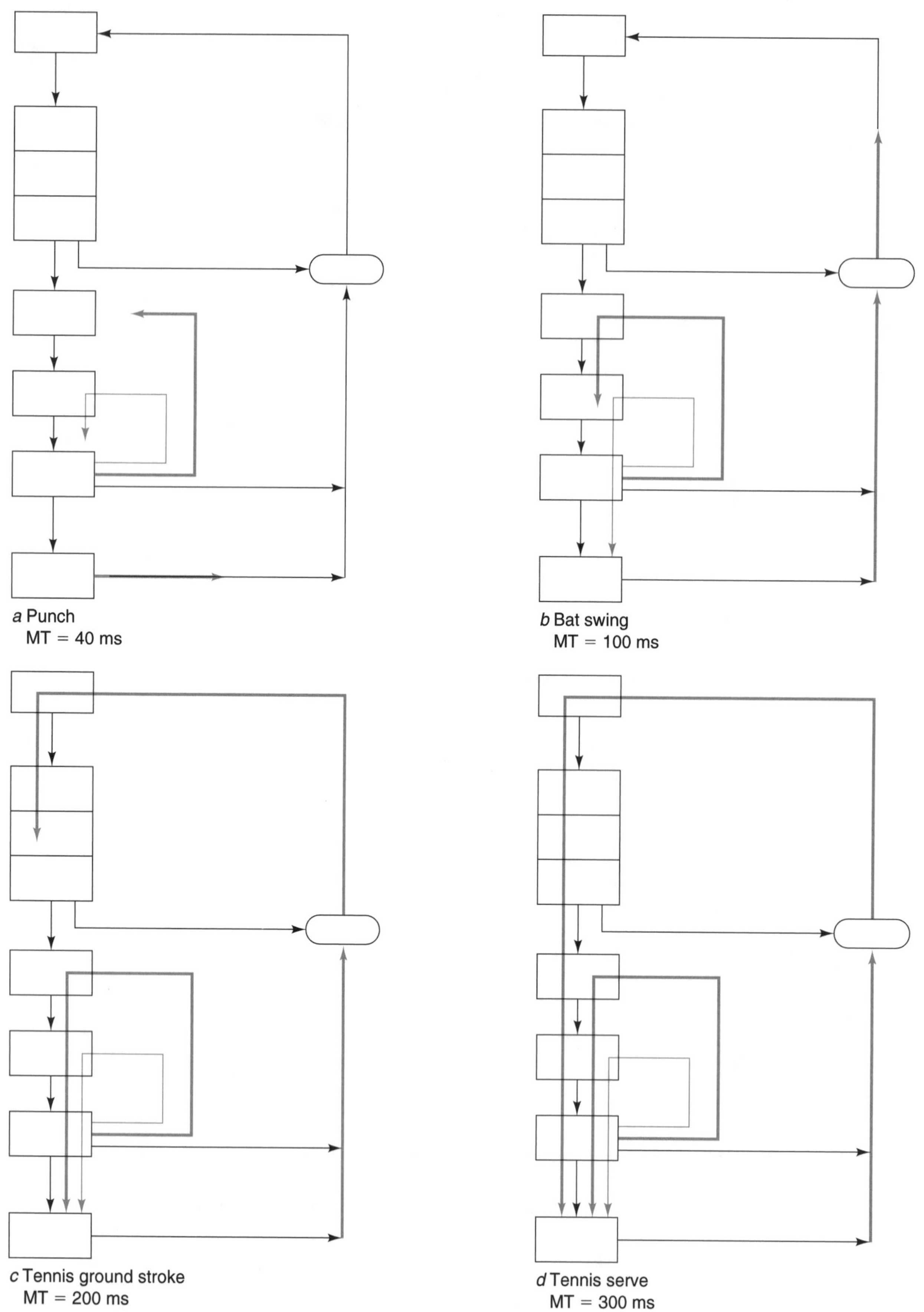


Figure 4.6 The progress of the various feedback loops after movements of different durations. The lowest-level reflex activities are completed first, and the highest-level responses are completed last.

Even the M1 response (with a latency of 30 ms to 50 ms; shown as the thin green line) has only enough time to begin influencing the muscles near the end of the movement.

Movements that take a longer time to be completed, such as a baseball swing, which lasts 100 ms or so, are more likely to be influenced by the M1 response. As shown in figure 4.6b, in 100 ms the M1 response has the potential of reaching the level of the muscles, thereby influencing the movement and the environmental outcome. However, in that time the M2 response reaches the level of only the motor program, the spinal cord, and perhaps the muscles. The outer, conscious loop has no influence; the information leaving the comparator (as indicated by the thick green line) has not yet reached the executive.

These movements that take longer than 100 ms allow both the M1 and M2 responses sufficient time to contribute to all levels of the action, from the level of the motor program (for the M2 response) to that of the environmental results. The forehand tennis stroke lasts about 200 ms (see figure 4.6c). Still, information in the outer, conscious loop is only able to reach the stages of processing within 200 ms, and the information remains essentially incapable of influencing the action.

Only when the duration of the movement is 300 ms or longer is there potential for the outer loop to be involved in amending the movement. A tennis serve takes about 300 ms to complete (see figure 4.6d; note how all loops reach all the way to the environmental results of the action). Thus, for movements that take longer than 300 ms for individuals to complete, closed-loop control is possible at several levels at the same time.

Generally speaking, as movement time increases, there is greater potential for the M1 and M2 responses to contribute to the originally intended action. Given this observation, it should not surprise us that movement time is one of the most important variables influencing the way we control our movements. Specifically, movement time dictates the kinds of feedback-based corrections that are possible and the relative contribution of these modifications to the original movement commands.

### *Choices Among Modes of Control*

In many cases the performer is in a position to choose a mode of movement control. If the movement is sufficiently long in duration, such as a slow component of a dance routine, a person can preprogram the control system, using only the fast, automatic feedback processes. The dancer may also choose to program only a small portion of the action, then modify it as needed by using feedback processed in the consciously controlled outer loop, as shown in figure 4.6d. However, this type of conscious, controlled information processing can sometimes cause problems. Teachers often see examples of this when they tell learners to "concentrate" on a particular part of the action or to "focus" on a particular source of movement feedback (e.g., the feel of the position of the feet). The result is that individuals choose to control

## WALKING ON ICE

A person walking along a sidewalk in winter might benefit from the activity of several of the responses shown in table 4.1. If the individual suddenly stepped on a dangerous patch of ice, she might have time to use the voluntary reaction response (M3) to regain balance. However, if she began to fall, the M1 response would initiate a righting reflex in the trunk and legs, while the M2 response would either contribute to the righting reflex or produce a "letting go" response, depending on the preference of the person. In the latter case, the lack of resistance might result in a more controlled fall.

## Feedback Processing in Ice Hockey

Applied research in ice hockey has demonstrated that players who are more skilled at skating can devote their attention to processing additional sources of feedback information. Leavitt (1979) examined the skating time of 6 groups of ice hockey players, differing in age (6–19 years old) and experience level (less than 1 year to over 15 years), under several skating conditions. In the simplest condition, participants skated as fast as they could for a distance of 50 ft (15.2 m). In another condition, they skated as fast as possible while attempting to control a puck with their hockey stick (referred to as "stickhandling"). Not surprisingly, the older, more experienced players had shorter movement times than the younger, less experienced players in both conditions. Of interest, however, was the additional finding that skating times for the two oldest and most experienced groups were virtually the same in both the "skating only" and the "skating plus stickhandling" conditions. As age and experience level decreased, the additional stickhandling task resulted in a greater slowing of skating speed. Since the task of skating is probably not as automated for younger, less experienced players as it is for their older, more experienced counterparts, it is likely that they have to rely on slower feedback-based control for both skating and stickhandling. In subsequent experiments, Leavitt found that beginning players who used larger pucks and ice hockey sticks with larger blades both skated and stickhandled faster than beginners who used smaller (regulation) pucks and junior ice hockey sticks with smaller blades. This is probably because larger pucks and sticks are easier to control and require less feedback processing.

their movements in a more conscious, effortful fashion, with their decisions about the action being handled in a slow, attention-demanding way. In such instances, their performance is usually hesitant and choppy. Interestingly, the general notion that paying attention to one's actions can impair performance has been around for years (Bliss, 1892–1893; Boder, 1935).

Gallwey's popular book *The Inner Game of Tennis* (1974) emphasizes that performers should allow their movements to "flow." Gallwey contends that individuals perform best when they simply let the learned capabilities of their motor system control the action, rather than when they attempt to intervene with conscious processes. Conscious intervention leads to an "overcontrolling" of the action, as seen in the

### IT DEPENDS . . .

Preprogrammed control relies on little, if any, of the slow, jerky, attention-demanding processes associated with outer feedback-loop operations (see figure 4.2). In fact, a person's overreliance on these types of conscious processes often results in a form of movement control that some have termed "paralysis by analysis." You can experience this phenomenon for yourself by attempting a skill you are familiar with (e.g., playing a musical instrument, performing a dance, throwing an object at a target) under two different sets of conditions. First, try to perform the skill by focusing only on the goal of the task (e.g., playing the song, staying in rhythm with the music, hitting the center of the target). After you do this, try to perform the skill by focusing on the movements themselves (e.g., the movements of the hands, the positioning of the feet, the mechanics of the throwing motion). Which set of conditions produces the better performance? Now, using the conceptual model shown in figure 4.2, see if you can explain what is happening under each set of performance conditions.

MIND GAMES

Sometimes competitive athletes use psychological tactics designed to make their opponents think about the control of their movements. For example, a tennis player might casually ask her opponent, "What are you doing differently with your serve today? You really seem to be hitting it well!" If the opponent begins to think about the things she might be doing differently, resulting in a shift to a more conscious form of movement control, she may begin hitting her serve less effectively.

performances of many beginners. Performers who allow their movements to flow likely do so by using preprogrammed operations that can be corrected by the inner feedback loops (see figure 4.6, a-c).

### *Let It Flow*

When asked to describe the characteristics of their better performances, athletes usually mention the sensation of being on automatic. Conscious control of the movement seems to be next to nonexistent. The performer's primary focus is on letting it happen or on a particular performance goal. Orlick and Partington give these examples, based on interviews with Canadian Olympic athletes (1986):

- *Rhythmic gymnast.* I'll just say, "Okay, now, you've got to do it, that's all there is to it. Go out, start it," and from then on it's great." (p. 60)
- *Alpine skier.* I don't like to think about "don'ts" before a race, like "don't do this or don't go too straight." Instead of saying that, you say, "Stay on line but go fast." I like to put it in a positive way, "Stay on line and go with the flow." (p. 66)
- *Pairs kayak athlete.* I used to look out over my partner's paddle when I was in the back of the boat because I found that was the easiest way to keep in stroke with her. I could see a "big look" by looking beyond her paddle. When I did that, I would feel myself move into "sync" with her. (p. 75)

# The Role of Two Visual Systems in Movement Control

To this point, we have treated all sources of sensory information as if they operated in essentially the same way during skilled action. In reality, one sensory system—vision—tends to dominate the others, and for this reason it deserves special mention for its unique role in movement control.

Over the past 20 years or so, it has become increasingly clear to scientists that two essentially separate visual systems underlie human functioning. Visual information is delivered from the retina of the eye along two separate pathways to two different places in the brain, and there is good evidence that these two pathways are used differently in the control of behavior (Trevarthen, 1968). More precisely, the two systems are

- focal vision, specialized for object identification, and
- ambient vision, specialized for movement control.

## Focal Vision for Object Identification

**Focal vision** is the system you are most familiar with as a result of personal experience. This system is specialized for the conscious identification of objects that lie

**focal vision**—The visual system people use to identify objects in the center of their visual field; it is conscious, biased by the movement of surrounding objects, and diminished in dim lighting.

primarily in the center of our visual field. Its major function seems to be providing answers to the general question What is it? In fact, you are using this system right now to identify images such as the words on this page. Focal vision contributes to our conscious perception of the objects we select for focus, leading to identification and perhaps action. It is severely degraded by dim lighting conditions, as we know from the experience of trying to read or to find a lost coin in the grass without adequate light. The essential features of focal vision are summarized in table 4.2.

**Table 4.2**
**Comparison of the Two Visual Systems**

| Feature | Focal vision | Ambient vision |
|---|---|---|
| *Visual field location* | *Central only* | *Central and peripheral* |
| *Awareness* | *Conscious* | *Nonconscious* |
| *Effect of low illumination* | *Degradation* | *Very little* |
| *General question resolved* | *What is it?* | *Where is it?* |

### Ambient Vision for Movement Control

**ambient vision**—The visual system people use to detect the orientation of their body in the environment; it is nonconscious, takes in all of the visual field, and is used for movement control.

A second, less-recognized visual system is **ambient vision**. Distinct from focal vision, ambient vision involves both central and peripheral portions of the visual field. Furthermore, it is not seriously degraded in dim lighting conditions. We often experience this when we walk on uneven terrain in the near-dark; we have no trouble making our way without tripping, even though the light is far too dim for reading a book.

Scientists believe that the ambient system is specialized for movement control. It functions to detect motion as well as the position of objects in the environment. Ambient vision also provides us with information about our own movements in relation to other objects. Thus, we use ambient vision to answer questions like Where is it? or Where am I in relation to it? Interestingly, our ambient system contributes to the fine control of movements without our being aware of it. This may be one reason we have so much difficulty appreciating the value of ambient vision.

## Visual Control of Movement Skills

How do we use visual information for movement control? And what factors determine its effectiveness? It is useful to divide this discussion into separate parts, particularly because it deals with the separate roles of the focal and ambient visual systems.

### Focal Vision and Movement Control

Although we primarily use focal vision for object identification, it is wrong to conclude that this system has no role in movement control. Focal vision has access to consciousness, so visual information handled by this system is processed through the information-processing stages (discussed in chapter 3). The processing of this type of visual information leads to action in much the same way as the processing of

## The Bridgeman, Kirch, and Sperling Experiment

Bridgeman, Kirch, and Sperling (1981) have provided some of the strongest evidence for the existence of an ambient system for movement control. In their experiment, participants sat in a darkened room in front of a screen. Projected on the screen was a rectangle (like a picture frame) with a spot of light located inside of it. Unbeknownst to the participants, the frame was moved back and forth a few degrees while the dot remained in a fixed position. Under these conditions, individuals experienced the illusion of the dot moving back and forth within the frame, rather than the frame moving back and forth. This phenomenon suggests that the focal visual system (the one with access to consciousness) can be "deceived": in this study it caused the participants to think they were seeing the dot move, when in actuality it remained stationary.

Next, Bridgeman and his colleagues attempted to manipulate the ambient system. In a second condition, participants were told that if the frame and dot were suddenly turned off, leaving the room in total darkness, they should immediately point to the position they last remembered seeing the dot. If the focal system is used to control the hand, and if participants' conscious perception was that the dot was moving back and forth, then the pointing movements should vary from right to left in coordination with the perceived movements of the dot. What Bridgeman and his colleagues found was that when the lights were turned off, participants pointed to where the dot actually was located, not to where they perceived it to be (i.e., they were not deceived by the movements of the frame). The investigators interpreted this to mean that people use their nonconscious ambient vision to control their limbs.

Taken together, the results of this investigation provide support for the existence of two separate visual systems: the focal system and the ambient system. The focal system, which is conscious, is used to locate objects in the center of the visual field (e.g., the dot) and is biased by movement of surrounding objects (e.g., the frame). The ambient system, which is nonconscious, is used for movement control and is not biased by the movement of surrounding objects.

any other information. In the conceptual model shown in figure 4.2 (and in figure 4.5), vision is represented as another source of exteroceptive information obtained from the environment. Therefore, the only way individuals can use focal vision for movement control is to process it through the stages. In one sense, this is obvious. You can look at a flying object, identify it as a bird, and observe that it is flying toward your head. Once you process this information, you probably decide to move your head in order to avoid a collision. Focal vision is important here, and the failure of a person to use it to accurately identify objects in the environment can lead to accidents or other serious errors. This is particularly a problem under conditions of dim lighting, such as in night driving, when the focal system's accuracy (visual acuity) is considerably degraded.

Before realizing that there could be an ambient system for movement control, scientists believed that a conscious focal system was the only way visual information could influence action. According to this outmoded view, a baseball batter watching a pitch approaching the plate would only be able to use the relatively slow information-processing stages to visually detect the ball's flight pattern and initiate changes in the swing. This idea was supported by numerous experiments that revealed that it takes about 200 ms (or approximately the duration of visual reaction time) for an individual to process visual information (Keele & Posner, 1968) and that the visual control of action is particularly slow and cumbersome. However, recent information about the ambient visual system, together with the discovery of optical-flow processes in vision, has markedly changed our understanding of the ways people use visual information to control their movements.

## EXPERT AND NOVICE OPEN-SKILL PERFORMERS USE THEIR FOCAL VISION DIFFERENTLY

Given how much visual information many performers have at their disposal and knowing what we do about the limited capacity of humans for processing information, we can assume that the skilled performer pays attention to the most relevant cues for the task she is performing. Some interesting research suggests that the visual focus of experts is more effective and efficient than that of novices. Bard and Fleury (1981) used a special apparatus that permitted them to observe the eye movements of expert and beginning ice hockey goaltenders as these individuals responded to a shot on goal. The results of this study indicated that experts, compared with novices, had fewer visual fixations on the puck, and they initiated their blocking movements sooner. By focusing on stick-related cues to a greater extent than puck-related cues, experts were able to make their decisions prior to puck contact by the shooter. Other researchers report a similar use of advanced visual cues by experts when compared to novices in a variety of other skills.

## Ambient Vision and Movement Control

**optical flow**—The movement of patterns of light rays from the environment over a person's retina, allowing the individual to perceive motion, position, and timing.

The late James J. Gibson (e.g., 1966) prompted scientists to begin searching for aspects of visual information that performers process for movement control. A fundamental concept that stimulated their search was a phenomenon called **optical-flow** patterns.

### *Optical Flow*

When you look into a lighted, textured environment, each visible feature reflects rays of light that enter your eye at particular angles (see figure 4.7, a-b). Imagine that objects A and B in this environment each reflect light rays into your eye, located at position 1a or 1b (only one eye is shown at each position for simplification). As you (and thus your eye) begin to move toward position 2a or 2b, the angle at which the light from the object enters your eye changes over time. These changes are continuous and can be thought of as a flow of light across the retina. The important point is that this "optical flow" provides an observer with the following kinds of information about his or her movement:

- Stability and balance
- Velocity of the movement through the environment
- Direction of the movement relative to the position of fixed objects in the environment
- Movement of environmental objects relative to the observer
- Time until contact between the observer and an object in the environment

Assume that you are moving directly toward object A, as in figure 4.7a. You would sense forward motion (from position 1a to position 2a) by an increase in the angle between the light rays entering your eye coming from the two edges of object A. (Also, the rays of light from object B sweep across your retina.) If you are moving backward, these changes would be reversed, indicating opposite motion in the environment. You sense the speed of movement by the rate of change of the angles of the light entering your eye from the sides of objects A and B, with faster movement producing more rapid changes in these angles.

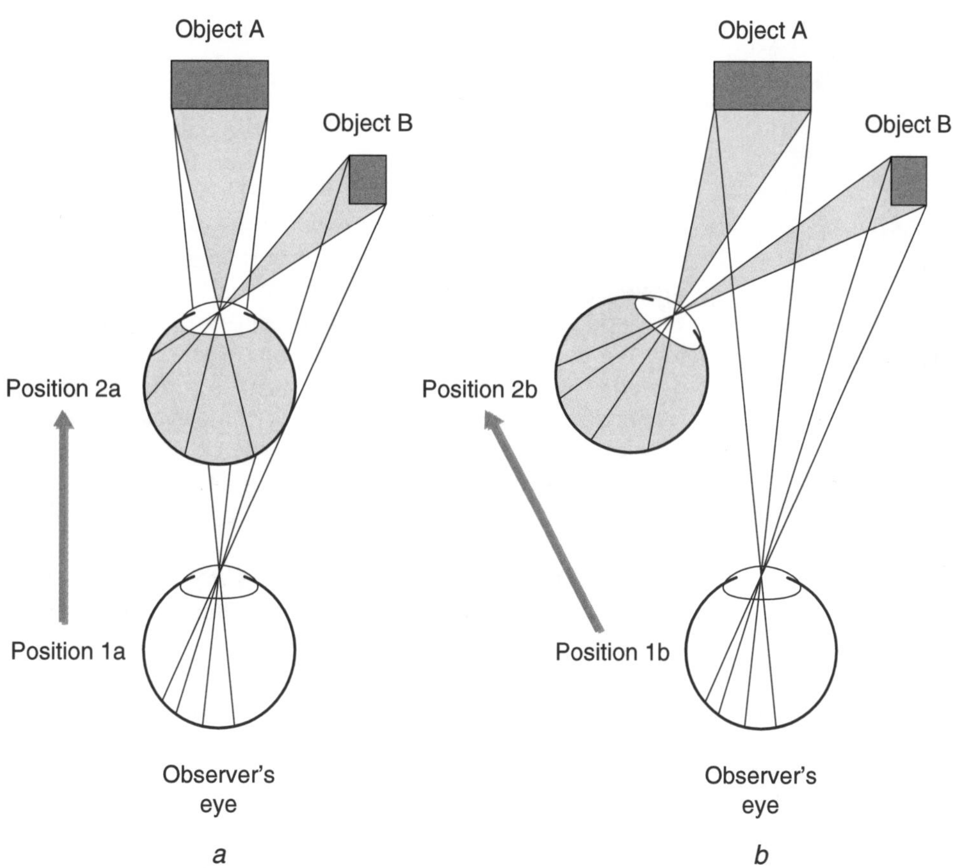


**Figure 4.7** Optical-flow information specifies the direction and speed of an observer's eye through an environment containing objects A and B.

In addition to providing information about the backward-forward dimension, optical flow provides information about subtle differences in the direction of travel. In figure 4.7a, the observer is moving directly toward object A, so the angles of the light from the object as they enter the eye are changing at the same rate across time. In general, a person perceives that he is moving directly toward or away from an object when the angles of light entering his eye from both sides of the object change in *opposite* directions at the *same* rate. The combined angle gets bigger if he is moving toward the object, and it gets smaller if he is backing away from the object. However, if the observer is moving so that the object is passing on his right side (see figure 4.7b), then the angles of light from both sides of the object entering the eye change in the *same* direction, with the one entering the eye from the right side of the object changing more quickly than the one entering from the left.

Presumably, a hiker knows how to walk through a forest or a rugby player knows how to avoid a tackler by processing information about the relative rates of change in the visual angles of light from those objects in those two environments. The term **visual proprioception**, suggested by D.N. Lee (1980), describes the type of sensory information that arises when vision, a form of exteroceptive information, provides performers with information about proprioception, the movement of one's body in space.

**visual proprioception**—Sensory information provided by the visual system about the proprioceptive aspects of a person's movements.

Visual proprioception may also occur in situations where an object, such as a ball, moves toward a motionless observer. In figure 4.8a the angles of the light rays entering the eye from the edges of the ball expand at the same rate from each side of the ball, indicating that the ball is coming directly toward the eye. In figure 4.8b the ball

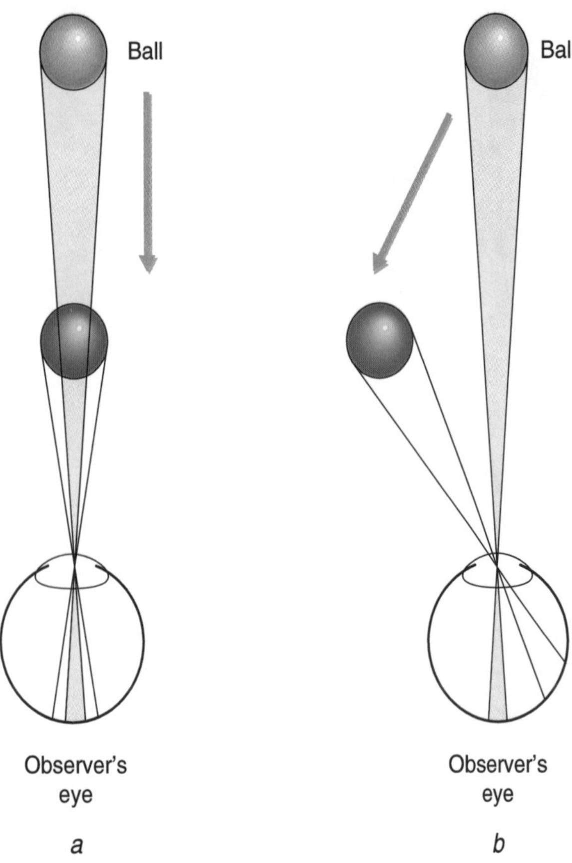


Figure 4.8 Optical flow provides information about a ball's speed and direction of travel relative to a fixed observer.

is not moving directly toward the observer, so the angles of the light entering the eye from both sides of the ball are all changing in the same direction, but the angles of those entering the eye from the left side of the ball are changing—that is, increasing—at a faster rate than those entering the eye from the right side of the ball. This information indicates that the ball is moving toward the observer's left side, possibly serving as input to the person's motor system to move the arm to the left to catch the ball.

A special case of visual proprioception can be frightening. We've all had this experience: an object suddenly hurtles directly toward our eyes—we're sure it's going to hit us. Our response is a nearly automatic blink of the eyes coupled with a jerk of the head to avoid being struck. Even a newborn baby shows this response when someone suddenly moves a hand directly toward the infant's face, even if the baby has never experienced being struck in the face before. This suggests that the response is relatively automatic, rather than one that is learned through experience. People probably have an innate capability of detecting particular patterns of optical flow that specify an impending threat; fortunately, our nervous system generates effective avoidance reactions in response to these patterns.

### Time-to-Contact Information

The pattern of optical flow produced by an approaching object, such as a ball, indicates the time remaining until the object reaches the plane of the observer's eye (Lee & Young, 1985). The retinal image of an approaching object expands as the object approaches. The rate of expansion indicates the speed of the approaching object. Images that expand on the retina more quickly are approaching at a faster rate. The optical variable **tau** is determined from this rate of expansion and is proportional to the time remaining until contact; tau is equal to the size of the retinal image at some moment divided by the rate of change of the image. Presumably tau is "computed" by the central nervous system on the basis of optical-flow information. Tau is important for individuals who perform interceptive actions or coincident-timing tasks (i.e., two objects or events coinciding), such as striking or catching a ball, or preparing the body for vertical entry into the water at the proper moment of a springboard dive. Tau may be critical in other situations as well, such as when an individual attempts to avoid a suddenly approaching car on the street.

**tau**—An optical variable proportional to time until contact, figured as the size of the retinal image divided by the rate of change of the image.

### Balance

Early scientific viewpoints emphasized the role of the proprioceptors in detecting postural sway and loss of stability. For example, when a person's body sways forward, the ankle joint is moved and the associated musculature is stretched, producing signals from the joint receptors and muscle spindles that indicate the body is moving. Also, vestibular receptors in the inner ear are sensitive to movements of the head, providing individuals with information about body sway.

More recently, however, research has indicated that the role of vision in balance may be far greater than previously believed. You can demonstrate this for yourself by looking straight ahead at an object on the wall. Without shifting your direction of gaze, move your head slightly forward and backward and pay attention to the changes in visual information. You will probably notice that the objects in your peripheral visual field seem to move and that this motion is dependent on the pattern of your head movement.

Lee and Aronson (1974) demonstrated that balance is strongly affected by varying the visual information presented to observers. In their experiment, the participant stood in a special room surrounded by suspended walls that did not quite touch the floor. The walls could be moved while the floor was kept still in order to influence the individual's optical-flow information. Moving the walls slightly away from the observer caused his body to sway slightly forward, and moving the walls closer caused a backward sway. With a toddler, an away-movement of the walls caused the child to stumble forward, and a toward-movement of the walls caused a rather ungraceful plop into a sitting position. Moving the walls toward or away from the observer generated optical-flow information that made the observer feel his head was moving in a direction opposite that of the walls. This created the perception of being out of balance and the feeling of falling in the direction opposite that of wall movement. The result was an automatic postural compensation in the same direction as wall movement. Such visually based compensations are far faster (with latencies of about 100 ms) than those requiring conscious processing by the focal visual system (Nashner & Berthoz, 1978). Experiments such as these suggest that optical-flow information and the ambient visual system are critically involved in the control of normal balancing activities.

This notion has strong implications for learned postures as well. In performing a handstand on the still rings, where it is important to remain as motionless as possible, the gymnast's visual system can signal very small changes in posture, providing a basis for tiny corrections in body position to hold the posture steady. It is probably important to train performers of tasks like this to fixate their gaze on a particular spot on the mat located on the floor below them so that they can see the changes in visual information more easily.

#### *Keep Your Eye on the Ball!*

It sometimes seems strange to hear a coach remind a golfer to "keep your eye on the ball" during the swing. This reminder makes more sense for baseball batters because by watching the approaching ball they are better able to detect last-moment information about its flight characteristics. But a golf ball is certainly not going anywhere until after it is hit, so why should watching it help the golfer's swing?

The role of optical-flow variables in balance can help us answer this question. It is important to hold the head in a constant position over the ball during the golf swing. Very small changes in head position during the swing are signaled by optical-flow information, just as they are during other movements requiring good balance. Small movements of the golfer's head backward during the backswing are detected rapidly, and small changes in muscle activities are generated to compensate for these unintentional movements. These compensatory movements can very well alter the swing enough to adversely influence the shot. As we explain in the next section, changes in a performer's musculature often occur as a result of the processing of optical-flow information by the ambient system. The resulting adjustments are nonconscious and are very fast—far faster than those produced by the focal visual system (as accomplished in the outer loop shown in figures 4.2 and 4.5).

## Vision in the Conceptual Model

We can now add these principles of visual information processing for movement control to the conceptual model, as shown in figure 4.9. Note that visual feedback from the focal system and the ambient system travels along different loops.

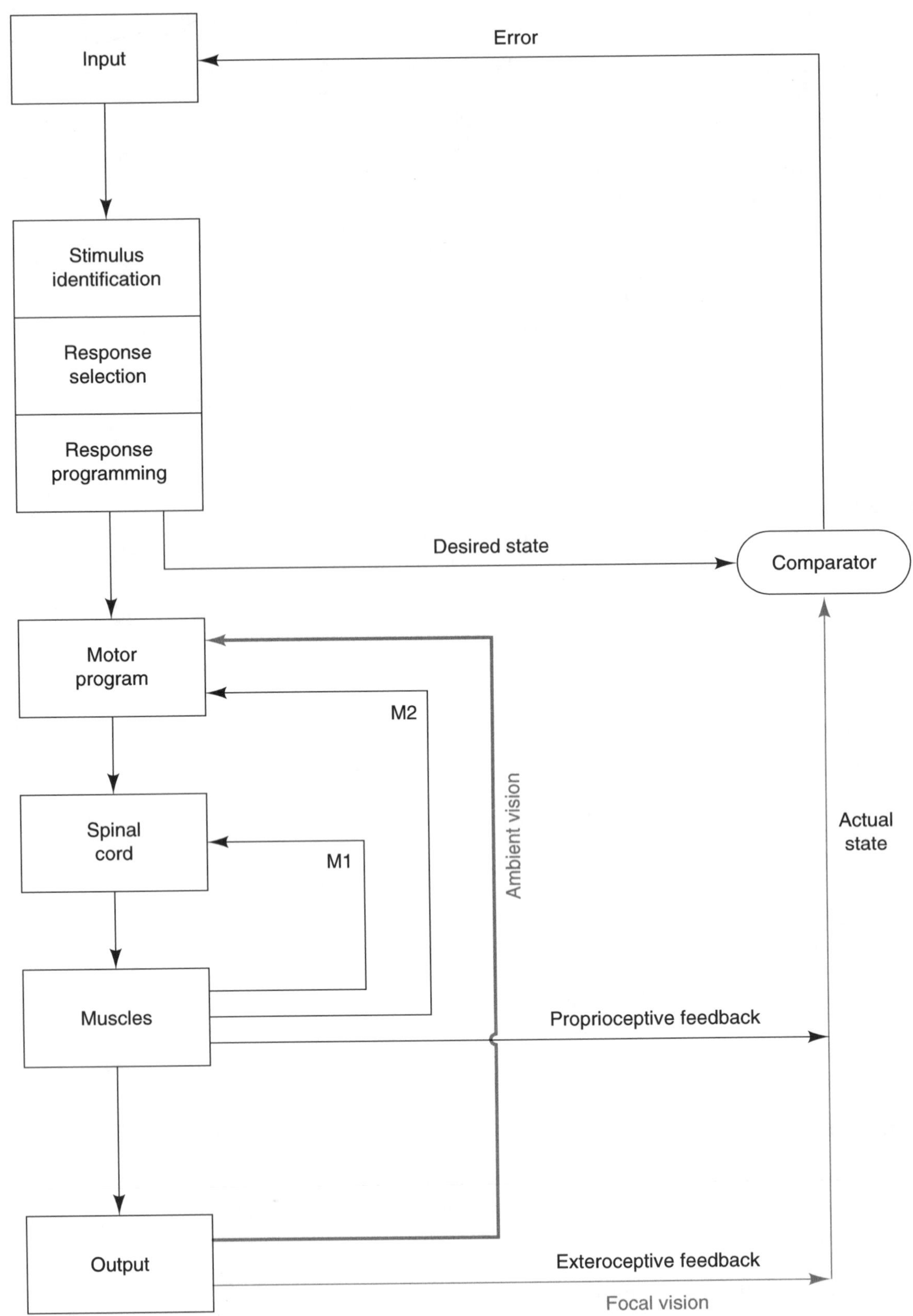


**Figure 4.9** The expanded conceptual model of human performance, here including the pathways for focal and ambient vision shown in green.

Information from the focal system is carried in the outer feedback loop (thin green line); the processing of this information is conscious, slow, and attention demanding, so it is logical that it is carried in the loop that passes through the stages of information processing. Information from focal vision can have effects on the control of a movement but only after relatively long delays. The loop for focal vision is, however, very flexible.

Second, there is the loop that transmits information from the ambient system, here shown by a thick green line. Because ambient information is handled in a nonconscious, relatively fast, and inflexible manner, it is routed to relatively low levels of the central nervous system, considerably "downstream" from the higher processes that select and initiate movement, but "upstream" from the muscles and the spinal cord. Thus, ambient vision operates at an intermediate level in the system, making minor adjustments in already programmed actions, such as compensations for head movements in the golf swing and alterations in posture to maintain balance on the still rings. The final common path to the muscles is based primarily on the originally programmed action—but notice that these commands can be supplemented by at least four different feedback loops that signal various features of the movement, the environment, or both.

## Visual Dominance and Visual Capture

Although vision can make powerful contributions to movement control, its influence is not always positive. Many performers choose to use other modes of control. For example, consider the race car driver or pilot who monitors engine performance by the sounds of the engine—instead of by the visual information provided by cockpit gauges. More often, however, performers opt to use vision, as it represents the most dominant sensory system (**visual dominance**) and has the power to unavoidably capture their attention (**visual capture**).

**visual dominance**—The tendency for visual information to supercede information coming from the other senses during the process of perception.

**visual capture**—The tendency for visual information to attract a person's attention more easily than other forms of information.

In situations where visual information is very important to task performance (e.g., coring an apple with a knife), this is not a problem. However, in other situations a person's overreliance on vision may cause an ineffective performance. Take, for example, the sport of sailboat racing, in which a sailor has rich visual information about the aerodynamic shapes of the sails and the way the wind is flowing over them. Although this plentiful visual information can yield good performance, a sailor who focuses exclusively on visual information may ignore other sources of information, such as the sounds the boat makes as it goes through the water, the action and position of the hull felt by the "seat of the pants," and the feel of the forces exerted on the tiller. Such sources provide additional useful information about speed—but only if the sailor is attending to them. Some sailors on the U.S. Olympic team, for example, use blindfolds during training in order to decrease their reliance on vision. When vision is prevented for a long time, the sailors presumably develop a heightened sensitivity to the less dominant sources of sensory information, such as sound and feel.

Looking again at the conceptual model (see figure 4.9), we see that focal visual information takes longer to process than kinesthetic information from the M2 loop does. If the performer uses focal vision in a conscious information-processing mode (i.e., the outer loop), processing is slow and attention demanding. On the other hand, if the individual uses kinesthetic information, routed through the M2 loop, the corrective response is speeded up noticeably. This phenomenon has also been reported in experiments on fencers (Jordan, 1972) where visual information has been shown to *slow* performers' responses by shifting their attention away from more relevant kinesthetic information.

In the same general way, performers who are instructed to concentrate (consciously) on certain visual events often perform more poorly as a result. Such a shift

## YOU DON'T SUPPOSE?

In 1998 an Australian sport fashion designer discovered that his golf game improved when he began wearing a wide-brim hat with a length of heavy wire wrapped around the rim ("Heavy hat credited with best golfing," 1998). The man decided to attach the wire after playing a particularly frustrating round of golf in a strong wind that kept blowing his hat off. "Before I knew it," he said, "my game started to get better in quantum leaps and I realized it could only be the hat." What do you think about the man's explanation? Could it be correct? If so, how would you interpret it using the conceptual model in figure 4.9? Can you think of any other explanations for the man's improved performance? How would you interpret them using the conceptual model?

to conscious processes shifts visual control from the relatively fast ambient system to the slower focal system (see figure 4.9). Thus, when baseball coaches instruct batters to watch the ball and then swing when the time "feels right," they may be offering greater assistance than when they tell batters to swing when the ball looks like it has reached a particular point in space (e.g., halfway to home plate). The feels-right instruction encourages the use of the batter's ambient visual system and time-to-contact information that is more reliably derived from optical flow (McLeod, McLaughlin, & Nimmo-Smith, 1985). The point-in-space instruction encourages the use of the individual's focal visual system and conscious control, resulting in poorer, rather than better, performance.

This is another example of the Bliss-Boder hypothesis—performance is sometimes impaired by instructions that encourage performers to engage in conscious activities demanding attention and controlled processing. This is particularly true for high-level performers who have developed many elegant, nonconscious processes for detecting and processing visual and kinesthetic information, along with very fast and effective processes for making corrections based on this information. If these individuals are forced out of these nonconscious modes of processing (by coaches' instructions, thoughts about not making mistakes, or whatever) and into the more conscious, controlled information-processing activities, their performance usually suffers.

**open skill**—A skill performed in an environment that is unpredictable or in motion and that requires individuals to adapt their movements in response to dynamic properties of the environment.

**closed skill**—A skill performed in an environment that is predictable or stationary and that allows individuals to plan their movements in advance.

## IT DEPENDS . . .

Two issues that confront individuals when they attempt to perform skilled movements are the goal of the movement and the most appropriate focus for achieving the goal. Whether the goal is to perform a gymnastics activity or to catch a ball, the performer needs to decide where the focus should be. When should it be on exteroceptive information? When should it be on proprioceptive information? Briefly describe the goal of an **open skill** or a **closed skill** you are familiar with. Under what circumstances might exteroceptive information be important for successful goal achievement? When might proprioceptive information be important? For each set of circumstances, how might focal vision and ambient vision be used to control the movement?

# Summary

The effectiveness with which individuals process various forms of sensory information often determines their overall performance level. Sensory signals from the environment are usually termed exteroceptive information, whereas those from within the body are referred to as proprioceptive or kinesthetic information. For human performance, it is useful to think of these signals operating within a closed-loop control system that contains an executive for decision making, an effector (i.e., muscles, joints, etc.) for carrying out the actions, feedback about the state of the environment, and a comparator for contrasting the actual state with the desired state determined by the system. In general, human closed-loop control systems that involve the three stages of processing have the following characteristics:

- They use many different sources of sensory information.
- They operate relatively slowly, allowing only three to five compensations per second due to limitations in processing speed.
- They are flexible and adaptable, and thus are effective in controlling slow, continuous actions, such as various types of tracking movements.

The expanded conceptual model, with the addition of closed-loop control processes, is particularly effective for understanding how people produce slower discrete actions as well as continuous tracking movements. Other reflexlike processes allow movement corrections without the involvement of information-processing stages. Moving from M1 reactions to M2 reactions to triggered reactions to M3 (or reaction-time) reactions, these processes become more flexible but slower. Vision is considered as a special case of closed-loop control. Two visual systems—a focal system for item identification and an ambient system for motor control—contribute in different ways to movement control.

Movement time, or the duration of a movement, is one of the most important variables in movement control; it has a strong limiting influence on the kinds of feedback that can be used to adjust movement commands during the course of an action. With respect to the issue of movement time and motor control, the following points should be kept in mind:

- The very quickest human movements have no possibility of any type of feedback-based correction until after the action is completed.
- Somewhat slower actions allow lower-level feedback control, with increased potential for modification as movement time becomes longer.
- Slow, continuous, or sustained actions allow the simultaneous involvement of a combination of hierarchically ordered feedback loops.

## From Principles to Practice

Check your understanding of the material in this chapter by responding to the following questions and then completing the application exercises. In each case, see if you can identify the most relevant questions or issues and then propose a solution based on the concepts and principles discussed in the chapter.

### Checking Your Understanding

1. What are the four essential components of any closed-loop control system? Describe how each of the components might function for a child who is using a crayon to color a figure in a coloring book.
2. Explain how movement time influences the type of control a person can use in performing a task. Discuss why it is problematic for a woodworker to sand surfaces or drill holes in a rapid fashion.
3. People are often told to pay attention to what they are doing. Under what conditions might paying attention to movements *hinder* the performance of a concert pianist? Why does this happen?
4. Describe how optical-flow information informs a badminton player about the time of arrival of a shuttlecock that is moving directly toward him. Does this process depend on either the size of the shuttle or the distance it must travel?
5. Define and describe the four principal responses involved in producing compensations for unexpected disturbances in a person's movement. How might each function for an individual who stubs her toe while walking along a sidewalk?

### Application Exercise #1

A volleyball coach notices that one of her better athletes seems to be "thinking too much" during crucial moments of competition. During those moments the athlete's movements are tentative and "choppy" looking.

*It Depends*

- What are the goals of the movements?
- Under what circumstances is "paralysis by analysis" occurring?
- Are the choppy movements being performed in an open or closed environment?
- What are the important sources of sensory information the athlete must use to achieve successful task performance?
- How long does it take the athlete to produce the movements (i.e., what is the average movement time)?
- What is the athlete's focus prior to and during the movements?

*Strategy*

Identify the athlete's focus during crucial moments of competition. Determine whether the athlete is utilizing the most effective and efficient form of movement control. Suggest a plan of action that maximizes the athlete's use of sensory information prior to and during performance.

*Response Example*

The athlete's movement time for the task must first be obtained in order to determine whether she has sufficient time to use the stages of processing to control the movement.

- If movement time is sufficiently long (e.g., 500 ms or longer), the athlete should be encouraged to identify (with the coach's assistance) those sources of sensory information that are most important to goal achievement. Once she does this, she should be instructed to attend to that information during performance.
- If movement time is short (e.g., less than 200 ms), the coach and athlete should discuss the movement plan in more detail in order to determine ways the athlete can successfully produce the movement in the absence of feedback processing.
- Once the strategies are determined, the athlete should practice them on a consistent basis and then use them during the crucial moments of competition.

## Application Exercise #2

A middle-aged man wants to learn how to dribble a basketball. Unfortunately, he is visually impaired, having lost most of the sight in both eyes as a result of a work-related accident.

*It Depends*

- What is the man's age?
- How much previous experience (i.e., prior to his accident) has the man had with other gross motor, eye-hand coordination activities (e.g., tennis, racquetball, volleyball)?
- How sensitive are the man's other senses (e.g., audition, proprioception, kinesthesis)?
- Does the man have any other impairments that are either genetic or a result of his accident?

*Strategy*

Since the man's primary goal is learning to dribble the basketball, modify the task and the environment to help maximize his processing of available sensory information and optimize his movement control.

## Application Exercise #3

A person is training to operate a robot using a remote control device. The robot is used to handle radioactive materials in an enclosed, lead-lined room. The controller's task is to manipulate the controls and watch the robot's movements displayed on a video monitor.

*It Depends*

- What forms of feedback are available to the controller?
- How does two-dimensional visual information (as seen on the video monitor) differ from the three-dimensional visual information the controller normally uses?
- What types of tasks are the robot expected to perform?

*Strategy*

Determine how the controller might use the feedback that is available to him to effectively operate the remote control device and safely manipulate the robot's movements.

## Application Exercise #4

A person wants to learn how to play his friend's favorite song on the piano so that he can perform it for his friend at a surprise birthday party.

*It Depends*

- How skilled is the person in playing the piano?
- Can the person read sheet music?
- How difficult is the song the person wants to play (i.e., does it involve simple or complex note sequences)?
- Can the person "carry a tune" (i.e., does he differentiate the pitch of sounds and can he match the sounds he produces on the piano with those of his friend's favorite song)?
- How rapidly does the person want to be able to play the song?

*Strategy*

Determine the person's piano-playing skill and his goal for performing the song. Identify the relevant sensory information the person would be able to use to achieve his goal. Determine whether the speed with which he wants to play the song allows him sufficient time to use visual feedback to hit all the correct notes.

# 5

# Movement Production and Motor Programs

## Chapter Outline



## Chapter Objectives

**When you have completed this chapter, you should be able to**

understand the concept of open-loop control for movement;

describe the rationale for and characteristics of motor programs;

understand how individuals might use generalized motor programs to produce various versions of a particular type of movement (e.g., long, medium, and short hops), including versions they have never attempted previously (e.g., a new hopscotch sequence); and

apply the principles of motor programming to practical performance situations.

## Preview

During a high-hurdles race in the sport of track and field, runners produce a number of separate actions almost simultaneously. At each hurdle they stretch forward with one leg (let's say it's the left) to clear the hurdle; bring the right arm forward, almost touching the toes; move the left arm backward with the elbow flexed; bring the right leg to the side with the knee sharply flexed to clear the hurdle; and then bring the left leg down sharply to the ground to initiate the next step. Runners execute this combination of clearly identifiable movements in an instant, with correct sequencing and a level of coordination that gives the impression of a single, fluid action. How do skilled athletes and other types of performers produce so many movements so quickly? How do they control the individual components and combine them to form a whole movement?

## Overview

In the last chapter we talked about the role of closed-loop processes in movement control. We learned that some forms of closed-loop control simply take so long that no corrections can be made in the movement before it is completed. Clearly, performers somehow control rapid acts of a discrete or serial nature, but it is unlikely that they use closed-loop processes to do so.

In this chapter we examine the idea of open-loop control and introduce the concept of the motor program, a structure that may be responsible for the control of rapid acts. We then discuss how motor programs might be used in conjunction with various reflex pathways (mentioned in the previous chapter) to give a more complete picture of central and peripheral contributions to movement control. Finally, we describe the concept of generalized motor programs, which, because of their flexibility, may be the sort of mechanisms that allow individuals to produce slight variations of particular types of movements (e.g., hopping different distances and speeds, on either leg).

## Motor Program Theory

For many actions, particularly those that are brief in duration and produced in stable and predictable environments (e.g., springboard diving, dropping a load of dirt from a front-end loader into a dump truck, dart throwing, hopping over a puddle of water), individuals usually plan the movement in advance, then trigger the action in such a way that it runs its course without much modification. There is very little conscious control over the movement once it is initiated; rather, the action just seems to "take care of itself." In this respect, humans are fortunate. The possible combinations of muscle and joint activity our bodies are capable of producing are so large in number that it would be virtually impossible for us to try to regulate them consciously while we are executing rapid, skilled actions. All of the independent components of a control system and the number of ways each component can act are sometimes called **degrees of freedom**. A challenge for performers is learning how to manage the degrees of freedom so that the desired action is produced in the most effective way.

**degrees of freedom**—The number of components of a control system and the possible ways each can perform.

**motor program**—A set of motor commands that is prestructured at the executive level and that defines the essential details of a skilled action; analogous to a central pattern generator.

**open-loop control**—A type of control that involves the use of centrally determined, prestructured commands sent to the effector system and run off without feedback; used by individuals to control rapid, discrete movements.

The question is how are all the degrees of freedom controlled for rapid movements? In many ways, this question is one of the most fundamental for students of motor behavior because it deals with the issue of how biological systems of all kinds control actions. In order to answer this question we must have some idea of how the central nervous system is functionally organized before and during action and how this organization contributes to the control of the unfolding movement. In chapter 4, we considered the ways sensory information might contribute to or modify movement production. However, we did not examine in much detail *what* the sensory information was modifying.

Most likely, sensory information modifies a set of prestructured movement commands, often referred to as the **motor program**, which defines and shapes the action being produced. The concept of the motor program, which is the central theme of this chapter, is based on a type of control system that is referred to as an **open-loop control** system. It is in some ways opposite the closed-loop system that we described in chapter 4.

## FUNCTIONAL ELECTRICAL STIMULATION: AN EXAMPLE OF OPEN-LOOP CONTROL

Many rehabilitation settings make use of functional electrical stimulation (FES), an open-loop control system. In FES systems, therapists program patterns of electrical stimulation that produce particular movements, such as the dorsiflexion of a patient's ankle on the swing leg that allows the foot to clear obstacles such as a step or a curb. Once the necessary open-loop programs have been developed, the patient may activate them by operating a hand switch that controls a small computer worn on the belt (Hausdorff & Durfee, 1991). Whenever the desired movement is required, the patient presses the hand switch and the computer triggers the programmed pattern of stimulation. The movement is then carried out without modification. Various types of FES systems are particularly useful for patients with hemiplegia, paraplegia, and quadriplegia.

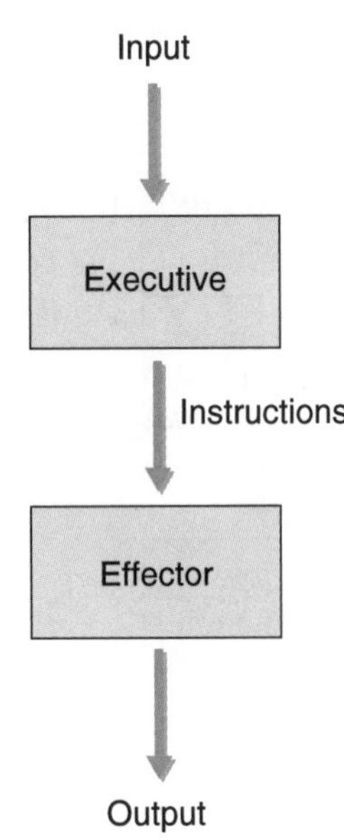


**Figure 5.1** Elements of an open-loop control system.

## Open-Loop Control

Figure 5.1 shows a diagram of a typical open-loop control system. It consists of essentially two parts: an executive and an effector. If you refer back to figure 4.1, you will see that these two components are also contained in the **closed-loop control** system. Missing from the open-loop control system, however, are the **feedback** loop and the **comparator** that determine errors. The system shown in figure 5.1 begins with input being delivered to the executive. This input is then processed and a decision is made about the action to be taken. Instructions regarding the production of this action are then transmitted to the effector, which carries them out. Once the action is completed, the open-loop system's work is finished. Without feedback, the system is "unaware" of whether the action was successful in achieving the environmental goal. Modifications to the action are not made while the movement is in progress.

This kind of control is used in a variety of real-world systems. For example, the open-loop mechanism that regulates traffic flow at many intersections often operates by illuminating a repetitive sequence of green, yellow, and red lights. If an accident should occur at the intersection, the system continues to activate the light sequence as if nothing had happened. Thus, one characteristic of an open-loop control system is that it is effective as long as the circumstances surrounding the action are unchanged, but it is inflexible in the face of unexpected changes.

Another example of an open-loop control system is a simple computer program, which some scientists believe is the basis for the idea of the motor program. Put simply, computer programs are sets of instructions that tell the computer what to do and in what order to do it. In some cases, the computer program also specifies the timing of the operations (i.e., what should be done when and for how long). Although many computer programs are sensitive to feedback (i.e., errors), the classical open-loop computer program is not. In such cases, the computer faithfully follows the instructions provided by the program without any regard for whether the actions are correct or whether the results have met the programmer's intended goals.

Open-loop systems are most effective for controlling operations that occur in stable, predictable environments where the need for modification of commands is low. Generally, the characteristics of a purely open-loop control system can be summarized as follows:

**closed-loop control**—A type of control that involves the use of feedback and the activity of error detection and correction processes to maintain the desired goal; used by individuals to control slow, deliberate movements.

**feedback**—Information about the actual state of a system.

**comparator**—The error detection mechanism contained in closed-loop control systems; compares the desired state to feedback about the actual state.

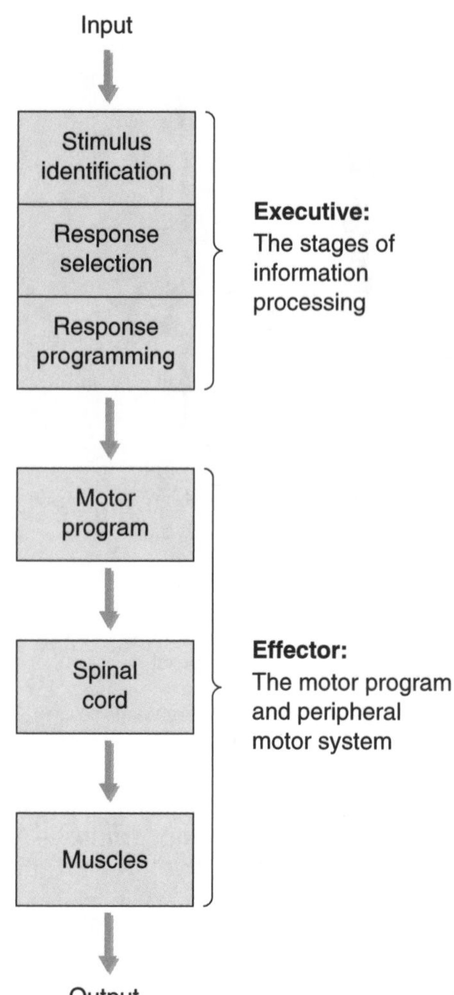


Figure 5.2 An expanded open-loop control system for human performance. The executive contains the stages of information processing, which determine what to do, while the effector carries out the movement.

- Advance instructions are given that specify the operations to be performed, as well as their sequencing and timing.
- Once the program has been initiated, the system faithfully carries out the instructions without modification.
- Because feedback is not being used during a completely programmed movement, there is virtually no capability for detecting or correcting errors.

## The Motor Program as an Open-Loop Control System

In a sense, much of our movement behavior—especially those actions that are quick and forceful, such as kicking and throwing—is controlled in an open-loop fashion and carried out without much feedback involvement. When performing these tasks we usually do not have time to process information about movement errors and must therefore plan the action properly before we initiate it. This is quite different from the style of control discussed in the previous chapter, in which slower movements could be modified by feedback processes of various kinds.

Open-loop control seems to be especially effective in environmental situations that are predictable and stable. Under such circumstances no changes in the planned movement are needed once the action is begun. The psychologist William James (1890) popularized this general idea over 100 years ago, and it continues to be one of the most important ways for us to understand movement control. Figure 5.2 illustrates this general idea of motor program control by combining the basic open-loop system shown in figure 5.1 with some of the processes we discussed in earlier chapters.

Consider a task such as hitting a pitched baseball. In the executive, the stages of information processing (see chapter 3) are activated to evalu-

In quick, forceful actions, movement behavior is largely controlled in an open-loop fashion, without much feedback involvement.

IT DEPENDS . . .

How fast can you spin a yo-yo? How do you think the spinning action is controlled? How does the type of control change when you perform "walk the dog" or allow the yo-yo to remain in a spinning mode at the end of the string? How would your movements be different in those two situations? How would your movement times be different? Which situations would require greater use of closed-loop control processes? Why?

ate the environment (stimulus identification), decide whether or not to swing (response selection), and, if the decision is made to swing, develop and initiate the motor program for doing so (response programming).

Control is then passed on to the effector mechanism for movement execution. Here the motor program is delivered to the spinal cord and then to the muscles where contraction takes place. If the resulting action (e.g., the bat swing) produces the intended outcome (i.e., contact with the ball), a change in the environment occurs (i.e., the path of the ball changes).

In this type of open-loop control system, the motor program determines which muscles should contract, as well as the order and timing of the contraction. The stages of processing are used to develop the motor program by determining the action to be initiated and, to some extent, the eventual form of the movement (e.g., the speed and trajectory of a swing). Movement execution, however, is carried out in the absence of direct conscious control.

Initially a program might be capable of controlling only a short string of actions. With practice, however, the program becomes more elaborate, controlling longer and longer strings of behavior, and perhaps even modulating various reflexive activities that support the overall movement goal. Once learned, these programs are stored in **long-term memory** and retrieved as needed to prepare (using the response-programming stage) future movements for execution (see figure 3.13).

**long-term memory (LTM)**—The memory system that holds information and experiences; believed to be vast in capacity and unlimited in duration.

One major advantage of motor program control is that not as much attention is needed for movement production. You have already learned that movement organization and initiation causes a bottleneck in the response-selection or response-programming (or both) stages of movement production (review figures 3.9 and 3.10 in chapter 3). With motor program control, entire sequences of action are run off without the need for additional organization. The more sophisticated the motor program, the longer it runs and the larger the chunk of skilled behavior it controls. When this happens, the response-programming stage is involved less often and attentional processes are freed up to perform other higher-order activities, such as the monitoring of movement form or style in gymnastics or dance, the development of strategic plans in tennis, or paying attention to safety hazards in operating earthmoving equipment.

## Open-Loop Control Within the Conceptual Model

How does the concept of open-loop control and the motor program fit into our conceptual model of human performance? Figure 5.3 shows the conceptual model used earlier in figure 4.9, only now the shaded portions represent the *open-loop* components shown in figure 5.2. The model can now be viewed as an open-loop control system, with feedback loops (i.e., the unshaded portion on the right side of the figure) that allow for the various types of closed-loop corrections we discussed in

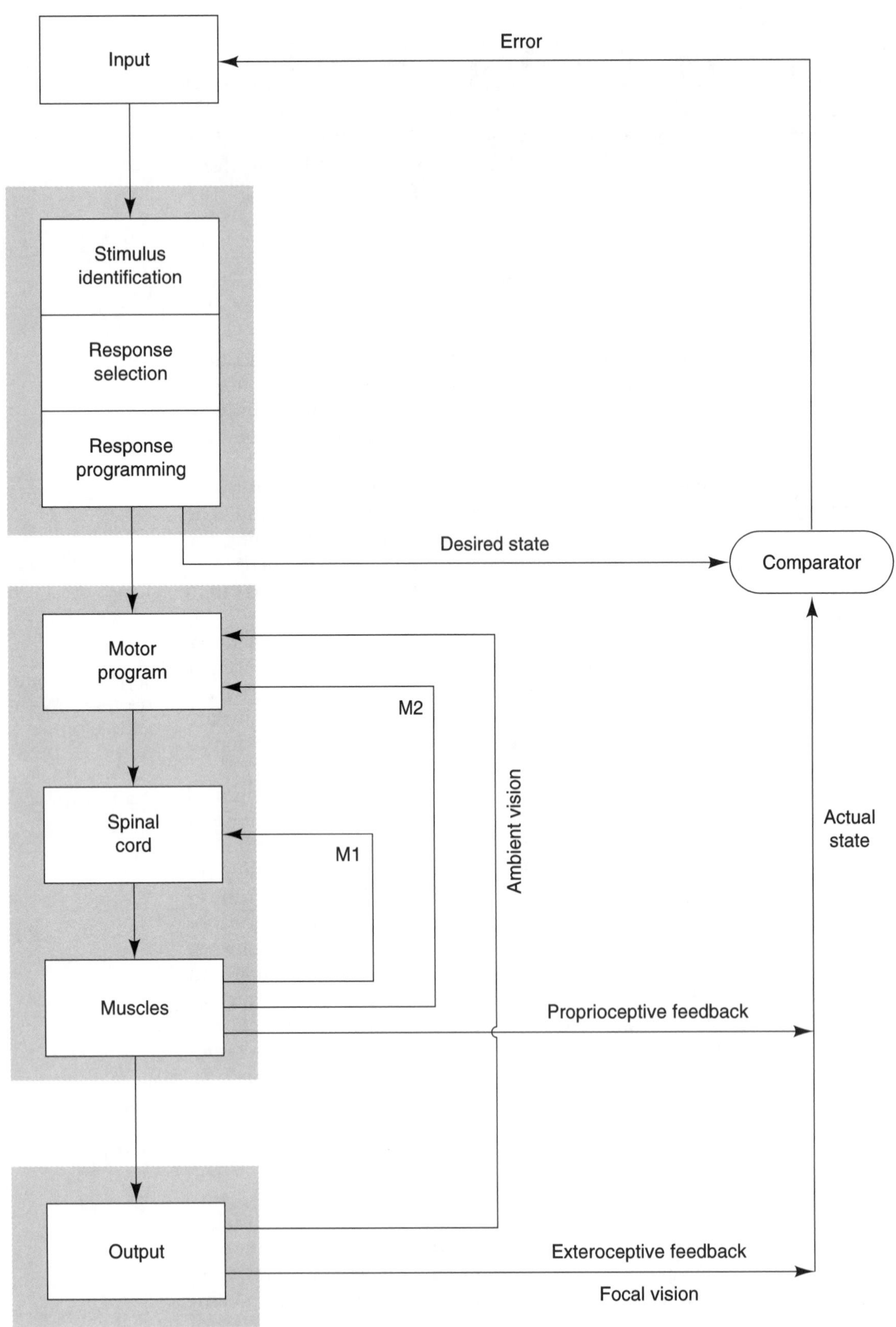


Figure 5.3 The conceptual model of human performance, with the open-loop components highlighted.

IT DEPENDS . . .

Fishing is a popular recreational activity for many people. Have you ever thought about how the various movements involved in this task might be controlled? Using the following continuum as a guide, mark an "X" along the line to indicate the extent to which you think closed-loop and open-loop processes are controlling each of the movements. For example, if you put an "X" on the line halfway between "closed-loop" and "open-loop" you would be indicating that the fisher is using both closed-loop and open-loop processes to the same extent to control that particular movement.

| | | | |
|---|---|---|---|
| Baiting the hook | Closed-loop | ——————————— | Open-loop |
| Casting the line | Closed-loop | ——————————— | Open-loop |
| Reeling in the line | Closed-loop | ——————————— | Open-loop |
| Netting the fish | Closed-loop | ——————————— | Open-loop |
| Taking the fish out of the net | Closed-loop | ——————————— | Open-loop |
| Throwing the fish back in the water | Closed-loop | ——————————— | Open-loop |

chapter 4. This more complete version of the conceptual model has the potential to operate in either of two basic ways, depending on the nature of the task. If the movement to be produced is very slow, control is dominated by the operation of feedback processes. If the movement is very fast, control is predominantly governed by the operation of open-loop processes. It is important to remember, however, that most motor behavior is a complex blend of both open- and closed-loop operations. Therefore, both types of control are often at work simultaneously or intermittently.

With very fast actions, the notion of motor programs offers a useful set of ideas and vocabulary for discussing how the motor system might be functionally organized. That is, if a movement appears to be organized in advance, is triggered more or less as a whole, and is carried out without much modification from sensory feedback, it is reasonable to label it "a programmed action." This type of language describes a style of motor control that involves central movement organization, where movement details are determined by the central nervous system and then sent to the muscles. This style of control contrasts sharply with that involving ongoing modification of a movement using peripheral feedback processes. Of course, both styles are possible and may even operate simultaneously to varying extents depending on the nature of the task, the time involved, and other factors.

A simple example of how we control movements using *both* open-loop and closed-loop processes is the game of bounce and catch. Stand in an upright position and bounce a tennis ball on the ground in front of you. As the ball rises from the ground, catch it. Repeat the task several times, bouncing the ball to a different height and catching it at a different point each time. Which aspects of this simple task are you controlling in an open-loop fashion? Which aspects are you controlling in a closed-loop fashion?

## Three Lines of Evidence for Motor Programs

Essentially three separate lines of research evidence converge to support the theory of motor program control of fast actions. This evidence includes studies examining the effects of movement complexity on reaction time, experiments on animals that

**electromyography (EMG)**—A device for recording the electrical activity in a muscle or group of muscles.

have undergone surgical elimination of feedback pathways, and research using **electromyography (EMG)** to analyze patterns of movements that are unexpectedly blocked.

### *Reaction Time and Movement Complexity*

**reaction time (RT)**—The interval of time that elapses from the presentation of an unanticipated stimulus to the beginning of a person's response.

**Reaction time (RT)**, you may remember from chapter 3, is the interval of time between a suddenly presented, unexpected stimulus and the beginning of a response. In 1960 Henry and Rogers examined the RT of participants who were asked to respond to a stimulus by initiating and then carrying out predetermined movements that varied in complexity (see the highlight box on page 131). What they found was that RT increased as the complexity of the movement to be produced increased. Since that time, several features of movements that make them more complex have been shown to lengthen RT:

- RT increases when additional elements are added to a movement. A brake press in a car with an automatic transmission requires a shorter RT than one in a car with a manual transmission, because the latter task also requires depression of the clutch.
- RT increases when movements require the coordination of a greater number of limbs. A one-handed blocking movement in judo or boxing is produced in a shorter RT than a more complicated two-handed movement.
- RT increases when the duration of the movement becomes longer. A bat swing that lasts 100 ms has a shorter RT than one lasting 300 ms.

The interpretation of these findings is that when the action is more complex (in any of the above-mentioned ways), RT is longer because more time is required to organize the system for movement initiation. This prior organization occurs in the response-programming stage. According to motor program theory, movements that are organized in advance should take longer to program if they are more complex. This longer "programming time" is presumably reflected in the longer RT found for more complicated actions.

### *Deafferentation Experiments*

**deafferentation**—A surgical procedure in which an afferent sensory pathway is cut, preventing nerve impulses from the periphery from reaching the spinal cord.

In chapter 4 we mentioned that sensory information from the joints and muscles is carried to the spinal cord. A surgical technique termed **deafferentation** involves a severing of the nerve bundle at the point where it enters the cord. Once this operation is performed, the central nervous system no longer receives sensory information from a particular portion of the periphery, such as an entire limb, or even several limbs.

A number of researchers have used the deafferentation procedure to examine the motor control characteristics of experimental animals. The question of interest is what types of movements are possible when animals are deprived of sensory feedback from their limbs. Films taken of monkeys with deafferented upper limbs show that they are still able to climb around, playfully chase each other, and groom and feed themselves. In fact, it is often very difficult for viewers to recognize that these animals have a total loss of sensory information from their upper limbs (Taub, 1976; Taub & Berman, 1968). The monkeys demonstrate some difficulty in fine motor control, such as in picking up a pea or manipulating small objects with their fingers. But on the whole, they show remarkably little impairment in most of their movement activities.

Studies of this kind clearly illustrate that sensory information from the moving limb is not critical for movement production, and in fact many movements can easily occur without it. This evidence suggests that theories of movement control that presume a need for sensory information from the responding limb are generally

## The Henry and Rogers Experiment

One of Franklin Henry's many important contributions to the field of motor behavior was a paper he and Donald Rogers published in 1960. The study they conducted was actually quite simple, as are many important scientific investigations. Participants were instructed to respond as quickly as possible to a stimulus (a gong sound) by making one of three different kinds of movements. However, since only one of the movements was tested during each set of trials, the study actually consisted of three different simple RT experiments. The three movements, designed to differ in complexity, were (a) a simple finger lift from a reaction key; (b) a simple finger lift plus a rapid hand movement that involved reaching forward and grasping a tennis ball suspended on a string; and (c) a simple finger lift followed by a series of movements requiring the striking of one suspended ball, reversing direction and touching a "dummy" button located next to the reaction key, and reversing direction again and striking a second suspended ball.

For each of these movements, Henry and Rogers measured the RT, that is, the interval of time between the gong and the finger lift. Their results revealed that RT increased as movement complexity increased. The finger-lift movement (a) had an RT of 150 ms, the reaching and grasping movement (b) had an RT of 195 ms, and the movement with two reversals in direction (c) had an RT of 208 ms.

It is important to remember that for each trial of this experiment, the stimulus to move (processed during stimulus identification) and the number of movement choices (response selection) were held constant (i.e., only one stimulus and only one response). The only factor that varied from one series of trials to the next was the complexity of the response. Henry and Rogers interpreted the lengthened RTs for the more complex movements as meaning that it was taking longer to program the action (in the response-programming stage) prior to movement initiation. This notion has had a profound effect on our understanding of movement organization processes, and has led to many additional studies of these processes. Most importantly, these data support the idea that people organize movements in advance, which is consistent with the motor program concept.

incorrect. Because feedback-based notions of motor control cannot account for the monkeys' movement capabilities, many theorists have argued that movements must be organized centrally in motor programs and carried out in an open-loop fashion.

This thinking is similar to several ideas we presented in chapter 4, specifically those dealing with the fact that some actions are performed too rapidly for feedback to be used in controlling them. Very quick movements are completed before performers can use the feedback produced by the action to alter its course (see figure 4.6). Thus, if the movement is fast enough, a mechanism like a motor program would have to be used to control the entire action, with the movement being carried out as though the performer were deprived of feedback. Our capability to move quickly gives additional support to the idea that we use some central program to handle that type of movement control.

### *Effects of Mechanically Blocking a Limb*

A third line of evidence supporting motor program control comes from experiments in which individuals are instructed to make a quick limb action (e.g., moving a lever to a target position as rapidly as possible). On some trials, participants initiate and complete the movement, while on others, unbeknownst to the individuals, they are prevented from completing the movement (e.g., by a mechanical block inserted by the experimenter to keep the lever from moving). Figure 5.4 shows an integrated electromyogram (EMG recording) of the muscle activity resulting from a quick

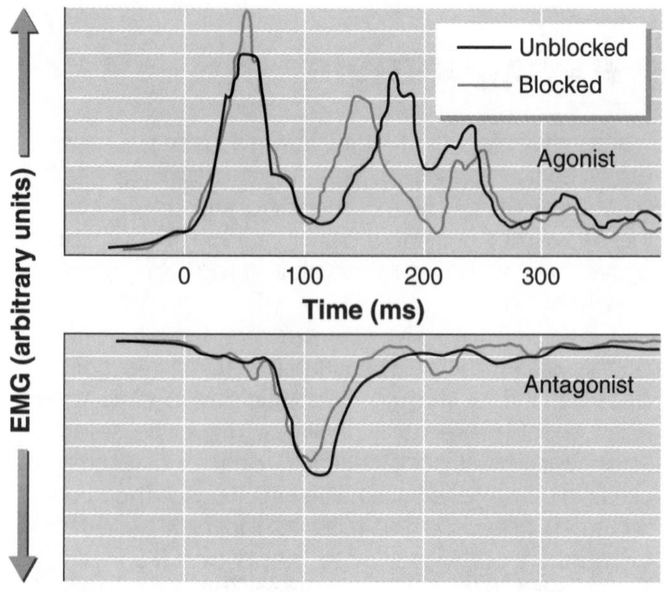


Figure 5.4 Agonist (triceps) and antagonist (biceps) EMG activity in a rapid elbow-extension movement. The green traces are from a movement which was mechanically blocked at the outset. (Reprinted, by permission, from W. Wadman et al., 1979, "Control of fast goal-directed arm movements," *Journal of Human Movement Studies* 5:10.)

elbow-extension movement to a target (Wadman et al., 1979). In the unblocked movement (black lines) there is first a burst of activity in the agonist (triceps) muscle, then the triceps turns off and the antagonist (biceps) muscle is activated to decelerate the limb. Finally, the agonist turns on again to stabilize the movement near the target. This triple-burst EMG pattern is typical of the way muscles turn on and off during quick movements of this kind.

The EMG pattern for trials in which the movement was unexpectedly prevented (green lines) reveals an initial pattern of muscular activity similar to that seen for the unblocked movement. Only after about 120 ms or so is there a slight modification of the patterning, undoubtedly caused by some of the reflex activities (e.g., stretch reflexes) we discussed in chapter 4. The most impressive finding is that the antagonist (biceps) muscle contracts at all in the blocked movement (since its function is to decelerate a *moving* limb!), not to mention that it contracts at the same time as in the unblocked movement.

Although feedback from the blocked limb is massively disrupted, EMG patterning is essentially the same as that for the unblocked movement, particularly during the first 100 ms or so. Data such as these contradict the idea that feedback from the moving limb (during the action) acts as a signal (a trigger) to activate the antagonist muscle at the proper time. Rather, these findings suggest that agonist and antagonist EMG activities are planned in advance and these signals are produced unmodified by sensory information for 100 ms to 120 ms, or at least until the first reflexive responses are activated.

## How and When Do Programs Contribute to Actions?

In the case of rapid movements, open-loop control allows the motor system to organize an entire action ahead of time. In order for this to occur, the programming process must include the following specifications:

- The particular muscles that are needed to produce the action
- The order in which these muscles are to be activated
- The relative forces of the various muscle contractions
- The relative timing and sequencing of these contractions
- The duration of the respective contractions

Most motor program theorists assume that a movement is organized in advance by a program that sets up some kind of neural mechanism, or network, containing time and event information—a movement script, if you will, that specifies certain essential details of the movement as it runs off over time. Some scientists even speak of performers "running" a motor program, which is clearly analogous to the processes involved in running a computer program.

A particularly useful analogy or model for the motor program is the old phonograph record. The record defines which sounds are to occur and in what order, the duration and timing (rhythm) of those events, and the relative intensities of the sounds. Unlike the phonograph record, the motor program does not specify every aspect of the movement, since reflexive activities are possible. Nevertheless, the motor program and the phonograph record operate conceptually in more or less the same way.

## Postural Adjustments Before Action

Imagine that you are a participant in an experiment in which you are instructed to stand with your arms at your sides and then, on command, raise your right arm as quickly as possible to shoulder level. Where do you think the first detectable muscular activity associated with this movement would come from? Most people would guess the shoulder muscles, but in fact those muscles are activated relatively late in the sequence of events. Actually, the first muscles to contract, some 80 ms before noticeable EMG activity occurs in the shoulders, are those in the lower back and legs (Belen'kii, Gurfinkel, & Pal'tsev, 1967).

This order of muscular activity may sound strange, but it is really quite "smart" for the motor system to operate this way. Since the shoulder muscles are mechanically linked to the rest of the body (e.g., the back and the arms), their contraction affects posture. If no preparatory compensations in posture were made, raising the arm would shift the center of gravity forward, causing a slight loss of balance. The motor system takes care of this potential problem by programming the appropriate postural modifications first, rather than requiring the body to make adjustments after the arm begins to move.

There is good evidence that these preparatory postural adjustments are really just a part of the motor program for arm movements (W.A. Lee, 1980). When arm movements are organized, the motor program contains instructions to adjust posture and then move the arm, so that the action is performed as a coordinated whole. Thus, we should not think of arm movement and posture control as separate events but simply as different parts of an integrated action that raises the arm while maintaining balance. Interestingly, these preparatory postural adjustments vanish from the EMG

A. Ramey/Unicorn Stock Photos

A one-handed blocking movement in judo or boxing is produced with a shorter RT than is a more complicated, two-handed movement.

record when individuals lean against some type of support prior to performing the arm movement. The "smart" system apparently realizes that advance preparation of posture is not needed for that type of situation.

## Central Pattern Generator

**central pattern generator**—A centrally located control mechanism that produces mainly genetically defined, repetitive actions; analogous to a motor program.

The idea of the motor program is similar to the concept of the **central pattern generator (CPG)**, which purports to explain certain features of repetitive action, such as locomotion in animals, swimming in fish, chewing in hamsters, and slithering in snakes (Grillner, 1975). For these species, some genetically defined (inherited) central organization is established in the brain stem or the spinal cord. When initiated by a triggering stimulus (sometimes called a "command neuron") in the brain, rhythmic, oscillating instructions are sent to the musculature. These signals define a sequence of alternating and repetitive activities (e.g., right-left-right-left limb movements) like those that occur during normal locomotion. Studies with nonhuman species indicate that the commands are forwarded even when sensory nerves are cut (deafferented), suggesting that this type of organization is truly central in nature.

Figure 5.5 shows an example of a simple network that could account for the alternating flexor-extensor pattern found in locomotion. Here, the input signal activates neuron 1, which activates neuron 2, as well as the flexor muscles. Neuron 2 activates neuron 3, which activates neuron 4, as well as the extensor muscles. Neuron 4 activates neuron 1 again, and the process continues to repeat itself. This is, of course, far too simple to account for all of the events in locomotion, but it shows how a collection of single neurons might be connected to each other in the spinal cord to produce an alternating pattern of motion.

While the notion of the CPG is almost identical to that of the motor program, there is an important difference. The CPG relates more to genetically defined activities, such as locomotion, chewing, and breathing, whereas the motor program involves learned activities that are centrally controlled (such as kicking and throwing).

## Integration of Central Organization and Feedback Control

Although it is clear that the central organization of movements is a major source of motor control, it is also obvious that sensory information modifies these commands in several important ways (see figure 5.3). Thus, the question becomes how and under what conditions the commands from programs and CPGs interact with sensory information to define the overall movement pattern.

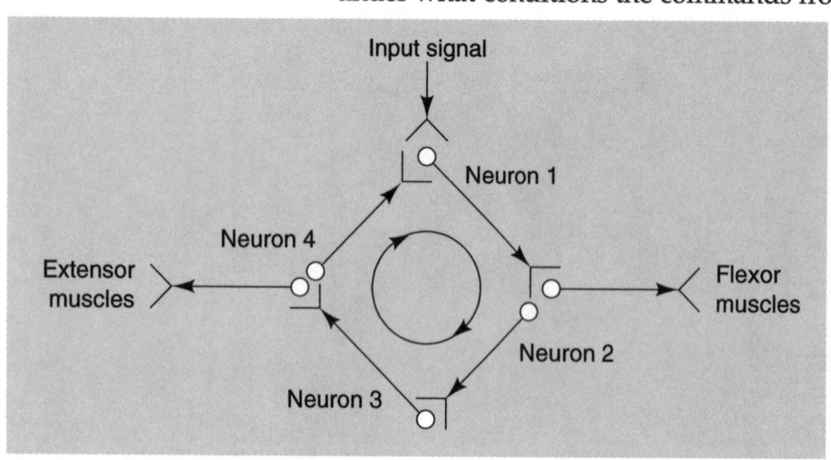


Figure 5.5 A simple network of neurons that could result in alternating flexor and extensor muscle movements in activities like locomotion. Such a network could form the basis of central pattern generators (CPGs).

We have already discussed various classes of reflexive activities that are capable of modifying originally programmed output (see figure 4.5). In addition to these feedback loops, there is another category of reflexive modulations that has a very different effect on movement behavior. In examining the control of locomotion in cats, experimenters have applied a light tactile stimulus to the top of the animal's foot while it walked on a treadmill. This stimulus has been found to have different effects on the movement at different locations in the step cycle. If it is applied at the moment the cat is placing its foot on the treadmill surface, the stimulated leg extends slightly, as if preparing to carry more load on that foot. This response has a latency of about 30 ms to 50 ms and is clearly nonconscious and automatic. If the same stimulus is applied when the cat is just lifting its foot from the treadmill surface in preparation for the swing phase, the response is very different. The leg flexes upward at the hip and the knee so that the foot travels above its usual trajectory.

**reflex reversal phenomenon**—A special case of reflex activity involving different responses to a tactile stimulus depending on the phase of the movement in which the stimulus is introduced.

This leg reflex, causing either an extension or a flexion depending on where in the step cycle the stimulus is applied, has been called the **reflex reversal phenomenon** (Forssberg, Grillner, & Rossignol, 1975). Most significantly, it challenges the usual conceptualization of a reflex, which is defined as an automatic, stereotyped response to a given stimulus. In the case of the reflex reversal phenomenon, the *same* stimulus generates different responses at different times.

Scientists believe that this variation in response occurs because of ongoing interactions among the movement program for locomotion, the CPG, and feedback that is carried along sensory pathways. As just discussed, the CPG is responsible for many of the major events that occur during locomotion and other rhythmical activities, such as sequencing and timing of muscle contractions. In addition, CPGs are now thought to be involved in the modulation of reflexes during repetitive action, producing the reflex reversal phenomenon. The logic is that the CPG determines whether and when certain reflex pathways are to be activated during the action, as diagrammed in figure 5.6, a and b. During the swing phase of locomotion when the cat's foot is being lifted from the ground (see figure 5.6a), the CPG activates the flexion reflex (i.e., by closing the circuit) and inhibits the extension reflex (i.e., by opening or "breaking" the circuit). If a tactile stimulus occurs during the swing phase, it is routed to the flexion reflex, not to the extension reflex. However, if the stimulus occurs during the stance phase, when the foot is being placed on the ground (see figure 5.6b), it is routed to the extension reflex, not to the flexion reflex. This process is repeated as long as the step cycle continues. If no stimulus occurs at any time during locomotion, there is no reflex activity at all, and the CPG produces the action uninterrupted.

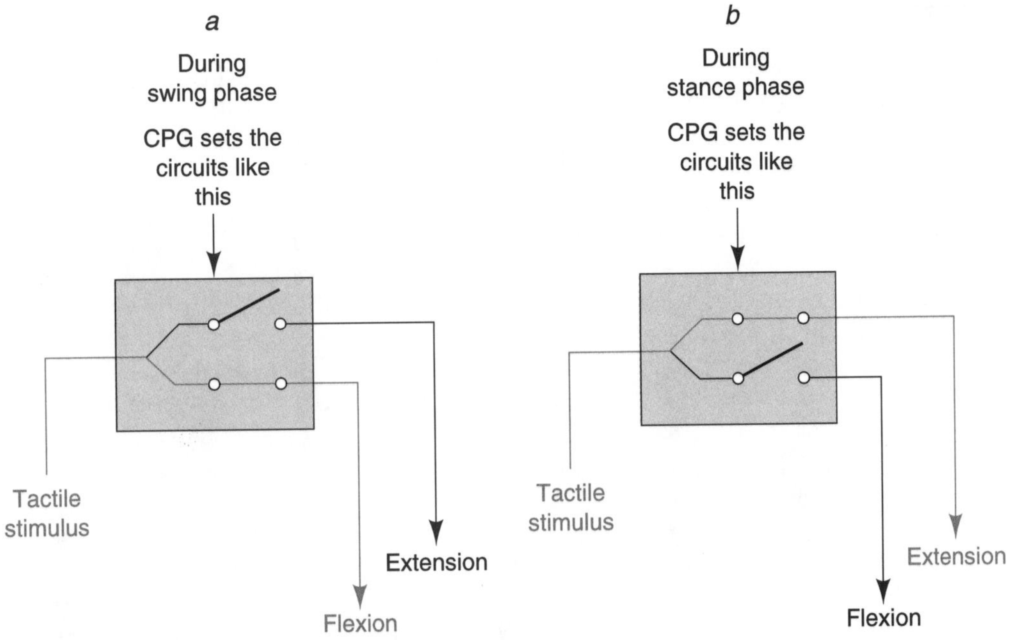

**Figure 5.6** In addition to controlling the leg motion during locomotion, the CPG can inhibit or enable flexion and extension reflexes, depending on the phase of the step cycle.

We are only beginning to understand these complex reflex responses, but they undoubtedly play an important role in providing flexibility to the control of skills. The organization of the cat's reflexes probably has an important survival role. Receiving a tactile stimulus on the top of the foot while it is swinging forward probably means that the foot has struck some object. The flexion reflex causes the foot to be quickly lifted in order to keep the cat from tripping. However, receiving the stimulus during the beginning of the stance phase causes an extension of the weight-bearing leg because the opposite-side leg is swinging at this time.

These responses can be thought of as temporary reflexes in that they exist only to modify individual segments of a particular action given certain sets of conditions. Such responses ensure that the goal is achieved even when a disturbance is encountered. It is likely that similar reflex responses operate during human locomotion when, for example, we catch our toe while walking along a sidewalk and immediately switch from swing to stance phase in order to avoid falling.

Analogous findings have also been reported in studies exploring the control of speech, where unexpected tugs on the lip musculature during the production of a sound cause rapid, reflexive modulations that allow the particular sound to still be produced (Abbs, Gracco, & Cole, 1984; Kelso et al., 1984).

## Motor Programs and the Conceptual Model

Motor programs are an important component of the conceptual model seen in figure 5.3. They operate within the motor system, sometimes in conjunction with feedback, to produce flexible skilled actions. The open-loop part of these actions provides the organization, or pattern, that may later be modified by feedback processes, if necessary. Motor programs also assist performers in regulating the many degrees of freedom in their movements. The concept of degrees of freedom, which we defined earlier in this chapter, pertains to the components of the motor system (e.g., muscles and joints) and all the ways in which each of the components can function. A simple example is to examine some of the ways you could choose to move just your index

### IT DEPENDS . . .

To visualize the concepts of "freeing" and "freezing" related to the degrees of freedom, stand next to your chair and put an object on the seat (e.g., a coin, a pen, a book). Your movement goal is to pick up the object with your left hand and place it in your right hand.

Attempt to perform this movement in three different ways. On the first attempt, keep your wrists and elbows locked. On the second attempt, bend your wrists and elbows, but keep all of your fingers, except for the thumb, locked and straight. On the third attempt, pick up the object any way you like. For which of the movements did you allow more degrees of freedom to vary? Give one example of a muscle or joint that you allowed the degrees of freedom to vary and one example of a muscle or joint you caused the degrees of freedom to "freeze."

For which of the following movements do you think performers would allow the degrees of freedom in their hands to vary more (rank order the movements with "1" indicating the task for which the performer allows the degrees of freedom in the hand to vary the most and "4" indicating the task for which the performer allows the degrees of freedom to vary the least): playing the piano, sculpting with clay, chopping wood with an axe, shooting a basketball free throw? For each of these tasks, explain why it is important for the performer to vary (or freeze) degrees of freedom in the hand.

## Motor Programs, Along With Feedback, Manage the Degrees of Freedom in Movement Control

Motor programs operate within the motor system, sometimes in conjunction with feedback, to manage the degrees of freedom of movements and produce flexible skilled actions. In a study by Steenbergen, Marteniuk, and Kalbfleisch (1995), seven right-handed individuals were seated and performed a task in which they reached forward a distance of 30 cm, grasped a Styrofoam cup, moved it a distance of 20 cm, and placed it in the center of a plate. During half of the movement attempts, the cup was empty; during the other half of the attempts, it was filled with cold coffee. Individuals performed half of the movements with their right hand (involving a leftward movement of the cup) and the other half with their left hand (involving a rightward movement of the cup). An analysis of movement patterns under the various conditions revealed that the speed of both the reaching and transporting phases of the participants' movements was slower when the cup was full than when it was empty—and when the task was performed with the left (nonpreferred) hand than when it was performed with the right. During these slower movements, individuals reduced the angular motion of their elbow and shoulder joints and increased the motion of their trunk. One interpretation of these results is that under the full-cup condition, the motor program "froze" selected joints (in this case the elbow and shoulder) in order to reduce the frequency of feedback-based corrections the performer needed to make while moving the cup full of liquid. It is also possible that the program selected the postural position for the full-cup condition because it is inherently more stable, is less susceptible to perturbations, or requires corrections of smaller amplitude.

finger. If you lock or "freeze" the top two (distal, near the fingertip) joints, you can move the finger in a forward-backward direction, a left-right direction, or rotate it clockwise or counterclockwise in a circle. This example illustrates just a few of the degrees of freedom you have in moving just one appendage.

A big challenge for performers is identifying the combinations of degrees of freedom that produce the most effective and efficient movements. Muscles and joints that a performer *allows to move* during an action (e.g., the plane in which the index finger is moving) are said to be "free" to vary, while those the individual *prevents from moving* (e.g., the top two joints of the index finger) are the ones she or he "freezes."

Another factor that appears to influence the way people program their movements is the anticipated final position of the limb or appendage. In a study by Rosenbaum (1989) participants performed a task in which they reached out and grasped a control handle and then rotated it to a target position. During the course of the experiment, individuals rotated the handle under a variety of conditions that involved a number of combinations of start and target positions. The results revealed that the way individuals oriented their hand prior to grasping the handle at the start position (in some cases the position seemed quite awkward and contorted) depended on the terminal or target position to which they would be moving. One interpretation of these results is that the system programmed the initial position of the hand in a way that ensured that the final position of the hand at the target position was always the same (and in the most comfortable position!).

The major roles of motor programs include the following:

- To define and issue the commands that ultimately determine which muscles to contract, when, and how forcefully
- To organize the many degrees of freedom of the muscles and joints into a single unit to produce an effective and efficient action

- To specify and initiate preliminary postural adjustments that performers need to support the upcoming action
- To modulate the many reflex pathways in order to ensure that the movement goal is achieved

## The Bernstein, or Dynamical, Perspective

There is an alternate view to the notion of the motor program for explaining the mechanisms of movement control. In fact, several theorists who have been critical of the motor program concept have countered with ideas that are usually referred to as the *Bernstein perspective* (after Russian physiologist N.I. Bernstein) or the *dynamical perspective* (Bernstein, 1967; Kelso, 1995). These dynamicists argue that the motor program concept places too much emphasis on the organization, control, and representation of every action in the central nervous system and that it ignores many of the dynamic features of movements, such as the springlike properties of contracting muscles and the preferred frequencies of oscillation of limb segments.

Proponents of the dynamical perspective hold that the regularities of movement patterns are not represented in motor programs, but rather emerge naturally (that is, physically) as the result of complex interactions among numerous connected elements. This idea is analogous to theoretical propositions explaining the organization and structure of many complex physical systems in the absence of a central program or set of commands. Examples of such "spontaneous" organization include the sudden transformation of still water to rolling patterns as it begins to boil and the ordering of water molecules into crystals when the temperature drops to freezing. Just as it would make little sense to postulate a central program for governing the patterns that emerge in boiling and freezing water, they argue, it is incorrect to think that motor programs are needed to control complex patterns of human action. Supporting evidence they point to includes research that shows that the exact dynamics of patterns of limb action during gait or locomotion are achieved by basic demands for stability (Hoyt & Taylor, 1981) and by the simple mechanical properties of the muscles in combination with gravitational forces (McMahon, 1984). Findings such as these suggest that an extensive motor program is not needed to govern the control of repetitive actions.

The debate of these issues continues in a healthy scientific fashion (T.D. Lee, 1998; Sternad, 1998; Walter, 1998). Perhaps one day we will find that the best explanation for movement control lies in some combination of the various viewpoints (Colley &

**dynamic systems theory**—An explanation for how people control coordinated movements that emphasizes the interaction of dynamical properties of the neuromuscular system and physical properties of environmental information.

### SELF-ORGANIZATION IN DYNAMIC SYSTEMS

One of the tenets of **dynamic systems theory** is called "self-organization," meaning that the human motor system is capable of spontaneously adjusting itself under certain controlled conditions. This concept was quite clearly illustrated in a study by Kelso and Schöner (1988). To experience the self-organization phenomenon for yourself, try the following task. Begin by placing your hands palms down on a flat surface in front of you (e.g., a desktop). Now begin tapping your two index fingers in an alternating fashion at a slow, steady pace. As you continue to do this, gradually increase the pace until you are moving your fingers at a maximum rate of speed. What happens? At some point, the motor system reorganizes the action, causing the fingers to tap at the same time ("in phase") rather than alternately ("out of phase"). We are only beginning to understand the implications of such self-organizing properties (see Kelso, 1995) but the research to date has uncovered some interesting features of coordination.

Beech, 1988). Nevertheless, thinking of the motor system as being driven by motor programs continues to be a helpful way to integrate many different types of research findings into a unified structure.

# Generalized Motor Programs

The theory of motor programs is very useful for understanding the functional organization of certain kinds of actions. However, simple motor program theory does not encompass several important aspects of movement behavior. Its most severe limitation is a failure to explain how people are able to produce novel movements and create flexible movement patterns.

## How Is a Novel Movement Produced?

Frequently we see a champion tennis player demonstrate an amazing capability to produce actions that appear completely novel (i.e., new and different). The player may be out of position, yet she is often able to return her opponent's shot with a shot of her own that looks extremely unorthodox and almost certainly could not have been practiced previously. When you consider the immense number of possible combinations of ball flight characteristics (i.e., speed, angle, trajectory, spin, unpredictable bounces), changes in court position of the two opponents, and so on, it is likely that each shot a player hits is essentially novel in that it has never been performed exactly that way before. In spite of all this, advanced players execute their movements with great style and grace, as if they are producing well-practiced actions.

Observations such as these raise problems for the formulations of a simple **motor program theory**. According to the simple view, each variation of the same general movement, such as the tennis swing, needs its own program because differences in ball flight characteristics, positioning of the opponent, and so on require a particular set of instructions, which are stored in long-term memory, to the muscles. Since there is likely an unlimited number of variations of some movements (e.g., kicking, throwing, striking, jumping), performers need to have a countless number of motor programs to produce all of these movements. As you may have probably surmised by now, the number of variations possible in tennis, not to mention in all other motor activities, creates the dilemma of an enormous number of programs being deposited in long-term memory; a problem Dick Schmidt has appropriately termed the **storage problem** (Schmidt, 1975; Schmidt & Lee, 1998).

In addition to the storage problem, simple motor program theory must also deal with the **novelty problem**. Before discussing this problem further, we dare you to try the following activity: From a standing position, jump up and rotate your body one-quarter turn to the left, and, while still in the air, touch your head with your right hand and your leg with your left hand. Were you able to do it? Although we doubt that you have ever attempted this movement before, our guess is that you were probably able to perform it effectively on the first or second try. Now the question is where does the specific program for this action come from? It could not have been learned and placed in long-term memory, unless you have practiced the movement before now. And it is not likely that the program was genetically determined, because such a movement would seem to have little biological significance, unlike those you need for locomotion or chewing, for example. Motor program theory is at a loss to explain the performance of such novel actions.

**motor program theory**—An explanation for how people control coordinated movements that emphasizes the role of prestructured motor commands organized at the executive level.

**storage problem**—A deficiency of simple motor program theory based on the notion that a vast memory capacity would be needed to store all the separate programs for controlling the nearly countless number of different movements people are able to produce.

**novelty problem**—A deficiency of simple motor program theory based on the notion that individuals should be unable to produce novel (i.e., new) movements or unpracticed variations of learned movements because they have not developed specific motor programs for producing the movements.

## How Can Motor Program Output Be Modified?

The storage and novelty problems motivated a search by scientists for alternative ways of understanding motor control. The result was an idea that emerged in the 1970s, one that characterized movement programs in a more general fashion. The

**generalized motor program**—A motor program that defines a pattern of movement rather than a specific movement; this flexibility allows performers to adapt the generalized program to produce variations of the pattern that meet altered environmental demands.

concept of the **generalized motor program** views the program as a stored movement pattern. However, unlike the pattern of the simple motor program, the generalized motor program is one that can be modified slightly when the program is executed, allowing performers to adjust the movement in order to meet altered environmental demands.

Over a half century ago, the British psychologist Sir Fredrick Bartlett (1932) wrote this about his tennis stroke: "When I make the stroke, I do not . . . produce something absolutely new, and I never repeat something old." (p. 202)

The first part of Bartlett's statement suggests that a movement is never totally new. All of his ground strokes resembled each other because they possessed Bartlett's own style of hitting a tennis ball (don't we all have our own individual and unique style of moving?). The second part of Bartlett's statement conveys the idea discussed in the previous section, that every movement is also novel in that it has never been performed exactly the same at any other time. What, then, are some of the features that performers can change when they produce the same type of movement in different ways?

### *Variations in Movement Time*

When we play throw and catch with a friend, sometimes we throw the ball faster and other times we throw it slower. That we are able to change the time or speed of our movements without significantly altering the pattern has been nicely demonstrated in an experiment by Armstrong (1970). He asked participants to move a control stick in a left-right-left-right-left motion, controlling the movement at the elbow joint. The solid black line in figure 5.7 illustrates the pattern these individuals were trying to produce. As you can see, the goal pattern required them to move the stick to the left for the first 0.75 s, then back to the right until 1.95 s, then back to the left until 2.90 s, then back to the right until 3.59 s, and finally back to the left to stop at the original position in a total time of 4 s.

Not surprisingly, participants were often unable to produce their movements in exactly 4 s. An example of one pattern is shown in figure 5.7 (green line). As you can see, this individual made the first reversal movement slightly sooner than that of the goal pattern (i.e., after 0.66 s, compared with 0.75 s) and produced subsequent reversals that occurred increasingly "early." However, it is clear that the participant's pattern was similar to the goal pattern in form even though it was produced too quickly (i.e., completed in closer to 3 s than to 4 s).

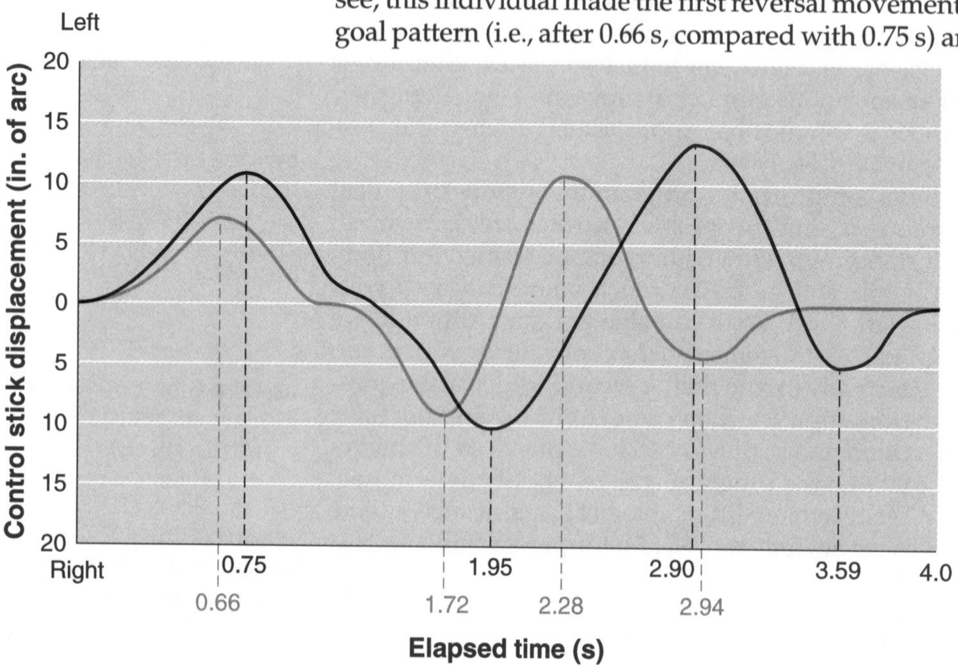

Figure 5.7 The position-time record of performance in an arm movement task. The black line is the goal movement, whereas a movement that is uniformly too rapid is shown by the green line. (Adapted by permission from Armstrong, 1970.)

Another way to think of this relationship is to imagine the participant's pattern in figure 5.7 being drawn on an expandable sheet that could be stretched to make the final peak of the participant's pattern (green line) line up with the final peak of the goal pattern (black line). If we did this we would see that all of the other peaks in the participant's pattern would be lined up with their respective peaks in the goal pattern. This illustration is similar to that of the phonograph record analogy of motor programs we discussed earlier. Just as a record can be played at a faster speed while still preserving the structure of the song, so too can a movement be produced in a shorter time (as shown in figure 5.7) while still preserving the fundamental pattern. In both cases, all aspects of the goal pattern are represented by a common underlying temporal (and sequential) arrangement that can be run off at different speeds.

### *Variations in Movement Amplitude*

The amplitude of movements is another feature individuals can change when performing the same action in slightly different ways. For example, you can write your signature in quarter-inch high letters on a bank check or in six-inch high letters on a blackboard. In both cases the signature is clearly yours (Merton, 1972).

Hollerbach (1978) studied the handwriting phenomenon more formally by asking individuals to write the word *hell* in different-sized letters. He then measured the acceleration patterns (i.e., changes in speed) of the actions exerted by their fingers. Patterns for two different-sized versions of the word are graphed in figure 5.8, the upward trace indicating that the movement is accelerating away from the body and the downward trace indicating that the movement is accelerating toward the body. Not surprisingly, when individuals wrote the word in larger letters (black line), the overall magnitude of the acceleration trace was larger than when they wrote it in smaller letters (green line). Of greater interest, though, is the fact that the *patterns* of acceleration for both versions were almost identical.

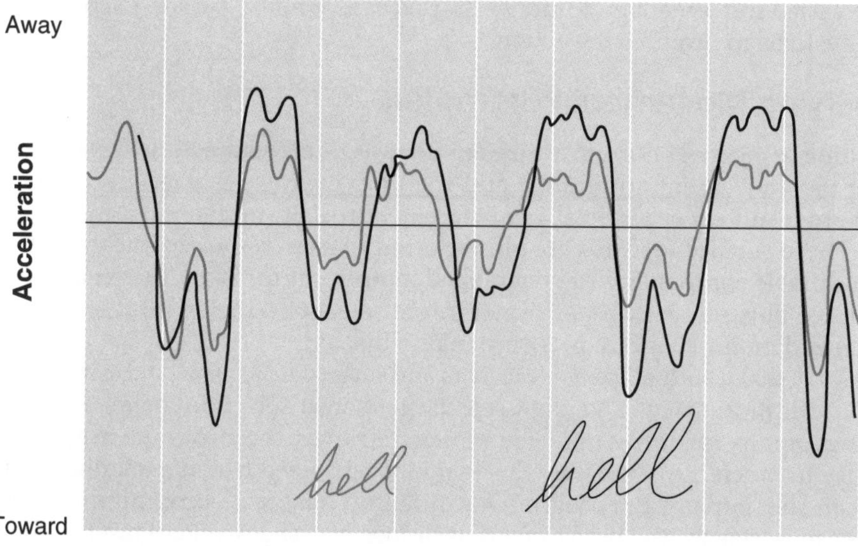


**Figure 5.8** Similar patterns of acceleration produced during the writing of the word *hell*, even though one example has twice the amplitude of the other. (Adapted by permission from Hollerbach, 1978.)

IT DEPENDS . . .

Notice how easily you are able to change movement time and movement amplitude when performing movements such as throwing or kicking. What happens to your movement time and movement amplitude when you want to throw or kick an object a short distance? A long distance?

Individuals can easily vary the amplitude of their movements (just as they can the time)—by uniformly increasing or decreasing the accelerations (forces) they apply—while still preserving the overall temporal pattern. Such variations appear to be possible for many kinds of movements. For example, we can hop various distances on one foot while using the same fundamental hopping action.

*Variations in Limb and Muscles Used*

A third way people can vary their movements while still preserving the fundamental pattern is by using a different limb or different muscles. In the signature example, writing on a blackboard involves very different muscles and joints than writing on a bank check. In blackboard writing your fingers are mainly fixed, and you do the writing using muscles that control the elbow and shoulder. In check writing, your elbow and shoulder are mainly fixed, and you do the writing by using muscles that control the fingers. Nevertheless, the pattern of your signature remains essentially the same. This indicates that people can produce the same movement pattern even when they use different effectors.

This phenomenon was studied by Raibert (1977), who attempted to write a palindrome (i.e., a sentence spelled the same way both forward and backward) using different effector systems. Raibert wrote the sentence "Able was I ere I saw Elba" by using his right (dominant) hand (A), his right arm with the wrist immobilized (B), his left hand (C), his teeth (D), and his foot with the pen taped to it (E). The resulting sentences, shown in figure 5.9, reveal an amazingly similar writing style even though they are written with different limbs and muscles (including those in the head and neck!). There is little doubt that the same person wrote all of them. Once again, the fundamental temporal structure of the movement appears to have been preserved under varied movement conditions—in this case when a person used different effector systems to produce the action.

## Identifying Movement Parameters

**surface features**—The easily changeable components of a movement, such as movement time or amplitude; also referred to as parameters.

**parameters**—The modifiable features of a generalized motor program, such as speed or amplitude of the movement; also referred to as surface features.

**parameter values**—The values assigned by a performer to the parameters of a generalized motor program (e.g., rapid movement time, short amplitude, right arm); allows individuals to adjust a movement pattern to meet specific environmental demands.

According to the theory of generalized motor programs, characteristics such as movement time, movement amplitude, and the limb or muscles used in producing the action are relatively superficial, or surface, features of fundamental movement patterns. These **surface features** are also referred to as **parameters**, meaning that they are modifiable components of generalized motor programs. In the remainder of this section we illustrate how a performer might select parameter values when using a generalized motor program in a particular situation.

Let's say that a softball player receives and interprets sensory information (stimulus-identification stage) and then selects (response-selection stage) a generalized motor program for throwing. The player retrieves the program from long-term memory in much the same way as she might retrieve a friend's telephone number, and then she prepares the program for initiation (response-programming stage).

Most importantly, the performer determines *how* she wants to modify the generalized throwing program for this occasion. Based on environmental information available immediately prior to the action, she determines the most appropriate throw (e.g., fast, slow, far, near, high, low) and perhaps the limb she needs to use. As she makes these decisions, the performer estimates **parameter values** (i.e., movement time, movement amplitude, limb) she needs to produce the desired throw. For example, if she decides to throw the ball a long distance in as short a time as possible, the performer selects a rapid movement time and a large movement amplitude. Since she is right-handed, the obvious limb choice for this type of throw is her right arm because it is presumably stronger. Once she has set these parameter values, the performer is ready to initiate and carry out the movement.

By using generalized motor programs, performers are able to modify already learned movement patterns in order to meet changing environmental demands. The

A Able was I ere I saw Elba

B Able was I ere I saw Elba

C Able was I ere I saw Elba

D Able was I ere I saw Elba

E Able was I ere I saw Elba

Figure 5.9 Similarities in writing with different effector systems. Line A was written by the right (dominant) hand, line B with the wrist immobilized, line C with the left hand, line D with pen gripped in the teeth, and line E with pen taped to the foot. (Reprinted by permission from Raibert, 1977.)

more individuals practice the process of parameterization (e.g., shortening or lengthening the time or amplitude of a movement), the better they become at determining parameter values that produce successful movements.

## Summary

When people want to produce rapid actions, meaning there is no time for the system to process feedback about errors and correct them, they must organize and produce the movements in an open-loop fashion (i.e., plan them in advance and execute them with minimal involvement of sensory information). The motor program is the structure that presumably carries out this action. Several lines of experimental evidence suggest support for the notion of motor programs:

- Reaction time is longer for more complex movements than for simple movements.
- Animals that are deprived of sensory information using a surgical process of deafferentation are still capable of producing relatively effective movements.
- Muscular activity patterns during the first 100 ms to 120 ms of limb movement remain the same even when a person's limb is unexpectedly prevented from moving.

Although the motor program is responsible for determining the major events in the movement pattern, there is considerable interaction with sensory processes. These sensory processes include various reflex mechanisms, which are organized to generate rapid corrections that enable goal achievement in the face of changing environmental demands. Finally, motor programs are thought to be generalized to allow the production of variations of a particular movement or class of actions (such as throwing). The following features characterize generalized motor programs:

- They allow performers to modify their movements along several dimensions, such as movement time, movement amplitude, and the effector system used to produce the action.
- They preserve the temporal pattern of the movement under various kinds of superficial modifications.

## From Principles to Practice

Check your understanding of the material in this chapter by responding to the following questions and then completing the application exercises. In each case, see if you can identify the most relevant questions or issues and then propose a solution based on the concepts and principles discussed in the chapter.

### Checking Your Understanding

1. What are the major components of an open-loop system? How does this type of control system differ from the closed-loop system? Describe how each of the components of the open-loop system might function for a person who is tossing an empty soft drink can into a recycling bin.
2. How do we know that motor programs exist? Discuss two of the three types of research evidence that suggest support for the motor program notion. How does each illustrate that individuals plan their movements in advance?
3. How do humans produce novel movements? Are such movements really "new"? Provide an example of a novel movement that might be produced by a shuffleboard player, a professional golfer, an airplane pilot, or a wheelchair basketball player.
4. What is the generalized motor program? Indicate how this concept allows us to explain the way performers adjust their movements to meet different sets of environmental demands. Using the example you selected in the previous question, explain how the generalized motor program might function to produce the performer's novel movement.

### Application Exercise #1

A senior has one of her hands amputated as a result of a diabetic condition. Unfortunately, the hand that is removed is the one she has predominantly used her entire life.

*It Depends*

- Does the senior have proper functioning of her other hand?
- Is she going to be fitted for a prosthetic device?
- Does she have any other physical impairments?
- What kinds of tasks does she want to be able to perform with the prosthetic device or with her other hand?

*Strategy*

Determine what kinds of hand movements the senior is motivated to perform either with the use of a prosthetic device or with her opposite hand. Determine which movements are primarily controlled in an open-loop fashion and which are controlled in a closed-loop fashion.

*Response Example*

- For movements controlled primarily in an open-loop fashion, determine how well the senior can produce them with different forces or at different speeds.
- For each open-loop movement, encourage her to concentrate on the force or speed that results in her best performance for different types of environmental demands (e.g., using more force to toss a towel into a laundry hamper, using less force to toss a tissue into a waste can).
- For movements she controls in a closed-loop fashion, determine which sources of exteroceptive feedback contribute the most to performance success.
- Explore ways to modify both types of tasks in order to improve the generalized program for controlling the rapid movements and the use of feedback in controlling the slower ones.

### Application Exercise #2

A man wakes up, gets out of bed, and walks to the kitchen to fix breakfast.

*It Depends*

- Which tasks does he control in an open-loop fashion?
- When does the man use feedback to control a movement?
- What types of adjustments does he need to make for movements he controls in an open-loop fashion?

- What is he planning to fix and eat for breakfast?

### *Strategy*

Starting with the task of getting out of bed and finishing with the task of putting the first bite of food in his mouth, describe four different movements the man must control. Indicate which of the movements are controlled in an open-loop fashion and which are controlled in a closed-loop fashion. For one of the open-loop movements, describe one parameter of the generalized program the man will probably need to modify. For one of the closed-loop movements, describe how the man might use feedback to adjust the action.

## Application Exercise #3

A teenager is going to play the snare drums for the first time.

### *It Depends*

- How well can she manipulate the drumsticks?
- What is her movement goal?
- What movements might she need to control in a closed-loop fashion, and what movements might she be able to control in an open-loop fashion?
- How might the teen integrate open-loop control and closed-loop control in producing a single rhythmic sequence?

### *Strategy*

Determine how well the teen is able to control the sticks when she is producing a slow sequence and when she is producing a rapid one. Identify those aspects of her performance that she controls in an open-loop fashion and those aspects she controls in a closed-loop fashion. Ask the teen to try to vary the parameter values of the generalized program she uses to produce the rapid movements. Also ask her to try to vary parameter values within an ongoing sequence. See if she can tell how and when she is able to change the control of her movements from open-loop to closed-loop and vice versa.

## Application Exercise #4

A golf coach notices that during competitive matches one of his players is both "accurate" and "consistent" when he is hitting full shots (i.e., swings that are performed using the full range of arm motion), but is "inaccurate" and "inconsistent" when attempting approach shots (i.e., swings performed with various amplitudes, each of which is less than the full range of motion).

### *It Depends*

- How are "accuracy" and "consistency" being defined by the coach?
- What factors, other than the way the golfer is *producing* the movement, might contribute to reduced accuracy and consistency of his approach shots?
- What aspects of the full swing and the approach shot are controlled in an open-loop fashion?
- What aspects of the full swing and the approach shot are controlled in a closed-loop fashion?

### *Strategy*

Determine the extent to which the golfer's difficulties are due to problems in stimulus identification (i.e., interpreting the environment), response selection (i.e., deciding what type of shot to hit), and response programming (i.e., producing the desired movement). Assuming that at least some of the problem is due to deficiencies in response programming, identify which aspects of each type of shot are controlled in an open-loop fashion and which are controlled in a closed-loop fashion. For those aspects of each movement that are controlled in an open-loop fashion, ask the athlete to produce variations of the shots by changing the parameter values of the generalized motor program (e.g., force, speed, etc.). For those aspects of each movement that are controlled in a closed-loop fashion, ask the athlete to try to produce the desired goal state (e.g., stopping at the same point at the top of a slow backswing) in a consistent fashion.

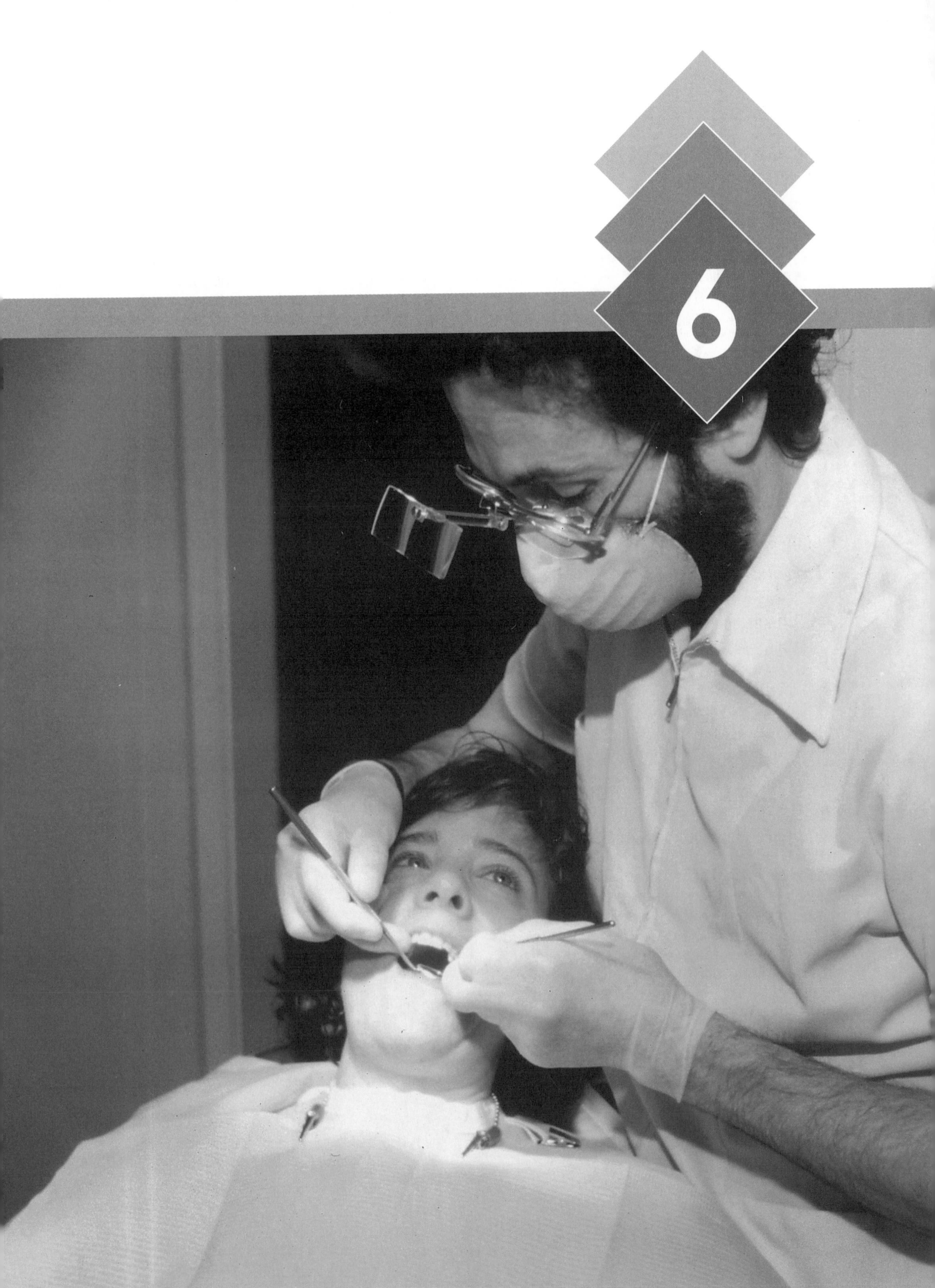
6

# Principles of Motor Control and Movement Accuracy

## Chapter Outline



## Chapter Objectives

**When you have completed this chapter, you should be able to**

understand the concept of invariance in motor control,

explain how the speed and amplitude of a movement influence movement accuracy,

understand the fundamental causes of inaccuracy in quick movements, and

apply the principles of rapid actions to real-world settings.

## Preview

It takes most dentists about two hours to complete a root canal operation. They accept the fact that the job is a slow and tedious one, yet they realize that in order to be successful they must execute their movements in a precise and accurate fashion. This is but one example of the kinds of tasks individuals must perform more slowly in order to achieve the desired outcome. Why is it that slower performance is better for many tasks? Does speed of performance always have to be sacrificed for accuracy? Does haste *always* make waste?

## Overview

In the previous chapter we discussed the concept of motor programs, focusing on the open-loop control of actions. An important aspect of our discussion dealt with how the surface features of fundamental movements may be altered, as when individuals throw snowballs various distances or jump over different-sized puddles. To tailor their movements to environmental demands, in those types of control situations, performers specify certain parameters of well-learned movement patterns (i.e., generalized motor programs for throwing or jumping).

In this chapter we continue our discussion of open-loop control and generalized motor programs. First we show how each generalized program has its own characteristic and fundamental timing structure. Then we discuss some of the most fundamental principles of movement production—analogous to the simple laws of physics—that govern the relationships among movement speed, movement distance, and movement accuracy. Last we examine some of the underlying causes of errors in movements and discuss several ways performers might minimize their movement errors.

## Invariant Features in a Generalized Motor Program

**invariant features**—The components of a movement that remain the same, or constant, when performers change the surface features of the movement.

**relative timing**—The temporal structure of action; the durations of various segments of an action divided by the total movement time.

**surface features**—The easily changeable components of a movement, such as movement time or amplitude; also referred to as parameters.

**parameters**—The modifiable features of a generalized motor program, such as speed or amplitude of the movement; also referred to as surface features.

**deep structure**—The fundamental structure of an action; comprised of the sequencing and relative timing (or rhythm) that defines the movement pattern.

In order to determine the way generalized motor programs are represented in memory, we must know which features of movements remain the same, or invariant, whenever individuals make alterations in flexible parameters (e.g., changing the speed of raking leaves by using more rapid motions). If some features of the motion did not remain invariant, we would not be able to distinguish a leaf-raking motion from the one we use to shovel dirt.

In the 1970s scientists began to search for possible **invariant features** of generalized programs. The most important invariant feature, or *invariance*, they discovered is one that deals with the temporal (or timing) structure of movement patterns. This invariance is termed *relative timing*.

## Relative Timing

If you look back to figure 5.7, you will see Armstrong's (1970) data showing what happens to a movement when it is produced at different speeds. Perhaps you remember our pointing out that there was something about the temporal pattern or timing of that action that remained constant, even though the actual duration of the movement was different on different attempts. The question now is "What *is* the feature that remains invariant?"

You can find the answer to this question in figure 5.7 by noticing that the timing of *all parts of the movement changed as a unit* whenever participants changed the timing of the *whole* movement. In other words, when individuals speeded up the whole movement, they uniformly speeded up *all* of the parts as well, not just some of them. This means that ratios of the time of each part to the total time of the movement remained the same. Put another way, the timing structure, or the **relative timing** of the parts, remained invariant (see Gentner, 1987, or Schmidt, 1985, 1988 for a more detailed discussion of this issue) regardless of the overall movement time.

Relative timing, then, is the fundamental temporal structure, organization, or rhythm of a movement pattern, and this structure remains the same even when individuals decide to make changes in the flexible features of their movements (e.g., movement time). The notion of relative timing is illustrated by the fact that a waltz fundamentally remains a waltz regardless of the actual speed that the music is playing. This is because the relative timing of the various waltz movements remains the same. Unlike the **surface features**, or **parameters**, of a movement that performers alter from one attempt to the next, relative timing is part of the movement's fundamental or **deep structure**. This deep structure is characterized by a temporal

## INVARIANCE IN THE RELATIVE TIMING OF MOVEMENT SEQUENCES

Research by Summers (1975) nicely illustrates the persistent invariance of relative timing in the production of well-learned movements. Participants in this study first learned a keypress task that involved depressing each of nine keys for a designated length of time, determined by the illumination of a stimulus light corresponding to the key (e.g., key 5: 500 ms; key 9: 100 ms; key 1: 500 ms; key 7: 500 ms; key 4: 100 ms; key 2: 500 ms; key 6: 500 ms; key 8: 100 ms; key 3: 500 ms). Following several hundred practice attempts, participants were instructed to produce the sequence as rapidly as possible and to disregard the relative-timing pattern they had learned. The interesting result was that, while these individuals were able to produce the sequence in a faster overall time, they were unable to disregard the learned relative-timing pattern. In other words, their keypresses looked like a speeded-up copy of the temporal structure they had previously learned, much like the results Armstrong reported in his study (1970), shown in figure 5.7. More recently, Summers et al. (1993) observed a similar pattern of control in people's performance of tasks involving the simultaneous production of different tapping rhythms with opposite hands.

## IT DEPENDS . . .

Relative-timing patterns are the temporal structure or "rhythm" of an action. These patterns not only appear to be important components of the deep structure of movements, but they are also difficult to change once they are well learned. If relative timing is an important feature of movements, what implications does this have for a coach who is helping a basketball player with her jump shot? For a physical therapist who is assisting an amputee trying to walk with a prosthetic device? For an elementary physical education instructor who is teaching children a country line dance?

organization or timing that remains invariant, even when performers produce the whole action with different speeds or amplitudes.

### Comparing Movements as a Set of Ratios

A more precise way to look at relative timing is as a *set of ratios* that defines the durations of several time intervals within the movement. Consider, for example, the two repetitions of a throwing movement illustrated in figure 6.1. The first repetition (movement 1) is performed in a shorter movement time than the second (movement 2). We can calculate the set of ratios (or relative timing) for each of these movements by first measuring and recording the duration of muscular activity (EMG) in three of the important muscles involved in the action and then dividing each measured duration by the total duration of the movement. The resulting set of ratios represents the deep structure or temporal organization of the throwing movement. Without actually doing the arithmetic, can you guess how the set of ratios for movement 1 would compare to the set of ratios for movement 2?

When the set of ratios is the same for two repetitions of the same general movement produced in different overall movement times, we can conclude that the relative timing of the movement is invariant. According to the theory of **generalized motor programs** introduced in chapter 5, the deep temporal structure of the two

**generalized motor program**—A motor program that defines a pattern of movement, rather than a specific movement; this flexibility allows performers to adapt the generalized program to produce variations of the pattern that meet altered environmental demands.

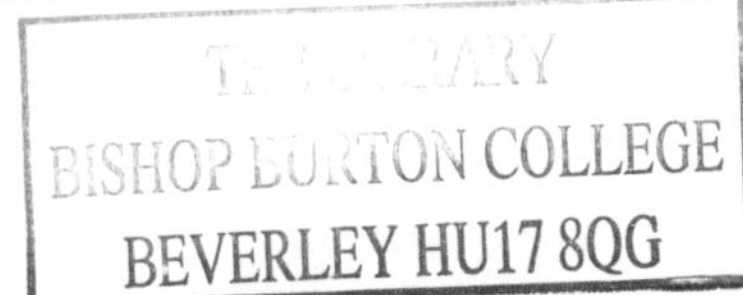

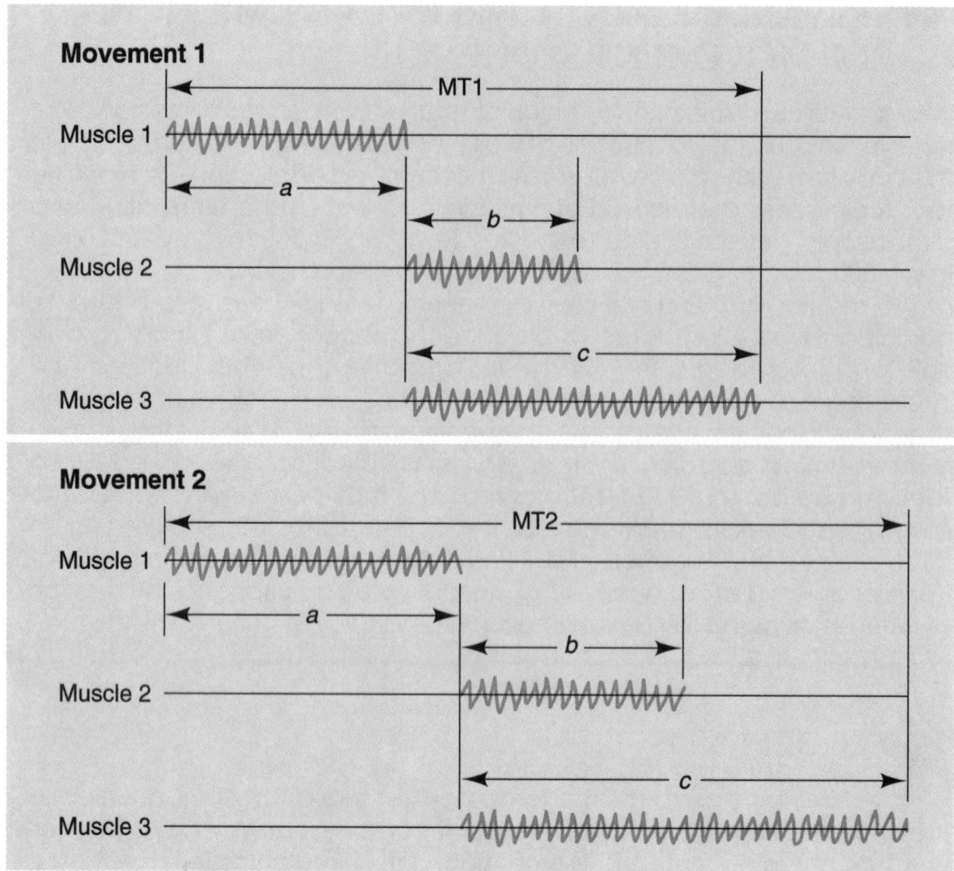


Figure 6.1 The duration of muscle activity (shown in a hypothetical EMG) for three important muscles involved in throwing is used to calculate the relative timing as a set of ratios for two movements (repetitions). (Reprinted by permission from Schmidt, 1988.)

movements represented in figure 6.1 remains the same because all parts of the action are either slowed down or speeded up as a unit. Differences in the two repetitions are due to differences in a surface feature (i.e., movement time).

One of the most important principles of movement control is that relative timing remains essentially invariant whenever performers change the

- speed of a rapid movement (e.g., a fast kick compared to a slow kick),
- size of the action (e.g., large handwriting compared to small handwriting),
- forces used to produce the action (e.g., throwing a tennis ball compared to throwing a basketball), or
- trajectory of the movement (e.g., the trajectory of the body after take-off when jumping over an aluminum can compared to jumping over a footstool).

Thus, the relative timing of an action can be thought of as a kind of "fingerprint" that is unique to all of the actions within a movement class. This allows individuals to preserve the form of movements (e.g., kicking, writing, throwing, or jumping) whenever they change any of a number of superficial features. While there is some controversy about whether relative timing is perfectly invariant (Gentner, 1987), there is little doubt that it is at least approximately invariant from one movement to the next—at least for movements that are brief in time.

## Invariant Relative Timing in Throwing Movements

An activity like throwing might be thought of as a class of movements containing numerous variations of the action (e.g., throwing overarm, underarm, or sidearm; throwing objects that differ in size and weight; throwing objects different distances). **General motor program theory** holds that this particular class of movements is represented by a single generalized program that has a specific, rigidly defined relative-timing structure. This program also has parameters that represent several flexible dimensions of the movement (movement time, movement amplitude, overall force), making it possible for individuals to produce an essentially limitless number of different throws. All of these actions, however, should possess nearly the same relative timing. Trained observers (e.g., coaches, gymnastics judges, movement therapists) can detect these invariances relatively easily (at least in general terms), allowing them to classify a movement according to its relative-timing structure rather quickly.

**general motor program theory**—An explanation for how people control coordinated movement; emphasizes the role of a single generalized program consisting of an invariant relative-timing structure and several flexible dimensions (e.g., movement time, movement amplitude, overall force) that allow individuals to produce different versions of the movement.

## Invariant Relative-Timing Differences for Walking and Running

Although general motor program theory postulates that relative timing is invariant within a class of movements (e.g., walking), it presumes that relative timing *differs* from one class of movements to another (e.g., walking vs. running). In order to test this notion, Shapiro et al. (1981) examined the relative-timing characteristics of human locomotion. They filmed people walking and running on a treadmill at speeds ranging from 3 to 12 kilometers per hour (km/hr). For each speed, they measured the duration of each of the 4 phases of the Philippson step cycle for the right leg (see figure 6.2). The intervals included the time between heel strike and maximum knee flexion (termed the extension phase and labeled $E_2$); between maximum knee flexion and toe-off (termed the propulsion phase and labeled $E_3$); between toe-off and the beginning of knee extension (termed the flexion phase and labeled F); and between the beginning of knee extension and heel strike (labeled $E_1$). Together, $E_2$ and $E_3$ comprised the stance phase, while F and $E_1$ comprised the swing phase of locomotion.

The data shown in figure 6.3 represent the set of ratios defining the duration of the four phases of the step cycle; in other words, the duration of each phase divided

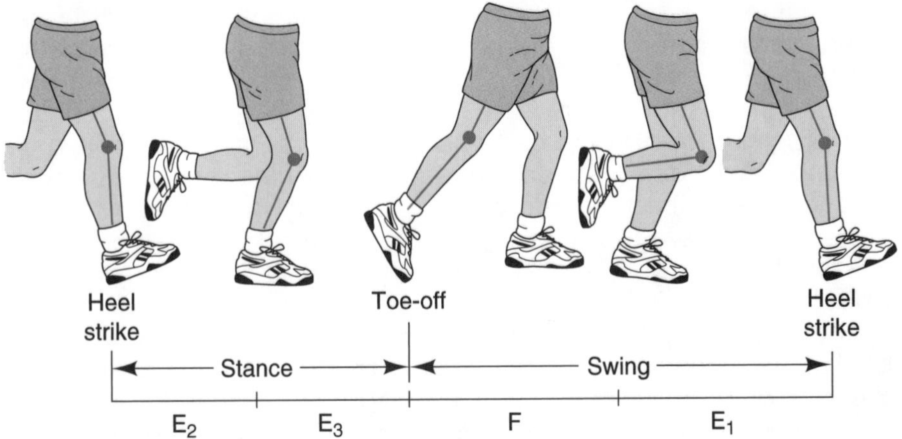


Figure 6.2 Dividing gait into phases (based on the Philippson step cycle). $E_2$ is the extension phase, $E_3$ is the propulsion phase, F is the flexion phase, and $E_1$ goes from the beginning of knee extension to the heel strike. (Reprinted by permission from Shapiro, Zernicke, Gregor, & Diestel, 1981.)

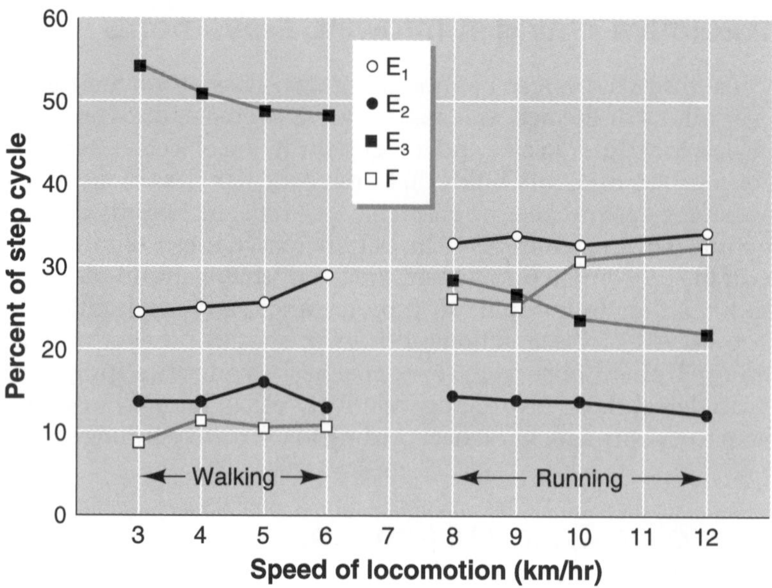


Figure 6.3 The step cycle in human gait, showing the proportion occupied by phases $E_1$, $E_2$, $E_3$, and F as the treadmill's speed is varied. Though the proportions differ for walking and running, they remain constant within each type of gait. (Reprinted by permission from Shapiro, Zernicke, Gregor, & Diestel, 1981.)

## The Phonograph Record Analogy for Generalized Motor Programs

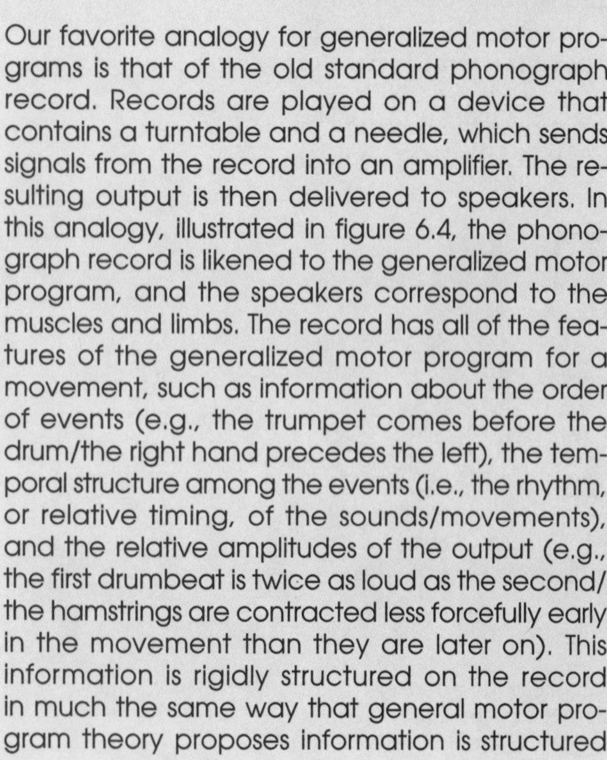

Our favorite analogy for generalized motor programs is that of the old standard phonograph record. Records are played on a device that contains a turntable and a needle, which sends signals from the record into an amplifier. The resulting output is then delivered to speakers. In this analogy, illustrated in figure 6.4, the phonograph record is likened to the generalized motor program, and the speakers correspond to the muscles and limbs. The record has all of the features of the generalized motor program for a movement, such as information about the order of events (e.g., the trumpet comes before the drum/the right hand precedes the left), the temporal structure among the events (i.e., the rhythm, or relative timing, of the sounds/movements), and the relative amplitudes of the output (e.g., the first drumbeat is twice as loud as the second/the hamstrings are contracted less forcefully early in the movement than they are later on). This information is rigidly structured on the record in much the same way that general motor program theory proposes information is structured in the generalized motor program. And, just as different records produce different types of music (rock, blues, classical, country, jazz, rap), so too different generalized motor programs (throwing, jumping, kicking, striking, hopping, catching) produce different classes of movements. In both cases, though, each different record or program contains a different pattern of stored information.

Notice again that the output of the record or the generalized motor program is not fixed: the speed of the music or of the movement can be increased (by increasing the speed of the turntable or the commands sent to the muscles), yet relative timing (rhythm) remains the same. Similarly, the amplitude of the output can be changed (by raising the volume or increasing the level of force). Even the "effectors" used can be changed (by switching the output from a set of speakers in the den to a second set located in the living room, or by using either the left or the right hand to produce a handball shot).

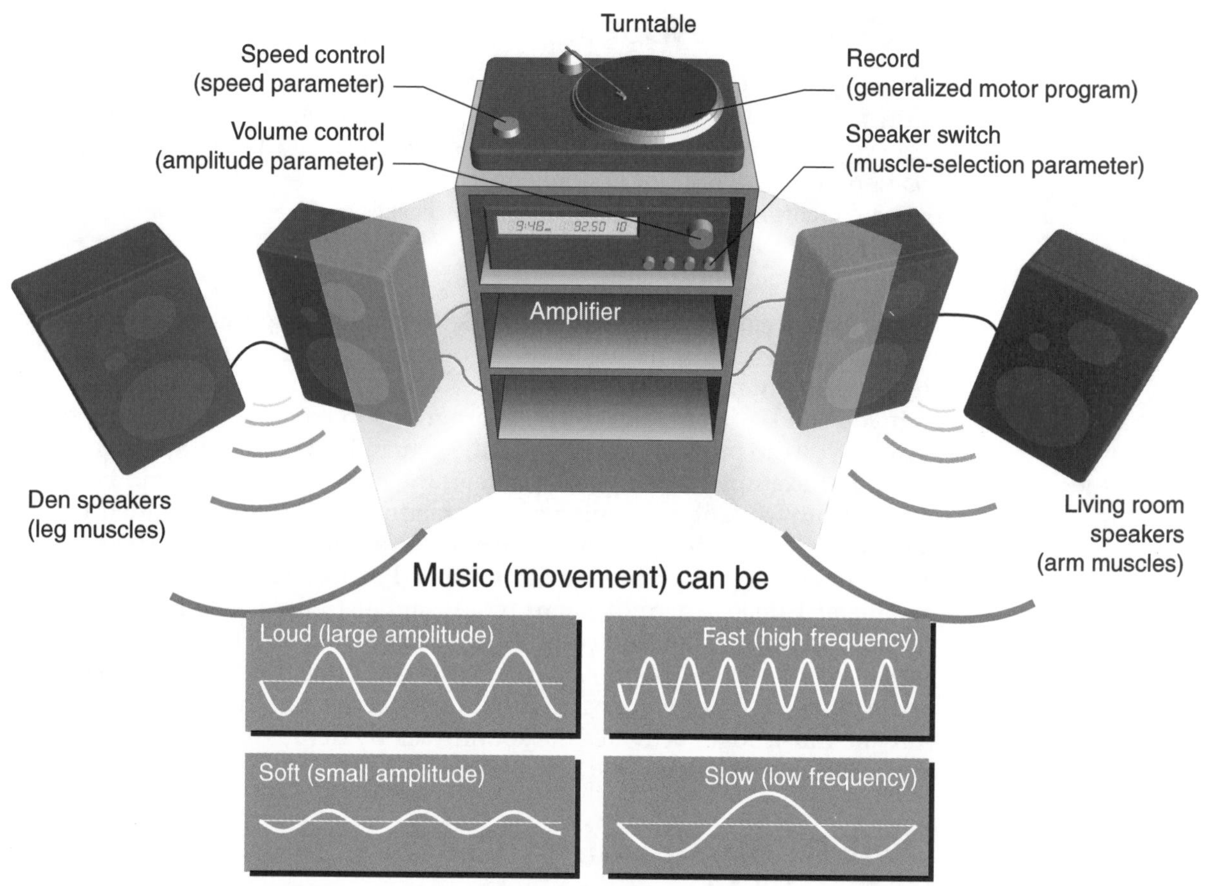


Figure 6.4 The phonograph record is like a generalized motor program. The program (record) has a fixed structure, which can be modified at output by the speed control (speed parameter), volume control (amplitude parameter), and speaker switch (muscle-selection parameter).

by the duration of the total step cycle (axis labeled "percent of step cycle" in the figure). When treadmill speed ranges from 3 to 6 km/hr (left side of figure), participants are walking. Notice that the relative timing of the four phases remains pretty much the same (as indicated by the relatively flat slopes of the lines) for all four walking speeds. Phase $E_3$ always lasts for about half of the step cycle, F and $E_2$ occupy around 10% each, and $E_1$ comprises about 28%. However, when treadmill speed is increased and ranges from 8 to 12 km/hr (right side of figure), all of the participants are running and, as you can see, the relative-timing pattern changes considerably. Now $E_1$ occupies the largest percentage of the step cycle (32%), closely followed by F (approximately 30%) and $E_3$ (approximately 28%). Only $E_2$ remains at a percentage similar to that for walking, but now this phase comprises the smallest portion of the step cycle. As in the case of walking, changes in treadmill speed while participants are running (i.e., 8 to 12 km/hr range) produce very little change in the ratios.

One interpretation of the results shown in figure 6.3 is that performers use different generalized motor programs for walking and running, each with its own pattern of relative timing. When treadmill speed increases, performers increase parameter values for all four phases of the step cycle uniformly, speeding up the entire movement but maintaining the pattern of relative timing. At a treadmill speed of about 7 km/hr, participants shift from a "walking program" to a "running program" characterized by a different pattern of relative timing. Another shift in the pattern of relative timing likely occurs when individuals transition from running to sprinting

Physical therapists examine relative-timing patterns during gait analysis in order to assess improvements in patients' locomotion due to developmental changes or therapeutic interventions (Ulrich et al., 1995). Can you think of other ways movement practitioners might use their knowledge of relative-timing patterns to assist performers and patients?

(Hay, 1993). Evidence from earlier studies with cats suggests that other locomotion programs (and relative-timing patterns) may exist for trotting and galloping (Goslow, Reinking, & Stuart, 1973).

If you think of generalized motor programs in concrete terms like phonograph records, you can probably understand the generalized motor program concept rather easily. For example, when participants in the study by Shapiro and her colleagues shifted from walking to running on the treadmill (see figure 6.3), their task became something like replacing a walking record on a phonograph with one that governs the act of running. Each time treadmill speed increased, performers had to change parameter values (e.g., movement time), similar to the way a music lover sets the volume, speed, and speaker controls prior to playing the soundtrack for the movie, *Schindler's List.* Once Shapiro's participants had done this, they initiated the appropriate movement (for walking or running) by activating the program, similar to the way the music lover activates the soundtrack by depressing the control that places the needle on the record.

# Determinants of Accuracy in Rapid Movements

**parameter values**—The values assigned by a performer to the parameters of a generalized motor program (e.g., rapid movement time, short amplitude, right arm); allows individuals to adjust a movement pattern to meet specific environmental demands.

So far we have discussed ways that individuals can plan and control their movements by applying a different set of **parameter values** (e.g., more speed or greater amplitude) to the generalized motor program. Now we consider how the act of modifying parameter values affects the performer's achievement of an environmental goal.

In this section we present the laws or principles of simple movements. These principles include how the time required for a movement changes as the distance to be moved increases and how the speed of a movement affects its accuracy. In many ways these principles are analogous to the simple laws of physics and mechanics that scientists use to define the behavior of physical objects in the world. As such, these basic principles of simple movements form the foundation of much of our knowledge about voluntary actions.

## Speed-Accuracy Trade-Offs in Rapid Continuous Movements

**Fitts' Law**—The law of movement control for rapid aiming tasks, holding that movement time is linearly related to the index of movement difficulty (ID); expressed mathematically as $\log_2(2A/W)$, where A = movement amplitude and W = target width.

Perhaps the most fundamental principle of human movement is the one dealing with the relationship between the speed and the accuracy of a movement. We all know that when we do things too quickly, we tend to do them less effectively or accurately. The old English saying "Haste makes waste" suggests that people have been aware of this relationship for a long time. Woodworth (1899) studied the speed-accuracy phenomenon early in the history of motor skills research, showing that as performers increased the length and speed of line-drawing movements, their accuracy diminished. Then in 1954 psychologist Paul Fitts made a major contribution to our understanding of this relationship by describing for the first time a mathematical principle concerning movement speed and accuracy. This principle eventually came to be known as **Fitts' Law**.

## Paul Fitts and Fitts' Law

In his landmark study, Fitts (1954) instructed participants to make movements with a handheld stylus between two target plates (see figure 6.5). In this task, which has come to be called the Fitts tapping task, the width of the targets (W) and the distance or amplitude between them (A) are varied to form different conditions of movement difficulty. In all cases, the performer's goal is to tap as quickly as possible between the targets without errors. A tap outside the target counts as an error. In Fitts' 1954 study, less than 5% of the participants' taps were errors. Fitts measured the number of taps that participants executed in a particular time, say a 20-s trial, and computed the average time taken per movement or, more simply, average movement time.

Fitts found, not surprisingly, that average movement time increases as the amplitude of the movement increases and as the width of the targets decreases. However, the major contribution of Fitts' study was the discovery that movement distance (amplitude), target width (required accuracy), and the resulting average movement time can be combined in a simple way that describes how these separate factors are related to each other. Specifically, Fitts found that average movement time (MT) is approximately constant whenever the ratio of two times the movement amplitude (2A) to target width (W) is constant. Therefore, very long movements to wide targets require about the same average movement time as very short movements to narrow targets. In addition, Fitts found that MT increases as the ratio of 2A to W increases, either by making amplitude longer, target width smaller, or both. Fitts combined these various effects into a single equation that is now referred to as Fitts' Law:

$$MT = a + b\,(\log_2(2A/W)).$$

In this equation, $a$ and $b$ are constants, and A and W refer to amplitude and width, respectively. The relationships between movement distance (A), required accuracy (W), and average movement time (MT) for one of Fitts' data sets are plotted in figure 6.6. The term "$\log_2(2A/W)$" is referred to as the index of movement difficulty (ID), and Fitts' Law states that MT is linearly related to the ID. Put simply, the average time it takes a person to tap between two targets lengthens as the ratio of movement distance to target width increases (i.e., as performers are required to move further, hit smaller targets, or both).

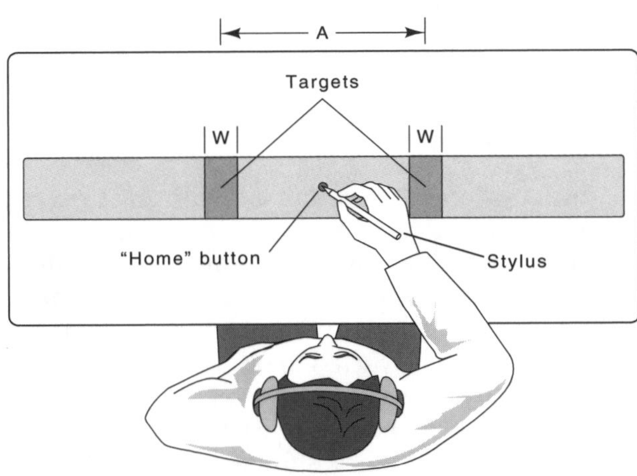


Figure 6.5 The Fitts tapping task. The subject taps as quickly as possible between two target plates of width W, which are separated by amplitude A. (Adapted from Fitts, 1954.)

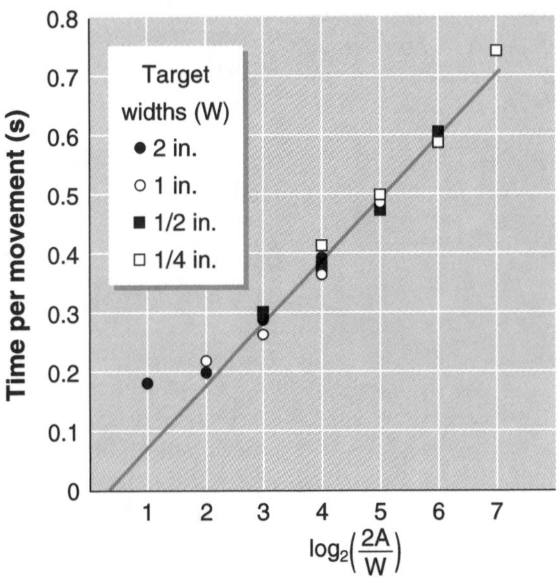


Figure 6.6 These tapping performances with very different amplitudes and target widths follow Fitts' Law. The time per movement is linearly related to the $\log_2(2A/W)$, or the index of movement difficulty. (Adapted from Fitts, 1954.)

**speed-accuracy trade-off**—The tendency for individuals to substitute accuracy for speed, or vice versa, in their movements depending on task requirements.

**Fitts' task**—An experimental task requiring performers to tap (using a stylus or other fine-pointed object) back and forth between two targets as rapidly and accurately as possible.

**open-loop control**—A type of control that involves the use of centrally determined, prestructured commands sent to the effector system and run off without feedback; used by individuals to control rapid, discrete movements.

**closed-loop control**—A type of control that involves the use of feedback and the activity of error detection and correction processes to maintain the desired goal; used by individuals to control slow, deliberate movements.

Fitts' Law illustrates an important point about performers when they are required to make fast and accurate movements—they make trade-offs between speed and accuracy. When the accuracy requirements of Fitts' task are relaxed (i.e., by using wide targets), performers' movement times are faster than when they are stringent (i.e., with narrow targets). The general notion of a **speed-accuracy trade-off**, the tendency of individuals to substitute accuracy for speed, or vice versa, depending on task requirements, is one of the most fundamental principles of movement behavior. This principle has been verified in many different settings (underwater as well as in a laboratory), for many different classifications of people (children as well as older adults), and in movements people perform using a number of different body parts (fingers, hands, arms). The trade-off has even been observed to operate during the performance of more modern-day movements, such as knob-controlled actions of a cursor across a computer screen (see Rosenbaum, 1991, chapter 6). Without a doubt, Fitts' Law is one of the most fundamental principles of movement control.

The movements scientists have studied using **Fitts' task** of alternate tapping are almost certainly blends of programmed actions with feedback processing added near the end. That is, the performer generates an initial segment of the action that is programmed to move the limb in the direction of the target. At some point in the movement, feedback about its accuracy is processed and one (or sometimes more) corrections are made to guide the limb to the target area. As we discussed in chapter 4, such visual compensations are probably processed through the ambient visual system and may not be performed under conscious control. Thus, Fitts' Law describes the effectiveness of combined **open-loop** and **closed-loop control** processes in producing fast and accurate kinds of actions. For such movements, all of the open-loop and closed-loop processes (see the conceptual model in figure 4.9) are potentially operating together.

It is reasonable to suspect that slower movements are more accurate, at least in part, because there is more time for the performer to detect errors and make corrections. Fitts' Law indicates that if the errors are too large, performers must slow down the movement to reduce them. In 1988, Meyer et al. introduced a more formal model of the processes involved when individuals trade off speed for gains in accuracy. However, a number of questions remain unanswered. For example, what causes movement accuracy to change if the performer attempts to produce the action more rapidly? And, for really quick actions, how can the performer's accuracy depend on the number of corrections when the individual presumably is not processing any feedback during the movement?

## Speed-Accuracy Trade-Offs in Very Rapid, Discrete Movements

Suppose that you have to make a quick movement of your hand with an object (e.g., an axe or a hammer) to a target, where spatial accuracy at the target is the major goal. How does your accuracy change as your movement time and movement distance change? Scientists have studied such factors by examining aiming movements, where participants attempt to make a single movement with a handheld stylus from a starting position to a target. The performer is instructed to produce the movement in a particular time, receiving feedback about the actual movement time after each attempt. In these studies the experimenter systematically varies the instructed movement time and movement distance. One set of results is shown in figure 6.7, where accuracy is expressed as the amount of variability, or inconsistency, of the performer's movement end points in the target area. This measure of spatial variability might be likened to the spread of axe marks on a log you are splitting or the pattern of holes surrounding the bull's-eye on a dartboard.

## IT DEPENDS . . .

If you performed Fitts' task, which variable do you think would influence your average movement time the most: target size or movement amplitude? You can answer this question by tapping back and forth as quickly as possible for 20 s on each of the pairs of targets shown below. Pairs "a" and "b" have the same movement amplitude (measured from the center of the targets) but they differ in target size (the size of the targets for "b" are twice the size as those for "a"). Pairs "a" and "c" have the same target size but differ in movement amplitude (the distance between the targets in "a" is twice that in "c"). For each pair of targets, begin by holding a pen or other pointed object and resting it in the center of one of the targets. Ask a friend to time you for 20 s. Count the number of taps you make for each pair of targets.

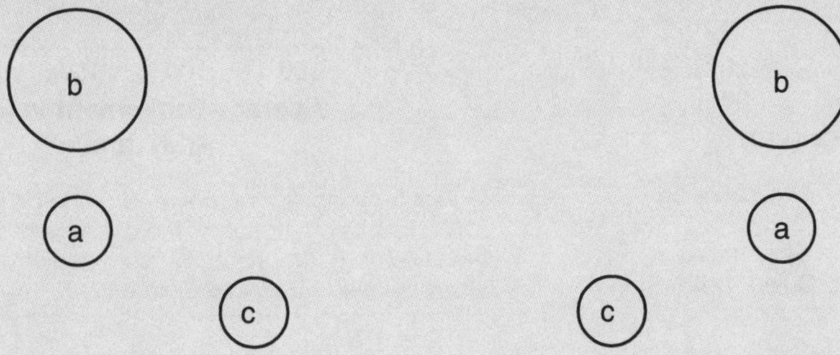


Now divide each of those numbers into 20 to obtain your average movement time for each of the pairs (remember, a smaller number means a faster average MT). For example, if you count 37 taps, your average movement time for that pair of targets is 20 ÷ 37 = 0.54 s/tap.

To test for speed-accuracy differences in target size, compare your average MT for pairs "a" and "b." To test for differences in movement amplitude, compare your average MT for pairs "a" and "c." Which difference is larger? How might the order in which you perform the three pairs of targets "contaminate" your results?

As you see, increases in movement amplitude produce only slight increases in movement time. In fact, if you double the movement distance (e.g., from 4 in. to 8 in.), movement time increases by only 30%. Thus, it appears that performers can increase the length of their movements without increasing movement time very much. This aspect of Fitts' Law has implications for the performance of a variety of tasks. For example, if a cricket batter lengthens his swing with very little increase in movement time, his movement velocity increases. This allows him to strike the ball with much greater impact. Other applications of Fitts' Law include the design of industrial workspaces, the organization of controls on the instrument panels of aircraft and cars, and the evaluation of head-controlled computer input devices (Radwin, Vanderheiden, & Lin, 1990).

Notice that all of these movements are rapidly produced, lasting 200 ms or less. From the previous sections, we would expect performers to control such movements by using open-loop processes or **motor programs**. Yet even with rapid movements such as these, where little or no feedback processing is possible, we see that increases in movement distance (from 10 to 20 to 30 cm) are accompanied by gradual increases

**motor program**—A set of motor commands that is prestructured at the executive level and that defines the essential details of a skilled action; analogous to a central pattern generator.

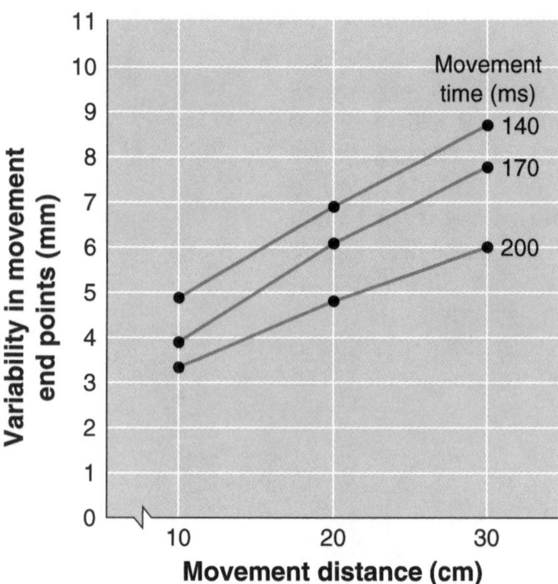


Figure 6.7 Variability (inconsistency) of movement end points in a rapid aiming task as a function of the movement time and distance. (Adapted by permission from Schmidt, Zelaznik, Hawkins, Frank, & Quinn, 1979.)

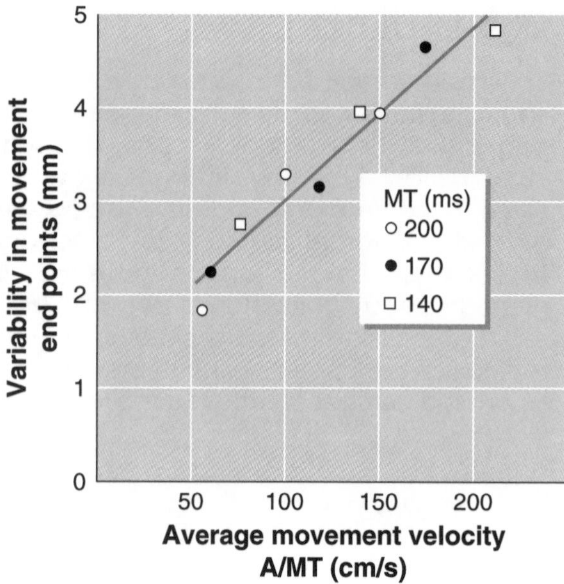


Figure 6.8 Variability of movement end points in an aiming task as a function of the average movement velocity (A/MT). (Reprinted by permission from Schmidt, Zelaznik, Hawkins, Frank, & Quinn, 1979.)

in the spread or variability of the movement end points. Also, we see that a decrease in movement time (i.e., a speeding up of the movement) from 200 ms to 140 ms increases the spread as well. This means aiming errors are influenced both by increases in movement distance and by decreases in movement time.

These effects of movement distance and movement time on aiming accuracy suggest that open-loop processes, which are used to produce the movement, are also subject to the speed-accuracy trade-off. In other words, when movement times are *very* short, decreases in accuracy are not simply due to the fact that there is less time for feedback utilization; these effects occur even when movements are too brief for *any* feedback modulations to be made. Thus, it appears that decreases in movement time also affect the consistency of the processes that generate the *initial* parts of the action: that is, they affect the open-loop processes necessary to produce a quick movement.

This is consistent with the principles of Fitts' Law and with the typical pattern of a person's performance on Fitts' task. In that situation, if participants try to make movements of a fixed distance too quickly, they tap outside the target area more frequently. Since they are told that such errors are unacceptable, performers slow down, decreasing the variability, or spread of movement end points, and hitting inside the target more often.

**effective target width**—The amount of spread, or variability, of a person's movement end points about their own mean position for repeated attempts of a rapid aiming task; abbreviated $W_e$.

We can combine into a single expression these separate effects of movement amplitude (A) and movement time (MT) on the accuracy of individual rapid-aiming movements, much the way that Fitts did for his alternate tapping task. In some of Dick Schmidt's research, he and his colleagues have found that the amount of movement error, or variability of movement end points at the target (sometimes termed the **effective target width**), is linearly related to the movement's average velocity—that is, to the ratio of amplitude to movement time or A/MT (Schmidt et al., 1979). You can see this relationship in figure 6.8, where the variability of movement end points is plotted against the average velocity of the movement (in centimeters per second, or cm/s). As the figure shows, the spread of movement end points (i.e., aiming error) increases as movement velocity increases. This principle is called the

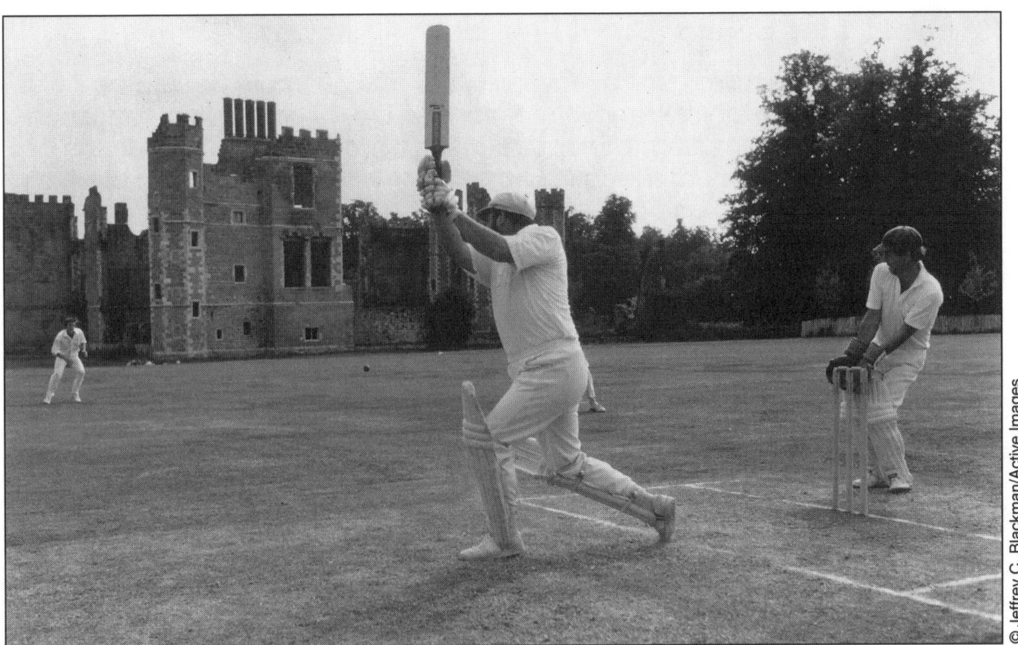


Aiming variability and spatial accuracy are important facets of many sports (such as cricket) and other movement tasks.

**linear speed-accuracy trade-off**, and it suggests that for various combinations of movement amplitude (or distance) and movement time, the resulting average velocity (i.e., A/MT) is associated with a particular spread of movement end points (i.e., aiming error). Thus, by decreasing the distance and increasing the time of aiming movements (i.e., moving slower), performers can trade off speed in order to maintain spatial accuracy.

**linear speed-accuracy trade-off**—The tendency for the spatial variability of movement end points ($W_e$) to increase as performers increase the velocity of rapid aiming movements.

## Sources of Errors in Quick Movements

Why is it that people have more errors even for quick aiming movements (when there is little time for them to process feedback and make corrections) when the movement distance increases or movement time decreases? We might look for the answer by examining processes in the central nervous system that translate the motor program's output into body movements. We have already explained that motor programs are responsible for determining the ordering of muscle contractions and the amounts of force that are generated in the respective muscles. The "location" of this activity is indicated by the area shaded in green in the conceptual model found in figure 6.9.

What is it about the activity in this area that diminishes the accuracy of a person's rapid movements? Scientists have known for some time that, even when a performer attempts to produce the same force over and over on successive trials, the individual exhibits considerable inconsistency in movement outcomes. Today scientists believe this variability is caused by the relatively "noisy" (i.e., inconsistent) processes in the central nervous system. These processes are responsible for converting nerve impulses into motor unit activation of muscles and the exertion of forces on bones through tendons. In addition, various reflex activities, such as the **M1 and M2 responses** (see figure 6.9), may contribute some variability to muscle contractions.

**M1 response**—The monosynaptic stretch reflex, with a latency of 30 ms to 50 ms.

**M2 response**—The polysynaptic, functional stretch reflex, with a latency of 50 ms to 80 ms.

Of course, the presence of these processes in the system means that the forces actually produced during a contraction are not always the ones that the system intended. This phenomenon can be illustrated by returning to the phonograph record analogy (see figure 6.4 again). You can see that "noise" could be introduced at

We can produce rapid aiming movements to a target more accurately if we move a shorter distance or move more slowly. Experience this phenomenon for yourself by attempting to produce a rapid movement with your pen or pencil at near maximum speed from the Trial # 1 starting position to each of the target lines (a, b, and c) shown below. You should perform at least five repetitions of each movement in order to determine the spatial variability of movement end points for each movement distance.

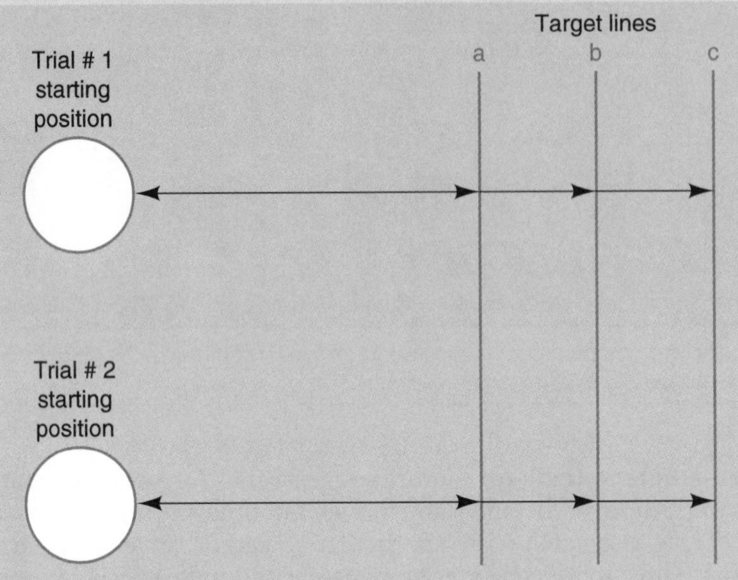


Now attempt the same rapid aiming movements, but this time perform them from the Trial # 2 starting position and produce them at about three-quarters of the speed you used before. How is the spatial variability of your movement end points influenced by decreases in movement distance (i.e., shorter distance)? By increases in movement time (i.e., slower time)?

several points in the system. For example, the electronics and wires lying between the turntable and the speakers might cause the sounds that the listener hears to be slightly different from the sounds that were originally recorded.

To complicate matters, these noisy processes in the nervous system do not operate consistently, but instead seem to change as the required amount of force changes. In other words, as the force of the desired contraction increases, the noise created by these processes increases, which in turn causes increased variability in the force that is eventually produced. Increases in this noise component generally increase force variability as the amount of force to be produced increases, up to about 70% of an individual's maximum force. Beyond 70%, the noise level and resulting force variability appear to level off and then decrease slightly for contractions that are near maximal (Sherwood, Schmidt, & Walter, 1988).

How does this information help us understand the way error is generated in a routine movement? Consider an action like striking a ball positioned on a tee situated at waist height. Using a bat, you try to make a horizontal swing with your arms and hands. In order to achieve this goal, many muscles operate in the shoulders and the trunk to produce forces against the bones that are used to direct the arms and bat

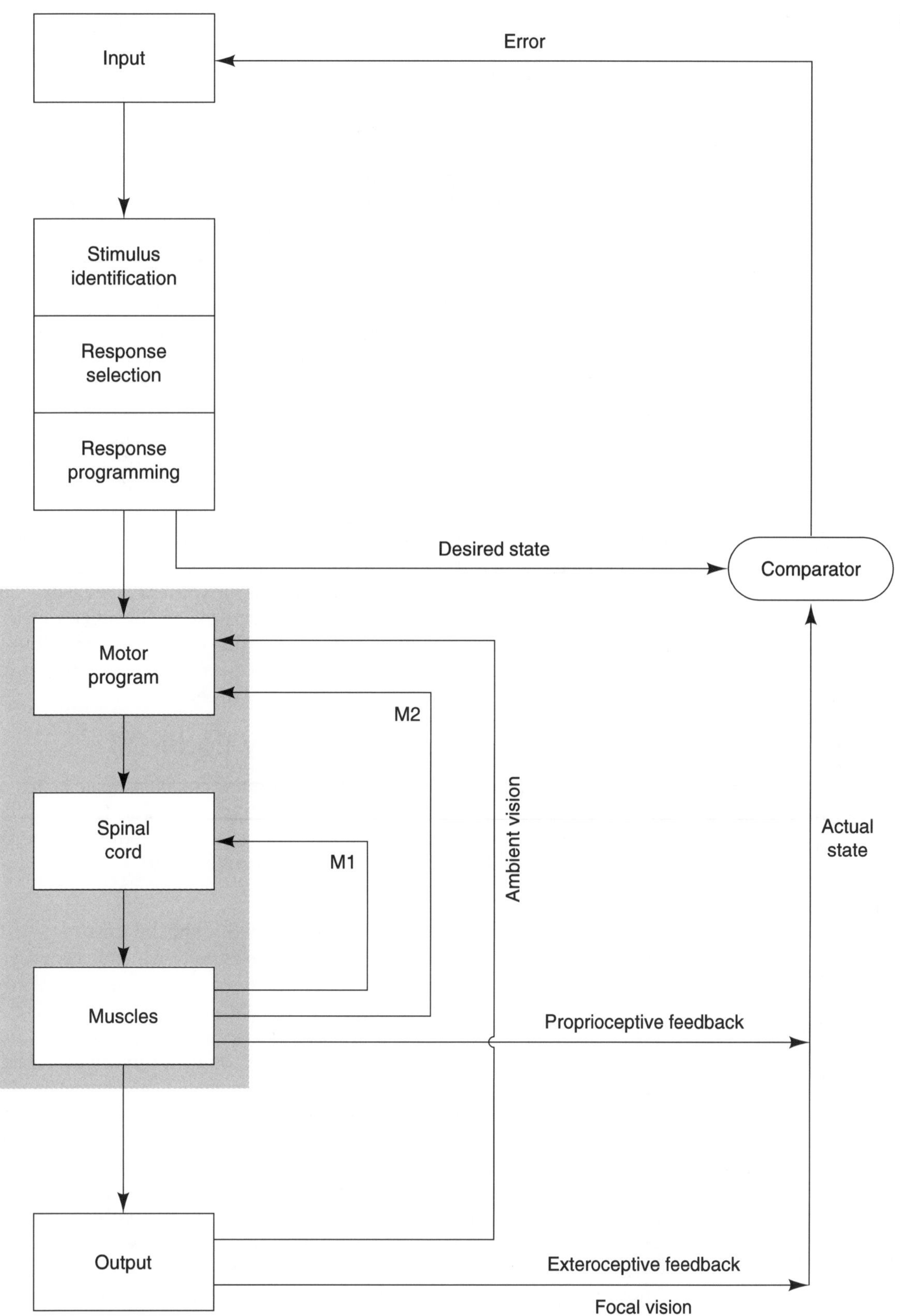


**Figure 6.9** Conceptual model with the location of motor program activity responsible for ordering muscle contractions highlighted.

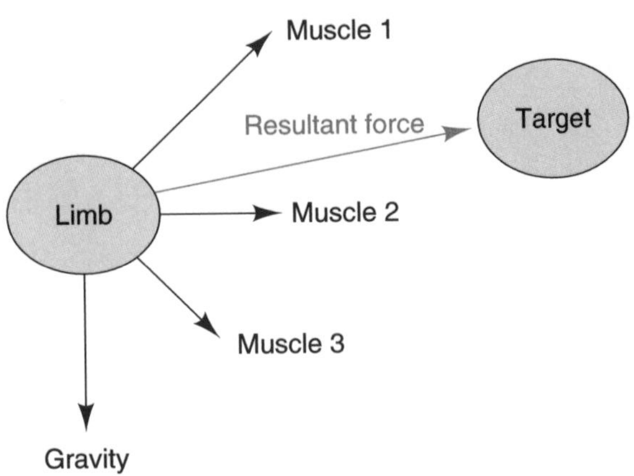


Figure 6.10 A limb being moved by three muscles and gravity toward a target. The eventual trajectory is a product of the many forces acting at a joint.

toward the ball. The direction of action of some of these muscles is in line with the intended movement, but the direction of action of many others is not, and instead they form various angles relative to the line of movement, as shown in figure 6.10. In many actions *gravity* represents an additional contributing force. To complete the swinging action perfectly, the various muscles must contract in coordination with each other so that they achieve just the right amount of force. If this happens, the final combination of forces (the *resultant force*) should be in line with the intended movement. Of course, if there is an error in any of these forces, say an excessive contraction of muscle 1 in figure 6.10, the direction of the movement would be altered, some amount of error would be introduced, and, if the error is large enough, the bat might even miss the ball.

What would happen if you made the movement more rapidly? Of course, as movement time decreases (i.e., the movement gets faster), the forces exerted against the bones of the arm increases. As these forces increase (up to about 70% of maximum force), the noisiness of the forces increases as well. This has the effect of adding some amount of error to the contraction of each of the muscles, causing each to respond slightly differently than specified in the motor program. The less these actual forces are coordinated with each other, the more likely the movement will be inaccurate (i.e., the bat will miss the ball). Thus, the inaccuracy of a movement increases as movement time decreases (i.e., the movement speeds up), primarily because of the increased noise that is generated in producing stronger muscle contractions. It is likely that some of this diminished accuracy occurs when you feel pressured to perform quickly or when you know your performance is being evaluated.

**spatial accuracy**—The type of accuracy required of aiming movements for which spatial position of the movement's end point is important to task performance.

## "Violations" of the Speed-Accuracy Trade-Off

As common as the speed-accuracy trade-off phenomenon seems to be for movement behavior, there are situations when it does not appear to hold true, or at least when the principles work somewhat differently. These situations involve the production of timing movements that are extremely rapid and forceful.

**temporal accuracy**—The type of accuracy required of rapid movements for which accuracy of the movement time is important to task performance; more commonly referred to as timing accuracy.

### *Timing Errors*

We have already discussed situations in which the **spatial accuracy** of the movement is an important goal. However, many skills have **temporal accuracy**, or **timing accuracy**, as the goal. For these skills of timing, performers must execute their movements so that the movement finishes at a particular instant or coincides in time with an external object or event, such as the task of a boxer trying to block a punch or an arcade game player trying to press the flipper button on a pinball machine at just the right fraction of a second.

**timing accuracy**—The type of accuracy required of rapid movements for which accuracy of the movement time is important to task performance; also referred to as temporal accuracy.

Still other skills have both temporal and spatial goals, intermixed in complicated ways. For example, batting a pitched baseball requires spatial accuracy in terms of the movement plane through which the bat must swing to meet the ball, as well as timing accuracy in producing the beginning of the swing and the required duration. Knowing or predicting the duration of the swing allows the batter to determine *when* to initiate the action so that the bat arrives in the hitting zone at the same time the ball does. So, being able to make a fast movement that consistently occupies a certain amount of time (in order for the batter to predict it) is a critical factor in batting effectiveness.

In this section we address the temporal component of rapid actions, restricting our attention to the factors that affect timing accuracy. The temporal component of rapid tasks can be isolated somewhat by requiring performers to produce a particu-

If you have a stopwatch or a digital watch that has a stopwatch function, try the following timing task. Without looking at the face of the watch, click it twice so that it starts and then stops at exactly 2 s. Repeat this task nine more times, noting the amount of error you make on each trial (i.e., the deviation in tenths of a second from 2 s). Now repeat the task, but this time try to stop the watch at 4 s. After a little bit of practice on both tasks, you will probably find that your timing error is about twice as high when estimating 4 s than when estimating 2 s. This is because the noise in the system that determines these durations increases, or accumulates, primarily as the duration of the interval or event increases. As long as goal movement *time* is held constant, increasing the forces that are necessary (e.g., for moving a greater distance) has little influence on the *timing* of motor programming processes.

lar movement *time* as accurately as possible. Scientists have studied this type of timing accuracy by using tasks that require individuals to make linear movements of the finger, hand, or arm under different conditions of movement distance, movement time, and several other factors. The results of these studies indicate that skills with temporal accuracy goals follow somewhat different principles than those with purely spatial accuracy goals (Schmidt et al., 1979).

What happens when individuals are asked to produce a rapid movement of a given distance in different times (e.g., 300 ms vs. 150 ms)? We might expect that if the velocity of the movement is faster, it would have more timing error, as illustrated in figures 6.7 and 6.8. Not so. In fact, decreasing the movement time results in a *decrease* in timing error, making the movement *more accurate* in time rather than less. We see this effect in figure 6.11, where the timing of the movement becomes less consistent (i.e., higher temporal variability) with increases in goal movement time (i.e., slower times). This relationship is almost proportional; doubling the goal movement time (within limits) almost doubles the timing error.

**movement time (MT)**—The interval of time that elapses from the beginning to the end of a person's movement.

Researchers have also found that when movement distance increases while goal movement time stays the same, thus increasing the movement's velocity, timing error hardly increases at all unless the movement is extremely short (Newell et al., 1980). Therefore, for skills in which the performer's goal is to minimize timing error, the main factor seems to be **movement time**; individuals are able to produce shorter movement times more accurately than longer movement times. This effect is exactly the opposite of the one we find for skills in which spatial accuracy is the main goal, as can be seen if you compare figures 6.7 and 6.8 with figure 6.11 (see Schmidt et al., 1979).

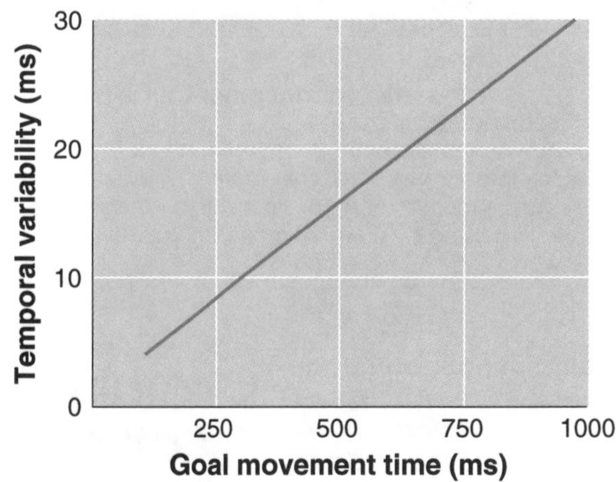


Figure 6.11 Temporal variability as a function of the instructed movement time. As movement time increases, the movement becomes less temporally stable. (Adapted by permission from Schmidt, Zelaznik, Hawkins, Frank, & Quinn, 1979.)

### *Producing a Very Forceful Movement*

Many human movements, including those required in a variety of sports (e.g., kicking a football or hitting a racquetball) or manual labor tasks (e.g., using a sledgehammer or an axe), involve extremely forceful contractions of muscles, leading to nearly maximal movement speeds. Making these movements at nearly maximal speed is often only a part of the challenge for a performer because the movement must be produced with high levels of spatial and temporal precision as well. It turns out that for movements like these, alterations in movement speed produce effects that are somewhat

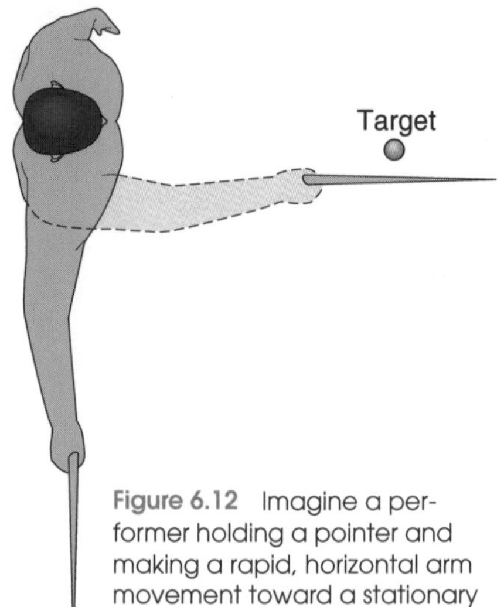


Figure 6.12 Imagine a performer holding a pointer and making a rapid, horizontal arm movement toward a stationary target.

different from those found for many of the less-forceful actions we have discussed so far.

Consider a task in which the performer holds a pointer and makes a rapid, horizontal arm movement toward a stationary target, like the task of batting in the child's game of T-ball, where the ball to be batted rests on a tee near waist level. In a study by Schmidt and Sherwood (1982), seated participants produced rapid, horizontal arm movements, attempting to strike a small (16 mm) stationary target suspended in front of them. Each attempt began with the arm extended out to the right (elbow locked) at approximately shoulder height (see figure 6.12). When ready, the performer moved his arm forward about 90° and attempted to contact the target (with a follow-through allowed).

In order to determine the effects of increased force on spatial accuracy, Schmidt and Sherwood instructed participants to perform their movements in progressively faster times. This would be like requiring baseball or cricket batters to swing the bat harder and harder, with maximum force being determined by each batter's own force capabilities. Speed-accuracy trade-off principles might lead us to believe that the movements with shorter goal movement times would be less spatially accurate. This was true—but only up to a point. As you can see in figure 6.13, when goal (or instructed) movement time decreased from 158 ms to 102 ms (and a higher percentage of the individual's force capabilities, labeled *% Maximum torque,* was needed), spatial errors increased. However, with further reductions in movement time to 80 ms, spatial errors began to decrease. This progression produced a kind of inverted-V effect, with very rapid (i.e., 80-ms) and very slow (i.e., 158-ms) movements having the least spatial error and those of moderate speed having the most. These findings are contrary to the strict view of the speed-accuracy trade-off, in which faster movements are always less spatially accurate.

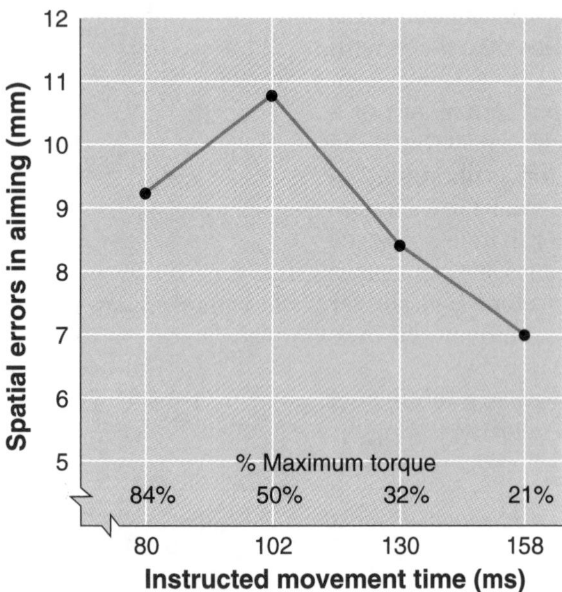


Figure 6.13 Spatial errors in aiming as a function of the instructed movement time. The estimated percentage of maximum torque (force) is indicated above the X-axis. (Adapted by permission from Schmidt & Sherwood, 1982.)

How can these movements be so fast yet so spatially accurate at the same time? Returning to figure 6.10, we are reminded that several muscles operate to determine the limb's trajectory. We also know that when forces are very large (i.e., greater than 70% of maximum force), force *variability decreases*. Therefore, the nearly maximal force participants used to produce the 80-ms movement in figure 6.13 is probably within a range for which force production is more consistent. The lower variability of this very forceful action makes it quite consistent spatially. However, this effect is based on the results of a small number of studies using simple and linear arm movements. Therefore, we must use caution when attempting to generalize the effect to more complicated actions.

**coincidence anticipation**—A type of task that requires performers to produce movements that coincide in time, space, or both with an external object or event (e.g., catching or hitting a moving ball); sometimes referred to as anticipation timing.

# Combining the Principles: A Batting Example

It may seem like there are a dizzying number of sometimes-contradictory principles involved in rapid actions. To help clarify things, let's see how the various principles simultaneously apply in the performance of a common task requiring both speed and accuracy. One **coincidence anticipation** task that serves the purpose nicely is hitting a pitched baseball. This skill requires several of the processes we have dis-

## MAKE THOSE SWINGS FAST AND FORCEFUL

Many American baseball players think that to improve their chances of contacting the ball, batters need to slow down their swings. Coaches shout out the instruction, "Just swing easy and try to meet the ball." This adage may be flawed, however, as some research by Schmidt and Sherwood (1982) suggests. Their results indicate that when individuals produce timing movements with nearly maximal (84% of max) forces, they are almost as accurate spatially as when they produce movements with forces that are not even half as large (32% of max). These findings suggest that batters may be able to swing the bat much faster without sacrificing spatial accuracy in hitting the ball. And this notion is further supported by popular media reports indicating that the two greatest home run hitters of all time, Mark McGwire and Sammy Sosa, produce more *rapid* bat swings than most other professional baseball players.

cussed, such as anticipation and timing, predicting a moving object's spatial trajectory and arrival time at the coincidence point (i.e., the point in space and time where contact with the object is to be made), and quick movements that performers must produce both forcefully and accurately.

Some facts about hitting a baseball are graphically summarized in figure 6.14. Pitchers in professional baseball can throw the ball at speeds exceeding 80 mph, and even 90 mph. In the example shown in figure 6.14, the pitch is moving at a speed of 89 mph. Since the distance between the pitcher and the batter is about 60 ft 6 in., we can estimate that the ball would travel from the pitcher's hand to the coincidence point (i.e., home plate) in about 460 ms (bold green line). The normal movement time of the swing for professional baseball batters is about 160 ms (Hubbard & Seng, 1954). We know from evidence presented earlier that the internal signal to trigger a movement occurs about 170 ms before the action starts (Slater-Hammel, 1960; review the highlight box on page 98 and figure 4.3).

Together, these facts suggest that batters must send the signal to trigger the bat swing at least 330 ms *before* the ball arrives at the plate, allowing them 170 ms to prepare the swing and 160 ms to carry it out. Therefore, batters must make all decisions about whether or not to swing before the ball has traveled about one-third of the way to the plate, or after only 130 ms of ball flight! Although batters may make minor modifications in their movements using the visual processes discussed in chapter 4, they must plan most of their actions in advance so that they are initiated by the central nervous system some 330 ms before the ball arrives.

Movement time is an important determiner of timing accuracy. So let's look at what would happen if the batter decides to decrease the movement time of his swing,

## IT DEPENDS . . .

If someone is attempting to strike an object as hard as possible with an implement (e.g., driving a golf ball off the tee, hitting a ball in baseball or cricket, serving in tennis, chopping wood, driving steel spikes into railroad ties), is it better for the individual to use a heavier implement (i.e., golf club, bat, tennis racket, axe, sledgehammer) or a lighter one? If the performer produces a very rapid movement with the light implement and then produces the same movement with the heavy implement, which movement would be more accurate? Why?

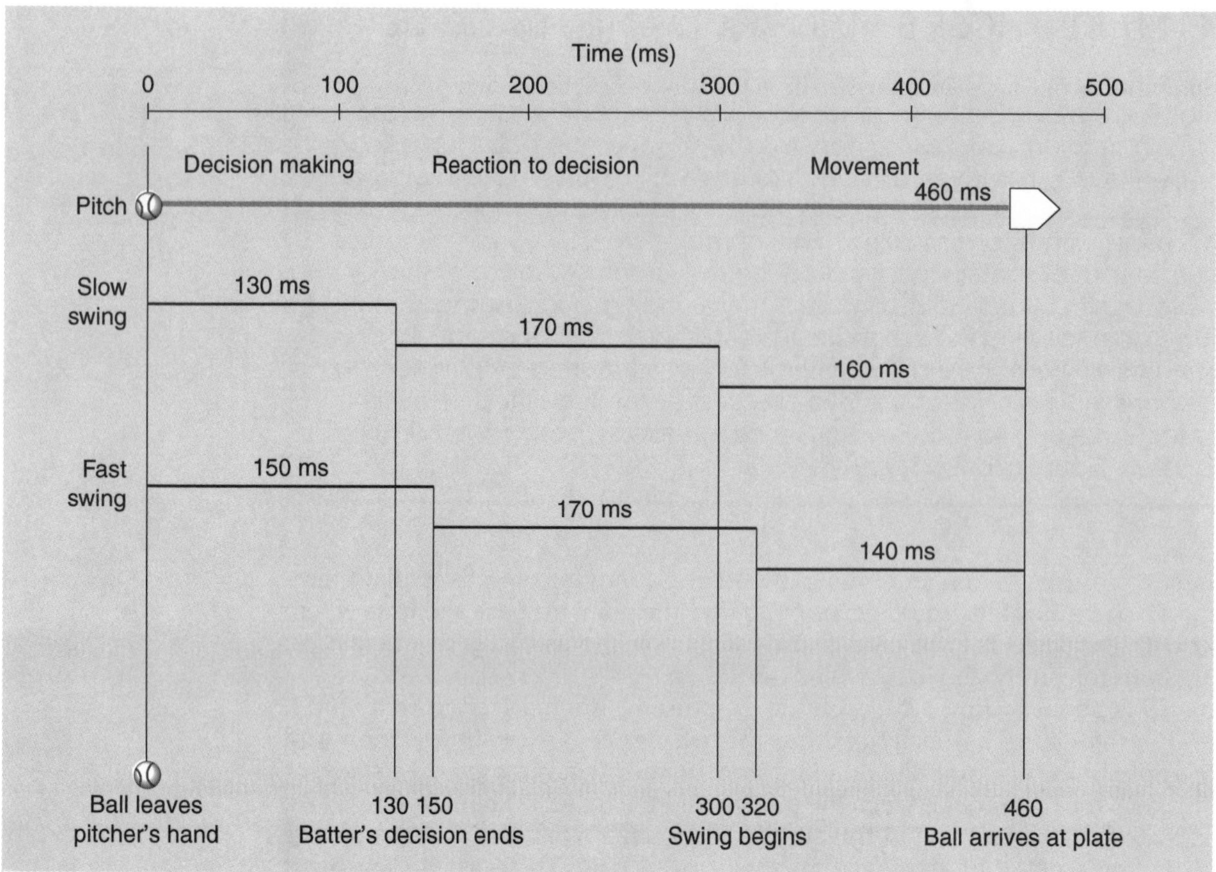


**Figure 6.14** Time line showing the critical events in hitting a pitched baseball. The movement time is 160 ms for the slow swing, 140 ms for the fast swing.

say from 160 ms to 140 ms. In order to reduce movement time, the batter could shorten the length of his swing slightly, use a lighter bat, or change the style of his movement in various ways. By reducing his movement time, the batter would also be altering the following aspects of his performance: the processing of visual information, timing the start of the swing, timing the swing itself, spatial accuracy, and the force of hitting the ball.

## Processing Visual Information

Figure 6.14 shows that when the batter shortens his movement time from 160 ms to 140 ms, he is able to shift the beginning of his swing to a position later in the ball's flight (i.e., at 320 ms). This extra 20 ms of information (from 130 ms to 150 ms, or about 3 ft of ball flight) comes at a point that is maximally useful—when the ball is closer to the plate. This gives the batter additional time to view the ball's speed and trajectory and to determine the time and place of contact (i.e., decision making). Therefore, his anticipation of when and where the ball is going to arrive should be more accurate. In summary, then, batters can improve their visual information processing and anticipate flight characteristics of the ball more effectively by shortening the time of their swing.

## Timing the Start of the Swing

When batters shorten their movement time, they are able to delay their decision about when to start the movement. In an experiment using a simulated batting task,

Dick Schmidt (1969) found that when participants shortened their movement time, their initiation time stabilized. Therefore, it appears that when the batter shortens his swing time, he becomes more *consistent* in the time he starts his swing. This would allow him to produce swings that arrive at the coincidence point more consistently, which should yield greater movement-timing accuracy.

## Timing the Swing Itself

One thing a batter must be aware of in planning a swing is the duration of his own bat movement (i.e., movement time). Therefore, the batter must select a movement time and then initiate the action far enough in advance to assure that the bat's time of arrival coincides with that of the ball. If the actual movement time is different from the estimated movement time, the swing will arrive too early or late, causing timing errors in hitting the ball. Based on our previous discussions (see also Schmidt, 1969) we know that individuals are able to time their movements more consistently when they produce them in shorter times (see figure 6.11). Therefore, if a batter shortens the time of his swing, he should be able to produce that movement time more consistently, resulting in greater timing accuracy at the end.

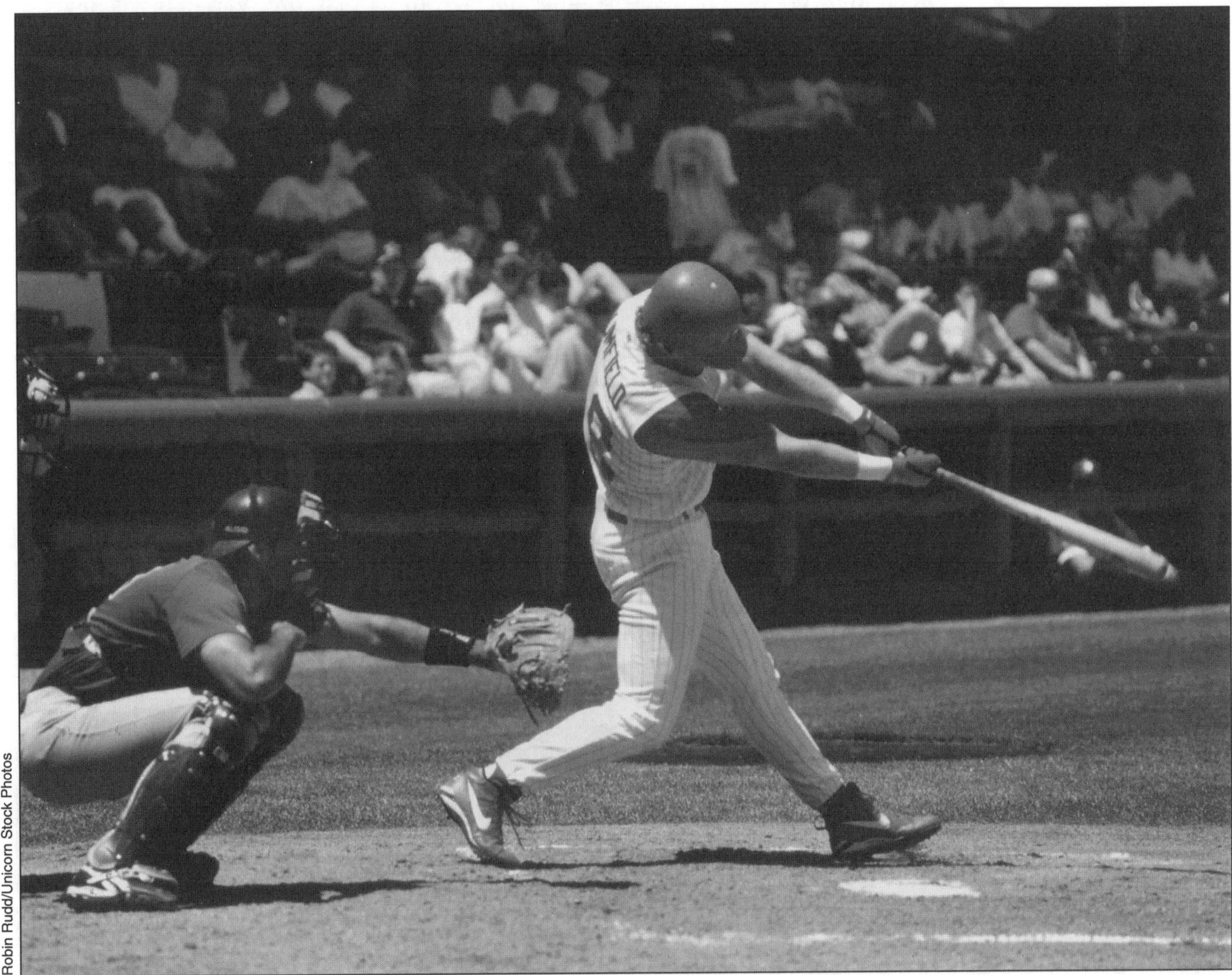

Robin Rudd/Unicorn Stock Photos

A batter selects movement time and prepares the swing to coincide with the ball's arrival.

## SKILLED BATTERS WHO SWING FASTER . . .

- increase their viewing time of the ball's flight, enhancing their anticipation of the pitch,
- increase the stability of their movement initiation time,
- increase the consistency of their movement time,
- increase the timing accuracy of ball contact,
- increase the spatial accuracy of ball contact (if they produce the swing with nearly maximal force), and
- increase the impact of ball contact.

### Achieving Spatial Accuracy

Since most skilled batters produce their swings very rapidly, they are probably near their limit of force production (certainly beyond 70% of maximum force). Therefore, if they reduce their swing time even further, the spatial accuracy of the swing should tend to increase—not decrease—because we know that force variability is lower in this range (see figure 6.13). Therefore, it appears that a batter can improve the spatial accuracy of his swings, promoting more frequent ball contact, if he shortens his movement time in a way that produces nearly maximal force.

### Hitting the Ball Hard

The batter who swings faster is able to impart more force to the ball, a critical factor in the game of baseball. If a batter is able to use a heavier bat without slowing movement time, he should be able to hit the ball harder without diminishing spatial accuracy (Schmidt & Sherwood, 1982).

Nearly every factor associated with decreases in movement time discussed in this section would be expected to improve a batter's chances of hitting the ball solidly. Therefore, we should not be surprised when we see high-performance professional baseball players (e.g., Mark McGwire, Sammy Sosa) swinging the bat at nearly maxi-

## How Do Experienced Batters Use Vision to Control Their Movements?

An interesting study conducted in the early 1950s showed how skilled batters use vision in controlling their swing. In this research, Hubbard and Seng (1954) filmed the movements of batters from three major league baseball teams: the Chicago Cubs, the St. Louis Browns, and the St. Louis Cardinals. A mirror, positioned to the side of the batter, provided a simultaneous view of the pitcher, the flight of the ball, and the face and body movements of the batter. In general, batters tended to synchronize the beginning of the stride with the release of the pitch, finish the stride, and begin the swing progressively later for slower speed pitches than for faster speed pitches, and to maintain the same swing speed or duration regardless of the speed of the pitch. There was no evidence that batters watched the ball up to the moment of contact (see also Bahill & LaRitz, 1984). Thus, it appears that these highly skilled individuals used vision of the ball to control only two aspects of their batting movements: the duration of the stride and the initiation of the swing.

mal speeds. Of course, such a strategy may not be as beneficial for inexperienced individuals or children, particularly if it results in clumsy, uncoordinated, inaccurate movements.

## Summary

Invariance is an important concept in motor control. Invariant features of a movement pattern are those that remain essentially unchanged while other features are changing. One prominent source of invariance is relative timing, a set of ratios among temporal intervals in the action that characterizes the temporal structure of a class of movements. Patterns of relative timing

- are the basis for generalized motor programs that performers use to produce movements of various classes (e.g., throwing, kicking, striking, running);
- are different for different classes of movements (e.g., throwing and walking);
- represent the deep, fundamental structure of movement classes, whereas modifiable aspects of the movements (e.g., movement time, movement amplitude, overall force, and the limb and muscles used) represent surface features; and
- remain invariant, even though movements within a class may be produced with different surface features.

Rapid movements controlled by generalized programs display a speed-accuracy trade-off. Research investigating the speed-accuracy trade-off in rapid skills suggests that

- unless movements are extremely rapid, increases in movement speed or decreases in movement time usually diminish spatial accuracy,
- decreases in movement time usually enhance temporal or timing accuracy, and
- errors are caused by relatively "noisy" low-level processes in the spinal cord and muscles, which produce contractions that are slightly different from those that were originally intended.

## From Principles to Practice

Check your understanding of the material in this chapter by responding to the following discussion questions and then completing the application exercises. In each case, see if you can identify the most relevant questions or issues and then propose a solution based on the concepts and principles discussed in the chapter.

### Checking Your Understanding

1. Explain the concept of relative timing. How might practitioners use this concept to determine differences between classes of movements? How might the relative-timing structure of dart throwing differ from that of putting the shot (hint: think of the difference in terms of the relative speeds of the wrist, lower arm, and upper arm in the two movements)?
2. What do movement scientists mean when they say that relative timing is an invariant feature of the generalized motor program? What implications does this have for performers who practice their movements at different speeds (e.g., dancers, jugglers, rhythmic gymnasts, drummers)?
3. Under what conditions are a performer's movements more spatially accurate as the person decreases his or her movement time? What implications might this have for an elementary physical education instructor who is teaching children how to throw or kick a ball toward a target?
4. Explain how an error in a low-level central nervous system process might cause a player throwing darts to miss the target area she is aiming for.

### Application Exercise #1

A factory worker has a job that requires him to assemble telephones as quickly and accurately as possible. The worker's primary task involves reaching out and picking up a number of different component parts, one at a time, and inserting them into various places in the housing of the telephone.

*It Depends*

- How big are the component parts?
- What is the shape of each part?
- How big are the various places in the housing of the telephone?
- What is the distance between the parts and the housing?
- How important is it for the worker to maintain 100% accuracy?

*Strategy*

Assist the worker in creating a workspace that allows him to pick up each part and insert it as quickly as possible into the housing.

*Response Example*

- Parts that are larger should be arranged on the work table a greater distance from the worker. This would allow him to move his hand at a faster rate when picking them up without sacrificing spatial accuracy.
- Parts that are smaller should be arranged on the work table a shorter distance from the housing. This would allow the worker to move more slowly when inserting them into the housing.
- If the housing (i.e., target) site is considerably larger than the component part, the worker can move at a faster rate.
- The more complex the shape of a part or the less accessible the location of the housing target site, the more the worker would have to trade off speed for accuracy or use slower feedback-based processes to control insertion movements.

### Application Exercise #2

Two people want to become accomplished square dancers so that they can enjoy country-western couples' dancing with their friends at a local club.

*It Depends*

- How spatially precise do the couple's movements have to be?

- How important is accurate timing of each person's movements to the other person's movements?
- How important is accurate timing of the couple's movements to the rhythm of the music?
- How fast is the tempo of the dances they want to learn?

*Strategy*

Since the couple's goal is to become a highly skilled pair of dancers, they must identify those aspects of their movements that involve possible speed-accuracy trade-offs. For movements requiring greater speed, they must find ways to perform the actions quickly without sacrificing accuracy (e.g., by increasing "target size" or decreasing "movement distance"). Practicing the dances at different tempos should help them identify the relative-timing structure of the various movements.

## Application Exercise #3

A baseball coach is having a difficult time with one of his pitchers. The pitcher throws his pitches with very high velocity, but his control is poor—in other words, the pitches lack spatial consistency.

*It Depends*

- How fast are the pitcher's pitches?
- Is he throwing the ball as hard as he can (i.e., maximum force)?
- What is the pitcher's visual focus when he throws the ball?
- Does the pitcher release his pitches at approximately the same point in his throwing motion?
- What other factors might be contributing to the spatial variability of the pitches?

*Strategy*

Using a radar gun and a video camcorder, determine the speed of the pitcher's pitches, the spatial variability of his release point, and the spatial variability of his pitches at the target. Ask the pitcher about the strategy he is using to be sure that it is as consistent as possible. For example, if his visual focus is not consistent, he might be reminded to focus on the point he expects the ball to go each time he throws a pitch. See what happens to the spatial variability of his pitches as the pitcher attempts to throw them at various percentages of maximum force (e.g., maximum, approximately 90% of maximum, etc.).

## Application Exercise #4

An 88-year-old female lives in a nursing home. A physical therapist comes to the home once a week to lead residents in upper-body toning activities. The only activity that the woman experiences difficulty with is throw and catch.

*It Depends*

- Does the woman have any visual impairments?
- Does the woman have past experiences that involved throwing and catching?
- What type of object is she expected to throw and catch (i.e., type of material, size, weight, etc.)?
- Does the woman have equal difficulty in throwing and catching?

*Strategy*

Assist the woman in developing a strategy for throwing and catching that allows her to experience modest success at the activity and reap the benefits of increased upper-body muscle tonus. Experiment with different types of objects (size, weight, texture), different throwing and catching distances, and different object speeds to determine the combinations that produce the highest frequency of successful throws and catches.

# PART III

# Principles of Skill Learning

7

# Preparing for the Learning Experience

## Chapter Outline



## Chapter Objectives

**When you have completed this chapter, you should be able to**

discuss the concept of the learning experience,

explain the role of the movement practitioner in defining learning experiences,

describe several characteristics of learners that practitioners should be aware of,

explain how movement practitioners might evaluate the progress of learners, and

◆

assist individuals in developing a "blueprint" for a motor learning experience.

## Preview

In Lewis Carroll's classic children's story, *Alice's Adventures in Wonderland* (1994 version), Alice and the Cheshire cat have the following verbal exchange:

*Alice:* Could you tell me which way I should go from here?

*Cheshire cat:* Well that depends a good deal on where you want to go.

*Alice:* Oh, I don't much care where.

*Cheshire cat:* Then it doesn't matter which way you go.

# Overview

In many ways, learners are like Alice and movement practitioners are like the Cheshire cat. For learning experiences to be rewarding and productive, learners must know where they want to go, and movement practitioners must be able to assist them in their efforts to get there. In chapters 3 through 6 we introduced a conceptual model of human performance. This model contains a variety of systems that underlie people's processing of information and their production of voluntary movements. By now you should have a pretty good understanding of the mechanisms of motor performance, as well as some of the basic principles of motor control and movement accuracy. In chapters 7 through 10 we turn our attention to the process of motor skill learning and the factors that influence people's acquisition of skills. In chapter 7 we discuss the concept of the learning experience and some of the factors movement practitioners should consider when preparing to assist learners. Then, in the next few chapters, we discuss instructional techniques practitioners can use when assisting learners (chapter 8), ways practitioners can structure the practice of tasks during learning sessions (chapter 9), and some things practitioners must remember when providing feedback for learners (chapter 10).

We take an approach to motor learning that conceptualizes learning in the way it typically seems to occur, not as an event artificially produced in a laboratory, but as an experience that takes place under everyday conditions, which are often "messy." There is considerable scientific literature on the factors that influence people's motor learning, and much of it represents useful information. We present the research that is most relevant for practitioners and learners in everyday situations.

In this chapter we discuss several concepts practitioners might want to consider when preparing to provide instructional assistance. These include goal setting, transfer of learning, learner characteristics, and the process of performance assessment.

**abilities**—Stable, enduring traits that, for the most part, are genetically determined and that underlie individuals' skilled performance.

**capabilities**—Characteristics of individuals that are subject to change as a result of practice and that represent a person's potential to excel in the performance of a task.

**motor learning**—Changes in internal processes that determine an individual's capability for producing a motor action. The level of an individual's motor learning improves with practice and is often inferred by observing relatively stable levels of the person's motor performance.

**learning experiences**—Situations in which people make deliberate attempts to improve their performance of a particular movement or action.

# Defining the Learning Experience

The capability to learn is essential to biological existence. It allows organisms to adapt to the particular features of their environment and to profit from their experiences. For humans, learning is crucial. Think of the difficulty individuals would have if they were forced to go through life equipped with only the **abilities** they inherited at birth. If that were the case, people would be relatively simple beings indeed; unable to walk, talk, write, or read, much less perform the complex movement skills involved in sport, the performing arts, or even in everyday settings.

Many factors contribute to a person's capability for skilled performance. As children mature and grow, their performance **capabilities** increase. Similarly, as people get stronger or improve their cardiovascular endurance, they sometimes can perform certain activities more effectively (e.g., ditch digging, wrestling, rappelling). However, maturation and fitness levels are not always related to skill levels. A major factor that does seem to be consistently related to skill level is that which comes as a direct result of practice of a task—the experience of learning.

In many ways, human learning seems to occur almost continuously, as if everything individuals do today generates knowledge or capabilities that affect how they do other things tomorrow and beyond. In chapter 1 we defined **motor learning** as changes in internal processes that determine an individual's capability for producing a motor task. More specifically, we restrict our view of skill learning to situations in which people make deliberate attempts to improve their performance of a particular movement or action, and we refer to those situations as **learning experiences** (or what some people term "deliberate practice"). We emphasize that learning expe-

A young girl tells her brother that she wishes she knew how to juggle, so he decides to help her. What are some things her brother might want to consider before he begins assisting his younger sister?

riences can take place in a variety of settings, involving an individual or a group of learners. Most of the time, although certainly not always, an instructor, a therapist, or a coach is present to guide the learning experience and assess the progress of the learner.

One issue practitioners should consider before assisting learners is the purpose of an individual's learning experience. It is important for practitioners to remember that the experience belongs to the *learner*. Every learner approaches a new skill learning situation with some idea of what he or she wants to accomplish. Our view is that practitioners should conceptualize the learning experience as an interaction between instructor and learner that has as its focus the successful achievement of the learner's goal. Two concepts practitioners find helpful when preparing to assist learners are goal setting and transfer of learning.

## Goal Setting

As we suggested in the preview to this chapter, an important prerequisite for productive learning is a clear understanding of the learner's intended goal or destination. Where does the learner want to go? What skills does the learner want to master? Under what conditions does the learner want to be able to perform the skills? Effective movement practitioners are able to assist learners in achieving *their* goals, but in order to do this they must first know what the learners' goals are!

Some learners approach learning situations with their goals clearly in mind; others do not. Practitioners should encourage all learners to set goals so that they can identify the specific skills and behaviors the learner wants to achieve, and so that the practitioner will have a reference point for assessing the learner's progress. **Goal setting** has been used successfully in many environments, particularly in industry, and it has strong implications for skill learning in other instructional settings (Locke & Latham, 1985). For the most part, goal setting is a highly individual matter. In other words, one person's goals are likely to be different from those of another. When learners participate in the goal-setting process, they are more committed to goal achievement, and they usually have a better understanding of the purpose of different learning activities (Tubbs, 1986).

**goal setting**—The process of establishing targets for future performance.

The research on goal setting indicates that goals that are challenging, attainable, realistic, and specific can have a beneficial effect on people's performance (Gould, 1998). And because goals that meet these criteria give participants an achievable target to shoot for, they serve to increase the quality of the learning experience.

Sometimes individuals set **outcome goals** that involve comparisons with other people's performance (e.g., beating a friend in tennis, winning a conference championship, leading the league in field goal percentage). While this is certainly okay, learners should be encouraged to set two other types of goals as well (Gould, 1998).

**outcome goals**—Targets for performance that focus on the end result of the activity.

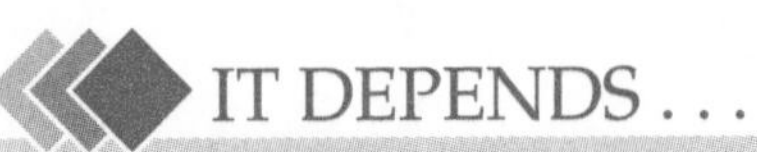


Two individuals want to learn how to play table tennis. In order for a practitioner to assist each person in setting goals that are challenging, attainable, realistic, and specific, what are some things the practitioner needs to know?

## CARS

You can easily remember four of the key elements of successful goal setting by remembering the acronym comprised of the first letters of each word: CARS

**C**hallenging

**A**ttainable

**R**ealistic

**S**pecific

**performance goals**—Targets for performance improvements relative to the individual's previous performance.

**process goals**—Targets for performance improvement that focus on the quality of movement production.

**target skills**—The tasks an individual wishes to be able to perform.

**Performance goals** are goals that focus on performance improvements relative to an individual's past performance (e.g., a basketball player's performance goal of increasing her free throw percentage from 70% to 75%). **Process goals** are those that emphasize particular aspects of skill execution (e.g., pumping the arms while running the 100-m dash, leading with the healthy leg when crutch walking up a flight of stairs). A tennis player might set a performance goal of improving his first first-serve percentage from 50% to 60% *and* a process goal of focusing his eyes on the seams of the ball every time he serves. Because performance and process goals focus the learner's attention on self-referenced improvements, they tend to be more motivating than outcome goals that involve comparisons with other people's performance. Examples of outcome goals, performance goals, and process goals are shown in table 7.1.

As we have previously suggested, an important advantage of goal setting is that it allows people to identify the skills they want to develop during their learning experience. For our purposes, we call these skills **target skills**. Target skills are the actual tasks individuals need to acquire in order to achieve their goals (e.g., keeping a tennis ball in play, knocking down 10 pins with a bowling ball, playing basketball with a prosthetic limb). Target skills for a person who wants to be a successful tennis player, for example, might include hitting ground strokes that land within the boundaries and within 5 ft of the opponent's baseline, hitting volleys that land beyond the opponent's service line, and hitting serves with good pace that land within 1 ft of the opponent's service line.

**Table 7.1**

**Examples of Outcome Goals, Performance Goals, and Process Goals for Different Activities**

| Activity | Outcome goals | Performance goals | Process goals |
|---|---|---|---|
| *Rifle shooting* | *Finish first in a local shooting competition.* | *Improve bull's-eye percentage from 60% to 70%.* | *Exhale slowly prior to each trigger squeeze.* |
| *Waterskiing* | *Qualify for the regional championships.* | *Increase average number of successful buoy passes from 4 to 5.* | *Visually focus on outside of buoys.* |
| *Volleyball* | *Win the conference title.* | *Improve blocking percentage from 40% to 50%.* | *Penetrate the plane of the net on each blocking attempt.* |

For *one* of the following pairs, suggest two target skills that might be the same for each activity and two target skills that might be different: bowling and croquet, tennis and squash, snow skiing and water skiing, cycling and canoeing, ballet dancing and ballroom dancing, surgery and dentistry, physical therapy and athletic training.

Once target skills are identified, practitioners must determine the observable behaviors that are associated with successful performance of those skills (e.g., watching the ball, keeping the wrist firm, turning the shoulders). For our purposes, we call these **target behaviors**. For the tennis ground stroke, target behaviors might include keeping the eyes on the ball, early racket preparation, and an exaggerated follow-through after ball contact. During instruction, practitioners should encourage learners to focus on one or more of these behaviors until each becomes a consistent characteristic of the individual's movements.

**target behaviors**—The actions individuals must be able to produce in order to successfully perform target skills in target contexts.

Third, practitioners must consider the **target context**, or the environmental context in which learners want to be able to produce their target skills. The target context for a tennis player might be a highly competitive tournament; for a recreational golfer it might be a round of golf with a few friends at a public course. The target context for a stroke patient learning to feed himself with his nonpreferred hand might be the home environment in the presence of concerned family members. Examples of target skills, target behaviors, and target contexts are shown in table 7.2.

**target context**—The environmental context in which individuals want to be able to perform a skill.

By encouraging learners to follow sound goal-setting principles in determining their outcome goals, performance goals, and process goals, practitioners should be able to get a clear picture of the learner's intended destination. Then practitioners can assist the learner in identifying the target skills and target behaviors that need to be developed in order to achieve the desired goals and produce effective movements in the target context.

## Transfer of Learning

Another concept practitioners consider when preparing to offer instructional assistance is the **transfer of learning**. In experiments on transfer of learning, researchers attempt to determine the influence of prior experiences on the individuals' learning of a new task. They do this by using an experimental design (see table 7.3) in which

**transfer of learning**—The gain or the loss of a person's proficiency on one task as a result of previous practice or experience on another task.

**Table 7.2**
**Examples of Target Skills, Target Behaviors, and Target Contexts for Different Activities**

| Activity | Target skills | Target behaviors | Target contexts |
|---|---|---|---|
| *Playing the piano* | *Error-free performance of a Mozart piece.* | *Proper hand and finger alignment.* | *Regional piano competition.* |
| *Basketball* | *Effective rebounding technique.* | *Use of body to block out opponent on each shot.* | *Junior varsity basketball game.* |
| *Surfing* | *Ride a moderately difficult wave.* | *Appropriate adjustments of body and feet.* | *At a local beach with friends.* |

**Table 7.3**
**A Common Experimental Design for Transfer of Learning Experiments**

| | | |
|---|---|---|
| **Experimental group** | *Experience with first task.* | *Experience with second task.* |
| **Control group** | *No experience with first task.* | *Experience with second task.* |

some participants perform or learn an initial task prior to the learning of a second task. A control group receives no experience, however, on the initial task and, therefore, represents a comparison condition for examining the effects (i.e., transfer) of the initial task on the learning of the second task. When prior experience on the initial task is beneficial to second-task learning, *positive transfer* is presumed to have occurred. If the prior experience is detrimental or has no influence, *negative transfer* or *no transfer*, respectively, is assumed.

Sometimes it can be difficult to see the real-world applications of transfer of learning experiments. In this section, therefore, we discuss several aspects of the transfer concept that we find particularly relevant for practitioners in assisting individuals in achieving their movement goals. Perhaps the most important transfer concern deals with the relationship between what an individual learns during practice sessions and what the person can do when required to perform the skill in the target context. A second aspect of the transfer concept deals with the potential impact of foundational motor learning on the future learning of other skills. Finally, there is the question of whether practicing simpler versions (or parts) of a task actually transfers positively to an individual's subsequent performance or learning of the whole task. In the following paragraphs we discuss each of these practical applications of the transfer concept in more detail.

**generalization**—A type of transfer of learning that occurs from one task to another very similar task or situation; also referred to as near transfer.

**near transfer**—A type of transfer of learning that occurs from one task to another very similar task or situation; also referred to as generalization.

**far transfer**—A type of transfer of learning that occurs from one task to another very different task or setting.

Perhaps the most important aspect of the transfer concept that practitioners should keep in mind is the notion of **generalization**, sometimes referred to as **near transfer**. With respect to the design of learning experiences, generalization promotes the near transfer of skill performance from the instructional setting to other situations, such as an athletic contest, a piano recital, the construction site or, for the therapy patient, the home environment (i.e., target contexts). In some cases this means that the performer adapts the target skill to meet the particular demands of another situation, such as when the basketball player puts more arc on the jump shot she has learned in order to clear the outstretched arms of a taller defender during a game. In other cases, near transfer means that the performer produces essentially the same movement that has been learned, but under a different set of environmental conditions, such as when the therapy patient with a prosthesis picks up food objects in the home environment after learning how to pick up similar objects in a clinical setting.

Another way practitioners can apply the transfer notion is in helping learners develop more general capabilities for producing a wide variety of actions in the future, a transfer concept sometimes referred to as **far transfer**. Perhaps the best-known technique for developing far transfer is the movement-education approach used by many elementary school instructors. Instructors who use this method encourage children to attempt a variety of fundamental movement activities, such as throwing, jumping, running, and skating. According to this view, children who learn to produce these kinds of basic movements are preparing themselves for future performance of other activities involving these fundamental movements. For example, throwing is important for baseball pitching and tennis serving, jumping is essential for hurdling and playing basketball, running is needed for soccer and football, and skating is a prerequisite for ice hockey and ice dancing.

Still another application of the transfer of learning concept concerns the question of whether modifying a skill—in order to make it easier for learners to practice—facilitates the performance or learning of the whole skill. For example, relatively long-duration serial skills, such as certain gymnastics routines, might be broken down into shorter elements for practice. Before deciding to do this, practitioners should consider whether having a learner practice various parts of a task in isolation is going to be beneficial when it's time for the person to resume performance of the whole task. We address the issue of part-whole practice in more detail in chapter 9.

# The Learner

The central figure in every learning experience is the learner, and to create the most effective learning experiences, movement practitioners must be aware of some of the important characteristics of learners. These characteristics include a person's motivation, abilities, past experiences, and present stage of learning.

## Motivation

Anyone who has taught another person something will testify that the key ingredient for productive learning is the learner's motivation (Deci & Ryan, 1985). Highly motivated people devote greater effort to the task, are more conscientious during learning sessions, and are willing to practice for longer periods of time. Individuals who are not motivated to learn do not practice or, at best, make only half-hearted attempts.

The general context of motor learning is achievement oriented. Therefore, it is reasonable to presume that the motivation of most learners is related to their *perceptions of success* in achieving their goals (i.e., **achievement motivation**). Individuals can make judgments about their success in one of two ways: with respect to improvements in their performance of the task itself (i.e., task-referenced judgments) or with respect to improvements in their performance as it compares with the performance of others (i.e., norm-referenced judgments). As long as learners feel they are competent or successful, they will continue to be motivated (Duda, 1993; Nicholls, 1989).

**achievement motivation**—The direction and intensity of a person's effort to reach a performance goal, either for task mastery or for surpassing others.

People feel more highly motivated when they see the relevance of the learning activity in their lives. With the popularity of movies like *Swing Kids* and *Dance Fever*, certain dance forms have become popular. The recent interest in retro swing movements as seen in the Gap commercials, for example, leads to requests for dance instruction. It is a pleasure for both students and teachers when interested dancers flock to class and are eager to develop their skills and express their emotions.

Unfortunately, there are also instructional situations in which learners are not so enthusiastic. High school students who are required to take physical education classes may not see the personal relevance of the activities they are being asked to perform. Sometimes injured athletes or stroke patients are so discouraged about their physical condition that they have a difficult time mustering the energy to attend therapy sessions. To enhance the motivation of individuals such as these, effective instructors or therapists must find creative ways to *forge a connection between the learner and the skill to be learned*. Fortunately, there are a variety of helpful techniques available (e.g., videos, group discussions, presentations by skilled performers, encouragement, and praise), some of which we describe in more detail in the next chapter.

One effective way practitioners can enhance learner motivation is to involve learners in the goal-setting process. The keys to motivation are *personal relevance* and a *process orientation*. When learners are given the opportunity to select their own goals and then are encouraged to evaluate their success in reaching those goals, they are always in a position to see themselves as competent performers. And as long as people feel successful about their own goal achievement, they continue to be highly motivated to learn.

## Past Experiences

Practitioners often use the transfer of learning concept to design learning experiences, as we explained previously. Let's look more at the aspect of this transfer of learning concept as it deals with the possible transfer of previously learned elements to the learning of a new task. All learners bring some movement experiences with them to the learning situation. If, among those experiences, are previously learned tasks containing motor, perceptual, or conceptual elements similar to those of the task to be learned, practitioners might emphasize those similarities as they provide instructional assistance (see Schmidt & Young, 1987). For example, individuals who want to learn to in-line skate might be reminded of the similar elements in other tasks they have already learned, such as ice skating, roller skating, or skateboarding.

The earliest discussions of the transfer concept dealt with the notion of "identical elements" between tasks (Thorndike, 1914). Two tasks that share a greater number of similar elements are expected to transfer more highly. When this is the case, individuals can capitalize on their previous task experiences when learning new skills. Elements that might be identical, or at least very similar, between tasks include movement elements, perceptual elements, and conceptual or strategic elements. Examples of similar elements that tasks might share are shown in table 7.4.

**movement elements**—Those aspects of a task that deal with the motor patterns or actions associated with correct performance.

**Movement elements** deal with the movement patterns of various actions. For example, throwing a baseball and casting a fishing lure involve movement patterns that are quite similar. Therefore, practitioners could remind learners who have had previous experience throwing baseballs that the casting action is "similar to throwing a baseball." Individuals who have not had prior experience throwing might be encouraged to practice throwing in order to get a better feel for the movement pattern used in casting. (Remember that the notion of fundamental, underlying movement patterns was an important part of our discussion of generalized motor programs in chapters 5 and 6).

**perceptual elements**—Those aspects of a task that deal with the individual's interpretation of stimuli that leads to correct performance.

**Perceptual elements** are task-related stimuli that individuals must be able to interpret in order to assure successful performance. For example, the sports of

### HELPFUL COMMENTS

It is often obvious to experts, but not necessarily to beginners, that a particular skill being learned for the first time resembles other skills learned previously. Helpful instructors and therapists point out possible similarities, using statements such as, "The arm action in this tennis serve is very similar to the kind of action you use in an overarm throw" or "The kip action here on the rings is just like the kip action you use on the horizontal bar." A patient who is attempting to stand for the first time following a leg amputation might be reminded of how it feels to balance on one leg or to play the game of hopscotch. By reminding individuals of action patterns they have experienced or learned previously, practitioners can assist them in grasping the concept or feel of a new skill, which can be particularly helpful during the initial stage of learning.

**Table 7.4**
**Examples of Similar Movement Elements, Perceptual Elements, and Conceptual Elements for Different Movement Activities**

| Activities | Movement elements | Perceptual elements | Conceptual elements |
|---|---|---|---|
| *Tennis and badminton* | *Shoulder rotation prior to shot.* | *Visual tracking of ball or shuttlecock.* | *Vary shot selection.* |
| *Bowling and shuffleboard* | *Follow through in direction of target.* | *Accurate judgment of target location.* | *Effective placement of object.* |
| *Ice hockey and soccer* | *Maintain balance while in motion and while manipulating an object.* | *Accurate interpretation of opponents' movements.* | *Maintain proper spacing with teammates.* |

## USING THE SAME MOVEMENT PATTERN FOR DIFFERENT ACTIVITIES

Some movement patterns appear to be inherent in the performance of a variety of actions. A good example is the so-called overarm throwing pattern that underlies the performance of throwing a baseball, serving a tennis ball, spiking a volleyball, casting a fishing lure, and many other actions. Each of these movements requires a forceful overarm action that a performer typically uses to strike or project an object. All of the movements involve rotation of the hips and shoulders and ballistic actions of the shoulder, arm, and wrist, ending with a wrist-hand action appropriate for the particular goal of the movement. In the sport of gymnastics, athletes apply certain fundamental actions (e.g., the sharp hip extension in the kip) in the performance of a number of apparatus events. In both of these examples, it is reasonable to expect that the practice of one of the tasks containing the fundamental movement pattern transfers to the learning of any of the other tasks that use that pattern.

racquetball, squash, paddleball, and handball require a perceptual awareness of the way the ball rebounds off the walls and floor. Practitioners can promote transfer of learning by either calling learners' attention to previous experiences they have had with these tasks or by allowing learners to practice tasks containing similar perceptual elements.

Some motor tasks contain similar **conceptual elements**, such as strategies, rules, guidelines, or concepts. Maintaining a narrow focus on the target is an important guideline for individuals who perform activities like setting a diamond, threading a needle, or suturing a wound. Some sports have similar rules (e.g., baseball and softball, gymnastics and diving, racquetball and paddleball); some have similar strategic elements (e.g., controlling or defending an area of the field, court, or ice in the games of basketball, rugby, soccer, ice hockey, field hockey, and lacrosse). Transfer of conceptual elements can be enhanced if learners have had previous experience with tasks having similar conceptual elements or if individuals are encouraged to practice activities having similar conceptual elements.

**conceptual elements**—Those aspects of a task that deal with principles, guidelines, or strategies of performance.

Practitioners should remember that the transfer of common elements is more pronounced when individuals are just beginning to learn a skill. For example, the person who is just beginning to practice her tennis serve might benefit from additional experiences of overarm throwing, since the arm motion is similar to that needed for the serve. However, once the individual has learned the basic serving motion, she should spend more time hitting different serves than practicing her throwing. As skill levels improve, a greater proportion of the individual's learning experience should be devoted to performance of the target skill in situations that resemble the target context (e.g., serving the tennis ball to an opponent in a gamelike situation). Indeed, the **specificity of learning** principle (Henry, 1968) holds that the best practice is that which approximates most closely the movements of the target skill and the environmental conditions of the target context. Although there may be exceptions to this principle, it is for the most part a sound one that practitioners should keep in mind when providing instructional assistance.

**specificity of learning**—The notion that the best learning experiences are those that approximate most closely the movement components and environmental conditions of the target skill and target context.

Sometimes practitioners are concerned that a learner's previous experiences might transfer negatively to the individual's performance or learning of a new skill. For example, the tennis instructor might feel that a person's previous experiences in racquetball or badminton could degrade the person's performance or learning of tennis skills. The assumption here is that the actions necessary for racquetball and badminton are just different enough from those needed for tennis that, if a performer experiences them to any great extent, her tennis skill is going to be susceptible to negative transfer.

The laboratory research suggests that the phenomenon of negative transfer is virtually nonexistent in the realm of motor skills. Only during the very early stages of learning, when the level of a person's skill is more general in nature, might she or he

© Dennis Curran Photography

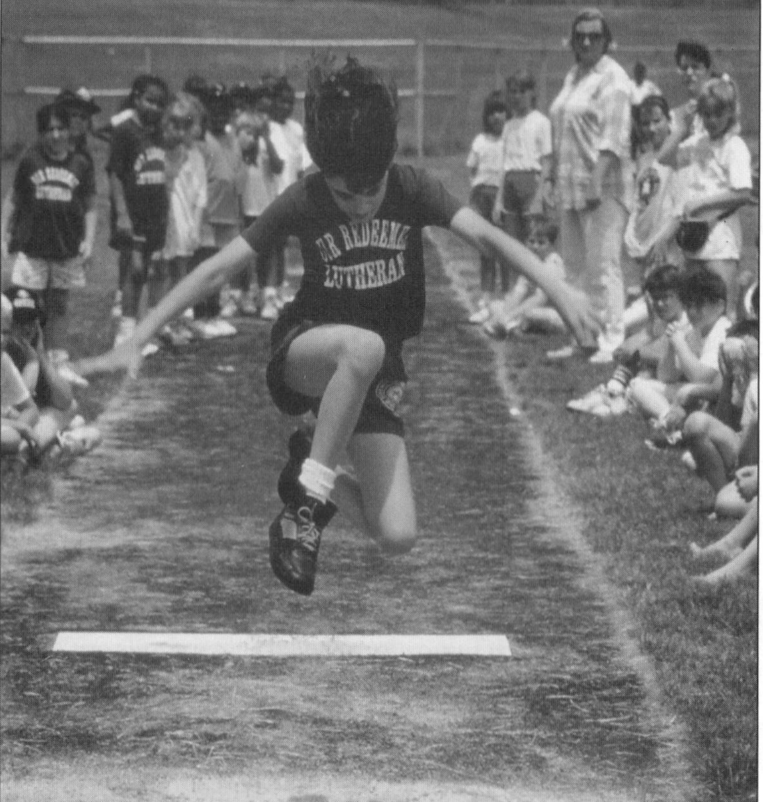

© Jeff Greenberg/Unicorn Stock Photos

A child leaping between rocks can transfer skills developed in doing the broad jump.

### CATEGORIES OF SIMILAR ELEMENTS IN MOTOR SKILLS INCLUDE THE FOLLOWING:

- Movement elements
- Perceptual elements
- Conceptual elements

### IT DEPENDS . . .

See if you can suggest one similar movement element, one similar perceptual element, *and* one similar conceptual element for *any two* of the following activities: archery, bowling, croquet, dentistry, engine repair, fencing, golf, horseback riding, ice skating, jai alai, kickboxing, leaf raking, moonwalking, nail filing, oboe playing, painting, quarterbacking, racquetball, sewing, tap dancing, urinalysis, vivisection, welding, xylophone playing, yo-yo playing, zoysia planting.

be susceptible to the negative influence of prior learning. Even here, though, the research suggests that most transfer between motor skills is at least mildly positive. Moreover, practitioners can avoid problems by pointing out to learners the aspects of a new skill (e.g., swinging a tennis racket with a firm wrist) that are different from those of a previously learned one (e.g., swinging a fly swatter with a flexible wrist), thus minimizing the potential for negative transfer.

## Abilities

As we discussed in chapter 2, all individuals inherit a variety of different abilities that predispose them to the successful performance and learning of different tasks. For example, a person who inherits a high level of gross body coordination might be expected to experience relatively more success, at least initially, in activities such as soccer, ballet, and kickboxing. There is little doubt that learners have an advantage if they bring with them to the learning situation high levels of the abilities important to successful task performance. For those who don't, including those who may have their abilities impaired due to accident, illness, or genetic predisposition, performance goals should probably be less rigorous and the number of repetitions of the learning task higher to assure goal achievement.

Many people hold the common misconception that fundamental abilities can be improved by practicing various drills. For example, some sport practitioners feel that even the best athletes can profit from exercises designed to strengthen certain abilities. Coaches sometimes use balancing drills to increase athletes' general balancing ability or use eye-movement exercises to improve athletes' vision. The most popular kind of drills seems to be the "quickening" exercises designed to improve athletes' quickness. If all these activities accomplished what coaches think they do, it would be great news for the many athletes who would love to improve their balance, vision, or quickness. Unfortunately, the available evidence suggests that exercises such as these do little more than improve individuals' performance of the drills themselves. Thus, if practitioners want to promote learning, they should encourage learners to spend the bulk of their time practicing the skills specific to goal achievement.

## Stages of Learning

**stages of learning**—Relatively distinct and sequential phases of the learning process; see verbal-cognitive stage, motor stage, and autonomous stage.

As we just mentioned, individuals bring with them to the learning situation different levels of motivation, types of experience, and inherited abilities. They also begin their learning experiences at different levels or **stages of learning** (not to be confused with the stages of information processing discussed in chapter 3). As mentioned in chapter 1, a number of authors have discussed the concept of learning stages (Adams, 1971; Fitts & Posner, 1967; Gentile, 1972), and although they give different labels to the stages, the characteristics they assign to learners in each of the stages are quite similar.

In this section, we discuss again the three relatively distinct stages of the learning process in more detail and describe the distinguishing characteristics of learners in each stage. We say "relatively distinct" because some overlap usually exists between the stages, and learners may demonstrate characteristics of different stages at different times. The three stages are (a) the verbal-cognitive stage, (b) the motor stage, and (c) the autonomous stage.

### *Verbal-Cognitive Stage*

Learners in the verbal-cognitive stage are confronted with an entirely unfamiliar task. Their challenge, as Gentile (1972) has suggested, is to get a general idea of the movement. For example, a person trying to use a sailboard for the first time must learn how and where to stand, how to hold the sail, and how to balance. As you go through this stage, you might find yourself fascinated (as Dick Schmidt did) simply by the many different ways you can manage to fall off a sailboard!

As the label implies, learners in the verbal-cognitive stage spend a lot of time talking (verbal) to themselves about what they are going to try to do and thinking (cognitive) about strategies that might work. Questions they tend to ask themselves deal with such issues as identifying the goal (i.e., "What am I trying to accomplish?"), deciding what to do or not do, figuring out how to perform the movement, perhaps determining when to perform it, and evaluating what they did (i.e., "What went wrong?" "Did I get that right?"). Some learners engage in a great deal of self-talk during this stage, verbally guiding themselves through their actions. This activity demands a lot of attention and prevents individuals from processing other information, such as appropriate strategies and the elements of form. While verbal-cognitive activity can be effective in helping learners grasp the general idea of the skill, it should drop out as individuals become more experienced with the task. As might be expected, verbal and cognitive abilities dominate during this stage. Therefore, individuals who are good at figuring out what to do and how to go about doing it have a distinct advantage.

Gains in performance proficiency in this verbal-cognitive stage tend to be rather large and occur rapidly, indicating that individuals are quickly discovering and using more effective strategies for performance. However, teachers and therapists should expect the performance of individuals to also be halting, jerky, uncertain, and poorly timed to objects and events in the external environment.

Instructions, demonstrations, and other types of verbal and visual information (see chapter 8) are particularly beneficial for learners in this stage. One goal of instructions is to help individuals see how something they have learned or experienced in the past is similar in some way to the new skill they are trying to learn. Practitioners sometimes capitalize on the concept of transfer of learning, therefore, by pointing out the similarity of elements between previously learned tasks and the new task. In another vein, a demonstration or visual model provides learners with a picture of the desired movement pattern, which they can then attempt to reproduce with their own actions.

### *Motor Stage*

Eventually, learners progress to the motor stage. Having solved most of the strategic or cognitive problems and having achieved a general idea of what the movement is like, the learner's focus now shifts to refining the skill by organizing more effective movement patterns to produce the action. Fitts and Posner (1967) call this stage the "associative stage," and Gentile (1972) labels it the "fixation/diversification stage," suggesting that the learner's focus is to "associate, fixate, or diversify" or whatever else is needed for skill refinement. When Dick Schmidt reached this stage in his sailboarding experience, he displayed a much more consistent stance and control, his confidence improved, and he started to work on the finer details of the task.

An individual's skill refinement is slightly different for quick movements than for slower ones. If the skill requires quick movements (e.g., the tennis stroke, the cricket swing, beating an egg, chopping vegetables), the individual begins to build the motor program for accomplishing movement requirements. If the skill involves slower movements (e.g., balancing in gymnastics, driving a car, cross-country skiing, threading a needle), the learner becomes more adept at processing and using movement-produced feedback to control the action. In a similar vein, refinement is different for **closed skills** (e.g., golf, bowling, chopping wood) and for **open skills** (e.g., soccer, cricket, white-water rafting). If movements are performed in a predictable environment, learners can "fixate" on reproducing the same actions each time. However, if movements must be adapted to meet the demands of a changing environment, learners must begin to "diversify" their actions in response to varied environmental conditions.

**closed skill**—A skill performed in an environment that is predictable or stationary and that allows individuals to plan their movements in advance.

**open skill**—A skill performed in an environment that is unpredictable or in motion and that requires individuals to adapt their movements in response to dynamic properties of the environment.

Several factors change markedly during the motor stage, most of which are associated with producing more effective movement patterns. Learners demonstrate more consistency as their strategies for skill refinement become more subtle and their movements become more "grooved" and "stable." They become more efficient in producing their movements; at times they appear to be performing almost effortlessly. Self-talk becomes less frequent. As individuals discover regularities in the environment (e.g., the speed of an approaching ball, the tendencies of an opponent to do certain things at certain times), their anticipation and timing develops, making their movements appear smoother and less rushed. In addition, performers begin to monitor their own feedback and detect their own errors.

This stage generally lasts somewhat longer than the verbal-cognitive stage, perhaps for several weeks or even months, if the task is extremely complex. Instructional assistance and feedback become somewhat less important during this stage. When feedback is provided, it should be more precise and target those aspects of the movement the learner is attempting to refine.

### Autonomous Stage

After extensive practice, some learners enter the autonomous stage where they are able to produce their actions almost automatically with little or no attention (see chapter 3). These individuals develop their **motor programs** to such an extent that they can use them to control their actions for longer periods of time. Thus, they don't have to think about every component of the skill they are performing. For example, an accomplished gymnast is able to run off several seconds of a high bar routine or a skilled typist or concert pianist produces longer strings of words or notes. By programming longer sequences, highly skilled individuals don't have to activate as many programs. This decreases the demands on performers' attention that occur when they have to initiate their movements more frequently (see chapter 3). Though Dick Schmidt never quite entered the autonomous stage in sailboarding, he has seen others who have clearly reached this stage, displaying very skillful sail handling in high winds, with plenty of attention left over to contemplate strategies for a race or determine creative ways to surf large waves.

**motor program**—A set of motor commands that is prestructured at the executive level and that defines the essential details of a skilled action; analogous to a central pattern generator.

Individuals in this stage also demonstrate increased automaticity in their sensory analysis of environmental patterns. Thus, for example, race car drivers recognize subtle characteristics of traffic flow patterns, white-water rafters notice shifts in water currents

**IT DEPENDS . . .**

Three friends decide to sign up for a badminton class. The first is one of the top players in her age group, the second has played for several years and has a pretty good command of the basic shots, and the third has never played the game at all. These individuals are obviously at different stages of learning. What are some of the things the instructor might keep in mind in order to create an effective learning experience for each individual?

and the presence of potential obstacles, and open-skill sport performers (e.g., squash players) identify aspects of their opponent's movements that indicate the use of a particular strategy. This capability frees expert performers to engage in higher-order cognitive activities, such as split second shifts in strategy or spontaneous adjustments in the form or style of a movement in dance or in figure skating. Famed professional basketball player Michael Jordan has repeatedly said that he creates his most incredible movements in a spontaneous fashion as the action is unfolding.

During the autonomous stage, self-confidence increases, and the capability to detect errors in movements becomes highly developed. Individuals engage in very little self-talk while producing their movements. In fact, advanced performers who self-talk usually suffer performance breakdowns (e.g., a concert violinist playing Mozart missing a series of notes when she begins to analyze the movements of her fingers and arms). Self-talk may be evidenced with respect to higher-order aspects of the task (e.g., adding emphasis or expression during the performance of a figure skating routine or a jazz dance routine).

Performance improvements are more difficult to detect during this stage because individuals are reaching the limits of their capabilities. However, their movements are characterized by increased automaticity (or automatic processing), reduced physical and mental effort, and improved style and form. Moreover, their learning may be far from over. This fact is perhaps best illustrated in a classic industrial study conducted by Crossman (1959). He investigated the performance of production line workers in a cigar factory and found that the time it took these workers to make each cigar continued to decrease even after seven years of practice—that's after approximately 100 million repetitions! Clearly, the role of the movement practitioner is more difficult to define when individuals reach the autonomous stage of learning.

## Assessing Progress

In order to determine the effectiveness of instruction and provide feedback to learners about their performance and their level of goal achievement, practitioners need to decide how progress will be assessed. Two important issues related to the assessment of progress are the goals of the learner and the aspects of performance that represent the best indicators of skilled action. Since most skill learning takes place with a particular goal in mind, the assessment of progress must be made in a way that indicates something about the level of the individual's goal achievement. And because learning must be inferred from performance observations, it is important that the aspects of performance practitioners choose to assess are those that accurately reflect the qualities associated with successful goal achievement. In the case of the stroke patient, the therapist may decide to simulate various environmental situations (e.g., the individual's home) and then assess the patient's **skill** in entering rooms in which the door must first be opened, in moving on various types of surfaces (e.g., gravel, tile, hardwood floors, carpet, grass, asphalt pavement), and in navigating around a variety of obstacles (e.g., chair, table, bed).

**skill**—The capability of producing a performance result with maximum certainty, minimum energy, or minimum time; developed as a result of practice.

When it comes to assessing the progress of learners, movement practitioners should ask themselves, "How is the assessment I am about to conduct indicative of the level of progress this individual has made toward her or his intended goal?" If the answer to that question is "That's a good question" or "I'm not really sure," then the decision to assess performance should probably be postponed. It would be an inefficient use of instructional time to schedule assessments that fail to reflect some level of goal achievement.

## Selecting Valid Indicators of Skill

Assuming that the learner and the practitioner have clearly determined the goal of learning, they must then decide which aspects of performance or target behaviors should be assessed in order to determine the learner's progress. In order to be of any value, target behaviors must, first, be valid indicators of the desired action. A measure is "valid" if it allows the practitioner to make a correct inference or conclusion about the level of the learner's skill. For example, valid measures of a person's archery skill might include the distance of the arrows from the center of the target and the "tightness" of a grouping of arrows. Valid measures also reflect something about the learner's capability of producing the desired skill *in a particular context*. The target context for an individual who is learning archery might be a particular competition conducted under specified conditions.

Practitioners who are able to identify appropriate target behaviors and select valid measures of performance are in the best position to assess the progress of learners. Generally speaking, there are two categories of performance measures practitioners can select from: outcome measures and process measures.

### *Outcome Measures*

**Outcome measures** indicate something about the *results* of a person's movements (e.g., a 100-m dash time of 11 s, 15 service aces in a set of tennis, 35 consecutive bounce-and-catch movements without an error). They include measures of time (e.g., how long it takes to perform the movement), distance (e.g., how high or far the person moves), frequency (e.g., how many attempts it takes to achieve the goal), accuracy (e.g., how close to the center of the target the object lands), and consistency (e.g., the percentage of attempts that hit the target). In the example of a stroke patient, outcome measures might be the time it takes her to move from her car to the front door of her house or the number of stops that she makes to adjust her walker. Practitioners should think carefully about the outcome measures they select and periodically evaluate the measures to determine which ones provide the most valid indication of progress.

**outcome measures**—Performance observations that indicate some aspect of the end result of performance.

### QUESTIONS TO ASK BEFORE ATTEMPTING TO ASSESS A LEARNER'S PROGRESS

Assessing the progress of learners is not a simple task for movement practitioners. Before conducting a performance assessment, practitioners might consider the following questions:

- What are the learner's goals?
- What am I going to learn from this performance assessment?
- What is the learner going to learn from this performance assessment?
- How am I going to use the information I obtain from this assessment to assist the learner in achieving his or her goals?

## The Woodchoppers' Ball

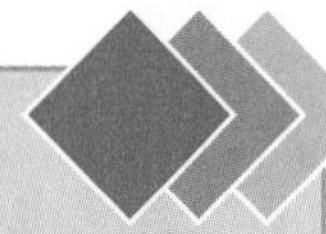

What are the characteristics of skilled performance? This is a question movement practitioners must be able to answer to assess learners' progress. An entertaining fable (Johnson, 1961) relates the story of a group of citizens in a small town in the great northern woods who came face-to-face with this question. It seems that a considerable debate existed among the townspeople as to which of two highly skilled individuals was "the most skilled woodchopper in the land." To determine the true champion, the townspeople decided to hold a contest. The first test was of speed. Each contestant attempted to split 10 cords of wood in the shortest time possible. As it turned out, the two choppers struck their final blows at exactly the same moment. The second test was of accuracy. Contestants alternately tried their hand at splitting everything from straws to buckshot. Again the result was a draw. Next, the choppers were tested for efficiency. Each was given all the wood he wanted and asked to "Chop 'til you drop!" As with the first two tests, the outcome was declared a tie—two loud "thuds" sounded simultaneously as the two collapsed at exactly the same instant. Just when it appeared there would be no winner, a bearded old sage stepped forward and suggested a final test. The sage correctly pointed out that in all of the previous tests, the woodchoppers had performed standard cutting tasks using their own axes. "Now," the sage said, "let's see how adaptable they are." So the combatants were required to chop wood of various lengths, under various conditions, using a variety of axes. Under these conditions, the contest was finally decided. One of the brawny individuals chopped masterfully under all of the required conditions, whereas the other was able to do no better than would be expected of any ordinary woodchopper. Therefore, the moral of the fable is that in some types of skilled performance one defining characteristic is adaptability, or generalizability.

### Process Measures

**process measures**—Performance observations that indicate something about the quality of movement production; involve the use of sophisticated instrumentation or the subjective evaluation of an expert.

**electromyography (EMG)**—A device for recording the electrical activity in a muscle or group of muscles.

**electroencephalography (EEG)**—A device for recording the electrical activity in different regions of the brain.

**Process measures** indicate something about the *quality* of the actions themselves (i.e., the process of moving). In the laboratory or the therapy clinic, movement scientists or therapists can use sophisticated instrumentation, such as **electromyography (EMG)**, which measures patterns of muscle activity, or **electroencephalography (EEG)**, which measures brain activity. If adequate instrumentation is available, instructors or therapists can examine changes in a variety of movement characteristics *as they occur* with skill practice or with improvements in an individual's coordination.

In most practical learning situations, sophisticated instruments are not available. Even if they are, the equipment may not be portable enough to allow practitioners to assess aspects of movement quality in the target context (e.g., at home, at the mall, at a music recital, during a squash competition). Therefore, practitioners typically use less precise alternatives. Of these, practitioners probably use expert ratings of movement form most often (e.g., a tennis instructor's rating of the components of a person's movement form during the serve).

Skilled practitioners (e.g., instructors, therapists, coaches, or human factors engineers) who are able to observe learners' movements directly or on videotape can make judgments about the quality of those movements. In order to assure that the process measures they select are valid, practitioners first must identify the components of the learners' movements that most accurately reflect the target behavior. See table 7.5 for an example of criteria that might be used to assess the quality of an individual's gait (Knudson & Morrison, 1997). Then they must decide the best means of observing those components (e.g., front view, side view, back view) and how to assess them in an appropriate fashion (e.g., individual movement components could be rated and summed, or an overall form rating could be assigned).

## Measuring Aiming Movements

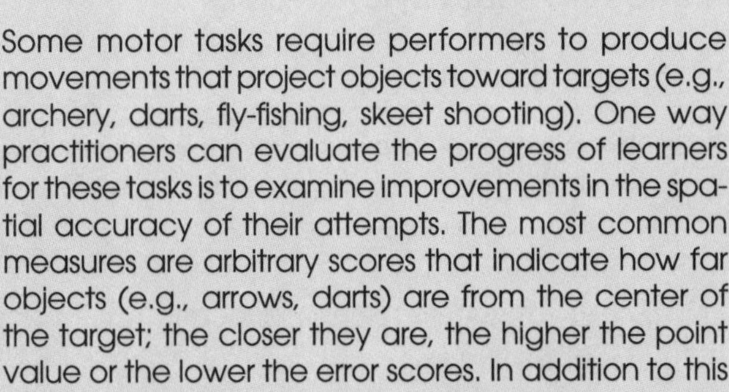

Some motor tasks require performers to produce movements that project objects toward targets (e.g., archery, darts, fly-fishing, skeet shooting). One way practitioners can evaluate the progress of learners for these tasks is to examine improvements in the spatial accuracy of their attempts. The most common measures are arbitrary scores that indicate how far objects (e.g., arrows, darts) are from the center of the target; the closer they are, the higher the point value or the lower the error scores. In addition to this global measure of accuracy, there are several other ways practitioners can assess the pattern of learners' errors.

For tasks like dart throwing, where a series of throws is attempted and then the score is calculated, practitioners can visually examine and perhaps record the spatial configuration of the darts. Figure 7.1 shows a spatial configuration of five darts that have landed above the target center. If there is time for more precise measurement, the practitioner could determine the exact extent of unidimensional (in this case above or below the target) directional bias and inconsistency of the spatial configuration of the darts. The practitioner draws a horizontal line through the center of the target to distinguish above-bull's-eye errors from below-bull's-eye errors. For the example shown in figure 7.1, all darts are assigned a positive value because they all landed above the line. If any darts had landed below the line, they would have been assigned a negative value.

The practitioner measures the distance of each point from the line and calculates the average **constant error (CE)** by adding the values and dividing the total by the number of darts thrown. In the figure 7.1 example, the CE value is +3 in. (7.6 cm; see the arithmetic for this example in table 7.6). This means that the thrower's spatial configuration of darts has a positive (i.e., above-bull's-eye) *directional bias* of 3 in. (7.6 cm) on the average. Other examples of CE might be a golf putt that stops 3 in. (7.6 cm) past the hole; a baseball swing that delivers the bat through the hitting zone 200 ms before the ball arrives. Average CE represents the average deviation of the results of several movement attempts (e.g., 3 putts that stop an average of 2.8 in. (7.1 cm) past the hole).

In order to determine the *spread,* or variability, of the grouping of darts, the practitioner calculates **variable error (VE)** by (a) subtracting the average CE from *each* value, (b) squaring *each* difference, (c) adding the squared differences, (d) dividing that total by the number of attempts, and (e) taking the square root of that number. The result (i.e., VE) is the standard deviation of the performer's throws (in this case approximately 1.4 in., or 3.6 cm) from her average CE (in this case, 3 in.). Three golf putts with an average CE of 0 in. and a VE of 5 in. are more inconsistent than 3 golf putts with an average CE of +2.8 in. and a VE of 1 in.); the lower the VE value, the more consistent the movement production.

The practitioner might then use this information to instruct the learner to change her release point or perhaps apply less force when attempting her next series of dart throws. By keeping a record of periodic changes in the CE and VE of the individual's throws, the practitioner and the learner can determine which types of adjustments to make to produce the most dramatic reductions in bias (i.e., CE) and inconsistency (i.e., VE).

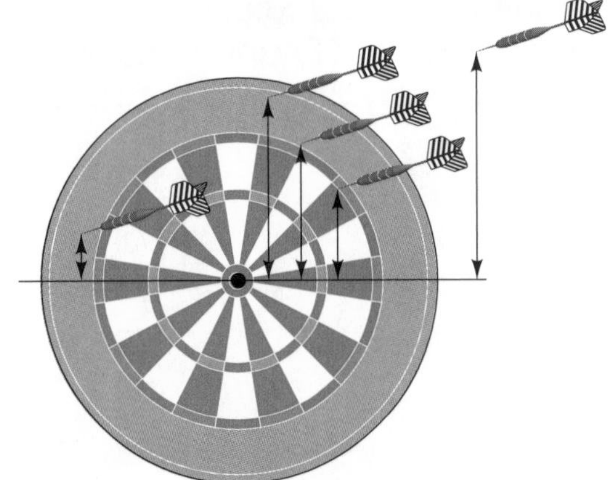

**Figure 7.1** Measure the distance the five darts landed above the target center to use in calculating the CE and VE.

**constant error (CE)**—The deviation, with respect to amount and direction, of the result of a person's movement relative to some target value. Average CE represents the average deviation of the results of several movement attempts.

**variable error (VE)**—The inconsistency of results of several movements with respect to the average constant error of the movements.

**Table 7.5**

**Movement Criteria for Assessing Human Gait**

| Criterion | Cues to watch for |
|---|---|
| *Minimal sway* | *Body is over base of support.* |
| *Arm opposition* | *Uses opposite arm and leg.* |
| *Minimal rise* | *Makes smooth recovery; smooth push-off.* |
| *Cushioning* | *Gives with the leg.* |
| *Leg support* | *Pushes down and backward.* |
| *Push-off* | *Presses with toes.* |

Adapted by permission from Knudson & Morrison, 1997.

**stimulus-identification stage**—The first stage of information processing; during this stage the individual recognizes and identifies the input.

**response-selection stage**—The second stage of information processing; during this stage the individual decides what, if any, response should be made.

**response-programming stage**—The third stage of information processing; during this stage the individual organizes the motor system to produce the desired movement.

## Some of the Observable Products of Learning

Learning can occur at all levels of the central nervous system, but the levels highlighted in figure 7.2 are probably the ones where the biggest changes take place. Some examples are (a) the increased use of automatic processes in analyzing sensory patterns (**stimulus identification**) that indicate the activity of external objects or events (e.g., the speed of an approaching object, the movements of other performers); (b) the improved selection (**response selection**) and parameterization (**response programming**) of movements (e.g., a shot on goal in ice hockey, driving a car in heavy traffic); and (c) the development of more effective motor programs and effector processes in the spinal cord (e.g., for advanced performance of activities like juggling, kayaking, and playing a musical instrument).

When practitioners see changes in observable performance characteristics, they can infer that changes have occurred at one or more of these levels and, therefore, in the learner's performance capability or skill. A number of observable characteristics change as people learn motor tasks (Magill, 1998). In the following paragraphs, we briefly summarize each of these and suggest some ways practitioners might examine them in assessing the progress of learners.

**Table 7.6**

**Arithmetic Calculations of Average Constant Error (CE) and Variable Error (VE) for the Dart-Throwing Example in Figure 7.1**

| Attempt | CE | VE |
|---|---|---|
| *1* | *+5* | $(+5) - (\mathbf{3}) = 2^2 = 4$ |
| *2* | *+3* | $(+3) - (\mathbf{3}) = 0^2 = 0$ |
| *3* | *+4* | $(+4) - (\mathbf{3}) = 1^2 = 1$ |
| *4* | *+1* | $(+1) - (\mathbf{3}) = -2^2 = 4$ |
| *5* | *+2* | $(+2) - (\mathbf{3}) = -1^2 = \underline{1}$ |
| | *Avg CE = +15/5 =* **3** | $VE = \sqrt{10/5} = \sqrt{2} = 1.4$ |

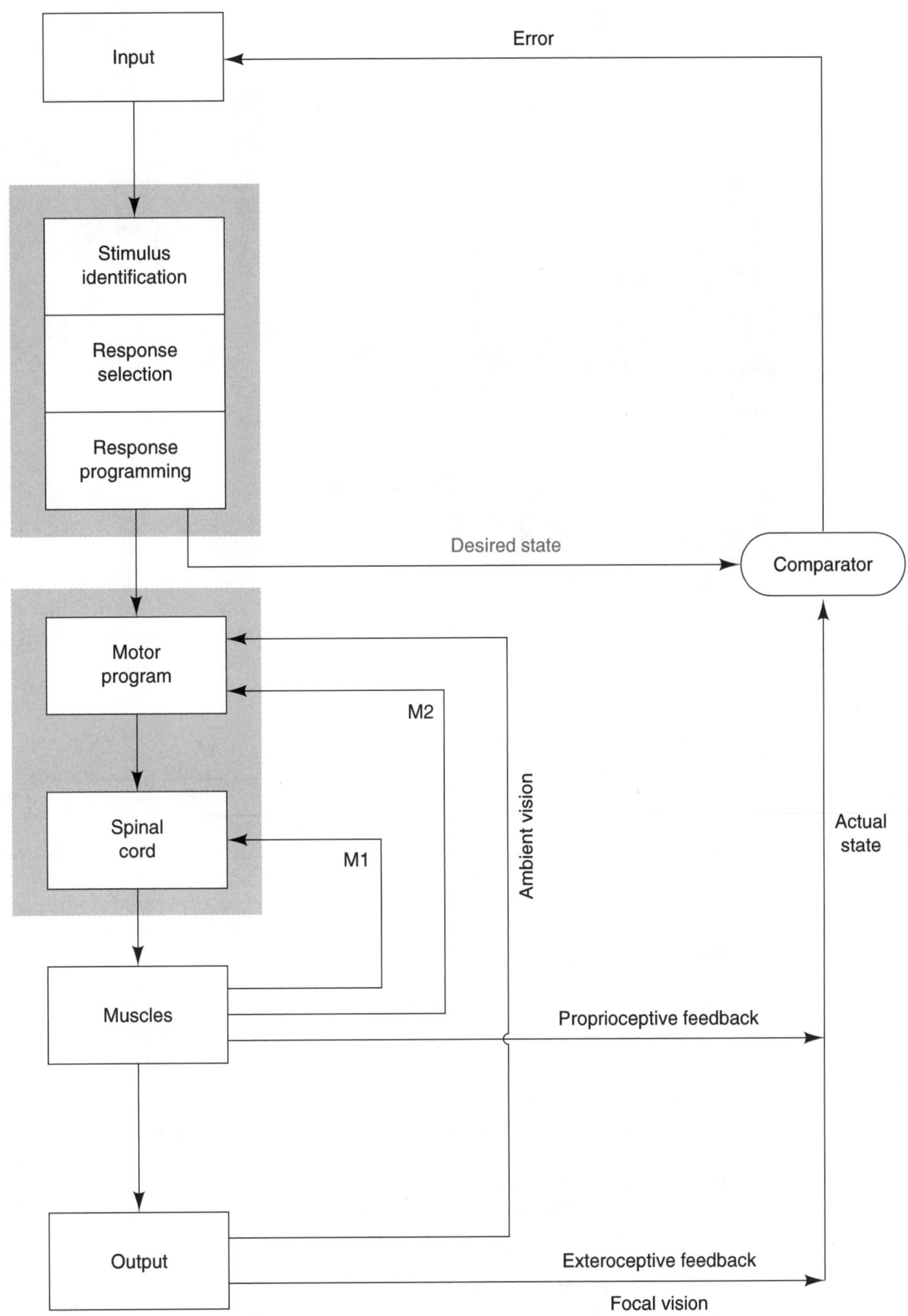


**Figure 7.2** The conceptual model of human performance, highlighting some of the major processes subject to alterations during practice.

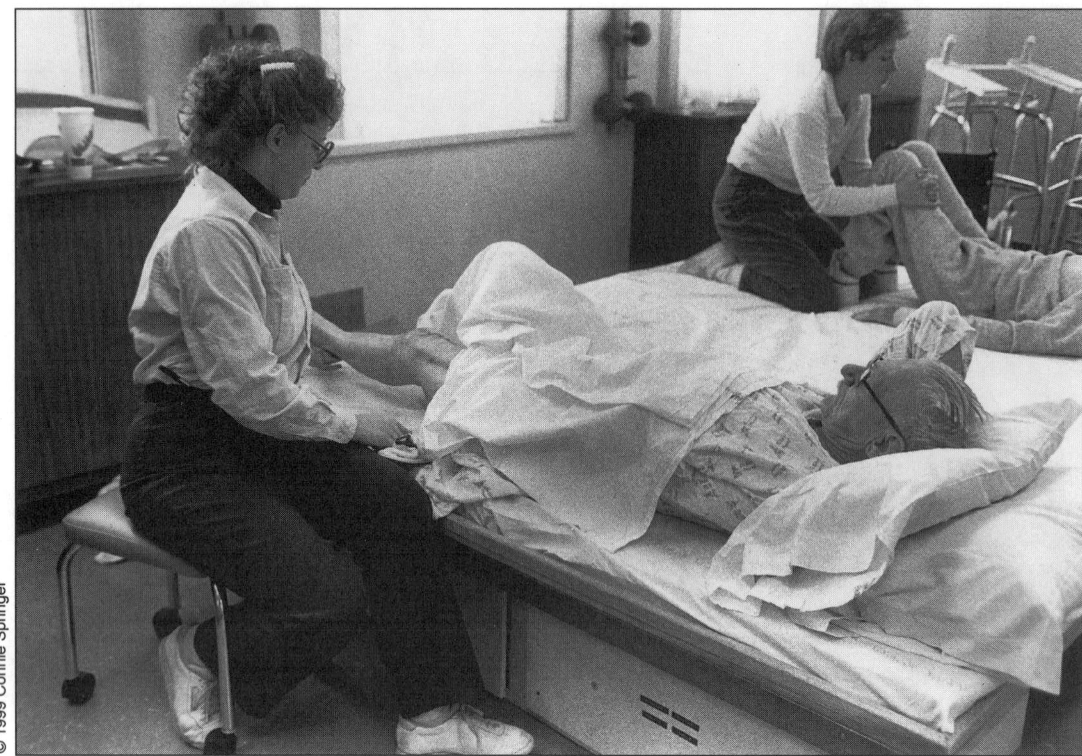


A therapist can measure range of motion and observe improvement in limb flexibility.

### Knowledge of Concepts

One characteristic of skilled performers is an understanding of the rules, strategies, and finer points of the activity. An advanced or expanded knowledge of these concepts allows accomplished individuals to assess task demands, determine the most appropriate actions, and effectively analyze the results of their performance. Put simply, skilled learners have a more sophisticated conceptual understanding of "what's going on" and "what needs to be done" as compared with novices, who may be able to comprehend a number of isolated facts but are not able to integrate them in a meaningful way (Housner, 1981; Tenenbaum & Bar-Eli, 1993). As the learners' knowledge improves, the instructors should be able to detect more rapid and appropriate decision making. One way to measure this is by charting the types and number of correct decisions or response-selection errors the learners make while performing in the target context.

### Control and Coordination

The movements of skilled individuals are characterized by a flowing quality that suggests more efficient control and a smoother coordination of joints and muscles. Research examining changes in control and coordination shows that individuals' movements become less stiff-looking after practice. In one study, Southard and Higgins (1987) examined changes in the coordination pattern of learners' backswings for the racquetball forehand shot. Initially, the pattern was characterized by similar limb velocities for the upper arm and forearm and by comparable joint angles at the elbow and wrist. After 10 days of practice, however, the pattern showed a higher limb velocity in the forearm than in the upper arm (indicating a more "whiplike" action) and an increase in joint angle at both the elbow and wrist (suggesting a more pronounced "bending" of the two joints). Instructors should notice an increase in the speed and "smoothness" of learners' movements as their control and coordination improves. The expert practitioner can assess these characteristics by using form ratings.

### Muscles Used

In addition to shifts in control and coordination, changes in the patterns of muscle activity also occur over practice. EMG studies have typically shown that learners initially demonstrate a pattern of activity characterized by the *simultaneous* contraction of agonist muscles (i.e., those that produce the action) and antagonist muscles (i.e., those that oppose the action), sometimes referred to as "co-contraction." With practice, however, the pattern shifts to one of sequential contraction, with agonists and antagonists, respectively, contracting only at the appropriate and necessary times (Moore & Marteniuk, 1986). Behaviorally, learners' movements should appear more fluid over practice as the amount of co-contraction is diminished. Again, form ratings may be the best way for practitioners to assess the quality of "smoothness."

### Movement Efficiency

Not surprisingly, the energy costs of learners' movements diminish with practice as well (Sparrow & Irizarry-Lopez, 1987). As control, coordination, and the patterns of muscle activity become more efficient, the amount of energy required to perform the movement is reduced. Perhaps this is one reason why accomplished performers are able to produce effective actions for extended periods of time. Behaviorally, individuals should appear progressively less fatigued during performance bouts or be able to sustain their performance for longer time periods. A possible outcome measure of efficiency might be the length of time individuals are able to continue performing a standard amount of activity. Practitioners might also ask individuals to rate their perception of exertion at the end of a learning session, particularly when task performance includes a significant endurance component.

### Attention

An important characteristic of skilled performers is their attentional proficiency (Abernethy, 1993). Accomplished individuals are not only able to sustain attention for longer periods of time, but are also adept at identifying and attending to those cues that are most essential to successful performance. Behavioral indicators of improved attention include more rapid recognition of and response to complex patterns of environmental stimuli (e.g., different movements of an opponent, unfamiliar traffic patterns, playing with a new band), an "unhurried" appearance when performing open skills, and the capability of adjusting quickly to unexpected events (e.g., the "bad bounce" of a ball). Practitioners might assess the progress of learners by measuring their reaction times in particular situations or by subjectively rating their overall recognition capability during a performance bout. As performers improve their skills, the attention demands of their movements diminish. Such reductions are often evidenced by more free-flowing and fluid movements and by the capacity to do several things at once.

### Error Detection and Correction

As individuals become more proficient in producing their movements, they also become more adept at recognizing and correcting errors that occur (Liu & Wrisberg, 1997). Errors may be due to faulty movement selection (e.g., the dancer who confuses or transposes several parts of a sequence) or to improper execution of the intended action (e.g., the diver who fails to completely extend the arms prior to entry into the water). With practice, learners begin to pay more attention to relevant feedback information, both proprioceptive (e.g., joint position) and exteroceptive (e.g., vision and audition), which they use to detect performance errors (e.g., the sight, sound, and feel of an errant shot in darts, tennis, or ice hockey). Behaviorally,

© Curt Beamer

As performers improve their skills, the attention demands of their movements diminish and their capacity to do and observe several things simultaneously improves.

individuals performing continuous skills (e.g., driving a car, in-line skating, skiing) should demonstrate the capacity to adjust their movements more effectively during the action. Discrete skill participants (e.g., kicking, throwing, striking) should be able to provide an accurate assessment of their mistakes after the movement is completed and explain how they intend to correct them on the next attempt.

## Deciding When and How Often to Assess Progress

There are really no hard and fast rules for determining when and how often practitioners should assess the progress of learners. As we mentioned previously, the best evaluations are those conducted in contexts similar to the ones in which the learned action must eventually be produced (e.g., at home for the patient, in a jam session for the musician, in a mixed doubles match for the tennis player). Therefore, practitioners should attempt to simulate the target context as much as possible when assessing learners' performance. Instructors should also be aware of temporary factors (e.g., mood, fatigue) that might alter learners' performance and attempt to evaluate performance under conditions that minimize the influence of such factors. The practitioner's goal is to conduct evaluations under the kinds of circumstances that allow the most valid assessments of skill.

To some extent decisions about when and how often to assess a person's skill depend on the needs of the individual learner. In some cases, individuals may wish to have an initial assessment of their performance in order to determine those areas in need of particular attention and to serve as a reference point for subsequent performance improvements. The best time for initial assessment is probably after the learner acquires a basic capability for producing the goal movement. After that, practitioners might conduct periodic evaluations to determine the effectiveness of instructional interventions and to provide learners with helpful information about their progress toward goal achievement.

## Summary

Learning experiences take many forms, and movement practitioners need to be aware of a number of factors when attempting to design experiences that are productive for learners. Two concepts that can be helpful to practitioners are goal setting and transfer of learning. Once learners know which movements they want to be able to perform (target skills) and where they want to be able to perform them (target context), the process of goal setting can begin. Some of the key aspects of goal setting are summarized as follows:

- Learners should have input in the goal-setting process.
- Goals should serve as road maps to successful performance of the target skill(s) in the target context(s).
- Goals should be challenging, attainable, realistic, and specific (CARS).
- Learners should be encouraged to set performance goals (focused on self-referenced improvement) and process goals (focused on correct movement execution) in addition to outcome goals (focused on the achievement of some external standard of performance or favorable comparisons with other individuals).

To enhance transfer of learning, practitioners should do the following things:

- Direct learners' attention to elements of previously learned tasks that may be similar to those of the target skill
- Provide opportunities for learners to practice tasks that contain elements that are similar to those of the target skill
- Allow learners to practice the target skill in situations that are similar to the target context

Practitioners need to remember that learners differ with respect to level of motivation, types of past experiences, types of abilities, and stage of learning. Practitioners should maximize each individual's learning experience by

- designing experiences that are relevant to the needs and interests of the learner,
- allowing the learner to experience successful goal achievement,
- encouraging the learner to focus on the improvements in their own skill level rather than on comparisons between their performance and that of others, and
- considering the individual's stage of learning when providing instructional assistance.

When assessing learners' progress, practitioners should remember to select measures that

- represent observable characteristics of the target skill,
- are valid indicators of goal achievement,
- reflect both outcome and process aspects of the target skill, and
- provide learners with meaningful feedback about their skill improvements and level of goal achievement.

## From Principles to Practice

Check your understanding of the material in this chapter by responding to the following questions and then completing the application exercises. In each case, see if you can identify the most relevant questions or issues and then propose a solution based on the concepts and principles discussed in the chapter.

### Checking Your Understanding

1. What are four important goal-setting principles practitioners should keep in mind when assisting an individual who wants to learn a particular skill? How might a practitioner apply each of the principles in assisting a person who is learning how to roller skate?
2. Discuss the relationships among target skills, target behaviors, and target contexts. For one of the following activities, give an example of a target skill, a target behavior, and a target context: fly-fishing, billiards, using a prosthetic hand while eating a baked potato, piloting an airplane, shooting a basketball.
3. Sometimes the past movement experiences a person brings to a learning situation can help the individual pick up the new skill more quickly. Discuss three categories of elements that might be shared by two motor skills and then give an example of each type of element that might be similar for one of the following pairs of skills: white-water canoeing and snow skiing, operating an automobile and operating a speedboat, wheelchair basketball and wheelchair floor hockey.
4. When assessing learners' progress, practitioners should select both outcome and process measures that are valid indicators of performance. Give an example of a valid outcome measure and a valid process measure for one of the following activities: hang gliding, bocci, rappelling, operating a lathe, reading braille, playing the flute, shuffling a deck of playing cards.

### Application Exercise #1

A teenager wants to learn how to perform a back handspring.

*It Depends*

- How much experience has the person had with other gymnastics activities?
- Where does the individual want to be able to perform the back handspring (i.e., what is the target context)?
- What are the information-processing demands of the target skill?
- What are the observable movement characteristics that accompany successful performance of the task?
- How strong and flexible is the individual?

*Strategy*

Define the target skill and the target context. Determine the types of past experiences the person has had that might transfer to the learning of the back handspring. Determine the information-processing demands of the task. Determine the observable movement characteristics associated with successful performance and the possible ways they might be measured accurately. Set process goals, performance goals, and outcome goals that can be used to assess the individual's progress.

*Response Example*

- Determine the stimulus-identification, response-selection, and response-programming demands of the back handspring.
- Identify movement elements, perceptual elements, and conceptual elements the individual might transfer from previous movement experiences to the learning of the back handspring.
- Encourage the learner to set process and performance goals that are challenging, attainable, realistic, and specific.
- Identify outcome and process characteristics that are valid indicators of skill improvement.
- Determine how, when, and under what circumstances assessments of progress might be made.

### Application Exercise #2

A varsity golfer on his college team is convinced that he needs to make some major changes in his swing mechanics in order to "take his game to the next level."

*It Depends*

- How long has the individual been playing golf?
- How long has the individual been using his current swing pattern?
- What other aspects of his game (e.g., stimulus identification, response selection) might be preventing the person from improving his level of play?
- How observable are the aspects of his swing mechanics that he wants to improve?

*Strategy*

Define the target skill (i.e., what the golfer wants to be able to do with the desired swing pattern) and the target behaviors (i.e., observable characteristics of the desired swing pattern). Determine whether other factors besides swing mechanics might be contributing to unsatisfactory outcomes (e.g., insufficient stimulus identification, competitive anxiety, anger, inconsistent mental focus). Identify process and performance goals that focus the individual's attention on the desired swing pattern. Decide which outcome and process measures to use when assessing the player's progress, as well as where and how often assessments should take place.

## Application Exercise #3

A wheelchair patient, paralyzed from the waist down, wants to obtain his driver's license. He has purchased a car that has the necessary control devices for safe operation.

*It Depends*

- Does the individual have any other physical or mental impairments?
- How long has the individual been paralyzed?
- Does the individual have any previous driving experience (i.e., prior to being paralyzed)?
- Which information-processing demands are the most problematic?
- In what contexts does the individual want to be able to drive the car?

*Strategy*

Obtain a copy of the driver-training manual that describes the conditions a physically challenged person must satisfy to obtain a driver's license. Determine the target skills and target behaviors needed for the individual to achieve his goal. Set process and performance goals that focus the person's attention on effective performance (i.e., accurate stimulus identification, correct response selection, appropriate response programming). Decide when, how often, and under what circumstances assessments of progress should be made. Determine valid outcome and process measures for assessing the level of goal achievement.

## Application Exercise #4

A young woman has spent many hours and a considerable amount of her money on flying lessons. She has tried several times to obtain a pilot's license but each time she has failed to achieve the necessary score. The individual is frustrated and wonders what more she can do to improve her chances of passing the test.

*It Depends*

- Is the individual able to produce effective performance of the required tasks when she is not in the test situation?
- What aspects of the test have been difficult for the individual?
- Has the person had problems with the same things every time she has taken the test?
- How does the individual feel and what is she thinking about when she is taking the test?

*Strategy*

Identify the factors that are contributing to the woman's subpar performance on the tests. Determine whether she needs to develop additional skills (e.g., arousal adjustment) to enhance her performance in the test situation. Create practice conditions that closely simulate those of the test situation (i.e., target context).

8

# Supplementing the Learning Experience

## Chapter Outline



## Chapter Objectives

**When you have completed this chapter, you should be able to**

discuss instructional techniques movement practitioners can use to supplement individuals' learning experiences and to assist them during practice sessions;

explain the concepts of attention control and arousal regulation, and describe how practitioners might assist learners with each;

discuss the value of balancing practice and rest periods during and between learning sessions;

explain the function of instructions and demonstrations, and discuss the principles practitioners should keep in mind when providing these forms of assistance;

describe the advantages and disadvantages of guidance procedures; and

discuss several techniques of physical rehearsal and mental rehearsal that individuals might use during skill learning.

# Preview

A young woman asks a skilled skier to help her learn to water ski. The skilled individual obviously knows what it feels like to ski correctly, yet he also remembers how difficult it was to "get over the hump" when he was first learning. He wants to help the novice skier but isn't exactly sure how to go about it. What should he tell her? Should he demonstrate the skill for her? What other types of instructional assistance should he provide? When should he allow her to rehearse the movement in an unassisted fashion?

# Overview

The questions the skiing expert is asking himself are like those all movement practitioners ask when they are preparing for instruction. Most practitioners want to help learners without becoming a distraction to them. Formal learning experiences are cooperative efforts between learners and practitioners. Learners must be able to identify the skills they want to learn and the contexts in which they want to be able to perform them. Practitioners must be able to assist learners in achieving the goals they set.

Once learners have set their goals and have identified appropriate target skills, they must be introduced to the learning task and be given sufficient opportunity to practice it. In this chapter we examine a number of instructional techniques practitioners might use to supplement an individual's learning experience. First, we suggest several issues instructors should consider when attempting to create a learning atmosphere that is open and nonthreatening for learners. These include familiarizing learners with the instructional situation, opening communication, directing learners' attention to task-relevant information, creating optimal arousal levels, and balancing practice and rest. After that, we discuss ways instructors can assist individuals in achieving a general idea of the learning task. These include instructions, demonstrations, and guidance procedures. Finally, we describe several forms of physical and mental rehearsal techniques that practitioners might incorporate during skill instruction.

# Preliminary Considerations

The difference between good teachers and great teachers, it has been said, is that great teachers pay more attention to details. Some of the "details" that contribute to effective instruction include familiarizing learners with the learning situation, developing open communication with learners, directing learners' attention to sources of important task-related information, and diminishing learners' anxiety. In addition, effective instructors give some consideration to balancing practice and rest periods, particularly if fatigued performance might put learners at risk.

## Familiarizing Learners and Opening Communication

Effective public speakers use a simple sequence: They begin their presentations by outlining what they intend to say. After that, they say what they said they were going to say, and then they conclude by reiterating what they have just said. By preparing their audiences in this way, speakers increase the receptivity of listeners to the content of their presentations. In a similar vein, movement practitioners can increase the receptivity of learners by familiarizing them with the instructional process. Taking the time to alert individuals to what they can expect during learning sessions can go a long way in diminishing their uncertainty and alleviating their concerns.

Let's face it. Most of us are apprehensive when we encounter unfamiliar situations. It's natural to ask ourselves, what is this going to be like? Will I do the right things? Is this instructor going to embarrass me if I make a mistake?

Instructional situations provide individuals with many opportunities to experience success, and most people are motivated by success. However, formal learning experiences may also be threatening for some people if they are afraid of making mistakes. These individuals approach new learning with a cautious attitude; they don't want to take risks that may lead to failure and personal embarrassment (Ames, 1992). When individuals are familiarized with the learning situation and made to feel that they can expect support and encouragement from the practitioner, they are more willing to take the kinds of risks that lead to improvements in performance.

*Familiarization*, in addition to alleviating the concerns of individuals, can establish an open line of *two-way communication* between the practitioner and the learner. When practitioners establish this type of communication, they send a message to learners that they are concerned about providing the best instructional assistance possible. Learners who have questions or concerns feel more free to communicate them to the practitioner. When they do, the practitioner is able to provide the kind of assistance that is best suited to the learner.

Let's say that the skiing instructor in this chapter's preview scenario feels he first needs to explain the main points of waterskiing and then demonstrate several components, so that the learner can get a picture of the actions she should try to produce. If he has established open communication with the learner, she should feel free to let him know whether this is going to be helpful or whether she would like some other form of assistance. Based on what we know about the limited attentional capacity of humans, it is possible that giving both a verbal description and a visual demonstration represents more information than the learner can handle all at once. Practitioners need to remember that more information may not necessarily be better, and that the person who is in the best position to determine how much information is "too much" is the learner. Therefore, it is important for practitioners to establish the type of open two-way communication that maximizes the efficiency of instruction.

**attentional focus**—The act of directing attention to information sources or the object of an individual's attention. A person can direct his or her focus to external or internal sources of information and can narrow or broaden the focus to include few or many stimuli.

## Directing Attention

Since the attentional capacity of individuals is limited and this capacity is diminished even further when performers are anxious, it is important for practitioners to be able to assist learners in directing their **attentional focus** to the most relevant sources of task information at all times. Nideffer (1995) has suggested some helpful guidelines for doing this.

According to Nideffer, there are two dimensions of attention that individuals have the capability of controlling (see figure 8.1). The first dimension deals with the *direction* of attentional focus—an **external focus** is used when individuals attend to cues or information in the environment, whereas an **internal focus** is employed when people attend to their own thoughts or feelings. The second dimension concerns the *width* of attentional focus—a **narrow focus** is one that encompasses a small amount of information, whereas a **broad focus** is one that is sensitive to a large number of cues at the same time.

In learning situations, practitioners can instruct individuals to direct their attention to any of a number of internal or external sources of information. A therapy patient might be asked to direct his attention to the feeling in his left knee (internal-narrow focus) as he attempts a particular strengthening exercise, a golfer might be instructed to close her eyes and attend to the feel of the full swing (internal-broad focus), a softball pitcher might be told to focus on the center of the catcher's glove

**external focus**—The act of attending to sources of information in the environment.

**internal focus**—The act of attending to internal information (e.g., thoughts, feelings, kinesthetic cues).

**narrow focus**—The act of attending to a narrow range of information at one time.

**broad focus**—The act of attending to a wide range of information at one time.

| Direction of focus / Width of focus | Narrow | Broad |
|---|---|---|
| Internal | Feeling in the left knee | Feel of the full golf swing |
| External | Center of the catcher's glove | Movements of opposing players |

Figure 8.1 Nideffer (1995) conceptualizes two dimensions of attention: direction (internal and external) and width (narrow and broad).

(external-narrow focus), and a rugby player might be encouraged to focus on the movements of opposing players attempting to advance the ball (external-broad focus).

The challenge, of course, for practitioners is to determine the optimal focus for each task. Landin (1994) suggests that when someone gives instructional cues for **open skills**, the teacher should direct learners' attention to important environmental information (i.e., an *external focus*), which then "triggers" the necessary motor response. Consistent with Landin's suggestion, Wulf, Höß, and Prinz (1998) found that directing individuals' attention to an environmental cue (i.e., the wheels of a slalom ski simulator, a narrow-external focus) during practice sessions produced better learning of this open skill than did directing the participants' attention to the forces exerted by their feet (i.e., a narrow-internal focus).

Practitioners can also encourage learners to direct their attention to different aspects of the target skill at different times. For example, a golfer might be instructed to first focus her attention on the environment in order to determine (*assess*) the conditions for the next shot (*analyze*), then to shift her attention to the possible ways she might hit the shot, then to narrow her attention on the image of the exact shot she intends to hit (*rehearse*), and finally to shift her focus to the point on the golf ball that she intends to strike with the club head (*perform*).

**open skill**—A skill performed in an environment that is unpredictable or in motion and that requires individuals to adapt their movements in response to dynamic properties of the environment.

By assisting learners in identifying task-relevant cues and then encouraging them to direct their attention to the most appropriate cues or information at all times, practitioners are encouraging the development of attention control. With practice,

Learners may view instruction as threatening or as an opportunity for improvement. Good two-way communication can reassure individuals and open doors to helpful assistance.

learners become more adept at managing their attention, which in turn contributes to their goal achievement.

## Managing Arousal

As we mentioned earlier, learners often perceive formal instructional settings to be threatening. The available research suggests that people's anxiety is particularly high when they feel that their performance is being evaluated (see Wrisberg, 1994). For individuals in the early stages of learning, elevated **anxiety** and **arousal** can contribute to the production of ineffective movements. Fortunately, there are a couple of things practitioners can do to assist learners in maintaining arousal levels that do not seriously impair their performance.

First, the practitioner might emphasize **process goals** rather than **outcome goals**. For example, learners in activities like tennis, golf, bowling, soccer, cricket, and curling might be encouraged to set a goal that involves following through on every movement attempt. This type of goal is likely to produce less anxiety than one that requires individuals to achieve some external performance standard (e.g., 7 out of 10 shots landing within 20 cm of the target). Second, practitioners might assure that each learner sets goals that are realistic. What is realistic for one learner may be unrealistic for another. As long as individuals perceive that their capabilities are sufficient to meet the demands of the task, they are going to be less anxious when performing.

**anxiety**—A person's uneasiness or distress about future uncertainties; a perception of threat to the self. Often characterized by elevated arousal levels.

**arousal**—The level of activation or excitement of the central nervous system; varies from extremely low levels during sleep to extremely high levels during intense physical activity and excitement.

**process goals**—Targets for performance improvement that focus on the quality of movement production.

**outcome goals**—Targets for performance improvement that focus on the end result of the activity.

## Balancing Practice and Rest

The scheduling of practice is another concern of practitioners who are designing a program of instruction. Practitioners may need to decide how many days per week

### SHORTER PRACTICE SESSIONS SPREAD OUT ARE BETTER THAN LONGER ONES BUNCHED TOGETHER

The results of a study by Baddeley and Longman (1978) indicate that there is some upper limit to the amount of practice individuals can effectively perform per day. In this study, postal trainees receiving 60 hours of practice learned how to operate mail-sorting machines far more effectively when their practice sessions were shorter and more spread out (1-hour sessions once a day for 12 weeks) than when they were longer and bunched together (2-hour sessions twice a day for 3 weeks). It is possible that individuals who practiced according to the more spread out or "spaced" format learned better because after the longer layoff they had to devote more attention to "relearning" the material each day, and therefore learned it better (we explore the possible learning benefits of spaced repetitions in greater depth in the next chapter).

Another reason shorter practice periods may be more effective is that they are less tiresome for learners. When practice sessions are longer, practitioners need to find ways to sustain learners' interest and attention (e.g., coaches may rotate athletes from individual skill rehearsal to small group rehearsal, to large group rehearsal, to discussions of strategy). If the practitioner is successful in doing this, learners may be able to practice for longer periods of time without reducing their efficiency.

learners should practice, whether to provide days in which there is no practice, how much learners should practice each day, and how much learners should rest during a practice period so that fatigue does not become a problem. Some of these issues have been studied in laboratory settings, and the results have several interesting and useful implications.

When supervising the long-term practice of movement skills, as in coaching an athletic team or monitoring the recovery of a stroke patient, instructors might first decide how often per week learners can practice. In some cases, there is a limit to the amount of time that is available for instruction. For example, coaches may be restricted by the rules of their sport to a certain number of weeks of practice prior to the competitive season, or therapists may be limited by the terms of a health insurance policy to a certain period of time for patient rehabilitation. However, the available research suggests that practice sessions that are shorter and more spread out are more effective than those that are longer and bunched together (e.g., Baddeley & Longman, 1978).

**massed practice**—A practice schedule in which the amount of rest between practice attempts or between practice sessions is relatively shorter than the amount of time spent practicing.

**distributed practice**—A practice schedule in which the amount of rest between practice attempts or between practice sessions is relatively longer than the amount of time spent practicing.

Researchers have devoted more time to the study of performance-rest ratios *within* practice sessions than *between* sessions. Depending on the relative amounts of performance and rest provided, experimenters have defined practice sessions to be either *massed* or *distributed* in nature. There is no fixed dividing line between massed and distributed practice, but **massed practice** usually means less rest between performance attempts, whereas **distributed practice** means more.

Researchers interested in the influence of massed and distributed practice schedules on skill learning (see Lee & Genovese, 1988, for a review) have looked at the effects of physical and mental fatigue on learning processes. Generally speaking, the effects of the various performance and rest schedules seem to be different for discrete and continuous tasks. For discrete tasks, such as shooting a basketball, fielding a baseball, or fastening a button, reducing the rest time between performance attempts has little or no influence on learning, and in some cases less rest may even be beneficial.

For continuous skills, such as handwriting, beating eggs, swimming, cycling, skiing, and skating, fatiguelike states are more apt to build up within a performance bout, so practitioners might expect that decreasing the amount of rest between performance attempts would hurt learning more. The bulk of the laboratory research suggests support for this notion—less rest between performance bouts degrades performance and has a relatively permanent influence on learning (i.e., performance on subsequent occasions).

There are several practical implications of this research. First, because even very little rest between practice attempts of discrete tasks does not seem to diminish learning, fatigue during practice sessions should not be a worrisome problem. Thus, for practices that last a short period of time, instructors should encourage learners to perform as many repetitions of the task as possible. The challenge here is to increase the number of repetitions without becoming repetitious in a boring or mechanical way, and practitioners can achieve this goal by giving careful thought to the structure of practice sessions (see chapter 9). Second, for continuous tasks or for tasks that contain an element of physical risk (e.g., gymnastics activities or, for elders, certain balance tasks), fatigue can be a problem, generating a sloppy performance that could lead to reduced learning or a serious accident or fall. In these situations, instructors and therapists should assure that sufficient rest is provided between practice attempts.

What factors determine the performance-rest balance that is most effective for learning? One important factor is the energy requirements of the task. Practitioners should analyze the physical demands of tasks they are teaching in order to tailor practice conditions to the energy requirements of the movements. Instructors should also be sensitive to the fitness levels of learners when teaching tasks that place individuals at risk when performed in a fatigued state.

## Graw's Experiment on Optimal Practice-Rest Ratios

In 1968 Graw studied different combinations of practice and rest on two balance tasks, making the percentage of time actually spent in physical practice either 20%, 30%, 40%, 57%, or 77% of the total 30-min practice period. He examined this schedule with the stabilometer balance board task and the Bachman ladder task (see figure 8.2, a-b). Then he tested for learning by administering a transfer test, which he gave on the second day. For the stabilometer task, the optimal condition for learning occurred when 57% of the time was spent practicing. For the Bachman ladder task, the 30% practice condition was best. It is clear from these results that there is no single optimal practice-rest ratio for all learning tasks: the ladder task was learned most effectively when more time was spent resting, whereas the stabilometer task was learned best when more time was spent practicing.

Some task differences determine which schedule is most effective for learning. Energy cost, for example, is one important factor. The energy costs with the Bachman ladder task are relatively large (the learner must climb a free-standing ladder quickly, over and over, during the trial's duration). In the stabilometer task, in contrast, less energy is required for balancing (little movement occurs in the major muscle groups). These differences suggest that instructors should first analyze the requirements of a task in order to determine the optimal practice-rest ratio.

Figure 8.2 The stabilometer balance board (*a*) and the Bachman ladder-climb task (*b*).

# Skill Presentation Techniques

In discussing the stages of learning in the last chapter, we emphasized that a knowledge of learner characteristics in each stage can help practitioners design beneficial learning experiences. The primary goal of people during the initial stage of learning is to acquire a general idea of the movement. The challenge for practitioners, then, is to provide learners with the types of assistance that allow them to achieve this goal.

For the young woman learning to water ski (see this chapter's preview scenario), the general idea of waterskiing probably includes some image of the elements of correct form, a sense of what a person needs to do to achieve a general approximation of this form, and an awareness of the pattern of sensory feedback that arises during successful performance attempts. The instructor's job, then, is to select and implement instructional methods that assist the learner in her efforts. And there are a number of techniques practitioners can use to introduce individuals to the learning situation and help them acquire a general idea of the desired movement(s). These methods are grouped under the categories of instructions, demonstrations, and guidance procedures.

## Selecting the Right Types of Instructional Assistance

Instructional assistance is important for skill improvement in many tasks. However, not all assistance appears to be of equal value. In a recent study (Beek & van Santvoord, 1992), young adult volunteers were taught to juggle three balls in a cascade, or figure-8, pattern. Prior to practice, all participants received the following sequence of instructions:

1. Take one ball and throw it from one hand to the other. Throw it from about waist height to a point level with the top of your head.
2. Hold one ball in each hand. Throw the right-hand ball in an arc toward your left hand. As it peaks, throw the second ball in an arc underneath it toward the right hand. Catch the first ball in your left hand and the second in your right.
3. Hold two balls in your right hand and one in your left. Throw the first ball in your right hand toward your left one. As it peaks, throw the ball in the left hand toward the right. As the second ball peaks, throw the final ball from your right hand. Catch none of the balls.
4. Do as before, but now catch the balls and throw them as the previously thrown ball peaks. Keep on repeating the sequence, and you are juggling (p. 88).

Participants practiced these tasks for three half-hour sessions on separate days and then were divided into two groups for a final seven sessions. One group continued practicing as before, while the other group attempted to synchronize their throws (or catches) in time with a metronome that was set at a preferred rhythm by each participant.

The researchers used a high-speed motion picture camera and film motion analyzer to evaluate the progress of participants. The results revealed that improved skill seemed to be associated with the identification of fixed points in space. Once participants determined these points, their performance became more accurate, consistent, and flexible. In some cases individuals added their own stylistic "flair." The metronome proved to be of little or no additional assistance, possibly because the participants had not achieved sufficient levels of juggling skill to allow them to match the tempo of their movements to that of the metronome. Nevertheless, these findings suggest that instructions offering information about spatial anchors in the environment (see how many you can find by looking again at the instructions) can be quite helpful initially for individuals learning closed skills like juggling.

## Instructions

© Terry Wild

Juggling balls in a cascade.

Instructions are a feature of nearly every formal teaching setting. Practitioners usually provide them in spoken form, although they might be written, and the instructions typically contain general information about the fundamental aspects of the skill. Such aspects might include how the skill is used in particular situations (e.g., in a group activity, in sport competition, with a partner), tips on where and how to move, points concerning how to hold a piece of apparatus or other implement (e.g., a ball, a guitar, a walker, a javelin, a welding torch), what to pay attention to (e.g., the seams of the ball, the frets on a guitar, hand position or posture for an elderly person learning to use a walker to assist locomotion), and what to do (e.g., press and hold, extend the arms, keep the wrists firm).

Practitioners can also use instructions to emphasize similarities between skills, a concept we discussed in chapter 7. A *verbal cue* or phrase, such as "Throw the racket head at the ball," is a useful instruction that alerts a person learning how to serve a tennis ball to the similarity between the arm action of the overarm throw and the arm action of the serve (Landin, 1994). In other activities it is helpful for instructors to use consistent labels for similar skills: for example, emphasizing that "kips" on the horizontal bar, rings, and mat are really the same movement and then referring to all these movements as kips, regardless of the gymnastics event individuals are practicing. Many skills have similar mechanical principles that practitioners can emphasize in their instructions (e.g., shifting body momentum when throwing, keeping the head still when striking an object, or maintaining a wide base of support when balancing or lifting). Used in these ways, instructions can serve as helpful reminders of previously experienced principles that individuals can apply to the learning of a new activity.

Instructions can also provide learners with information about what they might expect when performing the skill (e.g., "You should feel a firm tug in your shoulders during this movement"). Instructions that contain information like this help raise the awareness of beginners, facilitate improvements in their skill, and boost their confidence. Simple, direct statements that start people off on the right track can serve them effectively in the long run as well. An axiom in the construction industry states that the most important part of a structure is its foundation. In a similar vein, helpful instructions are an important part of the foundation of skill learning.

Instructions can be ineffective, though. One problem with words is that sometimes they fail to describe the subtle aspects of movements. For example, biomechanical or physical principles of movements, dealing with concepts such as the transfer of momentum and action-reaction, are not always clearly communicated in

### INSTRUCTIONS ARE SOMETIMES DIFFICULT TO CONVEY IN SPOKEN FORM

Try to describe the process of tying shoelaces, opening a combination lock, peeling an apple, or doing a cartwheel. Which instructions are easier to convey in spoken form? Which are more difficult? Why?

words. Verbal descriptions of this kind of information may be useful, but they presume that individuals understand the principles well enough to apply them to the new skill they are trying to learn. And even when they do, there is no guarantee that this knowledge is helpful for performance (Wulf & Weigelt, 1997).

Practitioners can also provide too much information in their instructions. When this happens learners have trouble remembering everything that was said—particularly if some time elapses between when learners hear the instructions and when they must attempt the movement. Recall from chapter 3 that our **short-term memory** for once-presented materials is limited in capacity to just a few items, that forgetting is rapid (occurring in about 30 s), and that information in short-term memory is subject to interference from other inputs (e.g., the sight of an emergency vehicle or the reminder from a friend to pick up a can of tomatoes on the way home). Therefore, instructions that contain more than one or two key points are usually forgotten by the time the learner gets around to attempting the skill for the first time.

**short-term memory (STM)**—The memory system that allows individuals to retrieve, rehearse, process, and transfer information to long-term memory; believed to be limited in capacity and brief in duration.

All of this strongly implies that practitioners should keep their instructions brief and to the point, emphasizing no more than one or two major concepts at a time. In order to make instructions more meaningful to learners, teachers and therapists should try to relate them to things the individual has previously learned, which can be transferred to the new skill. For example, a therapy patient who is trying to learn to lift his feet when walking on a thick carpet can be reminded of the kind of foot movements he used to use when walking through high grass. Spacing instructions throughout the first few minutes of practice—giving only the most elementary information first, then adding finer details—minimizes forgetting. All of these considerations are particularly relevant for young and elderly learners, as well as for those who are mentally challenged, because they have a more **limited attentional capacity** for processing information.

**limited attentional capacity**—The notion that humans can only concentrate on a small amount of information at one time; curtails the ability to process information.

## Demonstrations

Good companions to instructions are various forms of visual information, such as still pictures of proper actions; film clips or videotapes of successful performances; and demonstrations provided by the instructor, the therapist, or some other skilled individual (sometimes referred to as **modeling**). The familiar adage "A picture is worth a thousand words" seems to be particularly true when it comes to the learning of motor skills, because movement information can often be more easily transmitted by a visual demonstration than by a verbal description.

**modeling**—A practice procedure that involves the demonstration of a skill for the benefit of a person who is trying to learn the skill.

In many ways, much of our movement learning comes as the result of attempts to reproduce what we see. Observing an action prior to attempts to reproduce it is known as **observational learning**. How observational learning works prior to actual movement is a question that has stimulated considerable debate. Nevertheless, there is little doubt that a considerable amount of learning, particularly early in practice, comes from studying and imitating the actions of others. Effective movement practitioners regularly capitalize on this phenomenon in instructional settings.

**observational learning**—The process by which learners acquire the capability for action by observing the performance of others.

### IT DEPENDS . . .

A lot can be learned by simply physically experiencing a movement. However, to do this, learners sometimes need a few instructions that point them in the direction of goal achievement. What few basic instructions might you give an individual who wants to *begin* experiencing what it's like to play a guitar? Shoot an arrow at a target? Hit a pitched ball with a bat?

How would you know if your instructions were effective?

## IT DEPENDS . . .

Sometimes instructions can contain concepts that individuals have previously experienced, which they can then transfer to the learning of a new task (e.g., "Hit the handball just as if you were throwing it"). Can you think of some transferable concepts that a practitioner might use to assist a person learning to drive a car? Head a soccer ball? Throw a Frisbee? Do a front dive?

## INFANT IMITATION

Researchers at the University of Otago in New Zealand ("Memory study," 1997) have demonstrated that infants as young as 6 months of age are able to mimic actions they have seen a day earlier. In this study, 6-, 12-, and 18-month-old babies watched an adult pull a mitten off a hand puppet, jingle a bell that was hidden inside the mitten, and then put the mitten back on the puppet's hand. When offered the puppet a day later, all three groups of babies were able to reproduce the action they had seen previously. However, only the 12- and 18-month-old babies were able to reproduce the action after longer periods of time (up to 1 month for the 18-month-olds) and in different places.

Apparently, whether the model is an unskilled peer or a skilled teacher/therapist is of only minor importance (McCullagh, 1986, 1987). The main thing is that the actions of the model must display some of the essential features of the skill. Of course, demonstrations and modeling cannot be effective if observers are not paying attention or if they are unable to view the model from a perspective that is helpful. For example, a side view of a model demonstrating a dance step may not be as helpful as a front view or a rear view. Modeling can also be used in conjunction with instructions, with the teacher pointing out critical features of the action as it unfolds. As an example, a therapist might emphasize how the hands of the model move or how the model's feet are coordinated with the hands during a particular phase of crutch walking.

© Terry Wild

Parents model all sorts of behaviors for their children, who may observe them to learn essential features of motor skills.

Given the recent boom in instructional technology, it is possible for practitioners to provide models and demonstrations through the use of videotape or computer simulations of the desired action (Seat & Wrisberg, 1996). The available research suggests that such demonstrations are sometimes helpful. Schoenfelder-Zohdi (1992) found that, when people watched a videotape of a skilled model before beginning their own practice attempts on a ski simulator, they learned the task faster and demonstrated better coordination than learners who received only verbal instructions. Pein (1990) reported similar results in a study examining people learning the badminton long service. In addition, individuals who viewed the model only when they requested to see it during practice still learned and performed the serve on a level that was comparable with that of participants who viewed the model prior to every practice attempt. Pein's findings suggest that the interest of learners in seeing a videotape demonstration of the skill is at least as important as how often the demonstration is given.

As in the case of instructions, the use of models and demonstrations can sometimes provide too much information for the learner. Therefore, it is wise for instructors to use cueing techniques that direct the learner's attention to important aspects of the model's movements. For example, a golf instructor might say, "Watch how his hips lead the action of his arms." Remember also that the kinds of movement cues to emphasize for beginners are different from those for more advanced performers. Individuals in the later stages of practice may be instructed to attend to more precise aspects of a model's movements (e.g., how the golf club contacts the ground slightly after the ball is hit in order to achieve backspin when the ball lands on the green).

**guidance**—A procedure used to physically, verbally, or visually direct learners through task performance in an effort to reduce errors or dispel the individual's fear of performing dangerous movements.

## Guidance Procedures

Professionals or practitioners often assist individuals in the early stages of physical rehearsal by guiding them through the movement pattern in various ways. **Guidance** methods vary widely in different settings. Some methods provide the learner

## Delaying the Imitation of Modeled Actions Enhances Learning

Demonstrating the actions of a skilled model is a common technique used by practitioners to help learners get an idea or representation of the movement they are attempting to produce. Recent research by Weeks, Hall, and Anderson (1996) indicates that observational learning is enhanced when learners are instructed to *delay* their imitations, compared to performing them concurrently with the model. In this study, three groups of beginners attempted to reproduce the one-hand gestures of a skilled model, who performed a series of letters from the American manual alphabet (see figure 8.3). During practice, one group imitated each of the model's actions as it was being demonstrated. A second group observed groupings of three different actions and attempted to imitate them during a 10-s delay *following* the observation. A third group practiced a combination of concurrent and delayed imitations; participants imitated the model's actions in a concurrent manner during the first half of practice and in a delayed fashion (three actions at a time) during the second half. Retention of each of the groups was examined 5 min and then 48 hr after the conclusion of practice.

Expert ratings of the quality of participants' imitations revealed that performance was significantly lower for the delayed group than for the other two groups at the beginning of practice. However, this difference disappeared by the end of practice. While no difference in the performance of the groups was observed during immediate retention (after 5 min), the performance of the delayed group was significantly superior to that of the concurrent group when they were tested 2 days later ("delayed retention"). The scores of the combination group were between those of the other two groups. These findings suggest that observational learning conditions that increase the *cognitive effort* of learners during practice (in this study delayed-imitation participants had to retain, retrieve, *and* produce the three-action sequences, whereas the concurrent-imitation individuals only had to coordinate their imitations with the actions of the model) enhance skill retention in the absence of the model (we discuss the concept of increased cognitive effort and the structuring of the learning experience in greater detail in the next chapter). Fortunately, in most situations when skills are learned, modeling does occur in a delayed-imitation format (i.e., learners view the model first and then attempt to imitate the action).

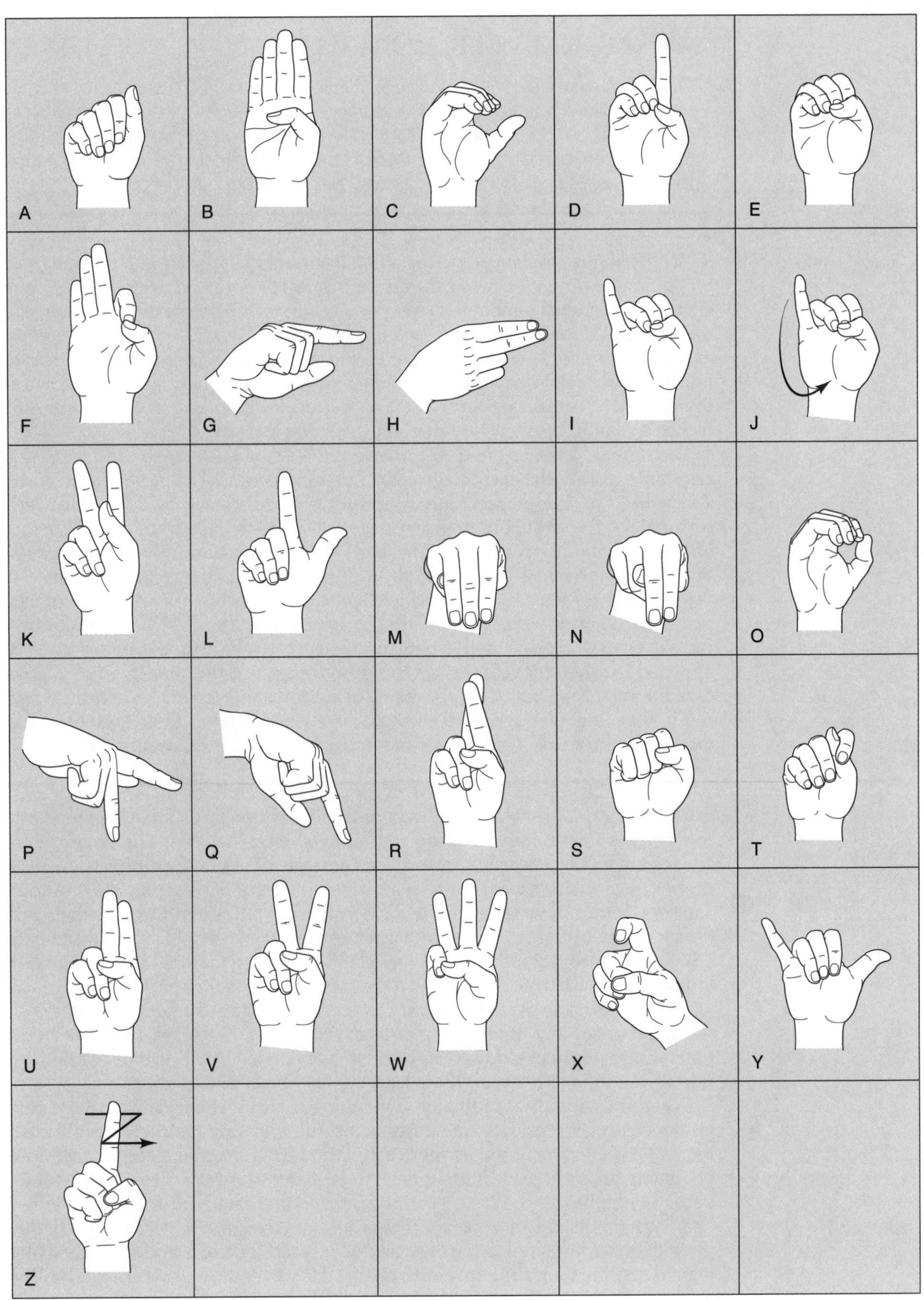


Figure 8.3 The American manual alphabet, which has been used to study effects of delaying imitation.

## MONKEY SEE, MONKEY DO

Observe the behavior of preschool children at a nearby playground or community park. What types of individuals are the children imitating? What types of actions are the children imitating? What aspects of the children's imitations are similar to those of the person they are imitating? How relevant are the children's imitations to successful performance of the action?

with only slight assistance, such as when the therapist talks a patient through a rehabilitation movement or when the dance instructor offers occasional verbal reminders to help students remember a new step sequence. Other forms of guidance are far more restrictive and invasive. For example, a therapist might grasp a patient's hands in order to provide assistance with walking and to minimize the chances of a serious fall. There are also many mechanical performance aids that physically constrain individuals' movement patterns, such as the training wheels that are sometimes attached to children's bicycles when they are first learning to ride.

Each method is designed to provide the learner with some kind of temporary assistance during the early stages of physical rehearsal. The hope is that learning, a s measured by the person's unaided future performance, will be enhanced. Unfortunately, the available research suggests that physical guidance is *not* a very effective technique for enhancing learning (see the highlight box on page 215). First of all, physical guidance can modify the feel of the task; the movement feels different when a learner produces it with the assistance of an instructor or therapist than when the learner performs it unassisted. In addition, decision-making processes may be different when the instructor tells the learner what to do, as opposed to when the learner has to figure things out for herself. Finally, guidance can diminish the learner's experience of performance errors. When this happens, individuals are also deprived of opportunities to correct their own errors, either during the production of slower movements or on the following attempt of more rapid ones.

None of this would be a problem if guidance techniques were always available during performance. However, most individuals must at some time perform their movements in situations that do not allow such assistance. The patient does not always have the therapist there to assist him in walking to the dining room. Athletes do not have their coaches with them when they are performing in a competition. Dancers do not have their instructors onstage to talk them through their routines during a performance. Since the **target context** for many learning tasks is one in which guidance techniques are unavailable, it is essential that learners acquire the kinds of skills they need to perform the task in the absence of guidance.

**target context**—The environmental context in which individuals want to be able to perform a skil.

So far our discussion of guidance procedures suggests that practitioners should not use them at any time during physical rehearsal. However, there are two situations where physical guidance appears to be beneficial: during early periods of task rehearsal and in situations where learners may be at risk of injury.

When individuals are initially developing their most basic ideas about the task, guidance procedures can sometimes be useful. A sailing instructor might place her hands on the hands of the learner to illustrate fundamental steering techniques, or the therapist might place his hands on those of a patient practicing rising to stand in order to emphasize the best location to place the hands on the arms of the chair. Temporary assistance such as this helps learners recognize basic features of the skill, gives them a rough indication of what they should try to do, and starts them on their way to making their first unaided attempt. However, these aids should be removed as quickly as possible, probably when the learner or patient begins to demonstrate the capability of performing the task independently.

## How Effective Is Guided Practice?

A classic experiment was conducted by Annett in 1959. In this study, participants tried to learn how to apply a particular amount of pressure to a hand-operated lever. During the practice phase, one group received additional guidance in the form of a visual display that indicated the amount of pressure they were applying at all times. The other group did not receive this guidance, but rather was told how well they did (i.e., how close they came to the desired amount of pressure) after each trial. Not surprisingly, the guidance group performed better during training because they always stopped at the correct point. However, when the visual guidance was removed, this group performed very poorly compared to the no-guidance group, with some individuals pressing so hard on the apparatus that it was damaged! Clearly, the participants who had practiced this task with the aid of visual guidance were unable to apply the correct amount of pressure to the lever when the guidance was taken away.

These results illustrate an important principle of guided practice. Guidance, almost by definition, is usually effective for performance when it is added to regular practice. The beginning golfer whose swing is aided by the instructor will produce a more correct-looking action, make fewer errors, feel more confident, and so on. The real test of guidance effectiveness, though, is seen in the level of performance produced by individuals when they are no longer given assistance, and here is where guidance procedures often fail. This phenomenon brings to mind the specificity hypothesis we discussed in chapter 2. If guided practice changes the task requirements markedly, then the task the individual is practicing is not really the same as the one the person must produce under unguided conditions.

Guidance procedures may also be necessary in learning situations that contain an element of fear or that place individuals at risk of injury. Therapists must position themselves to assist patients who are practicing reaching tasks, standing balance, walking, and stair climbing. As the performer gains proficiency, the amount of guidance can gradually be reduced, although in some cases, instructors need to remain present to provide quick assistance if necessary.

Physical guidance plays a prominent role, of course, in gymnastics. For many gymnastics activities, instructors use safety belts attached by ropes to support structures to prevent slips or falls that could cause serious injury. If belts are not available, instructors or other students provide physical guidance by offering the support of their hands and arms at critical points in the movement (e.g., when the gymnast is first learning to bring her legs over her head during a back handspring). Learners who are confident that they will not be injured can concentrate more effectively on the movement pattern and how it should be produced more smoothly and efficiently. For example, Wulf, Shea, and Whitacre (1998) found that individuals who were allowed to use poles during practice on a slalom ski simulator developed a more efficient coordination pattern and eventually performed better under no-guidance conditions than did individuals who learned without poles from the beginning.

### IT DEPENDS . . .

Sometimes movement practitioners attempt to assist learners by moving the individual's limbs in order to simulate a particular action. With the cooperation of a partner, attempt each of the following movements with and without partner assistance: tossing a coin back and forth from one hand to the other, drawing a straight line on a piece of paper, and balancing on one foot with your eyes closed. What differences did you notice in the two conditions? Was the guidance helpful? In what sense?

# Forms of Rehearsal

All learning requires some form of rehearsal. The very concept of *skill* is based on the assumption that some period of practice or rehearsal precedes task mastery. The rehearsal of motor skills can occur at many different times and places, under a variety of conditions. Sometimes it happens almost unintentionally (e.g., when a child repeatedly places variously shaped objects through correspondingly shaped holes in a cube or when an elderly individual uses a new walker during locomotion). Sometimes it is highly purposeful (e.g., the aspiring young athlete who spends almost every waking moment of his summer vacation practicing the same movements over and over). Other times rehearsal is highly guided and structured (e.g., when a musician rehearses under the watchful eye of a maestro conductor or a stroke patient attempts a movement that is being evaluated and corrected by a therapist). Rehearsal can even occur in covert ways (e.g., when the learner thinks about how she is going to modify her next movement attempt).

In the remaining sections of this chapter, we examine some of the ways individuals might rehearse the movements they are trying to learn. First we describe various types of physical rehearsal, and then we discuss the concept of mental rehearsal. When assisting learners in achieving the goals they have set for themselves, practitioners must decide which forms of rehearsal are the most effective at different times.

## Physical Rehearsal Techniques

Whoever said "Practice makes perfect" knew that skill improvement requires repetition. However, repetition alone does not guarantee improved skill but only more-permanent behavior. Therefore, the old adage might be more accurately phrased "Effectively designed practice makes perfect." The experience of physical rehearsal can, however, take many forms. In this section, we discuss some of the techniques practitioners might use to alter the effectiveness of the learner's experience of physical rehearsal. These techniques include simulator practice, part practice, slow-motion practice, and error detection practice.

### *Simulator Practice*

**simulator**—A training device that mimics various features of a real-world task.

A **simulator** is a physical rehearsal device that mimics certain features of a real-world task. Simulators are often elaborate, sophisticated, and expensive, such as the devices that are used to train pilots to fly aircraft. But simulators need not be elaborate at all. Craig Wrisberg's dad has a small pressure-sensing platform in his office that he uses whenever he wants to practice his golf putting skills. When the ball lands on the pressure sensor (located under a simulated "hole"), it is projected back toward the performer. Simulators can be an important part of instructional programs, especially when the learning task is expensive or dangerous (e.g., learning to fly a jetliner), when the availability of facilities is limited (e.g., a putting green at a golf course), or when normal practice is not feasible (e.g., when pitchers are fatigued, a pitching machine might be used for extra batting practice).

**target skills**—The tasks an individual wishes to be able to perform.

The overall goal of simulation is the transfer of learning with the simulator to performance on the **target skill**. Thus, a simulator is only effective when substantial transfer occurs. Because transfer between any two tasks increases as the similarity between the tasks increases (see chapter 7), it is important that simulators present the task in a way that is as realistic as possible; the simulated task should possess as many of the motor, perceptual, and conceptual elements of the target skill as possible. Not surprisingly, the creation of simulators is usually a very expensive undertaking. However, simulators that lack the essential features of the target skill or that require different processes for movement control cannot be expected to produce much transfer.

A more practical concern has to do with the amount of transfer that is produced by the simulator in relation to the amount of time it takes to use it. If simulator practice results in greater improvement on the target skill than practicing the target skill itself, then it makes sense to use the simulator. If this is not the case, the learner would be better off spending the entire practice time on the target skill, if that is feasible.

Besides the element of time, there may be other relevant factors that practitioners should consider before deciding to use a simulator. For example, the effectiveness of a simulator must also be judged according to the relative cost of simulator practice and target skill practice, the availability of resources and facilities, learner safety, and so on. Compared to the cost of practicing in a flight simulator, practice in an actual jetliner would be staggering, not to mention the additional concerns for the safety of people and equipment.

Task simulation is in some ways similar to guidance procedures. It can sometimes be a helpful instructional technique during the early stages of practice, when individuals are learning rules, strategies, and other cognitive and decision-making aspects of the target skill. However, as soon as learners demonstrate more consistent patterns of movement control, the effectiveness of simulators drops off considerably, unless simulator practice is nearly identical to that of the target skill.

### *Part Practice*

Some skills are enormously complex, such as those that make up many gymnastics routines and the various activities that are part of the game of baseball; even pole vaulting and javelin throwing seem very complex to beginners. Clearly, for tasks such as these, physical rehearsal cannot contain all aspects of the skill at once, because learners would be overwhelmed. In some cases, instructors can break tasks down into parts for rehearsal. Once learners become proficient at **part practice**, they can begin practicing the entire target skill. The three types of part practice mentioned in the motor learning literature—**fractionization**, **segmentation** (or progressive part practice), and **simplification**—all represent techniques instructors can use to reduce the complexity of skill practice (Wightman & Lintern, 1985). For example, a swimmer practicing the leg kick by itself, using a kickboard, is an instance of fractionization. Someone practicing the tennis serve by first working on just the toss, and then combining the toss and the racket swing is using segmentation. A child hitting a Wiffle ball with an oversized plastic bat is learning through simplification.

**part practice**—A procedure involving the practice of a complex skill in a more simplified form; the three types of part practice are fractionization, segmentation, and simplification.

**fractionization**—A type of part practice in which two or more parts of a complex skill are practiced separately.

**segmentation**—A type of part practice in which one part of a target skill is practiced until it is learned, then a second part is added to the first part, and the two are practiced together, and so on until the entire target skill is practiced; also referred to as progressive part practice.

**simplification**—A type of part practice in which the difficulty of some aspect of the target skill is reduced (e.g., slow-motion practice or the use of an oversized ball for the tennis serve).

## ABOVE REAL-TIME TRAINING

A simulation technique that has been successfully used to train airplane fighter pilots is called above real-time training (ARTT). This type of training requires individuals to perform standard tasks in a cockpit simulator, but each scenario takes place in a time that is faster than would occur during an actual flight segment (e.g., a 5-min air intercept task is completed in 2 or 3 min). Thus, trainees must make their decisions and their movements in shorter times than they would under normal flight conditions. Pilots who experience this type of training report that ARTT provides greater realism than conventional simulation, making actual flight conditions less fatiguing. The results of studies using ARTT also indicate that this simulator technique increases pilot performance and decreases training time (Miller et al., 1997).

Important questions dealing with the issue of part practice include how the subunits of skills should be created and how they should be practiced for maximum transfer to the whole skill. It may be a simple matter to divide skills into parts. Gymnastics routines can be separated into several component stunts; the pole vault can be divided into run-up, pole-plant, and vault segments. Each of these subparts can be divided even further. But the real question is does part practice, regardless of how it is structured, contribute to the learning of the whole target skill? That is the ultimate goal.

Before using part practice, practitioners should ask the following questions:

- Will practicing a simplified version of the target skill transfer positively to performance of the whole target skill?
- How much (if any) practice time should the learner spend on part practice?
- Would the learner's time be more effectively spent practicing the whole target skill?

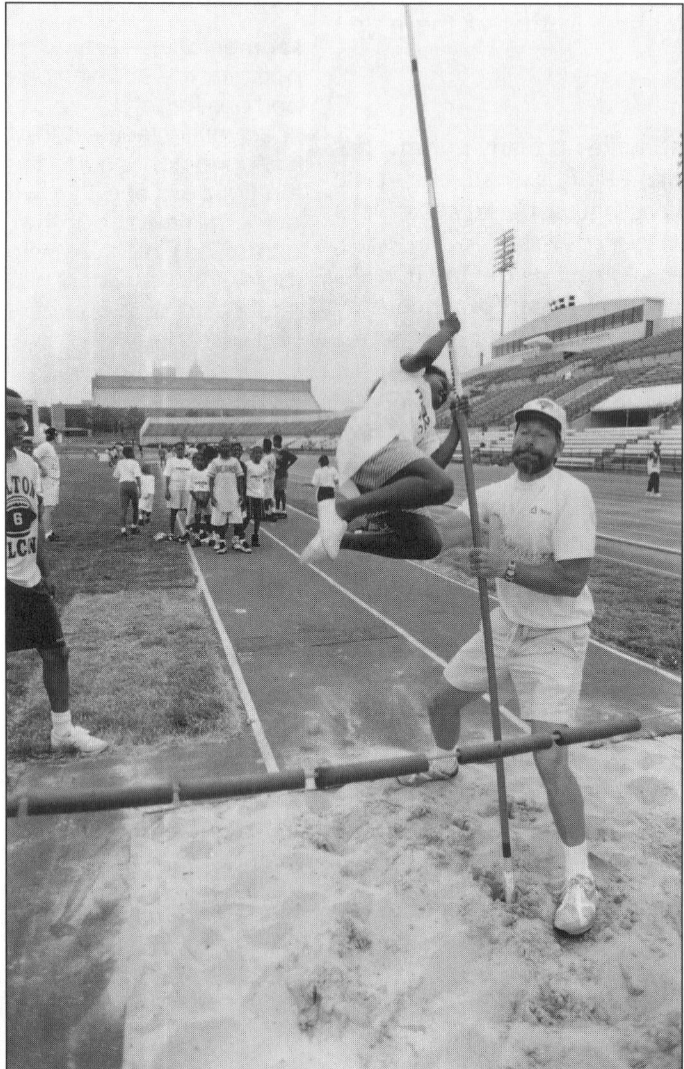

© Victah Sailer

Instructors may break practice into parts to help people learn complex skills such as pole vaulting.

At first glance, the answers to these questions seem obvious. In some cases, practicing a part of the task in isolation or in a simplified way seems the same as practicing the whole target skill (e.g., beating an egg, chopping nuts, sifting flour, and then doing all three when preparing to bake a cake). When this is the case, transfer of part practice to whole-skill performance should be almost perfect. However, there are some situations in which part-whole transfer is less than perfect, or even nonexistent.

Differences in the effectiveness of part practice usually depend on the nature of the target skill that is being learned. As suggested in the previous cake-baking example, part practice works best for serial tasks, where the actions (or errors) involved in one part do not influence the actions involved in the next. For example, passing the baton is a component of relay races in track and field that is generally independent of the running phases of the race. In tasks such as relay racing, learners can devote more time to the practice of troublesome parts (e.g., the baton pass) without having to practice the easier elements (e.g., running) every time.

In some serial sport skills, however, performance on one part of a task *does* influence performance on the next part. If the ski racer comes out of a turn too low and fast, this affects his approach for the next turn. Small positioning errors on one move on the balance beam determine how the gymnast must perform the next move. If the relationship between two parts of a task is high, performers must be able to quickly adjust an entire action if their performance of an early part is ineffective. A ballet dancer must sometimes be able to modify her later steps if she slips during an earlier part of her routine. Unfortunately, adjustments between parts of the entire

## IS PART PRACTICE OF WALKING BENEFICIAL?

Therapeutic literature suggests that part practice does not always lead to improved performance of the whole target skill. In tasks like walking, for example, encouraging the patient to practice stepping forward and back repeatedly with one foot in a rocking type of motion is probably not very helpful. Separated from the typical gait of stepping forward and moving into the stance phase, repeated stepping forward and back changes the dynamics of the walking action. The natural walking pattern uses substantial momentum to facilitate movement, whereas the forward and back pattern produces little momentum (i.e., hip and knee flexion with eccentric contraction of the hamstrings to hip and knee extension with concentric contraction of the hamstrings). Thus, the dynamics of the forward step during part practice differ markedly from those of the forward step produced in the context of normal locomotion.

target skill cannot be practiced and learned when individuals practice the parts in isolation. Therefore, mastery of individual parts of a serial skill does not guarantee effective performance of the whole skill unless individuals also practice making adjustments in some components based on the action of previous ones. The relationship between the degree of interaction among the components of a task and the effectiveness of part practice is depicted in figure 8.4.

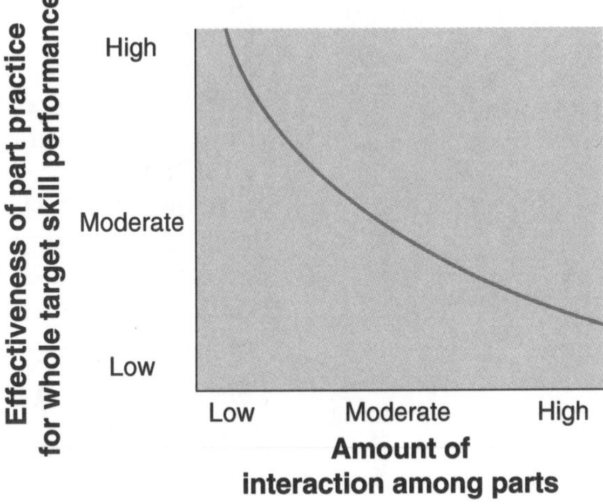


**Figure 8.4** Part practice effectiveness decreases markedly as the interaction among task components increases.

Research suggests that when rapid discrete actions are broken down into arbitrary parts, these parts become so changed from the way they operate in the whole task that practicing them in isolation contributes little to whole-task performance (e.g., Lersten, 1968; Schmidt & Young, 1987). In a task such as hitting a golf ball, for example, practicing the backswing separately from the forward swing changes the dynamics of the action at the top of the swing. Stopping the backswing at that point eliminates the active lengthening of the muscles, which, by the action of their springlike properties, produce a downswing that is smooth and powerful. Therefore, the dynamics of the backswing when practiced in isolation are quite different from those of the same backswing when the individual performs it in the context of the whole swing.

You may recall from studying the **motor program** concept that quick actions are controlled in an essentially open-loop fashion, with decisions about the action's structure being specified in advance. If only a part of a programmed action is practiced, particularly if the part has different dynamics performed in isolation (e.g., the

**motor program**—A set of motor commands that is prestructured at the executive level and that defines the essential details of a skilled action; analogous to a central pattern generator.

## IT DEPENDS . . .

Your friend's little brother wants to learn to swim the freestyle. His swimming teacher sees that the boy is unafraid of the water and "drownproofed," but also observes that he is having a difficult time practicing all of the parts of the movement (i.e., arm movement, leg kick, breathing) at the same time. How might the instructor schedule part practice of the task? What parts of the whole skill might the boy need to practice together? Why?

backswing in golf), compared with being performed as part of the whole task, a different program must be used (i.e., one that is responsible for producing only the part). Practicing this "part program" contributes to the learning of the isolated part, but it does not contribute to the learning of the program for producing the whole movement.

**specificity of learning**—The notion that the best learning experiences are those that most closely approximate the movement components and environmental condition of the target skill and target context.

**generalized motor program**—A motor program that defines a pattern of movement rather than a specific movement; this flexibility allows performers to adapt the generalized program to produce variations of the pattern that meet altered environmental demands.

### *Slow-Motion Practice*

One method practitioners use to simplify the learner's practice of a target skill is slow-motion practice. A relevant question to ask here is whether the slow-motion version of the target skill is really the "same" in some sense as the normal-speed version. Of course, the **specificity of learning** notion would argue that the slow-motion version differs too much from the normal-speed version to be of much use.

However, from the perspective of the **generalized motor program**, slow-motion practice may yield some benefit. One parameter of the generalized motor program is overall speed, the value of which performers vary depending on how slowly or quickly they decide to execute their movement pattern. If individuals slow their movement down slightly, they use the same generalized motor program as when they produce it at faster speeds. Slow-motion practice of this type can be useful to individuals early in the learning process. By practicing in slow motion, they should be able to control their movements more effectively, thereby reducing errors in the fundamental movement pattern.

Practitioners need to be careful, however, in advocating very slow motion. If individuals slow their movements down too much (e.g., a throwing motion that lasts for 20 s), they change the essential dynamics of the movement. If learners become comfortable with the slowed-down version, they may choose to forsake the use of the normal-speed program in favor of one that accomplishes the particular slow-motion goal. Unfortunately, a slow-motion program of this type would not help individuals much if the target context is one that requires normal-speed movements (e.g., a cricket match, a tennis match, a golf tournament).

### *Error Detection Practice*

Physical rehearsal can include more than the production of movements themselves. As individuals proceed through the stages of practice (see chapter 7), they become

## NOT TOO SLOW

In some activities, learners initially produce slower movements in an attempt to achieve more accuracy (e.g., badminton, squash, tennis). Research by Woods (1967) shows that this strategy may actually result in *less* accuracy when individuals switch to a more rapid speed. Three groups of adolescent males with no previous tennis experience were taught to hit the forehand ground stroke. They were instructed to emphasize rapid ball velocity, ball placement accuracy, or both rapid velocity and placement accuracy. Halfway through the learning sessions, participants in the first two conditions were instructed to switch their emphasis (i.e., from rapid velocity to placement accuracy, or from accuracy to velocity). The individuals who had the most difficulty were those who tried to increase their ball velocity after initially emphasizing placement accuracy. When these learners tried to hit the ball with greater velocity, their accuracy was poorer than that of participants in either of the other two groups. While swing dynamics were not analyzed in this study, it is possible that by initially emphasizing accuracy, these individuals developed a slower-speed program that was different than the one they needed to hit the ball with greater velocity.

more adept at detecting errors in their movements. Learning to detect errors is a bit like learning to produce movements, although the two involve somewhat different processes. The golfer who is able to detect her own errors must be sensitive to the wide range of information produced by the movement itself. Such information can be kinesthetic—feelings associated with the movements and forces in the muscles and joints, with ball contact, and with shifts in balance. Information can also be visual—seeing the movements of the limbs in relation to each other and to the environment. It can sometimes be auditory—hearing the sound of the club against wind resistance and the click that accompanies ball contact (or the "whoosh" sound that occurs when the ball is missed). Other tasks produce different sensations, but almost all are richly associated with various forms of movement-produced feedback that can inform individuals about the quality of their actions.

**error detection capability**—The learned capability of individuals to detect errors in the movements they produce by becoming adept at interpreting the feedback that arises from those movements.

In order for individuals to improve their **error detection capability**, they must become sensitive to the particular patterns of movement-produced feedback that are related to performance outcomes. The feel of the steering wheel when the car is turning a corner may indicate that the tires are not in proper balance. Through physical rehearsal and experience, accomplished drivers learn which sensations are reflective of good and bad performance (either by the person or the car or both) and which are irrelevant.

Practitioners can enhance the development of learners' error detection capability by encouraging them to become sensitive to movement-produced feedback. Individuals usually don't monitor this type of feedback unless someone draws their attention to it. One way instructors might do this is to ask individuals to describe, or estimate, what they feel happened when they moved—before the instructor gives them any additional information.

Learners can be asked to describe, or subjectively estimate, various aspects of their movements. For example, therapy patients might be instructed to describe the movement sensations that accompany a loss of balance caused by therapist-controlled perturbations. Archers might be asked to guess the location of the arrow on the target or to describe certain features of the movement just produced (e.g., elbow straightness or whether the finger release of the bowstring was "clean"). Having individuals estimate characteristics of their movements (Liu & Wrisberg, 1997) or the outcomes they produced (Hogan & Yanowitz, 1978) requires them to devote attention to the feedback that arises from the action. This more effortful processing

## MOVING WITH AND WITHOUT VISION

One way to sharpen your experience of the feel of a movement is to perform it with your eyes closed. Obviously, this is not a good idea in all cases (e.g., driving a car), but for some closed skills it can be very illuminating.

Here's a task to experiment with: Stand an arm's distance from a wall and pick out a spot on the wall that is about chest height. Now in one continuous motion, move your hand toward the wall until your finger rests on the spot.

Repeat this movement five times with your eyes open and five times with your eyes closed. Each time you attempt the movement with your eyes closed, try to guess how close you are to the target before opening your eyes. What feedback do you become aware of when you move with your eyes closed that you aren't aware of when you move with your eyes open? How might the eyes-closed movement experience benefit your performance of the eyes-open movement?

helps increase learners' familiarity with such feedback, leading to an improved capability of detecting errors.

Practitioners should not, however, instruct individuals to attend to movement-produced feedback *while* they are performing the action, for this may cause them to attend to sources of information that are inappropriate for goal achievement. The patient who is thinking about her balance may stumble because she is not paying attention to changes in the platform she is standing on. The archer who is thinking about the straightness of his arm may not be sufficiently focused on the bull's-eye. Once their movements are completed, though, individuals can be asked to describe some of these features—thereby directing their attention to sensations that the action has just produced.

Movement outcomes are often obvious—individuals can see whether the basketball went into the basket, how close the car is to the curb, or if the brush stroke covered the desired area with paint—shortly after the movement is produced. Therefore, asking performers to guess obvious outcomes is an essentially meaningless exercise. Moreover, this type of activity likely diverts their attention away from more relevant feedback produced by the movement. But what if individuals are prevented from obtaining outcome information? What if the free throw shooter is asked to close her eyes just after she releases the ball or the golfer is instructed to close his eyes during a practice swing? In the sport of sailing, individuals who are learning to operate the helm are often blindfolded while doing so (not to worry—a nonblindfolded person accompanies them in the boat). This forces the learner to detect information about the boat's performance based on kinesthetic, rather than visual, feedback. Such procedures require individuals to process their own (less obvious) movement-produced feedback, leading to improvements in their error detection capability.

Once individuals learn to detect their errors, their problem shifts to learning how to correct them. The patient who recognizes that her balance is easily disturbed must learn to focus on cues that promote improved stability. Some types of adjustments are more effective than others, and an inappropriate adjustment could lead to diminished, rather than improved, performance. Thus, it is important for instructors and therapists to be able to assist individuals in developing the capability of both detecting their own errors and of correcting them effectively.

## Mental Rehearsal Techniques

**mental rehearsal**—A procedure in which individuals think through or about performing a motor skill in the absence of overt movement.

Because people set aside time to practice or rehearse their movements doesn't mean they have to spend all of that time moving (i.e., physically rehearsing). Some of this time can be devoted to **mental rehearsal**—that is, thinking about or mentally imaging certain aspects of the skill they are learning, without engaging in any kind of actual movement. The question is, Can *mental* rehearsal actually contribute to *movement* learning? Until a few years ago, scientists in the field of motor learning had very much doubted that motor skill acquisition could actually be enhanced through mental rehearsal. Their general understanding of practice and learning was that overt physical action was essential if motor learning was to take place. It was difficult for them to comprehend how any learning could occur if there was

Which sources of movement-produced feedback might learners be instructed to attend to when physically rehearsing the following tasks: brushing teeth, chopping wood, eating spaghetti, or walking with a cane? How might this feedback assist individuals in learning to detect and correct their errors?

## MENTAL REHEARSAL IN THERAPY SETTINGS

Mental rehearsal would appear to be particularly useful in therapy settings with patients who are unable to engage in large amounts of physical rehearsal due to fatigue factors (e.g., multiple sclerosis, cardiac disease, myasthenia gravis). Support for this notion has come from Linden and colleagues who found that mental rehearsal, as compared to no rehearsal, improved the equilibrium characteristics of elder women (ages 67–90) on a task that required walking while carrying an object in each hand (Linden et al., 1989).

no actual movement, active practice, or movement-produced feedback that signaled errors.

The overwhelming evidence (e.g., Hird et al., 1991), and probably our own personal experience, tells us that physical rehearsal is superior to mental rehearsal when it comes to the learning of movement skills. However, in some instances, mental rehearsal has been shown to produce results that are nearly as good as those found for physical rehearsal (see Feltz & Landers, 1983, for a review of this research). Moreover, mental rehearsal is almost always superior to no rehearsal, which makes it an effective technique for use with patients whose physical activity is restricted or for individuals who sustain an injury that prevents them from physically rehearsing (Warner & McNeill, 1988).

During mental rehearsal, individuals might remind themselves of procedural or symbolic aspects of the skill (e.g., the sequence of steps in a dance routine or the reminder to follow through when throwing a ball), sometimes referred to as **mental practice**, or they might try to see and feel themselves actually performing the skill (e.g., throwing a dart that results in a bull's-eye), sometimes referred to as **mental imagery**. We discuss each of these types of mental rehearsal in the following sections.

**mental practice**—A mental rehearsal procedure in which performers think through or about the cognitive, symbolic, or procedural aspects of a motor skill in the absence of overt movement.

**mental imagery**—A mental rehearsal procedure in which individuals imagine themselves performing a motor skill from either a first-person perspective or a third-person perspective.

### *Mental Practice*

The earliest theory of mental rehearsal was formulated by Sackett (1934), who proposed that this type of no-movement practice facilitated the cognitive-symbolic elements of the skill. For example, a military trainee could mentally rehearse the sequence of steps involved in the assembly of a rifle, or a beginning swimmer could remind herself of the stretch and reach that is part of the arm movements in many swimming strokes. These cognitive elements were originally thought to be important only during the very early stages of learning (i.e., the **verbal-cognitive stage**). However, when Feltz and Landers (1983) conducted an extensive review of the research literature, they found that, regardless of the skill level of participants, mental practice was more effective for tasks that contained a greater number of cognitive-symbolic components. This makes sense, really, when we consider the kinds of mental activity that take place when people think about producing effective movements. Certainly strategies, focus cues, and general instructional information fall under the category of "cognitive-symbolic elements" of a skill. And they would be something all performers and learners should be able to mentally practice with little difficulty.

**verbal-cognitive stage**—The initial stage of learning, in which verbal and cognitive processes dominate the learner's activity.

The mental practice of cognitive, symbolic, or procedural elements of a task requires no apparatus and allows a large group of learners to engage in the activity at the same time. There is considerable evidence that, for less experienced individuals, alternating mental practice with physical practice is an effective strategy for improving movement performance (Etnier & Landers, 1996; Gabriele, Hall, & Lee, 1989; McBride & Rothstein, 1979). The clever instructor or therapist should be able to find ways to intertwine the two rehearsal modes to promote maximal performance gains.

### WHERE DOES MENTAL REHEARSAL FIT IN THE CONCEPTUAL MODEL?

Mental rehearsal could have an effect at several places in the motor system, as indicated in the conceptual model shown in figure 8.5. Any combination of the following hypotheses could correctly explain the benefits of mental rehearsal. Whatever the final explanation, though, it is clear that mental rehearsal enhances skill learning.

- Mental rehearsal could involve practice of the cognitive, symbolic, and decision-making aspects of the skill.
- Mental rehearsal could allow the learner to image possible actions and strategies, estimating the probable outcomes in the actual situation.
- Mental rehearsal could be accompanied by minute muscular activity, far too small to produce action, which involves the muscles that are used during the real movement.
- Mental rehearsal could help focus the attention of performers on task-relevant cues, which could be helpful for subsequent physical performance.

#### *Mental Imagery*

A special type of mental rehearsal is often referred to as mental imagery. During mental imaging, individuals try to see and feel themselves actually performing the skill. Imagery can occur from either an *internal perspective* (the way the movement

### Practicing Mental Imagery

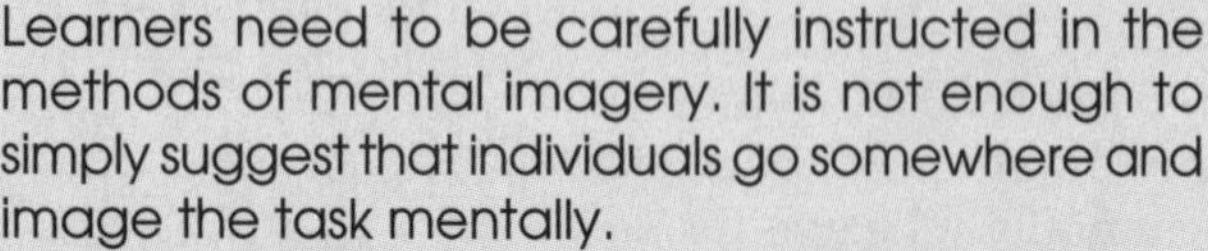

Learners need to be carefully instructed in the methods of mental imagery. It is not enough to simply suggest that individuals go somewhere and image the task mentally.

Initially, learners should move to a quiet, relaxing place and focus clearly on the movement task. This in itself requires some practice, because it is difficult to be calm and focused on command. One helpful method for achieving a state of physical relaxation is to focus simply on the breathing process, saying the word *relax* each time a breath is released. Once individuals are able to achieve a relaxed state, they should imagine the event in as vivid a way as possible, even in color and with all of the sounds and other sensations of the actual movement.

Sometimes it helps to practice initially by mentally imaging a simple generic experience, such as taking a lemon out of the refrigerator, slicing it in half, and slowly squeezing the juice on the tongue. Once learners become comfortable with simple scenes, they can attempt the mental rehearsal of movement skills. The action should be allowed to unfold in real time, the sequence of activities being imagined clearly as they become more and more a part of the skill. Finally, learners should imagine successful execution of the movement, avoiding images of failure (for additional tips on maximizing mental rehearsal, see Orlick, 1986, 1990).

Performed in this general way, mental imagery is a particularly effective way for individuals to rehearse skills. Imagery can take place almost anytime; for example, between performance attempts, between days of physical rehearsal, while relaxing at home, and when lying in bed at night. As with any skill, mental imagery becomes better the more individuals practice it. Therefore, learners should set aside specific times in the day for systematic mental imagery of the skill. For the best results, sessions should last no more than 10 to 15 min at a time, with emphasis given to quality rehearsal (i.e., creating vivid, lifelike images), rather than quantity.

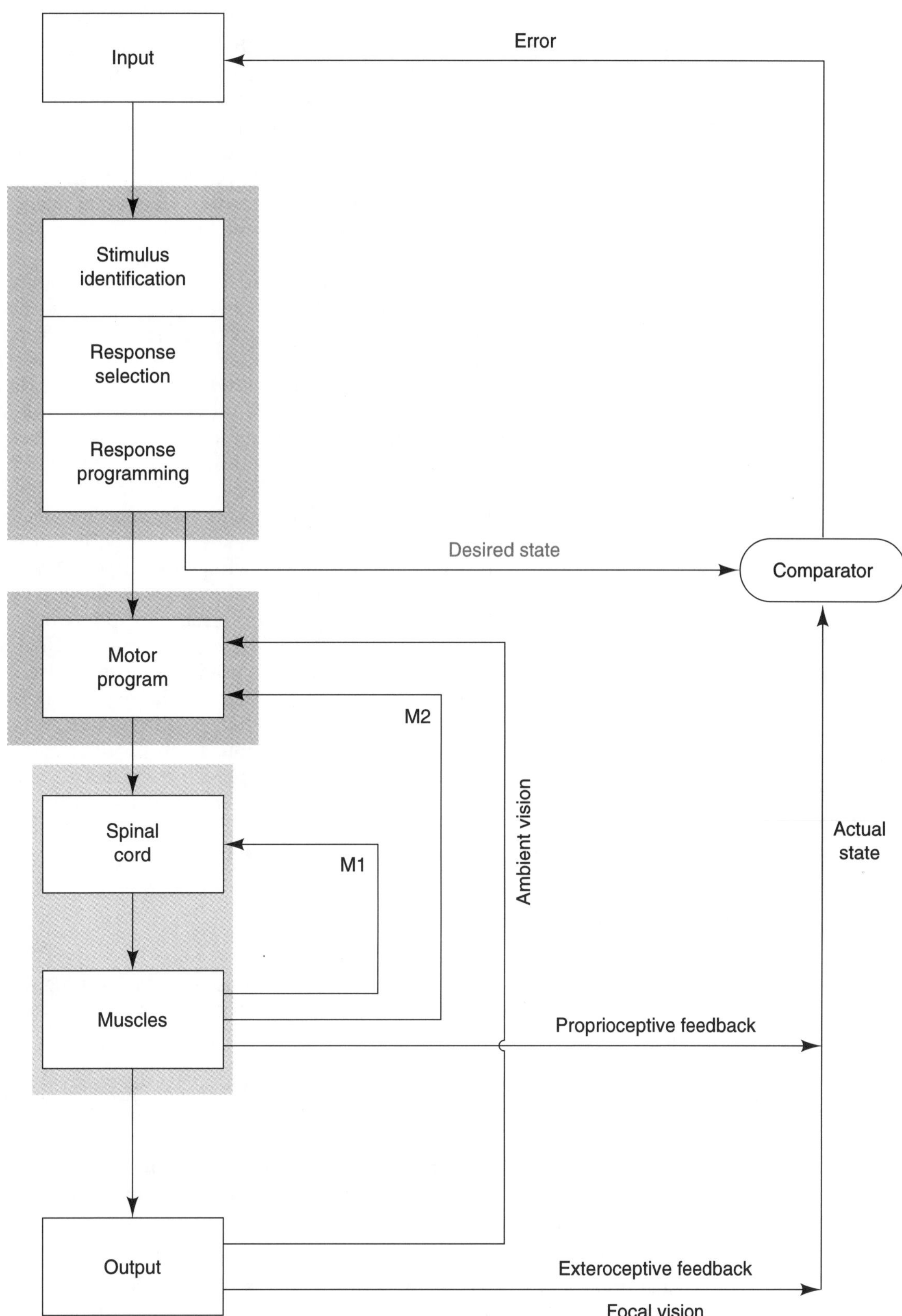


**Figure 8.5** The conceptual model of human performance, highlighting the major processes where mental practice is thought to have an effect.

and the movement environment are experienced when the individual is physically performing the action) or an *external perspective* (the way the movement is experienced when it is videotaped and replayed to the person). The perspective that works best appears to depend on the type of skill, although there also appears to be individual preferences (Smith, 1987). For example, a person imaging the free throw shot in basketball might benefit more from an internal perspective, and a diver might benefit more from an external perspective, particularly if she is imaging a triple somersault! The most effective imagery, regardless of perspective, stimulates both the look and feel (and sometimes even the sound and smell) of the actual movement (Hardy, 1997).

The earliest support for the connection between mind and movement during mental imagery came from Jacobson (1930). He observed that, when individuals mentally image a movement, weak electrical activity (EMG) occurs in the participating musculature, although the activity is far smaller in size than that necessary to produce the action. Thus, Jacobson proposed that, when people image themselves moving, a plan of action is carried by the central nervous system to the muscles, providing a form of "rehearsal" in the absence of actual body motion. Closer inspection of Jacobson's EMG patterns, unfortunately, indicates that they are not much like those that accompany physical performance of the actual movements.

A more recent explanation of the benefits of imagery has been proposed by MacKay (1981). According to MacKay, muscle units are "primed" for action during mental imagery, and the extent to which this priming benefits subsequent physical performance depends on the previous amount of physical practice or experience the person has had with the task. This view receives considerable support from studies in the sport psychology literature, which show that high-performance athletes benefit considerably more from mental rehearsal than do novice performers (see Vealey & Greenleaf, 1998). Presumably, the mental imagery of muscular or proprioceptive (i.e., "feel") components of a task is more effective when performers are very familiar with those components—a former collegiate gymnast can profit from the mental rehearsal of advanced gymnastics stunts, whereas someone who has never attempted a gymnastics event in his life cannot. According to MacKay's view, the priming of muscle units during mental imagery should become more effective as learners become more familiar with the physical properties of the task.

## Summary

Practitioners can use a variety of techniques to supplement the learning experiences of individuals. Here are some techniques practitioners can use prior to providing instructional assistance:

- Familiarize learners with the learning situation to diminish their anxiety and allow them to focus more readily on the process of performance improvement.
- Open communication with learners to encourage them to express their needs and provide information about the types of assistance they find most helpful.
- Assist learners in determining the most relevant attentional focus for various tasks and situations.
- Encourage learners to practice shifting their attentional focus between internal and external cues and between a larger number of cues (broad focus) and a smaller number of cues (narrow focus).
- Instruct learners to focus on process goals in order to diminish performance anxiety.

- Assist learners in setting realistic performance goals so they feel capable of achieving them and are able to perform with less anxiety.
- Schedule shorter practice sessions that are more spread out rather than ones that are long and bunched together.
- Balance the amount of practice and rest within a rehearsal period according to the fitness level of learners and the energy requirements of the movement.

When presenting the target skill, practitioners should be able to do the following:

- Provide instructions that are brief and simple—emphasizing no more than one or two points at a time.
- Give instructions that emphasize concepts learners are familiar with and that remind them of previous experiences they have had that they can transfer to the learning of the target skill.
- Provide demonstrations that convey the essential features of the target skill.
- Direct beginners' attention to the key features of a demonstration to enhance their picking up of the information.
- Use physical guidance procedures, if necessary, to present learners with a basic idea of the target skill.
- Remove physical guidance as soon as learners achieve an understanding of the basic movement pattern.
- Consider using physical guidance procedures when introducing learners to tasks that put them at risk of injury.

Learners can engage in both physical and mental rehearsal during task practice. Practitioners should encourage learners to combine the two types of rehearsal in order to obtain a deeper appreciation of the various dimensions of movement production. Practitioners might supplement the physical and mental rehearsal of learners in these ways:

- Using simulators for physical rehearsal, but only when they convey the essential features of the target skill
- Providing opportunity for part practice, but only when the target skill is too complex to be rehearsed as a whole
- Using slow-motion practice to increase learners' control and consistency of movement production
- Avoiding overly slow-motion practice that can develop a motor program that is different from the one learners need for faster-speed performance of the target skill
- Directing learners' attention to movement-produced feedback to encourage their development of error-detection capabilities
- Encouraging learners to mentally rehearse cognitive strategies and movement images that are related to successful physical performance of the target skill

## From Principles to Practice

Check your understanding of the material in this chapter by answering the following questions and then completing the application exercises. In each case, see if you can identify the most relevant questions or issues and then propose a solution based on the concepts and principles discussed in the chapter.

### Checking Your Understanding

1. Explain why it is important for practitioners to familiarize learners with the instructional situation, and then discuss how this might be helpful for a therapist working with an elderly nursing home resident who is trying to learn how to use a motorized bed.
2. Describe the process of two-way communication, and explain how a coach might use it to provide more effective instruction for a collegiate gymnast who is trying to learn the elements of a balance beam routine.
3. Briefly describe Nideffer's four categories of attentional focus, and indicate which category you think is most appropriate for each of the following tasks: threading a needle, driving a car on a busy interstate, remembering a friend's phone number, and plotting a strategy for defeating a racquetball opponent.
4. List three features of effective instructions, and illustrate how each feature might be evidenced in the instructions an adult gives to an 8-year-old child who is trying to learn how to do a headstand.
5. Explain the purpose of demonstrations during skill learning, and then discuss two features of a coin-flip motion that a person might point out to a friend prior to demonstrating the action.
6. Discuss the concept of part practice, and then describe how an instructor might use it with a person who is learning how to drive a stick shift car.
7. Describe the concept of error detection practice, and then explain how a practitioner might assist a dart thrower in developing the capability of detecting errors.
8. Explain the difference between mental practice and mental imagery. Give an example of each type of mental rehearsal by a person who is learning how to ballroom dance.

### Application Exercise #1

A young soccer player is having difficulty learning how to head the ball. Her coach thinks that the player is just afraid of the ball and that once she overcomes her fear she should be able to do it.

*It Depends*

- How old is the player?
- How much experience has the player had with other eye-hand or eye-foot coordination activities?
- Does the player have a fear of the ball?
- If so, what is the basis of her fear?

*Strategy*

Physical rehearsal should be structured in a way that allows the player to achieve success at the skill, gradually overcome any fear she might have, and eventually be able to perform the target skill of heading a ball in the target context of a soccer game.

*Response Example*

- Establish open communication between the player and coach so that the player understands and is comfortable with the things she is being asked to do.
- Determine the types of instructional cues and demonstrations that allow the player to get a basic idea of the movement.
- Modify physical rehearsal so that the player can focus on coordinating her head movement with the moving ball and achieve head-ball contact without the fear of being injured.
- Teach the player to mentally image correct execution of the heading action and supplement periods of physical rehearsal with mental rehearsal.

## Application Exercise #2

A college student who is hearing impaired wants to learn how to play racquetball.

*It Depends*

- What other kinds of movement or sport experiences has the student had?
- Is the student physically fit?
- Does the student have any other impairments?
- What are the student's goals for racquetball?
- Is the student able to lip-read, or must an instructor be able to communicate in sign language?

*Strategy*

Establish communication with the student to determine the kinds of assistance he would like during the course of learning. Determine the types of instructions and demonstrations that might help the student achieve a basic idea of the different racquetball shots. Give particular emphasis to visual and kinesthetic cues and direct the student's attention to those cues that are most important for different types of shots and situations.

## Application Exercise #3

An individual has just entered dental school, and his dream is to be a specialist who performs root canals. He wonders whether he will be able to learn the necessary skills and worries about the fact that most root canal operations take almost two hours.

*It Depends*

- Does the person have good vision (or at least near vision that is corrected to 20/20)?
- Does the individual have good fine motor coordination?
- Has the student had previous experience with any other complex, fine motor skills?
- What is the individual's anxiety level: low, moderate, or high?

*Strategy*

Assist the individual in establishing goals for learning the necessary fine motor skills and for managing his attentional focus. Provide physical rehearsal experiences that require him to make the appropriate evaluations and decisions regarding the course of treatment for each patient, attend to the appropriate cues while performing movements, and move at a controlled pace.

## Application Exercise #4

A 7-year-old girl wants her mother to teach her how to in-line skate so that she can enjoy skating with her friends. Her mother knows how to roller skate, but has never tried in-line skating.

*It Depends*

- Is the mother willing to learn how to in-line skate herself?
- How similar are in-line skating and roller skating?
- Does the mother have any friends who know how to in-line skate?
- Does the daughter have a fear of falling?
- What previous kinds of movement experiences has the young girl had?

*Strategy*

The mother needs to familiarize herself with the activity of in-line skating and, if possible, learn the activity before attempting to provide instructional assistance for her daughter. The mother should provide instructions, demonstrations, and physical rehearsal opportunities for her daughter that are simple and brief, and that allow the youngster to get a basic idea of the movement and enjoy some initial success. The mother might consider whether physical guidance procedures would be helpful during the first few sessions of practice. As the daughter's skill improves, she can be encouraged to perform the movement in a situation that is similar to the target context (i.e., on neighborhood sidewalks in the presence of other skaters).

# 9

# Structuring the Learning Experience

## Chapter Outline



## Chapter Objectives

**When you have completed this chapter, you should be able to**

discuss the concept of practice structure, and explain its importance to goal achievement and to people's performance of target skills in the desired target context(s);

describe the difference between blocked- and random-practice schedules for situations in which individuals are attempting to learn a number of different tasks;

provide several explanations for the advantages of random-practice schedules in people's learning of a number of different tasks;

describe the difference between constant- and varied-practice schedules for situations in which individuals are attempting to learn how to adapt a particular movement to a variety of target contexts;

contrast random- and varied-practice schedules, and explain how practitioners might combine the two during motor skill learning; and

explain the difference between consistent and varied stimulus-response mapping, and explain how practitioners might assist learners in automating their responses for each type of mapping.

## Preview

Two skill practitioners are puzzled and concerned. They have been supervising volleyball instruction for a group of preadolescent individuals at a summer camp. For several weeks the campers have practiced a variety of different skills in a series of 12 one-hour sessions. During each session, campers practice one skill for a while, then shift to a second skill and practice it, then move to a third skill, and so on. The instructors think that by structuring practice in this way they are encouraging the campers to concentrate more fully on each skill, and this should allow them sufficient repetitions to achieve a good level of mastery. When the campers practice this way, they seem to be getting better; they are performing most of the skills pretty well. However, each time they attempt to play an actual game of volleyball, the campers appear confused and seem to have lost much of the skill they had previously demonstrated.

The instructors wonder what is happening. Are they failing to give their learners enough practice. Should they wait longer before introducing the campers to the game situation? Have they chosen the wrong type of practice schedule for the campers? How else might they structure practice sessions to improve the campers' transition from skill rehearsal to game performance?

## Overview

It almost goes without saying that the most important contributor to motor learning is the act of proper physical rehearsal itself. Certainly, the extremely high skill levels demonstrated by accomplished performers are achievable only because of the amount of time, effort, and rehearsal these individuals have devoted to their preparation. Kottke et al. (1978) estimate that during their respective 15-yr professional sport careers, a typical quarterback in American football throws 1.4 million passes and a typical basketball player attempts a million shots! Clearly, individuals who desire to be accomplished performers must also be prepared to spend incredible amounts of time practicing their skills.

But the amount of time a person spends practicing is not the only concern here. Certainly, the *quality* of practice sessions is crucial as well. An individual can exert considerable effort during many hours of ineffective practice, with little to show for it except boredom, frustration, or perhaps a type of skill performance that is not appropriate for the target context. With this in mind, instructors must be diligent and organize and structure practice sessions in an effective manner.

There are countless ways to organize physical rehearsal. Understanding the pros and cons of all of these variations and the ways they affect learning is a challenging problem for practitioners. Yet, the scientific literature is full of studies dealing with several features of practice sessions. Understanding how these features affect learning can be extremely beneficial to movement practitioners who are interested in devising effective practices. In this chapter we turn our focus to the actual structure of practice sessions, showing how individuals can rehearse two or more tasks together to facilitate learning and how people's practice of variations of a single task can increase their capability to adapt movements to meet the demands of new situations. We conclude the chapter by discussing ways practitioners might structure the practice of rapid, open tasks that require performers to match their responses to environmental demands.

## Practicing Several Different Tasks

In many real-world settings, the instructor's goal is to teach more than a single skill during a fixed period of time, often within a single practice session. Most sport practices include the rehearsal of a variety of activities. For example, a tennis practice might involve rehearsal of the forehand and backhand ground strokes, the volley, and several types of serves, not to mention the numerous variations of spin or placement that individuals might practice. Rehabilitation sessions that are designed to assist stroke patients in the recovery of manual skills might include activities like buttoning a shirt, tying shoelaces, opening a can of tuna, and threading a needle. The question confronting teachers and therapists is how to sequence the practice of a number of tasks within a session in order to maximize learning. Two variations of sequencing, or practice scheduling, have been shown to have powerful effects on learning: blocked practice and random practice.

## Blocked Practice and Random Practice

Suppose that an individual wants to learn three tasks (tasks A, B, and C) in a practice session, and that these tasks are reasonably different, such as three different gymnastics stunts or three manual activities (e.g., hammering a nail, cutting out a dress pattern with a pair of scissors, and opening a bottle of wine with a corkscrew). A commonsense approach to scheduling would be to devote a fixed block of time for the learner to practice the first task before moving on to the next. Then the learner would spend a period of time on the second task before moving on to the third. This approach to scheduling, where the learner's entire rehearsal time is spent on one task before beginning practice on the next, is referred to as **blocked practice**. Blocked practice is typically seen during drills, with individuals attempting the same movement over and over. This kind of practice seems to make sense in that it allows learners uninterrupted time to concentrate on the performance of each task, so that they can engrain, refine, and, if necessary, correct one skill before proceeding to the next.

Sometimes an individual practices several tasks in a single session. In **random practice**, for example, the order of rehearsal of a number of different tasks is intermingled, or mixed, during the practice period. Learners rotate continually among the tasks and, in the most extreme case, they never perform the same task twice in a row.

What are some of the effects of these two different practice schedules (random and blocked) on learning? They may not be what you would expect. Numerous experiments have generated very surprising findings that seem to contradict standard views of practice. In 1979, Shea and Morgan conducted the first of these studies (see the highlight box on page 234) and reported that learning proved superior when practice had occurred under random conditions than under blocked conditions. Their findings have been reproduced several times in other highly controlled laboratory experiments (Lee & Magill, 1983; Shea, Kohl, & Indermill, 1990; Tsutsui, Lee, & Hodges, 1998), as well as in studies conducted in more everyday instructional settings (Boyce & Del Rey, 1990; Goode & Magill, 1986; Hall, Domingues, & Cavazos, 1994; Wrisberg & Liu, 1991) and in rehabilitation environments (Hanlon, 1996).

**blocked practice**—A practice sequence in which individuals repeatedly rehearse the same task.

**random practice**—A practice sequence in which individuals perform a number of different tasks in no particular order, thus avoiding or minimizing consecutive repetitions of any single task.

## Why Random Practice Is So Effective

Most research has shown that when individuals randomly practice a variety of movements, their performance during practice is less successful than that of individuals practicing movements in a blocked fashion. However, when participants resume performance at a later time, those who originally practiced under random conditions demonstrate superior retention compared to those who originally practiced under blocked conditions. Thus, in contextual interference studies we find one of those counterintuitive phenomena of human learning: poorer initial performance (in practices) leads to better learning! This pattern of results, termed the **contextual interference effect**, challenges conventional wisdom (that learning will be better if individuals are more proficient during practice, which usually is the case during

**contextual interference effect**—The phenomenon that arises from experimental research comparing the effects of random- and blocked-practice schedules on the learning of several tasks; specifically, although blocked practice produces better performance than random practice during initial rehearsal, when performance is compared on later retention tests, random practice produces better learning than blocked practice.

## The Shea and Morgan Experiment

John Shea and Robyn Morgan (1979) conducted a groundbreaking experiment that revolutionized the way movement scientists think about the processes involved in task rehearsal. Following some of the original ideas of William Battig (1966), Shea and Morgan placed individuals in two groups that practiced three different arm and hand movements (tasks A, B, and C), the goal being to move as fast as possible on each attempt. During the "practice phase," one group of participants performed the three movements in a blocked order; that is, they completed all of their attempts on task A before moving to task B, and then completed all their attempts on task B before moving to task C. Individuals in the other group practiced the three movements in a random order, with their attempts on the three tasks being randomly intermingled. Both groups performed all three movements the same number of times during the practice phase.

In order to determine how the two different practice schedules influenced skill learning, Shea and Morgan required participants to perform the movements again on two other occasions in what they called the "retention phase." The first occasion occurred just 10 min after individuals completed their last attempt of the practice phase, and the second occasion took place 10 days later (see figure 9.1). During the retention phase, each group (those who had practiced under random conditions and those who had practiced under blocked conditions) was asked to perform the movements in both a blocked and a random format. The results of this study revealed that in the practice phase, the blocked group produced movements that were far faster (i.e., lower movement times) than those of the random group. However, in the retention phase, there was a large advantage for the participants who had learned the task under random conditions.

These results indicate that, while blocked practice may produce better immediate performance, random practice produces better learning. Shea and Morgan's findings surprised scientists in the field who had previously assumed that consecutive repetitions of the same movement would produce better learning than nonconsecutive repetitions of several movements. Ever since the publication of this study, the challenge for researchers has been to understand how random-practice conditions, which seem to produce *poorer* initial performance, can actually lead to *better* long-term learning.

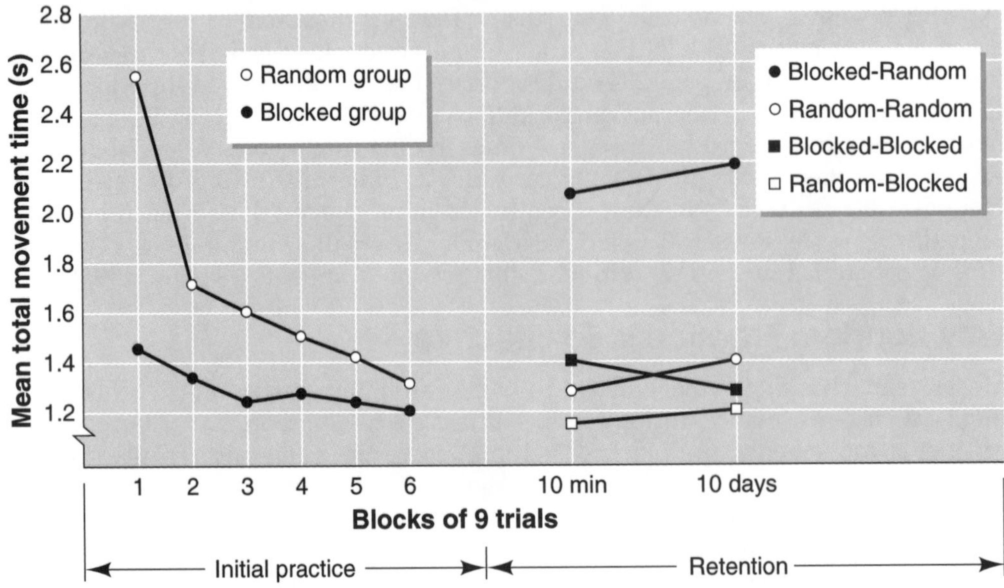


Figure 9.1 Performance on movement-speed tasks under random and blocked conditions. The relative amount learned by each group during initial practice (left side of figure) is shown by their retention performance under random and blocked conditions (right side of figure). (Reprinted by permission from Shea & Morgan, 1979.)

## A MATHEMATICAL ANALOGY TO THE FORGETTING EXPLANATION

Cuddy and Jacoby (1982) have suggested a mathematics example of the difference between blocked practice and random practice that is analogous to the forgetting explanation for the contextual interference effect in motor learning. Suppose that you are a 10-year-old who wants to learn to do long division in your head; the three problems you are asked to solve during practice are 21 ÷ 7, 18 ÷ 2, and 12 ÷ 4. If you are practicing under blocked conditions, the instructor might ask you for the answer to 21 ÷ 7 first, and you would struggle to come up with it—3. When the instructor asks you to come up with the answer to 21 ÷ 7 again, you simply remember the previous answer, 3, without going through the mental processing that you used to generate the solution the first time. This repetition of the same solution would continue to occur for as long as the instructor asked you to solve 21 ÷ 7. Your performance would be essentially perfect because you would have to do nothing more than repeat the same solution each time.

If you are practicing under random conditions, on the other hand, you would be asked for the answer to 21 ÷ 7, followed by the answer to 18 ÷ 2, and then the answer to 12 ÷ 4. After that you might be asked for the answer to 18 ÷ 2 or 21 ÷ 7 again, which by now you would probably have forgotten. Thus, you would be forced to come up with the solution once again. Improvements in your performance would come much more slowly and with considerably more difficulty than if you had learned under blocked-practice conditions, but your long-term learning and retention would be enhanced because you would be forced to generate solutions to the problems more frequently.

blocked practice). Two interesting hypotheses have been proposed to explain the contextual interference effect. Let's look at each.

### *More Meaningful and Distinctive Learning*

Shea and Zimny (1983) interpreted the beneficial effects of random practice in terms of an increased meaningfulness or distinctiveness of the movements, sometimes referred to as the **elaboration hypothesis**. They argued that, when individuals change from one task to another during a random-practice session, they begin to appreciate the distinctiveness of the different tasks, making each task more meaningful in their long-term memory. More meaningful or distinctive memories are presumably more durable and, therefore, more easily recalled for use at a later time.

**elaboration hypothesis**—One explanation for the contextual interference effect; states that random practice during early rehearsal causes individuals to appreciate the distinctiveness of different tasks, whereas blocked practice allows individuals to bypass such comparisons and produce the separate tasks automatically.

Shea and Zimny interviewed participants in one of their experiments, and the comments people made supported the researchers' interpretation. Random-practice individuals spoke of elaborate relationships they had noticed between the spatial pattern of the different movements they were producing, as well as between those movement patterns and the patterns of other familiar objects and shapes. For example, some random-practice individuals noticed that the pattern for movement A was essentially the same as that for movement C, except that the first part of the movement was reversed. One particular individual even observed that the spatial pattern of one of the movements was similar in shape to that of a mirror image of the letter Z. Comments such as these suggested to Shea and Zimny that individuals in the random-practice condition derived greater meaningfulness and distinctiveness from the movements they were practicing. Participants in the blocked-practice condition, on the other hand, talked of producing their movements more or less automatically. Apparently, the repetition of single movements during separate series of attempts did not cause these individuals to notice similarities and differences among the several movements or between those movements and others with which they were familiar.

### Spacing of Movements: The Forgetting Hypothesis

Another explanation for the benefits of random practice is the **forgetting, or spacing, hypothesis**. According to this hypothesis, when random-practice individuals shift from task A to task B, they forget what they did on task A while they are trying to figure out what to do on task B. Therefore, when it's time for them to attempt task A again, they have to generate the plan for that task all over. For this reason, the forgetting hypothesis is sometimes referred to as the *action plan reconstruction hypothesis* (Lee & Magill, 1985). Because random-practice individuals are continuously being challenged to produce the appropriate plans for different movements, their performance during initial practice is relatively poor. However, they benefit from this more rigorous form of practice when they resume task performance at a later time.

On the other hand, blocked-practice individuals are able to apply the same plan that they use on the first attempt of each task for all subsequent attempts. Not surprisingly, the performance of these individuals is quite good—all they do is remember and repeatedly execute a single plan. Unfortunately, longer-term learning is not as good, presumably because of the minimal experience these individuals have in generating different plans during their rehearsal of the various tasks.

The act of repeatedly generating task solutions or movement plans is one way to understand how random practice (compared to blocked practice) actually enhances learning. This is sometimes referred to as **retrieval practice**, because individuals are forced to practice the skill of retrieving necessary performance information from long-term memory (Bjork, 1975, 1979; Landauer & Bjork, 1978). The extensive retrieval practice that occurs during random practice presumably leads to more effective performance in future situations requiring these retrieval operations.

How might we use the conceptual model of human performance (see figure 9.2) to explain the way people repeatedly retrieve task solutions or movement plans? Remember that whenever individuals decide to produce a rapid, goal-oriented movement, they must retrieve a **generalized motor program** from **long-term memory** (using the *response-selection* stage). Once they have done this, individuals select **parameters** (using the *response-programming* stage) that dictate how the specific action should be executed (i.e., how rapidly, forcefully, long, etc.). The act of selecting the appropriate generalized program and determining the desired parameters represents a type of task solution. During random practice, individuals must retrieve a program and "parameterize" it prior to each movement, because they are producing different movements (requiring different *desired states* and *motor programs*) from one practice attempt to the next. During blocked practice, individuals can use the same program and parameters (almost without modification) for a series of movement attempts, thereby avoiding the effortful process of retrieval and **parameterization** which is important for learning.

**forgetting, or spacing, hypothesis**—One explanation for the contextual interference effect; states that random practice during early rehearsal causes individuals to generate, or reconstruct, the action plan for a movement task each time it is rehearsed because they forget the action plan while they are producing other tasks; also referred to as the action plan reconstruction hypothesis.

**retrieval practice**—The act of retrieving a motor program and its parameters from long-term memory; facilitated by a random-practice schedule.

**generalized motor program**—A motor program that defines a pattern of movement rather than a specific movement; this flexibility allows performers to adapt the generalized program to produce variations of the pattern that meet altered environmental demands.

**long-term memory (LTM)**—The memory system that holds information and experiences; believed to be vast in capacity and unlimited in duration.

**parameters**—The modifiable features of a generalized motor program, such as speed or amplitude of the movement; also referred to as surface features.

**parameterization**—The act of assigning parameter values to the parameters of a generalized motor program (e.g., more force, left hand, shorter movement time) that allows the performer to achieve a particular movement goal.

## Practical Implications of Blocked and Random Practice

One of the most important implications of the research on blocked and random practice concerns the impact of movement repetitions on skill learning. How often have you heard people say that learners need to practice a task "over and over until they get it right," as if a massive number of repetitions is somehow going to stamp the correct movement into the learners' brains?

The concept of repetition is deeply rooted in many traditional training methods. Serious students of piano, violin, and dance are required to devote countless hours of repetition to the fundamental movement patterns considered to be essential to performance. Athletes practice some of their movements hundreds of times, often in

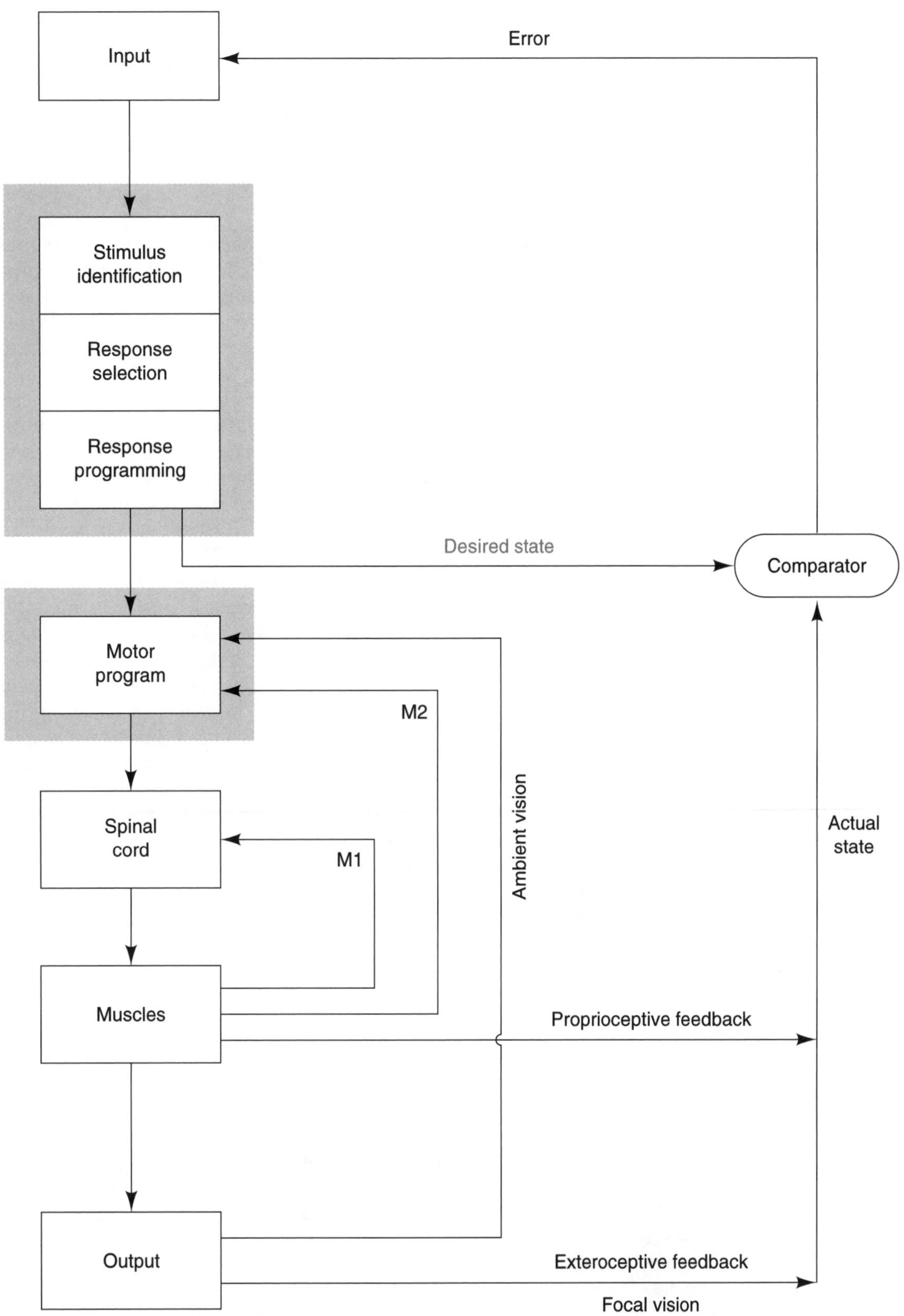


**Figure 9.2** The conceptual model of human performance, highlighting the processes where practice effects are thought to occur.

IT DEPENDS . . .

Do you agree with what Joe Gibbs, former Washington Redskins head coach, said in a televised interview in 1991? "The main reason we have football practice is so that we can run the same play over and over and over again." Is there a difference between repetitions and repetitiveness? Please explain your answer.

a single practice session, in order to engrain the correct action (e.g., free throw shots in basketball, serves in tennis, chip shots in golf). Therapy patients attempt the same actions over and over during rehabilitation sessions in an effort to recover the control of functional movements (e.g., feeding, locomotion, dressing). Typically, practice in these types of situations occurs in a blocked fashion, which we now know is relatively ineffective for long-term learning.

The paradox of blocked-practice scheduling is that it produces effective performance during initial rehearsal but does not create lasting learning. Individuals achieve good performance because they are practicing in an environment that is very stable and predictable, and they are able to fine-tune the movement parameters from one attempt to the next. Blocked practice may also be favorable for some of the minor, temporary factors that contribute to consistent performance (such as an optimal level of arousal and an appropriate focus of attention). The result is an artificially high level of performance that gives individuals a false sense of accomplishment.

Many of our golfing friends tell us they can "do anything" during blocked practice at the driving range, implying that their skills have risen to some new level. However, when these folks take their skills back out onto the golf course, they perform no better than they did before their driving range experience. In a similar way, patients may experience temporary performance improvements during therapy sessions but then become frustrated when the skills they thought were getting better disappear in the target context—at home or in other everyday environments. Why?

One answer is that, during blocked practice, people either fail to practice the **target skill**, or they practice the target skill in a context that is not the same as that of the **target context**. For example, during concerts, musicians and dancers are usually expected to perform movements that are in synchrony with those of other performers—while still maintaining their own degree of expressiveness—rather than repeat isolated sequences of fundamental movement patterns in an almost robotlike fashion. Similarly, during competition, athletes are often called upon to produce a single repetition of a particular movement in any of a number of different situations (e.g., one basketball free throw shot with two seconds left in the game and the shooter's team down by one point)—quite different from producing numerous repetitions of the movement in the same situation. The **specificity of learning** notion (see chapter 7) suggests

**target skills**—The tasks an individual wishes to be able to perform (e.g., keeping a tennis ball in play, knocking down 10-pins with a bowling ball, playing basketball with a prosthetic limb).

**target context**—The environmental context in which an individual wants to be able to perform a skill (e.g., keeping a tennis ball in play during a singles match with a friend at a local recreational facility).

**specificity of learning**—The notion that the best learning experiences are those that approximate most closely the movement components and environmental conditions of the target skill and target context.

IT DEPENDS . . .

Consider the following quote from former Tampa Bay Buccaneers head coach Sam Wyche: "I told our players I don't know what happens on Friday night and Saturday, because we see a whole different team on Sunday from what we see during the week. It's frustrating to me as a coach because I don't have an explanation. . . . I take the blame for it. For some reason, this team doesn't play as well as it practices." (Los Angeles Times, October 25, 1993)

Coach Wyche noticed a difference in his team's performance during practices and in games. What are some of the things this coach might have been doing during practices that could have contributed to the problem?

that the best practice experiences are those that bring individuals as close as possible to the conditions of the target skill and the target context. Such conditions are often negligible or absent in many blocked-practice situations.

Many tasks require individuals to produce movements in the target context in ways that are quite different from how they produce them during blocked practice. In table 9.1, we summarize some of the features of skill performance in the target context that may be different during blocked practice.

The fact that blocked practice does not include the almost-random characteristics of many target skills is not the only factor operating here. Recall from the highlight box on page 234 that, in the Shea and Morgan (1979) study, random-practice conditions during initial rehearsal produced more effective performance at a later time than did blocked-practice conditions, even when individuals were instructed to perform the skill at a later time under blocked conditions (see figure 9.1). In practical terms, these results suggest that, even when skills are performed in a target context that is blocked in nature (e.g., 100 repetitions of a rifle shot from a fixed distance, piecework on an assembly line, shoveling dirt), it is still slightly more effective for individuals to practice the task under random conditions. And when the target skill must be produced in a target context that includes random conditions, random practice is far more effective than blocked practice.

The target skill involves decisions about where to hit the ball, which club to use, how to adjust the stance depending on the slope of the ground, and how far to take the backswing back.

## How to Use Blocked and Random Practice During Instruction

For the first few attempts at a new skill, individuals in the verbal-cognitive stage of learning may benefit more from blocked-practice conditions than from random-practice conditions (Shea, Kohl, & Indermill, 1990), perhaps because they

**verbal-cognitive stage**—The initial stage of learning, in which verbal and cognitive processes dominate the learner's activity.

**Table 9.1**

**Features of a Skill Performed in the Target Context and in Blocked Practice**

| Target context | Blocked practice |
|---|---|
| *Preceded by regular varied conditions.* | *Not preceded by regular varied conditions.* |
| *Requires the generation of a solution on each attempt.* | *Requires the generation of a solution only on the first attempt.* |
| *Allows only one chance for success.* | *Allows many chances for success.* |
| *Same movement is not repeated on successive attempts.* | *Same movement is repeated on successive attempts.* |
| *Corrections are not allowed on next attempt.* | *Corrections are allowed on next attempt.* |

## HOW EFFECTIVE IS BLOCKED PRACTICE ON THE GOLF DRIVING RANGE?

On the golf course (i.e., the target context for most golfers), an individual rarely hits the same shot twice in a row (unless the ball goes into the lake on the first shot!), and most shots are preceded by a long walk (or maybe a search for the ball). The target skill involves a series of decisions about where to hit the ball, which club to use, how to adjust the stance depending on the slope of the ground, how far to take the backswing back, and so on. The target context (i.e., a round of golf on the golf course) requires a solution to a *particular* movement problem for *each* shot, not minor changes in a shot that has just been attempted a few seconds earlier. Furthermore, golfers (at least those who adhere to the rules of the game) get only one chance to make each shot, with no opportunity to modify that shot on the next attempt. In light of all this, blocked practice at the driving range does not simulate the target skill for golf very well.

need a number of repetitions in order to produce the action successfully just once. However, as soon as learners acquire a rough approximation of the movement, they should shift their practice to a random schedule (see table 9.2 for a sample progression). For therapy patients, who almost always have some knowledge of and experience with the tasks they are practicing (e.g., putting on a shirt, brushing teeth, walking), blocked practice may never be appropriate.

**motor stage**—The second stage of learning, in which motor programs are developed and the individual's performance becomes increasingly consistent.

By the time individuals reach the **motor stage** of learning, they should be avoiding repetitious blocked practice as much as possible. One way they can do this is to practice several tasks in the same session, rotating from one task to the next on a continuous basis. Springboard divers, for example, practice a different dive on each successive attempt, rotating through the various dives that are scheduled for practice that day. Athletes in team sports like basketball, football, volleyball, and team handball should practice different plays rather than the same play over and over. Golfers should practice hitting a different shot each time, even on the practice range. A former conference golf champion prepared for competition by mentally imaging the layout of the course he was going to play in his next tournament and then hitting the sequence of shots he planned to hit on each hole (except for putts). While this type of practice-range rehearsal did not simulate the golfer's target skill exactly (e.g., walking long distances to the ball, hitting balls positioned at different locations on

**Table 9.2**

**Gradual Progression From Blocked Practice to Random Practice for Volleyball Skills**

| | |
|---|---|
| *Blocked:* | *Spike, spike, spike, spike, spike, spike*<br>*Block, block, block, block, block, block*<br>*Pass, pass, pass, pass, pass, pass* |
| *Mixture of blocked and random:* | *Spike, spike, block, block, pass, pass*<br>*Block, block, spike, spike, pass, pass*<br>*Spike, spike, pass, pass, block, block* |
| *Random:* | *Spike, pass, block, pass, block, spike*<br>*Pass, block, spike, block, pass, spike*<br>*Block, pass, spike, pass, spike, block* |

## A COMMENT BY BERNSTEIN ON THE PROCESS OF LEARNING

The late Russian physiologist N.I. Bernstein (1967), known especially for his contributions to our understanding of the neurological basis of learning, said this about the learning process:

"The process of practice towards the achievement of new motor habits essentially consists in the gradual success of a search for optimal motor solutions to the appropriate problems. Because of this, practice, when properly undertaken, does not consist in repeating the means of solution of a motor problem time after time, but in the process of solving this problem again and again." (p. 134)

## PREPARING PEOPLE FOR THE TARGET CONTEXT

Former Princeton University coach Pete Carril offered the following comment about the relationship between practice structure and the target context for the sport of basketball:

"There is a whole bunch of dribbling drills, but my complaint about some of them is that they aren't connected to the actual skill and situation in a game. No drill is any good unless it's used in some form in the game." (Carril & White, 1997, p. 44)

the course, hitting out of the rough or out of sand), it did allow him to practice a variety of shots, changing the club each time, in a shorter time frame.

It appears that a random-practice structure is particularly effective when individuals are performing tasks that are less similar to each other. In fact, some research evidence (see Magill & Hall, 1990) suggests that the benefits of random practice are enhanced if the differences between the tasks individuals perform on successive attempts are larger. Thus, a therapy patient might benefit considerably from the random practice of several very different everyday skills (e.g., buttoning a shirt, tying a shoe, opening an aluminum can, brushing teeth). Practitioners need to remember, however, that learners may resist this type of practice because they aren't experiencing as much immediate success as they do in a blocked format. But, as Bjork and his associates point out, practice conditions (like those found with a blocked format) that keep "multiple aspects of the task environment fixed and predictable are conditions that, in effect, deny learners the opportunity to learn what they don't know" (Jacoby, Bjork, & Kelley, 1994, p. 72). The key to successful practice is allowing learners to experience the conditions they can expect to see in the target context—even when this means more frequent errors and slower performance improvements. Learners need to know that it is okay to make mistakes, and perhaps also why the mistakes are occurring. More importantly, they need to be assured that, though their performance during random practice may not be as good as they would like it to be, it is going to be much better when it's time for them to perform the tasks in the target context.

## Practicing Several Versions of the Same Task

Sometimes individuals want to learn just one task that they can perform in a variety of ways. For example, the task of throwing involves a collection, or class, of

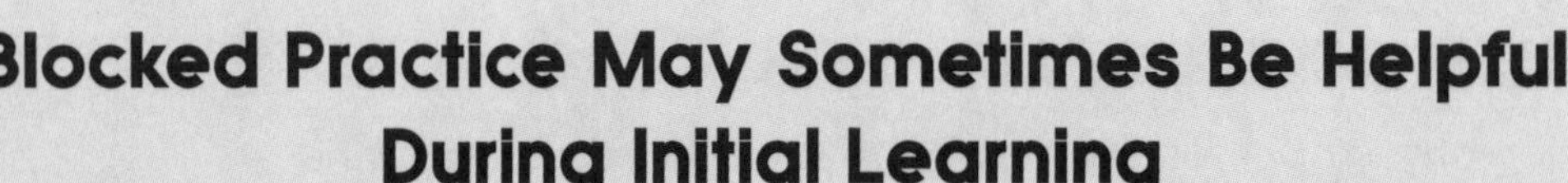

## Blocked Practice May Sometimes Be Helpful During Initial Learning

How much the practice of a number of tasks should be randomized during initial skill learning depends on, among other things, the age and skill level of learners. Individuals who are younger (Wrisberg & Mead, 1983) and less skilled may need to be given more opportunity to experience repetitions of one movement before practicing another. However, for older learners or for those who have achieved a higher level of skill, random practice may be more appropriate. In a recent study by Landin and Hebert (1997), moderately skilled college students (having already had two years of competitive high school basketball experience but no intercollegiate experience) practiced the basketball set shot from six different locations that varied in their distance from and their angle to the basket. Participants in the study were assigned to three practice conditions, which differed according to the number of repetitions individuals attempted at one location before moving to the next (1, 3, or 6). Following initial practice, participants were tested to determine shooting accuracy under each of the following conditions: four attempts from each of three locations in a blocked format, four attempts from the same locations in a repeating format (i.e., 1, 2, 3, 1, 2, 3, etc.), and 10 pairs of free throw shots with a brief rest between each pair. The results revealed that the performance of the group that had initially practiced three successive repetitions at each location was significantly more accurate than that of the other two groups. These findings add further support to the notion that the extent to which practitioners should use a blocked-practice format during the initial rehearsal of tasks depends on the skill level of learners. For these moderately skilled individuals, an intermediate level of random-practice structure proved to be the most beneficial.

movements that people can perform in various forms. If an individual's goal is to be skilled at throwing, she must develop the capability to throw objects of different sizes, shapes, and weights over different distances, with parabolic and flat trajectories, to stationary and moving targets—not to mention other possible variations.

**invariant features**—The components of a movement that remain the same, or constant, when performers change the surface features of the movement.

Individuals control different versions of the same class of movements by using a generalized motor program (see chapters 5 and 6). The generalized motor program is characterized by a number of fundamental **invariant features**. For example, the program for throwing might include the way the object is gripped, the stepping action and hip rotation, the arm action, the wrist movement, the follow-through, and so on. The way we can tell that a movement is a member of a particular class of actions (e.g., throwing) is that each time a person produces a version of the movement (e.g., throwing a baseball), we see the same invariant features as in other versions (e.g., throwing a newspaper). In addition, the invariant features for one class of movements (e.g., throwing) differ from the invariant features for other classes of movements (e.g., kicking, striking, hopping, catching).

### IT DEPENDS . . .

A woman who recently underwent double amputation is learning how to use the prosthetic devices that have been made for both her arms. Her goal is to be able to perform as many common movements as possible (e.g., feeding, drinking, card playing, bathing) both in the context of her home environment and in a variety of other social situations. How might a physical therapist structure the woman's practice sessions to allow her to achieve her goals?

## WHAT IS EFFECTIVE TRAINING?

"The effectiveness of a training program should be measured not by the speed of acquisition of a task during training or by the level of performance reached at the end of training, but rather by learners' performance in the posttraining tasks and real-world settings that are the target of training" (Druckman & Bjork, 1991, p. 47).

Once individuals have learned a generalized motor program, say for throwing, they can use it in many different situations. A helpful way of understanding how they might do this is illustrated in the conceptual model of human performance we have developed (see figure 9.2, on page 237). Let's say that a person needs to produce a particular throwing movement, such as throwing a damp, dirty sweatshirt into a laundry hamper. First, the individual evaluates (in the **stimulus-identification stage**) the present environmental conditions (e.g., size of the hamper, weight of the sweatshirt, distance it must be thrown, height of the ceiling, location of possible obstacles between the thrower and the hamper). Next, the person decides (in the **response-selection stage**) what kind of throw is needed (e.g., an overarm throw of a particular trajectory). Finally, the individual programs (in the **response-programming stage**) the parameters needed to produce the required movement (e.g., force, velocity, release point, etc.).

**stimulus-identification stage**—The first stage of information processing; during this stage, the individual recognizes and identifies the input.

**response-selection stage**—The second stage of information processing; during this stage, the individual decides what, if any, response should be made.

**response-programming stage**—The third stage of information processing; during this stage, the individual organizes the motor system to produce the desired movement.

An important question for movement practitioners is what type of practice structure most effectively promotes the development of generalized motor programs. In the next section, we address two types of practice structure that scientists have examined in research studies, then we discuss the relative merits of each type of structure in promoting generalized program development.

### Constant Practice and Varied Practice

Determining the type of practice structure that promotes development of the individual's capacity to produce a variety of actions from the same movement class is a fundamental issue for practitioners who are assisting individuals in the learning of generalized motor programs. Throwing is one example of such an action (e.g., throwing balls at different speeds to different locations in the games of baseball and football, throwing darts at different areas of a target, throwing different types of objects into trash receptacles of different sizes, and using various throwing motions to cast fishing lures toward targets). Practitioners could have learners repeatedly rehearse a single movement version (i.e., using blocked practice). This form of practice is sometimes referred to in the scientific literature as **constant practice**.

**constant practice**—A practice sequence in which individuals rehearse only one variation of a given class of tasks during a session.

## CHARACTERISTICS OF A GENERALIZED MOTOR PROGRAM FOR A CLASS OF MOVEMENTS

A class of movements is characterized by the following elements:

- Common sequencing among the elements of the action
- Common temporal, or rhythmical, organization (i.e., relative timing)
- Variable **parameters**, or surface features, (e.g., speed) that individuals specify prior to each movement attempt, depending on goal requirements

**parameters**—The modifiable features of a generalized motor program, such as speed or amplitude of the movement; also referred to as surface features.

## Random Practice and Stroke Patients

Little research has been conducted to determine how the practice structure affects stroke patients' learning, but a recent study by Hanlon (1996) suggests that a random-practice schedule may be superior to a blocked-practice schedule in improving the limb function of such individuals. In Hanlon's study, 24 patients with hemiparesis (semiparalysis to one limb) resulting from a cerebral stroke practiced a functional task (opening a cupboard door, grasping a coffee cup by the handle, lifting the cup off the shelf, placing it on a counter, and releasing the grasp) under one of two practice-structure conditions. Successful performance was defined as three consecutive correct attempts. Both a random-practice group and a blocked-practice group attempted the task 10 times daily until they achieved the performance criterion. Between each practice attempt on the primary task, random-practice participants performed three additional tasks with the semiparalyzed limb (pointing, touching objects, touching spots on a flat surface) while blocked-practice participants rested. A control group practiced neither the functional tasks nor the additional tasks. All three groups were given retention tests (involving five attempts on the functional task each time) two and again seven days after the practice phase.

No difference was found between the random- and blocked-practice groups in the number of attempts individuals needed to achieve the performance criterion. However, compared with both the blocked-practice group and the control group, the random-practice group performed a significantly greater number of successful attempts during both retention tests. These findings suggest that, for stroke patients, a random-practice schedule, which includes additional experiences with a number of motor tasks, produces better retention of a functional task than does repetition of the task alone. These findings have strong implications for rehabilitation.

**varied practice**—A practice sequence in which individuals rehearse a number of variations of a given class of tasks during a session; also referred to as variable practice.

However, if the goal of learning is to produce a number of versions of the movement class, it makes more sense to have learners attempt different versions of the action while they are practicing. This type of rehearsal is referred to as **varied practice**.

A particular strength of varied practice is that it allows learners to develop competence in parameterizing different dimensions of the action. An example of how this might work for the throwing action is illustrated in figure 9.3. On the horizontal axis are several possible distances an individual might throw an object during a practice session, with 40 m being the maximum distance. Regardless of which distance the person chooses, she would use the same generalized motor program. For any particular distance, the individual would specify the parameters needed (e.g., force, velocity) to produce the desired throw. For a 10-m throw, the individual would select parameter values in a lower range (i.e., less force and velocity); for a 40-m throw, she would select higher values (i.e., more force and velocity). If the performer selects the wrong parameter values, her throws will be too long or too short. Skilled performers are those more adept at selecting values that match task demands.

You may think that varied practice is just commonsensical. For example, if the fisher's only requirements are to cast lures that cover distances of 5 m and 10 m, then wouldn't it be smart to practice casting at distances of only 5 m and 10 m? This type of practice would also be consistent with the specificity of learning notion, which advocates the learning of specific actions to accomplish specific goals. Put another way, practice sessions should be structured so that rehearsal conditions resemble those of the target context as much as possible. This means that therapy patients learning to feed themselves should be given practice with different types of foods and utensils, dental students learning to insert fillings in cavities should be given practice with different shapes of teeth and mouths, and hockey goalies should be given practice stopping different types of shots.

But there is more to varied practice than the learning of specific movement versions. Assume you are teaching a child to throw a ball, and during practice sessions you instruct her to throw the ball three different distances (e.g., 10, 20, and 40 m). You know that someday the child will need to be able to throw balls different distances than these and you want her to be able to do it. Let's say that after the child has had considerable varied-practice experience, she is placed in a target context (e.g., playing catch with her brother at a family picnic) where she needs to produce a 30-m throw. In a sense, this might be considered a novel (i.e., new) task for her, because the child has never attempted a throw of this particular distance before. At the same time, this task should not be novel at all for her, because she has practiced throwing the ball a number of distances that are both less than and greater than the 30-m distance.

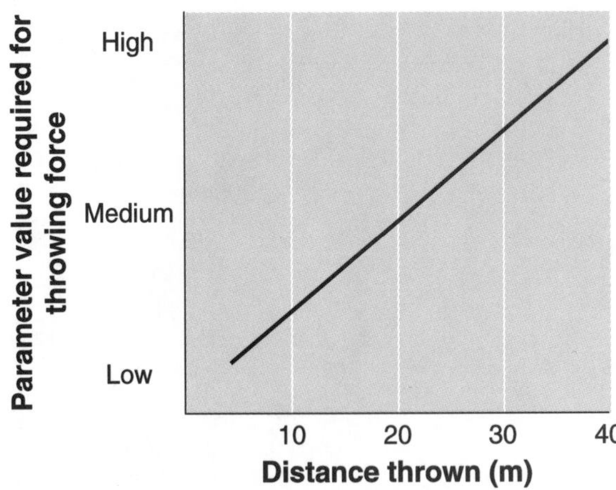


Figure 9.3 Hypothetical force parameter values for throwing an object different distances. Higher parameter values for force produce longer throws.

Laboratory research (e.g., Carson & Wiegand, 1979; Kerr & Booth, 1978) and our own experience tells us that the child should have little difficulty producing the 30-m throw. However, in this case, the research and our experience would be in conflict with the specificity of learning view. Remember that a strict specificity interpretation predicts that people learn exactly what they practice. According to this view, the child should be able to accurately perform throws for the particular distances she has practiced (i.e., 10, 20, and 40 m), but she should not be able to produce the novel (i.e., 30-m) throwing distance very effectively. The fact that individuals *are* able to successfully perform novel versions of a movement, however, indicates that, when they engage in varied practice, they acquire *much more* than the capability of producing those specific actions. Rather, what they develop is some *general capability* of producing many different variations of a *class* of actions, a capability that is not strongly tied to any particular version of the movement. The question becomes what the person is developing that allows her to do this. One answer to this question is a "schema."

## Schema Development: Motor Programs and Parameters

When people practice a number of specific throwing distances, they learn something that allows them to generalize this experience to the performance of many throwing distances. One conceptualization that has been proposed to account for this phenomenon is the **schema** (Schmidt, 1975). According to schema theory, when individuals practice a particular class of movements, they acquire a set of rules, the "schema," that they use to determine the **parameter values** necessary to produce different versions of the action (e.g., throwing an object different distances).

**schema**—A set of rules relating the various outcomes of an individual's actions (e.g., short distance of a throw) to the parameter values the individual chooses in order to produce those outcomes (e.g., small amount of force).

Figure 9.4 illustrates how an individual might use the schema to determine the values for the parameter of force he needs to produce throws of different distances. Suppose this individual begins by generating a force with a value of A, which leads to a throw that travels a distance of 15 m. On the next attempt, he chooses a force value of B, which produces a throw of 36 m. This is followed by a force value of C, which results in a throw of 24 m, and so on. With each throw, the individual begins to associate the specific force values he chooses with the actual distances the thrown object travels. With practice, this process of association becomes the basis for a set of rules, or schema, that governs a general relationship between force values and distances thrown. The schema is represented by the diagonal line in figure 9.4 that comes closest to passing through the black dots. With each successive throw, the individual updates the schema, so that by the time he has produced hundreds or thousands of

**parameter values**—The values assigned by a performer to the parameters of a generalized motor program (e.g., rapid movement time, short amplitude, right arm); allow individuals to adjust a movement pattern to meet specific environmental demands.

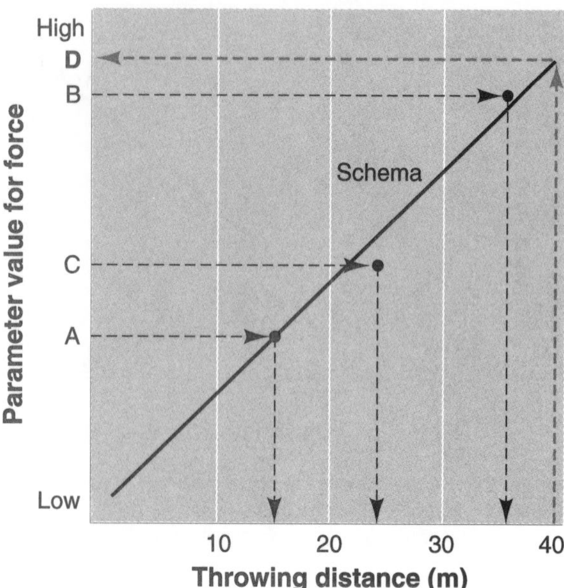


**Figure 9.4** The schema relating force parameter values to throwing distances. To produce a throw of 40 m, the performer uses the schema to select a force with a value of D.

throws, he has established a set of stable and strong rules relating force values to distances thrown.

How might the individual use the schema once it is developed? Say he decides to throw a ball to a friend and estimates that the required distance is 40 m. Once he does this, the individual uses the throwing schema (in the response-programming stage) to estimate the parameter value of force he needs to propel the ball that distance. Referring again to figure 9.4, we see that, theoretically, the individual does this (follow the green line) by connecting the estimated distance (40 m) to the point on the diagonal line representing the set of rules, or schema, that governs throwing. He then connects this point to the force value (D) that he needs in order to produce a throw that will travel this distance. He then delivers the parameter value of D to the generalized motor program, indicating the amount of force he wants to use for the throw, and then he produces the movement.

Using this process, the individual generates a throwing movement with parameter values (for force, as well as for other dimensions, such as movement time and movement distance) based on his past experience with the program. Viewed in this way, it is not too difficult to understand how individuals are able to effectively produce skilled movements they have never specifically practiced before.

## The Role of Varied Practice in Schema Development

Considerable research evidence suggests that varied practice plays a role in the development of schemas. In typical experiments examining this issue, two groups of participants practice under different sets of conditions. An equal number of individuals in a constant-practice group attempts one of several versions of the movement class (e.g., either a 20-, 30-, or 40-m throw). Participants in a varied-practice group perform all of the selected versions (e.g., 20-, 30-, and 40-m throws) an equal

### YOUNG LEARNERS MAY NEED TO MIX CONSTANT AND VARIED PRACTICE

Wrisberg and Mead (1983) examined the learning of four groups of 6- to 8-year-old children on a **coincidence anticipation** task, which involved watching a moving light pattern and tapping a padded panel at the same moment that a target bulb illuminated. Two constant-practice groups trained with a single-speed light pattern (one group practiced with a fast-speed pattern, and one with a slow-speed pattern), and two varied-practice groups trained with four different light speeds (one group practiced the speeds in a random order, while the other group performed a set of six consecutive repetitions with one speed before performing a set of six repetitions with the next). When the groups later switched to light speeds they had not previously experienced, the varied-practice group that had experienced consecutive repetitions of each training speed during initial practice demonstrated the best overall timing performance. These results suggest that young children may benefit from some repetition of a stimulus during the varied practice of an **open skill**

**coincidence anticipation**—A type of task that requires performers to produce movements that coincide in time, space, or both with an external object or event (e.g., catching or hitting a moving ball); sometimes referred to as anticipation timing.

**open skill**—A skill performed in an environment that is unpredictable or in motion and that requires individuals to adapt their movements in response to dynamic properties of the environment.

number of times. Individuals in both groups perform the same number of practice attempts, but their experiences differ with respect to the variability of practice attempts and the number of attempts with each of the movement versions. For example, if both groups attempt 75 throws, individuals in the constant-practice group attempt one of the versions (with an equal number of the individuals practicing each of the versions) for all 75 throws, while all participants in the varied-practice group attempt each of the three versions an equal number of times (i.e., 25 attempts for each version).

The results of these studies show that the constant-practice group outperforms the varied-practice group during initial rehearsal. This is not surprising, since each of the constant-practice individuals is producing a single movement version and does it more effectively than the varied-practice participants, who are producing the three versions in an intermingled fashion. The results of studies with adults (Catalano & Kleiner, 1984) generally indicate that the group that practices under varied conditions performs at least as well as, and frequently better than, the group that practices under constant conditions when both groups transfer to a novel version of the movement (e.g., 25- or 35-m throws). Studies with children show that the varied-practice group outperforms the constant-practice group to an even greater extent on the novel movement versions (e.g., Kerr & Booth, 1978).

One interpretation of these research findings is that individuals acquire movement schemas when they practice, and varied practice enhances the development of these schemas. Therefore, varied-practice individuals perform the novel task more effectively than do their constant-practice counterparts. Put another way, varied practice enhances the flexibility or adaptability of movement production, allowing individuals to apply what they have learned during varied practice to the performance of similar actions they have not specifically attempted before (e.g., Catalano & Kleiner, 1984).

## VARIED PRACTICE WITHIN THE BOUNDARIES OF THE SCHEMA

When organizing varied practice, instructors and therapists should be sure that learners do not exceed the boundaries of the generalized motor program they are developing. A given program's boundaries are exceeded if an individual's action pattern changes markedly near the extremes of a movement's range. For example, if an individual is required to throw a very short distance (less than 5 m) or a very long one (over 50 m), he might abandon the throwing program he has been developing and substitute a different one for producing these extreme range movements. Programs for producing throws of extremely short or extremely long distances may have their own sets of parameter values. Therefore, practitioners should not expect much transfer between a program for producing midrange throwing distances and programs used for producing throws of extreme distances.

## IT DEPENDS . . .

A young person is thinking about applying for a job as a postal employee. The job requires individuals to lift packages from a moving conveyor belt and toss them into bins that are situated in various locations around the conveyor. How might the person practice this task so that he can improve his chances of getting the job?

## Random/Blocked Practice vs. Varied/Constant Practice

At this point, it may seem that the distinction between varied practice and constant practice is identical to that between random practice and blocked practice. However, there are some important differences between these two classes of practice schedules. And the related mechanisms influencing the learning process in each case seem to be quite different as well (Wulf & Schmidt, 1988).

Random practice and blocked practice usually involve the rehearsal of several distinct tasks (e.g., throwing, kicking, and catching). The major difference between random practice and blocked practice is the *order* in which individuals rehearse these tasks. In random practice, performers don't repeat a task on consecutive movement attempts. In blocked practice, they repeat one task numerous times before switching to the practice of the next task.

Varied practice and constant practice involve the rehearsal of different numbers of *variations* of the same skill. These variations represent instances of some dimension of a particular class of actions (e.g., kicking), such as force, speed, direction, or distance. In varied-practice sessions, learners attempt a number of selected movement variations (e.g., kicking speeds of 5, 6, and 7 m/s). On the other hand, constant-practice learners rehearse a single variation of a particular dimension (e.g., a kicking movement speed of 5, 6, or 7 m/s, but not all three).

Both random practice and varied practice are beneficial to learners—but for different reasons. Random practice is presumed to cause gains in learning due to the trial-to-trial forgetting of task solutions to the different movement problems, to the development of more meaningful and distinctive representations of the different tasks in memory, or to both. Varied practice is assumed to produce gains in learning because it promotes the development of a set of rules for moving (i.e., the schema), which allows individuals to determine the parameter values needed to produce movement variations that effectively match different sets of environmental demands (e.g., kicks of different speeds).

## Combining Random and Varied Practice

The benefits of random practice over blocked practice and of varied practice over constant practice can be combined to produce further learning gains. For example, individuals who are learning to throw a ball might be given 100 trials of varied practice using either of two practice orders—blocked or random. With a blocked-practice order, individuals might perform 20 throws at a distance of 20 m, 20 throws at a distance of 30 m, and 20 throws at a distance of 40 m. With a random-practice order, on the other hand, individuals might perform one throw at a distance of 20 m, the next at 30 m, the next at 40 m, the next at 20 m, and so on, until a total of 20 throws at each distance had been attempted. Research by Lee, Magill, and Weeks (1985) has shown that the gains in learning due to varied practice compared to constant practice are far greater when individuals experience varied practice in a random order than when they practice the variations in a blocked order. Perhaps this is because learners who practice several movement variations in a random order are forced to generate a different parameter value prior to *each* movement attempt, thus producing an increased capability of assigning parameter values.

Random and varied practice can be merged even further. Suppose that individuals are given a series of randomly ordered variations of a single class of movements, such as throwing. If these throwing variations are interspersed with the performance attempts for a second class of movements, say catching, the benefits are even larger (Lee, Wulf, & Schmidt, 1992). In situations like this, individuals must not only generate a different parameter value on each trial, they must also retrieve a different motor program (throwing versus catching). Presumably, these types of generation processes are extremely beneficial for learning. With the proper combination of varied practice and a random order of scheduling, individuals sometimes experience stronger gains in learning than if they attempt either mode of practice alone.

## Practicing for Consistent and Varied Stimulus-Response Mapping

Some skills require individuals to produce rapid responses to various sources of sensory information. Automobile drivers, for example, must move a foot quickly from accelerator to brake whenever a squirrel or a young child suddenly dashes into the street in front of them. Race car drivers must sometimes brake, sometimes accelerate, and sometimes coast in response to a particular movement by another vehicle. Athletes in racket sports must be able to return some shots in the same way each time and return other shots in a variety of ways.

For some skills, the same response is required each time a stimulus is presented. Saying the word *yes* when these three letters are presented, pressing the *enter* key when computer commands are completed, or switching off your alarm clock when it sounds in the morning are all examples of this type of task. These skills are organized so that, when the stimulus information is presented, the same response is always produced. This is called **consistent mapping** in the motor skills literature, meaning that the mapping (or assignment) of stimuli to responses is always the same.

**consistent stimulus-response mapping**—A performance condition for which a given stimulus pattern always requires the same response.

For such skills, high levels of practice produce profound gains in performance. In early practice with these tasks, the mapping between stimuli and responses is not well acquired, so the individuals use the stages of processing (see figure 9.2)

### Training a Football Player for Rapid Responding

Many American football coaches use films and videos to familiarize their players with the tendencies and mannerisms of opposing teams. It is generally assumed that this type of training improves players' stimulus identification and response selection. In 1990, Christina, Barresi, and Shaffner used a modified video-training procedure to improve the response-selection accuracy of a defensive player from a college football team. Prior to training, as the coaches observed, this player responded quickly, but often incorrectly, during game situations.

The training task devised by Christina and his colleagues required the player to view a series of offensive plays that normally occurred in game situations. The plays were presented on a video monitor at a visual angle similar to one the player ordinarily experienced during competition. As soon as the player recognized the play, he made a quick arm movement in the direction the coaches wanted him to move. The player's coaches told him to focus on the movements of key individuals on the opposing team—the direction they moved was the direction he should move. During each training session, the player viewed 20 different plays, shown twice each in a random order. He participated in eight training sessions and eight test sessions in an alternating format.

After this training the player made progressively more correct responses (going from 25% to over 95% from the beginning to the end of training) with no slowing of response time. Perhaps more significantly, the player transferred his improved response-selection accuracy to actual game situations. These results suggest that a video-training procedure that incorporates both random practice and consistent stimulus-response mapping is a potentially effective supplement to normal physical rehearsal for defensive football players.

and the outer loop to produce the action. Naturally, this process is slow, effortful, serial (in the case of several such actions), conscious, and attention demanding (in that it interferes with other processes in response selection and response programming). In this sense, these tasks are produced with what has been called "controlled processing." This is in marked contrast to the kind of processing that occurs in this class of tasks after considerable practice. After several hundred trials or so under consistent-mapping conditions, individuals begin to produce what has been called "automatic processing." Such processing, when compared to controlled processing, is fast, effortless, done in parallel with other tasks (in that other tasks do not interfere with it), nonconscious, and not (very) attention demanding (see Shiffrin & Schneider, 1977, for early documentation of these kinds of effects). High levels of practice coupled with consistent-mapping conditions appears to build a kind of "special-purpose" information-processing device that functions very quickly and effortlessly to produce a given response when a given stimulus condition is presented. Reading aloud the words you are reading now is a good example, where the translation from printed stimulus information to spoken word is fast and nearly non-attentive, whereas reading the same words aloud for a third-grader is a clear example of controlled processing. For her, the "special-purpose" device has not been constructed yet.

The development of automaticity does not occur for tasks in which the stimulus does not specify completely or consistently the response that should be made. In these situations, the mapping from stimulus to response is variable from trial to trial, or from situation to situation—a configuration known in the literature as **varied mapping**. In many of these tasks, the action that is taken is dependent on several other factors that must be considered at the same time. For example, if an alarm is heard, we do not know whether to evacuate the building, get under the desk, or call the police because our car is being stolen. In baseball, receiving a ground ball at third base implies several different actions depending on the number of runners on base, where they are, the number of outs, and so on. In such situations, we hope to be able to speed up the processing of performers, making the actions not only faster but more accurate at the same time, but we should not expect them to become automatic in the sense just described.

**varied stimulus-response mapping**—A performance condition for which a given stimulus pattern requires different responses at different times or in different situations.

In designing practice, the practitioner needs to be aware of whether the tasks to be learned and practiced have varied- or consistent-mapping structures. Coaches in some sports include pattern-recognition activities in their practice sessions. For example, American football coaches commonly show their players game films of an opposing team. By watching those films, players are able to identify distinguishing patterns that lead invariably to certain outcomes (e.g., a certain formation and initial team movement always implies a running play to the right). If such consistencies can be identified (i.e., the mapping is consistent), players can be trained to recognize these patterns automatically and produce the appropriate actions far more quickly than if controlled processing were required. The problem is that, if the opposing team subsequently changes its way of operating, so that this pattern produces something other than the outcome that your team expected, your team members will make perhaps very serious errors by anticipating falsely. Other tasks may never have consistent-mapping conditions. Here, the practitioner needs to be clear that these will not be suitable for automatic responding, and should not be surprised or disappointed when performers resort to slow, controlled-processing strategies.

# Summary

Movement practitioners can promote the learning of skills by the way they structure learning experiences. One type of practice, which has been shown to be particularly effective, is random practice. During random practice, individuals attempt several different tasks in an intermingled order. Relative to blocked practice, in which individuals repeatedly perform a single task before moving to another, random practice produces far better retention and results in higher transfer, particularly when the target skill is performed under random circumstances. Some of the key aspects of random practice are summarized as follows:

- Random-practice conditions often lead to less effective practice performance than do blocked-practice conditions.
- The learning benefits of random practice over blocked practice are evidenced by the superior retention performance of individuals under either random or blocked conditions, but especially under random conditions.

An effective practice structure for individuals who are trying to learn how to produce variations of a particular task is varied practice. Varied practice involves the rehearsal of variations of the learning task, such as the practice of throws of different distances. Compared to constant practice, in which individuals practice a single version of the task, varied practice facilitates retention and adaptability, particularly when individuals have to produce a specific version of the task they have not previously attempted. The benefits of varied practice are thought to be due to the development of stronger schemas, which define the relationship between the parameters of a motor program and the desired movement outcome. Varied practice and constant practice may be distinguished from random practice and blocked practice in the following ways:

- Varied practice and constant practice involve different types of practice experiences within a single class of actions.
- Random and blocked practice both involve the practice of several different tasks, but the orders of rehearsal are different.
- Varied practice involves variations of a single class of movements (e.g., short, medium, and long kicks), whereas random practice involves different classes of movements (e.g., throwing, kicking, catching).
- Varied practice enhances learning by facilitating the development of more effective schemas (i.e., sets of rules), which individuals use to govern the production of movement variations of a particular class of actions.
- Random practice enhances learning because generalized motor programs are acquired more effectively during practice.

When learning requires the matching of responses to environmental stimuli, the task structure may consist of varied-mapping or consistent-mapping conditions. Varied-mapping conditions require learners to produce different responses to the same stimulus, while consistent-mapping conditions require individuals to produce a single response to each stimulus. Automatic responding is far more easily developed in consistent-mapping tasks, and may not be produced in varied-mapping tasks at all.

# From Principles to Practice

Check your understanding of the material in this chapter by responding to the following questions and then completing the application exercises. For each of the exercises, see if you can identify the most relevant questions or issues and then propose a solution based on concepts and principles we have discussed.

## Checking Your Understanding

1. Explain what it means to say that, compared to blocked practice, random practice is detrimental to performance but beneficial to learning. Why is this an important concept for movement practitioners to communicate to learners?
2. Discuss the relative merits of varied practice and constant practice for individuals who are trying to learn a task they must perform in a variety of ways. Describe how a practitioner might structure a practice session for a 10-year-old female who wants to learn the jump shot in basketball.
3. Explain how a coach might combine random practice and varied practice when teaching an individual to play soccer.
4. Discuss the difference between varied- and consistent-mapping of stimuli and responses. Which of these situations leads to automatic responding? Why?

## Application Exercise #1

A war veteran sustained damage to the nerves in his arms and hands. He wants to become a master chef, but knows he must learn a variety of skills (e.g., slicing, dicing, kneading, peeling) in order to achieve his goal.

*It Depends*

- How well is the man able to control his arms and hands?
- How well is he able to process proprioceptive feedback from his movements?
- Does he have any other physical impairments?
- What is the level of similarity among the tasks he wants to learn?
- What are the possible variations of each task?

*Strategy*

Structure practice experiences that enable the veteran to learn the necessary movements required of a master chef.

*Response Example*

- If the veteran has both motor and sensory impairment in his arms and hands, some amount of blocked practice may be necessary to promote his recognition of the relationship between each of the movements he attempts and its resulting feedback and outcomes.
- The amount of blocked practice might be reduced when the individual demonstrates improved consistency in performing each of the skills he is learning.
- The order of skill practice could be randomized in order to simulate the intermingling of movements required during food preparation.
- The individual could vary the practice of movements he performs in different ways depending on the type of food being prepared (e.g., stirring milk requires less force than stirring honey).

## Application Exercise #2

A woman is training to become a jeweler. The tasks she must learn include engraving on small surfaces, cutting stones, and setting stones in various types of jewelry.

*It Depends*

- How good is the woman's finger dexterity and arm-hand steadiness?
- How much movement variation is possible for each of the tasks she is learning?
- Will she always be using the same tools?
- How much variation is there in the work environment?

*Strategy*

Assist the woman in developing the various skills required of a jeweler, adapting her movements to different sizes and composition of materials, and performing tasks under a variety of working conditions (e.g., lighting, types of tools, level of noise, etc.).

## Application Exercise #3

An elementary school teacher has been assigned to supervise physical education for all of the first grade children at her school. She wonders what types of experiences might enhance the development of some of the children's motor skills.

*It Depends*

- How many children is the teacher going to be supervising at one time?
- What equipment does the teacher have at her disposal?
- How discrepant are the previous movement experiences of the children?
- How many different activities are the children going to be practicing?
- How much time does the teacher have during each physical education period?

*Strategy*

Suggest ways the teacher might maximize the children's skill development during the time she has with them. Consider how the teacher might structure practice so that the children are able to experience a variety of movements as well as the different ways they might adjust parameter values (e.g., force, distance, speed, etc.).

## Application Exercise #4

A soccer coach wants his players to be able to respond more quickly to different types of stimuli they confront during their games.

*It Depends*

- How automated are the players' movements?
- How old are the players?
- Which tasks require the same response to a given stimulus, and which tasks require different responses to the same stimuli at different times or in different situations?

*Strategy*

Design activities that simulate some of the different stimulus-response mapping conditions that exist in the game of soccer. Determine ways to rotate players among the different mapping conditions during practice to produce the most rapid response during soccer games.

# 10

# Providing Feedback During the Learning Experience

## Chapter Outline



## Chapter Objectives

**When you have completed this chapter, you should be able to**

discuss the difference between intrinsic and extrinsic feedback and give examples of each;

◆

explain the difference between knowledge of results and knowledge of performance and give examples of each;

◆

describe how instructional feedback can serve as a source of motivation, reinforcement, and error information;

◆

discuss the dependency-producing properties of instructional feedback;

◆

explain the principles practitioners should keep in mind when giving instructional feedback; that is, what type, how much, how precise, and how often; and

◆

apply the principles of feedback to a variety of real-world instructional settings.

## Preview

A physical therapist is frustrated and a bit bewildered. Her job is to oversee therapy for a number of stroke patients, who are trying to recover the functioning of their limbs. The therapist wants to provide as much assistance as possible, but given the number of patients she must work with, she is unable to provide a lot of feedback to any particular individual. As a result, the therapist's patients must spend most of the time practicing on their own.

How and when should the physical therapist provide feedback for her patients? What kinds of information should she convey to them about their performance? Should the therapist attempt to provide feedback about more than one aspect of a patient's movements at a time? When assisting a particular individual, should the therapist give feedback after each performance attempt, or wait until after the person makes several attempts before providing feedback?

# Overview

In this chapter, we continue our discussion of the decisions practitioners must make regarding the nature of the learning environment. In chapter 8, we discussed some factors practitioners should consider when organizing the rehearsal experiences of learners. In chapter 9, we focused on the issue of practice structure and examined the different ways practitioners might structure the rehearsal of movements during a learning session. In chapter 10, we turn our attention to the topic of instructional feedback and examine its effect on learning. First we classify the two major categories of feedback—intrinsic and extrinsic—and then we distinguish between two types of extrinsic feedback: knowledge of results and knowledge of performance. Next we examine the motivational, reinforcing, informational, and dependency-producing properties of extrinsic feedback. Finally we address several questions practitioners need to consider when providing learners with instructional feedback, such as what type of feedback to provide, how much information to include in feedback, how precise to make feedback, and how often to give feedback.

# Classifying Feedback

The term feedback was originally popularized near the end of World War II when scientists developed the concepts of the servomechanism and closed-loop control systems (e.g., Wiener, 1948). In the context of those discussions, feedback was characterized as sensory information that indicates something about the actual state of a person's movements (e.g., proprioceptive feedback about the feel of the movement). It was assumed that performers compare this actual feedback to the expected feedback of the desired, or goal, state in order to determine the amount of error in the movements. As long as error exists, performers attempt to amend the movement in order to reduce or eliminate the discrepancy between actual state and expected state (see chapter 4). While the error-reducing function of movement-produced feedback continues to be a prominent theme of motor control discussions, contemporary definitions of feedback refer to it more broadly as any kind of sensory information pertaining to the movement.

One of the most important ways practitioners can influence the learning process is by providing individuals with feedback about their actions. Some forms of feedback are a natural consequence of movements, as when an individual sees the plastic bottle he has thrown land in the recycling bin, or when a carpenter feels the impact of the hammer she is holding as it comes into contact with a nail. Feedback sometimes occurs in more "artificial" forms, such as when judges provide their ratings of a diver's performance during competition, or when a therapist evaluates the gait of a stroke patient trying to walk while using a cane.

One way we can differentiate categories of feedback is by classifying the various forms of sensory information that might represent feedback sources. An example of a classification system for sensory information is shown in figure 10.1. In most performance situations, there is a great deal of sensory information "out there," only some of which is related to the movement a person may be producing. When learning to drive a car, a person might notice the color of the dashboard, the smell of the upholstery, and the sounds of music on the radio. However, these sources of sensory information would not be as relevant to driving as those that tell the driver something about the feel of the steering wheel, the location of traffic signs, and the motion of vehicles seen in the rearview mirror.

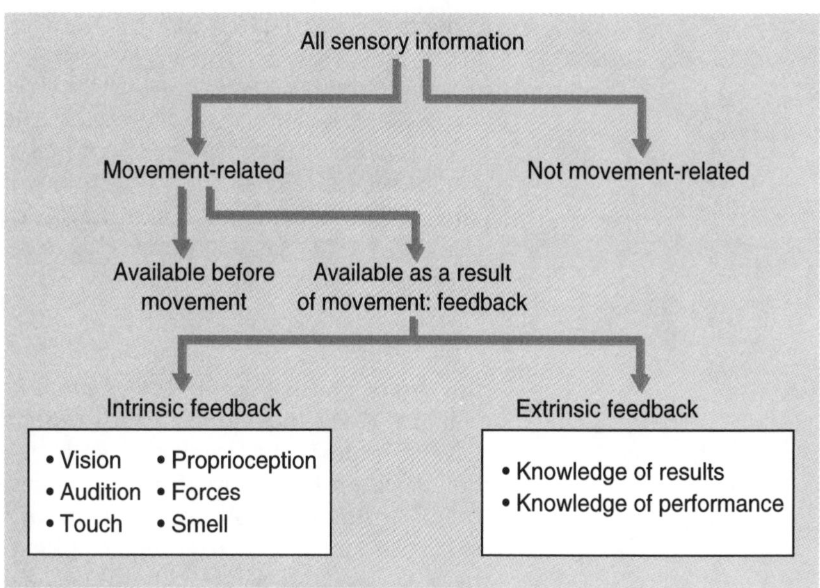


Figure 10.1 A classification system for sensory information.

Of the sensory information that is relevant to performance, some is available before the movement is executed (e.g., the speed and location of other vehicles), and some is available after the movement is completed (e.g., the view of the car centered in the proper lane of traffic after completing a turn). Information that is available before the action is produced is important for movement planning, and it affects anticipation, decision making, parameter selection, and so on. However, information that arises as a result of the movement (and is *fed back* to the performer) is technically the information that scientists refer to as "feedback." This class of information may be divided into two main categories: intrinsic feedback and extrinsic feedback.

**intrinsic feedback**—Sensory information that normally occurs when individuals produce movements; it can come from sources outside the body (exteroception) or inside the body (proprioception).

## Intrinsic Feedback

Sometimes called inherent feedback, **intrinsic feedback** is the sensory information that arises as a natural consequence of producing a movement. As we discussed in chapter 4, intrinsic feedback comes from sources outside a person's body (**exteroception**) or from within the body (**proprioception**). Perhaps you remember that this type of feedback (which we initially referred to as response-produced feedback) was an early addition to our conceptual model of human performance. Individuals are able to perceive intrinsic feedback more or less directly, without special assistance from other sources (e.g., instructors or mechanical devices). When the patient lifts a cup of tea to her mouth, she hears the sound of the cup leaving the saucer, feels the weight of the object, sees ripples in the liquid, and feels the warmth of the tea against her lips and tongue. When a squash player hits a shot, he feels the contact between the racket and the ball, sees the ball traveling toward the front wall, and hears it hit his opponent in the back (sorry!).

**exteroception**—Sensory information that comes primarily from sources outside a person's body.

**proprioception**—Sensory information arising from within a person's body that signals body and limb position and movement; similar to kinesthesis.

## Extrinsic Feedback

Now we finalize the conceptual model by adding the other category of information that follows movement completion (see the highlighted section in figure 10.2). **Extrinsic feedback**, sometimes called enhanced feedback or **augmented feedback**, consists of information that is provided to the learner by some outside source, such as the comments of an instructor or therapist, the digital display of a stopwatch, the handmarked score of a judge, the film of a game, the videotape replay of a movement, and so on. Thus, extrinsic feedback is information about the outcome of the

**extrinsic feedback**—Sensory information provided by an outside source and in addition to that which normally occurs when individuals produce movements (i.e., intrinsic feedback); sometimes referred to as augmented feedback.

**augmented feedback**—Another name for extrinsic feedback.

## IT DEPENDS . . .

Depending on the nature of the task and the goal of learning, individuals may be able to improve their performance based on intrinsic feedback alone. However, sometimes improvements are difficult or impossible without extrinsic feedback. For each of the following tasks or movement goals, list some of the sources of intrinsic and extrinsic feedback that individuals would need for learning to occur: riding a bicycle, roller skating, snow skiing, throwing a Frisbee, pitching horseshoes.

movement that is supplied *in addition to* the intrinsic information that is normally available when individuals produce their movements.

Most importantly, extrinsic feedback is information that is under the control of the instructor or therapist; thus, it can be provided at different times, in different forms, or not at all. When scientists in motor learning refer to feedback, they are usually talking about augmented, or extrinsic, feedback as defined here, and that's the way we will refer to feedback as well. Some scientists also differentiate two categories of extrinsic feedback, knowledge of results and knowledge of performance.

**knowledge of results (KR)**—Augmented, usually verbalizable information provided after the action is completed that indicates something about the degree to which the performer achieved the desired movement outcome or environmental goal.

### *Knowledge of Results (KR)*

**Knowledge of results (KR)** refers to extrinsic, usually verbal (or verbalizable), information that tells learners something about the success of their actions with respect to the intended environmental goal. For example, the therapist might tell a patient, "You buttoned that button in less than five seconds." In many real-world tasks, KR is redundant with (i.e., contains the same information as) intrinsic feedback. A classic example of feedback redundancy is when the parent tells the child, "You spilled your milk." Similar redundancies may also occur during movement instruction. A coach may say to an athlete, "You missed the shot" or a music teacher may tell his student, "That note was flat." KR that duplicates the intrinsic feedback individuals can pick up and interpret on their own is of little value and may even be irritating for learners.

Some types of KR are not redundant with intrinsic feedback. Gymnasts, divers, and dancers must wait for the judges' scores to know exactly how their performance was evaluated. Golfers sometimes hit shots that travel to targets they cannot see (e.g., approach shots to elevated greens), so they must receive extrinsic KR if they want augmented feedback. Therapy patients who are sorting objects into categories may need extrinsic KR indicating how many of each type object were successfully sorted during a given practice period. In cases such as these, KR is more important for performance and learning because the available intrinsic feedback is insufficient. Extrinsic feedback is also essential when a person's intrinsic feedback sources are diminished or distorted, as in the case of some patients who suffer from neurological impairment.

The effect of KR on motor performance and learning has received considerable attention in the research literature. In most of these studies, the experimenter is the one who determines the type and frequency of intrinsic and extrinsic feedback available to participants. Using this general method, researchers have examined how feedback processes influence learning. Early research was often conducted using very simple tasks that prevented participants from detecting their errors by themselves, such as drawing a 3-in. line while blindfolded. Not surprisingly, the results of these experiments generally showed that, without KR, there was no improvement or learning at all (e.g., Trowbridge & Cason, 1932). On the other hand, when KR was provided following movement attempts, rapid improvement occurred over practice and

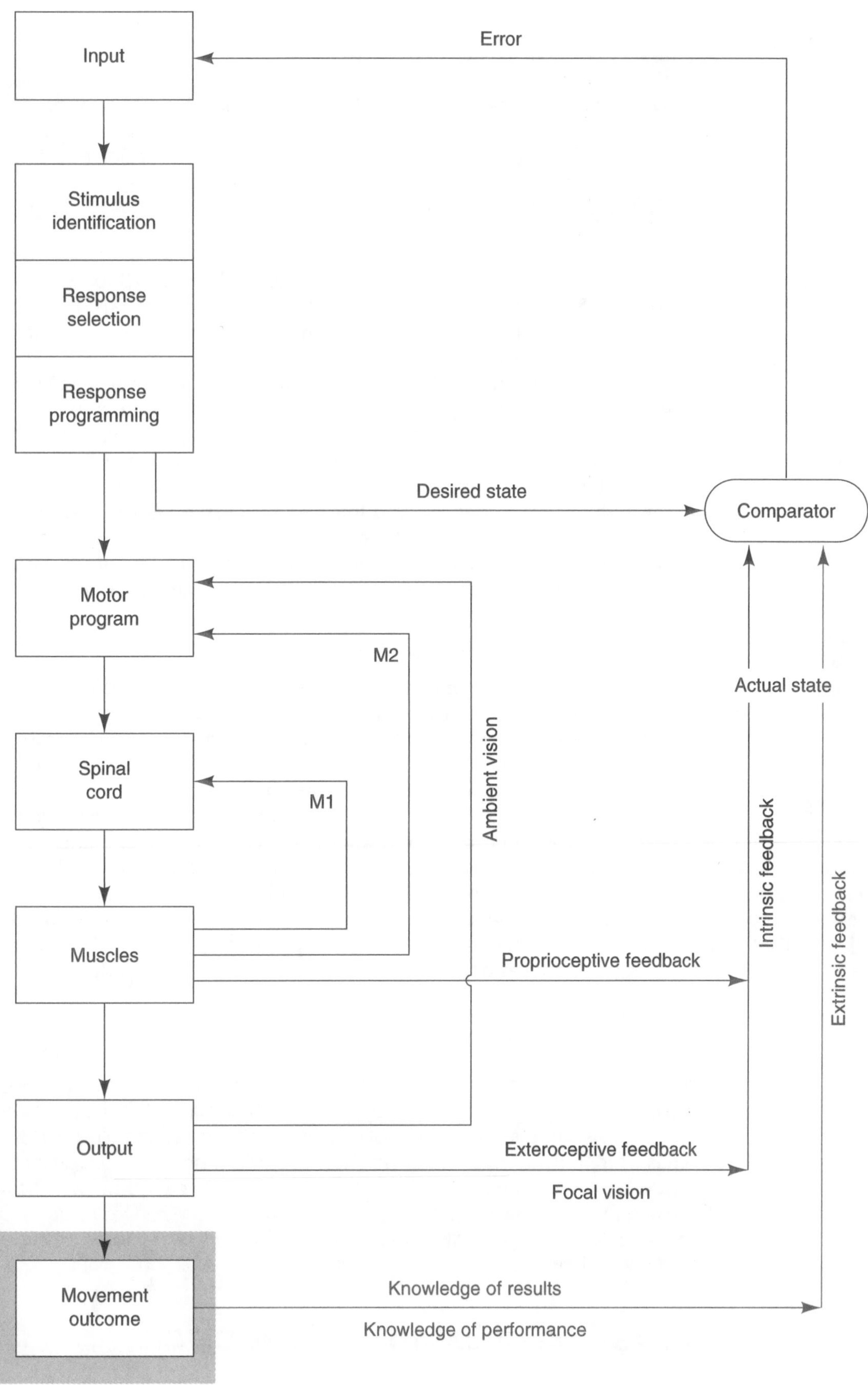


**Figure 10.2** The conceptual model of human performance, highlighting the sources of extrinsic information that follow movement production and provide additional information about the actual state of the system.

IT DEPENDS . . .

Sometimes KR can be redundant with the intrinsic feedback that individuals are able to pick up on their own. For each of the following tasks, list several examples of KR that might be redundant with the intrinsic feedback available to performers: playing miniature golf, bowling, digging a post hole, mowing a lawn, feeding an infant.

persisted during retention tests when KR was withdrawn (Bilodeau, Bilodeau, & Schumsky, 1959). These results suggested that, when individuals do not have sufficient intrinsic feedback to detect their own performance errors, they are unable to learn unless KR is provided.

Clearly, this is not to say that people cannot learn tasks in the absence of KR. During your own lifetime, you have learned many tasks without extrinsic KR from an instructor (e.g., throwing darts, shooting free throws, pouring water into a glass). For each of these tasks, you received goal achievement information (i.e., where the dart hit the target, whether or not the ball went into the basket, when the glass was full) through intrinsic feedback, and this feedback served as the basis of your learning. Taken together, then, the experimental evidence and our own experience tell us that, for learning to occur, individuals must receive some type of error information, either from intrinsic or extrinsic sources. This is one of the most important principles of learning.

**knowledge of performance (KP)**—Augmented feedback that provides information about the quality of the movement a performer has produced; sometimes referred to as kinematic feedback.

**kinematic feedback**—Feedback about the displacement, velocity, acceleration, or other aspects of the movement itself; see knowledge of performance (KP).

### *Knowledge of Performance (KP)*

Another type of extrinsic, or augmented, feedback provides performers with information about the pattern of their movements. **Knowledge of performance (KP)**, sometimes referred to as **kinematic feedback**, is frequently used by instructors and therapists in real-world settings. Coaches might provide these kinds of KP: "That punch was a little too slow," "Your tuck was not tight enough," or "Your backswing was too long." Therapists might make KP statements such as these: "Your step was too short" or "You did not lift your knees high enough." Each of these examples of KP contains information about the kinematics (pattern or speed) of the movement. Notice that KP information, unlike that provided by KR, does not necessarily indicate anything about the level of goal achievement. Rather, KP informs individuals about the quality of the *movement* they are producing. Some of the important similarities and differences between KR and KP are summarized in table 10.1.

IT DEPENDS . . .

While KR is an important source of feedback for learners, individuals can often obtain KR without the assistance of the practitioner. This is less true for KP because beginners are usually not capable of interpreting the kinematic properties of their movements. For each of the following tasks, suggest some examples of KR and KP that learners might be able to pick up on their own and some for which they would probably need help from the instructor: kicking a soccer ball, playing shuffleboard, shooting arrows at a target, and performing a back handspring.

## Properties of Extrinsic Feedback

In many learning situations, extrinsic feedback is under the direct control of the instructor or therapist and is usually provided in verbalized, or spoken, form. Practi-

**Table 10.1**

**Comparison of Knowledge of Results and Knowledge of Performance**

| Knowledge of results (KR) | Knowledge of performance (KP) |
|---|---|
| | ***Similarities*** |
| | *Verbal, or verbalizable*<br>*Extrinsic*<br>*Postresponse* |
| | ***Differences*** |
| *Information about outcome in terms of environmental goal.* | *Information about movement production or patterning (kinematics).* |
| *Often redundant with intrinsic feedback.* | *Usually distinct from intrinsic feedback.* |
| *More useful in the laboratory.* | *More useful in real-world tasks.* |

tioners who provide such feedback can convey a variety of messages, which influence the learning process in different ways.

Consider these feedback examples:

- Halfway through a long and frustrating learning session, the therapist says to her patient, "Keep it up—you're doing fine."
- After a daring, but successful, pass to an open teammate under the basket, a basketball player hears, "Good work!" from her coach.
- When one of her violin students finally performs a piece correctly, the high school music teacher stops criticizing him.
- After a beginning tennis player completes a forehand ground stroke, her instructor says, "You need to lengthen your backswing and take the racket back sooner."
- Following each rehearsal attempt, the ballet instructor informs a student about the height of her leap.

Each of these feedback situations illustrates a different property or function of feedback that can influence the performance and learning of individuals. On the positive side, instructional feedback can serve as motivation, reinforcement, and information for learners. Conversely, it can sometimes create a dependency, which diminishes learning. In this section, we examine the motivational, reinforcing, informational, and dependency-producing properties of extrinsic feedback.

## Motivational Properties

Motivation is strongly linked to goal achievement. When individuals are making progress toward the goals they set for themselves, their motivation is further increased. Certainly, one important function of extrinisic feedback is to provide individuals with information about the progress they are making so that they will continue to strive to achieve their goals. Early research revealed that for boring, repetitive tasks of long duration, the addition of feedback produced an immediate increase in performance proficiency, as if the feedback were a kind of stimulant that got individuals going again. Learners who are given **motivating feedback** during

**motivating feedback**—Augmented feedback about an individual's progress toward goal achievement that energizes and directs the person's behavior.

## THE FUNCTIONS OF EXTRINSIC FEEDBACK

When practitioners provide extrinsic feedback for learners, the feedback can serve at least four possible functions. These functions, which are often produced simultaneously and are therefore difficult to separate, include the following:

1. Motivation, which energizes individuals to increase their efforts to achieve the goals they have set for themselves
2. Reinforcement, which causes individuals to repeat the actions they have produced; or, in the case of punishment, to avoid repeating the actions
3. Information, which indicates, either directly or indirectly, the kinds of things individuals should do to refine their movement patterns and correct their errors
4. Dependence, which causes individuals to rely too heavily on instructional feedback; produces diminished performance when the feedback is later withdrawn

task practice say that they enjoy what they are doing more, that they try harder, and that they are willing to practice longer. Unless practitioners overdo the provision of feedback, learners seem to like it. Even when instructors have other reasons for giving feedback (e.g., to assist individuals in correcting their errors), the motivational properties of feedback information often provide added benefits.

Instructors and therapists can capitalize on the motivational feature of feedback during practice sessions if they can think of ways to give individuals the kind of feedback that keeps them motivated. Generally speaking, instructors should not allow too much time to elapse before providing individuals with feedback. Learners like to know how they are doing. Without feedback, learners' motivation can sag and their practice can become inefficient or even cease altogether. Keeping learners informed of their progress usually translates into greater effort during task practice. And, as most practitioners know, individuals who give greater effort during practice generally experience better learning down the road.

Extrinsic feedback can also be a helpful source of motivation when learners are making minimal progress toward achieving their goals. Let's suppose a patient is having a difficult time and is feeling frustrated. The therapist sees that the patient is making progress and lets him know it. She says to her patient, "Keep it up—you're doing fine." Sometimes, individuals are doing the right things in practice, but they fail to see much improvement in the results. A javelin thrower, for instance, may be doing a better job keeping his shoulders back prior to release—even though he is throwing the javelin no farther. Or perhaps a patient is increasing the consistency of her aiming movements, even though her accuracy is not yet improving. In situations like these, it is important for instructors and therapists to provide learners with feedback about the process characteristics of their movements or the good effort they are giving. Hearing the verbal praise of an instructor or therapist for progress they are making on a particular component of the task or for a good effort can motivate individuals to try even harder.

### Reinforcing Properties

Consider the example of the basketball coach who shouts, "Good work!" when the player completes a daring pass. This coach and player illustrate a second major function of feedback—**reinforcement**. When learners receive positive feedback from instructors after performing a movement, the feedback has a reinforcing function. The purpose of reinforcement is to increase the probability that an action will be repeated under similar circumstances.

**reinforcement**—An event that follows an individual's response and increases the likelihood that the person will repeat the response under similar circumstances.

The primary objective of reinforcement is to *increase* the probability that an action is repeated in the future. The intent of punishment is exactly the opposite—to *decrease* the chances of a response being repeated again. While punishment does not always influence behavior in a predictable fashion (see Adams, 1978, for a discussion of the uncertain effects of punishment), **positive reinforcement** produces rather consistent and beneficial changes in performance.

**positive reinforcement**—An event that follows an individual's response and, due to its pleasant nature, increases the likelihood that the person will repeat the response again under similar circumstances.

Practitioners may provide reinforcement and punishment in both verbal (i.e., spoken words) and nonverbal (i.e., facial expressions or visual symbols) forms. In fact, a smile or a frown on the face of a practitioner sometimes conveys clearer feedback to a learner than do words. In order to increase the effectiveness of reinforcing feedback, instructors should send verbal (e.g., "Nice job") *and* nonverbal (e.g., a smile) messages that convey the same meaning (i.e., approval) to learners.

A common misconception is that punishment and **negative reinforcement** are one and the same thing. However, we know that reinforcement and punishment are designed to achieve opposite purposes. Unlike punishment, negative reinforcement *increases* the probability that a response will be repeated again in the future. However, negative reinforcement operates in a slightly different way than does positive reinforcement. Let's assume that the basketball player is having a bad day and has made a number of errant passes, each of which has prompted the coach's comment, "That's terrible!" Now assume that the player makes a correct pass. Her coach is now in a position to provide negative reinforcement for that action. He does this by simply remaining silent. By withdrawing his critical (negative) comments, the coach *reinforces* the player for the correct pass she has made. The behavior of the violin teacher mentioned on page 261 is another example of negative reinforcement.

**negative reinforcement**—An event that follows an individual's response and consists of the removal of an unpleasant stimulus, thereby increasing the likelihood that the person will repeat the response again under similar circumstances.

## IT DEPENDS . . .

Instructional feedback is more motivating for learners when it informs them about the progress they are making in achieving their goals. An expert is teaching a beginner how to kayak and, after several practice sessions, the instructor notices that the learner is not responding as enthusiastically to his feedback as she did previously. What are some possible reasons the learner may be less motivated by the expert's feedback?

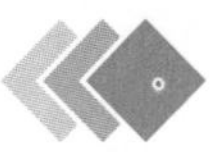

## THE LAW OF EFFECT

Psychologists who study instrumental learning are interested in the effects of reinforcing stimuli on the learning of actions. More specifically, they are concerned about how reinforcement produces correct actions more frequently and incorrect actions less frequently. Scientists have long realized that the nature and timing of feedback have a marked influence on the instrumental learning of a goal response. This influence is best summarized in Thorndike's (1927) *empirical law of effect:*

"An action elicited by a stimulus and followed by pleasant, or rewarding, consequences tends to be repeated when that stimulus appears again; an action followed by unpleasant, or punishing, consequences tends not to be repeated."

The available research indicates that positive reinforcement produces the greatest improvements in learning, followed by negative reinforcement, then by punishment. Moreover, the effects of negative reinforcement and punishment are less predictable (Adams, 1978). Perhaps the reason that negative reinforcement and punishment are not as effective as positive reinforcement is that they provide learners with feedback that is more difficult to interpret. Punishing feedback tells individuals that the action they produced is not acceptable, but it doesn't tell them why. The withdrawal of unpleasant (negative) feedback tells the basketball player that her most recent pass is not as bad as her earlier ones, but doesn't tell her why. It is also possible that the coach's silence is due to the fact that he was not watching the player when she made the correct pass. Positive reinforcement, on the other hand, clearly conveys the message that the action someone produced is acceptable and encourages them to repeat it in the future.

**intermittent reinforcement**—A schedule of reinforcement in which feedback is given only occasionally.

One principle of instrumental learning (see the law of effect element on page 263) is that feedback that is given only occasionally (i.e., **intermittent reinforcement**) is generally more effective for learning than feedback that is given after every performance attempt. The effects of reinforcement are best seen when the reinforcing feedback is removed. The results of studies examining the effects of various schedules of reinforcement show that participants who receive intermittent reinforcement during practice continue to perform at higher levels when the reinforcing feedback is withdrawn than those who receive reinforcement after every practice attempt. Apparently, when it is given too often, feedback loses some of its reinforcing power.

One effective way practitioners can provide intermittent reinforcement is by using a *fading procedure,* in which they gradually reduce the frequency of reinforcing feedback as individuals become more adept at performing the task. For skilled performers, the timing of reinforcement is an important issue. Less frequent reinforcement can be quite effective when it follows performances the individual believes are particularly exceptional.

## Informational Properties

In most motor learning situations, the learner's problem is not to perform a correct action more frequently than an incorrect action, but to perform a particular action *more effectively*. The learner is trying to create a pattern of movement that accomplishes a single, clearly defined goal. In a therapy situation, there is no question that the stroke patient wants to recover the skill of feeding himself, but the challenge is to come up with the necessary limb movements that will enable him to accurately transfer food from the plate to his mouth. Similarly, a baseball pitcher who wants to learn how to throw a curveball in the strike zone must acquire a movement pattern that allows him to generate a throwing action that imparts high velocity and the required degree of accuracy to the ball.

In light of all this, it might be argued that the most important function of feedback during motor skill instruction is to provide learners with information about their patterns of action. Feedback that is informational gives people the kind of direction

An instructor is helping a piano student practice her finger positioning. During one particular lesson, the student makes many mistakes, and the instructor spends a lot of time telling her, "That's wrong." Finally, the student produces an effective movement sequence and immediately looks at the instructor. She sees him silently sitting there with a smile on his face. What are some ways the student might interpret the instructor's silence and smile?

### THE USE OF NEGATIVE REINFORCEMENT TO CORRECT A SWIMMER'S STROKE

An interesting case study illustrating how a practitioner might use negative reinforcement to alter the movement pattern of an individual was reported by Rushall (1967). Working in collaboration with a competitive swimmer and his coach, Rushall determined that at least seven components of the swimmer's stroke were inefficient. Since the swimmer said that he was intrinsically reinforced by correct performance, Rushall decided that providing positive reinforcement for correct performance would be an ineffective method. Therefore, he employed a negative-reinforcement technique that involved shining a flashlight in the swimmer's face until he made the required change in the designated stroke component. Once the coach determined that the swimmer was executing the component in a consistently acceptable fashion, the flashlight was turned off. This process of negative reinforcement was repeated until the swimmer had satisfactorily altered all seven components.

they need to correct their errors and modify their future performance. Moreover, the provision of such feedback is what makes instructors and therapists such an important part of the learning process. Skilled instructors know the proper patterns of action; therefore, they are able to provide individuals with the type of feedback information needed for effective learning.

Consider now the example of feedback we listed earlier, in which the instructor told the beginning tennis player that she should try to lengthen her backswing and take the racket back sooner. This example of **information feedback** tells the player something about the desired correctness of her movement and clearly defines two things that she is doing wrong. It also becomes the basis for the player to make corrections on the next movement, thus helping her bring her backswing closer to the level of quality that characterizes the most effective backswings. By providing information feedback, practitioners can help learners keep their errors to a minimum, correct them more quickly, and bring their movement patterns closer to the goal.

**information feedback**—Feedback that provides performers with error correction information; either descriptive or prescriptive.

The fact that extrinsic feedback is mainly informational in nature raises many interesting and important questions for instructors and therapists. These questions deal with the kinds of information practitioners should provide as feedback (e.g., information about limb position, movement timing, coordination), the amount and precision of information feedback that is most effective, and the frequency of feedback presentation (e.g., following every attempt, after only certain attempts). Because each of these questions involves a number of important issues, we discuss them in more detail in the section of this chapter that discusses practical considerations when providing information feedback.

## Dependency-Producing Properties

Recently, scientists have realized that feedback containing error correction information can have a dependency-producing function. In the earlier ballet example, the ballet instructor provides the dancer with error correction information following each of her leaps. When instructors give this type of feedback on a frequent basis, it tends to guide the learner's actions in the direction of the goal movement, much the same way as physical guidance does. Just as with physical guidance, augmented information feedback allows individuals to maintain their movements near the intended goal by enabling them to correct their errors quickly and preserve the

Bud Syms

World-class athletes, such as John McEnroe, have used on-court video feedback to make adjustments in technique. Here McEnroe corrects his famed service motion with tennis coach John Yandell.

desired form or outcome. Again, as with physical guidance, individuals can become dependent on the feedback if practitioners provide it too often, using it to generate their movements and keep them on target, rather than relying on the more valid and reliable internally generated feedback processes. Unless learners develop the capability of producing the movement on their own, their performance suffers markedly when extrinsic feedback is removed. Fortunately, there are a number of ways practitioners can structure feedback in order to minimize its dependency-producing effects, and we discuss several of these techniques in the next section.

## Practical Considerations When Providing Information Feedback

For individuals to achieve their learning goal, they often need feedback from movement practitioners. However, learners must eventually be able to perform movements in the desired target context without assistance from the practitioner. Good instructors and therapists know how to provide feedback in a way that prepares individuals for unassisted performance. In this section, we discuss several questions practitioners should consider when providing information feedback for learners.

### Determining Whether to Give Feedback

When it comes to providing feedback, the first question practitioners must address is whether feedback should be provided at all. After all, there are many

IT DEPENDS . . .

A person wants to learn to play golf. Her instructor decides that the learner should start by going to the practice range and hitting a bucket of balls. The instructor shows the learner how to hold the club and then demonstrates the swing for her. The learner begins hitting balls; after each shot she receives feedback from the instructor about the speed of her swing (e.g., too slow, too fast, much too slow, much too fast). The learner repeatedly adjusts the speed of her swing according to the instructor's feedback until, by the end of the lesson, she is producing swings that are close to the correct speed. The next night, teacher and student return to the range, but unfortunately the instructor has developed laryngitis (from all the talking he did the night before). The learner tries her best to produce the correct swing speed, but she has little success. The learner worries that she has let her instructor down. What is another interpretation of the learner's diminished performance?

## Providing Feedback When the Learner Requests It

In most skill learning, individuals are able to see and feel something about the movements they are performing. If learners are throwing a ball, they can see where it lands and feel the temporary sensation in their arm and shoulder. If learners are jumping, they can roughly judge how high or far they jumped and feel the sensation in their legs and feet. If learners are playing a musical instrument, they can hear the pleasant- and not-so-pleasant-sounding notes they produce and feel the sensation in their mouths and fingers. In light of the fact that some amount of intrinsic feedback is always available during task performance, practitioners must carefully consider how and when to provide additional feedback that is useful for learners.

In a recent study by Janelle et al. (1997), participants attempted to learn a task that involved throwing a tennis ball with their nondominant hand a distance of nine meters to a target. The ball was always coated with chalk so that the participants could see where the ball struck the target. During the practice phase of the study (200 throws), some of the participants received additional feedback (videotape replay of the throw and verbal comments or suggestions from an expert) about certain aspects of their movement form, but other participants did not. Of those individuals who received additional information, some received it following each group of five throws; others received it only when they requested it. Later on, all participants were given a retention test in which they attempted 20 more throws in the absence of additional feedback information.

The results of the final 20 throws revealed that the throwing form and accuracy of individuals given additional information during learning was better than that of participants who received no additional feedback. Moreover, those individuals who had received additional information *only when they asked for it* during learning performed the best.

sources of sensory information that learners can pick up for themselves (i.e., intrinsic feedback). We also know that feedback dependency can become a problem if learners receive extrinsic information too often. In addition, recent studies have shown that instructional feedback is more effective when learners request it than when it is given more frequently.

What, then, should the practitioner's purpose be in providing extrinsic feedback for learners? Flach, Lintern, and Larish (1990) have suggested an answer to this question that is consistent with our view of motor learning (see chapter 7). These researchers propose that, for every task, there is a hierarchy of relevant intrinsic information that individuals must be aware of to produce effective movements. One purpose of instructional feedback, then, is to channel the search of learners for this relevant task information. Once individuals are able to identify the relevant intrinsic information and produce effective movements on their own, they should have little or no need for additional feedback.

Whiting and Vereijken (1993) suggest that the issue of what individuals must learn should be addressed by practitioners *before* they decide whether or not to provide augmented feedback during skill practice. In several experiments using a ski-training apparatus, these researchers determined that "what" individuals needed to learn was to delay the forcing of the platform until it passed the center point of the apparatus, termed "phase lag." They found that a discovery-learning group (receiving no feedback from the instructor) improved their performance over four days of practice to the same extent as (and in some cases more than) groups that received instructor feedback. Since experimental participants were not tested later under no-feedback conditions, the effect of the various feedback conditions on more permanent learning of the skill was not determined. Nevertheless, the results suggest that in some cases, practitioners might want to allow individuals time to discover the person-task-environment relationship before providing feedback. Once learners have a general idea of task requirements, they might benefit more from the provision of augmented feedback.

When practitioners do feel it is necessary to provide information feedback, they might next consider its content, amount, precision, and frequency. In the following sections, we address each of these questions in greater detail.

## Determining What Information to Give

One of the first questions practitioners might ask themselves before deciding to give feedback is, "What features of the individual's movements should I provide information about?" It is important for feedback to address features that are under the learner's control. It is also helpful for instructors and therapists to have some understanding of how individuals control their movements. Knowing these things allows practitioners to provide more effective feedback for learners.

### *Program Feedback and Parameter Feedback*

Individuals who are trying to learn generalized motor programs sometimes struggle because they are unable to adjust the program in the most effective ways. For example, a tennis player may be producing forehand ground strokes that are characterized by an arm swing that begins too early relative to the beginning of hip rotation. We know it is much more difficult for individuals to adjust the underlying timing or temporal structure of their movements than it is for them to change parameter values, such as movement speed, that influence the entire action.

The processes involved in making changes in temporal structure are not well understood, but there are a few guidelines practitioners can keep in mind when providing **program feedback** about this dimension of movements. As we mentioned earlier, instructional feedback is more helpful when it addresses movement features that individuals can control. In the tennis example, the player is able to control the moment when she triggers a new unit of action (e.g., when she starts the arm swing) or the length of time she takes to produce the backswing (i.e., making it shorter or longer). On the other hand, she may have more difficulty generating a particular timing pattern of muscular force, because these patterns are chiefly determined by the properties of muscle tissue. Even more difficult may be adjustments in the relative timing of her arm movement and hip action, because these features occur almost simultaneously. When practitioners are providing program feedback about the timing structure of movements, they can remind learners that progress can be quite slow. Learners can also be informed that the timing structure of movements sometimes takes a long time to acquire and that they should try to be patient when their performance is not as smooth or consistent as they would like it to be.

**program feedback**—Feedback that provides learners with error information about the fundamental pattern of their movement (i.e., the generalized motor program).

Fortunately, there are other ways people can change their movements that are easier for them than adjusting the timing structure of the generalized motor program. Remember that once individuals decide on the generalized motor program (regardless of how well the timing structure is developed), they then specify the parameters (such as duration, direction, and amplitude) that define the superficial features of the movement. Performers can usually do this quickly and easily, as when the tennis player swings faster, then slower, then faster again on consecutive forehand ground strokes.

Instructional feedback that leads to parameter adjustments is almost always useful as long as the individual's overall movement pattern is essentially correct. For example, **parameter feedback** statements such as "Swing the arm faster," "Make the swing longer," or "Hit the ball harder" are helpful because they tell individuals how

**parameter feedback**—Feedback that provides learners with error information about the parameter values (e.g., amplitude, speed, force) they are selecting to make their movement fit environmental requirements.

to select parameter values more effectively. An important part of motor learning is discovering the rules dealing with parameter selection. Parameter feedback that tells learners about the appropriateness of the parameter values they are selecting (i.e., faster, slower, longer, shorter, higher, lower, etc.) can be extremely beneficial.

In general, it is better for practitioners to initially give feedback that helps learners correct errors in their fundamental movement patterns (i.e., the generalized motor program), rather than in the parameter values they are selecting. For example, the patient who is learning to walk with a cane might first be given program feedback about the coordination of his arm and leg movements, the function of the cane as a stabilizing device, and so on. If individuals are allowed to practice ineffective movement patterns that lead to the learning of an improper action, the pattern may become difficult for them to change later.

Once learners have achieved an approximation of the correct movement pattern, they can be given feedback about parameter selection. For example, a patient could be given parameter feedback about the speed with which he is moving, the amplitude of his steps, or other parameter values (e.g., walk faster, take longer steps, veer to the right and then back to the left).

### Visual Feedback

While practitioners present the content of most information feedback in a verbal (i.e., spoken) form, there are a few other nonverbal forms of feedback—most of them visual—instructors can provide to assist learners in program development and parameter selection. Probably the most common form of visual feedback is videotape replay. Soon after video recorders became commercially available in the 1960s, gymnastics coaches began using them to provide nearly immediate feedback to athletes during practice sessions and also to record athletes' performances during competition. Videotape solved many of the problems associated with using films: individuals could view feedback about the entire performance after only a few seconds of tape rewinding, and they could see the patterns of their movements in relatively good detail and, more recently, in color and with sound.

While early video technology was not particularly portable, recent visual systems, including portable camcorders and computer software, allow practitioners to record performance in field settings. With these systems, the camcorder serves as the recording and video input device, and a computer monitor feeds back visual information about the efficiency and form of the performer's actions, allowing on-the-spot analysis (Seat & Wrisberg, 1996).

Before using videotape as feedback, practitioners need to remember several things (Rothstein & Arnold, 1976). Perhaps most important is the fact that beginners can attend to only a limited amount of information at their time. In addition, learners can change only one or two movement features on their next attempt. Therefore, it is important for instructors to initially point out specific cues contained in a video display so that learners can process and use the feedback more effectively. For example,

#### IT DEPENDS . . .

The content of the practitioner's feedback statements should initially emphasize characteristics of the basic movement pattern. Once learners have demonstrated that they can generally produce the desired action, they can be given feedback about parameter selection. For each of the following tasks, suggest one example of program feedback and one example of parameter feedback that a practitioner might give to a learner: throwing a ball, skipping, playing shuffleboard, rowing a boat.

## IT DEPENDS . . .

Instructors present most augmented feedback in a verbal form, although in some cases, they are able to provide visual feedback. Assuming a practitioner has the luxury of giving feedback in either form, how might he or she provide verbal and visual feedback for someone who is trying to learn each of the following tasks: a social dance routine, driving a stick shift car, making a pizza. Which of your feedback examples would assist the learner in program development? Which would promote more effective parameter selection? Which would facilitate the learning of procedural information?

## SPLIT-SCREEN VISUAL FEEDBACK

Occasionally, instructors can display videotape feedback of an individual's movements alongside a visual model of the correct action. This is called a split-screen display. How might the use of a split-screen display enhance a learner's program development? Parameter selection?

a physical therapist might direct the patient's attention to the position of her chin during locomotion. As individuals become more skilled at producing their actions and recognizing the key movement components, less of the instructor's cueing is necessary.

**descriptive feedback**—Feedback that describes the errors an individual makes during the performance of a skill.

**prescriptive feedback**—Feedback that describes the errors an individual makes during the performance of a skill and suggests something the learner might do to correct the errors.

### *Descriptive and Prescriptive Feedback*

The content of a practitioner's feedback statement can be either descriptive or prescriptive in nature. A **descriptive feedback** statement merely indicates something about what the learner did, as in the tennis instructor's comment, "Not so good that time," which conveys little useful information, or "Your backswing was too long that time," which is somewhat more precise but still presumes that the learner knows what to do on the next attempt. **Prescriptive feedback** provides learners with information they can use to make more effective corrections in their subsequent movements (Newell & McGinnis, 1985). Such feedback "prescribes" a solution to the individual's movement problem, in much the same way as the physician prescribes medicine for the patient's problem. For example, the tennis instructor might say, "Next time shorten your backswing." Research suggests that prescriptive feedback is more useful to learners than descriptive feedback.

## Determining How Much Information to Give

**attentional cueing**—Prescriptive feedback that directs learners' attention to the most pertinent information for correcting a particular performance error.

**transitional information**—A progression of prescriptive feedback that directs learners' attention to more advanced performance information as their skill level improves.

Because practitioners sometimes find themselves in a position to give feedback about countless features of an individual's movements, they have the potential to over-

## PROVIDING PRESCRIPTIVE FEEDBACK

Janelle and colleagues (1997) developed an **attentional cueing** protocol (referred to as **transitional information**) that they used to provide prescriptive feedback to participants who were trying to learn a throwing task with the nondominant hand. Their cueing protocol is shown in table 10.2, and samples of the transitional feedback statements they used are presented in table 10.3.

**Table 10.2**

### An Attentional-Cueing Protocol Used During Feedback Delivery for a Nondominant-Hand Throwing Task

1. *Focus on the initial position of the body.*
2. *Focus on the initial movement of the trunk.*
3. *Focus on the left arm during the preparatory phase of the left arm swing.*
4. *Focus on the right foot during the throwing phase.*
5. *Focus on the hips during the throwing phase.*
6. *Focus on the shoulders during the throwing phase.*
7. *Focus on the upper arm and elbow during the throwing phase.*
8. *Focus on the left hand and the ball during the throwing phase.*
9. *Focus on the left arm at the point of ball release.*
10. *Focus on the left arm during the final phase of the throw.*

*Good throw (correct form).*

**Table 10.3**

### Transitional Information Used During Feedback Delivery for a Nondominant-Hand Throwing Task

1. *(a) Align your body so that the right shoulder faces the target area.*
   *(b) Place your feet close together, parallel to each other, and at a 90-degree angle to the target area.*
2. *Rotate the hips 15–20 degrees from right to left during the initial phase of the throw.*
3. *Begin the arm backswing with initiation of the right foot stride.*
   *(a) Keep the left arm relatively straight during the backswing.*
   *(b) During the backswing, raise the left arm until even with the shoulder.*
   *(c) At the end of the backswing, flex the elbow and allow the hand and ball to drop down behind the back.*
4. *Stride forward with the right foot toward the target area.*
5. *Rotate the hips from left to right during the throwing phase.*
6. *Rotate the shoulders left to right during the throwing phase.*
7. *Lag the movement of the upper arm and elbow behind the rotation of the shoulders during the throwing phase.*
8. *Lag the movement of the hand and ball behind the upper arm and elbow during the throwing phase.*
9. *Extend the arm at ball release.*
10. *(a) Release the ball earlier in the movement.*
    *(b) Release the ball later in the movement.*
    *(c) Keep the left arm extended as you follow through down and across to the right side of the body.*

*Good throw (correct form).*

## Including the Desired Outcome in Visual KR

Research by Newell, Carlton, and Antoniou (1990) suggests that movement practitioners should consider the previous experience of learners and the complexity of the task to be learned when deciding what type of visual KR to provide. In this study, individuals attempted to draw shapes that were either familiar (i.e., a circle) or unfamiliar (i.e., an irregular form). Participants' movements were made on a white Formica surface, which prevented them from using specific spatial cues to produce their drawings. After each practice attempt, participants received one of three types of visual KR: a number representing the difference in the area of the shape they drew and that of the correct shape (termed *absolute integrated error,* AIE), AIE plus a computer-generated representation of the shape they drew, and AIE plus a computer-generated representation of the shape they drew superimposed on a representation of the correct shape. After 70 practice attempts with augmented feedback, participants in each group attempted to draw the shapes 30 more times without feedback. The results revealed that the KR that included the participant's drawing superimposed on a representation of the correct shape was beneficial only when learners were drawing figures that were *unfamiliar* to them. These findings suggest that, early in the practice of unfamiliar movements, learners might benefit from visual KR that includes a portrayal of the desired outcome along with the outcome of their own movement.

Figure 10.3 Feedback should be clear, direct, and limited to avoid an information overload.

load learners with too much information. As we know, this can be a problem because the information-processing and memory capabilities of humans—particularly those who are young or mentally challenged—is limited (see chapter 3). Feedback messages like those given by the tennis instructor in figure 10.3 are probably too difficult for most learners to translate into an effective correction.

## When Prescriptive Feedback Helps More Than Descriptive Feedback

An important issue for movement practitioners is determining what type of augmented feedback best promotes skill learning. One study by Kernodle and Carlton (1992) suggests that prescriptive feedback that focuses learners' attention on important movement cues or on movement transitions produces larger performance gains than descriptive feedback that informs learners about the outcome of an action or that consists of a videotape replay of the movement.

In this experiment, participants attempted to learn to throw a Nerf ball as far as possible with their nondominant hand. An opaque partition prevented learners from seeing how far their throws went. During practice, learners received one of four types of augmented feedback after each throw. Two groups of participants received descriptive feedback only: the distance thrown in feet and inches (KR) or a videotape replay of the movement (KP). The other two groups received descriptive feedback plus a prescriptive statement. Either they received a videotape replay plus attentional cueing (e.g., "Focus on the hips during the throwing phase," that is, KP-with-cue) or a videotape replay plus transitional information (e.g., "Rotate the hips from left to right during the throwing phase," that is, KP-with-transition).

Participants in the prescriptive feedback conditions improved their distance thrown and their movement form to a significantly greater extent than did participants in the descriptive feedback groups. These findings suggest that prescriptive feedback can be beneficial to learners during motor program development. The challenge for practitioners is to identify the important focus cues, or transitional information, to convey to learners as prescriptive feedback.

When providing feedback for program development, an instructor might consider the *one* feature of the learner's movement that is most fundamental for task improvement and restrict his or her feedback to that feature. For example, an instructor who is teaching the tennis serve might provide feedback that promotes development of the learner's coordination of the ball toss and the racket swing. Once an individual has mastered that feature, the instructor can provide transitional information about the next most important feature (e.g., the coordination of hip and shoulder rotation), and so on, until the learner is producing the entire movement pattern in an effective fashion.

On the other hand, in giving feedback for parameter selection, which is more easily modifiable, instructors can occasionally provide information about more than one parameter at a time. For example, an individual who has already developed an effective generalized motor program for the javelin throw might be told, "Move your left leg faster *and* farther next time."

### IT DEPENDS . . .

When providing feedback for program development, practitioners must know the relative importance of different movement features and first provide feedback about the most important feature. Once learners master that feature, the practitioner can provide feedback about the next most important feature, and so on. For each of the following tasks, suggest one feature a practitioner might emphasize first when providing feedback for program development: operating a stick shift car, three-ball juggling, dancing the waltz.

## MAXIMAL INFORMATION WITH MINIMAL WORDS

One way to maximize the information in a feedback statement is to first develop a list of words and phrases that characterize the essence of what learners should do. Using this list, practitioners can provide feedback statements that are brief and to the point and that enable learners to make the necessary corrections in their movements. An example from the sport of basketball is "Put your hand in the basket," which is intended to convey to the shooter an image of the position of her hand after she releases the ball. Can you think of a similar phrase for some other motor skill you are familiar with? What information or image would this phrase convey to the performer?

**summary feedback**—Feedback given after a series of performance attempts that provides the learner with information about each of the attempts in the series.

### *Summary Feedback*

Practitioners can maximize the amount of feedback they give, while minimizing the dependency-producing effects of feedback, by providing learners with **summary feedback**. The instructor does this by withholding feedback for a particular number of practice attempts—say from 5 to 20—and then providing it in summary form. For example, a tennis instructor who is helping an individual learn to hit serves closer to the service line might ask the person to hit 15 serves. If the instructor records the location that the ball lands for each of the 15 serves, the graph might look something like the one shown in figure 10.4. After the individual's last practice attempt, the instructor shows the person the graph. In this case, the learner receives feedback about all 15 attempts, but not until he completes the entire number of attempts.

Dick Young/Unicorn Stock Photos

"Put your hand in the basket" is an example of a concise feedback statement conveying information about a particular component of the motor program, that is, the follow-through.

The potential benefits of summary feedback were first discovered by Lavery (1962) in a series of experiments investigating the learning of simple laboratory tasks (see the highlight box on page 275). Lavery found that, compared with giving feedback after every practice attempt, summary feedback produced poorer performance during practice but better performance later on, when the extrinsic feedback was withdrawn.

How many performance attempts should practitioners include in a summary feedback statement? Recent evidence suggests that there is an optimal number, with either too few or too many attempts decreasing learning. If instructors provide feedback after every attempt, learners are guided strongly to the movement goal, but they also become more dependent on the feedback. On the other hand, if instructors summarize too many attempts (say 100), learners become less dependent on the feedback, but they are also less strongly guided toward the goal.

Schmidt, Lange, and Young (1990) explored the effects of different lengths of summary feedback statements on the learning of a timing skill. In this study, participants practiced a laboratory task that resembled the skill of baseball batting. During practice, participants received summary feedback about their timing accuracy after 1, 5, 10, or 15 attempts. As you can see in figure 10.5, the five-

## Lavery's Experiment on Summary Feedback

The Canadian scientist J.J. Lavery (1962; Lavery & Suddon, 1962) examined several kinds of feedback schedules during the learning of simple laboratory motor tasks, such as striking a small ball with a special hammer to propel it up a ramp to a target. All participants performed the skill the first day without any feedback; then for the next five days, they received different schedules of feedback. One group received immediate feedback after each practice attempt. A second group received summary feedback following 20 attempts in a manner similar to that shown in figure 10.4. A third group received both kinds of feedback, that is, feedback after each attempt and summary feedback after each set of 20 attempts. Following the five days of practice, all groups were tested without any feedback on each of the next four days, as well as 1one month and again three months later.

During the practice stage, the summary group performed much worse than did either of the other groups. However, during the no-feedback tests, this group performed better than the other groups on all but the three-month test. Thus, Lavery concluded that, while summary feedback may produce poorer performance during practice, it leads to better learning.

attempts summary feedback statement produced the best learning, as measured by a no-feedback retention test.

The number of performance attempts practitioners should summarize in a feedback statement probably depends on the complexity of the learning task. For very simple tasks, such as those used in Lavery's experiment, a relatively large number of attempts (e.g., 20 or more) can be included in the summary feedback statement. However, for more complex tasks, like the one used in the study by Schmidt, Lange, and Young (1990), fewer attempts (e.g., five) should be summarized. For extremely complex tasks, the optimal number may approach a single attempt, at least until learners master the essential movement elements. Generally, as the complexity of the task increases, practitioners should summarize fewer attempts if they want to assist learners in achieving the proper action. We depict this general trend in figure 10.6.

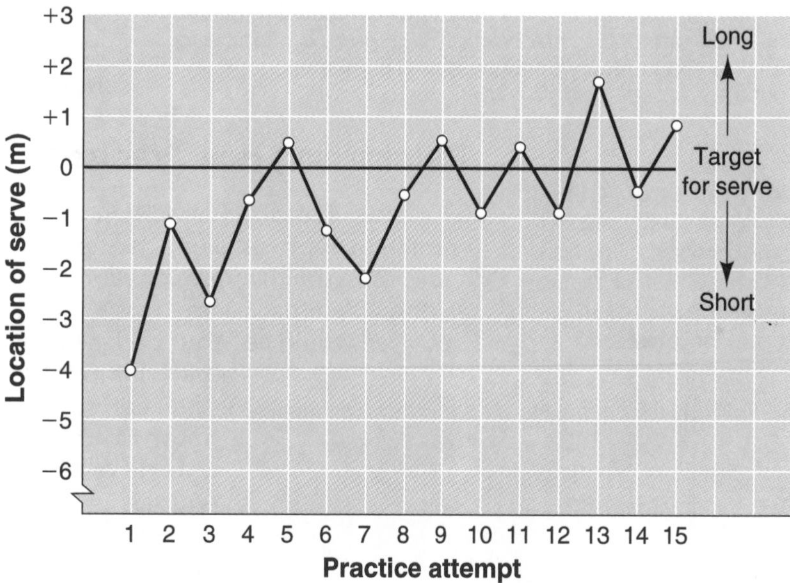


Figure 10.4 Summary feedback in learning a tennis serve. Scores are plotted on a graph, which is shown to the learner only after the last attempt is completed.

Lavery's experiment produced another interesting result. Specifically, the group that received *both* immediate feedback and summary feedback during practice performed as poorly when feedback was withdrawn as the group that received immediate feedback only. Why did this happen if summary feedback is supposed to be so beneficial? The most likely reason is that the participants in the combined group ignored the summary feedback in favor of the more immediate, dependency-producing feedback.

### *Average Feedback*

One variation of summary feedback is called **average feedback**. With this method, the practitioner again provides feedback information after a series of performance

**average feedback**—Feedback given after a series of practice attempts that provides learners with information about their average performance in the series.

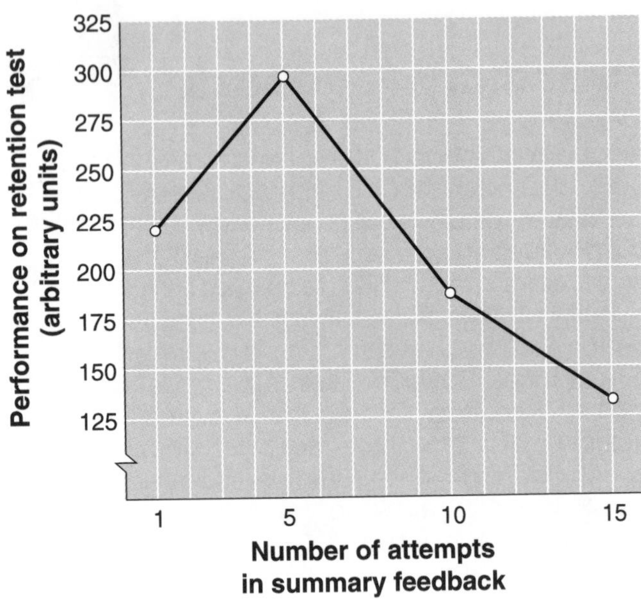


Figure 10.5 Performance on a retention test as a function of the number of attempts used for summary feedback in acquisition. The 5-attempts summary length was the most effective for learning. (Reprinted by permission from Schmidt, Lange, & Young, 1990.)

attempts, but the feedback in this case represents an estimated average, rather than a summary, of performance. In the tennis example shown in figure 10.4, the instructor might say to the student, "Your serves were (on the average) about one meter short of the service line." Young and Schmidt (1992) found that average kinematic feedback provided after a series of five performance attempts was more effective for the learning of a simulated batting task than feedback given following each attempt.

Very likely, average feedback and summary feedback function in a similar fashion—by blocking the detrimental, dependency-producing effects of giving feedback after each performance attempt. Moreover, average feedback is probably easier for instructors and therapists to administer than is summary feedback. When giving average feedback, practitioners are able to form a better idea of the learner's general movement pattern and filter out the occasional extreme errors. In this way, instructors can provide learners with more reliable information about the prominent features of their movements and the aspects they need to change during the next series of attempts.

## Determining How Precise to Make Feedback

**constant error (CE)**—The deviation, with respect to amount and direction, of the result of a person's movement relative to some target value.

The issue of feedback precision concerns the degree to which reported feedback information approximates actual performance. For example, an instructor might provide only a rough approximation of a movement feature (e.g., movement length), by saying, "Your backswing was a little too long." A more precise feedback statement, however, would be "Your backswing was 5.5 cm too long." Generally speaking, feedback information does not have to be very precise to be effective. Early in practice, learners' errors are so large that precise information about their exact size simply does not matter (Magill & Wood, 1986). At a high level of skill, however, individuals may benefit from somewhat more detailed feedback because they want to make more precise adjustments in their movements.

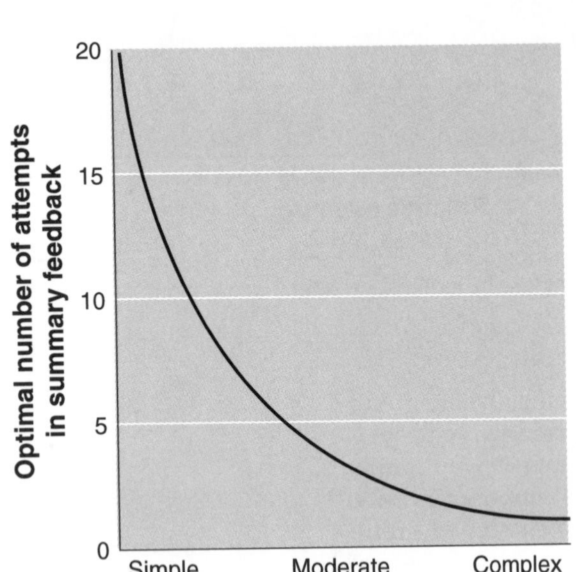


Figure 10.6 The probable relationship between task complexity and the optimal number of movement attempts to include in summary feedback.

Sometimes practitioners might provide learners with information about directional errors in their movements (e.g., early or late, high or low, left or right). In addition to direction information, instructors might also give individuals feedback about the magnitude of their errors. For example, an archery instructor might indicate that "The arrow landed two centimeters to the left of center," or a therapist might observe "Your first step was six inches shorter than it should be." You may recall from chapter 7 that **constant error** is the deviation of a person's movement relative to some target value (e.g., a golf putt that stops 3 in. past the hole; a baseball swing that delivers the bat through the hitting zone 200 ms before the ball arrives). Average CE represents the average deviation of the results of several movement attempts (e.g., three putts that stop an average of 2.8 in. past the hole). Of the two aspects of constant error, direction information

## HOW DOES SUMMARY FEEDBACK WORK?

How might the benefits of summary feedback be explained? Any or all of the following reasons appear to be viable explanations:

1. Learners must perform in an independent fashion for a number of practice attempts before they finally receive feedback. When they receive summary feedback, learners use this information to make corrections in their general movement pattern on the next series of attempts. For example, the tennis player looking at the graph of his serves shown in figure 10.4 would see that he tended to hit his serves short of the service line, at least initially; therefore, he might try to increase the force of his shots during the next series of attempts.
2. Summary feedback produces more stable movements. Because learners perform a number of attempts before receiving summary feedback, they have no reason to change their movements very much from one attempt to the next.
3. Summary feedback encourages learners to analyze their own movement-produced (kinesthetic, visual, etc.) feedback. Since they receive summary feedback less often, learners are encouraged to become familiar with intrinsic feedback and to develop their own error detection skills.

is more important than magnitude information. In fact, feedback about magnitude is of little use to individuals unless they are also informed about the direction of their errors.

One type of feedback information that speaks to the issue of precision is **bandwidth feedback** (Sherwood, 1988). With this method, the instructor only gives feedback when an individual's movements fall outside some acceptable level of correctness, or bandwidth. For example, let's say a therapist is working with a patient who is practicing rising to a standing position by first placing her hands in certain positions on the armrests of a chair. The therapist would not give feedback unless the patient's hand placement was outside some predefined bandwidth (e.g., more than 2 cm from the center position). We illustrate bandwidth feedback in figure 10.7, which shows a graph of the patient's hand positions during 10 hypothetical attempts to stand. The bandwidth is represented by the shaded area in the figure and spans the center of acceptable hand positions. In the example here, the therapist would give feedback about the direction and extent of the patient's hand placement error only after the first, second, sixth, and ninth attempts.

**bandwidth feedback**—Feedback given to learners only when their errors exceed a certain tolerance level.

The bandwidth feedback method has several advantages. First, it decreases the dependency of learners on extrinsic feedback as they become more skilled. When individuals are just beginning to practice, their movements tend to fall outside the acceptable bandwidth of correctness, requiring more frequent feedback from the instructor. However, as their skill improves, learners' movements fall within the bandwidth more often. Therefore, the practitioner gives extrinsic feedback less frequently, and intrinsic feedback becomes more important. Second, learners receive negative reinforcement, a reward, when error feedback is not given, resulting in further repetition of the correct movement. Finally, the absence of extrinsic feedback information during advanced performance fosters the production of more consistent actions, since individuals are receiving no information that suggests they should change anything. This allows them to strengthen their permanent memory of the action.

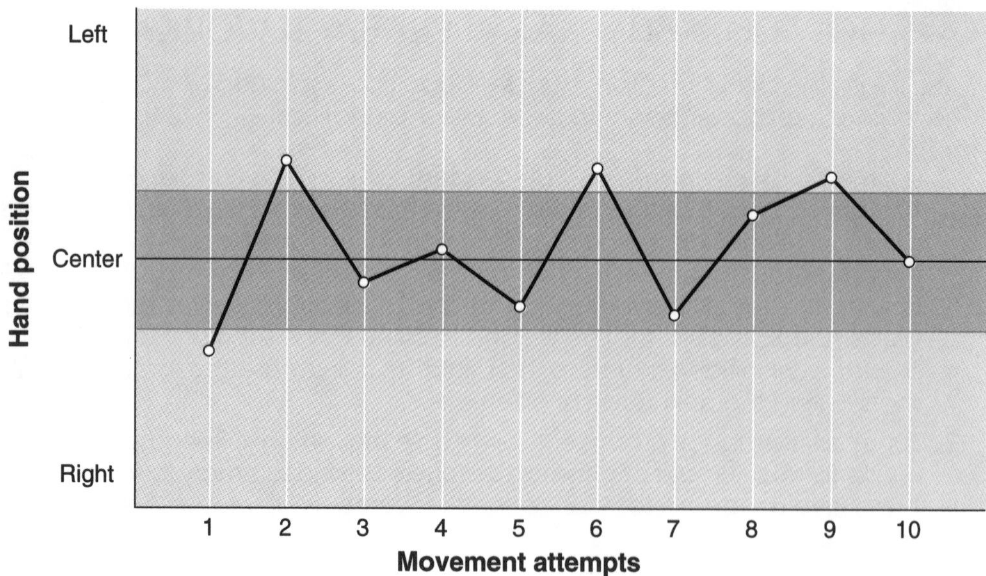


Figure 10.7 Bandwidth feedback is effective for learning. Feedback is given only if the performances fall outside the band of correctness.

## Determining How Often to Give Feedback

The frequency of providing feedback is an issue that is related to the amount and precision of feedback. Earlier in the 20th century, the understanding of how feedback operated for skill learning was largely based on Thorndike's law of effect. Because Thorndike believed that learning involved the strengthening of the bond between a stimulus and a response, and that extrinsic feedback increased the strength of that bond, he assumed that feedback should be presented as often as possible. Thorndike proposed that, if feedback was not presented after a movement attempt and learners could not determine the outcome from their own intrinsic feedback, no strengthening of the bond would occur.

Over the next few decades, scientists discovered little that contradicted Thorndike's viewpoint. Therefore, a "more is better" notion of feedback emerged, and it was assumed that feedback information that was more immediate, more precise, more frequent, more informationally rich, or more useful in general would be beneficial for learning. More is better seemed to make such good sense—giving more information to the learner "had to" benefit learning.

**absolute feedback frequency**—The total number of feedback presentations given for a series of performance attempts.

In time, though, scientists began to discover that more is not always better. With respect to the "how often" issue, researchers began to realize that feedback frequency could be viewed in two ways. One way involved **absolute feedback frequency**, which refers to the number of feedback presentations given to an individual during a practice session. If a person attempts 300 repetitions of a movement and the instruc-

When providing bandwidth feedback, instructors must make some decision about the level of a learner's performance that will be considered outside the bandwidth. What are some things instructors might keep in mind when determining the bandwidth for giving feedback to a child who is learning to swim? A therapy patient who is learning to use crutches? A middle school student who is learning to dance the Macarena?

tor gives feedback on 100 of them, the absolute feedback frequency is 100. **Relative feedback frequency**, on the other hand, refers to the number of feedback presentations divided by the number of movement attempts (multiplied by 100 to arrive at a percentage). In this example, 100 feedback presentations divided by 300 movement attempts and then multiplied by 100 yields a relative feedback frequency of 33%; that is to say, the instructor delivers feedback after 33% of an individual's performance attempts.

**relative feedback frequency**—The proportion of performance attempts for which feedback is given; equal to absolute feedback frequency divided by the number of performance attempts and multiplied by 100.

What are the principles that describe the roles of absolute and relative feedback frequency for learning? In general, increasing the absolute frequency of feedback enhances learning. This is especially true for learners who cannot detect their own errors without feedback because they cannot see or feel the outcome (e.g., the score in archery or the time in a running or swimming event) or because the outcome must be computed in another way (e.g., average stride length or a judge's rating of movement form). There are, however, limitations to this rule.

Consider the following situation: A group of individuals practices a task for which errors are difficult to detect without extrinsic feedback (e.g., archery, welding, knitting, adjusting brakes on a car). Because the instructor is busy rotating among them, the learners do not receive feedback information often. In other words, the relative feedback frequency is quite low. Does infrequent instructor feedback impair the learning of these individuals?

Research has shown that practice attempts followed by no feedback can actually be beneficial for learning, even when participants cannot detect their errors for themselves. In one study, Winstein and Schmidt (1990) found that individuals who received extrinsic feedback after 50% of their practice attempts improved at the same rate as those who received feedback following every attempt (100% relative frequency). Moreover, immediate retention of the skill (10 min after practice ended) performed in the absence of feedback was the same for both groups. Results such as these challenge Thorndike's assumption that movements followed by no extrinsic feedback produce no learning.

But there is more. When Winstein and Schmidt tested participants again two days later, the group that had received less frequent feedback (50% relative frequency) during practice performed *better* than the group that had received feedback after every attempt (100% relative frequency). How could less feedback during practice produce more learning? One answer may be that, when individuals don't receive feedback, they engage in different kinds of information-processing activities than when they do. In addition, it is likely that, when learners are not given feedback on a frequent basis, they are less likely to become dependent on the feedback. The result is more effective learning and better retention of the movement.

One way practitioners can reduce the dependency-producing processes inherent in feedback is to gradually reduce the relative frequency of feedback provision. A **faded feedback** approach begins with the instructor providing feedback after most of the learner's initial practice attempts (essentially 100% of the time). With this information, the learner can achieve the goal pattern quickly and repeatedly experience the sensations associated with it. However, once the learner

**faded feedback**—A schedule for providing extrinsic feedback in which relative frequency of feedback presentation is high during initial performance attempts and diminishes during later learning.

## IT DEPENDS . . .

One thing practitioners should keep in mind when reducing the relative frequency of feedback presentations is the learner's motivation. Assume that a physical education instructor is teaching a student how to hit a badminton drop shot, and the instructor is giving feedback after every tenth attempt. What else could the instructor do during the time between feedback statements that might help the student sustain motivation?

## HOW FREQUENTLY DO LEARNERS NEED INSTRUCTIONAL FEEDBACK?

In the study we described in the highlight box on page 267, Janelle and colleagues (1997) reported that individuals who received augmented feedback only when they requested it outperformed participants who received feedback following every practice attempt. The surprising result was that the group that requested feedback did so only 11% of the time—with most of the requests coming during the first 50 practice attempts (out of a total of 200). This finding is consistent with the notion that when it comes to feedback frequency, less may actually be better.

has reached a satisfactory level of proficiency, the instructor can gradually reduce or "fade" the relative feedback frequency. After considerable practice, the instructor can withdraw feedback entirely without diminishing the learner's performance. If for some reason performance proficiency should drop off, the instructor can give feedback again for one or two attempts to bring the learner's performance back to the target level. Once this is accomplished, the instructor can withdraw feedback again.

With the faded feedback method, instructors can adjust feedback scheduling to the proficiency level and improvement rate of each learner. The ultimate goal of this approach is to facilitate the development of the learner's capability to produce the required action on his or her own, without the need for extrinsic feedback. Even though instructors can enhance learning by providing feedback while individuals are developing and engraining the goal movement pattern, they must eventually remove it to enhance permanent skill learning.

One issue related to the frequency of feedback provision concerns the timing of feedback presentation. Regardless of how frequently instructors give feedback, they need to consider how long to wait after the learner completes a movement before providing feedback. As we mentioned earlier, the KR-delay period is a good time for individuals to process their own feedback and estimate their own errors. Laboratory research has shown that when experimenters give extrinsic feedback immediately after participants complete their movements, as opposed to delaying it a few seconds, learning is diminished. In a study by Swinnen et al. (1990), participants attempted to learn a simulated batting task. One group received **instantaneous feedback** after each movement, whereas another received **delayed feedback** a few seconds after they completed the movement. The instantaneous group turned out to perform more poorly than the delayed group on the second day of practice and on several retention tests administered over a four-month period. One reason instantaneous feedback may have been detrimental to learning is that it prevented individuals from processing their own response-produced feedback (i.e., how the movement felt, sounded, looked) and estimating their own errors. Ideally, practitioners should probably allow learners enough time for both activities before providing feedback.

**instantaneous feedback**—Feedback provided to learners immediately following movement completion.

**delayed feedback**—Feedback provided to learners several seconds or more following movement completion.

## IT DEPENDS . . .

A person is helping his friend learn to bowl. What are some things the individual might look for in his friend's performance that would help him determine when to begin reducing the relative frequency of his feedback?

## MORE FREQUENT FEEDBACK MAY BE NEEDED FOR COMPLEX SKILL LEARNING

In a recent series of experiments by Wulf, Shea, and Matschiner (1998), three groups of individuals attempted to learn to perform on a slalom-type ski simulator (see figure 10.8). During the practice phase, two of the groups received different frequencies of continuous **knowledge of performance** about the foot forces they exerted on the platform. One group received this feedback on 100% of their practice attempts, while the other group received it on 50% of their attempts. A third group received no knowledge of performance during skill practice. After the practice phase, a retention test was administered under conditions of no continuous feedback. The results of this test revealed that the group that had received feedback on 100% of their practice attempts outperformed the groups that had received feedback on 50% of their attempts or not at all. These findings suggest that, for complex tasks like the slalom-type ski simulator, a higher relative frequency of continuous knowledge of performance may be more effective for skill learning than a reduced frequency, at least until individuals reach an acceptable level of expertise. Thus, it appears that practitioners might want to consider the type of feedback they are giving and the relative difficulty of the task (i.e., the learner's capability relative to the complexity of the task) when determining optimal feedback frequency for skill learning.

**knowledge of performance (KP)**—Augmented feedback that provides information about the quality of the movement a performer has produced; sometimes referred to as kinematic feedback.

**Figure 10.8** The ski simulator apparatus. (Reprinted from Vereijken, Whiting, and Beek, 1992.)

A collegiate athlete is helping her younger brother learn how to throw the discus. She decides to let her brother think about each of his throws for a few moments before she gives him feedback. Why is this a good instructional strategy? What else might the athlete encourage her brother to do between the time he completes a throw and the time she gives him feedback? Why?

## Summary

A learner can receive various kinds of sensory information during skill rehearsal, but augmented, extrinsic feedback about errors provided by the instructor is one of the more important sources of information. Instructors often present feedback verbally (i.e., telling individuals what they did correctly and incorrectly), but they can also present feedback in other forms, such as visually (e.g., videotape replays). Instructional feedback is best when it is simple and when it refers to only one movement feature at a time, particularly when that feature deals with something that the learner controls.

Extrinsic feedback can serve the following simultaneous functions:

- Energize individuals and increase their motivation.
- Reinforce learners for correct performance or discourage incorrect performance.
- Provide learners with information about the nature and direction of their errors and suggest ways of correcting them.
- Make learners so dependent on the feedback that their performance suffers when the information is withdrawn.

When providing feedback, practitioners might want to keep the following questions in mind:

- What information should the feedback contain?
- How much information should the feedback contain?
- How precise should the feedback information be?
- How often should the feedback information be presented?

These are some considerations concerning the type of information given in feedback:

- Feedback about the timing or sequencing of a movement pattern leads to changes in the fundamental structure of the generalized motor program.
- Feedback about program features (e.g., the relative timing of arm and leg movements) is sometimes difficult for individuals to use, but is crucial for modifying faulty movement programs.
- Feedback about parameters (e.g., movement speed) and parameter values (e.g., slow, medium, and fast speeds) leaves the program's structure intact, and learners can easily use this information to match their movements to the current environmental demands.
- Prescriptive feedback that informs learners about specific changes to make in their movements is more effective than descriptive feedback that simply tells individuals about the errors they made.

These are two observations or issues dealing with the amount of information that might be contained in feedback:

- The optimum amount of information instructors should include in their feedback decreases as the complexity of the task increases.
- Summary feedback and average feedback are particularly effective ways of providing learners with an optimal amount of information without creating a feedback dependency.

Some important principles dealing with the precision of feedback information include the following:

- Increasing the precision of feedback enhances learning only to a point (e.g., saying that an individual's follow-through was slightly left of center is better than saying that the follow-through was not very good); beyond that point, further increases in feedback precision result in little additional learning.
- Feedback about the direction of learners' errors is more useful than feedback about the magnitude of their errors.
- Bandwidth feedback is an effective way to manipulate feedback precision and reduce the learner's dependence on feedback information.

Issues dealing with the frequency and timing of feedback presentation are summarized as follows:

- Instructors can present feedback more frequently early in learning but should then reduce (or fade) the relative frequency of feedback as learners become more skilled in task performance.
- Instantaneous feedback degrades learning, probably because it interferes with the individual's intrinsic feedback processing and development of error detection capability.

## From Principles to Practice

Check your understanding of the material in this chapter by responding to the following questions and then completing the application exercises. In each case, see if you can identify the most relevant questions or issues and then propose a solution based on the concepts and principles discussed in the chapter.

### Checking Your Understanding

1. Explain the difference between intrinsic feedback and extrinsic feedback and between knowledge of results and knowledge of performance. Give an example of each type of feedback information for a golf instructor giving a beginner a lesson.
2. Describe the four ways that extrinsic feedback can act to modify an individual's behavior, and then discuss how a diving coach might utilize each of the four functions in teaching a child how to do a back dive.
3. Discuss three advantages and three disadvantages of instructor feedback for a person who is learning how to play the piano.
4. Explain the difference between descriptive feedback and prescriptive feedback, and give two examples of each that an instructor in a driving school might give to a student driver.
5. Discuss two procedures a therapist might use to reduce the dependency-producing properties of feedback when teaching a person recovering from ACL knee surgery how to correctly perform a leg-strengthening exercise.

### Application Exercise #1

A young man enrolls in a class to learn how to operate a forklift. The demands of this task include driving the forklift and operating the steel prongs that pick up, move, and stack objects of different sizes and weights.

*It Depends*

- What is the individual's present skill level?
- Does he have 20/20 vision?
- Is the instrument panel on the forklift easy to interpret?
- What is the maximum number of control movements an operator must be able to perform at any one time?
- What aspects of the control movements are more complex?

*Strategy*

Prioritize the various components of the task with respect to their order of importance for successful performance. Determine a practice and feedback schedule that allows the individual to become familiar with the essential control movements and to develop a generalized motor program for operating the steel prongs (i.e., successfully manipulating objects of various weights and sizes).

*Response Example*

- Encourage the learner to request feedback anytime he feels he needs it and, whenever possible, to request the type of information that is most helpful for him.
- Provide program feedback initially to assist the individual in learning the general movement pattern for operating the forklift.
- Once the individual acquires the basic movement pattern, structure practice so that he must lift and move objects of different weights and sizes, providing parameter feedback as needed.
- Provide feedback less frequently as the individual's performance improves.

### Application Exercise #2

A woman wants to learn judo and enrolls in a judo class.

*It Depends*

- What are the program and parameter requirements of judo?
- Can the woman recognize the timing characteristics of the various movements by observing the instructor's demonstrations?
- How well is the student able to imitate the instructor's movements?
- What types of feedback does the student need most?

### Strategy

Identify the basic movement patterns for each of the fundamental judo movements. Determine the forms of feedback that are most helpful for the learner. Develop a feedback schedule that provides the learner with the types and frequency of feedback she needs.

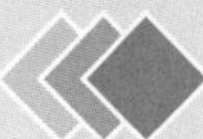

## Application Exercise #3

A gymnastics coach is trying to teach an athlete a new routine on the still rings.

### It Depends

- How long has the athlete participated in gymnastics?
- What is the athlete's level of competition?
- Does the routine contain movements the athlete has never attempted before?
- What type of feedback is most helpful for the athlete?

### Strategy

Devise a strategy for practice and feedback that enables the athlete to progressively develop and assemble the skills required for the new rings routine and be able to perform it in competition.

## Application Exercise #4

A man has recently lost the sight in both eyes as a result of an industrial accident. In order to maintain his aerobic fitness level, he needs to learn how to swim using the freestyle stroke.

### It Depends

- Is the man "drownproofed"?
- Does he have any impairments in addition to his visual deficit?
- Can the instructor communicate verbal feedback in a way that the man can comprehend?
- Are there any nonverbal forms of feedback the instructor might provide?

### Strategy

Determine the type of feedback that helps the man achieve a close approximation of the correct mechanics of the freestyle stroke. Request his assistance in determining the types and frequency of feedback that are motivating and reinforcing for him, and that provide necessary information for error correction.

# PART IV

# Integration and Applications

11
22

# Facilitating Learning and Performance

## Chapter Outline



## Chapter Objectives

**When you have completed this chapter, you should be able to**

integrate the conceptual model of human performance and the various principles presented in the book, and be able to apply them when teaching skills in applied settings;

appreciate how different kinds of learners, tasks, and situations influence the design of effective learning experiences; and

determine appropriate instructional strategies for a variety of learning experiences.

## Preview

How many classes have you taken in school for which you diligently copied lecture notes, memorized them along with other facts from the textbook, "regurgitated" as much of the information as you could on exams (perhaps even earning an "A" in the course), and yet didn't have a clue as to what you were talking about? Or, if you did have a clue, how much of the material did you forget once the course was over? Our hope is that this will not happen when it comes to the concepts you have learned in this book. Certainly, the problem-based approach you have used for the various application exercises is one that should prove helpful to you in the future.

One day you may find yourself in a therapeutic setting where you are expected to assist individuals in the recovery of skills they have lost as a result of an accident or stroke, skills these people once produced with ease, but that now require their best effort to achieve at the crudest level. Perhaps you will have the opportunity to teach or coach individuals who want to play the violin, tune the engine of a car, swim the freestyle, or throw darts. When your time comes to assist others in the learning or relearning of skills—and be assured your time *will* come—what kind of approach will you take? What will you do to make each individual's learning experience efficient, interesting, and productive? How will you organize practice sessions? How and when will you provide feedback? How will you assess the quality of each learning experience?

## Overview

To design an effective plan of instruction, practitioners must know something about the background, abilities, and experiences of learners (see chapter 2); the underlying mechanisms of human performance (see chapters 3–6); the learning goal and target context (see chapter 7); and the important principles of practice organization (see chapter 8), structure (see chapter 9), and feedback (see chapter 10). In this book, we have presented scientific literature dealing with all of these issues. Many times, the research provides clear direction for practitioners. Sometimes the evidence still is either inconsistent or nonexistent.

Regardless of the amount of supporting evidence at their disposal, practitioners must be able to design learning experiences that optimize learners' chances of goal achievement. For those situations in which relevant scientific evidence is partial or incomplete, practitioners must exercise due caution and be prepared to make adjustments in the instructional plan as needed.

In this chapter, we pull together a number of key themes we have discussed throughout the book. Our purpose is to suggest and demonstrate how you might use the material you have learned to devise effective solutions to a variety of instructional challenges you are apt to face in the future. First, we propose a working strategy that combines the conceptual model of human performance with many of the principles of skill learning. In the rest of the chapter, we present case studies, giving four varied scenarios that illustrate how practitioners might use the strategy to design learning experiences that help individuals achieve their goals.

## A Working Strategy for Providing Instructional Assistance

As with most large projects in life (e.g., earning a degree, teaching a class, or writing this book), the hardest and frequently the most important part is preparing a plan of action. Preparation is agonizing for most of us because of all the issues that need to be considered, making the task seem at times almost overwhelming. However, once we come up with an effective plan, even if it is not exactly perfect, execution of the plan becomes a relatively easy task, leaving us wondering why we had so much difficulty preparing it in the first place.

The plan of action or *working strategy* for skill instruction we propose begins with the conceptual model of human performance we have developed in this book (shown in finalized form in figure 11.1). Regardless of the types of instructional challenges you might face as a practitioner, you should always keep in mind the fundamental mechanisms of human performance that underlie skill learning. Knowledge of these mechanisms allows you to determine things like the possible effects of task demands on the three information-processing stages, the extent to which performers can make feedback-based adjustments in their movements, and the types of intrinsic and extrinsic information learners need to improve their skills and develop their error detection capabilities.

The remainder of our working strategy consists of the various concepts and principles presented in this book. Many of these statements or principles are not hard-

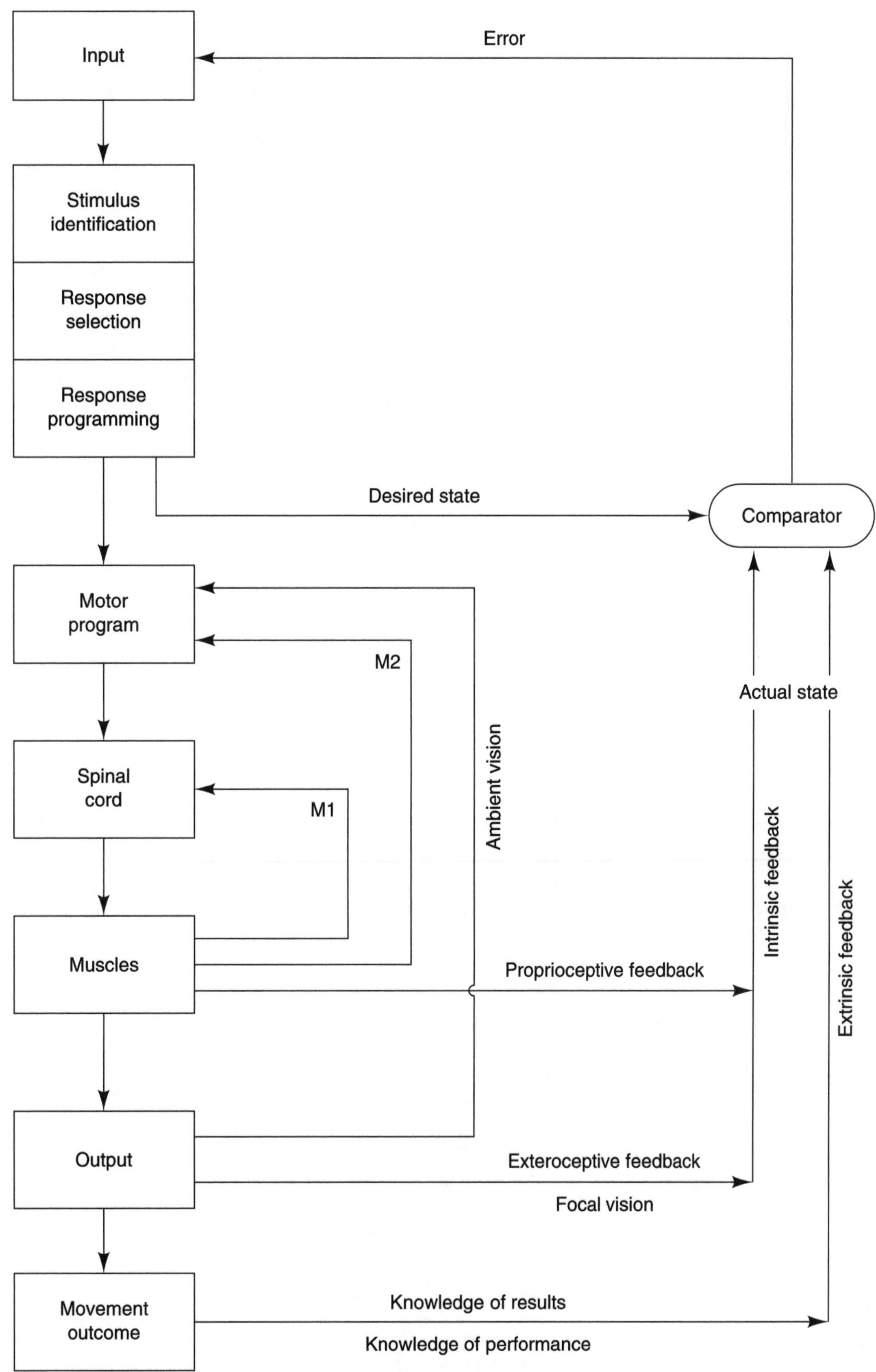


Figure 11.1 The completed conceptual model of human performance, which is used here as a basis for the organization of effective practice.

and-fast rules. Rather, they include qualifying phrases such as "in the early stages of learning" or "when dealing with a complex task." The reason for this is that the solution to most problems of performance or learning *depends* on answers to such questions as "Who is the learner (a child, an athlete, a rehab patient, a senior citizen)?" "What is the target skill (handwriting, using a wheelchair, hitting a ball, driving a car)?" and "Where is the target context in which an individual must ultimately perform the skill (in the home environment, during the finals of a sport tournament, during a physical education class, at a musical recital)?" To be consistently effective, a working strategy must provide you with reasonable answers to these and other relevant questions.

In table 11.1, we present a checklist of items you can refer to when diagnosing the learning experience prior to devising your own instructional strategy. For each question, we list a number of factors you might consider. As you review this table, you might be able to think of other items to include. If so, we encourage you to add them. You should, however, be able to provide supporting rationale and, wherever possible, scientific evidence for any additions you propose.

Once you have completed the checklist in table 11.1, you can decide what types of instructional assistance you would provide. In table 11.2, we present a checklist for determining the most effective types of assistance. Again, you might be able to think of other items to add to this list and, if so, we encourage you to do so.

Viewed as a whole, the conceptual model of human performance, along with the checklists of factors for diagnosing and designing the learning experience, provides a working strategy you should be able to use for just about any instructional situation. In the remainder of this chapter, we present four hypothetical case studies to illustrate how practitioners might do this.

**Table 11.1**

**A Checklist for Diagnosing the Learning Experience**

| WHO? | WHAT? | WHERE? |
|---|---|---|
| **Learner characteristics** | **Task (target skill) characteristics** | **Target context** |
| ☐ Age | ☐ Discrete/Serial/Continuous | ☐ Recreational |
| ☐ Previous experience | ☐ Motor/Cognitive | ☐ Competitive (athletic) |
| ☐ Motivation | ☐ Closed/Open | ☐ Clinical |
| ☐ Stage of learning | ☐ Closed-loop control | ☐ Home |
| ☐ Abilities | a. Exteroceptive feedback | ☐ Presence or absence of others |
| ☐ Attention | b. Proprioceptive feedback | |
| ☐ Arousal | ☐ Open-loop control | |
| ☐ Memory | a. Motor programs | |
| ☐ Information-processing capability | b. Generalized motor programs | |
| **Goal(s) of learning** | ☐ Speed-accuracy trade-offs | |
| ☐ Program learning | a. Spatial accuracy | |
| ☐ Parameter learning | b. Temporal accuracy | |
| ☐ Error detection and correction | ☐ Object manipulation | |
| ☐ Skill refinement | ☐ Information-processing demands | |
| ☐ Generalization | a. Stimulus identification | |
| | b. Response selection | |
| | c. Response programming | |
| | ☐ Risk of injury | |

**Table 11.2**
**A Checklist for Designing the Learning Experience**

| PRACTICE PREPARATION | PRACTICE PRESENTATION | PRACTICE FEEDBACK |
|---|---|---|
| ☐ Goal setting<br>a. Outcome goals<br>b. Performance goals<br>c. Process goals<br>☐ Stage of learning<br>☐ Transfer of learning<br>☐ Target skills<br>☐ Target behavior<br>☐ Target context<br>☐ Performance measures<br>a. Outcome<br>b. Process | ☐ Clarifying expectations<br>☐ Managing arousal<br>☐ Focusing attention<br>☐ Instructions<br>☐ Demonstrations<br>☐ Guidance<br>☐ Physical rehearsal<br>a. Simulators<br>b. Part practice<br>c. Slow-motion practice<br>d. Error detection practice<br>☐ Mental rehearsal<br>a. Procedures<br>b. Imagery | ☐ Intrinsic feedback<br>☐ Extrinsic feedback<br>a. Knowledge of results<br>b. Knowledge of performance<br>☐ Instructional decisions<br>☐ Type of feedback<br>a. Program/Parameter<br>b. Visual/Verbal/Manual<br>c. Descriptive/Prescriptive<br>☐ Amount of feedback<br>a. Average feedback<br>b. Summary feedback<br>☐ Precision of feedback<br>☐ Frequency of feedback |
| **PRACTICE STRUCTURE** | | |
| ☐ Schema development<br>a. Constant practice<br>b. Varied practice<br>☐ Facilitating transfer<br>a. Blocked practice<br>b. Random practice<br>c. Consistent and varied S-R mapping | | |

# Four Case Studies

For each of the following case studies, we present a hypothetical scenario, a sample solution, and two variations of the scenario, which require slight alterations in the solution.

## Case Study #1: Teaching the Backhand Ground Stroke in Tennis

Bill is a 50-year-old male who has played tennis recreationally for many years but has never developed a satisfactory backhand ground stroke. During his matches, Bill's strategy is usually to avoid hitting backhands whenever possible. Recently, however, Bill decided he's tired of that strategy and wants to learn how to hit the backhand correctly so that he can produce the shot with confidence during competition. Bill asks his friend Liz, an experienced player, to teach him. How might Liz approach this task?

### *Problem Assessment*

Using the checklist for diagnosing the learning experience (see table 11.1), Liz makes the following notes:

**Learner characteristics.** Bill is a 50-year-old male with 25 years of previous tennis experience. Bill appears to have average to better-than-average levels of the important abilities for playing tennis (i.e., multilimb coordination, motor timing, perceptual timing, and force control). He is physically fit and has no obvious handicapping conditions. He is highly motivated to improve his backhand ground stroke. For the most part, Bill is in the motor stage of learning (*skill refinement*), but he may need to do some of the things associated with the verbal-cognitive stage of learning if he intends to seriously revamp his stroke.

**Goal of learning.** Since Bill's current backhand requires serious adjustment and possibly a complete overhaul, program learning is a primary goal. Bill also needs to be able to produce a variety of backhand shots (*parameter learning*) and to generalize his performance from practice settings to competition situations (*generalization*). A final goal is the development of error detection and correction capability, which Bill needs in order to make appropriate adjustments in his backhand on his own.

**Characteristics of the target skill.** The tennis backhand is a discrete, open skill involving both large and small muscles. The task also requires object manipulation: Bill must control the racket in order to produce different angles and spins with his shots. Speed-accuracy trade-offs are a consideration, since Bill must hit the ball with pace while, at the same time, keeping it within the boundaries of the court. There is an abundance of intrinsic feedback available, including vision of the ball's trajectory, angle, and speed; proprioception of limb movements and the racket-ball impact; and audition of the racket-ball impact. Information-processing demands exist for each of the three stages of processing: stimulus identification, response selection, and response programming. There is little risk of injury unless Bill uses incorrect mechanics, which could produce tennis elbow.

**Nature of the target context.** Since Bill's goal is to hit the backhand ground stroke within the context of competitive tennis matches, an evaluative audience will eventually be present, including other players and perhaps spectators. Time pressure is also a part of the target context, since Bill must occasionally produce the backhand shot with very little time for preparation. Possible distractions include his fear of failure as well as an overemphasis on the importance of the match, the score, and how others evaluate him. The primary strategy demands include selecting and producing a variety of backhand shots in different situations.

Once Liz summarizes all this relevant information, she uses the conceptual model of human performance in figure 11.1 and the checklist for designing the learning experience (see table 11.2) to devise the following instructional strategy for helping Bill.

### *Instructional Strategy*

Liz decides Bill's biggest problem is that, over the years, he has developed an inappropriate program for producing the backhand ground stroke. Therefore, Liz decides the most important thing Bill must do is change the fundamental structure of his backhand (*program learning*). Liz decides to introduce the stroke in the same way she would for a beginner who had never played tennis before. She begins by verbally explaining (*instructions*) and visually demonstrating (*demonstrations*) the proper grip, stance, and swing.

When Liz is sure that Bill understands this preliminary information, she describes and demonstrates the most important temporal component of the swing (i.e., one flowing motion of the arm, wrist, and racket in a straight path). Then Liz asks Bill to produce the component in isolation (*part practice*). Bill performs repetitions of the component, and Liz provides *verbal feedback* and a *visual demonstration* whenever Bill requests it. When Bill asks for feedback, Liz offers *prescriptive information* that alerts Bill to possible changes he might make in the swing component (e.g., "the head of the racket should lead the wrist and arm"). Otherwise, Liz lets Bill perform repetitions of the action without interruption. Occasionally, Liz asks Bill to rehearse the component with his eyes closed so that he gets a better feel of the movement (*intrinsic proprioceptive feedback*). Once Liz notices that Bill is producing the component on a consistent basis, she introduces the next most important movement component (i.e., keeping the shoulders level with the court throughout the entire stroke) and asks Bill to practice it in combination with the previous component (*segmentation*, or *progressive part practice*). Liz repeats this process until Bill demonstrates he can produce the fundamental pattern of the entire swing on a consistent basis.

Now Liz decides to create a situation where Bill must produce the newly learned pattern while hitting a tennis ball (*open skill practice*). Since Liz knows that automation of the pattern will require many more repetitions, she is careful to minimize *stimulus-identification* and *response-selection* demands. Liz does this by suspending the ball from a string with a Velcro band and asking Bill to focus only on the swing and on ball contact (*directing attention*). She tells Bill not to be concerned with the accuracy of ball placement (*speed-accuracy trade-off*), but to focus on hitting his strokes at full speed.

Bill's rehearsal continues like this for several days until he demonstrates that he can consistently produce the new backhand pattern and strike the ball firmly. At this point, Liz decides to increase *stimulus-identification* demands by using a ball machine to project the balls at a constant speed and location to Bill's backhand side. Now Bill must identify the speed, trajectory, and direction of the approaching ball. Again, Bill is told to focus only on producing the correct pattern and making solid contact with the ball. Liz provides occasional *prescriptive feedback* for program adjustment (e.g., "shoulders level"), but *reduces feedback frequency* as Bill continues to progress.

Once Liz sees that Bill is consistently striking the ball with the correct pattern, she shifts her instructional emphasis to *parameter learning*. Liz does this by asking Bill to hit backhands to several targets located at different distances and locations on the court. The targets are numbered, and Liz calls out a different sequence of numbers as Bill hits shots in a *varied-practice format* under *varied stimulus-response mapping conditions* (e.g., Bill attempts to hit a variety of returns for each of a variety of shots hit to him). With practice, Bill becomes quite adept at producing variations of the backhand pattern, resulting in shots that travel at different angles and speeds to different locations. Occasionally, Liz asks Bill to create his own sequence of shots and challenges him to see how many different ways he can produce the fundamental pattern (*retrieval practice* and *parameter selection*). When Bill produces an erroneous shot, Liz asks him to tell her what he thinks

went wrong (e.g., backswing preparation was too late) and what he feels he should do on the next shot to correct the error (*error detection and correction*).

Once Liz sees that Bill is able to produce a variety of backhand shots using the ball machine, she has him attempt his backhands while rallying with a partner. Liz instructs Bill to focus on the approaching ball while continuing to hit variations of the backhand shot. In time, Bill is hitting his backhand so consistently that Liz allows him to combine it with his forehand and volley in a *random-practice format*. In this way, Bill must select the most appropriate shot (*response selection*) and produce it (*response programming*) in a way that maximizes his chances of winning each point.

Liz now feels that Bill is ready to test his new backhand ground stroke in competition. Before doing so, Liz encourages Bill to set goals (*goal setting*) for each game that include hitting a certain percentage of backhands that travel over the net and inside the boundaries, using a *process focus* on each shot (e.g., watch the ball and make solid contact) and hitting a variety of backhand shots. In order to help Bill deal with distractions, Liz creates additional practice opportunities that are more matchlike in nature (*random practice*), using a variety of opponents and tennis court locations that include other players and spectators. In this way, Bill practices his shots under real-world competitive conditions (*generalization*).

### Variations in the Scenario: Relearning the Backhand and the Volley

Let's say Bill wants to relearn the volley in addition to the backhand. How does Liz adjust her instructional strategy? Liz still emphasizes program learning initially, but blocks Bill's practice (*blocked practice*) of each stroke until he demonstrates that he can produce both the volley and backhand actions on a consistent basis. At that point, Liz shifts Bill to a *random-practice format*. She then begins to provide *average feedback* and *summary feedback* so that Bill understands the types of adjustments he needs to make in the general pattern of each movement. For example, after Bill hits a sequence of backhands and volleys, Liz says, "Your weight was generally too far forward on your volleys" (*average feedback*) and "Your backswing preparation was too late for the first few backhands, but better timed for the rest of them" (*summary feedback*). As Bill's performance continues to improve, Liz fades the frequency of feedback (*reduced feedback frequency*).

### Variations in the Scenario: Reverting to Old Habits in Competition

When individuals confront stressful situations, they tend to revert to familiar habits. For Bill, this happens when he is playing a close tennis match and suddenly hits one of his "old" backhand ground strokes. Liz is not surprised when this happens, because she realizes that Bill has had many more repetitions of his ineffective backhand than he has had of his new backhand pattern. How, then, does Liz help Bill when she sees him reverting to his old backhand?

One thing Liz does is provide Bill with a *verbal cue* (e.g., "lead with the racket head") that helps him redirect his focus to the new movement pattern (*prescriptive feedback*). Liz also encourages Bill to occasionally rehearse a key component of the movement pattern in isolation (*part practice*). Sometimes Bill does this with his eyes closed, in order to reinforce the feel and timing of the correct pattern (*intrinsic proprioceptive feedback*). Liz also asks Bill to tell her what he thinks went wrong and what he thinks he should do to correct the mistake (*error detection and correction*). When Bill returns to competition, Liz encourages him to set a goal of focusing more on correct execution of his new backhand pattern (*process goal*) and less on winning the point (*goal setting*). This type of *process focus* reduces Bill's competitive anxiety and enhances his game performance (*generalization*). As Bill becomes more adept at producing the new pattern in practice and in competition, his relapses become less frequent, and when they do occur, Bill is better able to recognize them and correct them on his own.

## Case Study #2: Preparing a Collegiate Springboard Diver for Competition

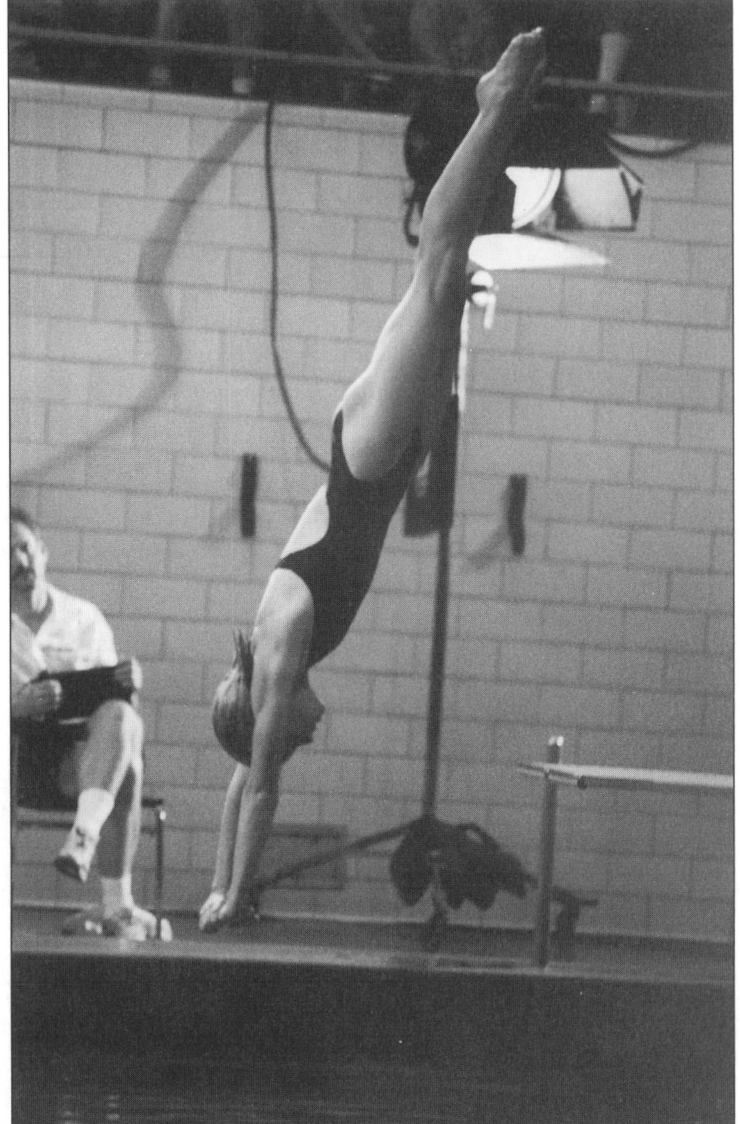
Paul Martinez/Photosport

Tracy is a 17-year-old female collegiate athlete who aspires to win the conference championship in 3-m springboard diving. Tracy's event requires her to perform a sequence of 10 dives of differing levels of complexity. Prior to entering the sport of diving, Tracy was a successful competitive gymnast. However, a shoulder injury forced her to give up that sport when she was 14 years old. Tracy's coach, Dave, feels that she has the physical abilities to compete for the championship. During training sessions, Tracy produces each of her dives in an effective fashion. However, during competition Tracy's performance is less consistent, particularly when she receives a low score on one of the first two or three dives in her program. Tracy also seems to struggle with two particular dives: the reverse two-and-one-half in the pike position and the reverse two-and-one-half in the tuck position. Dave's challenge is to provide Tracy with the kind of instructional assistance that allows her to produce all of her dives as effectively in competition as she does in practice.

### *Problem Assessment*

Using the checklist for diagnosing the learning experience (see table 11.1), Dave makes the following notes:

**Learner characteristics.** Tracy is a 17-year-old female with 3 years of previous competitive diving experience at the junior national level. Prior to that Tracy competed in gymnastics for 7 years. Tracy appears to have high levels of the relevant abilities for the sport of diving (i.e., gross body coordination, explosive strength, and dynamic flexibility). Tracy's prior shoulder injury has healed sufficiently for her to experience success in diving. Tracy is highly motivated to achieve the goal of winning the conference championship. Tracy's stage of learning varies from the motor stage to the autonomous stage, depending on the particular dive.

**Goal of learning.** Tracy's primary goal is to be able to effectively execute all of her dives in competition situations the same way she does in practice.

**Characteristics of the target skill.** All of the dives in Tracy's routine are classified as discrete or serial closed skills, primarily requiring the activity of large muscles. Relevant intrinsic feedback consists of kinesthetic and proprioceptive information about body and limb movements. Response programming is the only real information-processing demand. There is always the risk of injury in competitive diving (which may be a significant issue for Tracy, given her previous experience of injury).

**Nature of the target context.** Tracy must perform her dives in the presence of an evaluative audience (i.e., other divers, swimmers, officials, spectators, media).

Possible distractions include the importance of the score, the success of other competitors, a noisy environment, and an unfamiliar diving board. In the midst of all this, Tracy must execute each of 10 dives in the most effective way.

After Dave summarizes the relevant information pertaining to Tracy, the task of diving, Tracy's learning goal, and the target context, he uses the conceptual model of human performance and the checklist for designing the learning experience (see table 11.2) to devise the following strategy.

### Instructional Strategy

Dave and Tracy decide that there are two primary differences between Tracy's training and competition experiences: the frequency of Dave's feedback, and the structure of Tracy's performance attempts. During training, Dave provides Tracy with verbal feedback after each of her dives. In addition, he requires Tracy to perform each of her dives in a blocked format (i.e., five consecutive attempts for the first dive, five consecutive attempts for the second dive, etc.). During competition, Dave is not allowed to provide feedback, and Tracy is required to perform her dives in a serial format (i.e., one attempt for each of the 10 different dives).

To make Tracy's training experiences more similar to her competition experiences, Dave decides that Tracy must begin practicing her dives in a serial format (*random practice*) and with less immediate feedback (*reduced frequency of feedback*). After each sequence of 10 dives, Dave provides Tracy with *summary feedback* (i.e., one feedback statement for each dive), which she then uses to make necessary adjustments during her next sequence of dives. Dave also encourages Tracy to briefly evaluate her own kinesthetic and proprioceptive feedback following each dive (*error detection and correction*). After each sequence of dives, Dave asks Tracy to report the feedback she remembers about each dive and provide him with an estimate of the score she thinks the judges would give her.

Dave realizes that Tracy must learn to assume more control of her performance preparation during competition. Therefore, he refers Tracy to the team's sport psychology consultant, who helps her develop a mental plan for competition. A key component of Tracy's mental plan is a pre-dive mental routine that includes a breathing technique for adjusting her arousal level (*managing arousal*), *mental imagery* of each dive performed correctly, and the repetition of a simple verbal cue that reminds her of the appropriate focus for successful execution of the dive (*directing attention*). For example, the verbal cue "kick tight" reminds Tracy to come out of the tuck position quickly on the reverse two-and-one-half.

Once Tracy incorporates her pre-dive routine into her training sessions, she notices that the quality of her performance seems to be related to her arousal level. Tracy performs her simpler dives better at higher levels of arousal, but performs her more complex dives better at lower arousal levels. When Tracy shares this perception with Dave, he immediately wonders whether differences between her arousal level in practice and in competition are contributing to differences in her performance in those two situations. As a result, Dave instructs Tracy to pay more attention to her arousal levels in training and in competition to see if she detects any differences (*directing attention*). Tracy rates her arousal level for each dive on a scale of 1 to 3, where 1 means "low arousal," 2 means "intermediate arousal," and 3 means "high arousal." Almost immediately, Tracy notices that her arousal levels are higher during competition than they are during training, particularly if she competes against highly skilled opponents or performs in front of large audiences.

Dave and Tracy also notice that the two dives she has the most difficulty producing in competition are her two most complex dives. During training sessions, when Tracy's arousal levels are lower, she performs those dives without difficulty. However, during competition, when her arousal levels are higher, Tracy produces the two dives less effectively. Dave and Tracy believe that if she is to overcome this problem, she must learn to manage her arousal (*managing arousal*) so that, during competition, she can lower her arousal level for the more complex dives.

After several more sessions with the sport psychology consultant, Tracy is able to raise and lower her arousal level using a simple breathing technique. During training, Dave begins to incorporate distractions (e.g., noisy conditions) and competition stressors (e.g., reminders of the scores of highly regarded opponents), which usually elevate Tracy's arousal level during competition. Then Tracy uses her pre-dive mental routine to adjust her arousal level in the appropriate direction for each dive. With repeated practice, Tracy gets better at managing her arousal. Most significantly, she becomes adept at lowering her arousal level prior to the two complex dives. Tracy is excited because she realizes that her training is equipping her for competition and, with continued rehearsal, she begins to perform her two complex dives more effectively and consistently in competition.

As the season progresses, Dave creates more challenges for Tracy by requiring her to perform her sequence of dives in a different format each time (*random practice*) and by introducing a greater variety of possible distractions (e.g., warm and cool air temperature, unexpected performance delays, an occasional "unfair" judge's rating, varying noise conditions). By the time the conference meet arrives, Tracy knows she is ready for just about anything (*generalization*), and she is confident that she will respond with her best performance ever.

### Variations in the Scenario: Adjusting to Unfamiliar Diving Boards

Let's say that Tracy dives well in practice because she is familiar with the diving board. Tracy likes the level of spring in the board and knows exactly how it will respond during each of her dives. As a result, Tracy is relaxed prior to each dive and is able to focus all of her attention on correct execution. However, when she travels to competitions in other locations, Tracy is anxious, because she knows that the boards always feel different than the one at her home pool.

In order to assist Tracy in dealing with this problem, Dave decides she must learn how to make necessary adjustments to the diving board by herself. Prior to each practice, Dave alters the tension of the board (to a low, medium, or high level) and then challenges Tracy to adjust the tension until she achieves the level that feels comfortable to her (*closed-loop control*). Initially, Dave provides *knowledge of results* (regarding whether the tension level she sets is less than, equal to, or greater than her usual preferred level). After a few days of practice, however, Dave begins to *fade feedback frequency* and provide *summary feedback* after each sequence of Tracy's adjustments. This exercise directs Tracy's attention (*directing attention*) to the *intrinsic proprioceptive feedback* associated with the feel of different levels of board tension and helps her make the appropriate adjustments in the tension of the board without Dave's assistance (*error detection and correction*).

Dave then develops a *random-practice* format that requires Tracy to adjust the board to the appropriate tension level prior to each of her dives. In this way, Tracy develops a more sophisticated understanding of the level of tension that is optimal for each dive. Once Tracy becomes adept at adjusting the board in her home pool, Dave takes her to other pools in town so that she can generalize what she has learned while attempting to adjust the unfamiliar boards (*generalization*). As Tracy's proficiency increases, Dave introduces other variables that might influence the sensitivity of Tracy's board-tension adjustments (e.g., fatigue, crowd noise, air temperature, telling Tracy that she has to produce a high score to win the competition). With increased practice in a *varied and random format* of dives and distractions, Tracy learns how to adjust any board to an optimal level for all of her dives, regardless of the environmental circumstances. As a result of the practice experiences Dave has created for her, Tracy develops a more sophisticated understanding of the relationship between diving board tension and the performance of her dives under a variety of environmental conditions. Tracy is also more confident during competition because she knows she is able to make the appropriate adjustments in board tension any time and any place (*generalization*).

### Variations in the Scenario: Synchronized Diving

Synchronized diving is a fairly new event in the sport of competitive diving. In this event, two divers attempt to execute the same dive on adjacent boards in a synchronized fashion. The pair's performance is evaluated both with respect to the quality of the dives and the extent to which the two divers execute their dives in a synchronous fashion. Tracy and one of her teammates, Kathy, ask Dave to help them learn synchronized diving. Dave knows that while both women are accomplished divers, each executes her dives in a unique way.

Dave begins by asking Tracy and Kathy to attempt each of their dives in a synchronous manner on two adjacent boards. Dave *videotapes* all of their dives and then replays the dives in a *split-screen* format. In this way, Dave and the divers are able to identify the elements of each dive that are not synchronous. After several replays of each dive, Dave, Tracy, and Kathy agree on the adjustments in form and timing that each diver needs to make to produce two simultaneous dives in a synchronous fashion. Since Tracy is taller than Kathy, she must make adjustments (*parameter learning*) that produce a compression of her form and a reduction in the total time of the dive. For Kathy, the challenge is just the opposite—she must find ways to elongate her form and increase the total time of her dives.

Dave assists Tracy and Kathy with *verbal cues* that *direct their attention* to respective aspects of the dives that each individual must modify. Dave also provides *verbal and visual prescriptive feedback* that suggests changes the divers should make in their movements. With the assistance of the team's sport psychology consultant, Tracy and Kathy develop individual pre-dive routines for each dive that include *arousal adjustment*, *imagery* of the dive, and a simple *focus cue* (e.g., "stay in line in the press" or "throw over the top" are appropriate cues for executing the inward two-and-one-half in the tuck position). After some discussion, the divers agree that Tracy should be the one to verbalize the spoken commands they use to initiate each dive in a synchronized fashion.

Since synchrony is the primary goal of learning, Dave conducts practices that involve only synchronous rehearsal. Initially, he uses a *blocked-practice format* and provides *split-screen videotape feedback* and *verbal prescriptive feedback* (e.g., "throw over the top") after each dive. As the level of synchrony begins to improve, Dave *fades feedback frequency* and provides *summary feedback* at the end of each block of five attempts. In addition, Dave asks Tracy and Kathy to estimate their own errors prior to showing them the videotape feedback (*error detection and correction*).

Once Tracy and Kathy demonstrate that they can perform each dive with a considerable level of synchrony, Dave shifts the structure of practice sessions to a *random format*. Initially, Dave provides *visual and verbal feedback* after each dive, but gradually he *fades feedback frequency* until he presents it only at the end of each sequence of dives. Following each sequence, Tracy and Kathy evaluate their performance before Dave shows them the videotape feedback. Working together, Tracy and Kathy continue to detect and correct their errors and determine the types of adjustments that either or both need to make in order to maximize their collective performance.

The final stage of learning involves practicing under varied environmental conditions (*generalization*). Tracy and Kathy do this by rehearsing their entire sequence of dives at different pools, on different boards, under a variety of conditions of noise and other distractions, and by asking Dave to simulate some of the pressures of competition (e.g., telling them that their closest competitors have just achieved a high score). The two divers know they are now ready for their first synchronized diving competition, and they approach the event with a high level of confidence and excitement.

## Case Study #3: Teaching a Child With Cerebral Palsy to Walk Up and Down Stairs

Jennie is an 8-year-old female with cerebral palsy (spastic diplegia). Jennie can ambulate independently with modified ankle and foot orthoses and bilateral straight canes, but she doesn't do so spontaneously. When she is at home, Jennie prefers to crawl. If she does try to walk, Jennie is able to come to a standing position without being pulled up but must place her hands on the floor to do so. Once Jennie achieves a vertical posture, she prefers to place her hands on furniture and other objects to balance herself during locomotion. Jennie can stand independently to perform routine tasks like washing her face or throwing a ball.

Lisa is a physical therapist who has been assisting Jennie with independent walking. Now Jennie's mother asks Lisa to help Jennie learn how to walk up and down stairs using a railing. Lisa knows that Jennie prefers crawling to independent walking, even when it comes to climbing stairs. Jennie loves candy, and Lisa uses her favorite sweets to reinforce her attempts at independent walking. However, Lisa realizes that, for Jennie to *choose* independent walking when ambulating at home or in a variety of nonclinical settings, she must first become more intrinsically motivated. One potentially influential factor is time efficiency—if Jennie is able to get from one place to another faster by walking than by crawling, she is more likely to choose independent walking as a means of locomotion.

### *Problem Assessment*

Using the checklist for diagnosing the learning experience (see table 11.1), Lisa compiles the following profile:

**Learner characteristics.** Jennie is an 8-year-old female with spastic diplegia. Her lower extremities are often in a state of extreme flexion or extreme extension, and she demonstrates scapulohumeral association (i.e., the tendency to hold extremities close to the midline of the body). Jennie's previous movement experiences include crawling, independent standing, and occasional independent walking with ankle-foot orthoses and bilateral straight canes. Jennie possesses average to below-average levels of the abilities relevant to stair walking (i.e., an active range of motion in the lower extremities; range of motion in the upper extremities, especially scapulohumeral dissociation; trunk strength and control; dynamic balance; and strength in the lower extremities, especially the quadriceps, hip extensors, and pelvic stabilizers). Jennie has only low-level motivation to learn stair walking. She prefers crawling to independent walking, unless she knows she is going to receive candy for attempting to walk independently. Since stair walking is a new activity for Jennie, her learning stage is primarily verbal-cognitive.

**Goal of learning.** Jennie's goals include program learning, parameter learning, and task generalization. She is still in the process of developing a consistently effective program for locomotion; she needs to be able to adapt the locomotion program when walking up and down stairs while using a railing; and she needs to be able to climb stairs of various heights or textures and at various locations (e.g., at the clinic, at home, in the homes of family and friends).

**Characteristics of the target skill.** The task of stair walking is a closed, serial skill that primarily requires the activity of large muscle groups. There is no object manipulation, although Jennie must use straight canes and a stair railing to assist locomotion. Intrinsic visual and proprioceptive feedback is available, but is sometimes unreliable due to Jennie's inability to inhibit inappropriate reflex activity.

The primary information-processing demands are those dealing with response programming. There is a risk of injury, and Jennie is extremely afraid of falling.

**Nature of the target context.** An evaluative audience is often present at the clinic and in the home (e.g., parents, therapists, staff, and other patients at the clinic; parents, siblings, and occasionally friends and other family members at home). There is no time pressure to perform the task unless Jennie perceives pressure from others (e.g., parents, siblings). Possible distractions include Jennie's fear of failure, fear of injury, impatience, and short attention span.

Once Lisa summarizes the foregoing information, she uses the conceptual model of human performance and the checklist for designing the learning experience to devise the following instructional strategy for helping Jennie.

### *Instructional Strategy*

As a result of extensive physical therapy, Jennie achieves sufficient levels of lower-extremity active range of motion, upper-extremity range of motion, and lower-extremity strength (quadriceps, hip extensors, pelvic stabilizers). Knowing that Jennie has a short attention span and that she is not intrinsically motivated to use independent walking, Lisa limits the length of each instructional session to no more than 5 or 10 min (*distributed practice*).

One day Lisa introduces Jennie to the stair-stepping task by asking her if she would like to try something different. When Jennie says, "Maybe. . . . What is it?" Lisa shows her the simulated staircase (consisting of 5 steps, each 6 in. high, and a hand railing) and asks Jennie if she thinks she can walk up the first step. In this way, Lisa assists Jennie in setting a goal that is realistic for her (*goal setting*). If Lisa sees that Jennie is apprehensive about the height of the step, she creates a modified stepping task (*part practice*) that is less threatening for her (e.g., stepping onto a curb in the parking lot).

Initially, Lisa uses manual cueing (*physical guidance*) by placing her hands on Jennie's legs in order to assist her in getting an idea of the stepping motion and to alleviate her fear of falling. As Jennie lifts her right foot onto the step, Lisa says, "Up right." Then as she lifts her left foot, shifting her entire weight onto the step, Lisa says, "Up left" (*verbal cues*). Jennie smiles and looks at Lisa. She is smiling, too, as she says to Jennie, "That's great." Then Lisa asks Jennie if she thinks she can step down. She nods cautiously and then with Lisa's assistance steps down one foot at a time ("Down right, down left"). Lisa praises Jennie's effort (*motivational feedback and positive reinforcement*) and tells her that maybe they can play the stepping game again the next time she comes to the clinic. Jennie is so excited (*intrinsic motivation*) that she forgets to ask Lisa for candy as a reward for her performance.

The next time Jennie asks to play the stepping game, Lisa provides less manual cueing by diminishing the pressure she places on Jennie's legs. Lisa also begins to use *verbal cues* and *prescriptive feedback* that help Jennie understand what she should try to do in order to play the stepping game better. For example, when Lisa wants Jennie to stand more erect she says, "Higher, higher, pants on fire." When Jennie's weight is too far up on her toes, Lisa says, "Flea, fly, flat feet" to get her to come down. Jennie likes these phrases and tries to respond by doing what Lisa asks her to do.

As Jennie's performance gradually improves, Lisa asks her if she thinks she can walk up and down two steps, then three, then four, and eventually five (*goal setting*). With each level of progression, Lisa provides appropriate *verbal cues* and *prescriptive feedback* to help Jennie preserve her balance, shift her weight, and use the handrail (e.g., "reach and lift"). As Jennie's errors diminish, Lisa gradually reduces the frequency of the feedback (*faded feedback frequency*). However, she always praises Jennie for her effort (e.g., "You look just like a mountain climber!") and gives her a hug before she leaves each day (*intermittent positive reinforcement*).

Lisa assists Jennie in improving her functional efficiency by asking her to set movement time (*outcome*) goals (e.g., "How fast can you walk up and down one step? Two steps?"). Each time Jennie sets a movement time goal (*goal setting*), Lisa times her performance and provides her with *motivational feedback* (e.g., "You climbed that step in only eight seconds!"). After several months, Jennie is able to successfully walk up and down all of the steps at the clinic on a consistent basis. Soon after that, Lisa asks Jennie if she'd like to play the stepping game somewhere else (*generalization*). Over the next several weeks, Lisa introduces Jennie to other staircases at the clinic that vary in the number of steps, step height, surface material, and location of the handrail (*varied practice*). Lisa also reminds Jennie that she can play the stepping game at home any time she feels like it.

Lisa begins to combine Jennie's practice of stair climbing and other independent walking activities with the rehearsal of other functional activities, such as brushing teeth and putting on shoes (*random practice*). To reinforce independent walking even further, Lisa asks Jennie to set movement time goals for walking different distances and for climbing up and down different sets of stairs (*goal setting*). Occasionally, Jennie attempts the combined tasks of independent walking and stair climbing in a variety of other situations (e.g., at her grandparents' home, at the local Little League baseball stadium). As her sense of accomplishment increases, Jennie walks independently under a wider variety of circumstances (*generalization*). For Jennie, crawling is no longer an attractive option.

### Variations in the Scenario: Reluctance to Abandon Crawling as the Preferred Mode of Locomotion

While Jennie's independent walking and stair-climbing performance continues to improve with practice, she still chooses to crawl when moving in her home environment. Lisa learns from Jennie's mother that her brothers tease her about being so slow when she tries to move from one place to another. Since Jennie can crawl faster than she can walk independently, she continues to crawl when she is at home because she doesn't want to be teased (*negative reinforcement*). Lisa also notices that Jennie's mother seems to offer little praise when Jennie tells her about her accomplishments at the clinic. Her mother either minimizes them ("That's all you did today?") or reminds her daughter of what she still has not accomplished ("I still haven't seen you walk up the stairs at home."). Lisa realizes that something more must be done to create rehearsal experiences for Jennie that reinforce independent walking and discourage crawling in the home environment (*generalization*).

Lisa decides to meet with Jennie's mother and brothers and request their assistance in helping Jennie. She believes that if Jennie's family members are systematically involved in the therapy process, they can become a source of *positive reinforcement* for Jennie. Lisa asks them to think about some games Jennie could be encouraged to play at home that would stimulate her use of independent walking. She shows them a videotape of Jennie's activities at the clinic in order to give them a few ideas. Lisa reminds Jennie's mother that Jennie responds better to short periods of activity than she does to longer sessions (*distributed practice*). Lisa also stresses the importance of randomizing Jennie's activities (*random practice*), perhaps by mixing stair walking, playing with a puzzle, and throwing a ball, and of giving Jennie encouragement for attempting to climb the stairs (*motivational feedback*), regardless of how many steps she actually climbs each time.

Lisa meets weekly with Jennie's mother and brothers to see how things are going. She obtains feedback from them about Jennie's progress and asks them to explain the things they are doing to encourage her independent walking. The strategy seems to be working. For example, one of Jennie's brothers, Aaron, observes that Jennie has to climb 15 steps at home in order to make it all the way to the second floor but only has to climb 5 steps at a time at the clinic. Lisa compliments Aaron for his observation and asks him if he can think of ways to help Jennie achieve the ultimate goal of walking up all 15 steps at home (*goal setting*). After some discussion, Lisa and Jennie's family members develop a progression of short-term goals (e.g., climb 5 steps in 30 seconds, climb 7 steps in 45 seconds, etc.) that can help Jennie achieve the long-term goal of climbing all 15 steps using independent walking.

Initially, they encourage Jennie to climb the first five steps at home using independent walking and then allow her to crawl the remainder of the way. With continued practice and *positive reinforcement* for effort, Jennie gradually walks up more and more steps before she switches to crawling. Finally, after several weeks of rehearsal, Jennie makes it all the way to the top of the stairs without crawling. Jennie is excited about her accomplishment, and her family is pleased that they have had a role in Jennie's learning.

Lisa continues to communicate with Jennie's family and asks them to think of ways they might encourage Jennie to use independent walking in other functional contexts, like walking from the kitchen table to the living room sofa or walking from the house to the family car (*varied practice and generalization*). Lisa also suggests that family members allow Jennie to attempt tasks with less supervision and feedback (*faded feedback*), reinforcing her only when she shows genuine excitement over some new accomplishment (*intermittent reinforcement*)—for example, when Jennie walks all the way from the downstairs living room to her upstairs bedroom without crawling. The entire family is gratified by the progress Jennie makes as a result of her learning experiences at the therapy clinic and at home.

### *Variations in the Scenario: Independent Walking in Other Functional Environments*

Once Jennie achieves a satisfactory level of independent walking at the clinic and at home, she must generalize the walking action to a wider variety of functional target contexts (*generalization*). Variations of independent walking include moving up and down different types of stairs, up and down handicapped-accessible ramps, walking alone and in the midst of other walkers, walking around obstacles, and walking on various types of surfaces (e.g., carpet, vinyl, gravel, asphalt, hardwood, ceramic tile, brick, and stone). Jennie must also walk in various types of inclement weather (e.g., windy or rainy conditions). While Lisa exposes Jennie to some of these contexts in the clinical setting (e.g., walking on carpet and vinyl floor surfaces, walking up and down stairs, walking around obstacles), she takes Jennie outside the clinic to experience other situations (e.g., walking on a rainy sidewalk).

Two functional contexts that are particularly difficult for Jennie are walking up and down open stairs and walking in the midst of other pedestrians. Jennie's problem in each case is due to her perception of the situation and her fear of falling. With open stairs, Jennie perceives that she is higher off the ground than she really is, which feeds her fear of falling. This in turn alters Jennie's perception of the height of each step and causes her to overshoot or undershoot the step with her climbing movements. In the presence of other pedestrians, Jennie perceives they don't see her and is afraid they are going to bump into her.

In order to assist Jennie in generalizing independent walking to these two situations, Lisa employs a combination of techniques. First, she alerts Jennie to the nature of the situation (open stairs or an approaching pedestrian) beforehand so that she is not caught by surprise (*instructions*). Next, Lisa directs Jennie's attention to relevant environmental cues (*directing attention*) to focus on in each situation (e.g., the top of each successive step or the eyes of the approaching pedestrian).

Like most children, Jennie has a vivid imagination, so Lisa capitalizes on this capability by instructing Jennie to picture herself walking exactly the way she intends to walk in each situation (*mental rehearsal*). Sometimes Lisa tells Jennie to close her eyes and imagine that she is watching herself walking on television. Other times she asks her to close her eyes and try to see and feel herself walking up the open stairs or walking past the approaching pedestrian (*mental imagery*). To enhance the vividness of Jennie's imagery, Lisa occasionally asks her to tell her what type of shirt she is wearing in her mental picture or what the imaginary steps look and feel like.

Initially, Lisa blocks out separate time for Jennie's practice of each task (*blocked practice*) but, as she becomes more skilled in performing the tasks, she shifts Jennie to a *varied- and random-practice* format (e.g., walking in the midst of other pedestrians, climbing open stairs, walking alongside a single person, climbing open stairs while another person is descending the stairs). Eventually, Jennie learns to adapt her independent walking to a variety of functional contexts consisting of both open and closed environments (*generalization*) and requiring subtle alterations of the generalized motor program (*parameterization*), for example, climbing steps of different heights at different speeds.

## Case Study #4: Training a Level-I Firefighter

Ellen is a 27-year-old volunteer firefighter who is training to meet the fire-related performance objectives of the National Fire Protection Association. For the past five years, Ellen has been a fitness instructor at a local health club. Prior to that, she was a competitive collegiate athlete in soccer and softball at her university. Ellen's goal is to achieve the level of Firefighter I; that is, a person "who is minimally trained to function safely and effectively as a member of a fire-fighting team under direct supervision" (Wieder, Smith, & Brackage, 1996, p. 1). During the past two years, Ellen has achieved minimum performance requirements for most of the basic fire-fighting tasks (e.g., donning self-contained breathing apparatus, handling ladders, rescuing and extricating victims, loading and coupling hoses). However, Ellen has not yet learned how to advance hoselines.

Advancing hoselines is typically the last task firefighters perform prior to applying water to a fire. Once firefighters have moved hoselines from the truck and laid them out, they advance the hose into the final position. In addition to learning the basic technique for advancing hoselines, firefighters must also know how to adapt this technique when advancing hose to different destinations (e.g., up stairways, down inside and outside stairways, up ladders, from a standpipe). It is easier for firefighters to advance a hoseline before it is charged with water (because it is lighter); however, sometimes they must advance hoseline that is already charged. Firefighters must also be aware of a variety of potential dangers when advancing a hoseline (e.g., backdraft, flashover, structural collapse).

Jerry is a veteran firefighter who is responsible for supervising the training experiences of firefighter candidates. Jerry knows the essential tasks of fire fighting and the performance-based objectives required of level-I firefighters. Jerry is also aware of the varied demands of fire-fighting situations. How might Jerry use the working strategy for skill instruction presented in this chapter to assist Ellen in achieving her learning goal?

### *Problem Assessment*

Using the checklist for diagnosing the learning experience (see table 11.1), Jerry makes the following notes:

**Learner characteristics.** Ellen is a 27-year-old female with a considerable amount of previous movement experience, including participation as a collegiate athlete in soccer and softball, employment as a fitness instructor, personal involvement in a variety of strength and endurance activities, two years of service as a volunteer firefighter, and demonstrated competence in performing most level-I fire-fighting tasks. Ellen appears to have above-average levels of the abilities relevant to the performance of advancing hoseline (i.e., manual dexterity, static strength, dynamic strength, and stamina). She is highly motivated to learn the tasks necessary for her to achieve the status of a level-I firefighter. Ellen is physically, mentally, and emotionally fit. Since she has had previous experience loading and coupling hoseline, Ellen's stage of learning for advancing hoseline is late verbal-cognitive to early motor.

**Goal of learning.** Ellen's first goal is to learn the general procedures for advancing hoseline. Her second goal is to learn how to parameterize these procedures so that she can advance hoseline in a variety of ways (e.g., up stairways, down inside and outside stairways, up ladders, from a standpipe). A third goal is error detection and correction; Ellen must be able to recognize errors in her movements and make the appropriate corrections, sometimes under extreme time pressure. And Ellen must demonstrate that she can advance hoseline under a wide variety of environmental conditions.

**Characteristics of the target skill.** Advancing a hoseline is classified as a closed skill that can be either serial or continuous. It primarily involves the use of the large muscles, although small-muscle activity is sometimes needed to untangle a hoseline. Object manipulation is an important component of the task; Ellen wants to be able to achieve an optimal final position each time she advances a hose. To some extent, speed-accuracy trade-offs are part of the task; however, the weight of the hose naturally limits the speed with which the firefighter can move it. The amount of available intrinsic feedback varies (e.g., both vision of the problem situation and approach route can sometimes be reduced by extensive smoke, both audition and proprioception can be distorted by fire-fighting apparel). Information-processing demands include stimulus identification (particularly when visibility is poor), response selection (i.e., determining the best possible route), and response programming (i.e., modifying the generalized procedure to meet the demands of each situation). The risk of injury is high and performance mistakes can sometimes be fatal.

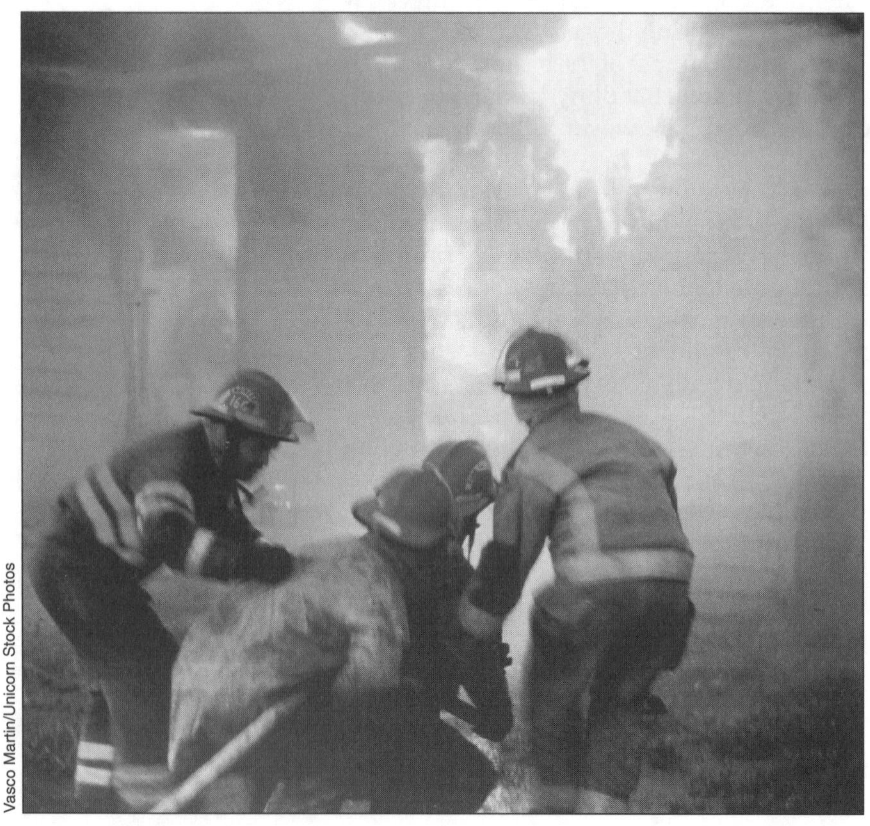
Vasco Martin/Unicorn Stock Photos

**Nature of the target context.** There is always an evaluative audience at a fire-fighting scene (e.g., other firefighters, police and other emergency personnel, fire inspectors, and occasionally media personnel and spectators). Firefighters usually operate under extreme time pressure. Other possible distractions include failure anxiety and equipment breakdown. Since no two fire-fighting situations are alike, firefighters must be able to devise innovative solutions for advancing hoseline at a moment's notice.

After Jerry completes his analysis of the relevant factors in Ellen's learning experience, he uses the conceptual model of human performance and the checklist for designing the learning experience to devise the following instructional strategy.

### Instructional Strategy

At first, Jerry introduces Ellen to the various techniques for advancing preconnected and unconnected hoseline. After describing (*instructions*) and demonstrating each technique (*demonstration*), Jerry lets Ellen practice the technique in a *blocked format*. Since Ellen has had previous fire-fighting experience, she produces each technique with only limited instructional assistance. She and Jerry decide that Ellen should receive *extrinsic feedback* only when she requests it. On those occasions, Jerry offers *prescriptive feedback* and occasionally provides an additional *visual demonstration*.

Once Jerry sees that Ellen is satisfactorily producing each of the techniques for carrying hoseline, he shifts Ellen to *varied practice* in a *random format*. During each session, Ellen performs the various hose-carrying techniques in a random order. Following each attempt, Ellen tells Jerry what she thinks of her performance (*error detection*) and then, if necessary, requests feedback. If Jerry observes no errors in Ellen's performance, he congratulates her (*positive reinforcement*). If Jerry detects an error, he offers *prescriptive feedback* (e.g., "Stay low and lock the arms") and perhaps a *visual demonstration* to indicate actions Ellen should try to change on the next attempt of that movement. After several rounds of this type of varied and random practice, Jerry *reduces the frequency of feedback* and begins to provide *summary feedback*. Jerry also reduces the frequency of reinforcement, providing it only after Ellen completes an error-free series of performance attempts (*intermittent reinforcement*).

After Jerry is satisfied that Ellen can effectively produce all of the hoseline-carrying techniques on command, he introduces her to the various situations that require firefighters to advance hoseline (*varied practice*). These include advancing hose up a stairway, advancing hose down inside and outside stairways, advancing hose up a ladder, and advancing hose from a standpipe. All these situations require a knowledge of both procedural guidelines and effective movement patterns. Realizing this, Jerry decides to combine Ellen's rehearsal of guidelines and of the movement patterns for each type of situation. For example, when Ellen practices advancing hoseline up a stairway, she must perform the three most appropriate hose-carrying techniques (shoulder carry, underarm carry, minuteman load and carry) and adhere to the following guidelines: carry rather than drag hose if it is uncharged, clamp the hose off before carrying it if it is charged, lay hose against the outside wall around stairways to avoid sharp bends in the line, and repeatedly toss sections of the excess hose up the stairs to make it easier to advance into the fire floor (*random practice*).

Jerry initially uses a combined practice structure that involves *blocked practice* of the situation (e.g., advancing hoseline up a stairway) but *varied practice* of each of the possible hose-carrying techniques. Ellen's challenge is to effectively produce any of the techniques on command while following the appropriate guidelines. Following each block of practice attempts, Ellen evaluates her own performance (*error detection*), then Jerry provides her with *summary feedback* about both the effectiveness of her movements and the degree of adherence to the appropriate guidelines.

Jerry repeats this procedure for each of the different hose-advance situations. When he sees that Ellen can produce the proper hose-carrying techniques and follow the recommended guidelines for each situation, Jerry shifts her to a *random- and varied-practice format*. During rehearsal sessions, Ellen advances hoseline in all four situations in a random order. Prior to each attempt, Jerry tells Ellen which situation to respond to and which hose-carrying technique to use. After each series of attempts, Jerry asks Ellen for her self-evaluation (*error detection*) and, if there are errors, for a proposed correction (*error correction*). Then Jerry provides Ellen with *summary feedback* about both the effectiveness of her movements and the degree of adherence to proper guidelines for all of the situations in the series.

The more of this type of practice Ellen gets, the more automatically she advances hoseline (using a variety of appropriate techniques and the recommended guidelines) for each of the four situations. Ellen is pleased and confident, and she thanks Jerry for his helpful assistance in preparing her to achieve her goal.

### Variations in the Scenario: Integrating Fire-Fighting Skills

Once Ellen meets the fire-related performance objectives for all of the skills required of level-I firefighters, she needs to be able to integrate and automate those skills. During intermittent lulls in fire-fighting activity, Ellen asks Jerry to structure *random-practice* sessions that require her to perform a variety of different fire-fighting skills (e.g., cardiopulmonary resuscitation, donning and doffing protective breathing apparatus, changing cylinders, coiling a rope for service, lone rescuer lift and carry, one-firefighter ladder raise, advancing hoseline up a stairway). Sometimes Jerry asks Ellen to perform two or three skills in a random order; at other times he asks her to produce several variations (*varied practice*) of the same skill (e.g., proper lifting and lowering of hoseline). Occasionally Jerry spontaneously asks Ellen to attempt a single skill chosen at random.

By practicing this way, Ellen becomes more adept at producing all the essential fire-fighting skills on command at any time. In addition, Ellen and Jerry set goals (*goal setting*) that challenge her to achieve a performance standard that minimizes both performance errors and movement time (e.g., advancing a hoseline up a ladder in less than 30 seconds). Now *extrinsic feedback* begins to function as *motivation* and *reinforcement*, as well as for *error correction*. Ellen continues to improve her *error detection and correction* capability by providing Jerry with a self-evaluation following each of her practice sessions. Soon Ellen starts challenging Jerry to contests to see which person can perform a randomly selected fire-fighting task with the fewest errors in the shortest time. Occasional games like this sharpen Ellen's skills and bolster her confidence as a firefighter.

### Variations in the Scenario: Adapting to Different Fire-Fighting Situations

The ultimate test of the firefighter's skill comes at the scene of the fire. Regardless of the situation, firefighters are expected to accurately assess the conditions and perform the most appropriate sequence of skills in a smooth, deliberate fashion. This can be a challenge for firefighters when they encounter situations that are extremely dangerous or that include the physical and psychological burden of extricating victims from the structure.

Like any good firefighter, Ellen wants to be able to perform her duties effectively at the scene of a fire, regardless of the type of situation she encounters. She asks Jerry for assistance in achieving this most important goal. Jerry uses his knowledge of the essentials of fire-fighting, the conceptual model of human performance, and the working strategy of skill instruction to design several learning experiences for Ellen.

One of the first factors Jerry addresses is the arousal-performance relationship. Jerry knows that high arousal and anxiety can be a problem for novice firefighters and that Ellen must be able to *manage arousal*, or she will place herself at risk at the scene of a fire. High levels of anxiety produce an increase in the rate of respiration, which causes a more rapid depletion of the available air supply in a protective-breathing apparatus. In addition, anxiety produces a narrowing of attentional focus, which can lead to serious errors in judgement. Jerry knows that Ellen's self-confidence in her fire-fighting skills is high and that this should reduce the likelihood of her experiencing increased anxiety in a fire-fighting situation. Nevertheless, Jerry realizes that if Ellen is to be optimally prepared to fight fires, she must rehearse under conditions that simulate those of actual fires as closely as possible (*generalization*).

Fortunately, Jerry has access to local facilities that allow him to introduce Ellen to a variety of simulated fire-fighting situations. At these facilities, Jerry simulates different conditions, while Ellen performs a variety of fire-fighting skills in much the same way she does in the station environment. As a result of *random and varied* exposure to a number of simulated situations (e.g., high and low visibility, advancing charged and uncharged hoseline), Ellen learns which techniques are most appropriate under different sets of circumstances.

Since fire fighting consists of both *consistent* and *varied stimulus-response mapping* conditions, Jerry also exposes Ellen to challenges that require her to produce the same response to some stimuli (e.g., before entering any fire area, always bleed the air out of the hoseline) and to vary the responses to other stimuli (e.g., when advancing a hoseline down a flight of stairs, charge the hose first if there is the chance of intense heat—but don't charge the hose first if there is not, since advancing hoseline is easier if the hose is uncharged). With repeated exposure to a variety of simulated situations, Ellen develops the capability to be innovative when the conditions are less predictable and to be deliberate, smooth, and systematic when they are more predictable.

Each time Jerry provides Ellen with a simulated experience, he asks her for a self-evaluation (*error detection and correction*) prior to giving her *summary feedback*. Jerry's feedback entails several performance characteristics, including the quality of Ellen's motor performance, the appropriateness of her decisions, and the level of composure she demonstrates under stress. Jerry also teaches Ellen a *mental rehearsal* technique that combines relaxation (*managing arousal*) and *imagery*. Ellen soon learns to use the technique, and with repeated rehearsal, she is able to quickly create vivid mental images of herself producing appropriate responses in specific fire-fighting situations.

The occasional experience of simulated fire-fighting conditions and the more regular and systematic use of mental rehearsal provide Ellen with a great deal of self-confidence. Ellen knows she is ready to respond appropriately and effectively to just about any fire-fighting situation she might encounter. Both Ellen and Jerry are proud of her accomplishments, and they look forward to working together for many years.

## Assessment of Learner Progress

In each of the case studies presented in this chapter, the hypothetical practitioner had to decide how he or she should assess the learner's progress. In several places, we mentioned specific measures (e.g., at one point the practitioner in case study #4 measured the time it took the volunteer firefighter to perform various tasks). In other places, we said only that the practitioner made instructional decisions based on the progress he or she observed in the learner's performance. Obviously those observations had to be based on something the practitioner was looking for that indicated the learner was improving.

As we discussed in chapter 7, assessment is an important component of any learning experience. A practitioner must measure an individual's performance in order to determine the extent to which the individual is making progress toward goal achievement and to assess the effectiveness of instructional strategies. However, determining how and when to assess learner performance is no simple matter.

How should instructors and therapists—not to mention the learners themselves—assess the quality of learning experiences? What measures should they obtain? How often should formal assessment take place? To a large extent, the answers to these questions depend on the goals of the learner and on the outcomes and behaviors that most clearly reflect goal achievement. For a tennis player learning a new serve, a valid outcome measure might be the percentage of successful first serves performed in one set of tennis. For an aspiring carpenter it might be the number of hammer blows needed to drive a dozen nails. Valid process measures in the tennis-serving and nail-hammering situations might involve practitioner ratings of arm extension during ball contact and follow-through and of wrist and forearm action during nail-striking movements, respectively. Regardless of the instructional situation, the skilled practitioner knows which outcomes and behaviors to look for and how to assess them accurately and reliably.

Determining how often skill assessment should take place is another difficult decision for the practitioner. Learners want to know whether they are making progress, but they are not always excited about formal evaluations. At what points during skill learning should a person's performance be formally assessed? Sometimes practitioners are required to perform assessments at predefined intervals (e.g., skills testing in school physical education classes). In other cases, the frequency of assessment may be the result of a joint decision by the practitioner and the learner. As is the case with other types of instructional feedback, formal assessments are probably more helpful to learners when they have a desire to know, "How am I doing?" Practitioners who maintain good communication with learners and who are sensitive to the individual's needs are usually more adept at determining the optimal timing and frequency of assessments. In any case, the evaluation should be separated in time from the specific procedures you have used during practice, as these often mask or distort performance gains (e.g., physical guidance, frequent feedback, etc.).

Of course, the ultimate moment of assessment comes when learners must perform the skills they have learned in the desired target context. In sports, the context might be the game, match, meet, or race. In rehabilitation settings, the context is more often the home or work environment. In recreational pursuits, the context may be at the lake, in the mountains, or on a bike trail. Regardless of the person, the target skill, or the target context, the best learning experience is ultimately one that turns out to be the one that is most *useful* to the learner.

In the next and final chapter, you are given the opportunity to test your own ability to apply the principles and concepts you have learned in this book to a hypothetical situation that is relevant and interesting to *you*. We hope you enjoy the experience.

## Summary

Instructors and therapists are constantly faced with the challenge of providing individuals with interesting and beneficial practice experiences that are consistent with the scientific principles of motor learning and performance. In this chapter, we propose a working strategy for skill instruction based on the conceptual model of human performance and the principles of motor performance and learning discussed throughout the book. Using the conceptual model as a backdrop, we compile two checklists for practitioners to use in assessing the factors that are relevant to individual learning experiences and in determining the types of instructional assistance that might be provided.

Practitioners should consider the following factors when diagnosing learning experiences:

- Characteristics of the learner (e.g., age, previous experiences, stage of learning, handicapping conditions, etc.)

- The goal of learning (e.g., program learning, parameter learning, generalization, error detection and correction, etc.)
- Characteristics of the target skill (e.g., types of information-processing demands, level of environmental stability, speed-accuracy trade-offs, risk of injury, etc.)
- Nature of the target context (time pressure, evaluative audience, possible distractions, strategy demands)

Practitioners should be prepared to provide any of the following types of instructional assistance:

- Prepractice assistance in the form of goal setting, instructions, and demonstrations
- Early practice assistance, such as physical guidance and attention focusing
- Special types of physical practice experiences, such as simulator practice, part-whole practice, slow-motion practice, and error detection practice
- Appropriate practice structure (i.e., constant practice, varied practice, blocked practice, random practice)
- Development of supporting skills, such as arousal control and mental rehearsal or imagery
- Augmented feedback of the appropriate type, amount, precision, and frequency

To illustrate how the working strategy might be used by practitioners, we present hypothetical case studies that describe four different instructional scenarios. The scenarios differ with respect to factors such as the age and experience of the learner, the goal of learning, characteristics of the target skill, and the nature of the target context. For each case study, we offer a proposed instructional strategy and then illustrate how the practitioner might change the strategy if the scenario is altered in two different ways.

In order to assess the progress of learners and determine the effectiveness of instructional strategies, practitioners must decide how and when to measure performance. When measuring performance, practitioners should consider the following issues:

- The goal of learning, the target skill, and the target context
- The outcome and process characteristics that represent the most valid indicators of skill improvement
- The optimal timing and frequency of formal assessments
- The fact that formal assessment represents a type of augmented feedback and, therefore, should conform to the same principles that govern the process of effective feedback delivery (i.e., choosing the type, amount, precision, and frequency of feedback that is optimal for each learner, task, and situation)
- The recognition that evaluation should be separated from the practice phase of learning, where temporary factors influence performance and distort estimates of learning

12

# Applying the Principles of Skill Learning

## Chapter Outline



## Chapter Objectives

**When you have completed this chapter, you should be able to**

demonstrate your ability to integrate the conceptual model of human performance and the various principles presented in this book to assist an individual who is trying to learn or relearn a motor skill;

describe a hypothetical or real instructional scenario, and then demonstrate your capability of diagnosing, designing, and assessing the learning experience; and

provide supporting rationale and, where possible, research documentation for your decisions.

## Preview

By now you should have a pretty good understanding of the principles and processes underlying skilled performance and of the factors practitioners should consider when diagnosing, designing, and assessing learning experiences. However, the real test of your comprehension of this information will come when you attempt to provide instructional assistance for an actual learner. For some of you, that opportunity will arise when you try to help a patient relearn movements in a therapy setting. For others, it will come when you coach athletes or provide instruction for individuals attempting to learn a variety of recreational or job-related activities. For still others of you, the moment will come when you assist aspiring musicians or dancers who want to refine their skills.

Only when your instructional skills are tested "under fire" will you *really* be able to evaluate the effectiveness of your approach. How will *you* respond to the challenge? How will *you* diagnose the learning experience? How will *you* design the learning experience? How will *you* assess the learning experience? What types of rationale and research documentation will *you* offer in support of your decisions?

## Overview

Throughout this book we have challenged you to demonstrate your comprehension of concepts and principles of motor performance and learning by relating them in meaningful ways to movement tasks and situations you are familiar with. We now offer you a final opportunity to check your understanding of this information by creating your own instructional scenario and then indicating how you would go about assisting an individual in the pursuit of his or her motor learning goals. Hopefully, you will find the experience to be one that reinforces your confidence in the problem-based approach and of your practical knowledge of the field of motor learning and performance.

## Now It's Your Turn

In chapter 11 we presented four hypothetical instructional scenarios along with proposed solutions for each. Each scenario involved a specific learner and learning goal, unique task requirements, and particular situational demands. Each solution was based primarily on the motor learning concepts and experimental evidence we have presented throughout this book. Now it's your turn to create your own instructional scenario and then demonstrate how well you can diagnose, design, and assess a learning experience. In addition, we want you to provide supporting evidence for your decisions by referring to the concepts or research upon which each is based. In the following sections, we offer several guidelines you should follow as you respond to each of these challenges.

### Creating the Instructional Scenario

If you look again at the instructional scenarios in chapter 11, you will see that each represents an example of the kind of challenge different types of movement practitioners face every day. In much the same way, your scenario can take place in a setting that involves common motor skill instruction (e.g., sport skills, manual skills, dance and music performance), coaching, physical therapy assistance, or human factors operations (e.g., ergonomics or industrial skills, equipment operation, etc.).

When creating your instructional scenario, you might want to think about motor performance situations you are familiar with and the types of learning challenges individuals typically face when they try to learn or perform the skills necessary for that situation. Perhaps the scenario involves an individual who wants to learn a new skill or would like to refine an existing skill she or he has performed for years without noticeable improvement. It may be that the person needs to relearn a skill they have lost due to injury or partial paralysis. If you can anticipate these or other possible learning situations, using a skill you have had experience with yourself, you should be able to create your own instructional scenario without too much difficulty.

Another way you could approach the task of creating an instructional scenario is to interview an experienced movement practitioner for suggestions. This is what we did when we were putting together the scenarios in chapter 11 that dealt with the cerebral palsy patient and the volunteer firefighter. For the third case study, we interviewed a physical therapist and asked her to tell us about some of the patients she was currently working with and the skills she was trying to teach them. After several rounds of discussion with the therapist, we decided that the problem of teaching a young patient with cerebral palsy to climb stairs would be an interesting and representative scenario. For the fourth case study, we asked a local fire chief to tell us about some of the motor skill challenges that confront the average firefighter. In addition to sharing his experiential knowledge with us, the chief sent us a copy of a book, *Essentials of Fire Fighting* (Wieder, Smith, & Brackage, 1996), so that we could read about the different skills firefighters must learn and see pictures of the correct ways they are to perform them.

Regardless of how you do it, try to create a scenario you are comfortable with. Once you do this, you can begin the task of diagnosing the learning experience.

## Diagnosing the Learning Experience

In chapter 11 we introduced a working strategy for diagnosing, designing, and assessing an individual's learning experience. As you attempt to diagnose the experience of the learner in your scenario, keep in mind the components of the conceptual model of human performance that might be relevant to your instructional situation. For the most part, these components include the stages of information processing that are important during the learning process, the forms of intrinsic feedback that are available to the learner, and the types of extrinsic feedback you might provide.

Other aspects of your diagnosis deal with the items listed in table 11.1. These items address issues such as the following: Who is the learner? What is the learner's goal (i.e., what types of learning are required)? What is the target context (i.e., under what conditions will the task have to be performed)? For each of your questions, provide the accompanying descriptive information that is appropriate for your scenario.

Once you identify the relevant factors to keep in mind when assisting the learner in your scenario, it's time to decide how you will design the learning experience. In other words, what instructional options will you choose to promote the most effective goal achievement for your learner? Review the blueprint for providing instructional assistance that we presented in the preface (see figure 1, page ix).

## Designing the Learning Experience

As you design the learning experience, refer again to table 11.2. Consider questions like the following: How will communication be established? What types of goals will be set? How will arousal level be managed? How will attention be focused? What types of rehearsal will be provided? How will rehearsal be structured? For each of these questions, select items from the accompanying descriptive information, as well as other materials you can think of, that are appropriate for your scenario.

To check the appropriateness of each of your instructional choices, refer back to the information you compiled in diagnosing the learning experience. If you can see a clear connection between how you diagnosed the learning experience and how you are going to design the learning experience, that is a good sign. That means that the type of instruction you are providing the learner is appropriate to the characteristics you identified in your diagnosis. For example, if you diagnosed the learner as a beginner who is in the verbal-cognitive stage of practice, it is appropriate to design an experience that includes more frequent demonstrations and feedback or an initial practice structure that is blocked. Conversely, if you can't find a connection between a particular component of your instructional design and some feature of your diagnosis, consider whether the component is really necessary.

## Assessing the Learning Experience

The final piece of your instructional strategy concerns the issue of performance assessment. If you can accurately assess the performance of learners, you can then provide them with helpful information about their level of goal achievement, as well as with feedback about the kind of things they need to do to improve their performance.

Before deciding how you are going to assess the progress of your learner, remind yourself of the learner's goals. What does the learner want to be able to do and under what conditions does she or he want to be able to do it when instruction is completed? If the learner wants to be able to keep a tennis ball in play when participating in recreational doubles with her friends, your assessment will probably focus on different movement characteristics and performance outcomes than it would if the learner wants to be able to compete for the singles tennis championship at her local country club. Always remember that the purpose of your assessment is to provide learners with feedback about the extent to which they are making progress toward *their* goals. As long as your assessments accomplish this purpose, they serve as a helpful source of augmented information for the learner.

Once you remind yourself of the learner's goals, decide how to assess the learner's performance. Refer to the practice preparation and practice feedback sections of table 11.2, which address questions such as "Which measures will be used to assess learning?" and "How will feedback be provided?"

In order to accurately assess the learner's performance, you must be able to identify movement components and movement outcomes that are indicative of skilled performance. Once you do this, you must be able to measure each component or outcome reliably and accurately. To determine which aspects of performance to assess, you may need to consult instructional manuals or books that contain information about the pertinent components of the task(s) your learner is attempting to acquire. The components you select should include both process characteristics (e.g., movement form or quality) and outcome scores (e.g., distance from the target, movement time). If you attempt to rate the quality of the learner's movement form, you must know which movement criteria to look for and be able to reliably assess each component. If you have access to video recording equipment, you can videotape the learner's movements and check the reliability of your ratings by evaluating the same movement on separate occasions.

You also need to decide how you will share assessment information with the learner. Relevant feedback issues to consider include the most effective type (e.g., program/parameter, verbal/visual/manual, descriptive/prescriptive), amount (e.g., summary feedback, average feedback), precision level, and frequency of feedback. By maintaining open communication with the learner, you should be able to determine how to provide feedback in the most helpful way possible and at times when it will be most appreciated.

## Documenting the Instructional Strategy

Effective practitioners base their instructional decisions on the best evidence available. As a prospective practitioner you should be able to provide answers for people who might ask, "Why are you doing what you are doing to help learners achieve their goals?" Many instructional decisions are the result of conclusions based on a pattern of consistent findings from a series of experiments. For example, motor skills theorists are reasonably certain that a random-practice structure facilitates the retention and transfer of skills to a greater extent than does a blocked-practice format; that, compared with a constant-practice format, a varied-practice format promotes the individual's capability to select appropriate parameter values when using a generalized motor program; and that a reduced frequency of augmented feedback produces retention that is superior to that produced by a more frequent feedback schedule.

In the scenarios we presented in chapter 11, we indicated the principles or concepts that the various practitioners used when making their instructional decisions.

For your instructional scenario, provide similar documentation of your decisions. Even better, you should offer original experimental evidence whenever it is directly relevant to your scenario. For example, if you create a coaching situation in which you attempt to assist a college football player who is learning how to identify and rapidly respond to the movements of an opposing team, you might elect to use a visual reaction-time procedure similar to that employed by Christina, Barresi, and Shaffner (1990) in a similar study with a college football linebacker. In that case, cite the study as supporting evidence for your decision.

By providing supporting rationale and documentation for each of your instructional decisions, you demonstrate that you are aware of the relevant available evidence and that you are offering this evidence as the basis for your decisions. Where the experimental evidence is not as clear-cut, offer the best rationale possible and then indicate that your decision is more tentative in nature.

## A Final Comment

We hope you enjoy this project and that you find the material in this book to be helpful whenever you have opportunity to assist individuals in achieving their motor learning goals. The problem-based approach allows you to effectively diagnose, design, and assess any person's learning experience. As you become more and more adept at implementing this approach, you can expect to begin enjoying the ultimate reward of skill instruction—satisfied learners. Best wishes in your efforts to do this and in each of the professional challenges that awaits you.

# References


Abbs, J.H., Gracco, V.L., & Cole, K.J. (1984). Control of multi-joint movement coordination: Sensorimotor mechanisms in speech motor programming. *Journal of Motor Behavior,* 16, 195–231.

Abernethy, B. (1993). Attention. In R.N. Singer, M. Murphey, & L.K. Tennant (Eds.), *Handbook of research on sport psychology* (pp. 127–170). New York: Macmillan.

Abernethy, B., & Russell, D.G. (1984). Advance cue utilisation by skilled cricket batsmen. *Australian Journal of Science and Medicine in Sport,* 16, 2–10.

Abernethy, B., & Russell, D.G. (1987a). Expert-novice differences in an applied selective attention task. *Journal of Sport Psychology,* 9, 326–345.

Abernethy, B., & Russell, D.G. (1987b). The relationship between expertise and visual search strategy in a racquet sport. *Human Movement Science,* 6, 283–319.

Adams, J.A. (1971). A closed-loop theory of motor learning. *Journal of Motor Behavior,* 3, 111–150.

Adams, J.A. (1978). Theoretical issues for knowledge of results. In G.E. Stelmach (Ed.), *Information processing in motor control and learning* (pp. 229-240). New York: Academic Press.

Allard, F., & Burnett, N. (1985). Skill in sport. *Canadian Journal of Psychology,* 39, 294–312.

Amato, I. (1989). The finishing touch: Robots may lend a hand in the making of Steinway pianos. *Science News,* 135, 108–109.

Ames, C. (1992). Achievement goals, motivational climate, and motivational processes. In G.C. Roberts (Ed.), *Motivation in sport and exercise* (pp. 161–176). Champaign, IL: Human Kinetics.

Annett, J. (1959). *Feedback and human behavior.* Middlesex, England: Penguin Books.

Armstrong, T.R. (1970). *Training for the production of memorized movement patterns* (Tech. Rep. No. 26). Ann Arbor: University of Michigan, Human Performance Center.

Baddeley, A.D., & Longman, D.J.A. (1978). The influence of length and frequency of training session on the rate of learning to type. *Ergonomics,* 21, 627–635.

Bahill, A.T., & LaRitz, T. (1984). Why can't batters keep their eyes on the ball? *American Scientist,* 72, 249–253.

Bard, C., & Fleury, M. (1981). Considering eye movement as a predictor of attainment. In I.M. Cockerill & W.W. MacGillivary (Eds.), *Vision and sport* (pp. 28–41). Cheltenham, UK: Stanley Thornes.

Bartlett, F.C. (1932). *Remembering: A study in experimental and social psychology.* Cambridge, England: Cambridge University Press.

Battig, W.F. (1966). Facilitation and interference. In E.A. Bilodeau (Ed.), *Acquisition of skill* (pp. 215–244). New York: Academic Press.

Beals, R.P., Mayyasi, A.M., Templeton, A.E., & Johnston, W.L. (1971). The relationship between basketball-shooting performance and certain visual attributes. *American Journal of Optometry and Archives of American Academy of Optometry,* 48, 585–590.

Beek, P.J., & van Santvoord, A.A.M. (1992). Learning the cascade juggle: A dynamical systems analysis. *Journal of Motor Behavior,* 24, 85–94.

Belen'kii, V.Y., Gurfinkel, V.S., & Pal'tsev, Y.I. (1967). Elements of control of voluntary movements. *Biofizika,* 12, 135–141.

Bernstein, N.I. (1967). *The co-ordination and regulation of movements.* Oxford, England: Pergamon Press.

Bilodeau, E.A., Bilodeau, I.M., & Schumsky, D.A. (1959). Some effects of introducing and withdrawing knowledge of results early and late in practice. *Journal of Experimental Psychology,* 58, 142–144.

Bjork, R.A. (1975). Retrieval as a memory modifier. In R. Solso (Ed.), *Information processing and cognition: The Loyola Symposium* (pp. 123–144). Hillsdale, NJ: Erlbaum.

Bjork, R.A. (1979). *Retrieval practice.* Unpublished manuscript, University of California, Los Angeles.

Bliss, C.B. (1892–1893). Investigations in reaction time and attention. *Studies from the Yale Psychological Laboratory,* 1, 1–55.

Boder, D.P. (1935). The influence of concomitant activity and fatigue upon certain forms of reciprocal hand movement and its fundamental components. *Comparative Psychology Monographs,* 11 (article 54).

Boyce, B.A., & Del Rey, P. (1990). Designing applied research in a naturalistic setting using a contextual interference paradigm. *Journal of Human Movement Studies,* 18, 189–200.

Brace, D.K. (1927). *Measuring motor ability.* New York: A.S. Barnes.

Bridgeman, B., Kirch, M., & Sperling, A. (1981). Segregation of cognitive and motor aspects of visual information using induced motion. *Perception and Psychophysics,* 29, 336–342.

Carril, P., & White, D. (1997). *The smart take from the strong.* New York: Simon & Schuster.

Carroll, L. (1994). *Alice in wonderland and through the looking glass.* New York: Grosset & Dunlap. (Original work published 1865)

Carson, L.M., & Wiegand, R.L. (1979). Motor schema formation and retention in young children: A test of Schmidt's schema theory. *Journal of Motor Behavior,* 11, 247–252.

Catalano, J.F., & Kleiner, B.M. (1984). Distant transfer and practice variability. *Perceptual and Motor Skills,* 58, 851–856.

Christina, R.W., Barresi, J.V., & Shaffner, P. (1990). The development of response selection accuracy in a football linebacker using video training. *The Sport Psychologist,* 4, 11–17.

Colley, A.M., & Beech, J.R. (1988). Grounds for reconciliation: Some preliminary thoughts on cognition and action. In A.M. Colley & J.R. Beech (Eds.), *Cognition and action in skilled behavior* (pp. 1–11). Amsterdam: North-Holland.

Combs, A.W. (1981). What the future demands of education. *Phi Delta Kappan,* 62, 369–372.

Crossman, E.R.F.W. (1959). A theory of the acquisition of speed skill. *Ergonomics,* 2, 153–166.

Cuddy, L.J., & Jacoby, L.L. (1982). When forgetting helps memory. Analysis of repetition effects. *Journal of Verbal Learning and Verbal Behavior,* 21, 451–467.

Deci, E.L., & Ryan, R.M. (1985). *Intrinsic motivation and self-determination in human behavior.* New York: Plenum.

Deshaies, P., Pargman, D., & Thiffault, C. (1979). A psychobiological profile of individual performance in junior hockey players. In G.C. Roberts & K.M. Newell (Eds.), *Psychology of motor behavior and sport—1978* (pp. 36–50). Champaign, IL: Human Kinetics.

Dewhurst, D.J. (1967). Neuromuscular control system. *IEEE Transactions on Bio-Medical Engineering,* 14, 167–171.

Drowatzky, J.N., & Zuccato, F.C. (1967). Interrelationships between selected measures of static and dynamic balance. *Research Quarterly,* 38, 509–510.

Druckman, D. & Bjork, R.A. (1991). *In the mind's eye: Enhancing human performance.* Washington, DC: National Academy Press.

Duda, J.L. (1993). Goals: A social-cognitive approach to the study of achievement motivation in sport. In R.N. Singer, M. Murphey, & L.K. Tennant (Eds.), *Handbook of research on sport psychology* (pp. 421–436). New York: Macmillan.

Easterbrook, J.A. (1959). The effect of emotion on cue utilization and the organization of behavior. *Psychological Review,* 66, 183–201.

Etnier, J., & Landers, D.M. (1996). The influence of procedural variables on the efficacy of mental practice. *The Sport Psychologist,* 10, 48–57.

Feltz, D.L., & Landers, D.M. (1983). The effects of mental practice on motor skill learning and performance: A meta analysis. *Journal of Sport Psychology,* 5, 1–8.

Fitts, P.M. (1954). The information capacity of the human motor system in controlling the amplitude of movement. *Journal of Experimental Psychology,* 47, 381–391.

Fitts, P.M., & Posner, M.I. (1967). *Human performance.* Belmont, CA: Brooks/Cole.

Flach, J.M., Lintern, G., & Larish, J.F. (1990). Perceptual motor skill: A theoretical framework. In R. Warren & A.H. Wertheim (Eds.), *The perception and control of self motion* (pp. 327–355). Hillsdale, NJ: Erlbaum.

Fleishman, E.A. (1956). Psychomotor selection tests: Research and application in the United States Air Force. *Personnel Psychology,* 9, 449–467.

Fleishman, E.A. (1964). *The structure and measurement of physical fitness.* Englewood Cliffs, NJ: Prentice-Hall.

Fleishman, E.A. (1965). The description and prediction of perceptual motor skill learning. In R. Glaser (Ed.), *Training research and education* (pp. 137–175). New York: Wiley.

Fleishman, E.A., & Bartlett, C.J. (1969). Human abilities. *Annual Review of Psychology,* 20, 349–380.

Fleishman, E.A., & Parker, J.F. (1962). Factors in the retention and relearning of perceptual motor skill. *Journal of Experimental Psychology,* 64, 215–226.

Fleishman, E.A., & Stephenson, R.W. (1970). *Development of a taxonomy of human performance: A review of the third year's progress* (Tech. Rep. No. 726-TPR3). Silver Spring, MD: American Institutes for Research.

Forssberg, H., Grillner, S., & Rossignol, S. (1975). Phase dependent reflex reversal during walking in the chronic spinal cat. *Brain Research,* 85, 103–107.

Franz, E.A., Zelaznik, H.N., & Smith, A. (1992). Evidence of common timing processes in the control of manual, orofacial, and speech movements. *Journal of Motor Behavior,* 24, 281–287.

Gabriele, T., Hall, C.R., & Lee, T.D. (1989). Cognition in motor learning: Imagery effects on contextual interference. *Human Movement Science,* 8, 227–245.

Gallwey, T. (1974). *The inner game of tennis.* New York: Random House.

Gardner, H. (1975). *The shattered mind.* New York: Knopf.

Gentile, A.M. (1972). A working model of skill acquisition with application to teaching. *Quest Monograph* XVII, 3–23.

Gentile, A.M. (1987). Skill acquisition: Action, movement, and the neuromotor processes. In J.H. Carr, R.B. Shepherd, J. Gordon, A.M. Gentile, & J.M. Hinds (Eds.), *Movement science: Foundations for physical therapy in rehabilitation* (pp. 93–154). Rockville, MD: Aspen.

Gentner, D.R. (1987). Timing of skilled motor performance: Tests of the proportional duration model. *Psychological Review,* 94, 255–276.

Gibson, J.J. (1966). *The senses considered as perceptual systems.* Boston: Houghton Mifflin.

Gibson, J.J. (1979). *The ecological approach to visual perception.* Boston: Houghton Mifflin.

Goode, S., & Magill, R.A. (1986). The contextual interference effects in learning three badminton serves. *Research Quarterly for Exercise and Sport,* 57, 308–314.

Goslow, G.E., Reinking, R.M., & Stuart, D.G. (1973). The cat step cycle: Hind limb joint angles and muscle lengths during unrestrained locomotion. *Journal of Morphology,* 141, 1–42.

Gould, D. (1998). Goal setting for peak performance. In J.M. Williams (Ed.), *Applied sport psychology: Personal growth to peak performance* (pp. 158–169). Mountain View, CA: Mayfield.

Graw, H.M.A. (1968). *The most efficient usage of a fixed work plus rest practice period in motor learning.* Unpublished doctoral dissertation, University of California, Berkeley.

Grillner, S. (1975). Locomotion in vertebrates: Central mechanisms and reflex interaction. *Physiological Reviews,* 55, 247–304.

Guthrie, E.R. (1952). *The psychology of learning.* New York: Harper & Row.

Hall, K.G., Domingues, D.A., & Cavazos, R. (1994). Contextual interference effects with skilled baseball players. *Perceptual and Motor Skills,* 78, 835–841.

Hanin, Y.L. (1980). A study of anxiety in sports. In W.F. Straub (Ed.), *Sport psychology: An analysis of athlete behavior* (pp. 236–249). Ithaca, NY: Mouvement.

Hanlon, R.E. (1996). Motor learning following unilateral stroke. *Archives of Physical Medicine and Rehabilitation,* 77, 811–815.

Hardy, L. (1997). The Coleman Robert Griffith Address: Three myths about sport psychology consultancy work. *Journal of Applied Sport Psychology,* 9, 277–294.

Hausdorff, J.M., & Durfee, W.K. (1991). Open-loop position control of the knee joint using electrical stimulation of the quadriceps and hamstrings. *Medical Biological Engineering and Computing,* 29, 269–280.

Hay, J.G. (1993). *The biomechanics of sports techniques* (4th ed.). Englewood Cliffs, NJ: Prentice-Hall.

Haywood, K.M. (1993). *Life span motor development.* Champaign, IL: Human Kinetics.

Heavy hat credited with best golfing. (1998, January 9). *The Knoxville (TN) News Sentinel,* p. A2.

Henry, F.M. (1961). Reaction time-movement time correlations. *Perceptual and Motor Skills,* 12, 63–66.

Henry, F.M. (1968). Specificity vs. generality in learning motor skill. In R.C. Brown & G.S. Kenyon (Eds.), *Classical studies on physical activity* (pp. 331–340). Englewood Cliffs, NJ: Prentice-Hall. (Original work published 1958)

Henry, F.M., & Rogers, D.E. (1960). Increased response latency for complicated movements and a "memory drum" theory of neuromotor reaction. *Research Quarterly,* 31, 448–458.

Hick, W.E. (1952). On the rate of gain of information. *Quarterly Journal of Experimental Psychology,* 4, 11–26.

Hird, J.S., Landers, D.M., Thomas, J.R., & Horan, J.J. (1991). Physical practice is superior to mental practice in enhancing cognitive and motor task performance. *Journal of Sport and Exercise Psychology,* 8, 281–293.

Hogan, J., & Yanowitz, B. (1978). The role of verbal estimates of movement error in ballistic skill acquisition. *Journal of Motor Behavior,* 10, 133–138.

Hollerbach, J.M. (1978). *A study of human motor control through analysis and synthesis of handwriting.* Unpublished doctoral dissertation, Massachusetts Institute of Technology, Cambridge.

Housner, L.D. (1981). Expert-novice knowledge structure and cognitive processing differences in badminton [Abstract]. *Psychology of motor behavior and sport,* 1981, (p. 1). Proceedings of the annual meeting of the North American Society for the Psychology of Sport and Physical Activity, Asilomar, CA.

Hoyt, D.F., & Taylor, C.R. (1981). Gait and the energetics of locomotion in horses. *Science,* 292, 239–240.

Hubbard, A.W., & Seng, C.N. (1954). Visual movements of batters. *Research Quarterly,* 25, 42–57.

Hyman, R. (1953). Stimulus information as a determinant of reaction time. *Journal of Experimental Psychology,* 45, 188–196.

Ivry, R., & Hazeltine, R.E. (1995). Perception and production of temporal intervals across a range of durations: Evidence for a common timing mechanism. *Journal of Experimental Psychology: Human Perception and Performance,* 21, 3–18.

Jacobson, E. (1930). Electrical measurement of neuromuscular states during mental activities. *American Journal of Physiology,* 94, 22–34.

Jacoby, L.L., Bjork, R.A., & Kelley, C.M. (1994). Illusions of comprehensions and competence. In D. Druckman & R.A. Bjork (Eds.), *Learning, remembering, believing: Enhancing human performance* (pp. 57–80). Washington, DC: National Academy Press.

James, W. (1890). *The principles of psychology.* Vol. 1. New York: Holt, Reinhart & Winston.

Janelle, C.M., Barba, D.A., Frehlich, S.G., Tennant, L.K., & Cauraugh, J.H. (1997). Maximizing performance feedback effectiveness through videotape replay and a self-controlled learning environment. *Research Quarterly for Exercise and Sport,* 68, 269–279.

Johansson, R.S., & Westling, G. (1984). Roles of glabrous skin receptors and sensorimotor memory in automatic control of precision grip when lifting rougher or more slippery objects. *Experimental Brain Research,* 56, 560–564.

Johnson, H.W. (1961). Skill = speed × accuracy × form × adaptability. *Perceptual and Motor Skills,* 13, 163–170.

Jordan, T.C. (1972). Characteristics of visual and proprioceptive response times in the learning of a motor skill. *Journal of Experimental Psychology,* 24, 536–543.

Kahneman, D. (1973). *Attention and effort.* Englewood Cliffs, NJ: Prentice-Hall.

Keele, S.W., & Hawkins, H.L. (1982). Explorations of individual differences relevant to high level skill. *Journal of Motor Behavior,* 14, 3–23.

Keele, S.W., & Ivry, R. (1987). Modular analysis of timing in motor skill. In G.H. Bower (Ed.), *The psychology of learning and motivation,* vol. 21 (pp. 183–228). San Diego: Academic Press.

Keele, S.W., Ivry, R.I., & Pokorny, R.A. (1987). Force control and its relation to timing. *Journal of Motor Behavior,* 19, 96–114.

Keele, S.W., Pokorny, R.A., Corcos, D.M., & Ivry, R. (1985). Do perception and motor production share common timing mechanisms: A correlational analysis. *Acta Psychologica,* 60, 173–191.

Keele, S.W., & Posner, M.I. (1968). Processing of visual feedback in rapid movements. *Journal of Experimental Psychology,* 77, 155–158.

Kelso, J.A.S. (Ed.) (1995). *Dynamic patterns: The self-organization of brain and behavior.* Cambridge, MA: MIT Press.

Kelso, J.A.S., & Schöner, G. (1988). Self-organization of coordinative movement patterns. *Human Movement Science,* 7, 27–46.

Kelso, J.A.S., Tuller, B., Vatikoitis-Bateson, E., & Fowler, C.A. (1984). Functionally specific articulatory cooperation following jaw perturbations during speech: Evidence for coordinative structures. *Journal of Experimental Psychology: Human Perception and Performance,* 10, 812–832.

Kernodle, M.W., & Carlton, L.G. (1992). Information feedback and the learning of multiple-degree-of-freedom activities. *Journal of Motor Behavior,* 24, 187–196.

Kerr, R., & Booth, B. (1978). Specific and varied practice of motor skill. *Perceptual and Motor Skills,* 46, 395–401.

Klapp, S.T., Hill, M.D., Tyler, J.G., Martin, Z.E., Jagacinski, R.J., & Jones, M.R. (1985). On marching to two different drummers: Perceptual aspects of the difficulties. *Journal of Experimental Psychology: Human Perception and Performance*, 11, 814–827.

Knudson, D.V., & Morrison, C.S. (1997). *Qualitative analysis of human movement*. Champaign, IL: Human Kinetics.

Konzem, P.B. (1987). *Extended practice and patterns of bimanual interference*. Unpublished doctoral dissertation, University of Southern California, Los Angeles.

Kottke, F.J., Halpern, D., Easton, J.K., Ozel, A.T., & Burrill, B.S. (1978). The training of coordination. *Archives of Physical Medicine and Rehabilitation Medicine*, 59, 567–572.

Landauer, T.K., & Bjork, R.A. (1978). Optimum rehearsal patterns and name learning. In M.M. Gruenberg, P.E. Morris, & R.N. Sykes (Eds.), *Practical aspects of memory* (pp. 625–632). London: Academic Press.

Landers, D.M., & Boutcher, S.H. (1998). Arousal-performance relationships. In J.M. Williams (Ed.), *Applied sport psychology: Personal growth to peak performance* (pp. 170–184). Mountain View, CA: Mayfield.

Landers, D.M., Boutcher, S.H., & Wang, M.Q. (1986). A psychobiological study of archery performance. *Research Quarterly for Exercise and Sport*, 57, 236–244.

Landin, D. (1994). The role of verbal cues in skill learning. *Quest*, 46, 299–313.

Landin, D., & Hebert, E.P. (1997). A comparison of three practice schedules along the contextual interference continuum. *Research Quarterly for Exercise and Sport*, 68, 357–361.

Lavery, J.J. (1962). Retention of simple motor skills as a function of type of knowledge of results. *Canadian Journal of Psychology*, 16, 300–311.

Lavery, J.J., & Suddon, F.H. (1962). Retention of simple motor skills as a function of the number of trials by which KR is delayed. *Perceptual and Motor Skills*, 15, 231–237.

Leavitt, J.L. (1979). Cognitive demands of skating and stickhandling in ice hockey. *Canadian Journal of Applied Sport Sciences*, 4, 46–55.

Lee, D.N. (1980). Visuo-motor coordination in space-time. In G.E. Stelmach & J. Requin (Eds.), *Tutorials in motor behavior* (pp. 281–285). Amsterdam: North-Holland.

Lee, D.N., & Aronson, E. (1974). Visual proprioceptive control of standing in human infants. *Perception and Psychophysics*, 15, 527–532.

Lee, D.N., & Young, D.S. (1985). Visual timing of interceptive action. In D. Ingle, M. Jeannerod, & D.N. Lee (Eds.), *Brain mechanisms and spatial vision* (pp. 1–30). Dordrecht, Netherlands: Martinus Nijhoff.

Lee, T.D. (1998). On the dynamics of motor learning research. *Research Quarterly for Exercise and Sport*, 69, 334–337.

Lee, T.D., & Genovese, E.D. (1988). Distribution of practice in motor skill acquisition: Learning and performance effects reconsidered. *Research Quarterly for Exercise and Sport*, 59, 277–287.

Lee, T.D., & Magill, R.A. (1983). The locus of contextual interference in motor-skill acquisition. *Journal of Experimental Psychology: Learning, Memory, and Cognition*, 9, 730–746.

Lee, T.D., & Magill, R.A. (1985). Can forgetting facilitate skill acquisition? In D. Goodman, R.B. Wilberg, & I.M. Franks (Eds.), *Differing perspectives in motor learning, memory and control* (pp. 3–22). Amsterdam: North-Holland.

Lee, T.D., Magill, R.A., & Weeks, D.J. (1985). Influence of practice schedule on testing schema theory predictions in adults. *Journal of Motor Behavior*, 17, 283-299.

Lee, T.D., Wulf, G., & Schmidt, R.A. (1992). Contextual interference in motor learning: Dissociated effects due to the nature of task variations. *Quarterly Journal of Experimental Psychology*, 44A, 627–644.

Lee, W.A. (1980). Anticipatory control of postural and task muscles during rapid arm flexion. *Journal of Motor Behavior*, 12, 185–196.

Lersten, K.C. (1968). Transfer of movement components in a motor learning task. *Research Quarterly*, 39, 575–581.

Linden, C.A., Uhley, J.E., Smith, D., & Bush, M.A. (1989). The effects of mental practice on walking balance in an elderly population. *Occupational Therapy Journal of Research*, 9, 155–169.

Liu, J., & Wrisberg, C.A. (1997). The effect of knowledge of results delay and the subjective estimation of movement form on the acquisition and retention of a motor skill. *Research Quarterly for Exercise and Sport*, 68, 145–151.

Locke, E.A., & Latham, G.P. (1985). The application of goal setting to sports. *Sport Psychology Today*, 7, 205–222.

Lotter, W.S. (1960). Interrelationships among reaction times and speeds of movement in different limbs. *Research Quarterly*, 31, 147–155.

MacKay, D.G. (1981). The problem of rehearsal or mental practice. *Journal of Motor Behavior*, 13, 274–285.

Magill, R.A. (1998). *Motor Learning: Concepts and applications* (5th ed.). Dubuque, IA: Brown.

Magill, R.A. (in press). Knowledge is more than we can talk about: Implicit learning in motor skill acquisition. *Research Quarterly for Exercise and Science.*

Magill, R.A., & Hall, K.G. (1990). A review of the contextual interference effect in motor skill acquisition. *Human Movement Science*, 9, 241–289.

Magill, R.A., & Wood, C.A. (1986). Knowledge of results precision as a learning variable in motor skill acquisition. *Research Quarterly for Exercise and Sport*, 57, 170–173.

McBride, E., & Rothstein, A. (1979). Mental and physical practice and the learning and retention of open and closed skills. *Perceptual and Motor Skills*, 49, 359–365.

McCloy, C.H. (1934). The measurement of general motor capacity and general motor ability. *Research Quarterly*, 5(Suppl. 5), 45–61.

McCullagh, P. (1986). Model status as a determinant of attention in observational learning and performance. *Journal of Sport Psychology*, 8, 319–331.

McCullagh, P. (1987). Model similarity effects on motor performance. *Journal of Sport Psychology*, 9, 249–260.

McDavid, R.F. (1977). Predicting potential in football players. *Research Quarterly*, 48, 98–104.

McLeod, P., McLaughlin, C., & Nimmo-Smith, I. (1985). Information encapsulation and automaticity: Evidence from the visual control of finely tuned actions. In M.I. Posner & O.S.M. Marin (Eds.), *Attention and performance* XI (pp. 391–406). Hillsdale, NJ: Erlbaum.

McMahon, T.A. (1984). *Muscles, reflexes, and locomotion*. Princeton, NJ: Princeton University Press.

Memory study. (1997, October 29). *The Knoxville (TN) News Sentinel*, p. A8.

Merkel, J. (1885). Die zeitlichen Verhaltnisse der Willenstatigkeit. *Philosophische Studien*, 2, 73–127. (Cited in Woodworth, 1938)

Merton, P.A. (1972). How we control the contraction of our muscles. *Scientific American*, 226, 30–37.

Meyer, D.E., Abrams, R.A., Kornblum, S., Wright, C.E., & Smith, J.E.K. (1988). Optimality in human motor performance: Ideal control of rapid aimed movements. *Psychological Review*, 95, 340–370.

Miller, G.A. (1956). The magical number seven, plus or minus two: Some limits on our capacity for processing information. *Psychological Review*, 63, 81–97.

Miller, L., Stanney, K., Guckenberger, D., & Guckenberger, E., (1997, July). Above real-time training. *Ergonomics in Design*, 21–24.

Milner, B., Corkin, S., & Teuber, H.L. (1968). Further analysis of the hippocampal amnesic syndrome: 14-year follow-up study of H.M. *Neuropsychologia*, 6, 215–234.

Moore, S.P., & Marteniuk, R.G. (1986). Kinematic and electromyographic changes that occur as a function of learning a time-constrained aiming task. *Journal of Motor Behavior*, 18, 397–426.

Morgan, W.P. (1979). Prediction of performance in athletics. In P. Klavora & J.V. Daniel (Eds.), *Coach, athlete, and the sport psychologist* (pp. 173–186). Toronto: University of Toronto.

Nashner, L., & Berthoz, A. (1978). Visual contribution to rapid motor responses during postural control. *Brain Research*, 150, 403–407.

Newell, K.M. (1985). Coordination, control, and skill. In D. Goodman, R.B. Wilberg, & I.M. Franks (Eds.), *Differing perspectives in motor learning, memory, and control* (pp. 295–317). Amsterdam: North-Holland.

Newell, K.M., Carlton, L.G., & Antoniou, A. (1990). The interaction of criterion and feedback information in learning a drawing task. *Journal of Motor Behavior*, 22, 536–552.

Newell, K.M., Carlton, L.G., Carlton, M.J., & Halbert, J.A. (1980). Velocity as a factor in movement timing accuracy. *Journal of Motor Behavior*, 12, 47–56.

Newell, K.M., & McGinnis, P.M. (1985). Kinematic information feedback for skilled performance. *Human Learning*, 4, 39–56.

Nicholls, J.G. (1989). *The competitive ethos and democratic education*. Cambridge, MA: Harvard University Press.

Nideffer, R.M. (1995). *Focus for success*. San Diego: Enhanced Performance Services.

Orlick, T. (1986). *Psyching for sport: Mental training for athletes*. Champaign, IL: Leisure Press.

Orlick, T. (1990). *In pursuit of excellence* (2nd ed.). Champaign, IL: Leisure Press.

Orlick, T., & Partington, J. (1986). *Psyched: Inner views of winning*. Ottawa, Ontario: Coaching Association of Canada.

Pashler, H. (1993, January-February). Doing two things at the same time. *American Scientist*, 81(1), 48–49.

Pashler, H. (1994). Dual-task interference in simple tasks: Data and theory. *Psychological Bulletin*, 116, 220–244.

Pein, R. (1990). *The effect of different frequencies of model presentation on the acquisition, retention, and transfer of an applied motor skill*. Unpublished doctoral dissertation, University of Tennessee, Knoxville.

Pew, R.W. (1974). Levels of analysis in motor control. *Brain Research*, 71, 393–400.

Polanyi, M. (1958). *Personal knowledge: Towards a post-critical philosophy*. London: Routledge & Kegan Paul.

Radwin, R.G., Vanderheiden, G.C., & Lin, M.L. (1990). A method for evaluating head-controlled computer input devices using Fitts' law. *Human Factors*, 32, 423–438.

Raibert, M.H. (1977). *Motor control and learning by the state-space model* (Tech. Rep. No. AI-TR-439). Cambridge: Massachusetts Institute of Technology, Artificial Intelligence Laboratory.

Robertson, S.D., Zelaznik, H.N., Lantero, D.A., Gadacz, K.E., Spencer, R.M., Doffin, J.G., & Schneidt, T. (in press). Correlations for timing consistency among tapping and drawing tasks: Evidence against a single timing process for motor control. *Journal of Experimental Psychology: Human Perception and Performance*.

Rodionov, A.V. (1978). *Psikhologiia Sportivnoi Deiatel'nosti* [The psychology of sport activity]. Moscow.

Rosenbaum, D.A. (1980). Human movement initiation: Specification of arm, direction, and extent. *Journal of Experimental Psychology: General*, 109, 444–474.

Rosenbaum, D.A. (1989). *On the selection of physical actions*. Five College Cognitive Science Paper, #89-4.

Rosenbaum, D.A. (1991). *Human motor control*. San Diego: Academic Press.

Rothstein, A.L., & Arnold, R.K. (1976). Bridging the gap: Application of research on videotape feedback and bowling. *Motor Skills: Theory Into Practice*, 1, 35–62.

Rushall, B.S. (1967). *An evaluation of the effect of various reinforcers used as motivators in swimming*. Unpublished manuscript, Indiana University, Bloomington.

Sackett, R.S. (1934). The influences of symbolic rehearsal upon the retention of a maze task. *Journal of General Psychology*, 10, 376–395.

Schmidt, R.A. (1969). Movement time as a determiner of timing accuracy. *Journal of Experimental Psychology*, 79, 43–47.

Schmidt, R.A. (1975). A schema theory of discrete motor skill learning. *Psychological Review*, 82, 225–260.

Schmidt, R.A. (1985). The search for invariance in skilled movement behavior. *Research Quarterly for Exercise and Sport*, 56, 188–200.

Schmidt, R.A. (1988). Motor and action perspective on motor behavior. In O.G. Meijer & K. Roth (Eds.), *Complex movement behaviour: "The" motor-action controversy* (pp. 3–44). Amsterdam: North-Holland.

Schmidt, R.A., & Gordon, E.B. (1977). Errors in motor responding, "rapid" corrections, and false anticipations. *Journal of Motor Behavior*, 9, 101–111.

Schmidt, R.A., Heuer, H., Ghodsian, D., & Young, D.E. (1998). Generalized motor programs and units of action in bimanual coordination. In M. Latash (Ed.), *Bernstein's traditions in motor control* (pp. 329–360). Champaign, IL: Human Kinetics.

Schmidt, R.A., Lange, C.A., & Young, D.E. (1990). Optimizing summary knowledge of results for skill learning. *Human Movement Science*, 9, 325–348.

Schmidt, R.A., & Lee, T.D. (1998). *Motor control and learning: A behavioral emphasis* (3rd Ed.). Champaign, IL: Human Kinetics.

Schmidt, R.A., & Pew, R.W. (1974). *Predicting motor-manipulative performances in the manufacture of dental appliances* (Tech. Rep. to Heritage Laboratories, Romulus, Michigan). Ann Arbor: University of Michigan.

Schmidt, R.A., & Sherwood, D.E. (1982). An inverted-U relation between spatial error and force requirements in rapid limb movements: Further evidence for the impulse-variability model. *Journal of Experimental Psychology: Human Perception and Performance,* 8, 158–170.

Schmidt, R.A., & Young, D.E. (1987). Transfer of motor control in motor skill learning. In S.M. Cormier & J.D. Hagman (Eds.), *Transfer of learning* (pp. 47–79). Orlando, FL: Academic Press.

Schmidt, R.A., Zelaznik, H.N., Hawkins, B., Frank, J.S., & Quinn, J.T. (1979). Motor-output variability: A theory for the accuracy of rapid motor acts. *Psychological Review,* 86, 415–451.

Schoenfelder-Zohdi, B.G. (1992). *Investigating the informational nature of a modeled visual demonstration.* Unpublished doctoral dissertation, Louisiana State University, Baton Rouge.

Scripture, C.W. (1905). *The new psychology.* New York: Scott.

Seat, J.E., & Wrisberg, C.A. (1996). The visual instruction system. *Research Quarterly for Exercise and Sport,* 67, 106–108.

Shapiro, D.C., Zernicke, R.F., Gregor, R.J., & Diestel, J.D. (1981). Evidence for generalized motor programs using gait-pattern analysis. *Journal of Motor Behavior,* 13, 33–47.

Shea, C.H., Kohl, R., & Indermill, C. (1990). Contextual interference: Contributions of practice. *Acta Psychologica,* 73, 145–157.

Shea, J.B., & Morgan, R.L. (1979). Contextual interference effects on the acquisition, retention, and transfer of a motor skill. *Journal of Experimental Psychology: Human Learning and Memory,* 5, 179–187.

Shea, J.B., & Zimny, S.T. (1983). Context effects in memory and learning movement information. In R.A. Magill (Ed.), *Memory and control of action* (pp. 345–366). Amsterdam: North-Holland.

Sherrington, C.S. (1906). *The integrative action of the nervous system.* New Haven, CT: Yale University Press.

Sherwood, D.E. (1988). Effect of bandwidth knowledge of results on movement consistency. *Perceptual and Motor Skills,* 66, 535–542.

Sherwood, D.E., Schmidt, R.A., & Walter, C.B. (1988). The force/force-variability relationship under controlled temporal conditions. *Journal of Motor Behavior,* 20, 106–116.

Shiffrin, R.M., & Schneider, W. (1977). Controlled and automatic human information processing: II. Perceptual learning, automatic attending, and a general theory. *Psychological Review,* 84, 127–190.

Slater-Hammel, A.T. (1960). Reliability, accuracy, and refractoriness of a transit reaction. *Research Quarterly,* 31, 217–228.

Smith, D. (1987). Conditions that facilitate the development of sport imagery training. *The Sport Psychologist,* 1, 237–247.

Southard, D., & Higgins, T. (1987). Changing movement patterns: Effects of demonstration and practice. *Research Quarterly for Exercise and Sport,* 58, 77–80.

Sparrow, W.A., & Irizarry-Lopez, V.M. (1987). Mechanical efficiency and metabolic cost as measures of learning a novel gross motor task. *Journal of Motor Behavior,* 19, 240–264.

*Sports Illustrated Book of Baseball.* (1960). Philadelphia: J.B. Lippincott Company.

Steenbergen, B., Marteniuk, R.G., & Kalbfleisch, L.E. (1995). Achieving coordination in prehension: Joint freezing and postural contributions. *Journal of Motor Behavior,* 27, 333–348.

Sternad, D. (1998). A dynamic systems perspective to perception and action. *Research Quarterly for Exercise and Sport,* 69, 319–325.

Summers, J.J. (1975). The role of timing in motor program representation. *Journal of Motor Behavior,* 7, 229–241.

Summers, J.J., Rosenbaum, D.A., Burns, B.D., & Ford, S.K. (1993). Production of polyrhythms. *Journal of Experimental Psychology: Human Perception and Performance,* 19, 416–428.

Swinnen, S., Schmidt, R.A., Nicholson, D.E., & Shapiro, D.C. (1990). Information feedback for skill acquisition: Instantaneous knowledge of results degrades learning. *Journal of Experimental Psychology: Learning, Memory, and Cognition,* 16, 706–716.

Taub, E. (1976). Movements in nonhuman primates deprived of somatosensory feedback. *Exercise and Sport Sciences Reviews,* 4, 335–374.

Taub, E., & Berman, A.J. (1968). Movement and learning in the absence of sensory feedback. In S.J. Freedman (Ed.), *The neuropsychology of spatially oriented behavior* (pp. 173–192). Homewood, IL: Dorsey Press.

Tenenbaum, G., & Bar-Eli, M. (1993). Decision making in sport: A cognitive perspective. In R.N. Singer, M. Murphey, & L.K. Tennant (Eds.), *Handbook of research on sport psychology* (pp. 171–192). New York: Macmillan.

Thorndike, E.L. (1914). *Educational psychology: Briefer course.* New York: Columbia University Press.

Thorndike, E.L. (1927). The law of effect. *American Journal of Psychology,* 39, 212–222.

Trevarthen, C.B. (1968). Two mechanisms of vision in primates. *Psychologische Forschung,* 31, 299–337.

Trowbridge, M.H., & Cason, H. (1932). An experimental study of Thorndike's theory of learning. *Journal of General Psychology,* 7, 245–260.

Tsutsui, S., Lee, T.D., & Hodges, N.J. (1998). Contextual interference in learning new patterns of bimanual coordination. *Journal of Motor Behavior,* 30, 151–157.

Tubbs, M.E. (1986). Goal setting: A meta-analysis examination of the empirical evidence. *Journal of Applied Psychology,* 71, 474–483.

Ulrich, B.D., Ulrich, D.A., Coffer, D.H., & Cole, E.L. (1995). Developmental shifts in the ability of infants with Down syndrome to produce treadmill steps. *Physical Therapy,* 75, 14–23.

Vealey, R.S., & Greenleaf, C.A. (1998). Seeing is believing: Understanding and using imagery in sport. In J.M. Williams (Ed.), *Applied sport psychology: Personal growth to peak performance* (pp. 237–260). Mountain View, CA: Mayfield.

Vereijken, B., Whiting, H.T.A., & Beek, P.J. (1992). A dynamical systems approach to skill acquisition. *Quarterly Journal of Experimental Psychology,* 45A, 323–344.

Wadman, W.J., Denier van der Gon, J.J., Geuze, R.H., & Mol, C.R. (1979). Control of fast goal-directed arm movements. *Journal of Human Movement Studies, 5*, 3–17.

Walter, C.B. (1998). An alternative view of dynamical systems concepts in motor control and learning. *Research Quarterly for Exercise and Sport, 69*, 326–333.

Warner, L., & McNeill, M.E. (1988). Mental imagery and its potential for physical therapy. *Physical Therapy, 68*, 516–521.

Weeks, D.L., Hall, A.K., & Anderson, L.P. (1996). A comparison of imitation strategies in observational learning of action patterns. *Journal of Motor Behavior, 28*, 348–358.

Weinberg, R.S., & Hunt, V.V. (1976). The interrelationships between anxiety, motor performance, and electromyography. *Journal of Motor Behavior, 8*, 219–224.

Weltman, G., & Egstrom, G.H. (1966). Perceptual narrowing in novice divers. *Human Factors, 8*, 499–505.

Whiting, H.T.A., & Vereijken, B. (1993). The acquisition of coordination in skill learning. *International Journal of Sport Psychology, 24*, 343–357.

Wieder, M.A., Smith, C., & Brackage, C. (1996). *Essentials of fire fighting* (3rd ed.). Stillwater, OK: Fire Protection Publications.

Wiener, N. (1948). *Cybernetics or control and communication in the animal and the machine.* New York: Wiley.

Wightman, D.C., & Lintern, G. (1985). Part-task training strategies for tracking and manual control. *Human Factors, 27*, 267–283.

Williams, A.M., & Davids, K. (1998). Visual search strategy, selective attention, and expertise in soccer. *Research Quarterly for Exercise and Sport, 69*, 111–128.

Williams, A.M., Davids, K., Burwitz, L., & Williams, J.G. (1992). Perception and action in sport. *Journal of Human Movement Studies, 22*, 147–205.

Williams, H.G., Woollacott, M.H., & Ivry, R. (1992). Timing and motor control in clumsy children. *Journal of Motor Behavior, 24*, 165–172.

Williams, J.M., & Harris, D.V. (1998). Relaxation and energizing techniques for regulation of arousal. In J.M. Williams (Ed.), *Applied sport psychology: Personal growth to peak performance* (pp. 219-236). Mountain View, CA: Mayfield.

Williams, T., & Underwood, J. (1988). *My turn at bat.* New York: Fireside.

Winstein, C.J., & Schmidt, R.A. (1990). Reduced frequency of knowledge of results enhances motor skill learning. *Journal of Experimental Psychology: Learning, Memory, and Cognition, 16*, 677–691.

Woods, J.B. (1967). The effect of varied instructional emphasis upon the development of a motor skill. *Research Quarterly, 38*, 132–142.

Woodworth, R.S. (1899). The accuracy of voluntary movement. *Psychological Review,* 3 (Suppl. 2), 1–114.

Woodworth, R.S. (1938). *Experimental psychology.* New York: Holt.

Wright, D.L., Pleasants, F., & Gomez-Mesa, M. (1990). Use of advanced visual cue sources in volleyball. *Journal of Sport and Exercise Psychology, 12*, 406–414.

Wrisberg, C.A. (1994). The arousal-performance relationship. *Quest, 46*, 60–77.

Wrisberg, C.A., & Liu, Z. (1991). The effect of contextual variety on the practice, retention, and transfer of an applied motor skill. *Research Quarterly for Exercise and Sport, 62*, 406–412.

Wrisberg, C.A., & Mead, B.J. (1983). Developing coincident-timing skill in children: A comparison of training methods. *Research Quarterly for Exercise and Sport, 54*, 67–74.

Wulf, G., Höß, M., & Prinz, W. (1998). Instructions for motor learning: Differential effects of internal versus external focus of attention. *Journal of Motor Behavior, 30*, 169–179.

Wulf, G., & Schmidt, R.A. (1988). Variability in practice: Facilitation in retention and transfer through schema formation or context effects? *Journal of Motor Behavior, 20*, 133–149.

Wulf, G., & Schmidt, R.A. (1997). Variability of practice and implicit motor learning. *Journal of Experimental Psychology: Learning, Memory, and Cognition, 23*, 987–1006.

Wulf, G., Shea, C.H., & Matschiner, S. (1998). Frequent feedback enhances complex motor skill learning. *Journal of Motor Behavior, 30*, 180–192.

Wulf, G., Shea, C.H., & Whitacre, C. (1998). Physical guidance benefits in learning a complex motor skill. *Journal of Motor Behavior, 30*, 367–380.

Wulf, G., & Weigelt, C. (1997). Instructions about physical principles in learning a complex motor skill: To tell or not to tell. *Research Quarterly for Exercise and Sport, 68*, 362–367.

Young, D.E., & Schmidt, R.A. (1992). Augmented kinematic feedback for motor learning. *Journal of Motor Behavior, 24*, 261–273.

# Credits

## Figures and Tables

**Line drawing on page 61**—Adapted from C.W. Scripture (1905). *The new psychology*. New York: Scott.

**Table 2.3**—Adapted, by permission, from J.N. Drowatzky and F.C. Zuccato, 1967, "Interrelationships between selected measures of static and dynamic balance," *Research Quarterly for Exercise and Sport* 38:510. *Research Quarterly* is a publication of the American Alliance for Health, Physical Education, Recreation and Dance, 1900 Association Drive, Reston, VA 22091.

**Table 2.4**—Reprinted, by permission, from E.A. Fleishman, 1964, *The structure and measurement of physical fitness*. New York: McGraw-Hill.

**Figure 3.3**—Adapted from R.S. Woodworth, 1938, *Experimental psychology*. New York: Holt. Data obtained by J. Merkel, 1885, "Die zeitlichen verhaltnisse der willenstatigkeit," *Philosophische Studien*, 2:73–127.

**Figure 3.12**—Reprinted, by permission, from P.B. Konzem, 1987, "Extended practice and patterns of bimanual interference," Doctoral dissertation, University of Southern California.

**Figure 4.3**—Adapted, by permission, from A.T. Slater-Hammel, 1960, "Reliability, accuracy and refractoriness of a transit reaction," *Research Quarterly for Exercise and Sport* 31:226. *Research Quarterly* is a publication of the American Alliance for Health, Physical Education, Recreation and Dance, 1900 Association Drive, Reston, VA 22091.

**Figure 4.4**—Adapted, by permission, from D.J. Dewhurst, 1967, "Neuromuscular control system," *IEEE Transactions on Bio-Medical Engineering* 14:170.

**Figure 5.7**—Adapted, by permission, from T.R. Armstrong, 1970, *Training for the production of memorized movement patterns: Technical report no. 26* (Ann Arbor, MI: University of Michigan, Human Performance Center), 35.

**Figure 5.8**—Adapted, by permission, from J.M. Hollerbach, 1978, "A study of human motor control through analysis and synthesis of handwriting," Doctoral dissertation, Massachusetts Institute of Technology.

**Figure 5.9**—Reprinted, by permission, from M.H. Raibert, 1977, *Motor control and learning by the state-space model, Technical Report No. AI-TR-439* (Cambridge, MA: Massachusetts Institute of Technology), 50.

**Figure 6.1**—Reprinted, by permission, from R.A. Schmidt, 1988, *Motor control and learning: A behavioral emphasis*, 2nd ed. (Champaign, IL: Human Kinetics), 244.

**Figures 6.2 and 6.3**—Reprinted, by permission, from D.C. Shapiro, R.F. Zernicke, R.J. Gregor, and J.D. Diestel, 1981, "Evidence for generalized motor programs using gait-pattern analysis," *Journal of Motor Behavior* 13:38, 42.

**Figures 6.5 and 6.6**—Adapted from P.M. Fitts, 1954, "The information capacity of the human motor system in controlling the amplitude of movement," *Journal of Experimental Psychology*, 47, 381–391.

**Figures 6.7, 6.8, and 6.11**—Adapted (6.7 and 6.11) and reprinted (6.8), by permission, from R.A. Schmidt, H.N. Zelaznik, B. Hawkins, J.S. Frank, and J.T. Quinn, 1979, "Motor-output variability: A theory for the accuracy of rapid motor acts," *Psychological Review* 86:428. Copyright © 1979 by the American Psychological Association.

**Figure 6.13**—Adapted, by permission, from R.A. Schmidt and D.E. Sherwood, 1982, "An inverted-U relation between spatial error and force requirements in rapid limb movement: Further evidence for the impulse-variability model," *Journal of Experimental Psychology: Human Perception and Performance* 8:167. Copyright © 1982 by the American Psychological Association.

**Table 7.5**—Adapted, by permission, from D.V. Knudson and C.S. Morrison, 1997, *Qualitative analysis of human movement* (Champaign, IL: Human Kinetics), 155.

**Figure 9.1**—Reprinted, by permission, from J.B. Shea and R.L. Morgan, 1979, "Contextual Interference Effects on the Acquisition, Retention, and Transfer of a Motor Skill," *Journal of Experimental Psychology: Human Learning and Memory*, 5:183. Copyright © 1979 by the American Psychological Association.

**Figure 10.5**—Reprinted, by permission, from R.A. Schmidt, C.A. Lange, and D.E. Young, 1990, "Optimizing summary knowledge of results for skill learning," *Human Movement Science*, 9, 325–348.

**Figure 10.8**—Reprinted, by permission, from B. Vereijken, H.T.A. Whiting, and P.J. Beek, 1992, "A dynamical systems approach to skill acquisition," *Quarterly Journal of Experimental Psychology*, 45A: 323–344.

## Chapter Opener Photos

**Chapter 1**—Photo by Teresa Whitehead. Courtesy of Casa Colina Centers for Rehabilitation, Adaptive Sports.

**Chapter 2**—Photo © Martha McBride / Unicorn Stock Photos.

**Chapters 3, 4, 5, 7, 9, 11, and 12**—Photos by Tom Roberts.

**Chapter 6**—Photo © Richard B. Levine.

**Chapter 8**—Photo © SportsChrome.

**Chapter 10**—Photo © Terry Wild.

# Index

**Boldfaced** locators indicate glossary terms.
*Italicized* locators indicate figures and tables.

# About the Authors

Richard A. Schmidt

**Richard A. Schmidt**, PhD, is a principal scientist at Exponent Failure Analysis Associates, Inc., in Los Angeles, California, and a professor of psychology at the University of California, Los Angeles. Known as one of the research leaders in motor behavior, Dr. Schmidt has nearly 30 years' experience in this area and has published widely.

The originator of "schema theory," Dr. Schmidt founded the *Journal of Motor Behavior* and was its editor for 11 years. He authored the first edition of *Motor Control and Learning* in 1982 and *Motor Learning and Performance* in 1991 and has since followed up with new editions of both books. He received an honorary doctorate from Catholic University of Leuven, Belgium, in recognition of his work.

Dr. Schmidt is a member of the North American Society for the Psychology of Sport and Physical Activity, the Human Factors and Ergonomics Society, and the Psychonomic Society. He has served as president of the North American Society for the Psychology of Sport and Physical Activity, and he received the C.H. McCloy Research Lectureship from the American Alliance for Health, Physical Education, Recreation and Dance.

Dr. Schmidt's leisure-time activities include sailboat racing, running, and skiing.

Craig A. Wrisberg

**Craig A. Wrisberg**, PhD, is a professor of motor behavior and sport psychology at the University of Tennessee, Knoxville (UTK), where he has taught since 1977. During the past 25 years he has published numerous research articles on the topics of anticipation and timing in performance, knowledge of results and motor learning, and warm-up decrement in sport performance. He has received the Chancellor's Award for Research and Creative Achievement (1994) and the Brady Award for Excellence in Teaching (1982).

A past president of the North American Society for the Psychology of Sport and Physical Activity, Dr. Wrisberg is a fellow of both the American Academy of Kinesiology and Physical Education and the Association for the Advancement of Applied Sport Psychology.

In addition to his teaching and research, Dr. Wrisberg supervises the provision of mental training services for student-athletes in the Departments of Men's and Women's Athletics at UTK. In his work with athletes, he applies many of the important concepts and principles covered in this edition of *Motor Learning and Performance,* using the problem-based learning approach on a consistent basis.

Dr. Wrisberg enjoys several outdoor activities, including tennis, canoeing, and hiking in the Great Smoky Mountains.